QUICK *simple*

MICROSOFT® OFFICE 2000

Linda Ericksen

LANE COMMUNITY COLLEGE

PRENTICE HALL, Upper Saddle River, New Jersey 07458

Editor-in-Chief: Mickey Cox
Executive Editor: Alex von Rosenberg
Editorial Assistant: Jennifer Surich
Managing Editor: Susan Rifkin
Director of Strategic Marketing: Nancy Evans
Development Editor (for Windows 98, Word, and Excel): Cecil Yarbrough
Production Manager: Gail Steier de Acevedo
Project Manager: Lynne Breitfeller
Manufacturing Buyer: Lisa DiMaulo
Senior Manufacturing Supervisor: Paul Smolenski
Manufacturing Manager: Vincent Scelta
Design Manager: Patricia Smythe
Interior Design: Mary McDonald
Cover Design: Kevin Kall
Cover Illustration/Photo: Artville, Stephanie Carter
Composition: TSI Graphics, Inc.

Prentice-Hall International (UK) Limited, London
Prentice-Hall of Australia Pty. Limited, Sydney
Prentice-Hall Canada, Inc., Toronto
Prentice-Hall Hispanoamericana, S.A., Mexico
Prentice-Hall of India Private Limited, New Delhi
Prentice-Hall of Japan, Inc., Tokyo
Editora Prentice-Hall do Bràsil, Ltda., Rio de Janeiro

Printed in the United States of America

10 9 8 7 6 5 4 3

CONTENTS

Contents   v

CHECK POINT

UNIT 3
Relating Tables and Working with Data

UNIT 4
Querying the Database

CHECK POINT

POWERPOINT 2000

UNIT I
Getting Started

UNIT 2
Creating and Viewing Presentations

About the Author

Linda Ericksen teaches in the Department of Business Technologies at Lane Community College (LCC), Eugene, Oregon. Linda has a Master of Science degree in Computer Science Education from the University of Oregon and a Master of Arts degree in English from the University of Kentucky. Prior to teaching at LCC, she taught at both the community college and the university levels in the computer information systems department and in the English and communication departments. Linda started her teaching career as a Vista volunteer in a native Alaskan college-without-walls, developing curriculum and delivering courses in rural Alaska.

Linda is the author of 19 college-level computer textbooks on application software and the Internet. She is a past president of the Oregon chapter of the American Association of Women in Community Colleges and makes presentations at both the national and international levels. In her free time, Linda enjoys drawing, playing music, hiking, and camping in the Pacific Northwest.

An experienced author, Linda is delighted to come to Prentice Hall as the author of her own application series, Quick, Simple Microsoft Office 2000. For questions or comments, please contact Linda at www.cyber-writer.com.

WHAT Is Quick, Simple Microsoft® Office 2000 All About?

Quick, Simple Microsoft® Office 2000 is part of my new introductory application series for Prentice Hall. The series includes the Office 2000 text, along with

- Quick, Simple Microsoft® Windows® 98
- Quick, Simple Microsoft® Word 2000
- Quick, Simple Microsoft® PowerPoint 2000
- Quick, Simple Microsoft® Access 2000
- Quick, Simple Microsoft® Excel 2000

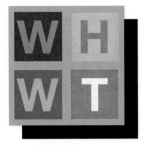

WHY Did I Write Quick, Simple Microsoft® Office 2000?

This book is written for students from the perspective of a teacher. I applied everything I have learned from teaching in the classroom and incorporated it into the series. Through teaching, I have noticed that most entry-level books are filled with case studies and stories that typically talk down to adults. Most students are frustrated by this. What they really want are exercises that are meaningful to them, and my series gives them this.

The difference between other texts on the market and my Quick, Simple Microsoft Office 2000 Series is that the "fluff" is gone and what remains is valuable, hands-on information. Every procedure is made perfectly clear.

For many students, a course in Microsoft Office can be very challenging. Not only is the vocabulary new to the students, but also the actual skills and application of the software can be overwhelming. Quick, Simple Office 2000 introduces the student to the entire environment first with a friendly, informal guide to buying and setting up a computer, defining all vocabulary as it is first mentioned. The student is further introduced to the overall user environment with units on Windows 98 and Internet Explorer, supplying students with skills that they will apply in all Office applications.

Each Office application is covered in detail with real-world examples, projects, exercises, and check points. The student masters each individual application, building on skills learned in previous units.

Quick, Simple Office 2000 goes one step further by providing a unit devoted to integrating the various software applications, using Object Linking and Embedding–OLE. For example, students link an Excel worksheet and chart to a report created in Word, create a hyperlink from an Office document to the World Wide Web, and use an Access database to create a Word mail merge.

Each unit starts with a list of objectives and is divided into discrete tasks that support those objectives. Each task is defined and each starts with the WHWT icon, which clearly states *what* the task is, *how* to perform it, *why* it is needed, and provides the user with a *tip*. Each task is explained in numbered steps with clear screen captures and contains a hands-on exercise that the student can use to reinforce the information. These exercises call for the student to print the results in case the instructor wants the student to submit them.

The end-of-unit material is rich and varied. Each unit includes:

- A **Summary** of all tasks
- A list of all **Key Terms** and the page where they are first encountered
- **True/False** questions
- **Multiple Choice** questions
- **Short Answer** questions—many that provide screens for identification of important elements
- **What Does This Do?** questions that ask the student to define the function of buttons or keystrokes
- **On Your Own** review exercises that the student will use to reinforce the tasks, but that can be used for practice rather than as an assignment
- **Projects** that require the student to apply the unit's material in the creation of new documents

Check Point projects are located at the end of every other unit starting with Unit 2. These projects pull together all information that the student has learned to that point in the text.

A **Wrap-Up** project is located at the end of the last unit of the text. This comprehensive project provides a review of the entire text by having the student create a number of real-world documents for an organization.

Further learning aids include:

- An alphabetized list of **Tasks and Commands**, in Appendix A
- The **toolbar** and **buttons** and their functions, in Appendix B
- A **Glossary** of key terms with their definitions, at the end of the book

If students are unable to type text for every project, the unedited version of all projects is available both on the instructor's resource disk and on the World Wide Web at www.prenhall.com/ericksen.

Quick, Simple Microsoft Office 2000 with all its features helps the student learn to use the software in an efficient way. This applied, task-oriented learning works equally well with on-campus students and with distance learners.

Formatting Documents

UNIT OBJECTIVES

- Use bold, italic, and underline
- Change the font, size, color, and other font attributes
- Change text alignment
- Change line spacing
- Indent paragraphs
- Set custom tab stops

Formatting is the structure and layout of a document and its individual parts. Documents can be formatted to call attention to important points, manage the space on the page, and make the documents more attractive. Formatting in Word takes place at four levels: the character, the paragraph, the page, and the section. In this unit you will learn character and paragraph formatting. Unit 6 explains page and section formatting. **Character formatting** applies to individual characters or selected text. You format characters to change the way the text looks on the page. **Paragraph formatting** applies to whole paragraphs. You format paragraphs to change how paragraphs line up and are spaced on the page.

HOW should you use the text in your classroom?

Each unit in the text opens with a detailed Unit Objective section that outlines for students the tasks they will undertake in the unit.

Each unit is made up of individual tasks, which are explained in steps illustrated with screens. Callouts point to key elements. I start each task in the text with a unique "What/How/Why/Tip" list offering one-sentence explanations of the skill to be learned and the reason for learning it. Many students never know "Why" they are learning a particular task. My organization explains What/How/Why at the beginning of each lesson.

TASK 1 | *Using the MIN Function*

What: Use Excel's built-in MIN function.
How: Choose Insert | Function or click the Paste Function button on the toolbar.
Why: MIN finds the smallest value in a range of cells.
Tip: MIN is short for "minimum." You might use this function to find the lowest airline fare from a list on the Web.

Excel provides excellent help in constructing functions so you don't have to memorize their arguments and type them from scratch.

THE PASTE FUNCTION DIALOG BOX

When you choose Insert | Function or click the Paste Function button on the Standard toolbar, the Paste Function dialog box opens, showing you all of the functions that are available. Click any function and the dialog box describes what it does.

To use one of Excel's built-in functions:

1. Click in the cell where you want the results to appear.
2. Click the Paste Function button on the Standard toolbar. The Paste Function dialog box opens, as shown in Figure 4.1.

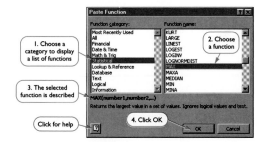

FIGURE 4.1   The Paste Function Dialog Box

3. Select a category in the *Function category* list and all of the functions in that category are listed in the *Function name* list.
4. Select a function in the *Function name* list.

- The selected function is described at the bottom of the dialog box.
- For more information about the function, click the Office Assistant button at the bottom left of the dialog box. Click the button for *Help with this feature* and then for *Help on selected function*. A Help window opens with details of the function's syntax and examples of its use.

5. Click OK to close the dialog box and open the Form...

Tasks include easy-to-follow **numbered** and **bulleted steps** along with **Pointer** boxes that caution the student about problems or provide extra information. **Key Terms** are boldfaced and defined in the body of the text. **Buttons** appear in the margin when they are used for the first time, so that the student will know the correct one to click.

Each task includes a clear, numbered **Exercise**. The numbered steps are followed by an exact explanation of what is happening on the student's screen.

In the end-of-unit objective reviews, I've included a **Summary**, and a **Key Terms** list with the page number of the definition, plus **True/False**, **Multiple Choice**, **Short Answer**, and **What Does This Do?** sets of reinforcement exercises.

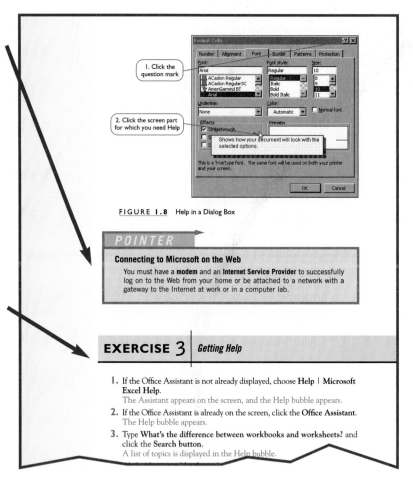

FIGURE 1.8   Help in a Dialog Box

POINTER

Connecting to Microsoft on the Web
You must have a **modem** and an **Internet Service Provider** to successfully log on to the Web from your home or be attached to a network with a gateway to the Internet at work or in a computer lab.

EXERCISE 3 | *Getting Help*

1. If the Office Assistant is not already displayed, choose **Help | Microsoft Excel Help**.
   The Assistant appears on the screen, and the Help bubble appears.
2. If the Office Assistant is already on the screen, click the **Office Assistant**.
   The Help bubble appears.
3. Type **What's the difference between workbooks and worksheets?** and click the **Search button**.
   A list of topics is displayed in the Help bubble.

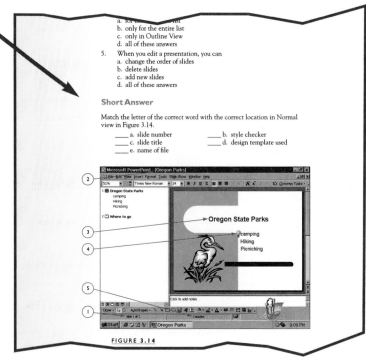

a. for each entire list
b. only for the entire list
c. only in Outline View
d. all of these answers

5. When you edit a presentation, you can
   a. change the order of slides
   b. delete slides
   c. add new slides
   d. all of these answers

Short Answer

Match the letter of the correct word with the correct location in Normal view in Figure 3.14.

_____ a. slide number   _____ b. style checker
_____ c. slide title   _____ d. design template used
_____ e. name of file

FIGURE 3.14

On Your Own

1. Search Access Help for information about primary keys.
2. Create a table for which you can set field properties to try them out.
3. Create a new database of your own choosing to organize some of your own data.
4. Search Access Help for information on field properties.
5. Print the structure of one of the tables in the Northwind database.

PROJECTS

1. As the owner of JRT Kennels you want to organize all your records into a database using Access 2000. You have lists of dogs and the people who have purchased them both in file cabinets and binders. One problem you notice is that, over the years, customers have purchased several dogs from you, and you have not been able to keep up-to-date records.

   List the following information in Word 2000 and group data about each subject into tables: customer's name, customer's complete address, dog's name, breed, date of purchase. Print the grouped data.

2. Create a database called JRT Kennels. Using your analysis of the data in project 1, create two tables—a customer table and a dog table. Remember to divide the data into the smallest unit, such as placing the customer name in two fields.

   Set the following field properties:

   • State/Prov.—size should be equal to two
   • Country—default value should be USA
   • Phone—use an input mask
   • Purchase Date—must be after 1985

   Create a primary key that uniquely identifies the data in each table. Make the primary key a text field. For example, create a Customer Number in the Customer table and input data, such as 111, 112, 113, and so on, for use in the following unit.

   Print the structure of the tables, using an Object Definition report.

   Input the following data, placing it in the correct tables:

   John Smith, 123 Orchard Dr., Walnut Creek, CA 98765, USA, (654)123-3456, Misty, Jack Russell Terrier, January 15, 1991.

   Sue Mason, 18 View St., Winooski, VT 05409, USA, (345)234-9876, Jessie, Mixed breed, February 9, 1992.

   Bob Jones, 567 Lake Dr., Denville, NJ 09876, USA, (202)341-9456, Toto, Yorkshire Terrier, August 15, 1994

   John Smith, 123 Orchard Dr., Walnut Creek, CA 98765, USA, (654)123-3456, Mickey, Jack Russell Terrier, September 5, 1993.

   Mary Lawrence, 987 Hill Dr., Calgary, AL, 87654, Canada, (345)345-9876, Hobo, Yorkshire Terrier, June 7, 1997

   Bob Jones, 567 Lake Dr., Denville, NJ 09876, USA, (202...

The student is also provided with On Your Own exercises to provide more hands-on practice.

End-of-unit hands-on Projects provide a setting for the use of the application. They let students show mastery of tasks using the software.

Check Points at the end of every other unit provide cumulative projects that allow students to pull together all that they have learned so far.

CHECK POINT

FOR UNITS 1-2

PROJECTS

1. a. Create the following profit and loss statement for Spread the Light Candles or open **Profit-Loss**:

	A	B	C	D
1	Spread the Light			
2	Profit/Loss Statement			
3				
4			Year 1	Year 2
5	Sales		110,000	150,000
6	Cost of goods		45,000	82,000
7	Gross margin			

The Wrap-Up project provides a way of testing all that has been learned in the text. Students create reports, worksheets, a database, a slide presentation, and a Web site as a final project.

Two Appendixes and a Glossary serve as quick reference guides.

Appendix A, Alphabetized List of Tasks, lists every task taught in the book and the commands for performing it. This feature gives students a single source of useful review information while eliminating the necessity of repeating the same instructions from exercise to exercise in the text. (A new Office user who can't remember how to save a file, for instance, can go to the list and find the commands needed.)

Appendix B, Toolbars and Buttons, provides images of the buttons students will encounter on the Office 2000 toolbars, with simple explanations of their functions.

A Glossary of the book's Key Terms and a comprehensive Index complete the reference section.

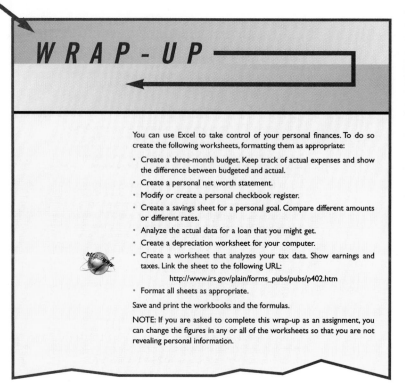

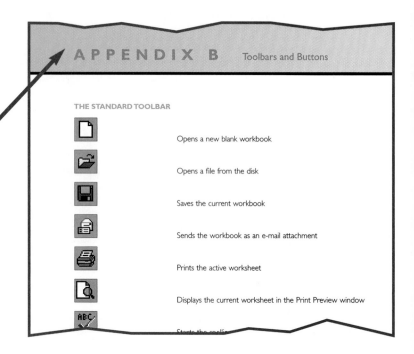

TIPS to use in the classroom

Quick, Simple Microsoft Office 2000 will be supported by a fully integrated technology package:

CBT Task-Based Tutorials

Prentice Hall has a strategic partnership with CBT Systems, a leading developer of interactive computer-based tutorials. CBT has developed a complete set of task-based tutorials for Microsoft Office that is fully certified at the Expert Level of the Microsoft Office User Specialist (MOUS) program. These tutorials are available to colleges and universities exclusively through Prentice Hall in conjunction with the Quick, Simple Microsoft Office series, which was designed to help ready students for this certification. Tasks covered will lead your students through the basic skills that are necessary for their successful completion of the Certification program.

Introducing SkillCheck Professional Plus
Performance-based assessment software for Microsoft Office 2000

Prentice Hall has developed a new alliance with SkillCheck, Inc., a leading international developer of fully interactive, fully validated computer-based testing for application software skills. This partnership enables Prentice Hall to bring a customized version of the SkillCheck Professional Plus skills-based assessment software exclusively to adopters of the Quick, Simple Microsoft Office Series. SkillCheck Professional Plus features fully interactive test items that allow examinees to answer questions by performing the tasks in any correct way the Office application program allows. Essential software features are fully simulated, so no additional software is required. In addition to independently validated student tests covering beginning, intermediate, and advanced levels, each SkillCheck Professional Plus system includes a database of over 100 interactive questions per Office application and offers the instructor the opportunity to customize tests, set testing parameters (timing, number of tries per question), and control reporting and feedback features.

To further enhance your class structure, the Quick, Simple Microsoft® Office series is also available from Prentice Hall's Right PHit custom binding program, enabling you to create the perfect textbook for your specific course structure. You can visit the companion Web site for Quick, Simple Microsoft Office located at **www.pren-hall.com/ericksen** for additional instructor resources and for an enriched learning experience for your students. Each volume in the Quick, Simple Microsoft Office series makes use of the World Wide Web so that students will have the most up-to-date information, even at this introductory level.

In addition to a strong technology package, Instructor Supplements include an Instructor's Manual, Data Disks, and Computerized Testing System. All of these supplements are available on one CD-ROM. Ask your local Prentice Hall representative for details.

ACKNOWLEDGMENTS

I want to thank many individuals who helped this series become a reality. I want to thank Amy June, my Prentice Hall Sales Representative, and Sally McPherson, Prentice Hall Western Regional Manager, for their help. I especially want to thank Cecil Yarbrough, my Development Editor. I also want to thank P. J. Boardman, Alex von Rosenberg, Executive Editor, and Susan Rifkin, Managing Editor. Thanks also to Karen Jeanne, whose final accuracy check was invaluable. In addition, I would like to thank Nancy Evans, Director of Strategic Marketing; Janet Feruggia, Marketing Communications Director; Pat Smythe, Design Director; Leanne Nieglos, Assistant Editor; Eve Adams, Advertising Director. Thanks also to Sande Johnson, Market Research Analyst, and Dennis Fernandez, Prentice Hall District Sales Manager. Thank you also to Don Cassell for his assistance in the writing of the Access manuscript, Emily Ketcham for her super reviews of late drafts, and to Scott Warner as developmental editor of the Access and PowerPoint manuscripts. I especially want to thank Lynne Breitfeller, Project Manager, for going the extra mile for these manuscripts.

Lastly I would like to thank the reviewers:

Bill Boroski	Trident Technical College
E. Sonny Butler	Eastern Kentucky University
Dan Christiansen	Iowa Western Community College
Susan DeMauro	New Hampshire Community Technical College
Glenda Dilts	DeVry Institute of Technology
Ed Eille	Delaware County Community College
Larry Jackson	Computer Learning Center
Marilyn Konnick	Albuquerque Technical Vocational Institute
William Kornegay	Miami-Dade Community College
Tammie Lancaster	Northwest Arkansas Community College
Jean Merenda	Pitt Community College
Kathleen E. Proietti	Northern Essex Community College
Kathleen Ryan	Community College of Spokane
Ken Steinkruger	DeVry Institute of Technology
Maggie Trigg	Arapahoe Community College, Regis University
Linda Volonino	Canisius College
Diane Ward	Pensacola Junior College

Introduction to
Microsoft Office 2000

Office 2000 is the latest and most powerful suite of office applications created by Microsoft. Office 2000 comes in several versions. Office 2000 Professional, for which this book was written, consists of Word, Excel, PowerPoint, Access, Outlook, and Publisher, plus dozens of small programs used to enhance these major applications. Each application is a powerful stand-alone software package. The individual applications gain even more power and flexibility when integrated with each other or with the World Wide Web, which you will learn about throughout this text and especially in the last unit of the book.

Microsoft Word 2000 is a word processing application. You use word processing for creating text-based documents such as letters, memos, reports, and résumés. You can format the text in a variety of ways, and you can include many enhancements such as graphics, tables, and charts. You can also do specialized activities such as merging address files with form letters, saving a document as a Web document, and creating envelopes and labels. (See Figures 1 to 3.)

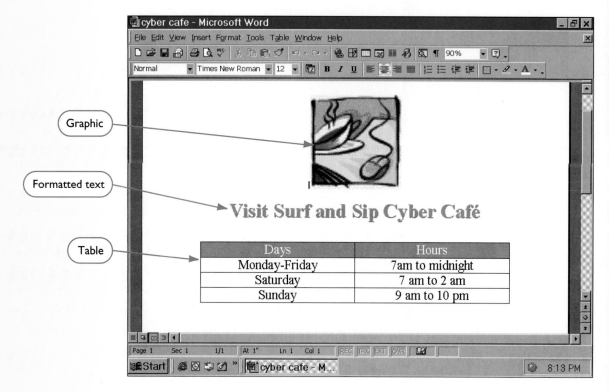

FIGURE **1**

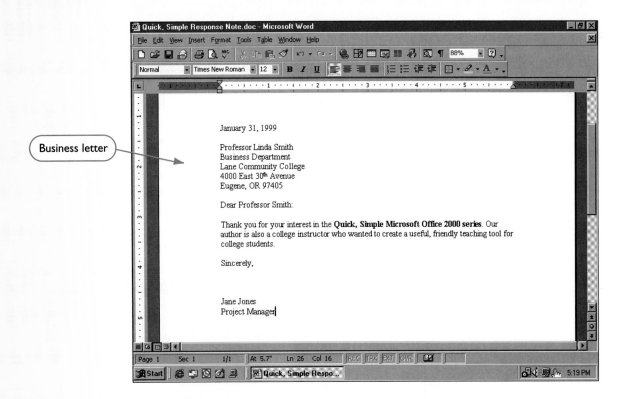

Business letter

FIGURE 2

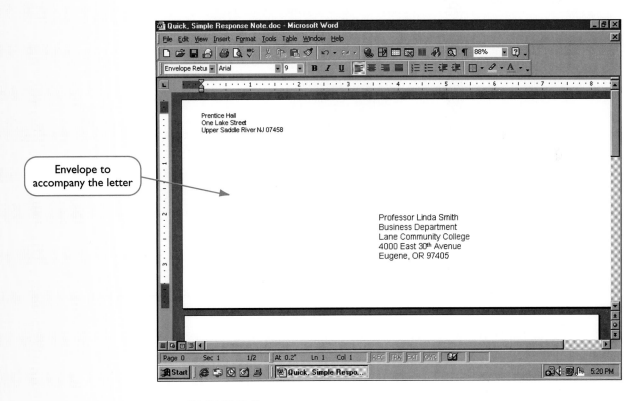

Envelope to accompany the letter

FIGURE 3

Microsoft Excel 2000 is an electronic worksheet application. You use worksheets for creating number-based documents such as budgets, checkbook registers, or loan calculations. Worksheets consist of columns and rows with numbers, text, and formulas placed into cells. You can enhance worksheets by formatting text and numbers and including such elements as borders or graphics. Once you have input data, you write formulas and use functions that are built into Excel to perform calculations. The numeric data can then be charted to see trends or to make comparisons. This powerful application is used extensively in businesses to analyze data. (See Figure 4.)

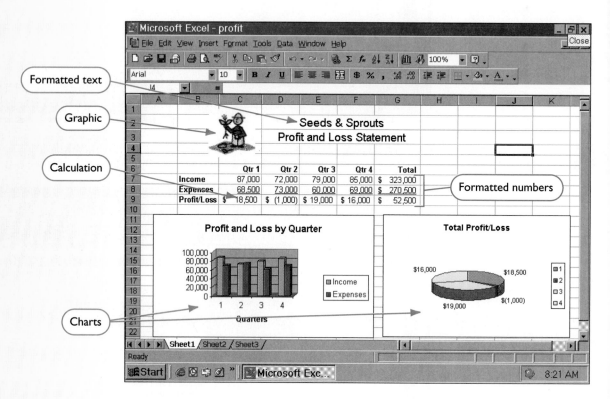

FIGURE 4

Microsoft PowerPoint 2000 is a presentation application used to create slide shows that can be viewed on a computer or as slides presented on an overhead or slide projector. PowerPoint lets you create attention-grabbing shows through the use of enhancements such as graphics, video, audio, animation, and text effects. Self-running computer-based PowerPoint presentations are used extensively as a way to provide information. Slide presentations can also be controlled by a speaker to provide an audience, class, or hiring panel with information. PowerPoint's audience and speaker notes can help to keep a presentation on track. (See Figures 5 and 6.)

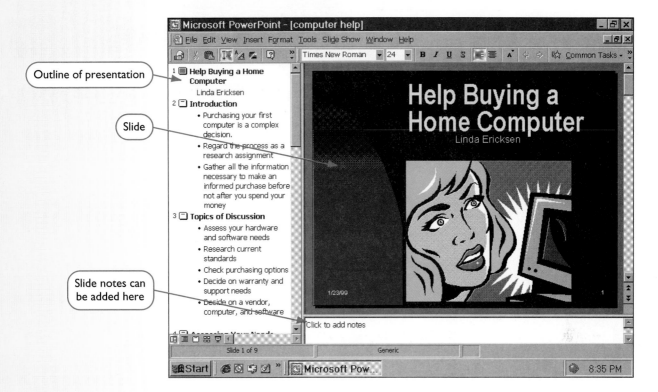

FIGURE **5**

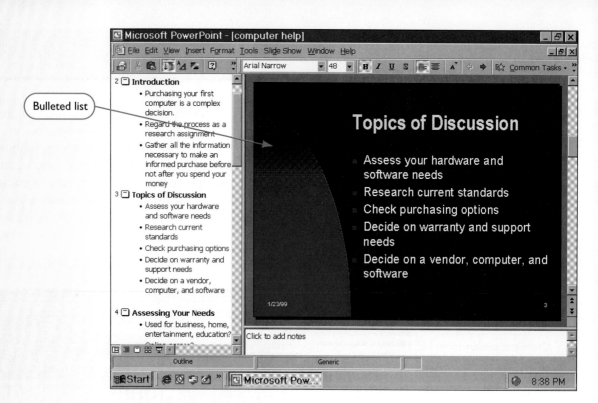

Bulleted list

FIGURE 6

Microsoft Access 2000 is a powerful relational database tool allowing businesses of all types to keep up-to-date records. Data is stored in tables that look a lot like an electronic worksheet. However, Access provides many features used specifically to manipulate and present data. You can store thousands of records in Access and use its powerful query feature to get the information you need. Access also provides reporting capabilities that present the data in a format that makes them easy to understand. (See Figures 7 to 9.)

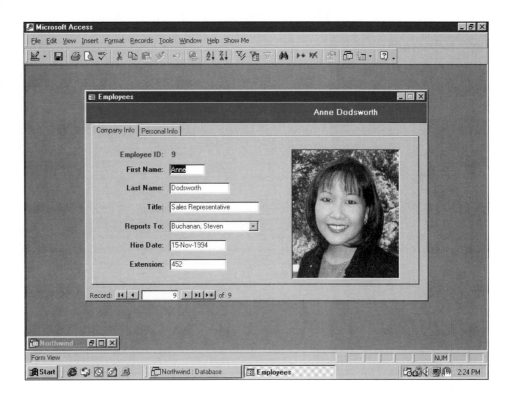

FIGURE 7

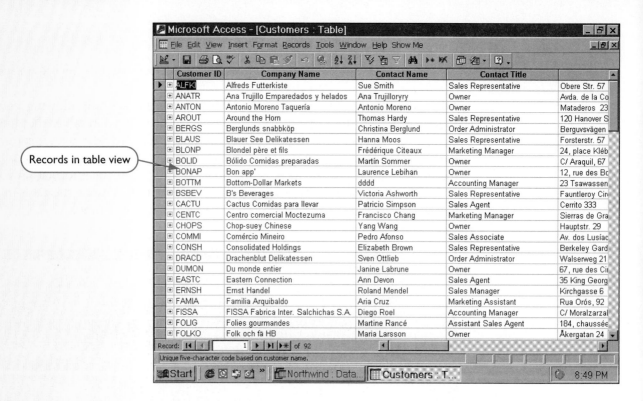

Records in table view

FIGURE 8

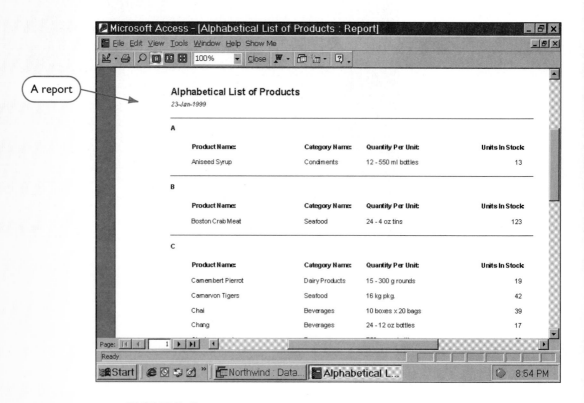

A report

FIGURE 9

Microsoft Outlook 2000 is a desktop information management and e-mail application. You use a desktop information management application to help you organize your day-to-day activities. You schedule meetings and appointments using Outlook's electronic calendar, and keep track of contacts with name and address information in a contact list. The contact list can then be used to create virtual business cards or to dial phone numbers automatically. You can also organize tasks both for yourself and others, assigning tasks and monitoring progress. You can use the e-mail application portion of Outlook to send and receive electronic mail, manage e-mail messages, and manage your address book. (See Figures 10 to 12.)

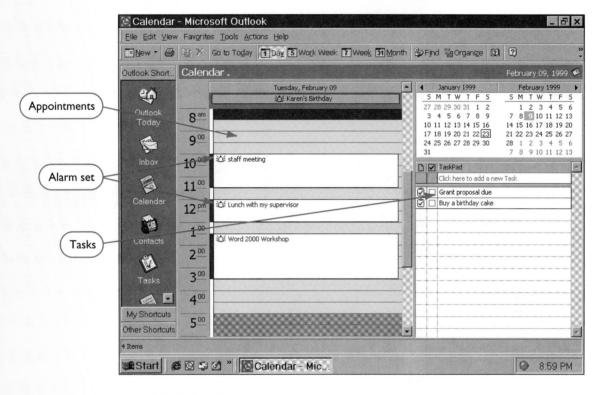

FIGURE 10

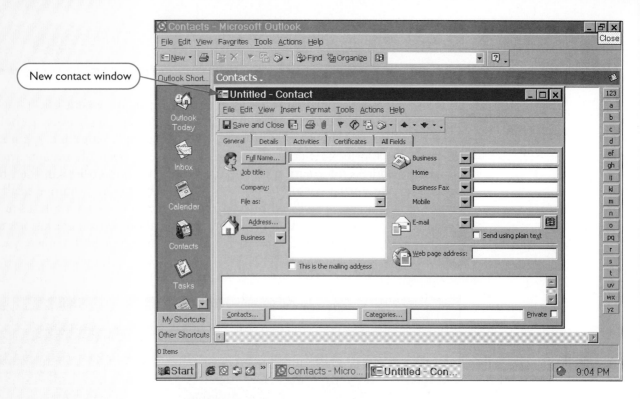

New contact window

FIGURE 11

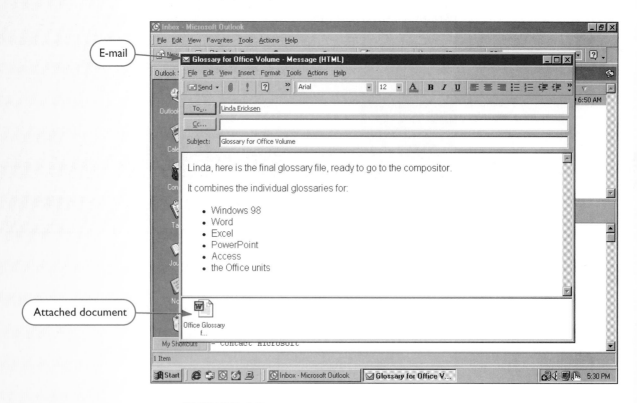

E-mail

Attached document

FIGURE 12

Introduction to Microsoft Office 2000

Microsoft Publisher 2000 is desktop publishing software that helps you create documents for publication. Publisher 2000 includes many wizards to walk you through the creation of documents ranging from newsletters, catalogs, flyers, and brochures, to greeting cards, menus, programs, and even origami and paper airplanes. Publisher 2000 provides help organizing your information and formatting the documents.

The *Quick, Simple Office 2000* text doesn't cover Microsoft Outlook 2000 or Microsoft Publisher 2000, because most college courses don't cover these two applications. However, after using *Quick, Simple Office 2000* and learning to use Microsoft Word 2000, Excel 2000, PowerPoint 2000, and Access 2000 along with Windows 98 and Internet Explorer 5, you should feel confident to experiment using these other applications. (See Figures 13 to 15.)

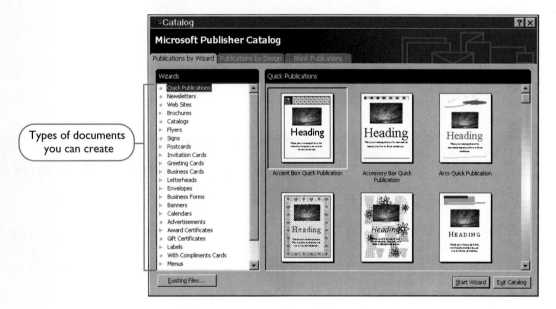

FIGURE 13

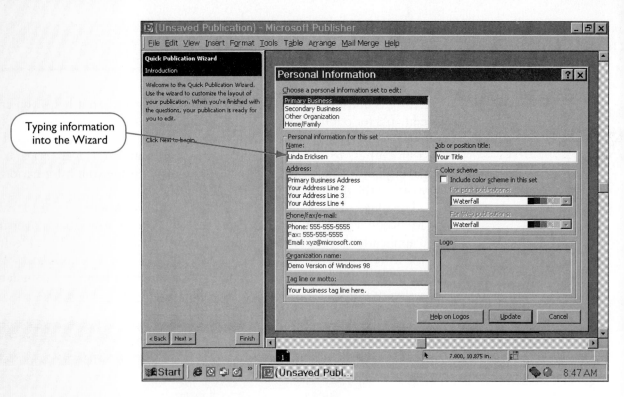

Typing information into the Wizard

FIGURE 14

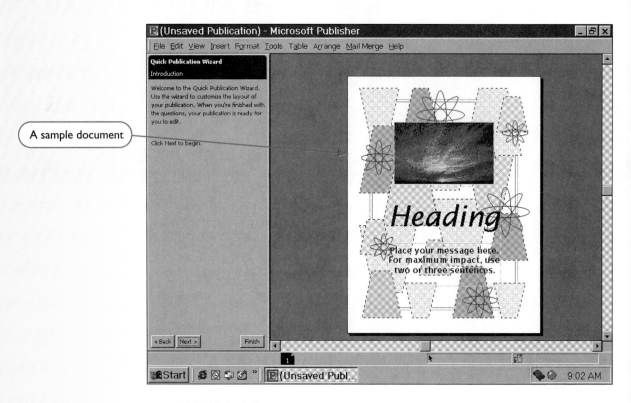

A sample document

FIGURE 15

A Personal Computer Guide

OBJECTIVES

- Define the parts of a personal computer
- Explain how a computer works
- Define your computing needs
- Compare vendors and understand the proper setup of a computer

Many people who use computers at work or school want to purchase a personal computer system for their homes but are unsure how to go about it. They want a system that will meet their present needs and be capable of expansion in the future. To purchase the right system, it is best to understand the parts of a personal computer system, to define your needs, and to learn enough terminology to understand computer ads.

Purchasing a computer is a lot like purchasing a car. You wouldn't buy a limousine to haul firewood or a sports car to go four-wheeling in the mountains. It's the same with a computer. If you are clear about your purpose and your needs, you can buy a computer with enough power to perform the tasks you need it to do, be flexible and expandable, and not cost any more than it has to.

TASK 1 | *Defining the Parts of a Personal Computer*

What: Identify the main elements of a computer system.

How: Read, talk to computer users, and shop around for information to become an informed consumer.

Why: Planning ahead for your hardware needs can help you avoid costly mistakes.

Tip: When shopping for a printer, always ask to see the actual printed output.

Computer systems are composed of two parts: **hardware**, the actual computer, and **software**, the programs that make the computer function. A **personal computer system** is made up of all the hardware components and programs that you would use in your home or small business. Most personal computer systems are stand-alone systems; that is, they are not connected to and dependent upon a network, as are the computers in colleges or large businesses.

Every computer system is made up of four types of hardware:

- **input devices**—used to get data into a computer
- **processing hardware**—used to perform operations on the data
- **output devices**—used to view the results of the processing
- **storage devices**—used to store programs and data

The next sections introduce the system unit, which contains the processing hardware, and then explain the main input, output, and storage devices. You'll learn about the actual processing hardware in the following task.

THE SYSTEM UNIT

When you think of a computer, your first image is probably that of a box. The box that contains the processing hardware is called the **system unit**. All of the other devices, known as **peripherals**, are contained in or attached to the system unit. The system unit can be a **desktop model** (lies flat on a desk), **mini-tower model** (stands vertically on a desk), **tower model** (stands under a desk), **laptop model** (portable with full keys on the keyboard), or **sub-laptop model** (smaller portable with reduced-size keys and fewer keys on the keyboard). Figure 1 shows typical mini-tower, desktop, and laptop computers.

> ## POINTER
>
> **CPU**
>
> The system unit is sometimes referred to as the central processing unit, or CPU, but that term is more often reserved for the microprocessor chip that does the actual computing.

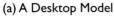

(a) A Desktop Model

(b) A Mini-Tower Model

(c) A Laptop Model

FIGURE I   Three Computer Models

Deciding which model of personal computer to purchase is one of the first choices to make.

- If you intend to use the computer in one location, a stationary model—a desktop, mini-tower, or tower—is the best choice. You will get more computing power per dollar spent and the advantage of a full-sized monitor.

- If you need expandability in a system, a tower or mini-tower is the best choice. Tower models have more free space inside them and larger power supplies to run more peripherals.

- If you plan to use the computer at home and at school or work, a laptop or sub-laptop is the way to go. The smaller models tend to sacrifice some usability for portability; that is, keyboards are smaller and screen display can be less clear than on a full-sized monitor. Also, disk drives to store files are usually smaller, and CPUs are slower than on a desktop or tower model.

You will learn about the processing components located inside the system unit in the following task.

INPUT DEVICES

Input devices are used to get information into the computer. The most common input devices are:

- keyboard
- mouse or other pointing device
- scanner
- digital camera
- microphone

Keyboards: The computer **keyboard** is an expansion of a typewriter keyboard that includes specialized keys. It is the most common means of inputting data into a computer. A keyboard is described by the number of keys it has. For example, newer keyboards have 104 keys, and keyboards advertised as Windows keyboards have an extra key on each side of the spacebar used to open the Windows Start menu.

Other newer keyboards include those based on ergonomic studies, which are designed to help avoid wrist stress for the typist. (**Ergonomics** is the science that studies the interaction of humans and technology.) Some keyboards, especially on laptops, may contain built-in pointing devices.

POINTER

QWERTY and Dvorak Keyboards

Keyboards are also described by the physical configuration of the keys on the keyboard. The traditional keyboard known as the *QWERTY keyboard* is named for the six top-left letter keys. This configuration was developed for the first manual typewriters to slow down the typist so that jamming keys could be avoided. A newer keyboard known as the *Dvorak keyboard* places the most commonly used keys on the home row, so that less finger movement is needed. Despite the fact that it is easier and faster to use, the Dvorak keyboard has not gained popularity because of the expense of training to implement it in schools and businesses.

Pointing Devices: The most common pointing device is the mouse. The mouse is connected to the computer either through its own port or through the serial port on the back of the computer. (A port is a plug, explained in the next task.) Inside the **mouse**, and exposed on its undersurface, is a rubber ball that rolls when you slide it on a flat surface. These movements are mirrored by the mouse pointer on the screen. The standard mouse has two buttons that you click to select screen elements, issue commands, and indicate the spot where you want to type. Some mice have a third, programmable button, and other mice have a wheel between the buttons, used for scrolling through documents. Alternatives to the mouse include the **trackball**, which contains the ball on top rather than underneath; the **touchpad**, which allows you to move your finger on a pad to move the pointer on the screen; and the **touchscreen**, which allows you to touch the screen directly. The **joystick** is a specialized pointing device used for playing computer games.

Scanners: Scanners read text or images and convert them to digital files that can be read and manipulated by computer software. A **scanner** connects to a computer through the parallel port or by means of an expansion card. A scanner works like a copy machine. You scan the original text or graphics to make a copy, but the copy is a digital file.

Digital Cameras: Digital cameras work like ordinary still or video cameras but record the images as digital files that can be loaded directly into computer software, without the need for scanning.

Microphones: Microphones work like ordinary mikes on cassette recorders or video cameras. The microphone plugs into the sound card through an expansion slot on the back of the computer.

OUTPUT DEVICES

The most common output devices include:

- monitor
- printer
- speakers or headphones

Monitors: The **monitor** is a video display device that shows the result of the input and processing on its screen. Physically, monitors are described by the size of the display. The standard size for a desktop model is 15″, and models from 17″ to 21″ are common. Most monitors use cathode ray tubes (CRTs) to display the image. These monitors are nearly as deep as they are wide. Newer flat-panel monitors that use liquid crystal displays (LCDs) occupy much less space on the desk but cost considerably more.

Color monitors are classified by industry standards that describe the number of colors and the amount of information they can display. Most of today's monitors can display from 16 to 16 million colors. Two color classifications commonly found are:

- High Color: 16-bit (65,536 or 64K colors)—useful for everyday work and entertainment
- True Color: 24-bit (16,777,216 or 16.8M colors)—necessary for professional graphic work

Resolution is defined by the number of **pixels**, short for picture elements, that are displayed on the screen. The more pixels or dots on the screen, the more information is displayed. Common display resolutions are:

- 640 pixels across x 480 pixels down
- 800 x 600 pixels
- 1024 x 768 pixels
- 1280 x 1024 pixels
- 1600 x 1200 pixels

The same 1280 pixels displayed on a 15-inch monitor will be smaller than on a 21-inch monitor, so the ideal resolution depends on monitor size. With a small monitor and a high resolution, text becomes so small that you can't read it. A resolution of 800 x 600 makes for readable text on most monitors.

> ### POINTER
>
> **SVGA**
>
> The video standard known as **SVGA (Super Video Graphics Array)** supports resolutions of 1600 x 1200 and up to 16 million colors. You will often see monitors described as SVGA monitors.

The inside of a CRT is coated with colored phosphors that glow when struck by a beam of electrons. The closer together these phosphors are on the tube, the sharper the image will be. The distance between two phosphors of the same color is known as the **dot pitch**. A dot pitch of 0.27mm (millimeters) is standard, and the smaller the number, the sharper the image.

> ### POINTER
>
> **Shadow Mask vs. Aperture Grill**
>
> The CRT display is produced in one of two ways: using a shadow mask or an aperture grill. The *shadow mask* is a metal plate punched with holes. It produces clear text and precise graphics. Standard dot pitch is usually 0.27mm between two phosphors of the same color. The *aperture grill* is a wire frame strung with vertical metal strings or stripes. It produces vibrant colors. The standard stripe pitch is 0.25mm.

Monitors are rated by how often they refresh or update the image on the screen. Slow refresh speeds can result in screen flicker that causes eyestrain. Vertical refresh rates of 70 hertz (70 times per second) or more are the standard.

Monitors are connected to the computer by a video adapter. The picture quality depends in large part on the specifications of this adapter, which is explained in the following section.

Printers: Printers produce a paper copy, also called a **hard copy**, of your documents. Printers connect to the computer through a parallel port. The two most common types of printers today are inkjet and laser. **Inkjet printers** work by spraying tiny droplets of ink onto paper to form text and graphics. Today most inkjet printers produce reasonably high-quality text and can produce excellent color graphics as well. The result is not waterproof, however, and must be handled with some care even after it has dried. **Laser printers** produce high-quality black-and-white hard copies and are usually faster than inkjet printers. The output is waterproof. Color laser printers are available, and though their prices are falling, they still cost more than a good PC.

Printers are rated by two measurements: the number of pages printed in one minute, and the resolution, measured in **dpi (dots per inch)**. You usually pay more for speed and higher resolution. Resolutions of 300 dpi can produce acceptable hard copies of text and screens, but 600 dpi produces noticeably better results. Going from 600 to 1,200 dpi doesn't produce much improvement in plain text but makes much clearer screens. For color graphics, resolution is important, but other elements can make just as much difference. Some inkjet printers come with special photo ink cartridges which, when used with high-quality papers, can produce stunning results. The price of the ink and paper can be high, however.

Speakers: PCs come with built-in speakers that are capable of producing the beeps and bells produced by most software. But to hear music or voice over a computer or the 3-D sound of some computer games, you need external speakers or headphones. Some monitors come with speakers attached, and most laptop computers have built-in speakers capable of reproducing music. Speakers are available that will rival the sound quality of low-end music sound systems. Many speaker systems have a left and right speaker and a subwoofer for low bass sounds. Some systems reproduce 3-D sound like that of home theater systems. Speakers are connected to the system through the sound card, explained later in the unit.

INPUT/OUTPUT DEVICES

Some hardware components may be used for both input and output. A **modem** (the word is shorthand for "modulate-demodulate") allows the computer to send and receive data over phone lines by converting the **digital signals** (discrete on/off signals) of the computer into **analog signals** (wave signals) that can be transmitted over phone connections. Modems are necessary to connect to the Internet from a personal stand-alone computer. They come in both internal and external models.

Most modems today are faxmodems, allowing you to send your documents to a fax machine or receive faxes using your computer and fax software.

> ### POINTER
>
> **Bits and Bytes**
>
> **Bit** is short for binary digit, which is equal to one "on" or "off" pulse or signal in the computer. By themselves, bits are practically meaningless; however, when combined in groups of eight, they form bytes, which represent a unit of meaningful data such as a number or letter. Bits are used to measure the number of pulses transmitted in a second. You'll see modems listed as 56Kbps, meaning that they are capable of transmitting 56 kilobits per second.

STORAGE DEVICES

Storage devices are used to store programs and to save computer files. The most common storage devices for personal computers are:

- hard disks
- floppy disks
- CD-ROM disks
- DVD-ROM disks
- removable media disks

Each type of storage device requires a peripheral attached to the computer to read the data stored on it. For example, if you are going to listen to CDs or install software that comes on CDs, you must have a CD-ROM drive; and to use a floppy disk, the system must contain a floppy drive.

Storage devices are categorized by the amount of data they can store, measured in bytes. A **byte** is made up of 8 bits of data and is equal to one **alphanumeric character** (any letter or number). Table 1 describes the units of measure.

Unit	Abbreviation	Amount
kilobyte	K, or KB	a thousand, actually 1,024
megabyte (called a *meg*)	M, or MB	a million, actually 1,048,576
gigabyte (called a *gig*)	G, or GB	a billion, actually 1,073,741,824
terabyte	T or TB	a trillion, actually 1,099,511,627,776

TABLE 1.1   Units of Measure

The **hard disk drive**, or fixed disk drive, is the main device used on personal computers to store programs and data. Most PCs come with a single hard disk drive. Hard disks of 25G were available when this text was written, and disks with larger capacities were being produced every few months. One rule of thumb for computers is that you can never have a hard drive that is too large, because today's programs use so much disk space. In fact, most people will not need a 25G hard drive, but the cost of big drives is not much more than that of small ones.

POINTER

Drive Speed and Disk Access

Hard disk drives run at different speeds and access data at different rates. Usually 7,200 RPM drives access data faster than 5,400 RPM drives. Drive access speed is measured in milliseconds (where lower numbers are faster), and you will see access speeds listed between 8ms and 12ms.

The **floppy disk drive** is used to copy data from the hard drive or to save files in a computer lab. The standard floppy disk is the 3½-inch high-density disk, which holds 1.44M of information.

CD-ROM (for Compact Disc Read-Only Memory) **drives** are used to read program and other data stored on compact disks. The disks look like music CDs and hold approximately 650MB of data. CD-ROM drives are rated by the speed with which they access the data on the CD. The first drives transferred data at 150K per second. Maximum transfer rates are measured by their multiple of that rate. Thus a 32X drive has a maximum transfer rate of 4800K per second. CD-ROM drives will read music CDs, but music CDs won't read CD-ROM disks. CD-ROM drives cannot write files; they are "read only." CD-R (CD-recordable) and CD-RW (CD-rewritable) drives exist that will both read and write files, and they are a useful way of backing up files on a computer system.

DVD-ROM drives read digital versatile disks and are similar to CD-ROMs but can hold up to 5.2G of data. They will probably replace the CD-ROM in the future.

Removable media drives are similar to floppies in that they can be used to transport data. The most popular removable media drive is Iomega's Zip drive. **Zip disks** hold 100M or 250M of data and are faster than a floppy disk but much slower than a hard disk drive. Sony and Imation also make drives of this size (the HiFD and the LS-120, or SuperDisk), and, unlike Zip disks, these will also read floppy disks. Iomega and other manufacturers also make larger-capacity removable drives. Iomega's Jaz drives hold 1G or 2G of data. Some of the drives come in both internal and external versions. The internal versions are faster, but some lower-end desktop computers don't have room for extra drives, and then the external ones are the only option. External drives also have the advantage of being movable.

POINTER

Backup Options

If you are storing a great amount of important information, a backup system is important to ensure against loss of data due to a hard disk crash or a natural event such as a fire or flood. **Tape backup drives** are specialized drives that are used to back up computer data on tape. For the average PC user, however, a dedicated tape backup system is cumbersome, slow, and a waste of money. Floppy disks are useful to back up documents but don't hold enough data to back up program files or other large files. Zip disks are very handy for this purpose, and Jaz disks even more so. Buying a second hard disk drive is another option. If you buy a second hard drive just like the first one, you can back up your whole system onto it.

TASK 2 | *Learning How Computers Work*

What: Learn how a computer works.

How: Read this text and then follow up with further reading or an Introduction to Computers course.

Why: Knowing how the parts of a computer work helps you decide what to buy and know what to expect of it once you own it.

Tip: If possible, try the keyboard and any pointing device you purchase to make sure that it feels comfortable to you.

To understand how a computer works, let's suppose that you sit down at a computer and type your name using the keyboard. Following the route of your name through the computer to the display monitor will help you understand how computers process data.

As you type the individual letters of your name using the keys on the keyboard, each keystroke is translated into a signal that is transmitted through the cable connected from the keyboard into a **port**, or plug, on the back of the computer. Your name is placed in a **RAM buffer**, or memory, which is a temporary holding area. It is transmitted along the bus, which consists of electrical circuits inside the **motherboard**, to be processed by the **CPU**, or **central processing unit**, the microprocessor chip that serves as the brains of the computer. The CPU translates and relays the signals that make up your name to the **video adapter card**, the **circuit board** (a board that contains electrical components) that controls the monitor display. The signal then travels along the cable from the video adapter card to the monitor, and your name is displayed.

If you take the cover off the system unit, you will see the components used to process and display your name. Figure 2 shows the inside of a mini-tower computer.

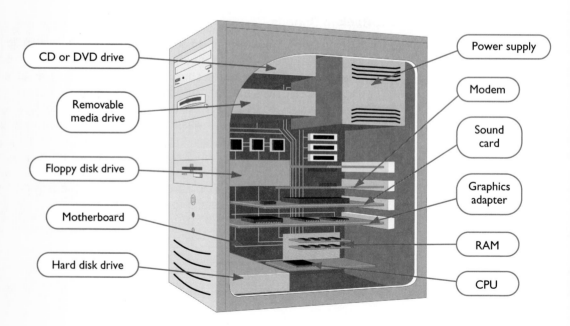

FIGURE 2   Inside a Mini-Tower Computer

MOTHERBOARD

The motherboard or system board is the main circuit board located along one wall of the system unit (in a desktop computer it's on the bottom.) The system board is the foundation that every computer component plugs into. All the data travel between the components that are plugged into the motherboard along a path known as a **bus**.

The type of bus determines how fast data can travel. Older buses, which carried 8 or 16 bits at a time, are likened to traveling along a two-lane country road, whereas newer buses, like a superhighway, carry 32 bits at a time.

- The **PCI** (Peripheral Component Interconnect) **local bus** is the current standard; it speeds up the computer's performance by linking the CPU with key components.
- The **AGP** (Accelerated Graphics Port) is not technically a bus, but it provides direct communication between the graphics chip and the system memory, speeding up video performance.
- The **USB** (Universal Serial Bus) is an external bus that allows up to 127 peripherals to use the same port at rapid speeds.
- Most of today's computers have the three buses listed above and also an **ISA** (Industry Standard Architecture) **bus** carrying 16 bits at a time. The ISA bus is being phased out.

Motherboards hold the central processing unit, ports and slots for the memory and peripherals, and the buses (the wires that connect the parts). Different motherboards contain different kinds and numbers of these parts. The greater the capacity, the more flexible the system is.

CENTRAL PROCESSING UNIT

The CPU is the microprocessor that processes all data in the computer system. Which CPU is contained in a computer has become so important that we refer to the entire computer system by its name—586, 686, AMD-K6, Pentium, Pentium II, Pentium III. The **Pentium**® processors are produced by the chip manufacturer Intel; other chips manufacturers (principally Cyrix and Advanced Micro Devices) produce similar chips but use other letter or number designations for their names.

The CPU determines the overall speed and power of the computer system. Some chips are like the four-cylinder engine in an economy car; others like a six- or eight-cylinder engine in a luxury or sports car. Chip speed is the rate at which the microprocessor processes data. This is determined by two factors: the speed of the system bus that delivers data to the processor and the speed at which the processor performs operations on the data. These speeds are measured in millions of cycles per second—**MHz**, that is, **Mega-Hertz**. The rate of the **system clock**, a circuit that paces the operations of the computer's circuits, determines how fast program instructions are executed. When this text was written, higher-end processors ran from 350MHz to 500MHz with a 100MHz bus speed. Lower-end models ran at 233MHz with a 66MHz bus speed.

RANDOM ACCESS MEMORY

RAM (Random Access Memory) is the temporary storage used to load programs and store data as you work on the computer. RAM is emptied when the computer is turned off. The amount of RAM a computer system has is a big factor in system performance because it determines the size of the programs and amount of data that can be processed without the computer's having to go back to the hard disk drive. RAM is measured in megabytes. Windows 98 programs will run slowly on computers with 32M of RAM but will run noticeably faster if 64M is available. Many memory-intensive software programs run better with 128M of RAM. RAM can be added to a system, but the amount can be limited by the number of RAM slots on the motherboard. The type of memory also affects the performance of the system. SDRAM—Synchronous Dynamic Random-Access Memory—is faster than DRAM—Dynamic Random-Access Memory. SDRAM synchronizes memory with the system clock. RAM chips come on small circuit boards called **DIMMs** (dual inline memory module) or **SIMMs** (single inline memory modules) with DIMMs being the standard for new computers.

CACHE

Cache is memory that is used to speed up the computer by placing recently executed instructions in a memory location. The cache can be physically located on the system board or even in the processor itself. Specialized caches, such as video cache, are located on adapter cards. Cache can be compared to placing papers that you need to refer to often on the top of your desk. If the information you need is not located on your desktop, you will search in the file cabinet. This is the same process used by the computer. When the CPU needs to execute an instruction, it searches for data in the cache. If it is there, the information is accessed faster than accessing it from RAM. However, if the instruction is not located in the cache, it is retrieved from RAM. Many computers today have a 512K **L2 cache** (Level 2 or secondary cache) external to the processor, while others have 128K of integrated cache.

PORTS

A port is a connector for attaching a device to a computer. PCs have internal ports for the floppy and fixed disk drives. They also have these external ports:

- parallel port—used for printers, removable media storage devices, scanners, and other peripherals; allows bits of data to pass through in groups of 8, 16, or 32
- serial port—can be used for many devices, including mice and modems; allows only 1 bit of data to pass through at time
- PS/2 port—a specialized port used for mice or keyboards

POWER SUPPLY

The **power supply unit** located inside the computer connects to the wall socket to provide the electricity necessary to run the computer. The power supply unit also converts AC electrical currents from the wall socket into DC voltages used by the computer. The power supply unit contains a fan used to cool the inside of the computer. A power supply of 200 watts is standard. Newer top-of-the-line computers have larger power supply units in order to run a lot of peripheral devices.

BIOS AND ROM

When the computer's on/off switch is turned to the on position and the computer **boots up** or powers up, the CPU contains no instructions and RAM is empty. Instructions about how to start the system are accessed from the **BIOS (Basic Input/Output System)** that is stored on the **ROM (Read-Only Memory)** chip. The ROM chip stores the start-up information even when the power is turned off, and it is read each time the computer is started.

EXPANSION CARDS AND SLOTS

Peripheral devices come with circuit boards called expansion cards. **Expansion cards** connect the device to the computer by plugging into **expansion slots** on the motherboard. Expansion slots are identified by the bus they use—ISA, PCI, or AGP—and expansion cards must match the slot type. The mini-tower computer shown in Figure 2 has a video card, sound card, and modem card attached to the motherboard.

The video adapter determines how fast the monitor loads graphic images and thereby helps determine the overall quality of the image on the screen. The card should be an SVGA to work easily with the SVGA monitor, and it should also contain as much memory as possible, with 2 megabytes as standard but with 8 megabytes desirable. Video adapters can be on their own circuit board or integrated with the motherboard. They plug into either a PCI slot or the dedicated AGP slot. (The Accelerated Graphics Port gives faster graphics performance.) Video adapter technology changes quickly. When this text was written, many new PCs were being offered with 128-bit graphics adapters with 8M or 16M of memory.

The **sound card** allows the computer to manipulate and output sounds. Nearly all computers today have a sound card, either as a separate expansion board Blaster®, or integrated with the motherboard. Cards with 32-bit sound produce sounds fast enough to sound real. The standard for sound is the one manufactured by Creative Labs, called the Sound Blaster®. Other manufacturers will describe theirs as Sound Blaster compatible. Sound cards are really multipurpose devices containing chips that perform several different functions. They have connectors for joysticks that are used to play computer games, for microphones that record sound, for CD-ROMs to play music CDs over the computer's speakers.

Modems are available in both internal and external models. External modems attach to one of the computer's serial ports. Internal modems are located on a circuit card placed in one of the existing expansion slots. Modems described as Windows modems rely on instructions built into the Windows operating system and will not work with other systems. Modems are rated by the speed that they transmit data. The standard today is 56 **Kbps**, or 56,000 **bits per second**. Most modems today are faxmodems, which enable you to send and receive faxes. The standard transmission rate for faxes is 14,400 Kbps, so you will see faxmodems listed as 56k/14.4.

Remember that in order to add new peripherals to your system, there must be open or unused expansion slots of the proper type.

TASK 3 | *Defining Your Needs*

What: Estimate your present and future hardware requirements.

How: List the uses you will make of your computer, and research the hardware needed to permit them.

Why: More people have purchased out-of-date computer systems that can't be upgraded than they have any other appliance or vehicle.

Tip: If you plan to expand your present system instead of replacing it with a new one when your needs change, be sure to buy a computer with free expansion slots and drive bays.

Before you get on the phone, start a Web browser, or walk into a computer store to buy a computer, you should narrow your requirements by defining your computer needs. If you don't know specifically what you plan to use a computer for, you may end up buying the equivalent of a VW bug to haul around your three Great Danes.

Talk to each person who will use the computer and ask what he or she would like to do with it. Here is a list of typical uses for the home or small business:

- write letters, envelopes, and labels
- merge addresses and correspondence
- write reports
- balance the checkbook
- prepare budgets
- fill out tax returns
- bring home files from school or work
- connect to the Internet
- send e-mail
- pay bills
- play games and simulations
- use educational software
- research genealogy
- keep track of payroll
- develop marketing materials
- keep personnel records

Using the lists you create, research what software and hardware you will need for each item. For example, if you want to use a flight simulator, you'll need a joystick; but if you are not interested in complex games or simulations, a mouse will be adequate. When you know what software you will be using, read the box it comes in to see what hardware it requires.

Then make a list of the hardware and specifications necessary for the system to meet your needs. Create a list of peripherals that are desirable though not necessary. Decide what you are willing to sacrifice to keep within your budget—an extra device, overall performance, a smaller hard disk, the ability to expand later.

Here are some tips on expandability:

- The processor, processor speed, and bus type are not easily upgraded and should be the first consideration when you are purchasing a system.
- Given a Universal Serial Bus or plenty of free expansion slots, you can add peripheral devices later.
- Given a free RAM slot, you can add RAM in the future.
- The only way to upgrade a hard drive is to replace the original or add another to the system.

Now look at computer ads for typical configurations, and use Table 2 to narrow the available options. Adapt the table to your needs.

Available Options	My Needs
Model—configuration	
CPU—type	
CPU—clock speed	
RAM—size and type	
RAM slots—number	
Hard disk drive—size	
CD-ROM or DVD-ROM drive	
Keyboard—style	
Mouse—style	
Expansion slots—number free	
Modem type—Winmodem? faxmodem? V.90?	
Sound card	
Speakers or headset	
Monitor—size, resolution, dot pitch	
Video adapter card—memory	
Printer—type, speed, resolution	
Other peripherals wanted	

TABLE 2 Computer System Options

The best rule is to buy a computer only after you have done enough research so that you feel like an informed user.

TASK 4 | *Purchasing and Setting Up a Computer*

What: Decide which computer system to buy and where to buy it.
How: Conduct your own research and read the fine print.
Why: If you buy in haste, you may have a long time to regret it.
Tip: If you find that many outlets have the same basic configuration, price, and warranty, check for extras like a printer cable and printer paper to get you started.

Deciding where to buy the system can be complex. Choices include electronics stores, department stores, discount stores, local resellers, PC superstores, office supply stores, ordering by mail, Internet shopping, and having a computer built to your specifications from a major manufacturer such as Dell, Gateway, or Micron. It's worthwhile to check several outlets. Be sure to check the reputation of vendors with friends and co-workers before you buy.

POINTER

Hardware-Software Bundles

Many special packages or **bundles** of hardware and software can save you money. However, be sure that the hardware meets the specifications you want and that the software includes current releases of programs you will use. Many higher-end systems offer a version of Microsoft Office as part of the package. Make sure that the version offered includes the software applications you plan to use. (For instance, if you plan to use Microsoft Access, you will need the Professional or Premium edition, which is not usually offered in a package.) As is true with all shopping, some specials can end up not saving you money.

Figure 3 shows specifications for two computers taken from recent ads. By now you should be able to read and understand the specifications they list, though you may not know all of the abbreviations. The ads you see in your own newspapers will not match these ads, because nothing changes much faster than computer specifications, with new and better products being offered for lower prices every month if not every week. There are plenty of under-$1,000 computers available today that offer good value, but for some users the expenditure of three times that much is worthwhile. Let's take a close look at the specifications.

As with most advertisements, it is not only what is said that's important, but also what's not said. Neither ad tells how many slots are available for expansion of memory or peripherals. In the desktop computer, no brand of chip or printer is

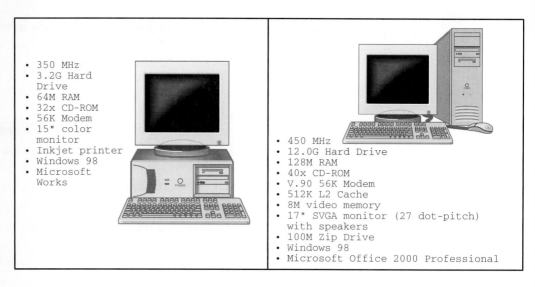

- 350 MHz
- 3.2G Hard Drive
- 64M RAM
- 32x CD-ROM
- 56K Modem
- 15" color monitor
- Inkjet printer
- Windows 98
- Microsoft Works

- 450 MHz
- 12.0G Hard Drive
- 128M RAM
- 40x CD-ROM
- V.90 56K Modem
- 512K L2 Cache
- 8M video memory
- 17" SVGA monitor (27 dot-pitch) with speakers
- 100M Zip Drive
- Windows 98
- Microsoft Office 2000 Professional

FIGURE 3   Two Computer Ads

specified. The ad doesn't mention the dot pitch for the monitor or whether the monitor is SVGA. The modem is not described as V.90. No mention is made of sound card or video memory, so these are probably integrated on the motherboard. The difference between Microsoft Works (a home-based integrated package offered with the desktop system) and Microsoft Office 2000 Professional is huge. But the desktop system includes a printer, and its specifications look adequate for doing word processing, creating ordinary worksheets, and browsing the Web. Though it may sound plenty big, a 3.2G hard drive may not be adequate if you plan to do a lot of work with graphics. The mini-tower system is probably more expandable, and it has a Zip drive for backing up files. From what you have learned in this unit, you would know what questions to ask a salesperson in order to evaluate the systems more fully.

WARRANTY

When purchasing a vehicle, the reputation of the dealer and the warranty are important considerations. The warranty is also an important consideration when you are purchasing a computer. Even though you purchase carefully and manufacturers have quality control standards, parts can break or malfunction. Ask to see the warranty in writing and then read it carefully and ask questions.

- Look first for the return policy, that is, for how long a period can you try the machine and return it for a full refund. Local vendors will probably give you 14 days or less. However, if you are buying through mail order, you should look for a 30-day full return without a restocking fee. You shouldn't expect a supplier to pay the return freight charge if you return a machine that isn't faulty.

- Second, check out the length of the overall warranty. What happens after the first 30 days? Who will repair it? Where will it be repaired? A 100% parts and labor warranty might sound adequate, but some manufacturers will simply mail you the part to install yourself. Does the dealer provide on-site service where a technician is sent to your home or office, or do you need to box up your system and mail it to an authorized repair shop? If you need to deliver or mail your system to a repair shop, is a loaner provided free of charge while your machine is being repaired? What is the average turnaround time on repairs?

- Third, find out about the availability and cost of an extended warranty and then decide whether you want it. Some people feel that computers become outdated so quickly that purchasing an extended warranty is a waste of money. Others plan to keep their computer and upgrade it, and prefer to have it under warranty for a longer time.
- Fourth, check technical support. If you have a question, does the dealer or manufacturer have 24-hour toll-free technical support, and what is the average wait on hold?

TIPS

Here are some final tips before you pick up the phone:

- Don't rely on brand name alone to determine what you purchase. Look at all the components in the system.
- Read ads carefully and then check out the system. An advertisement for a Pentium for under $400 might sound great, but that tells you very little about the overall performance of the system.
- Make sure that you receive all the manuals for the system you are purchasing.
- If purchasing by mail order, use a credit card to avoid fraud. Don't purchase from a reseller that wants only cash.
- Rely on your own reaction to salespeople and the reputation of the dealer.
- Ask questions to find out whether the salesperson knows what he or she is talking about. Remember that a computer salesperson's job is to sell computers.
- Make sure the computer comes with the operating system loaded. That is, Windows 98 should be installed on the hard drive, so that you can simply turn on the machine.
- If the system comes with software, make sure that it is the latest version. If it is already installed on the hard disk, does it come with manuals? Some software does not have printed manuals but instead has a CD-ROM disk on which the help files are contained. Make sure you receive all appropriate manuals.
- If training is included, find out when the next training session is, whether computers are provided for hands-on training, and where the session is held.
- If buying locally, check to see if the dealer is a certified repair facility for the brand you plan to purchase. Go into the repair shop to see that it is functional and staffed.
- Make sure you get all the cables you need to connect peripherals such as the printer to the computer.
- Buy a surge protector and a box of formatted floppy disks when you buy the computer system (or see whether you can get them included with the purchase). The reasons for this tip are explained in the next section.

SETTING UP THE SYSTEM

Connecting computer components is usually quite easy because most will have only one possible connection, and many manufacturers color-code them.

Don't plug your computer components directly into a wall socket. Instead, plug them into a surge protector, and plug the **surge protector** into the wall socket. Surge protectors protect the system against a power spike; some models provide a phone jack to protect your modem also.

When you turn on your computer the first time, you may see a message asking you to back up some system or utility files. Have a box of formatted floppy disks handy to perform this backup, and keep the backup disks in a safe place in case things go wrong.

Register your software and peripherals if asked to do so. Registering gives you access to customer support lines and may get you notification of upgrades. Read the registration form to see whether there's a spot where you can agree or refuse to be put on a mailing list or telemarketing list. It's easy to overlook such a check box, and the result can be unwanted calls.

It's a good idea to turn a new computer on and leave it running for a week or more. Many components will fail quickly if there is something wrong with them. Check out all the components and be sensitive to possible problems. The list below provides some things to watch out for.

- Does the screen flicker?
- Is the mouse very stiff?
- Does the system make a great deal of noise?
- Do keys stick on the keyboard?
- Does the system shut down when you are using it?
- Do you get thrown out of software as you are using it?
- Do you get an error message on startup?
- Do you get a recurring error message when you are using the system?

Remedy any of these or other problems as soon as possible by contacting your vendor.

REVIEW

SUMMARY

After completing this unit, you should be able to
- define the parts of a personal computer (page 2)
- outline how a computer works (page 10)
- define your needs (page 15)
- compare vendors and set up a computer (page 17)

KEY TERMS

AGP (Advanced Graphics Port) (page 11)

alphanumeric character (page 8)

analog signal (page 7)

BIOS (Basic Input/Output System) (page 13)

bit (page 7)

boot up (page 13)

bus (page 11)

byte (page 8)

cache (page 12)

CD-ROM drive (page 9)

circuit board (page 10)

CPU (central processing unit) (page 10)

desktop model (page 2)

digital camera (page 5)
digital signal (page 7)
DIMM (page 12)
dot pitch (page 6)
dpi (dots per inch) (page 7)
DVD-ROM drive (page 9)
ergonomics (page 4)
expansion card (page 13)
expansion slot (page 13)
floppy disk drive (page 9)
gigabyte (GB) (page 8)
hard copy (page 6)
hard disk drive (page 8)
hardware (page 2)
inkjet printer (page 6)
input device (page 2)
ISA bus (page 11)
joystick (page 4)
Kbps (page 14)
keyboard (page 4)
kilobyte (KB) (page 8)
L2 cache (page 12)
laptop model (page 2)
laser printer (page 6)
megabyte (MB) (page 8)
MHz (MegaHertz) (page 11)
microphone (page 5)
mini-tower model (page 2)
MMX (MultiMedia extensions) (page 12)
modem (page 7)
monitor (page 5)
motherboard (page 10)
mouse (page 4)
output device (page 2)

PCI local bus (page 11)
Pentium® (page 11)
peripheral (page 2)
personal computer system (page 2)
pixel (page 5)
port (page 10)
power supply unit (page 13)
processing hardware (page 2)
RAM buffer (page 10)
RAM (Random Access Memory) (page 12)
removable media drive (page 9)
resolution (page 5)
ROM (Read-Only Memory) chip (page 13)
scanner (page 5)
SIMM (page 12)
software (page 2)
sound card (page 14)
storage device (page 2)
sub-laptop model (page 2)
surge protector (page 19)
SVGA (Super Video Graphics Array) (page 6)
system clock (page 11)
system unit (page 2)
tape backup drive (page 9)
terabyte (TB) (page 8)
touchpad (page 5)
touchscreen (page 5)
tower model (page 2)
trackball (page 4)
USB (Universal Serial Bus) (page 11)
video adapter card (page 10)
Zip® disk (page 9)

TEST YOUR SKILLS

True/False

1. In order to expand a computer system, you must add a new disk drive.
2. All components in a computer system plug into the computer's motherboard.
3. Input devices display the result of processing.
4. A modem is necessary to connect a stand-alone computer to the phone lines.
5. A surge protector can help protect your system from power spikes.

Multiple Choice

1. The brains of a computer is its
   a. RAM   b. CPU
   c. L2   d. G
2. The internal memory used to store the programs and data as you work is
   a. RAM   b. CPU
   c. L2   d. G
3. The set of instructions used by the computer at start-up is the
   a. ROM   b. MMX
   c. DVD   d. BIOS
4. The current video standard is
   a. QWERTY   b. SVGA
   c. RAM   d. ROM
5. The individual picture element on a screen is
   a. pixel   b. PCI
   c. dot pitch   d. SVGA

Short Answer

Match the definition in the right column with the term in the left.

___ 1. MHz	a. measurement of display resolution
___ 2. DPI	b. measurement of floppy disk storage
___ 3. G	c. measurement of hard disk storage
___ 4. M	d. measurement of modem transmission speed
___ 5. Kbps	e. measurement of processor speed

What Does This Do?

Write a description of the function of each of the following:

1. RAM	6. expansion slot
2. CPU	7. L2 cache
3. ROM	8. CD-ROM
4. DVD	9. power supply
5. hard drive	10. surge protector

On Your Own

1. Go to the library and find an article about the current computer standards in a computer magazine.
2. Talk to several people who own computer systems and find out what they like or what they dislike about their models.
3. Visit a computer store and try out various brands or models.
4. Save computer ads for a month to see trends in the market.
5. Visit a software store to help you determine the exact software you want on a system.

PROJECTS

1. Table 3 gives specifications for two computer systems as found in recent ads. Write a brief explanation of which one you would purchase and why you would purchase it.

Computer A	Computer B
380MHz 64M RAM 8.0G Hard Drive 32x CD-ROM 56K V.90 Modem 4M 100MHz Video Memory SVGA 17" SVGA .28 dot pitch monitor Inkjet printer Windows 98	400MHz Pentium® with 512K L2 Cache 96M RAM 9.6G Hard Drive 3rd Generation DVD-ROM 56K V.90 Modem 4M 100MHz Video Memory SVGA 17" SVGA .28 dot pitch monitor with speakers 100 MB Zip drive Inkjet printer Windows 98

TABLE 3　Specifications for Two Systems

2. Use Table 4 to compile information about two competitive systems for sale at the current time. If you are working from real ads, attach the ads to your copy of the table.

Item	Computer A	Computer B
Model—configuration		
CPU—type		
CPU—clock speed		
RAM—size and type		
RAM slots—number		
Hard disk drive—size		
CD-ROM or DVD-ROM drive		
Keyboard—style		
Mouse—style		
Expansion slots—number free		
Modem type—Winmodem? faxmodem? V.90?		
Sound card		
Speakers or headset		
Monitor—size, resolution, dot pitch		
Video adapter card—memory		

(continued)

TABLE 4　Comparison Worksheet

Item	Computer A	Computer B
Printer—type, speed, resolution		
Other peripherals wanted		
Software		
Price		

TABLE 4   Comparison Worksheet *(continued)*

3. a. You have been given a loan for $1,000 to purchase a computer system for use in school. Find an actual system that meets all your needs. Write up a detailed specifications sheet of the computer.

   b. You are starting a small business in your home and want to keep customer lists, inventory, and budgets and to connect to the Internet. Write a detailed specifications sheet of the computer that is the result of your research.

4. If you have access to the Internet, research the following sites:
   - *PC Magazine* at http://www.zdnet.com/pcmag
   - *PC World Magazine* at http://pcworld.com
   - *Home Office Computing Magazine* at http://www.smalloffice.com
   - *Smart Computing Magazine* at http://wwwsmartcomputing.com
   - *c | net's Shoppers Guide* at http://www.shopper.com
   - Intel at http://www.intel.com
   - Microsoft at http://www.microsoft.com
   - IBM computers at http://www.ibm.com
   - Hewlett Packard computers at http://www.hp.com
   - Dell computers at http://www.dell.com
   - Gateway computers at http://www.gateway.com

Using Internet Explorer to Explore the World Wide Web

OBJECTIVES

- Be able to connect to the Internet and the World Wide Web
- Use Internet Explorer to explore the World Wide Web
- Search the World Wide Web

The World Wide Web is the most important communications phenomenon of the late 20th century. It has experienced explosive growth and continues to link people around the globe in greater numbers every day. The Web is important to personal lives, to businesses, and to governments. This unit presents information about the World Wide Web that will help you understand it and get started using it. You are introduced to Internet Explorer, software that allows you to explore or **browse** the World Wide Web, and you will also conduct searches, learning how to get to the information you desire.

What: Understand what the World Wide Web is and get connected to it.

How: Choose an Internet Service Provider that works for you.

Why: The World Wide Web is the largest storehouse of information on earth.

Tip: Remember that anyone can post to the World Wide Web, so check the source of the information you plan to use.

Many people think that the Internet and the World Wide Web are the same entity. The **Internet**, also called the **information superhighway**, is the network of computer networks that spans the globe. These networks are linked together through telephone lines, satellite links, cables, and other means. The Internet is a **distributed system**; that is, there is no central computer running the network, which means that if part of the network goes down, the rest can still function. This was a goal of the U.S. Department of Defense, the early developer of the Internet that linked computers at universities, research centers, and government installations. Today, the Internet has grown far beyond developers' dreams. From being used almost exclusively by computer experts at government agencies, research facilities, and universities, it has become a part of the daily lives of millions of private individuals and businesses.

The **World Wide Web** consists of all the documents, called **Web pages**, located on computers all over the Internet, consequently all over the world. Computers that host Web documents are known as **Web servers**. Web documents contain **hyperlinks**, "hot" references to other documents that can be text or graphics. When you click a hyperlink in a document, you are transferred to the referenced document because the hyperlink contains the address of that linked document. When a document contains "hot" text, or **hypertext**, it usually appears formatted as blue and underlined. The mouse pointer changes to a pointing hand when you point to a hyperlink in a document, indicating that the object is a link.

Many people refer to Web documents as home pages. A **home page** refers to the top or starting page in a related group of documents. These related documents that are linked together constitute a **Web site** for a company, individual, or organization.

In order to view Web pages, your computer must have specialized software known as a **browser**. Browsers can display documents created in **HyperText Markup Language (HTML)** the universal language of the Web. Microsoft has built the browser Internet Explorer right into the Windows 98 operating system, making for easy access. You will get started using Internet Explorer in the next task. Microsoft has also made conversion of Office 2000 documents into HTML very easy, and you will use this feature in software modules throughout this text.

There are two steps that you need to take before you are ready to sit down at your home computer and browse the World Wide Web.

- First, if your system didn't come with a modem, you will need to purchase one. Make sure the modem is "plug and play," so all you have to do is plug it in and turn on your computer (and, if Windows asks you to, insert the disk that comes with it into the drive). The current standard for modems is the V.90 standard. See "A Personal Computer Guide" elsewhere in this book for details.

- Second, you will need to contract with an **Internet Service Provider (ISP)**. An ISP is the most common way to connect personal computers to the Internet.

POINTER

Connecting to the Internet at School

Most schools today use computer networks to link all the computers in a building, location, or entire college. These networks provide Internet access through specialized computers known as gateways, so that you don't use a modem or a dial-up connection to connect to the Internet.

When a modem is installed in your system and you have contracted with an Internet Service Provider for a dial-up account, you dial the ISP, usually by clicking its icon on the desktop. The ISP then connects you via a high-speed link to the Internet. Your browser software starts, and you are ready to browse the Web or perform other Internet-related activities.

CHOOSING AN INTERNET SERVICE PROVIDER

Choosing the right Internet Service Provider can be a difficult task. Many people make their decision based solely on price. Price should be a consideration, but service, support, and speed should also be considered. Table 1 provides information to help you choose an ISP.

Question	Explanation
Is there a start-up fee?	Many ISPs charge no fee and give a month's free service; if a fee is charged, what does it provide?
Is there customer support for getting started and for problems after you are set up? Is it available 24 hours a day?	New users may need help getting set up, and even experienced users may encounter problems from time to time.
Can you access the ISP using a local number?	If the answer is no, you may end up paying long distance fees, and your phone bill can go through the roof.
Does the ISP have local phone numbers throughout the country? If not, is there a toll-free number for access away from home?	Access to your account while you are traveling is a desired feature.
What is the ratio of modems to users? One rule of thumb is 10 to 20 users per modem.	Few modems and a large number of users result in frequent busy signals.
Does the ISP provide space to host a Web site? If so, how much space?	Most ISPs offer space, but some offer as little as 2MB, which would not be enough space except for a very small personal site.

(continued)

TABLE I   Questions for an Internet Service Provider

Question	Explanation
What fee plans are available?	Some plans offer limited access for a low fee and charge hourly fees for extra use; other plans offer unlimited use for a fixed monthly fee.
Can you use the browser of your choice with the ISP?	If no, do you have to use a particular software package?
How fast is the ISP's access?	Does it offer 56Kbps access, and is your 56K modem compatible with its system?
Does the ISP offer a free trial period?	If yes, find out how to cancel the service before you sign up. Many require a credit card number before the trial service can begin, and then automatically bill the credit card account after the trial period.

TABLE I   Questions for an Internet Service Provider *(continued)*

Internet Service Providers come in all sizes. You can use large national service providers such as AOL (America Online) or MSN (Microsoft Network); mid-sized service providers that are usually regionally based; or small local providers. There are even service providers known as **freenets** that are staffed mostly by volunteers and are usually associated with a library or community center. Many new ISPs are springing up all the time, and established companies, such as cable TV and telephone companies, are expanding their services into this market. When you are ready to begin service, you should research current offerings.

POINTER

Internet Connection Wizard

Windows 98 contains the Internet Connection Wizard, which will present you with a list of some of the ISPs in your locality and let you sign up for one on the spot. To use the Wizard, click its button on the desktop or click the Start button and choose Programs I Internet Explorer I Connection Wizard.

EXERCISE 1   *Finding an Internet Service Provider*

1. Use the library, newspaper ads, or other sources to find the names of ISPs in your area.
2. Call local ISPs to determine level of service and price.
3. Use the **Internet Connection Wizard** to see what it offers in your area.

TASK 2 | *Using Microsoft Internet Explorer*

What: Use Internet Explorer to browse the World Wide Web.

How: Click the Internet Explorer icon on the desktop or click the Start button and choose Programs | Internet Explorer.

Why: To connect to the World Wide Web, you must use browser software such as Internet Explorer.

Tip: If you plan to spend a lot of time connected to the Internet, you might want to have a second phone line installed, so you aren't tying up your only phone connection.

Internet Explorer is the browser that comes as part of the Microsoft Windows 98 operating system.

To start Internet Explorer:

1. Click the Internet Explorer icon on the desktop or the Launch Internet Explorer Browser button on the Quick Launch toolbar. Your modem will dial the Internet Service Provider that you selected.
2. Internet Explorer will open on the desktop and display a Web page. The page shown will vary. Figure 1 shows the Internet Explorer 5 window with Microsoft's home page.

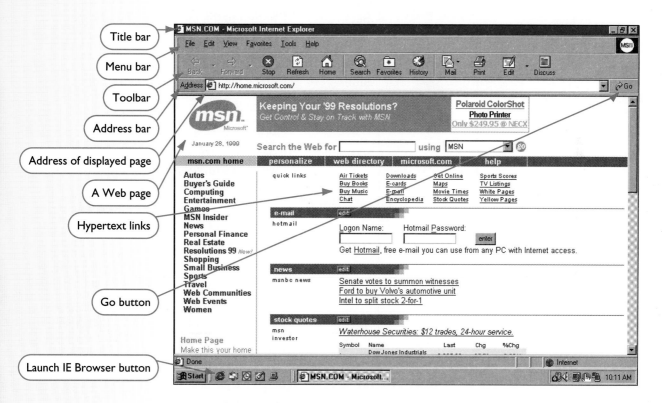

FIGURE I   The Internet Explorer Window

Using the browser Internet Explorer is quite easy. Table 2 describes the buttons on the Internet Explorer's Standard Buttons toolbar.

Button	Name	Description
Back	Back	Return to the previously viewed page
Forward	Forward	If you have gone back to a page, sends you forward again
Stop	Stop	Stops the current page from loading
Refresh	Refresh	Reloads the current page
Home	Home	Displays the page designated as your home page
Search	Search	Displays the Explorer bar's Search pane, with links to tools you can use to search for documents on the World Wide Web
Favorites	Favorites	Displays the Explorer bar's Favorites pane, with a list of pages you have indicated you want to return to
History	History	Displays the Explorer bar's History pane, with a list of pages you have visited in recent days or weeks
Mail	Mail	Opens Outlook Express or another Mail program, allowing you to read and send mail if you have an Internet e-mail account
Print	Print	Prints the open page
Edit	Edit	Opens the page to be edited in your Web page editor
Discuss	Discuss	Connects to a discussion server in order to connect to an online discussion

TABLE 2   The Internet Explorer Toolbar

You can display documents from around the world—doing research, checking business statistics, finding out about alternative health care, playing games, chatting with people online, planning a vacation or a move to a new city, or just browsing (called **surfing**). Just about anything you can think of probably has been posted to the World Wide Web. Once you find information that you want to keep, you can print a Web document that is displayed on the screen by choosing File | Print.

POINTER

Hypertext Colors Change When You Visit a Site

A hypertext link you haven't yet clicked is blue, but once you visit the site, the hypertext changes color (to purple by default) to let you know you've been there already.

ENTERING A WEB ADDRESS

If you know the Web address (the **Uniform Resource Locator**, or **URL**) of an Internet site, you can go directly to it by typing the address in the Address text box in Internet Explorer. For example, if you want to connect to World Wildlife Fund and you know that its address, or URL, is http://www.wwf.org, you can type the address in the Address bar's text box and click the Go button, and WWF's home page will open in your browser, as shown in Figure 2.

FIGURE 2   Entering an Address in the Address Bar's Text Box

Typing Internet Addresses

You must type a URL precisely in order to display the Web page. Note that the forward slash character is used instead of the backslash character. If the address uses a lowercase letter, you can't type a capital.

The parts of the URL that make up a Web address are shown in Table 3.

Component	Explanation
http://	**HyperText Transfer Protocol** (the communication standard used for Web documents) informs your browser that a Web page is being transmitted
www.wwf.org	The domain name, or address, of the server that stores the document (the *www* stands for *World Wide Web*; see Table 4 for an explanation of *org*)
index.html	The document name (the *html* stands for *HyperText Markup Language*)

TABLE 3   An Internet Address Explained: http://www.wwf.org/index.html

The three-letter domain name refers to the type of organization that owns the site. For example, the World Wildlife Fund is a nonprofit organization, so it has the top-level designation **org**. Table 4 lists six top-level domain names.

Domain Name	Type of Organization
edu	Educational institution
org	Nonprofit organization
gov	Government agency
com	Commercial or business entity
mil	Military organization
net	Network

TABLE 4   The Six Top-Level Domains

POINTER

Guessing Internet Names

If you want to connect to a business or organization but don't know its URL, you can try to connect using some guesswork. For example, if you want to connect to Microsoft, you might try *www.microsoft.com*. Notice that the company name is the name of the site and the *com* domain name works because Microsoft is a business.

To get a feeling for the size of the World Wide Web, go to the http://www.domainstats.com site, which provides up-to-date statistics on the World Wide Web. Figure 3 shows the home page of this site. Notice the number of .com sites, that is, the number of businesses using the Web.

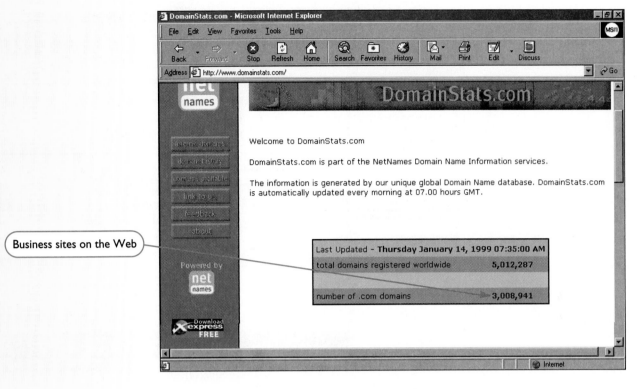

FIGURE 3 The DomainStats Home Page

FAVORITES

After you become familiar with browsing the Web, you may want to return to sites that you have already visited. You can save the addresses of pages you want to come back to in the Favorites list.

To add a page to your collection of favorite pages:

1. Display the page you want to add.
2. Choose Favorites | Add to Favorites. The Add Favorite dialog box opens, as shown in Figure 4.

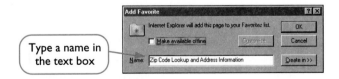

FIGURE 4 The Add Favorite Dialog Box

3. In the Name text box, type an easy-to-remember name for the page and click OK. The name you typed is stored in the Favorites folder, along with the URL of the site.

Later when you want to return to the site, click the Favorites button on the Internet Explorer toolbar. The Favorites pane opens with the list of shortcuts to the pages you want to return to. Click the name of the Favorite and you are taken to the page, as shown in Figure 5.

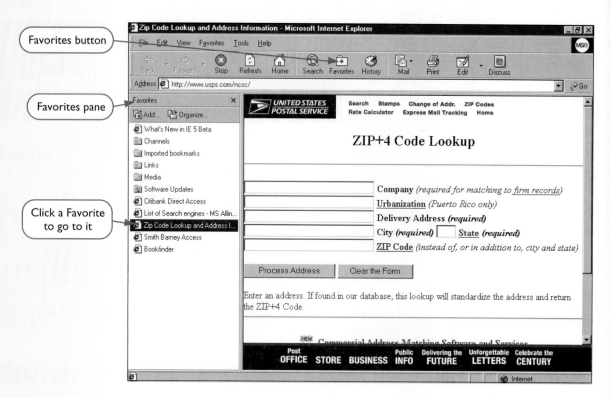

FIGURE 5   Using the Favorites Pane to Display a Favorite Web Site

After adding several Web sites to the Favorites folder, you may want to organize them by placing related sites in the same folder, deleting sites you no longer want to visit, or renaming the shortcuts listed in the Favorites pane.

To organize your favorite pages into folders, choose Favorites | Organize Favorites, and the Organize Favorites dialog box opens, as shown in Figure 6a.

- To create a new folder, click the Create Folder button. A new folder is created in the list. Type a name for the folder, just as you would do in a Windows Explorer window, and press Enter.

- To move a Favorite to a folder, select the Favorite; then click the Move to Folder button to open the Browse for Folder dialog box, shown in Figure 6b. Click a folder and then click the OK button. You can also drag a Favorite to a new position in the list. A heavy horizontal insertion point shows where it will be dropped when you release the mouse button.

- To rename or delete a Favorite, select it and click the appropriate button in the dialog box.

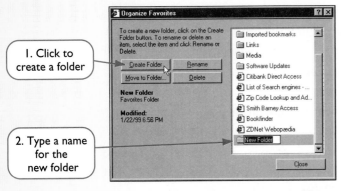

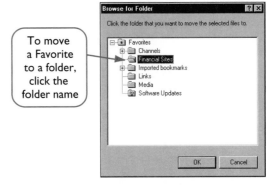

(a) The Organize Favorites Dialog Box   (b) The Browse for Folder Dialog Box

FIGURE 6   Organizing the Favorites List

POINTER

The History Pane

Internet Explorer provides a History pane that records Web sites that you have visited recently. To open the History pane, click the History button. Then click a site in the History list to be returned to it.

EXERCISE 2 | *Using Internet Explorer*

1. Start **Internet Explorer**.
   Click the program's desktop icon or the Launch Internet Explorer Browser button on the Quick Launch toolbar.

2. Click a **hypertext link**.
   Hypertext links are underlined. When you point to one, the pointer changes to a hand with a pointing finger. Scroll down the page if necessary to find a link.

3. View the page you are taken to, and then click the toolbar's **Back** button to return to the previous page.

4. In the Address bar's text box, type **www.sportsline.com** (type it exactly as shown), and then click the **Go** button.
   You are taken to the home page of CBS Sportsline. The actual address is http://www.sportsline.com, but Internet Explorer will let you leave off the http.

5. Choose **Favorites | Add to Favorites**.
   The Add Favorites dialog box opens.

6. Click in the text box and type **SportsLine**, then click the **OK** button.
   The name you typed is stored in the Favorites folder, along with the URL of the Web page.

7. Browse this site, clicking links that interest you. Stop after a few minutes.
   Don't worry about getting back home.

8. Click the **Back button's down arrow** to display a list of pages you have visited, and click the address you started with.
   You are taken back to your home page.

9. Click the **Favorites** button.
   The Favorites pane opens.

10. Click the shortcut to **SportsLine**.
    The site is again displayed on the screen.

11. Click the **Favorites** button.
    The Favorites pane closes.

12. Choose **File | Print**.
    The Print dialog box opens.

13. Click **OK**.
    The SportsLine home page prints on the default printer.

14. Exit from Internet Explorer.

TASK 3 | *Searching the World Wide Web*

What: Find useful information on the Web.

How: Learn to use the various types of search tools.

Why: Finding useful information on the Web can be a challenge.

Tip: Check the online help for each search tool you use regularly to find search tips for that particular tool.

Most people cite finding information as their number one Web-related activity; however, these same people cite locating valuable information as their biggest frustration. Because the Internet is a distributed system with Web documents located on servers all over the world, there is no central computer with a centralized database that lists the millions of publicly owned pages that exist. In order to find information, you must use a search tool.

There are two main types of search tools:

- **Directories** categorize Web sites by subject, using people to do the work.
- **Search engines** index Web sites by keyword, using software called **robots**, **worms**, or **spiders**, that travel the Web checking sites and recording their content.

Directories place Web sites in hierarchical categories. To find a document, you typically start with a broad category and then choose narrower subtopics that take you to the desired result. Directories are easy to use and are especially useful if you want information on a general topic. One thing to remember when you are using a directory is that any one of them will categorize only a small portion of available documents, giving you a smaller number of **hits**, or matching documents. Figure 7 shows the directory LookSmart. Follow the way the broad topic gets limited by choosing subtopics.

Search engines cover more of the Web because they employ software that follow links from page to page, cataloging each site. Use a search engine to find a specific concept, word, or phrase. To use a search engine, you type

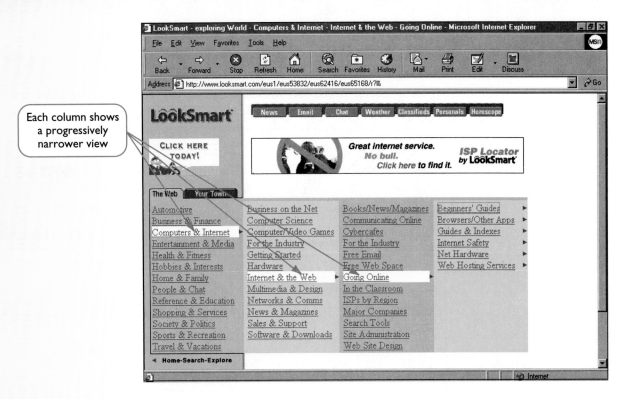

Each column shows a progressively narrower view

FIGURE 7 Using the LookSmart Web Directory to Limit a Search

keywords that describe the information you want. This approach can lead to too much information unless you learn to narrow your topics. Figure 8 shows the search engine AltaVista.

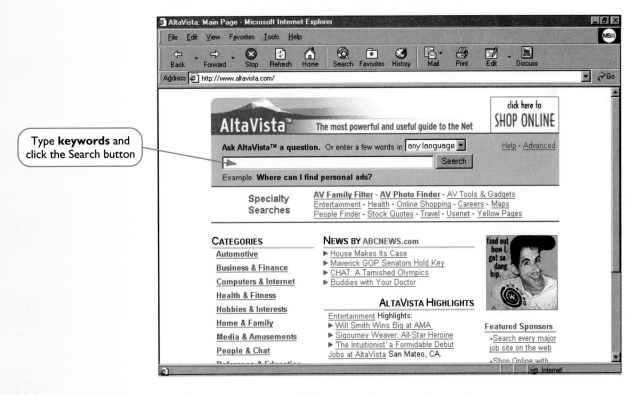

Type **keywords** and click the Search button

FIGURE 8 The AltaVista Search Engine's Home Page

Other types of search tools include:

- specialized search tools—find one type of information, such as people, e-mail addresses, and businesses
- **meta-search tools** or **multithreaded search engines**—search multiple search tools simultaneously. Figure 9 show the meta-search tool ProFusion. Notice all the search tools it searches to provide results.

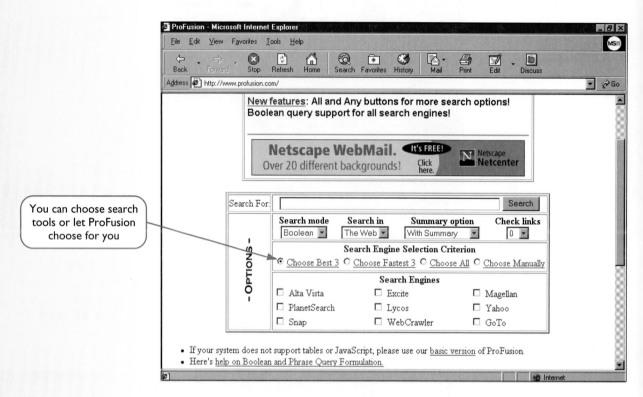

FIGURE 9   The ProFusion Meta-Search Engine's Home Page

Table 5 provides examples of the various types of search tools.

Search Tool	URL
Directories:	
Yahoo	http://www.yahoo.com
Magellan	http://www.magellan.excite.com
LookSmart	http://www.looksmart.com
Search Engines:	
AltaVista	http://www.altavista.com
Excite	http://www.excite.com
Infoseek	http://www.infoseek.com
HotBot	http://www.hotbot.com

(continued)

TABLE 5   Search Tools

Search Tool	URL
Meta-Search Tools:	
ProFusion	http://www.profusion.com
Dogpile	http://www.dogpile.com
MetaFind	http://www.metafind.com
MetaCrawler	http://www.metacrawler.com
Specialized Search Tools:	
To Find People:	
WhoWhere?	http://www.whowhere.com
BigFoot People Finder	http://www.bigfoot.com
To Find a Business:	
YellowPages AtHand	http://www.athand.com

TABLE 5 Search Tools *(continued)*

SEARCHING STRATEGY

In order to avoid great amounts of wasted time finding either nothing or thousands of useless documents, you should plan your search before you connect to any search tools.

To conduct a successful Web search, follow these steps:

1. Identify exactly what you are searching for. Ask yourself questions about the concept and identify the key elements.
2. Identify keywords and turn them into nouns. Search engines search predominately for nouns. Think of synonyms and other forms of the words. Use phrases wherever possible. Always place phrases in quotation marks so that the search engine regards the phrase as a single entity.
3. Start by running your search on a meta-search tool. This will provide you with information on your subject from a variety of search tools.
4. Select one or two of the search engines that provided good information in the meta-search and run the search again; or use a directory to limit the topic by categories; or use a specialized search tool.
5. If you are still not able to find the right information, try a search engine that supports **Boolean logic** to combine keywords, as shown in Figure 10. Boolean expressions use the logical operators AND, OR, and NOT to express relationships between two or more entities:

   - AND finds matches only when both terms are present. For example, searching for **Y2K AND bug** will find articles that have both words present.
   - OR finds documents that contain at least one of the specified words. For example, searching for **Y2K OR bug** will find all documents that contain the word *Y2K* and all documents that contain the word *bug*. This search would result in thousands of hits.

- NOT excludes documents containing the specified word. For example, searching for **Y2K NOT compliance** will find only those documents containing the word *Y2K* that do not contain the word *compliance*. (Some search tools require AND NOT used together. Check each tool's Help for details.)

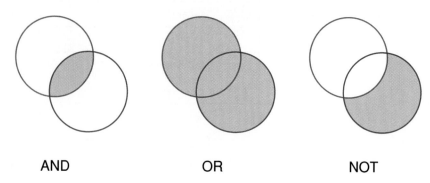

AND   OR   NOT

FIGURE 10   Three Boolean Operators

Table 6 describes these three Boolean operators. There are other Boolean expressions such as NEAR, FAR, and BEFORE. Use the help files of the search engines to get details.

Operator	Description
AND	Linking two keywords with AND narrows the search because only sites that contain both terms will be displayed.
OR	Linking two keywords with OR broadens the search because sites that contain either term will be displayed.
NOT	Using NOT excludes words from the search.

TABLE 6   Boolean Operators

POINTER

Typing Boolean Operators

You must type Boolean operators in all caps in order for the search engine to recognize them.

Figure 11 shows the Advanced Search screen for AltaVista. Notice the text box used to type keywords connected by Boolean operators.

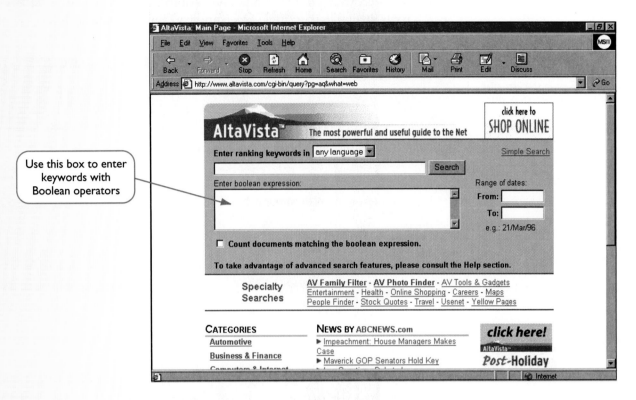

Use this box to enter keywords with Boolean operators

FIGURE 11 The AltaVista Advanced Search Page

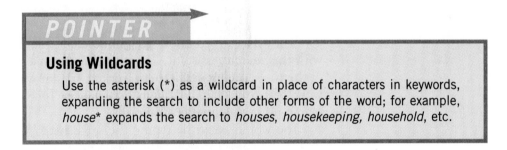

Using Wildcards

Use the asterisk (*) as a wildcard in place of characters in keywords, expanding the search to include other forms of the word; for example, *house** expands the search to *houses, housekeeping, household,* etc.

USING INTERNET EXPLORER TO SEARCH

Internet Explorer gives you access to all of the search tools described above, but you may prefer to use its Search pane to take advantage of some built-in search help. To do so, you click the toolbar's Search button (or choose View | Explorer Bar | Search) to display the Explorer bar's Search pane, shown for Internet Explorer 5 in Figure 12. This is the **Search Assistant**.

The Search Assistant lets you choose a type of search before you enter keywords, and then, based on your choice, chooses an appropriate search tool. If you specify that you want to find a Web page, for instance, the Search Assistant chooses a search tool, conducts the search, and displays the result at the bottom of the Search pane. If you don't find what you want, you can click the Search button again, and the next search tool on the list will be used.

If you click the Customize button at the top of the Search pane, you can customize the Search Assistant, choosing which search tools are used and the order in which they are searched. The Search Assistant makes a variety of search tools available in a single place and can simplify your search.

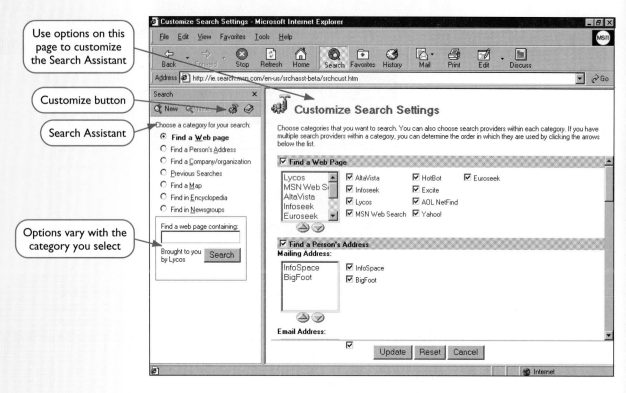

FIGURE 12   Using Internet Explorer 5's Search Assistant

You will want to know how to conduct searches on your own as well as with the Search Assistant. There's not room in a textbook for examples of all of the tools, and many of them work in similar ways. You'll learn which ones work best for you as you gain experience. To get started, look at a sample search using the directory Yahoo.

You would begin by typing the URL http://www.yahoo.com in the Address bar. Figure 13a shows the Yahoo home page.

1. Click a category, such as Society and Culture, to narrow your search.
2. Choose a subcategory, such as Environment and Nature. Yahoo's Environment and Nature page is shown in Figure 13b.
3. Narrow the search by typing keywords in the text box. In Figure 13b, the keyword *wolves* was typed in the box
4. Limit the search to documents Yahoo has collected in this category by selecting options from the drop-down box.
5. Click the Search button, and Yahoo searches for documents that match your criteria, that is, articles about wolves in the Environment and Nature subcategory of the Society and Culture category.

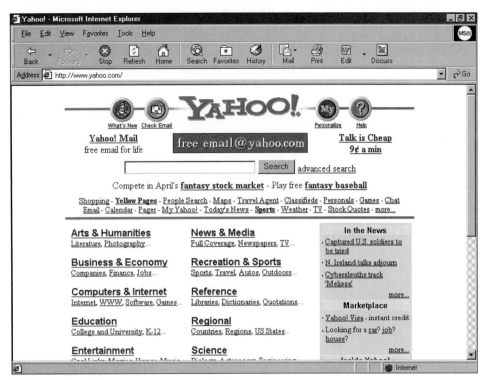

(a) The Yahoo Directory's Home Page

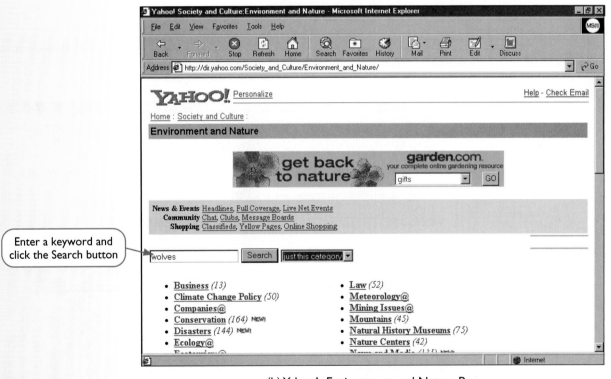

Enter a keyword and click the Search button

(b) Yahoo's Environment and Nature Page

FIGURE 13   Using Yahoo to Conduct a Search

When the search is completed (it doesn't take long), Yahoo displays a list of documents that match your criteria, as shown in Figure 13c.

You can click a hypertext link to go to the article you want to see. Figure 13d shows a page from the search in the example.

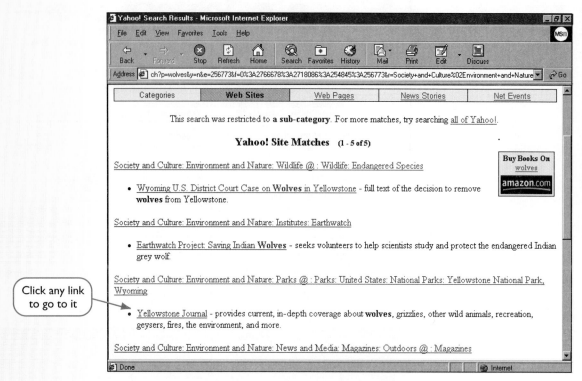

Click any link to go to it

(c) The Result of the Search

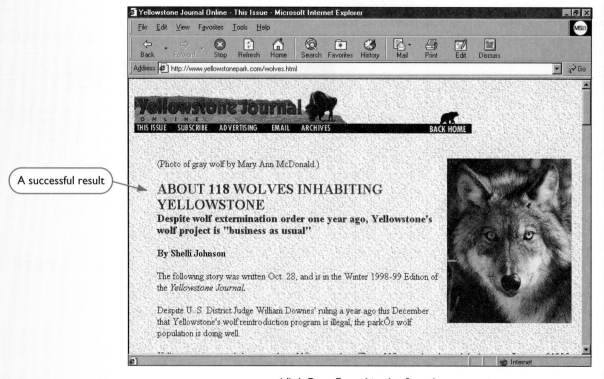

A successful result

(d) A Page Found in the Search

FIGURE 13 Using Yahoo to Conduct a Search *(continued)*

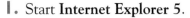

EXERCISE 3 | *Searching the World Wide Web*

1. Start **Internet Explorer 5**.

2. Click the **Search button**.
The Search pane opens, displaying the Search Assistant.

3. Click the option button to **Find a Person's Address**.
The search form changes to show option buttons and text boxes for addresses.

4. In the *Search For* list box, choose **mailing address**, and then fill in the *First Name*, *Last Name*, *City*, and *State/Province* text boxes with your own name and address or that of a person you wish to locate.

5. Click the list box's **Search button** and view the result.
If the search was unsuccessful, try to find someone else. A search for someone who has a listed telephone number is almost always successful.

6. Use the Search Assistant or one of the search tools described in this unit to locate the following information. When you have the information, print the Web site.

- The top three movies at the box office for the current week
- The Web site for your town or city
- Statistics about the growth of the Web
- The main zip code for Seattle, Washington

7. Exit from Internet Explorer.

R E V I E W

SUMMARY

After completing this unit, you should be able to
- describe the Internet and the World Wide Web (page 26)
- use Internet Explorer to explore the World Wide Web (page 29)
- search the World Wide Web (page 36)

KEY TERMS

Boolean logic (page 39)

directory (page 36)

distributed system (page 26)

freenet (page 28)

hits (page 36)

home page (page 26)

hyperlinks (page 26)

hypertext (page 26)

HyperText Markup Language (HTML) (page 26)

HyperText Transfer Protocol (http) (page 32)

TEST YOUR SKILLS

True/False

1. You need a modem to connect to the Internet unless you are connected through a network.
2. Search engines use software to index words on Web documents.
3. The World Wide Web is a network of computers.
4. A browser is the software necessary to surf the Web.
5. Hypertext is used as links in Web documents.

Multiple Choice

1. Links in Web documents
   a. cannot be viewed
   b. are generally represented as underlined and colored text
   c. are indicated by the cursor's changing to an arrow
   d. all of these answers

2. The World Wide Web
   a. is documents located all over the world
   b. can be accessed using a browser
   c. can be searched
   d. all of these answers

3. Internet Explorer
   a. is a browser
   b. is part of Windows 98
   c. displays Web documents
   d. all of these answers

4. The Boolean operator AND
   a. narrows a search
   b. expands a search
   c. must always be used with NOT
   d. is the same as OR

5. Before you can connect to the Internet, you need
   a. an Internet Service Provider
   b. a word processing program
   c. a printer
   d. all of these answers

Short Answer

Identify the parts of the Internet Explorer screen indicated in Figure 14:

___ a. URL for the current page
___ b. Hypertext
___ c. Lets you view the previous page
___ d. Allows you to type keywords for searching
___ e. Displays search tools

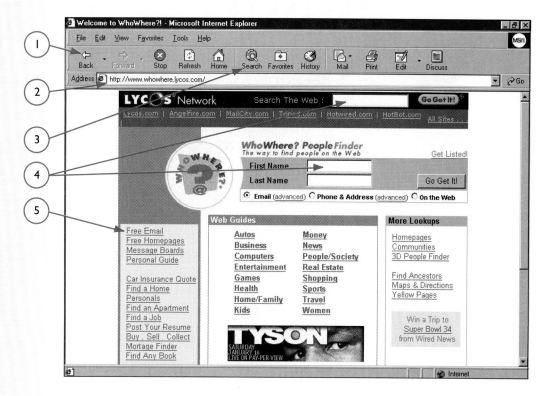

FIGURE 14

What Does This Do?

Write a description of the function of the following:

1.	AND	6.	.org
2.	Stop	7.	Favorites
3.	Back	8.	NOT
4.	.com	9.	Search
5.	OR	10.	Forward

On Your Own

1. Conduct a search using a meta-search tool for information that you are interested in or that you can use for another course.
2. Conduct the same search using a search engine.
3. Conduct the same search using a directory.
4. Search for a person or a product using one of the specialized search tools.
5. Search for a topic using Boolean operators.

PROJECTS

1. Start Internet Explorer and choose Help | Web Tutorial. Complete the tutorial.

2. Research the following sites that provide information about Internet Service Providers. Select two ISPs that you would be interested in using, and write a description of each and why you chose it.
   a. Mecklermedia at http://thelist.com
   b. c | net's ISP Guide at http://www.cnet.com/Contnet/Reports/ Special/ISP/index.html
   c. PC World at http://www.pcworld.com/interactive/isps/isps.html
   d. Celestin at http://www2.celestin.com/pocia/index.html
   e. Boardwatch (lists ISPs by area code) at http://boardwatch.internet.com/isp/ac/index.html

3. Type the following URLs in the Address text box to display the following Web sites; print the results.
   a. The College Board at http://www.collegeboard.org
   b. Student Loan Financing at http://www.nelliemae.com
   c. Campus Tours at http://www.campustours.com
   d. CNN Science and Technology at http://cnn.com/TECH/index.html
   e. PBS Deep Space at http://www.pbs.org/deepspace
   f. Search for Extraterrestrial Intelligence Institute at http://www.seto.org

4. Search for the following information; print the Web site where you find it.
   a. Find which are the top Web sites listed by one of the search tools.
   b. Find out if your Social Security records are correct and determine your likely benefits.
   c. Find your U.S. senators' e-mail addresses.
   d. Find the site of Dr. Koop, the former Surgeon General.
   e. Search for information on a topic that interests you.

Getting Started

UNIT OBJECTIVES

- Learn to use the mouse
- Become familiar with the Windows 98 interface
- Move and size windows
- Switch between open windows
- Arrange open windows
- Use the Windows 98 Help system
- Shut down Windows 98

Windows 98 is the latest version of Microsoft's most popular computer operating system. An **operating system** is the **software**, or programs, necessary to start the computer, run **application programs** such as word processors, open and save files, and make all the computer **hardware**, or physical components, work together. Even though you may not be aware of it, Windows 98 is working behind the scenes whenever you use your computer, enabling other programs to run. Windows 98 also contains a powerful group of **utilities**, software programs that perform housekeeping tasks, allowing you to work more easily and efficiently. In this book you will learn the skills necessary to use Windows 98.

What: Learn to use a mouse.

How: Point the mouse and click the left or right mouse button.

Why: The mouse is an input device found on most computers running Windows 98.

Tip: Not all mice are the same. Microsoft's IntelliMouse contains a wheel between the right and left mouse buttons. The wheel is used to scroll through documents on the screen. Whatever mouse you use, it will work more smoothly if you place it on a mouse pad.

The **mouse** is a hand-held **input device**—a part of the hardware that allows you to enter information into the computer system. A mouse is a standard feature on most desktop computers. To use it, place your right hand over the body of the mouse and your index finger on the left mouse button. When you move the mouse on your desktop or a mouse pad, the **mouse pointer**, or cursor, moves on the screen. The pointer assumes different shapes depending on what you are doing. It most often appears as an arrow, but when you point to a link, it changes to a hand with a pointing index finger.

Once you have pointed the mouse to the object you want, such as a menu or icon on the screen, you can click it, double-click it, right-click it, or drag it.

- To click it, press the left mouse button with your index finger and quickly release it.

- To double-click it, click the left mouse button two times in quick succession.

- To right-click it, press the right mouse button and release it. Right-clicking opens a shortcut menu, explained in Task 2.

- To drag with the mouse, point to an object, hold down the left button, and move the mouse. Dragging an object moves it or changes its size, as explained in Task 3.

- Instructions in this text to click or double-click the mouse always refer to the left mouse button. When an operation calls for you to right-click, the text will clearly specify the right mouse button.

In Task 6 you will learn how to use Windows 98's built-in Help system. Figure 1.1 shows a portion of the Windows 98 Help screen on clicking the mouse.

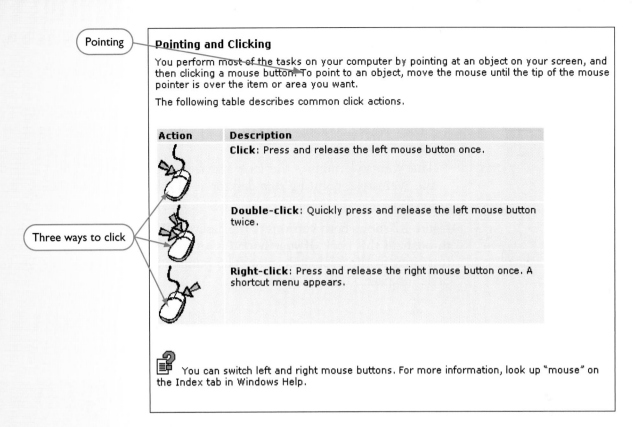

Pointing

Pointing and Clicking

You perform most of the tasks on your computer by pointing at an object on your screen, and then clicking a mouse button. To point to an object, move the mouse until the tip of the mouse pointer is over the item or area you want.

The following table describes common click actions.

Three ways to click

Action	Description
	Click: Press and release the left mouse button once.
	Double-click: Quickly press and release the left mouse button twice.
	Right-click: Press and release the right mouse button once. A shortcut menu appears.

You can switch left and right mouse buttons. For more information, look up "mouse" on the Index tab in Windows Help.

FIGURE 1.1   Pointing and Clicking the Mouse

TASK 2 | Becoming Familiar with the Windows 98 Interface

What: Learn to use the various parts of the Windows 98 desktop.

How: Use the mouse to explore.

Why: To use Windows 98 effectively, you need to be familiar with the Windows environment.

Tip: If you take time to feel comfortable with Windows 98, you will be more comfortable with your application software.

Windows 98 makes use of a **graphical user interface**, or **GUI** (pronounced "goo-ey"). That is, you communicate with the computer by selecting icons and other graphical screen elements on the desktop rather than by typing commands.

THE DESKTOP

When you turn on your computer, Windows 98 starts and displays the desktop environment. The **desktop** is the background area of your screen display. Just as you place items you want to work with on the top of your desk at school or work, Windows 98 places items such as icons and toolbars on its desktop.

Windows 98 has two versions of the desktop, the Classic style and the Web style.

- The Classic style is the style of previous versions of Windows. With the Classic style, clicking a desktop icon selects it and double-clicking it opens it.
- The Web style mimics the look and feel of the World Wide Web. With the Web style, pointing to a desktop icon selects it and single-clicking it opens it.

Figure 1.2 shows both versions of the desktop. We will be using the Web style throughout this book. If your system is set to the Classic style, you will want to switch to the Web style now. The pointer box "Changing the Desktop Style" on page 5 tells you how.

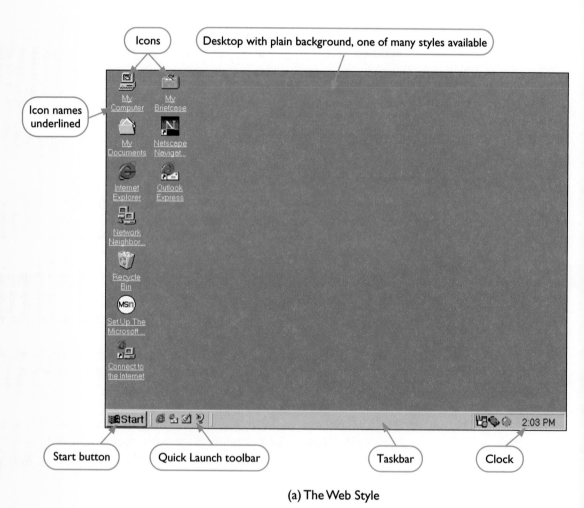

(a) The Web Style

FIGURE 1.2   The Windows 98 Desktop

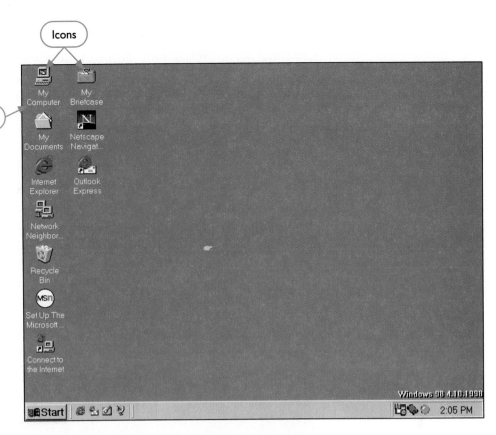

Icons

Icon names not underlined

(b) The Classic Style

FIGURE 1.2   The Windows 98 Desktop (continued)

POINTER

Changing the Desktop Style

Figure 1.2a shows Windows 98 with the Web-style desktop displayed. We will be using the Web style in this book, so if your display is set to the Classic style, you'll want to switch display styles now. Here's how:

1. Click the **Start button** at the bottom left of the Windows screen display.
2. Point to the word **Settings** in the menu that opens, and another menu will open.
3. On this menu, click the words **Folder options**, and a dialog box will open.
4. If necessary, click the **General tab** at the top left of this dialog box to bring it to the front.
5. In the Windows Desktop Update section of this tab, click the **Web style option button**.
6. Click the **OK button** at the bottom right of the dialog box, to close the box and change your desktop.

To switch back from the Web style to the Classic style, repeat these steps, clicking the Classic style option button. You will learn more about display features in Unit 7. Task 1 in that unit, for instance, on page 154, shows you how to change the desktop background.

ICONS

Icons are the small graphics displayed on the Windows desktop, shown in Figure 1.2. Each icon represents a program or document to which you have access. To open the program or document, point to the icon with the mouse and click (double-click in the Classic view).

TASKBAR

The Windows 98 **taskbar**, which appears along the bottom of the screen, displays the Start button, buttons for all open programs, and the clock. It may also contain toolbars such as the Quick Launch toolbar for quick access to the desktop and selected programs. At the left edge of the taskbar is the **Start button** used to open the Start menu. You will use the Start menu to start programs, access Help, find files, and shut down your computer. (Some keyboards have a Windows key on either side of the Spacebar that opens the Start menu.) The Start menu is shown in Figure 1.3.

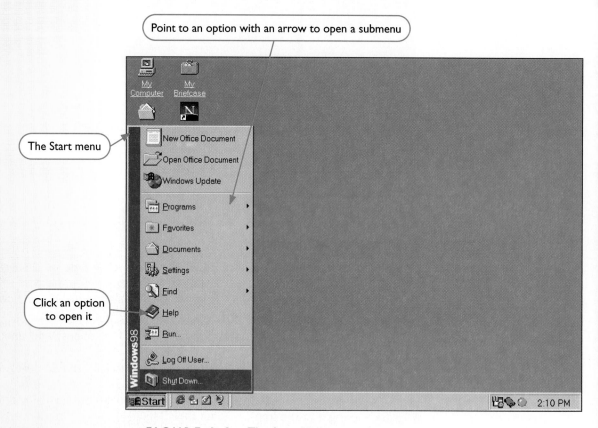

FIGURE 1.3 The Start Menu

Notice in Figure 1.3 that some menu names have right-pointing arrows next to them. Pointing to these items opens a submenu. To start a program, point to a menu name, point to a submenu name, and then click the program name. For example, to use the Calculator program:

1. Click the Start button to open the Start menu.
2. Point to Programs to open the Programs submenu.

3. Point to Accessories to open the Accessories submenu.
4. Click Calculator to start the Calculator Accessory program.

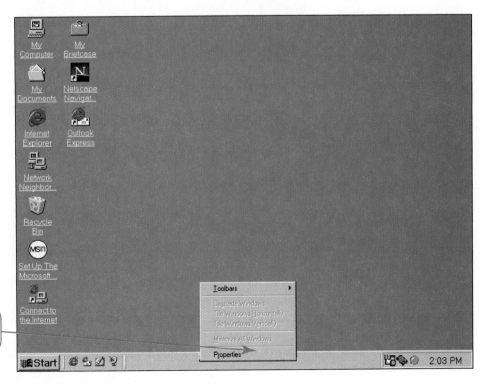

EXERCISE 1	*The Windows Interface: The Start Menu*

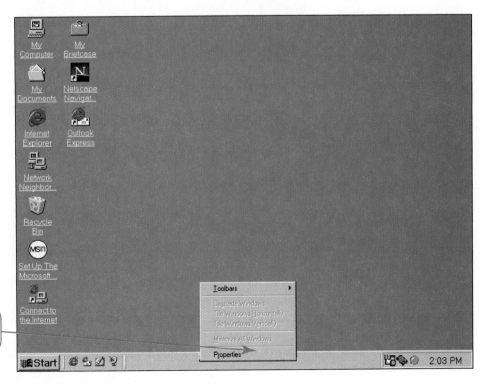

1. Turn on your computer.

   Windows 98 starts automatically and displays the desktop.

2. Click the **Start button**.

   The Start menu opens.

3. Point to **Programs**.

   A submenu opens showing programs available on your computer.

4. Examine the menu, and then click **an empty area on the desktop**.

   The menu closes.

SHORTCUT MENUS

Windows 98 provides **shortcut menus**, small menus that appear when you right-click the mouse on many objects. The contents of the shortcut menu will vary with the object you point to. Figure 1.4 shows the shortcut menu that opens when you click an empty area on the taskbar.

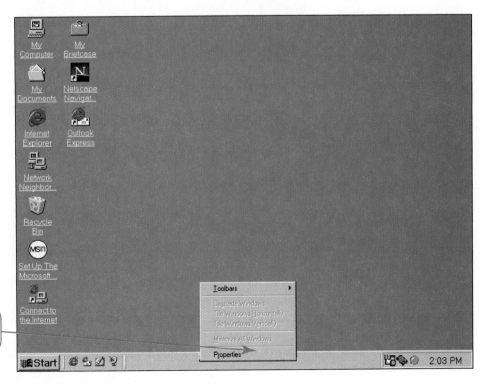

Right-click an empty area of the taskbar to open this shortcut menu

FIGURE 1.4   A Shortcut Menu

To select an option from the shortcut menu, point to it and click either the right or left mouse button. For example, you can change the taskbar display using the following steps:

1. Point the mouse to an empty area on the taskbar.
2. Click the right mouse button to open a shortcut menu.
3. Point to Toolbars on the shortcut menu to open a submenu.
4. Click Quick Launch on the submenu to toggle the Quick Launch toolbar display on or off.
5. Repeat steps 1 through 4 to toggle the display again.

If you decide that you don't want to make a selection from a shortcut menu, click outside the menu to close it.

WINDOWS

The Windows operating system is named for the **windows** that are a part of its graphical user interface. Windows are rectangular frames that can contain objects such as documents, programs, dialog boxes, or icons. Windows always have a title bar and may contain any or all of the elements shown in Figure 1.5. More than one window can be open at the same time, but only one can be active. You can switch back and forth between open windows. This is called multitasking and is explained in Task 4.

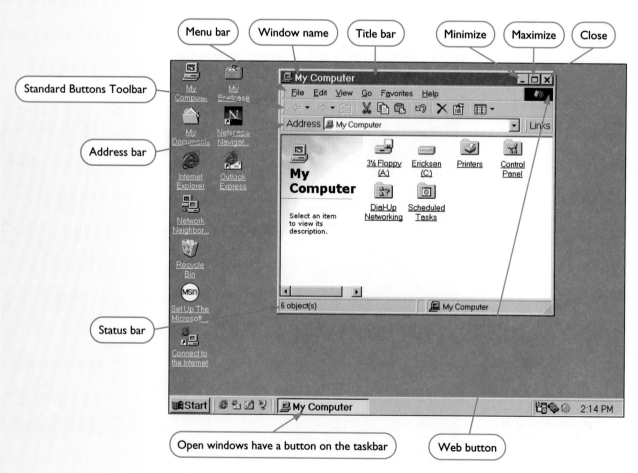

FIGURE 1.5 A Window Open on the Desktop

TITLE BAR

Every window has a **title bar** across the top. When more than one window is open, the title bar of the active window is displayed in a brighter or more intense color than that of other open windows (dark blue by default), as shown in Figure 1.6.

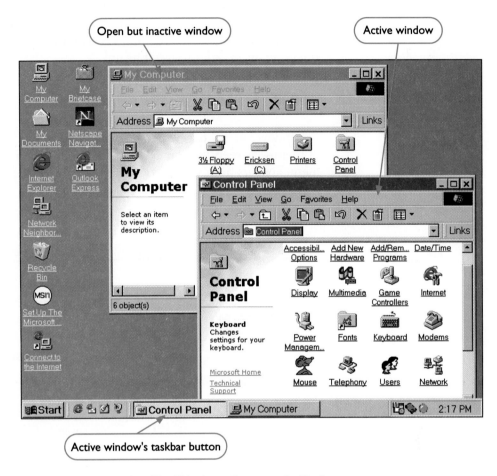

FIGURE 1.6 Two Windows Open on the Desktop

The title bar names the program or document contained in the window. It usually contains the buttons described in Table 1.1 at its right edge.

Button	Name	Description
	Minimize	Shrinks the open window to a button on the taskbar
	Maximize	Enlarges the window to fill the desktop
	Restore	In a maximized window, replaces the Maximize button, returning the window to its previous size
	Close	Closes the window

TABLE 1.1 Buttons That Close and Size a Window

Clicking the **Close button** closes the window. If the window is a program window, clicking the Close button exits from the program.

Most windows can be sized to occupy part or all of the desktop. Clicking the **Maximize button** expands a window so that it fills the desktop. When the window is maximized, the Maximize button changes to a **Restore button**. Clicking the Restore button shrinks a window back to its previous size.

The **Minimize button** keeps a program running in the background but reduces it to a button on the taskbar. You can display the window again by clicking the taskbar button. Minimizing rather than closing a program gives you quick access to the program; you don't have to wait for Windows to start the program in order to use it again.

MENU BAR

A window's **menu bar,** which is located below its title bar, displays the names of menus, as seen in Figure 1.5. When you click a menu name, a drop-down menu appears from which you select a command or other option, as shown in Figure 1.7.

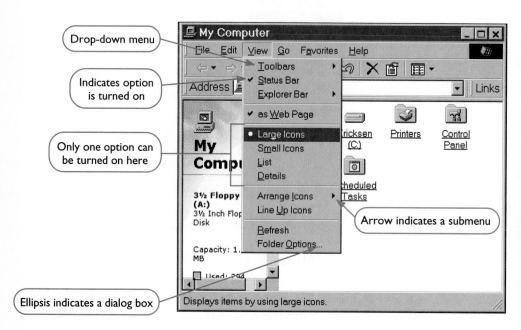

FIGURE 1.7   A Drop-down Menu

Instructions in this text to choose menu commands are shown as **Menu Name│Menu Command**. For example, "choose View │ Toolbars" means to choose View from the menu bar and Toolbars from the drop-down menu.

Notice that each menu choice in Figures 1.5 and 1.7 has an underlined character. Pressing this character on the keyboard (often while holding down the Alt key) has the same effect as clicking the choice with the mouse. For example, to open the File menu, you can click its name on the menu bar or hold down the Alt key and press the letter F. Once a menu is open, you can choose an item by clicking it or by typing the underlined letter.

To close a menu without choosing a command, either click the mouse outside the menu or press the Esc key on the keyboard.

The Web button is located at the right edge of the menu bar. Clicking this button starts your browser and connects you to the World Wide Web.

A menu choice on drop-down menus can appear:

- with a check mark (✔) in front of it—to indicate an option that is turned on in a group where more than one choice is permitted
- without a check mark (✔)—to indicate that the option is turned off
- with a dot (●) in front of it—to indicate the option that is turned on in a group where only one choice is permitted

- grayed-out—to indicate it is not available at the present time
- followed by a right-pointing arrow (▶)—to indicate that clicking it will open a submenu
- followed by an ellipsis (. . .)—to indicate that clicking it will open a dialog box like the one shown in Figure 1.8.

DIALOG BOXES

Dialog boxes are windows in which you provide Windows 98 with information needed to perform a task. Some dialog boxes, like the one in Figure 1.8, are **tabbed**, with each tab containing a group of similar options.

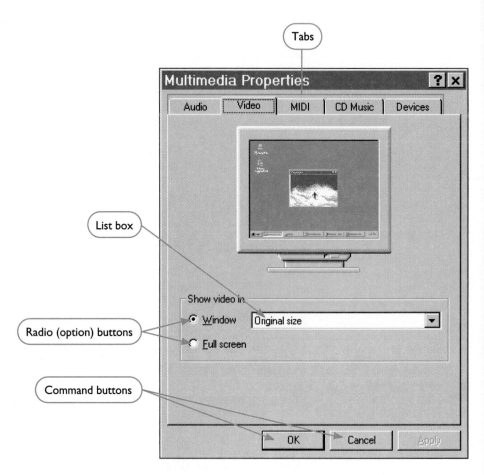

FIGURE 1.8   A Dialog Box

Dialog boxes contain **command buttons** that allow you to issue commands. Two common command buttons are the OK button and the Cancel button. When you have made the desired selections in a dialog box, you click the OK button. If you simply want to close the dialog box, click the Close button or the Cancel button.

When a dialog box contains a **text box**, you can type your response in the box provided. Other ways of selecting options in a dialog box include clicking a **radio button** (also called an **option button**) or **check box** or selecting items from a **list box**. Appendix B at the end of the book shows the buttons used in dialog boxes.

TOOLBARS

Three **toolbars** can be turned on or off by choosing View | Toolbars. They normally appear below the menu bar, but you can move them by dragging them to another position. Below the menu bar is the **Standard Buttons toolbar**, with buttons you can click to perform tasks. Some of the buttons are followed by a downward-pointing arrow (▼). Clicking the arrow opens a list box from which you can make a choice, as shown in Figure 1.9.

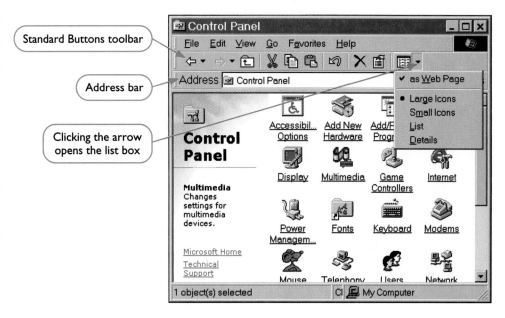

FIGURE 1.9   The Standard Buttons Toolbar Displaying a List Box

---

POINTER

Text Labels on Toolbars

The toolbar can be set to show buttons with or without text labels. To have it display labels identifying the buttons, choose View | Toolbars | Text Labels. If you point to a button on a toolbar or the taskbar, a little yellow box called a ToolTip will appear with information about the button.

Below the Standard toolbar is the **Address toolbar**, showing the address of the current document or selection.

POINTER

Folders and Subfolders

An address can appear to be long and complex because documents are stored in folders and subfolders. You will learn to understand addresses in Unit 3.

The Address bar is a powerful navigation tool. If you type the address of a document or a Web page into its text box and press Enter, Windows will take you to the address and open the document, whether it is on a local disk drive, a network drive, or on the World Wide Web. Figure 1.10 shows a Web address typed into the Address bar.

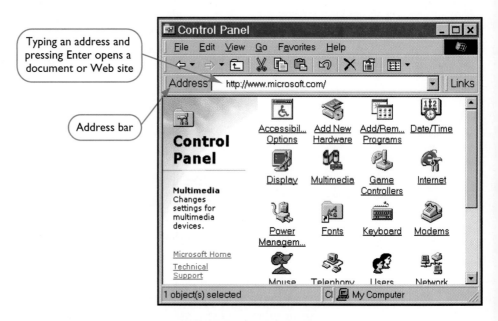

FIGURE 1.10   An Address Bar Displaying a Web Address

A third toolbar, the Links toolbar, is also available in Windows 98 for use with the World Wide Web.

Appendix B at the end of this book shows the Windows toolbars.

SCROLL BARS

If there is more information than can be viewed in a window, Windows 98 will place **scroll bars** at the right edge or bottom of the window that allow you to move through a window using the mouse. If the window has two sections or panes, each may have its own scroll bar, as shown in Figure 1.11.

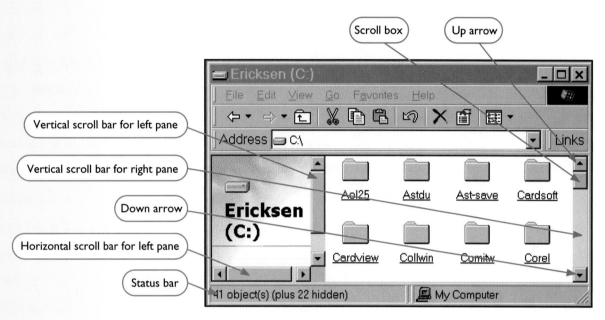

FIGURE 1.11 Scroll Bars and Status Bar

- Click the up and down arrow on the vertical scroll bar to move the display up or down one line.
- Click below the up arrow to move the display up one screen.
- Click above the down arrow to move the display down one screen.
- Click and drag the **scroll box** down or up to quickly scroll down or back up a window.

If the window has more horizontal contents than can be displayed, the window will contain a horizontal scroll bar that works just like the vertical scroll bar.

STATUS BAR

At the bottom of the window is the **status bar**, which displays information about the status of the window, such as how many icons or objects the window contains and the name of the window (see Figure 1.11).

1. With Windows 98 running on your computer, point to **an empty area on the taskbar** and click the **right mouse button**.

   A shortcut menu opens.

2. Point to **Toolbars** on the shortcut menu.

   A submenu opens, with a list of toolbars you can display on the taskbar.

3. If there is a check in front of Quick Launch, click outside the menu on the desktop to close the menu. If there is no check, click **Quick Launch**.

   The Quick Launch toolbar will be displayed on the taskbar, and the shortcut menu will close.

4. Point to the **My Computer icon** on the desktop and, when the pointer changes to a hand, click the **left mouse button**.

   The My Computer window opens.

5. Click the **Control Panel icon** in the My Computer window.

   The Control Panel window opens in the same window, replacing My Computer.

6. Click the **Back button** on the Standard Buttons toolbar.

   The My Computer window returns.

7. Click the **Close button** on the title bar of the My Computer window.

   The My Computer window closes.

TASK 3 | *Moving and Sizing a Window*

What: Move a window to a different screen location and change the size of a window.

How: Use the mouse to drag the window or to size the window.

Why: A window may cover an area of the screen that you want to see, or you may want to display more of a window's contents.

Tip: Dialog boxes and some other windows, such as the Calculator window, cannot be sized.

If an open window covers something else you want to see on the desktop, you can easily click and drag it to a different location on the screen. To move a window:

1. Point to the title bar of the window.
2. Click and drag it across the screen.
3. Release the mouse button to complete the action.

Click and drag is a method for moving and sizing objects. You click the object, hold down the left mouse button, move the mouse, then release the button. You can change the size of windows using the following steps:

1. Point to the edge of a window until the pointer changes to a two-headed arrow (↔).
2. Click and drag the mouse.
3. Release the mouse button when the window reaches the desired size.

If you drag the mouse away from the center of the window, the window will get larger, but if you drag toward the center of the window, the window will get smaller.

If you point to a corner of the window, the window will resize proportionally when you click and drag. But if you point to one edge of the window, then the window will enlarge only along that edge.

EXERCISE 3 | *Moving and Sizing Windows*

1. Open the **My Computer window**. If the window occupies the whole of the desktop, click the **Restore button** in its title bar to reduce its size.

2. Open the **Control Panel**.

    The Control Panel opens in the same window, replacing My Computer.

3. Click the **Regional Settings icon**.

    The Regional Setting Properties dialog box opens separately on the desktop, and may obscure part or all of the Control Panel window. Dialog boxes open separately from windows in the Web style.

4. Click and drag the **title bar** of the Regional Settings Properties dialog box.

    The dialog box moves as you drag it.

5. Close the **Regional Settings Properties dialog box**.

6. Point to the **bottom right corner** of the Control Panel window.

    The pointer turns into a two-headed arrow (↔).

7. Click and drag the mouse away from the center of the window.

    The window enlarges proportionately in both height and depth.

8. Click the **Maximize button** on the Control Panel title bar.

    The window expands to fill the desktop.

9. Click the **Restore button** on the Control Panel title bar.

    The window returns to its previous size.

10. Click the **Minimize button** on the Control Panel title bar.

    The Control Panel is reduced to a button on the taskbar.

11. Click the **Control Panel button** on the Windows taskbar.

    The Control Panel returns to its previous size.

12. Close the Control Panel.

TASK 4 | *Switching Between Open Windows*

What: Switch between windows.

How: Click the program button on the taskbar.

Why: When you have several programs open at the same time, only one can be active.

Tip: If you can see any part of the window you want to use, just point to the window and click it to place it on top as the active window.

The Windows operating system allows you to keep more than one program open at a time and switch between them. This is called **multitasking**. The taskbar displays a button for every open window, containing the name of the window or program and the active file. The taskbar button for the active window looks pushed in. When a button is too small to display the entire name, it shows a shortened form of the name and an ellipsis (**. . .**). Point to the button to display the full name, as shown in Figure 1.12.

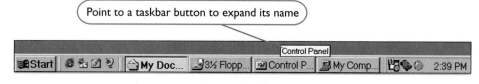

Point to a taskbar button to expand its name

FIGURE 1.12   The Taskbar with Shortened Names

To switch to a different program or window, click its button on the taskbar.

EXERCISE 4 | *Switching Between Open Windows*

1. Open **My Computer**.

2. Minimize **My Computer**.

My Computer appears only as a button on the taskbar.

3. Click the **Start button** on the taskbar.

The Start menu opens.

4. Choose **Programs | Accessories | Calculator**.

The Calculator program starts, and opens on the desktop.

5. Minimize the **Calculator**.

The Calculator appears only as a button on the taskbar.

6. Click the **My Computer button** on the taskbar.

The My Computer window is restored to its previous size.

7. Click the **Calculator button** on the taskbar.

The Calculator also displays.

8. Click anywhere inside the **My Computer window**.

My Computer comes to the front as the active window.

9. Click the **Calculator button** on the taskbar.

The Calculator comes to the front as the active window.

10. Close both windows.

TASK 5 | *Arranging Windows*

What: Display all open windows at one time.

How: Use the taskbar's shortcut menu.

Why: To see all open windows at once rather than switching between windows.

Tip: To minimize all open windows at one time, click the Show Desktop button on the Quick Launch toolbar on the Windows taskbar. Clicking the Show Desktop button a second time displays the windows again.

You can display all open windows on the screen at the same time. This feature allows you to compare the contents of two or more windows.

1. Open the windows separately.
2. Right-click an empty area of the taskbar to display the shortcut menu shown in Figure 1.13.

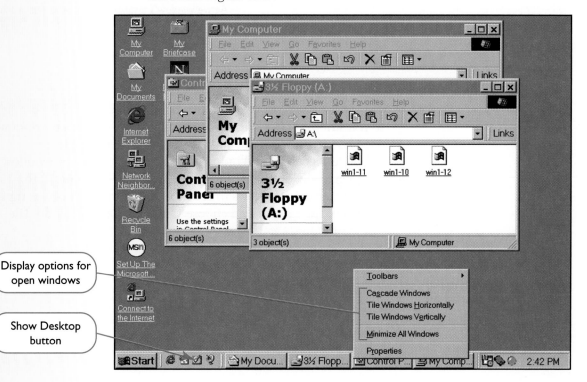

FIGURE 1.13   The Taskbar's Shortcut Menu

If you choose **Cascade Windows** from the shortcut menu, the open windows will overlap each other on the desktop, with the title bars of each showing, as can be seen in Figure 1.14.

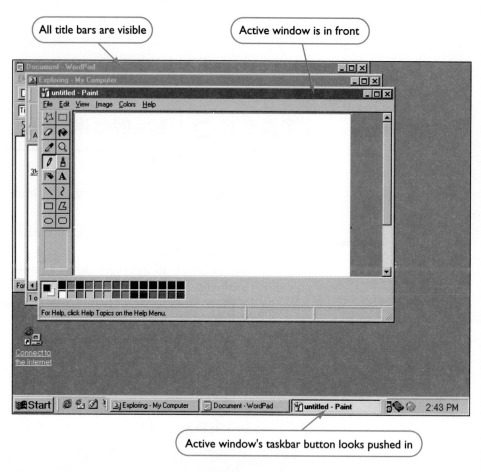

FIGURE 1.14   Cascaded Windows

To bring a window to the front and make it active, you click its title bar.

If you choose **Tile Windows Horizontally**, the open windows will be arranged horizontally on the desktop, as can be seen in Figure 1.15.

If you choose **Tile Windows Vertically**, the open windows will be arranged vertically on the desktop, as can be seen in Figure 1.16.

If you want the Windows to revert to their original display, right-click an empty area of the taskbar and choose **Undo Cascade** or **Undo Tile**.

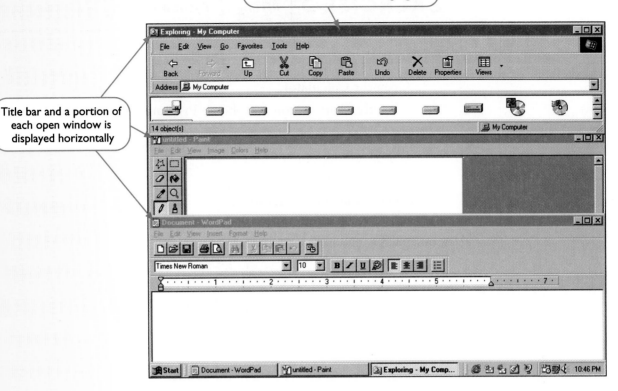

Active window's title bar is highlighted

Title bar and a portion of each open window is displayed horizontally

FIGURE 1.15 Windows Tiled Horizontally

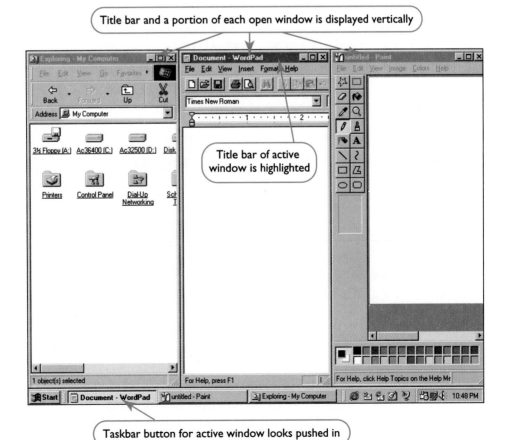

Title bar and a portion of each open window is displayed vertically

Title bar of active window is highlighted

Taskbar button for active window looks pushed in

FIGURE 1.16 Windows Tiled Vertically

1. Open **My Computer**.
2. Open the **Calculator**.
3. Click the **Start button** and choose **Programs | Accessories | Paint**.

   The Paint program starts and opens on the desktop.
4. Right-click **an empty area of the taskbar**.

   A shortcut menu opens.
5. Choose **Cascade Windows**.

   All of the open windows appear cascaded down the screen.
6. Click the **title bar** of a different window.

   The window moves to the front and becomes the active window. Its title bar changes color, and its taskbar button looks pushed in.
7. Right-click **an empty area of the taskbar**.
8. Choose **Undo Cascade**.

   The cascade is undone, and the windows revert to their previous state.
9. Right-click **an empty area of the taskbar**.
10. Choose **Tile Windows Horizontally**.

    The open windows are all displayed on the screen at once, divided horizontally.
11. Right-click **an empty area of the taskbar**.
12. Choose **Undo Tile**.

    The windows will no longer be tiled.
13. Close all open windows.

TASK 6 | *Getting Help*

What: Use Microsoft Help.

How: Click the Start button and choose Help.

Why: Microsoft provides documentation that is easy to use.

Tip: The Windows Help window has a Web Help button on its toolbar. If you click it, you get a Help screen with a link to Support Online. If you click this link, your browser opens and automatically dials Microsoft Technical Support.

Microsoft Windows 98 includes a Help feature so you can get answers to your questions as you work. To start Help, click the Start button and choose Help. Windows Help opens, as shown in Figure 1.17.

The Contents tab provides the main topics available through online Help. If you click the book icon before a topic, the topic expands to display subtopics.

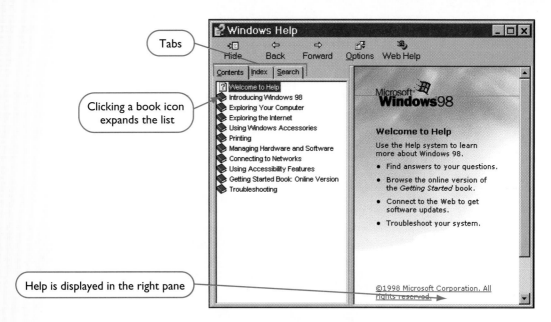

FIGURE 1.17 The Help Window's Contents Tab

Click a subtopic to display the topic list, then click a topic to see the help information in the Help window's right frame.

After you are finished with the help topic, you can close the Help window by clicking the Close button, or you can simply resume working and the Help window will remain open. You can resize the Help window if you want to use it while you work.

When you know what operation you want to perform but you simply can't remember the menu choices, use the Index tab. You can scroll down through the alphabetized topics (but this is tedious), or you can type the first few character of the word and the highlight will jump to that location in the alphabetized list. Then click the Display button to see the information you want.

The Search tab of the Windows Help window provides help by searching the Help files for keywords that you type, as shown in Figure 1.18.

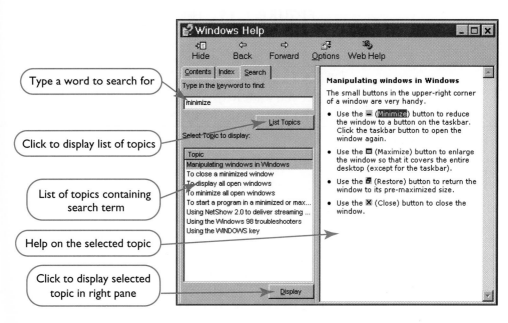

FIGURE 1.18 The Help Window's Search Tab

If you click the Options button on the Help toolbar and choose Print from the drop-down list, you will get a printout of the Help topic. You can also right-click inside the right frame of the window and choose Print from the shortcut menu.

If you need help while using a dialog box, click the question-mark button (?) in its title bar and then click the item you need explained. Help on that topic will be displayed in a pop-up box as shown in Figure 1.19.

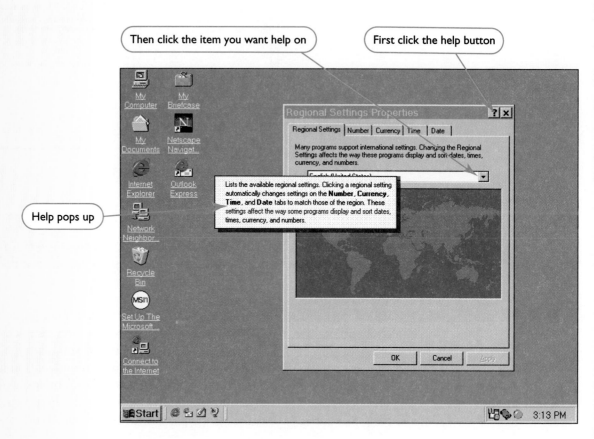

FIGURE 1.19 Help in a Dialog Box

Windows 98 also provides specific help on items on the screen. Point to the object you want help with and right-click the mouse. Click What's This? from the shortcut menu. Windows will provide help on the object.

EXERCISE 6 | *Using Help*

1. Click the **Start button** and choose **Help**.

   The Windows Help window opens.

2. On the Contents tab, click **Introducing Windows 98**.

   The display expands to show the subtopics.

3. Click the topic **How to Use Help**.

   The display expands to show the subtopics.

4. Click the topic **Find a Topic**.

   The topic is displayed in the right frame of the window.

5. Read the text of the Help topic, and then **right-click** inside the frame that contains it.

6. Choose **Print** from the shortcut menu.

   The Print dialog box opens.

7. Click **OK**.

   The topic prints.

8. Click the **Index tab** to display the index of help terms.

9. Type **Help** in the text box.

   The index scrolls to display the index entries for this term.

10. Double-click **History**.

    The text of this entry is displayed in the right frame.

11. Read the text to learn about the use of buttons on the Help toolbar.

12. Close Help.

TASK 7 | *Shutting Down Windows 98*

What: End your session.

 How: Click the Start button and choose Shut Down.

 Why: You should always shut down Windows 98 before turning off your computer.

  Tip: If you shut down Windows 98 while programs are running, a message asks whether you want to save any open documents.

When you finish working with the computer, you should shut down Windows 98 before turning off your computer. Failing to do this can damage files. To perform a proper shutdown, click the Start button and choose Shut Down.

The Shut Down Windows dialog box opens, as shown in Figure 1.20. Choose the option you want and click the OK button to proceed or the Cancel button to cancel the operation. Microsoft Windows will shut down and then display the message: *It's now safe to turn off your computer.*

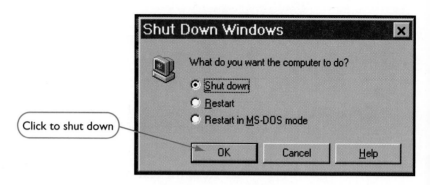

FIGURE 1.20   The Shut Down Windows Dialog Box

EXERCISE 7 | *Shutting Down Windows 98*

1. Click the **Start button** to open the Start menu.

2. Choose **Shut Down** from the Start menu.

The Shut Down Windows dialog box opens.

3. In the Shut Down dialog box, make sure that *Shut Down* is selected.

4. Click **OK**.

Windows will shut down, and a message will tell you that it is safe to turn off the computer.

S U M M A R Y

After completing this unit, you should
- know how to use a mouse
- be familiar with the Windows 98 interface
- be able to move and size windows
- be able to switch between programs
- be able to arrange open windows on the screen
- be able to use the Windows 98 Help system
- know the proper way to shut down Windows 98

K E Y   T E R M S

application program (*page 1*)
cascaded windows (*page 20*)
check box (*page 13*)
click and drag (*page 17*)
Close button (*page 10*)
command button (*page 12*)
desktop (*page 3*)
dialog box (*page 12*)
graphical user interface (GUI)
  (*page 3*)
hardware (*page 1*)
icon (*page 6*)
input device (*page 2*)
Internet Service Provider (ISP)
  (*page 11*)
list box (*page 13*)
maximize (*page 10*)
menu bar (*page 10*)
minimize (*page 10*)
modem (*page 11*)
mouse (*page 2*)
mouse pointer (*page 2*)

multitask (*page 18*)
operating system (*page 1*)
option button (radio button)
  (*page 13*)
radio button (*page 13*)
restore (*page 10*)
scroll bar (*page 15*)
scroll box (*page 15*)
shortcut menu (*page 7*)
software (*page 1*)
Start button (*page 6*)
status bar (*page 15*)
tabbed dialog box (*page 12*)
taskbar (*page 6*)
text box (*page 13*)
tiled windows (*page 20*)
title bar (*page 9*)
toolbar (*page 13*)
utility program (*page 1*)
window (*page 8*)
Windows 98 (*page 1*)

TEST YOUR SKILLS

True/False

1. The status bar is located at the top of a window and contains the name of the current window.
2. To shut down Windows 98, you use the Start button.
3. Windows 98 employs a graphical user interface.
4. Shortcut menus are accessed by right-clicking the mouse.
5. A button is displayed on the taskbar for every window and program that is open.

Multiple Choice

1. When you are using a dialog box and need help, you
   a. must cancel the operation and use the Search tab
   b. must cancel the operation and use the Help menu
   c. click the question-mark button [?] in the dialog box and then click the item you want help for
   d. exit the dialog box and find help using the Index tab

2. The scroll bars
   a. let you view information or icons that can't be displayed in the window
   b. contain a box that you can drag for quick changes in viewing
   c. are both horizontal and vertical
   d. all of these answers

3. To display all open windows as short windows across the screen, you would
   a. tile the windows
   b. cascade the windows
   c. move the windows
   d. switch the windows

4. The desktop in Windows 98
   a. has a title bar
   b. is the empty area that has icons placed on it
   c. has a status bar
   d. all of these answers

5. The Close button
   a. changes the size of the window
   b. keeps the program running in the background
   c. closes the window or program
   d. provides help on objects in the window

Short Answer

Match the letter of the correct word with the correct location in Figure 1.21:

___ a. Windows taskbar   ___ d. Status bar
___ b. Menu bar   ___ e. Active window
___ c. Icon   ___ f. Address bar

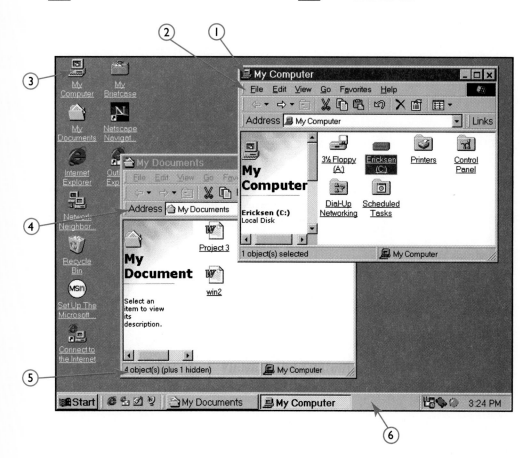

FIGURE 1.21

PROJECTS

1. (a) Open **Help**. Click the **Contents tab** and select **Getting Started Book: Online Version**. Choose **Microsoft Windows 98 Getting Started Book** and then click the link *Click here* in the right frame. Now click **Using a Mouse** and then **Dragging**. (b) Print the resulting topic.

2. (a) Open **Help**. Click the **Index tab** and type **left-clicking**. (b) Print the resulting topic.

3. (a) Open **Help**. Click the **Search tab** and type **switching**. Then click the **List Topics button**. From the Topic list select **Switching between programs** and then click the **Display button**. (b) Print the resulting topic.

4. (a) Click the **Start button** and choose **Programs | Accessories | System Tools | Welcome To Windows | Discover Windows 98 | Computer Essentials**. (b) Read the information.

Using Programs

UNIT OBJECTIVES

- Start a program
- Use the Calculator
- Use WordPad
- Use the Copy and Paste commands
- Save and print a document
- Use the Print Screen key
- Exit from a program
- Open a previously saved file
- Close a frozen program

You probably want to learn to use a computer so that you can create documents, get connected to the World Wide Web, or be entertained. Whatever program you plan to use, you'll start it from Windows 98. In this unit, you will use two handy programs that come with Windows 98: the Calculator, for performing calculations, and WordPad, for creating text documents. You will enter text and cut, copy, and paste between the two programs, using the Windows Clipboard. You will learn to save and print the documents you create and to open a document again. These procedures are the same in most programs that run under Windows 98. You will also learn to close programs properly when you have finished using them, and discover what to do if the computer you are working on quits functioning.

TASK 1 | *Starting a Program*

What: Start a program.

How: Use the Start button or the program icon.

Why: To use application software, you must start it.

Tip: When you are first learning to use Windows 98, the easiest way to start programs is from the Start menu.

As you saw in Unit 1, you can start programs easily using the Start menu, as shown in Figure 2.1:

1. Click the Start button.
2. Point to Programs.
3. If there is a submenu, point to it.
4. Click the name of the program you want to use.

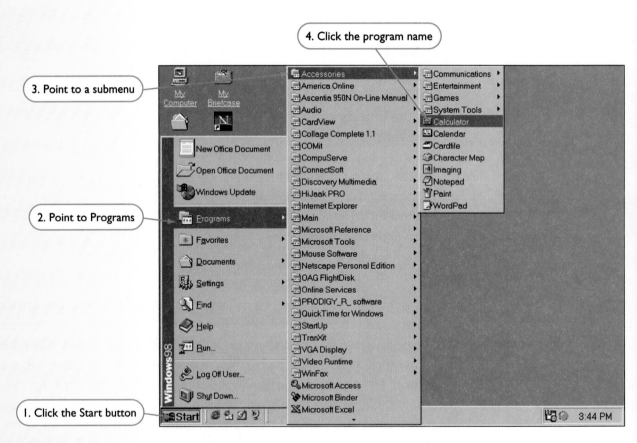

FIGURE 2.1   Starting a Program from the Start Menu

Windows 98 provides several ways to do most tasks, and there are other ways to start programs. Some methods not only start a program but also open a document in it. Here is a small sample. You will learn these methods as you go, so don't worry about mastering them now.

- If there is an icon on the desktop for the program you want to use, you can click it (double-click it in the Classic style) to start the program. Desktop icons are shortcuts, and you will learn how to place a shortcut on the desktop in Unit 6.

- Click the program's icon (double-click it in the Classic style) in a My Computer window, as illustrated in Figure 2.2. (This is what you did in Unit 1 when you opened the Control Panel from My Computer.)

- Click the Start button and point to Documents. The submenu that opens will contain the names of the fifteen documents most recently opened on your computer. Click a document name to start the program that created it and open the document.

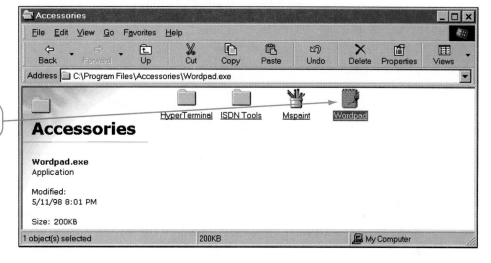

FIGURE 2.2   Starting a Program from a My Computer Window

POINTER

The Paint Program

Windows 98 includes the Paint accessory program for creating your own drawings. Paint is not taught in this book, but you can learn it from the Help screens if you are interested. You will see how to start the program in the following exercise.

EXERCISE 1 | *Starting a Program*

1. Click the **Start button** and choose **Programs | Accessories | Calculator**.

   The Calculator opens on the desktop.

2. Click the **Start button** and choose **Programs | Accessories | WordPad**.

   The WordPad program opens on the desktop, on top of the Calculator window.

3. Click the **Start button** and choose **Programs | Accessories | Paint**.

   The Paint program opens on the desktop, on top of the WordPad window.

4. Close **Paint**.

   Click the Close button on its title bar.

5. Close **WordPad**.

6. Minimize the **Calculator**.

   The Calculator is reduced to a button on the Windows taskbar, ready for use in the next exercise.

TASK 2 | *Using the Calculator*

What: Use the Calculator accessory program.

How: Click the Start button and choose Programs | Accessories | Calculator.

Why: The Calculator is a useful application either by itself or in conjunction with other programs.

Tip: If you need to do calculations while working in another program, don't forget to keep the Calculator running in the background.

In Task 1 you opened the Windows 98 Calculator accessory. This program functions just like any other calculator, but resides on your computer's desktop instead of on your actual desk.

To use the Standard Calculator, shown in Figure 2.3a, click the numbers and **operator** buttons (the symbols that represent the mathematical operations). For instance, to multiply 3 by 109, you would click 3, then *, then 1, 0, and 9, then =. As you click, the numbers and the result (327 in the example) appear in the calculator's text box. If you need help, choose Help | Help Topics | Performing Calculations.

If you need a scientific calculator, choose View | Scientific and the screen display will change to provide you with the Scientific Calculator shown in Figure 2.3b. Choose View | Standard to return to the Standard Calculator.

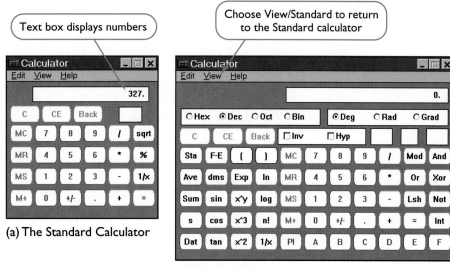

Text box displays numbers

Choose View/Standard to return to the Standard calculator

(a) The Standard Calculator

(b) The Scientific Calculator

FIGURE 2.3   The Calculator Accessory

POINTER

Use the Number Pad

Instead of clicking the Calculator's numbers with the mouse, you can press the numbers on the 10-key pad that is found at the right side of a standard keyboard. Be sure the Num Lock key is turned on, as indicated by a light on the keyboard.

EXERCISE 2 | *Using the Calculator*

1. Restore the **Calculator**.

   If you did not leave the Calculator minimized at the end of the last exercise, start it instead.

2. Using the mouse, point to and click these numbers on the Calculator: **4**, then **9**, then **3**.

   As you click the numbers, they are displayed in the Calculator's text box.

3. Click the Calculator's ***** **button** (the multiplication operator).

4. Click the number **6**.

5. Click the Calculator's = (equal) **button**.

   The operation is completed, and the number 2958 is displayed in the Calculator window—the result of the calculation 493 times 6.

6. Minimize the **Calculator**.

   The Calculator appears as a button on the taskbar. Don't close the Calculator, because you will use this calculation in Exercise 4.

TASK 3 | *Using WordPad*

What: Use the WordPad accessory program.

How: Click the Start button and choose Programs | Accessories | WordPad.

Why: You will use WordPad to complete the projects at the end of this and subsequent units.

Tip: Learning to use WordPad is an easy way to get started learning to use word processing software.

WordPad is a simple **word processor** built into Windows 98. It is best used to create small documents such as memos and letters. Because WordPad's main function is to create documents, the opening screen contains a blank document, as shown in Figure 2.4.

You will probably feel comfortable with most of the screen because it has the standard Windows interface that you became familiar with in Unit 1, with title bar, menu bar, toolbars, and status bar. Some toolbar buttons are different, but you can point to a button to display its name. The blank document that is displayed contains an **insertion point**—the blinking vertical line that marks the spot where you will begin typing. After you have typed text, you can move the insertion point to another location by pointing and clicking the mouse or by pressing one of the four arrow keys on the standard keyboard.

Editing in WordPad is simple.

- Press the Backspace key on the keyboard to erase characters to the left of the insertion point.

- Press the Delete key to erase characters to the right of the insertion point.

- To erase more than one character at a time, click and drag over the text to select it. **Selected text** is highlighted. Then press the Delete key to erase the selection.

- To replace selected text, just start typing. The first letter you type replaces the selection.

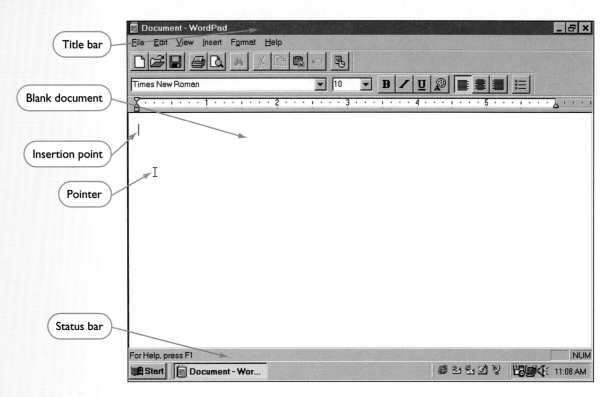

FIGURE 2.4 WordPad's Opening Screen

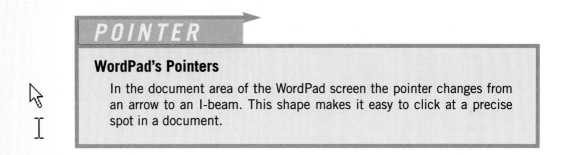

POINTER

WordPad's Pointers

In the document area of the WordPad screen the pointer changes from an arrow to an I-beam. This shape makes it easy to click at a precise spot in a document.

With a word processor, you don't need to press the Enter key at the end of a line, because the program automatically carries the text over to the next line, in a feature called **word wrap**. Pressing the Enter key begins a new paragraph. Therefore, you press the Enter key only at the end of a paragraph or when you want to end a short line such as a title.

Exercise 3 demonstrates three features of WordPad: Undo, Bullet Style, and Insert Date. To find out more about how WordPad works, use WordPad's Help feature. You will find the Help interface to be just like the one you used in Unit 1 to get help using Windows 98.

1. Start **WordPad**.

A new blank document opens.

2. Type your name and press **Enter** *twice*.

If you make a mistake, use the editing features described in this task to eliminate typing errors. Pressing Enter moves the insertion point to the next line.

3. Type **Learning to Use Windows 98** and press **Enter** *twice*.

The insertion point moves down each time you press Enter.

4. Type **Windows 98 is an operating system produced by Microsoft. Many people find using Windows 98 speeds up the performance of their computer and makes it easier to install new hardware because of its plug and play enhancements.** Press **Enter** *twice*.

When you get to the end of a line, WordPad wraps the text to the following line.

5. Type **WordPad is one of the accessory programs built into Windows 98. Two others are:** and press **Enter** *twice*.

6. Type **Calculator** and press **Enter**.

7. Type **Paint** and press **Enter** *twice*.

8. Type **At our school we have a site license for copies of Windows 98 running in our six labs.** Press **Enter** *three times*.

9. Choose **Insert | Date and Time**.

The Date and Time dialog box opens.

10. Click the down arrow in the dialog box's scroll bar to see the available date formats.

Today's date will be displayed.

11. Click the date that has the format **July 11, 1998** and then click the **OK button**.

The date is inserted into the document.

12. Position the mouse pointer at the beginning of the word *Calculator*, and click.

The insertion point is placed at the beginning of the paragraph.

13. Drag the mouse over the words *Calculator* and *Paint*, and then release the mouse.

The two paragraphs are highlighted, showing they are selected.

14. Press the **Delete key** on the keyboard.

The paragraphs are deleted.

15. Choose **Edit | Undo**.

The paragraphs are restored, and they remain selected. You could also have clicked the Undo button on the toolbar.

16. Choose **Format | Bullet Style**.

The selected paragraphs are formatted with bullets. You could also have clicked the Bullets button on the toolbar. Your document should look like the one in Figure 2.5.

17. Leave WordPad open for the next exercise.

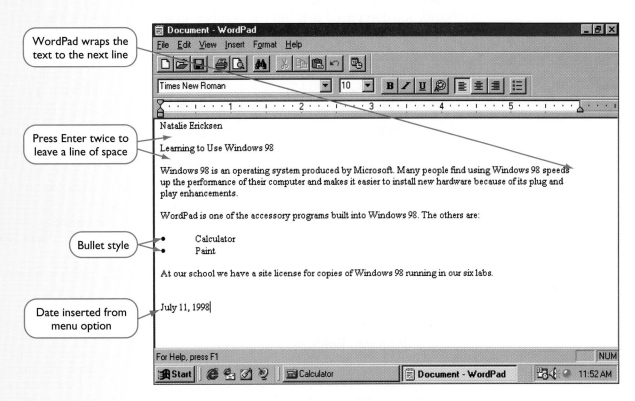

FIGURE 2.5 The Completed WordPad Document

TASK 4 | *Using Cut, Copy, and Paste*

What: Use Copy, Cut, and Paste between programs.

How: Choose Edit | Copy or Edit | Cut and then Edit | Paste.

Why: These commands let you make information created in one program available in another program.

Tip: It's a good idea to use the Copy feature (rather than Cut). The original stays intact and Windows makes a copy of it. You will then need to delete the original if you no longer want the text to appear in the original location.

Windows 98 has a storage area for material you copy or cut. It is called the **Clipboard,** and you can use it in any Windows program. To copy or cut material from a document:

1. Select the text to be copied or cut.
2. Choose Edit | Copy to leave the original and place a copy of it on the Clipboard, or choose Edit | Cut to remove the original and place it on the Clipboard.

To paste the contents of the Clipboard:

1. Start the program and open the document into which the material will be inserted.
2. Move the insertion point to the desired location.
3. Choose Edit | Paste.

When copying the results of a calculation from the Calculator to the Clipboard, you don't need to select the numbers in the Calculator text box before choosing Edit | Copy. Perform the calculation, then:

1. Choose Edit | Copy—the results will be stored on the Clipboard.
2. Start the other program, open the document, and move the insertion point to the spot where you want to insert the Clipboard contents.
3. Choose Edit | Paste.

The Calculator's Edit menu contains the Paste command. This allows you to copy a number from another program such as WordPad into the Calculator window so that you can perform a calculation on it:

1. In WordPad, select the number you want to use in a calculation.
2. Copy the number to the Clipboard, using Edit | Copy.
3. Switch to the Calculator by clicking its button on the taskbar.
4. Choose Edit | Paste and the number appears in the Calculator text box.

POINTER

The Clipboard Holds Only One Item

The Clipboard holds only the last information that you place on it, so if you copy or cut twice without pasting, the first contents are lost. However, you can paste the Clipboard contents again and again.

The Windows Clipboard is handy to use, but you should be aware of the way it works so that you don't lose valuable information.

POINTER

Saving the Clipboard Contents

The Windows Clipboard is cleared whenever you turn off your computer. If you want to save the contents of the Clipboard, you must paste it into a document and save the document before shutting down Windows and turning off the computer.

1. Click the **Calculator button** on the Windows taskbar.

The Calculator's text box still displays the result of the calculation in Exercise 2. If it does not, you can enter the number 2958 into it now.

2. Choose **Edit | Copy**.

The number in the Calculator text box is copied to the Clipboard.

3. Click the **WordPad button** on the Windows taskbar.

The WordPad window contains the document you created in Exercise 3.

4. Position the pointer just before the **c** in *copies* in the last sentence of the document in the WordPad window.

Be sure to place the pointer to the right of the space between *for* and *copies*.

5. Click the mouse to place the insertion point just before the word.

6. Choose **Edit | Paste**.

The result of the calculation is pasted into the WordPad document.

7. Press the **Spacebar** to insert a space.

Your document should look like one in Figure 2.6.

8. Leave WordPad open for the next exercise. Close the Calculator program if you like.

Paste the calculation here and press the Spacebar

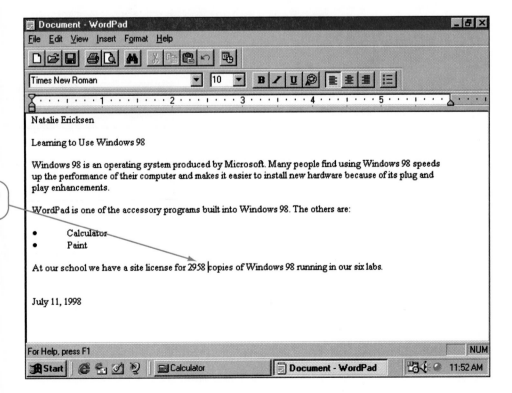

FIGURE 2.6 The WordPad Document After Pasting

What: Save a document to disk and print the document.

How: Choose File | Save As, File | Print.

Why: If you don't save your documents, you will have to retype them the next time you want them. To share them with others, you will want a hard copy.

Tip: Give your documents meaningful file names so that you will be able to find them again later.

If you exit from WordPad without saving a document you have created, it will be lost. If you need to change the document later, you will have to start from scratch by retyping it.

To save a document, choose File | Save As. The Save As dialog box opens as shown in Figure 2.7.

POINTER

Document versus File

You will find all kinds of documents referred to as files in Windows 98 dialog boxes. A **file** is simply a document you have given a name and saved on disk.

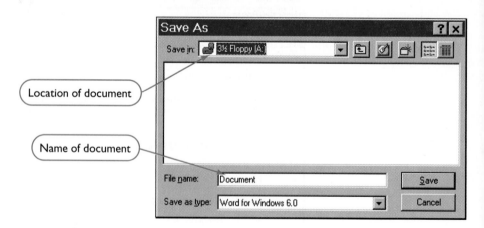

Location of document

Name of document

FIGURE 2.7 The Save As Dialog Box

Files are saved on disks in disk drives. Windows uses standard letters to designate the disk drives, as shown in Table 2.1.

Drive	My Computer Icon	Description
A		The first floppy drive
B		The second floppy drive (most computers don't have one)
C		The first built-in **hard disk drive**
D, E, F, etc.		The other disk drives: the CD-ROM drive, another hard disk drive, a removable drive, etc.

TABLE 2.1   Standard Disk Drive Letters

To choose the location where WordPad saves a file, click the downward-pointing arrow at the end of the Save in list box, as shown in Figure 2.8, and then click a drive letter.

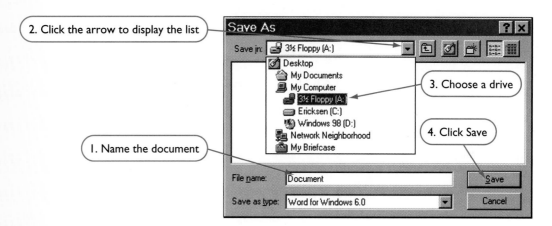

FIGURE 2.8   Choosing a Drive for Saving a Document

ORGANIZING FILES

Saving all of your files together on the C drive would be like randomly dumping papers into a file-cabinet drawer. Windows lets you organize files in folders so they will be easy to find. If you create **folders** on the drive like the hanging folders within a file drawer, you can organize your files in any way you like. Windows represents these folders with a little yellow folder icon next to the name you give them.

You can create subfolders within folders on a disk drive, just as you might have groups of related documents in folders within the hanging folders in a file cabinet. You will learn more about folders in Unit 3.

NAMING FILES

Besides selecting the folder in which to save the file, you must give the file a name. With Windows 98, you can name a file almost anything you like, but there are a few characters that can't be used in file names. Table 2.2 lists characters that can never be used in file names. Table 2.3 shows some sample file names.

Name	Character
Asterisk	*
Question mark	?
Less than	<
Greater than	>
Forward slash	/
Back slash	\
Quotation mark	"
Colon	:
Pipe		

TABLE 2.2   Invalid File Name Characters

POINTER

Don't Use Periods in File Names

Even though the period is a valid character in a file name, you should avoid using it because it can cause confusion. Windows automatically places a period at the end of a file name and a three-character extension after the period. The **three-letter extension** identifies the file type and the software that created the file. For example, Microsoft Word document files have a **.doc** extension after the file name, and Microsoft Excel spreadsheet (workbook) files have an **.xls** extension. Windows hides the extension in most screen views. If you are interested in the details, look up *extensions* in Windows Help.

File Name	Description
Oct-98 Mileage Report.xls	An Excel spreadsheet that computes mileage
JSmith-98 Evaluation.doc	A Word document that is the employee evaluation for J Smith
Index.htm	A Web document

TABLE 2.3   File Names and Extensions

PRINTING FILES

If you want a **hard copy**, that is, a copy on paper, then you need to print the document. In WordPad and other Windows programs, you can print a document by choosing File | Print. The Print dialog box opens, as shown in Figure 2.9.

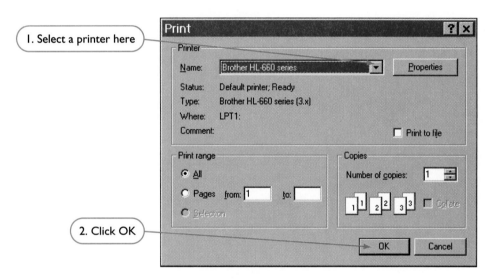

FIGURE 2.9   The Print Dialog Box

When you are just beginning to use programs, you will want to leave the printing options set to the defaults. If you are working at your own computer, attached to a single printer, you can just click the OK button in the dialog box, and the document will print. But if you are working in a lab, you will want to find out which printer you should use. The Print dialog box has a drop-down list box showing the names of all the printers attached to your system. Find out which printer you should use, and select that printer before you click OK.

Formatted Disk Needed

You will learn to format your own disks in Unit 3, but you need an already formatted 3½-inch floppy disk for Exercise 5. Be sure you have one before you start.

EXERCISE 5 | *Saving and Printing the WordPad Document*

1. With the document from Exercise 4 on your screen, choose **File | Save As**.

The Save As dialog box opens, with the default file name *Document* selected in the File Name text box.

2. Insert a formatted 3½-inch floppy disk into the A drive of your computer.

Check with your instructor to make sure this is where you should save your file.

3. In the File Name text box, type **Learning to Use Windows 98** as the name of your document.

When you begin to type, the default name is replaced.

4. Click the **downward-pointing arrow** at the right end of the Save In list box to see a list of drives like that of Figure 2.8.

5. Choose **3½ Floppy (A)**.

If your instructor wants you to save the file in a different location, choose that drive instead, and follow the instructions you have been given. This book assumes that you will use drive A, so if you use a different drive, be sure to keep the instructions handy.

6. Click the **Save button** in the dialog box.

The dialog box closes and the document is saved to the disk.

7. Click the toolbar's **Print Preview button**.

The document is displayed in Print Preview, showing you how it will look on the printed page. If you see errors, you can correct them before printing.

8. Click the **Close command button** in the Print Preview window's toolbar.

The Print Preview window closes, and you return to the document window.

9. With the document still on the screen, choose **File | Print**.

The Print dialog box opens.

10. In the Name section of the dialog box, check that the selected printer is the correct one.

11. Click **OK**.

The document is printed.

12. Close **WordPad**.

TASK 6 | *Using the Print Screen Key*

What: Copy an image of a Windows 98 screen or active window.

How: Choose Print Screen or Alt+Print Screen.

Why: To print out the contents of a window, you must copy the window to a document.

Tip: You will use the Print Screen key extensively throughout the rest of this text to provide hard copies of your work.

In Windows 98, the Print Screen key places an image of the entire screen on the Windows Clipboard, allowing you to paste it into a WordPad document or another application. This is a handy feature for those learning to use the operating system.

If you hold down the Alt key while pressing the Print Screen key (shown in this text as **Alt+Print Screen**), you will copy only the active window to the Clipboard.

POINTER

Why Is It Called the Print Screen Key?

Under older Microsoft operating systems, the Print Screen or PrtSc key automatically sent a copy of the text on the screen to the printer.

EXERCISE 6 | *Using the Print Screen Key*

1. Start the **Calculator** program.

2. With the Calculator as the active window, press **Alt+Print Screen**.

Hold down the Alt key and press the Print Screen key, then release both keys. An image of the Calculator window is copied to the Clipboard.

3. Start **WordPad**.

A new blank document opens.

4. Type your name and press **Enter** *twice*.

5. Type **Here is a copy of Microsoft's Calculator** and press **Enter** *twice*.

6. Choose **Edit | Paste**.

The image of the Calculator window appears in your document, and it remains selected.

7. Click **outside the Calculator image** or press the **right arrow key**.

The image is deselected. Until you deselect the image, anything you type will replace it in the document.

8. Click **inside the image** to select it again.

Little squares appear at the corners and edges of the image. You could click and drag these squares to resize the image on the screen.

9. Press the **Delete key** on the keyboard.

The image is removed from the document.

10. Choose **Edit | Undo**.

The deletion is undone and the image is returned to the document. Your document should now look like Figure 2.10.

11. Save the file as **Calculator** on the same disk where you saved the document in Exercise 5.

12. Leave WordPad and the Calculator open for the next exercise.

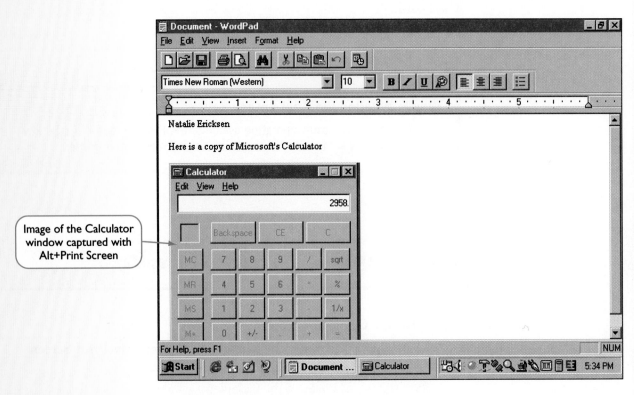

FIGURE 2.10 The Calculator Document

TASK 7 | *Exiting from Programs*

What: Exit correctly from programs.

How: Choose File | Exit.

Why: You can cause problems with your system if you don't exit from software before turning off the computer.

Tip: You can also use the Close button on the title bar to exit from programs.

To exit from a program, choose File | Exit or click the Close button on the title bar. If the document has not been saved, you will be asked if you want to save it.

POINTER

Exit Before Shutting Down

To keep Windows 98 and all your programs working properly, you should exit from (close) all open programs before shutting down Windows 98.

EXERCISE 7 | *Exiting from Programs*

1. With WordPad open from Exercise 6, choose **File | Exit**.

The WordPad program closes and its button vanishes from the taskbar.

2. On the Calculator window, click the **Close button**.

All active programs have been closed.

TASK 8 | *Opening a File*

What: Open a file.

How: In the application program, choose File | Open.

Why: Once you save a file, you will want to open it again at a later time.

Tip: If you can click a file name (double-click it in the Classic view) in a My Computer or Windows Explorer window, the program that created the file will start and open the file.

Once you save files, you will want to open them again to make changes, to print, or simply to review or reuse the information. To open a file in an application:

1. Start the application, such as WordPad.
2. Choose File | Open to open the Open dialog box, shown in Figure 2.11.
3. Select the name of the file in the file list box, or click the down arrow on the Look in box to select the correct location, and then select the file name.
4. Click the Open button.

Notice that the Open dialog box looks much like the Save As dialog box in Figure 2.8. Where the Save As dialog box has a Save in list box, the Open dialog box has a Look in list box. If you saved a document in drive A, then you will choose the 3½ Floppy (A) drive in the Look in list box when you want to open the document again.

In the following exercise you will open the WordPad document you saved in Exercise 5. You will open it from within WordPad, but then you will also see two other ways to open a document.

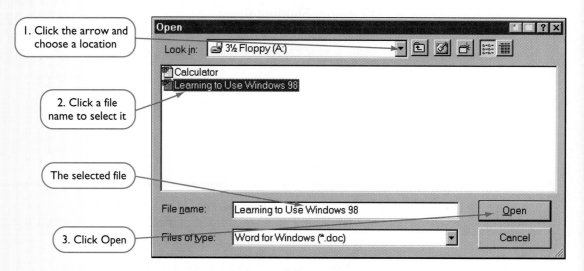

FIGURE 2.11   The Open Dialog Box

POINTER

Finding Files

Don't worry if finding the correct files sounds difficult. Windows 98 includes utilities that help you locate files. You will learn more about finding files in Unit 4.

EXERCISE 8 | *Opening a File*

1. Insert the disk containing the documents you saved in Exercises 5 and 6 into **drive A**.

You saved the *Learning to Use Windows* 98 document in Exercise 5 and the *Calculator* document in Exercise 6.

2. Start **WordPad**.

WordPad opens with a new blank document on the screen.

3. Choose **File | Open**.

The Open dialog box opens.

4. Check the **Look in text box**. If the **3½ Floppy (A) drive** isn't shown in the box, click the down arrow and click it to select it.

The file list changes to show the files saved in the selected location.

5. Select the **Learning to Use Windows 98 file name** in the file list.

Notice that you have to *click* the file name to select it—you can't just point to it. The Open dialog box uses the Classic view, not the Web view. When you select the file name, it is placed in the File Name text box.

6. Click the **Open button**.

The *Learning to Use Windows* 98 document opens on the desktop. If you wanted to print the document again, or change it and save the changes, you could do so.

7. Choose **File | Exit**.

WordPad closes.

8. Click the **Start button** and choose **Documents**.

A submenu opens listing the last fifteen documents that have been opened on your computer.

9. Click **Learning to Use Windows 98**.

WordPad (or Word, if it is installed on your system) starts, and opens the document.

10. Choose **File | Exit**.

WordPad (or Word) closes.

11. Open **My Computer**.

The drives on your system are shown.

12. Click the **3½ Floppy (A) drive icon**.

The contents of the floppy disk are shown.

13. Click the **Learning to Use Windows 98 file name** or **icon**.

WordPad (or Word, if it is installed on your system) starts, and opens the document.

14. Choose **File | Exit**.

WordPad (or Word) closes.

15. Close **My Computer**.

What: Close a program that stops functioning when you are using it.

How: Press Ctrl+Alt+Delete.

Why: This is the proper way to shut down the task or program that is not working.

Tip: Never just turn off a system; instead, use Ctrl+Alt+Delete to close and even shut down when there is a problem.

Sometimes when you are using software, the computer will freeze up; that is, it will stop responding to your mouse clicks or your keystrokes. When this happens, you need to end the task or program that is malfunctioning.

Instead of turning off the system, you should hold down the Ctrl key and the Alt key while you press the Delete key. The Close Program dialog box will open, as shown in Figure 2.12.

1. Choose the program to close

2. Click End Task

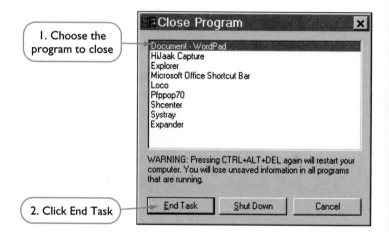

FIGURE 2.12   The Close Program Dialog Box

The top of the dialog box lists all open programs. Select the malfunctioning program and click the End Task button. This should clear up the problem. If the problem persists, repeat the same steps for all the open programs, and then choose the Shut Down button.

End Task, End Task, End Task

In Exercise 8 you close the Calculator program as if it were frozen. The exercise isn't totally realistic, because the Calculator isn't actually malfunctioning when you press Ctrl+Alt+Delete. When a program is actually malfunctioning, you sometimes have to click the End Task button more than once before anything happens. Then another dialog box opens, where you confirm that you want to end the task.

EXERCISE 9 | *Closing a Program as If It Isn't Responding*

1. Start the **Calculator**.
2. Press and hold **Ctrl**, press and hold **Alt**, and press **Delete**.

   The Close Program dialog box opens, with a list of all open programs.

3. If the Calculator program is not already selected, click the **Calculator program name** in the dialog box, and then press the **End Task button**.

   The Calculator program closes.

R E V I E W

S U M M A R Y

After completing this unit, you should
- be able to start Windows 98 programs
- be able to use the Calculator
- be able to use WordPad
- have learned to copy, cut, and paste
- be able to save a document
- be able to print a document
- have learned to use the Print Screen key to copy the entire screen
- have learned to use the Alt+Print Screen key combination to copy the active window
- have learned how to exit correctly from programs
- have learned to open a file in an application program
- have learned to close a frozen program using Ctlr+Alt+Delete

K E Y   T E R M S

Clipboard *(page 39)*
extension *(page 44)*
file *(page 42)*
folder *(page 43)*
hard copy *(page 45)*
hard disk drive *(page 43)*

insertion point *(page 36)*
operator *(page 34)*
selected text *(page 36)*
word processor *(page 36)*
word wrap *(page 37)*

T E S T   Y O U R   S K I L L S

True/False

1. Windows lets you organize disks into files and folders.
2. WordPad is used for creating text documents.
3. If you need a scientific calculator, you will need to buy a specialized software package.
4. If a program is frozen, try pressing Ctrl+Alt+Delete.
5. The Clipboard stores whatever you have copied to it even after you have shut off the computer.

Multiple Choice

1. The built-in hard disk drive is usually named
   a. B
   b. A
   c. F
   d. C

2. The floppy drive is usually named
   a. E
   b. A
   c. F
   d. C

3. The CD-ROM drive is usually named
   a. A or B
   b. B or C
   c. D or E
   d. A or F

4. When you are saving a file, you should never use which character in a file name?
   a. a colon
   b. a number
   c. a space
   d. a comma

5. The Print Screen key captures the contents of
   a. the Clipboard
   b. the screen
   c. the insertion point
   d. all of these answers.

Match the letter of the correct word with the correct location in Figure 2.13:

___ a. Operator   ___ d. Status bar

___ b. Menu bar   ___ e. Pointer

___ c. Document   ___ f. Insertion point

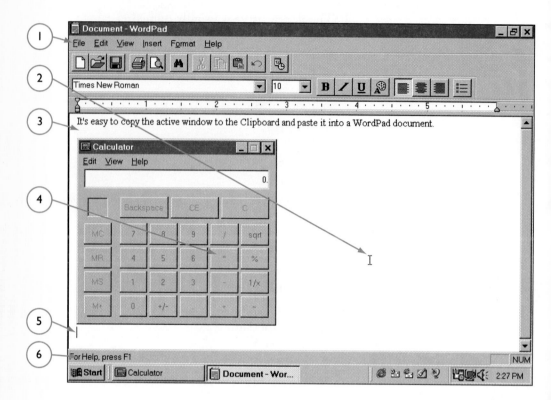

PROJECTS

1. (a) Open a new WordPad document. Type your name at the top of the document and leave a line of space. (b) Type: Learning to use Microsoft Windows 98 is actually fun and easy if you go step by step. Before you know it, you are using programs and creating documents. (c) Save the document as **Learning** on the disk in drive A and print the document.

2. (a) Perform the following calculation using the Calculator: **5** plus **146** minus **3** times **2** divided by **3**. Copy the result. (b) Open a new WordPad document. Type your name at the top of the document and leave a line of space. (c) Type **The result of the mathematical calculation for Project 2 is:** (d) Paste the result of the calculation. (e) Save the document as **Calculation Exercise** on the disk in drive A and print the document.

3. (a) Open a new WordPad document. Type your name at the top of the document and leave a line of space. (b) Paste a copy of the Control Panel window into the WordPad document. (c) Save the document as **Print Screen Exercise** on the disk in drive A and print the document.

4. (a) Paste a copy of the entire desktop into a new WordPad document and add your name below it. (b) Print the document and close it without saving it.

Working with Disks

UNIT OBJECTIVES

- Find out what is on a disk
- View the disk contents using icons or lists
- Sort the disk contents by file type, date, size, and name
- Format a disk
- Copy an entire disk
- Create a new folder on a disk

In Unit 2, you learned about saving files to disks. You were introduced to disk drives and folders, and you learned to distinguish a floppy disk drive from a hard disk drive. In this unit you will learn to work with disks; that is, see what's on them, view them in different ways so you can find what you are looking for, prepare disks for use, and copy disks. Windows 98 provides two ways for you to view and manage files—My Computer and Windows Explorer. Both utilities show you the folders, programs, and files that you have available on your computer system. A My Computer window displays the contents of a single drive or folder while the Explorer window has a second pane that shows the structure of your whole system.

What: See what files are on a disk.
How: Use Windows Explorer.
Why: To use your files, you need to know where they are.
Tip: You can also use My Computer to view disk contents.

When you opened My Computer from the desktop in Unit 1 (see Figure 1.5), you saw icons representing your computer's disk drives. You can view the contents of the individual drives from My Computer, but a quicker way is to use Windows Explorer. You open Windows Explorer from the Start menu. Figure 3.1 shows Windows Explorer open on the desktop.

Like the Windows 98 Help windows you opened in Unit 1, the Windows Explorer window is divided into two frames or panes. The left pane displays icons for the drives and folders on your computer system and the network (if any) to which it is attached. You can see all of the folders on your whole system in this left pane. In either the Web or the Classic view, you must *click* a folder name to select the folder in the left pane.

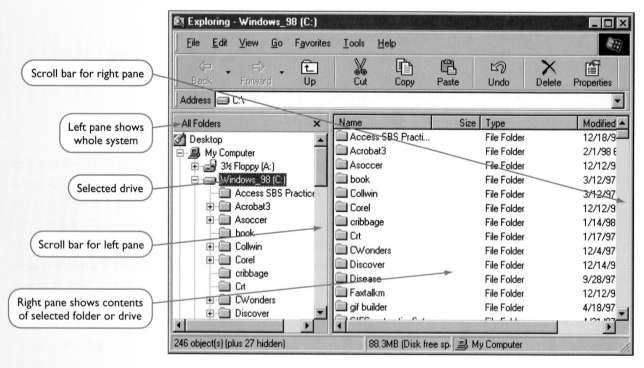

FIGURE 3.1   Windows Explorer

Disk Labels

To help you remember what is stored on a drive, you can attach an electronic label to it. The label for a hard disk drive is listed with the drive letter in a My Computer or Windows Explorer window. The C drive in the figures in this unit is labeled *Windows_98,* but the C drive on your system may not be labeled, or may have a different label. You will learn how to label drives and floppy disks in Task 4.

Each folder is represented by a folder icon and a name. Some folders in the list will have a plus sign (+) in front of the icon. The plus sign indicates that at least one subfolder is contained in that folder. When you click the plus sign, the folder expands to display the subfolders, and the plus sign changes to a minus sign (−), indicating that all the subfolders are displayed. If a subfolder appears with a plus sign (+), it also has at least one subfolder in it, as shown in Figure 3.2. You can click a minus sign (−) to hide the subfolders; the minus sign then changes to a plus sign.

Most computers have more folders than can be shown on the screen at one time. To move to another part of the list, you use the vertical scroll bar. (Remember from Unit 1 that each pane has its own scroll bar.)

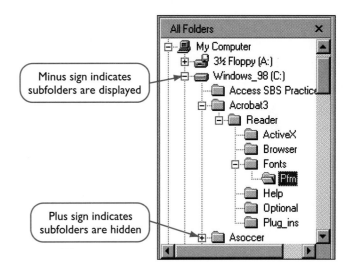

FIGURE 3.2 Expanding Folder Views

The right pane of the Windows Explorer window shows the contents of the folder or drive selected in the left pane. As you click different locations or folders in the left pane, the folders and files located there will be displayed.

Notice the folders located on drive A shown in Figure 3.3. The Address bar and the status bar in Figure 3.3 display information about the selected folder, and the title bar shows its name.

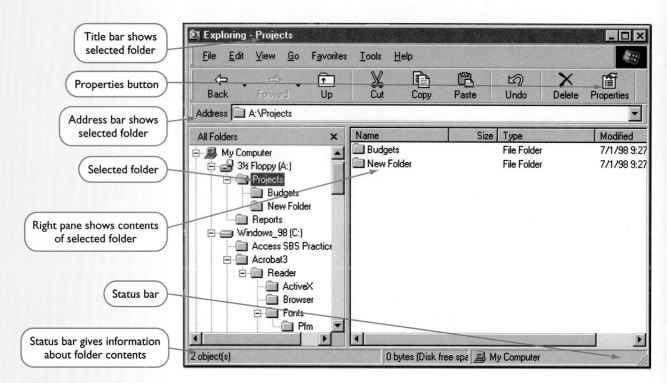

FIGURE 3.3 A Folder with Subfolders Displayed

Why Doesn't My Screen Match the Book?

The right pane of a Windows Explorer window can display disk contents in four different views. You'll learn how to change views in Task 2. In Exercise 1 you will be examining the left pane of the Explorer window, and so the view in the right pane doesn't matter.

You can see more information about a drive or folder by selecting it (either in the left or right pane) and then clicking the Properties button on the Standard Buttons toolbar. The General tab of the Properties dialog box provides information as shown in Figure 3.4.

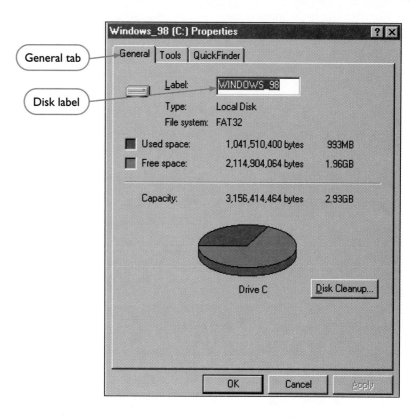

General tab

Disk label

FIGURE 3.4 Properties for a Disk Drive

EXERCISE 1 | *Viewing the Contents of Drive C*

1. Click the **Start button** and choose **Programs | Windows Explorer**.

Windows Explorer opens.

2. Click the **up scroll arrow** in the left pane's vertical scroll bar to scroll to the top of the pane.

The Desktop icon will be at the top, and you should see the icon for drive C.

3. If the icon for drive C has a plus sign (+) in front of it, click the **plus sign** to expand the view of the drive.

If the icon has a minus sign (−) in front of it, the view is already expanded.

4. Click the **Program Files folder** in the left pane of the window, scrolling down if necessary to find it.

Even though you are in the Web view, you must *click* a folder in the left pane of Windows Explorer to select it. You can't just point to it. The icon changes to an open file folder; the title bar and Address bar change to show the selection; and the contents of the Program Files folder are displayed in the right pane of the window.

5. If the Program Files icon has a plus sign in front of it, click the **plus sign** to expand the folder view.

6. In the list of subfolders below the Program Files folder, click **any folder name with a plus sign** (+) in front of its icon.

The contents of the subfolder are displayed in the right pane of the window.

7. Click the **Program Files folder's minus sign** (−).

The subfolders are no longer displayed, and the Program Files folder is again selected.

8. Click the **Properties button** on the Standard Buttons toolbar.

The Properties dialog box displays information about the folder.

9. Click the Properties dialog box's **OK button**.

The dialog box closes.

10. Close **Windows Explorer**.

TASK 2 | *Changing the Display of Disk Contents*

What: You can view more or less information about files on a disk.

How: Choose View | Large Icons, View | Small Icons, View | List, View | Details, View as Web Page, View | Refresh.

Why: Different views are best for different purposes.

Tip: Choosing a view from the Views button's drop-down list is faster than using the menu.

Windows 98 offers several different views of the disk contents. You can display a large icon for each folder or file, a small icon, a list, or details. Each of these views has its uses. You may have a hard time finding a file if the large icons are displayed; but at other times you may not want to see all the information provided by a detailed display. Figure 3.5 displays the same disk contents using the four views described in Table 3.1.

Option	Result
Large Icons	Displays a large icon with the name under the icon.
Small Icons	Displays a small icon with the name. The display extends horizontally across the window.
List	Displays a small icon with the name. The display extends vertically down the screen.
Details	Displays columns of information including the file name, type, size, and date the file was last modified.

TABLE 3.1   Four Views of Folders and Files

To change the display of the file contents, choose the View menu. The active display option appears on the drop-down menu with a • in front of it.

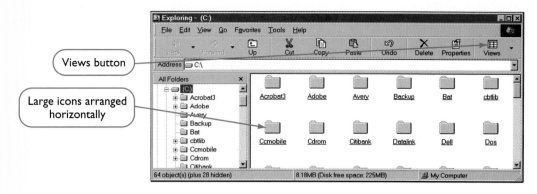

Views button

Large icons arranged horizontally

(a) The Large Icons View

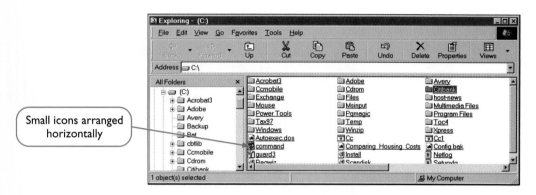

Small icons arranged horizontally

(b) The Small Icons View

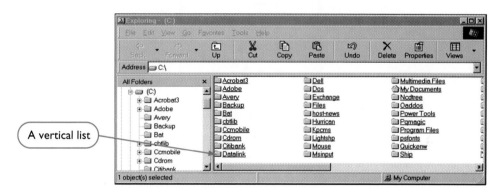

A vertical list

(c) The List View

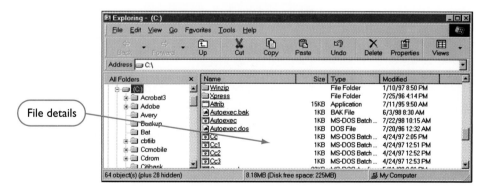

File details

(d) The Details View

FIGURE 3.5   Four Views of Disk Contents

To change to a different view, click its name in the list: Large Icons, Small Icons, List, or Details.

There are two other useful view options:

- **View as Web page**: With any of the views you can choose the *View as Web Page* option. Figure 3.6 shows the List view of a disk in drive A displayed as a Web page. This option adds a new frame giving information about the selected object (a text document in the figure).

- **Refresh**: When you perform an operation on the disk such as moving a file, the display may not immediately change to reflect it. Choose View | Refresh and the window will be updated to reflect the change.

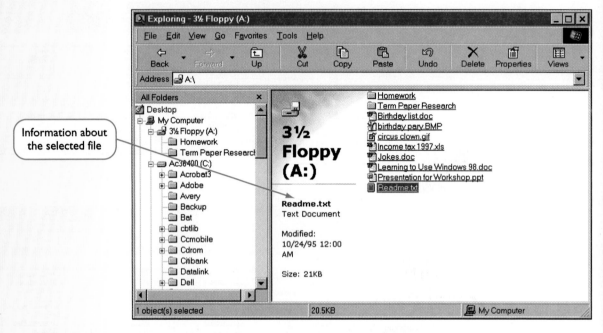

Information about the selected file

FIGURE 3.6   Viewing a Disk as a Web Page

POINTER

Why Do My Folders Open in Different Views?

If you choose View | Folder Options | View tab, you will find a list of Advanced settings. Expand the Files and Folders folder in the list and you will find a check box for "Remember each folder's view settings." If that box is checked, each folder will reopen in the view in which it was last closed. If the box is not checked, each folder always opens in the same view.

EXERCISE 2 | *Changing the View*

1. Open **Windows Explorer**.

2. In the left pane, click **drive C** and expand it to display its folders.

The contents of the C drive are displayed in the right pane. The title bar and Address bar display the new address.

3. In the left pane, open the **Windows folder**.

If a message warns you not to modify the contents of the folder, read it and click Show Files. The contents of the Windows folder are displayed in the right pane.

4. Choose **View | Details**.

The right pane displays the contents of the Windows folder with full details. We will use this view in the next exercise.

5. Choose **View | List**.

The view changes to a list running down the display. This view displays the greatest number of folders and files in a single window.

6. Choose **View | Large Icons**.

The view changes to large icons. This view is handy for a folder with few items in it.

7. Choose **View | Small Icons**.

The display changes to smaller icons running horizontally across the window.

8. Close **Windows Explorer**.

TASK 3 | *Sorting the Disk Contents*

What: Arrange the file list.

How: Choose View | Arrange Icons.

Why: When you are looking for a file, it can help to arrange the files by date or file type instead of by name.

Tip: You can arrange files in My Computer following the same method you use for Windows Explorer.

By default, the file list is arranged in alphabetical order by the name of the file. If you want to change that order to help you find a file, you can choose View | Arrange Icons and then select a sort order from the submenu. Figures 3.7 shows the same data sorted by date, type, size, and name. These sort orders are described in Table 3.2.

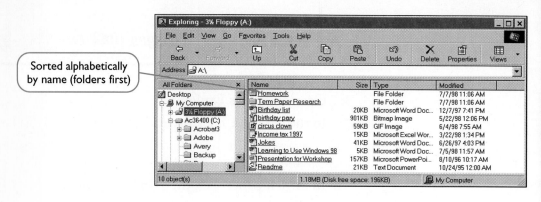

Sorted alphabetically by name (folders first)

(a) Sorted by Name

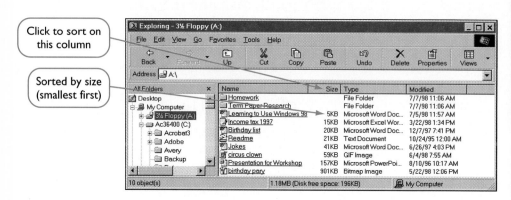

Click to sort on this column

Sorted by size (smallest first)

(b) Sorted by Size

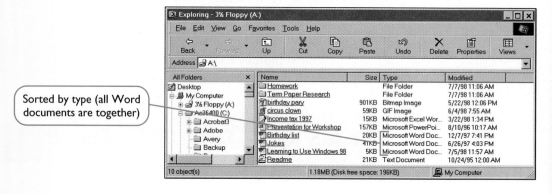

Sorted by type (all Word documents are together)

(c) Sorted by Type

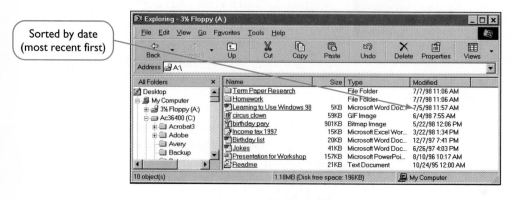

Sorted by date (most recent first)

(d) Sorted by Date

FIGURE **3.7**   Four Ways to Sort Files

Sort Order	Result
Date	The file list is sorted by date, with the newest date at the top. That is, the most recently created or modified file appears at the top of the list, and the oldest file appears at the bottom.
Type	The file list is sorted by three-letter extension, placing all files created by the same software application together in the listing.
Size	The file list is sorted by file size, with the smallest file at the top of the list and the largest file at the bottom.
Name	Files are sorted alphabetically by file name.

TABLE 3.2 Four Ways to Sort Files

One quick method for sorting files is to choose View|Details in either Windows Explorer or My Computer. The buttons at the top of the right pane in the Details view are more than headings for the columns. Clicking one of them sorts the files on that column. Clicking the button again reverses the order of the sort (for instance, to sort from Z to A instead of from A to Z).

POINTER

Folders Come Before Files

When you are sorting a window that contains both folders and files, you may become confused by the results. Folders, represented by small yellow folder icons, are sorted separately from files. They are displayed at the top of the list, or at the bottom if you reverse the sort. To see the files, accompanied by icons representing the software that created them, scroll down past all the yellow file folders.

EXERCISE 3 | *Sorting the File List*

1. Open **Windows Explorer**.
2. Display the contents of **drive C**.
3. Choose **View | Details**.
4. If necessary, scroll down past all yellow file-folder icons.

   The files on drive C are displayed.

5. Choose **View | Arrange Icons**.

6. Choose **by Date**.

The list is sorted by date.

7. Click the **Type button** at the top of the list.

The files are sorted by file type.

8. Click the **Name button**.

The files are sorted by file name.

9. Close **Windows Explorer**.

| Type |
| Name |

TASK 4 | *Formatting a Disk*

What: Prepare disks to work with Windows 98.

How: Choose File | Format.

Why: The operating system cannot read an unformatted disk.

Tip: Even though the 3½″ disks have a hard plastic case, they are still called **floppy disks**. Calling them hard disks is erroneous.

Disks have to be prepared for use before Windows 98 can read them. The process of preparing the disk is called **formatting** the disk. You can buy formatted disks, but you should learn how to format them yourself.

> ### POINTER
>
> **Formatting Can Be Dangerous to Your Computer's Health**
>
> The Format command can be a dangerous option if you don't know how to use it correctly, so you should do this exercise even if your floppy disks are already formatted.

WHAT FORMATTING DOES

When you choose the Format command, Windows electronically divides the disk into sectors and places tracks on the disk. The Format command also places a table of contents on the disk at the first track, called track 0 (zero). This table of contents is called the **File Allocation Table, FAT**.

The File Allocation Table keeps track of all files on the disk and their exact address by track and sector. For example, the file *June Report.doc* may be located at track 03, sector 04. This addressing scheme allows for direct and quick access of files. For example, when you are using Microsoft Word and want to open the *June Report.doc*, you don't have to wait a long time as Windows searches the entire disk from beginning to end to find the file. Instead, Windows searches the FAT, locating the *June Report.doc* at track 03 sector 04. The file is quickly accessed at that address and opened in the software.

FORMATTING A DISK

To format a floppy disk, place it in the floppy disk drive and open My Computer. Select (but do not open) the 3½ floppy (A) drive in the display.

- In the Web view, point to the drive icon.
- In the Classic view, single-click it.

With the 3½ (A) drive selected, choose File | Format. The Format dialog box opens, as shown in Figure 3.8.

POINTER

View Disks Before Reformatting Them

Formatting a disk wipes all files from the disk. Check the disk you are about to format by viewing its contents to be sure that you won't lose valuable information. Make sure you are formatting the disk in drive A, not drive C.

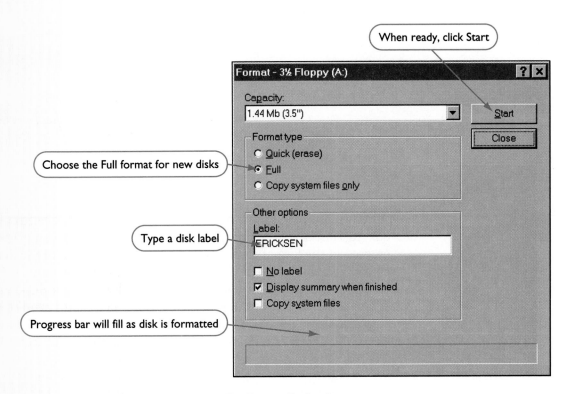

FIGURE 3.8 The Format Dialog Box

The Format dialog box is divided into sections.

- **Capacity**: The *Capacity* option allows you to format older disks that have a smaller capacity than the drive will accommodate. Use it to choose a 720 Kb disk only if you need to format such a disk. (It has only one square hole, whereas a 1.44 Mb disk has two square holes.)
- **Format type**: If the disk is brand new and has never been used, then you must select the *Full* format type, which checks the disk for errors and prepares it for use. If the disk has already been formatted and used to store files, you can choose the *Quick (erase)* option to erase all the existing files.
- **Label**: You can attach an electronic label to the disk by typing a name in the Label text box. Many people use this feature to help identify the department or person the disk belongs to. To see the label of a formatted disk, select the disk or open it and click the toolbar's Properties button.
- **Display summary when finished**: This option, which is selected by default, displays statistics about the disk when the format is complete, as shown in Figure 3.9.

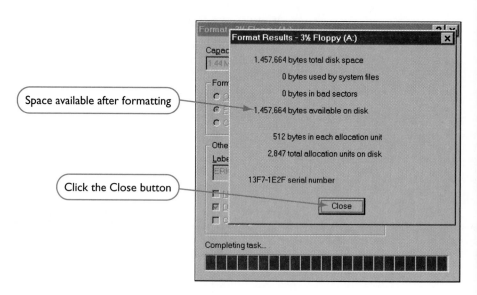

FIGURE 3.9   Displaying Format Results

When you have made all your selections, click the Start button in the dialog box to start the formatting process. As the disk is being formatted, the progress of the format is shown in the bar at the bottom of the dialog box (see Figure 3.9, where the bar is full at the end of the format).

After the disk is formatted, the Format Results box displays a summary. When you close the box, the Format dialog box remains open so that you can format another disk. Click its Close button when you are through. The formatted disk is ready to be used with any software running under Windows 98.

EXERCISE 4 | *Formatting a Disk*

1. Place a blank disk in **drive A**.

2. Open **My Computer**.

3. Select but do not open the **3½ Floppy (A) drive**.

   To select the drive, point to it in the Web style or single-click it in the Classic style. The drive label and icon will be highlighted.

4. Choose **File | Format**.

   The Format dialog box opens. If the File menu does not contain the Format option, you have not selected the drive or have opened it. Start again.

5. Choose **Full** in the Type section of the Format dialog box.

6. Type your **last name** in the Label text box.

   Later, when you want to see the label, you can click the Properties button on the toolbar.

7. Make sure the **Display summary when finished option** is selected.

8. Click the **Start button** in the dialog box.

   The progress bar at the bottom of the dialog box will fill as the disk is being formatted, keeping you informed of the format process. When the format is complete, the Format Results box will open.

9. View the format statistics.

   Bad sectors in a reformatted old disk may indicate a disk that will soon fail, so you may want to replace it.

10. Click the **Close button** in the Format Results dialog box.

11. Click the **Close button** in the Format dialog box.

    The disk is now ready to be used.

12. Close **My Computer**.

TASK 5 | *Copying a Floppy Disk*

What: Make an exact copy of a floppy disk.

How: Choose File | Copy Disk.

Why: If you want to make a backup of a floppy disk, you can copy the entire disk.

Tip: If you try to copy to an unformatted disk, Windows will prompt you to format the disk first.

It's a good idea to copy disks that contain valuable information, to ensure against lost data. To copy an entire disk to another disk, follow these steps:

1. Place the original disk (the disk you want to copy) in drive A.
2. Open My Computer.
3. Select but do not open drive A.
4. Choose File I Copy Disk, and the Copy Disk dialog box will open, as shown in Figure 3.10.
5. Click the Start button in the Copy Disk dialog box, and Windows will read the contents of the disk.
6. When a Copy Disk message box prompts you for the destination disk, remove the original disk from drive A and place a formatted disk in the drive (see Figure 3.11).
7. Click OK, and Windows copies the information that it read from the previous disk to the disk in drive A. The result is two floppy disks with the exact same information on each disk.

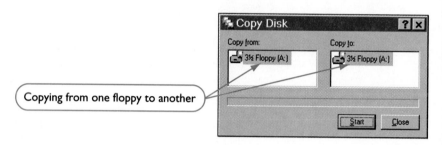

FIGURE 3.10   The Copy Disk Dialog Box

FIGURE 3.11   The Copy Disk Message Box

POINTER

Write-Protecting Floppy Disks

To protect the contents of a disk with important documents, you can write-protect the disk. To do so, open the sliding tab at one corner of the disk. Now you can read the documents on the disk, but you cannot change them or erase them.

EXERCISE 5 | *Copying a Floppy Disk*

1. Insert a disk with some files on it into **drive A**.

2. Open **My Computer**.

3. Select but do not open the **3½ Floppy (A) drive**.

   The disk icon and label are highlighted.

4. Choose **File | Copy Disk**.

   The Copy Disk dialog box opens.

5. Click the **Start button** in the dialog box.

   While the disk is being read, a progress bar begins to fill and the text "Reading source disk" is displayed in the dialog box.

6. When a message appears telling you to insert the disk you want to copy to, remove the **source disk** from the drive and replace it with **the disk you formatted** in the previous exercise.

   The copying process erases any data already on the destination disk, so you should be careful what disk you use.

7. Click **OK**.

   As the progress bar continues to fill, the dialog box now displays the text "Writing to destination disk." When the copy is complete, the text changes to "Copy completed successfully."

8. Click the **Close button** in the dialog box.

TASK 6 | *Creating a Folder on a Disk*

What: Create a folder to organize your files.

How: Choose File | New | Folder.

Why: You will have a difficult time finding your files if they aren't organized.

Tip: You can use either My Computer or Windows Explorer to create a new folder.

In Unit 2 you got a brief introduction to folders and subfolders. As you work with files, you will want to organize them in folders to keep track of them. You can create folders for projects you are working on, for instance, or keep your word processing files in one folder and your spreadsheet files in another. You can create folders within other folders. Your individual needs will determine the folder structure that works for you. (In the next unit you will copy and move files into folders to help you organize your disk storage.)

Remember this and you will not go wrong: *Windows creates new folders within whatever drive or folder you have open when you choose File | New | Folder.*

If you have the My Documents folder open on the C drive, any new folder you create will become a subfolder of My Documents. So the first step in creating a new folder is to open the drive and folder where you want the new folder to appear.

To create and name a folder:

1. Open My Computer and open the drive (and folder) in which you want the new folder to appear.
2. Choose File | New | Folder, or right-click to open a shortcut menu and choose New | Folder. Both methods place a new folder on the screen, named *New Folder*, as shown in Figure 3.12.
3. The name *New Folder* remains selected. To rename the folder, simply start typing. The words *New Folder* will be replaced by the name you type. Press the Enter key or click the mouse outside the selected text to make the name permanent.

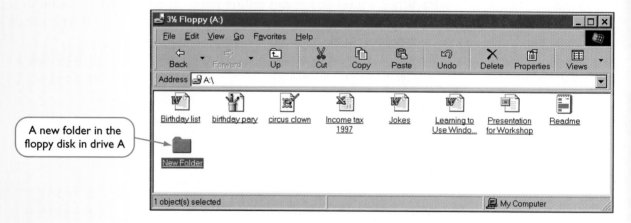

FIGURE 3.12 Creating a New Folder

Open the new folder just as you would any other folder, by clicking it (in the Web style) or double-clicking it (in the Classic style). When it is open, you can create a new folder within it, following the same steps.

POINTER

Typing Addresses of Folders and Files

Remember from Unit 1 that if you type a document address in the Address bar and press Enter, Windows will take you to the document. How do you type the address if a document is stored in a folder? To open the *Project 1* file stored in the *Homework* subfolder of the *My Documents* folder on drive C, you would type **c:\My Documents\Homework\Project 1**. Type the drive letter first, then the folder name, then the subfolder name, and finally the file name. Use the backslash character to separate the parts of the address, and put a colon after the drive letter. Internet addresses are typed differently. You'll learn about them in Unit 8.

Quick, Simple Microsoft Windows 98

EXERCISE 6 | *Creating Folders*

1. After placing a disk in drive A, open **My Computer**.

2. Open the **3½ Floppy (A) drive**.

The My Computer window for drive A opens, and its contents, if any, are displayed. The Address bar shows the address, and the title bar reads *3½ Floppy (A)*.

3. Choose **File | New | Folder**.

A new folder appears in the window with the name *New Folder* selected.

4. Type **Homework** and press **Enter**.

The folder is renamed *Homework*.

5. Open the **Homework folder**.

The Homework folder replaces the folder for the A drive in the My Computer window.

6. Right-click inside the window.

A shortcut menu opens.

7. Choose **New | Folder**.

A new folder is created within the Homework folder with the name *New Folder*.

8. Type **Projects** and press **Enter**.

The new folder within the *Homework* folder is renamed *Projects*.

9. Close **My Computer**.

SUMMARY

After completing this unit, you should
- be able to find out what is on a disk
- be able to view the disk contents using icons or lists
- be able to view the disk contents by file type, date, size, and name
- have learned to sort the files on a disk
- have learned to format a disk
- be able to copy an entire disk
- be able to create a new folder on a disk

KEY TERMS

disk capacity (*page 70*)
File Allocation Table (FAT)
  (*page 68*)

floppy disk (*page 68*)
formatting (*page 68*)

TEST YOUR SKILLS

True/False

1. Folders can't have subfolders in Windows 98.
2. You can sort files by date with the last files at the top of the list.
3. You can make a duplicate of a floppy disk using the Copy Disk command.
4. You can change the size of the icons that display in a file list.
5. Formatting prepares a disk for use.

Multiple Choice

1. The Quick Format option
   a. doesn't erase the contents of the disk
   b. must be used on a brand new disk
   c. erases the contents of the disk
   d. doesn't use a File Allocation Table

2. To view the contents of a disk with a display that includes the date last modified, you would choose
    a. View | Refresh
    b. View | List
    c. View | Date
    d. View | Details
3. New folders
    a. are created within the open folder
    b. are given the name New Folder
    c. are used to organize files
    d. all of these answers
4. Sorting by Type
    a. places all files saved on the same day together
    b. sorts all files created by the same software together
    c. sorts folders and files together
    d. all of these answers
5. To see the contents of a disk in one window, you would use
    a. Windows Explorer
    b. My Computer
    c. WordPad
    d. All of these answers

Short Answer

1. To locate a file you created last March, it would be helpful to sort by _____.
2. To see the type of files you are looking at, you would view _____.
3. Formatting electronically divides the disk into _____.
4. The _____ _____ _____ is the listing of all files and their location on the disk.
5. You should consider organizing your files into _____.

PROJECTS

1. (a) Format a disk, giving it the label **Practice**. (b) When the disk is formatted, create a new folder on the disk. Name the folder **Homework**. (c) View the contents of the disk and capture the display of the window. (d) In WordPad, create a document containing your name, the title **Project 1**, and the screen display. Save the document as **Project 1** on the *Practice* disk. Print the document.

2. (a) View the Windows folder on drive C. Scroll down below the folders until you can see the files, then enlarge the window so that you can see as many files as possible. Capture the display of the window.
(b) Print the results in WordPad in a document that also includes your name and the title **Project 2**. (c) Delete the screen image from

the WordPad document, so that it now contains only your name and *Project 2*. Save the WordPad document on the *Practice* disk, naming the file **Project 2**.

3. (a) Using the same display you opened in Project 2, sort the files by size, and then capture the display of the window. (b) Print the results in WordPad in a document that also includes your name and the title **Project 3**. (c) Delete the screen image from the WordPad document, so that it now contains only your name and *Project 3*. Save the WordPad document on the *Practice* disk, naming the file **Project 3**.

4. (a) Copy the entire *Practice Disk* to another disk, formatting the second disk if necessary. Label the new disk **Backup**. (Hint: Use the Properties button.) (b) Capture the display of the Properties dialog box for the *Backup* disk. (c) Print the result in WordPad in a document that also includes your name and the title **Project 4**. (d) Delete the screen image from the WordPad document, and then save it on the *Practice* disk (not the *Backup* disk), naming it **Project 4**. (e) Keep the *Practice* disk for use in subsequent projects.

CHECK POINT

PROJECTS

1. Using WordPad, type your name at the top of a document. On the next line type **Check Point for Units 1–3**, **Project 1**. Reduce the Word-Pad program window to Restored size so that it occupies only a part of the desktop, and then capture the contents of the entire Windows 98 desktop. Paste the results into the WordPad document and print the document. Then delete the screen image from the document and save it as **Review 1** on the *Practice* disk. Using a pen or pencil, write the name of every part of the screen that is displayed; however, don't label duplicate items.

2. Using WordPad, type your name at the top of a document. On the next line type **Check Point for Units 1–3**, **Project 2**. Display the contents of the *Practice* disk. Create a folder, and name it **Test**. Capture the contents of the window only, and paste the results into the WordPad document. Print the WordPad document, then delete the screen image. Save the document as **Review 2** on the *Practice* disk and print the document.

Working with Files

UNIT OBJECTIVES

- Select files
- Copy and move files
- Rename files
- Delete files
- Restore files from the Recycle Bin
- Find files
- Preview files
- Use the Classic desktop
- Change the background

Whenever you work on a computer, you are working with files. Some files are programs that allow you to perform specialized functions, and some are data files used to store information that you create. You arrange files in folders so that you can find them later when you need them. In this unit, you will learn to work with files—that is, to copy, rename, delete, find, and preview files. You will also see how to use the Classic view of the desktop and change the desktop background.

What: Select more than one file.

How: Use the mouse with the Shift and Ctrl keys.

Why: If you select several files, you can perform an action on all of them at once.

Tip: If you have trouble selecting several files, try a different view of the file list, such as the List view.

Before you can work with files, you must select them. To select a single file in the Web view, point to it and pause. When you point to a second file, it is selected, and the first file is deselected. Pointing to files will select only one file at a time.

To select more than one file in a folder, you have a choice of methods. To select **noncontiguous files**, that is, files that are not next to each other in the file list:

1. Point to the first file to select it.
2. Hold down the Ctrl key.
3. Point to another file and pause until it is selected. Selecting the new file does not deselect the first. Continue to point to files and they will be added to the selection. Figure 4.1 shows noncontiguous files selected.

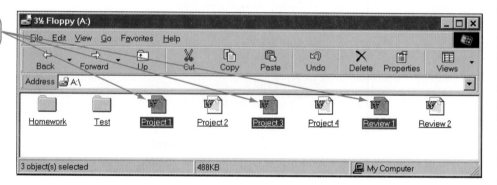

FIGURE 4.1 Noncontiguous Files Selected

To select a group of files that are **contiguous**, or next to each other, in the file list:

1. Point to the first file to select it.
2. Hold down the Shift key.
3. Point to the last file in the group and pause. The group of files is selected, as shown in Figure 4.2.

To select all of the files in the selected folder, choose Edit | Select All.

To deselect files:

• To deselect a file in a group of selected files, hold down Ctrl, point to the file, and pause. Only that file will be deselected.

• To deselect a group of selected files, click outside the selected area.

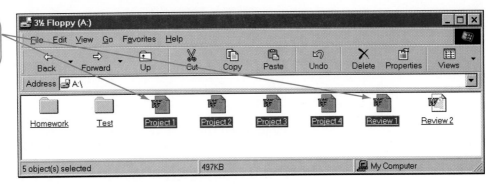

Select the first file, hold down Shift, and select the last file

FIGURE 4.2   Contiguous Files Selected

POINTER

Selecting Files in the Classic View

Remember that in the Classic view you click a file to select it and double-click it to open it.

- To select a single file, click it.
- To select noncontiguous files, click the first, then hold down the Ctrl key while you click each of the others.
- To select a group of contiguous files, click the first, then hold down the Shift key while you click the last.

EXERCISE 1 | *Selecting Files*

1. Place the **Practice disk** into drive A.

This disk contains the folders and files you created in Unit 3 and Check Point 1.

2. Open **My Computer** and then open **drive A**.

3. Choose **View | Large Icons** and then **View | Arrange Icons | By Name**.

Your screen should now look something like Figure 4.1, but no files are yet selected.

4. Point to the **Project 1 file** to select it, then hold down the **Ctrl key** and select **Project 3** and then **Review 1**.

Pause after pointing until each file is highlighted. A group of three noncontiguous files is selected.

5. Release the **Ctrl key.**

The files remain selected.

6. Click **outside the selected files**.

The files are no longer selected.

7. Choose **View | List**.

8. Select the **Project 1 file**.

9. Hold down the **Shift key** and select **Review 1**.

All of the files in between the first and last files you pointed to are selected.

10. Hold down the **Ctrl key**, point to **Project 3**, and pause.

The file is deselected. The rest of the files remain selected.

11. Choose **Edit | Invert Selection**.

What was selected is deselected, and what was not selected is now selected.

12. Choose **Edit | Select All**.

All of the files and folders are selected.

13. Click **outside the files**.

Everything is deselected.

14. Close **My Computer**.

TASK 2 | *Copying and Moving Files*

What: Make a copy of a file or a group of files on another disk or in another folder, or move a file or group of files to another disk or folder.

How: Select the files first, then use drag and drop with the shortcut menu.

Why: You may want to share a document with another person or make a copy for safekeeping.

Tip: When using Windows Explorer to drag and drop files, remember to scroll the left pane so that the destination drive or folder is displayed.

As you use your computer, you will find many reasons to move and copy files. You might want to move related files into the same folder. You might want to take a file to another computer, or you might want to have a backup copy of an important file.

You can use Windows Explorer or My Computer to copy or move files. It is particularly easy with Windows Explorer, because there you can see your whole system in a single window.

DRAG WITH THE RIGHT BUTTON

With Windows Explorer, you can simply drag and drop the files into the folder where you want them moved or copied. The easiest way is to use the right mouse button. If you learn this technique, you don't really need any other:

1. Open Windows Explorer, and open the folder that contains the file or files that you want to copy or move.
2. If necessary, scroll the left pane to show the drive or folder where the files will be copied or moved.
3. In the right pane, select the files to be copied or moved.
4. With the right mouse button, drag the selected files to the left pane until the mouse is over the drive and folder where you want to copy or move them. (The selected folder will be highlighted.)
5. Drop the files.
6. A shortcut menu will open giving you the choice of copying or moving the files, as shown in Figure 4.3. Click the option you want, and the files are copied or moved.

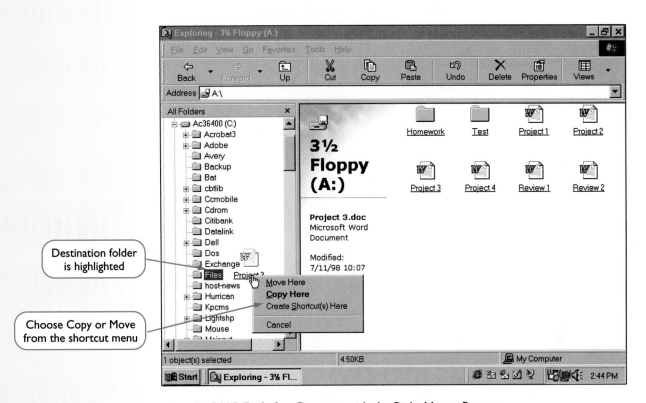

FIGURE 4.3 Dragging with the Right Mouse Button

DRAG WITH THE LEFT BUTTON

You can also drag with the left mouse button. What happens when you drop the files depends on whether the source and destination drives are the same.

- If you drag files to a different location on the same drive, the files will be moved.

- If you drag files to a different drive, the files will be copied. (A plus sign appears next to the pointer to let you know the files will be copied when dropped.)

- If you hold down the Ctrl key while dragging files, and release the Ctrl key after dropping them, the files will always be copied, not moved. (A plus sign appears next to the pointer to let you know, as shown in Figure 4.4.)

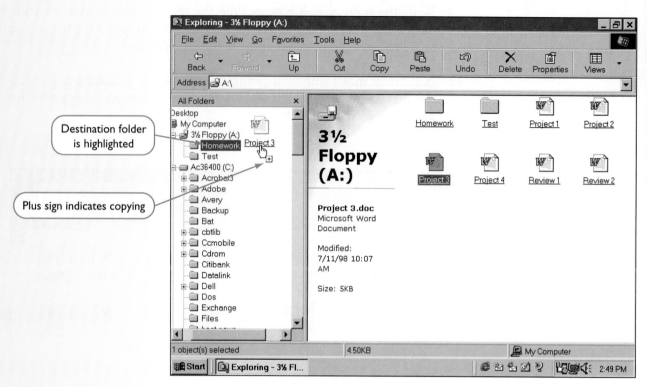

Destination folder is highlighted

Plus sign indicates copying

FIGURE 4.4   Dragging with the Left Button and the Ctrl Key

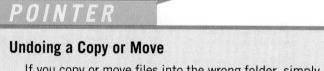

Undoing a Copy or Move

If you copy or move files into the wrong folder, simply choose Edit I Undo Copy or Edit I Undo Move and start over. You can also use the Undo button on the toolbar.

COPY (OR CUT) AND PASTE

You can use the copy (or cut) and paste technique, with drop-down menus, shortcut menus, or toolbar buttons.

1. Open Windows Explorer.
2. Open the folder containing the file or files that you want to move or copy.
3. If necessary, scroll the left pane to display the destination drive or folder.
4. In the right pane, select the files to be moved or copied.

Cut

Copy

5. Cut or copy the files to the Clipboard. You have three options:
   - Click the Cut or Copy button on the toolbar.
   - Choose Edit | Cut or Edit | Copy.
   - Right-click to open a shortcut menu and choose Cut or Copy.
6. In the left pane of Windows Explorer, select the folder where you want to move or copy the files.
7. Do any of the following:

Paste

   - Click the Paste button on the toolbar.
   - Choose Edit | Paste.
   - Right-click to open a shortcut menu and choose Paste.

When you move or copy a file, Windows 98 looks in the destination folder for a file with the same name. If it finds one, it asks you whether you want to replace the file (see Figure 4.5). This keeps you from accidentally copying the contents of one file over the other.

POINTER

Copying over a File with the Same Name

Each file in a folder must have a unique name. If you copy a file into a folder with a file of the same name, the copy will replace the original.

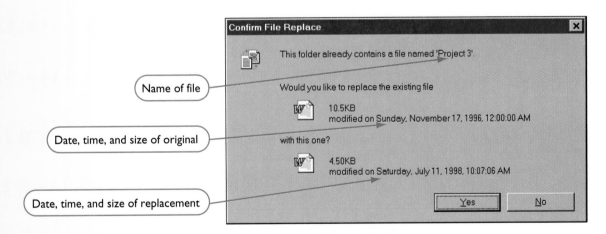

FIGURE 4.5   The Confirm File Replace Box

In the following exercises you will create a new folder on drive C. Then you will copy and move files into and out of the new folder from the *Practice* disk, using several techniques. Do all of the exercises and decide which technique you like best.

EXERCISE 2A | *Copying Files with Windows Explorer: Dragging with the Right Button*

1. Place the **Practice disk** into drive A and start **Windows Explorer**.

   First you will create a new folder to use in the exercise.

2. Select **drive C**.

3. Choose **File | New | Folder**.

   A new folder, named *New Folder*, is created on drive C and displayed in the right pane.

4. Rename the folder **Files**.

   You will copy and move files into this folder from the *Practice* disk.

5. In the left pane, select **drive A**.

   The folders and files on the *Practice* disk are displayed in the right pane.

6. Choose **View | List**.

   The files are displayed in a list.

7. If necessary, scroll the left pane until you can see the **Files folder**.

8. Select only **Project 2** and **Project 4**.

   Remember to use the Ctrl key to select noncontiguous files.

9. Press and hold the **right mouse button**, and drag the files to the **Files folder** in the left pane.

   As you drag the files past folder names in the left pane, the names are highlighted, to show you where the files would be dropped if you released the mouse button. Be sure the *Files* folder is highlighted.

10. Release the mouse button to drop the files into the **Files folder**.

    A shortcut menu opens giving you the option to copy the files, move them, create a shortcut, or cancel.

11. Choose **Copy here**.

    The files are copied to the *Files* folder.

12. Select the **Files folder** in the left pane.

    You can see the copied files in the right pane.

13. Choose **Edit | Undo Copy**.

    The files are deleted from the *Files* folder.

EXERCISE 2B | *Copying Files with Windows Explorer: Dragging with the Left Button*

1. In the left pane, select **drive A**, and then in the right pane select **Project 2**, **Project 3**, and **Project 4**.

   Remember to use the Shift key to select contiguous files.

2. Press and hold the **Ctrl key**.

3. Use the left mouse button to drag the files to the **Homework folder** of drive A in the left pane.

   You are dragging files from one location to another on the same disk. If you dragged without the Ctrl key, the files would be moved instead of copied. The plus sign next to the pointer shows that the files will be copied when dropped.

4. First release the mouse button to drop the files into the **Homework folder**, and then release the **Ctrl key**.

   The files are copied to the *Homework* folder.

5. Select the **Homework folder** in the left pane.

   The three copied files are displayed in the right pane.

6. Choose **Edit | Undo Copy**.

   You could also click the Undo button on the toolbar. The files are deleted from the *Homework* folder.

EXERCISE 2C | *Copying Files with Windows Explorer: Copy and Paste*

1. In the left pane, select **drive A**.

2. In the right pane, select **Project 3**.

3. Click the **Copy button** on the toolbar.

   The file is placed on the Clipboard.

4. In the left pane, select the **Files folder** on drive C.

5. Click the **Paste button** on the toolbar.

   The file appears in the in *Files* folder.

6. Close **Windows Explorer**.

MOVE OR COPY USING MY COMPUTER

To use My Computer to move or copy files in the Web view, you must:

1. Open My Computer.
2. Open the drive and folder that contains the files to be moved or copied.
3. Select the files.
4. Click the Cut or Copy button (see Figure 4.6), or right-click and choose Cut or Copy from the shortcut menu.
5. Use a toolbar button or the Address bar's drop-down list box to display the drive or folder where you want to move or copy the files. Refer to Table 4.1 for details.
6. Click the Paste button, or right-click and choose Paste from the shortcut menu.

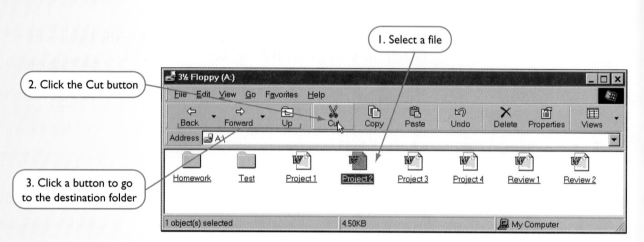

FIGURE **4.6** Cutting a File Using My Computer

Object to Click	Icon	Result
Address bar's down arrow	▼	Displays a list of of the drives on your system; click a drive to jump to it
Up button	Up	Move up one level, such as from drive C to My Computer (can be clicked repeatedly)
Back button	Back	Move back one step
Back button's down arrow	▾	Displays a list of addresses you have accessed earlier; click one of them to return to it
Forward button	Forward	Move forward one step (available after clicking the Back button)
Forward button's down arrow	▾	Displays a list of addresses you have gone back to; click one of them to return to it

TABLE **4.1** Navigating in My Computer

Copying and Moving in the Classic View

With Windows Explorer, the techniques for copying and moving are the same in the Web and Classic views. Just remember to click files in the right pane instead of pointing to them to select them. With My Computer, the techniques are different, because in the Classic view My Computer opens each folder in a separate window. To move or copy files from one folder to another, open a My Computer window for both folders, tile the two windows, and then drag the files from one window to the other.

EXERCISE 2D | *Moving Files with My Computer*

1. With the **Practice disk** in drive A, open **My Computer**.

2. Select the **3½ Floppy (A) drive**.

   The display changes to show the folders and files on the *Practice* disk.

3. Select **Project 2**.

   The file name and icon are highlighted.

4. Click the **Cut button** on the toolbar.

   The file is removed from the disk in drive A and placed on the Clipboard.

5. Click the toolbar's **Back button**.

   The screen display goes back one step, to My Computer.

6. Select **drive C**.

   The folders and files on drive C are displayed.

7. Select the **Files folder**.

   The contents of the *Files* folder are shown.

8. Click the **Paste button**.

   The *Project 2* file is placed in the *Files* folder.

9. Click the **Up button**.

   The display moves up one level, from the *Files* folder to drive C.

10. Close **My Computer**.

What: Change the name of a file or a folder.

How: Use the shortcut menu.

Why: You may think of an easier-to-remember file name, or you may want to copy a file to a folder that already has a file of that name.

Tip: Never rename a program file because it might not work with a different name.

Whenever you want to rename a file or folder, you can do so without changing its contents. Using either My Computer or Windows Explorer:

1. Select the file that you want to rename.
2. Choose File | Rename, or right-click to open a shortcut menu, and choose Rename. The file name is boxed in, with a blinking insertion point at the right end of the name, as shown in Figure 4.7.
3. Type a new name, or press the right or left arrow key to deselect the old name so you can edit it.
4. Complete the name change by pressing Enter or by clicking outside the file name.

If you change your mind in the middle of the operation, press the Esc key on the keyboard to return to the original name. If you change your mind right after making the change, click the Undo button on the toolbar.

The procedure for renaming a folder is the same as for renaming a file.

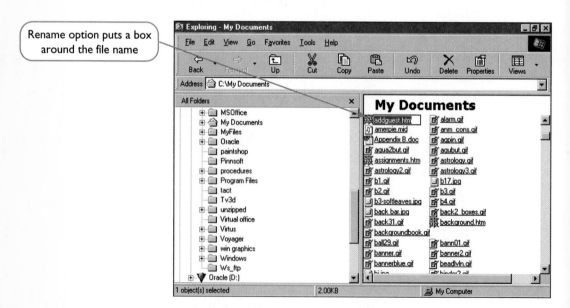

Rename option puts a box around the file name

FIGURE 4.7 A File Ready to Be Renamed

EXERCISE 3 | *Renaming a File*

1. Open **My Computer**.
2. Open **drive C** and open the **Files folder**.

   The folder contains the file you copied to it in Exercise 2.
3. Select **Project 2**.

   The file name is highlighted.
4. Right-click the mouse.

   A shortcut menu opens.
5. Choose **Rename**.

   Project 2 has a blinking insertion point in the file name box.
6. Type **Unit 3 Project 2** and press **Enter**. (If the file name reads *Project2.doc* type **Unit3Project2.doc** instead and press Enter.)

   The file is renamed.
7. Close **My Computer**.

TASK 4 | *Deleting and Restoring Files*

What: Delete files and folders that you no longer need.

How: Use the shortcut menu.

Why: Deleting unneeded files and folders makes it easier to find the ones you use.

Tip: Never delete a file unless you are sure it is the correct one.

Hard disks, like closets, can get full and need some housekeeping. You need to know how to delete files (and how to change your mind). Files deleted from hard disks are placed in the Windows **Recycle Bin**, a temporary storage location. In this task you will learn how to delete files. In the next task you will learn to restore files from the Recycle Bin.

Floppy Files Are Not Recyclable

Files that are deleted from floppy disks are not placed in the Recycle Bin—they are permanently deleted!

To delete files or folders, first select them in My Computer or Windows Explorer. Then do any of the following:

- Right-click to display a shortcut menu and choose Delete.
- Press the Delete key on the keyboard.
- Click the Delete button on the toolbar.
- Choose File | Delete.
- Click and drag the files to the Recycle Bin icon on the desktop (as shown in Figure 4.8) or in the left pane of Windows Explorer.

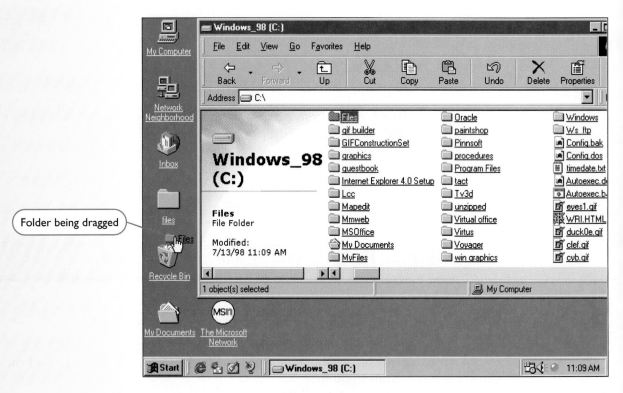

Folder being dragged

FIGURE 4.8   A Folder Being Dragged to the Recycle Bin Icon on the Desktop

When you drag files or folders to the Recycle Bin from a hard disk or use one of the other methods to delete files from the hard disk, Windows displays the Confirm File Delete message box, shown in Figure 4.9a. When you delete files from a floppy disk, the Confirm File Delete message box has a different wording, shown in Figure 4.9b, because the deletion will be permanent. And when you delete a folder from a hard or floppy disk, similar messages appear.

(a) For a File Being Moved to the Recycle Bin from a Hard Disk Drive

(b) For a File Being Permanently Deleted from a Floppy Disk

FIGURE 4.9   The Confirm File Delete Message Boxes

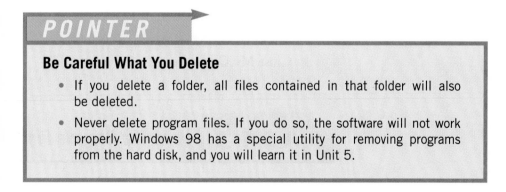

POINTER

Be Careful What You Delete

- If you delete a folder, all files contained in that folder will also be deleted.
- Never delete program files. If you do so, the software will not work properly. Windows 98 has a special utility for removing programs from the hard disk, and you will learn it in Unit 5.

1. Open **My Computer**, then **drive C**, then the **Files folder**.

   The files in the *Files* folder are displayed.

2. Size and position the window. If it is maximized, click the **Restore button**. Make sure you can see the **Delete button** on the toolbar, then move the window so that you can see the **Recycle Bin icon** on the desktop.

3. In the My Computer window, select **Unit 3 Project 2**.

   The file name and icon are highlighted.

4. Click the **Delete button** on the toolbar.

   The Confirm File Delete dialog box opens.

5. Click **Yes**.

   The file is deleted.

6. Select **Project 3**.

   The file name and icon are highlighted.

7. Right click the **file name**.

   A shortcut menu opens.

8. Choose **Delete** from the shortcut menu.

   The Confirm File Delete dialog box opens.

9. Click **Yes**.

   The file is deleted from drive C and moved to the Recycle Bin.

10. Click the **Back button**.

    The folders on drive C are displayed.

11. Select the **Files folder**.

12. Drag the **Files folder** to the **Recycle Bin icon** on the Windows 98 desktop and drop it, and click **Yes** if asked to confirm the action.

    The folder is moved to the Recycle Bin.

13. Close **My Computer**.

TASK 5 | *Using the Recycle Bin*

What: Use the Recycle Bin to restore files.

How: Open the Recycle Bin from the desktop or from Windows Explorer.

Why: The Windows Recycle Bin holds deleted files so that you can restore them.

Tip: The Recycle Bin is just temporary storage, so be careful what you delete.

You can restore files that have been deleted and placed in the Windows Recycle Bin, using the following method:

1. Click the Recycle Bin icon on the Windows 98 desktop. The Recycle Bin window opens, as shown in Figure 4.10.
2. Select the folder or files you want to restore.
3. Choose File | Restore, or right-click one of the selected items and choose Restore from the shortcut menu. The file or files are moved from the Recycle Bin back to their original location.

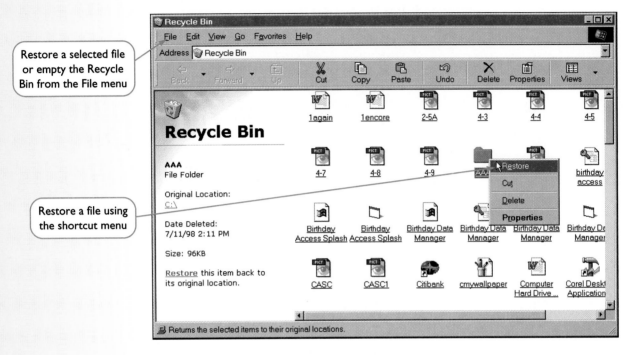

FIGURE 4.10 The Recycle Bin

Deleting files from the Recycle Bin removes them permanently. You can select a single file or group of files to delete, or you can delete all of the files at once by choosing File | Empty Recycle Bin. Because emptying the Recycle Bin permanently deletes its files, you should view the file list carefully before using this option.

By default, Windows 98 stores deleted files from all hard disks in a single Recycle Bin, to which it allocates 10 percent of your hard disk space. You shouldn't need to change these settings, but if you would like to view them, you can do so by right-clicking the Recycle Bin's icon on the desktop and choosing Properties from the shortcut menu.

> **POINTER**
>
> **Don't Forget the Floppy Disk**
>
> Do not place files in the Recycle Bin that you might want at a later time. When the Recycle Bin becomes full, Windows 98 automatically deletes the oldest files without giving any warning. If you need to keep old files and they are taking up too much room on the hard disk, remember that you can move them to a floppy disk or removable drive for future use.

EXERCISE 5 | *Using the Recycle Bin*

1. Click the **Recycle Bin icon** on the desktop.

The Recycle Bin window opens, and displays the contents of the Recycle Bin. It may contain dozens or hundreds of files, depending on when it was last emptied.

2. Select **Project 3**.

This is a file you deleted in Exercise 4. If you have trouble finding it, try switching to the Details view and sorting by Name or Date.

3. Choose **File | Restore**.

The file is restored to its original location, the *Files* folder on drive C. You dragged that folder to the Recycle Bin in Exercise 4, but when you restore the file, the folder will be restored too.

4. Right-click **Unit 3 Project 2**.

This is the other file you deleted from the *Files* folder on drive C in Exercise 4. A shortcut menu opens.

5. Choose **Restore** from the shortcut menu.

The file is restored to its original location.

6. Click the **Address bar's down arrow**.

A list of the drives on your system is displayed.

7. Select **drive C**.

A My Computer window displays the contents of the drive.

8. Select the **Files folder**.

The folder has been restored, and it contains the files you just restored from the Recycle Bin.

9. Click the **Delete button** on the toolbar.

The Confirm Folder Delete message box opens.

10. Click **Yes**.

The folder and its files are moved to the Recycle Bin again. (You won't need this folder again in this text, and it is good practice to delete unneeded files and folders.)

11. Close **My Computer**.

TASK 6 | *Finding Files*

What: Find files using the Windows 98 Find utility.

How: Click the Start button and choose Find | Files or Folders.

Why: Keeping track of documents you create can be a frustrating task.

Tip: Remember to give all files meaningful names to save you from lost time and lost files.

If you have difficulty finding a file that you have saved, you can use the Windows 98 Find utility to help you. Click the Start button on the taskbar and choose Find | Files or Folders. The Find dialog box opens.

The dialog box has three tabs. It opens to the Name and Location tab, as shown in Figure 4.11. Use this tab to specify search criteria as follows:

- **Named** text box: If you know the exact name, such as *Project 1*, or a part of the name, such as *Project*, you can type it here.
- **Containing** text box: If you know that the file (not the file name) contains specific text, such as *1997 Project Report*, you can type the text here.
- **Look In** text box: Displays the drives that will be searched. If the location shown doesn't include the drive you want Windows to search, you can click the down arrow and select a different option in the list.
- **Browse** button: To select a folder, rather than a drive, to start the search in, click the Browse button to open the Browse for Folder dialog box, shown in Figure 4.12. This dialog box shows a view of your system like that of the left pane of Windows Explorer. Select a folder or subfolder where you want to start the search.
- **Includes subfolders** check box: If you do not want to search subfolders, remove the check.

The *Date tab* of the dialog box lets you modify a search by looking for files modified, created, or last accessed within a certain time frame. The *Advanced tab* lets you specify a file type or size to search for.

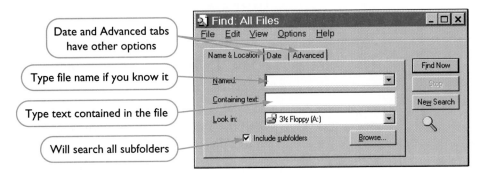

FIGURE 4.11 The Find Dialog Box's Name and Location Tab

When you have given Windows as much information about the file you are looking for as you can (using all three tabs if you like), click the Find Now button to start the search. Windows will display all matches to your criteria in the bottom of the dialog box, as shown in Figure 4.13. You can open a file directly from within the list.

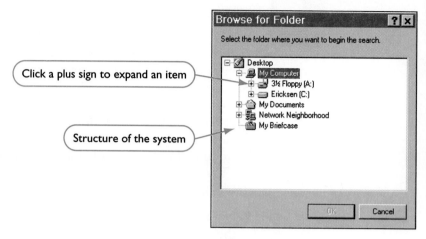

FIGURE 4.12   The Browse for Folder Dialog Box

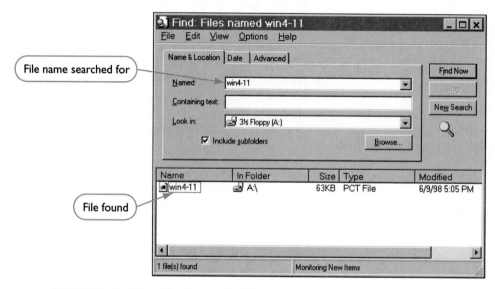

FIGURE 4.13   The Result of a File Search

EXERCISE 6 | *Finding Files*

1. With the **Practice** disk in drive A, click the **Start button** and choose **Find I Files or Folders**.

   The Find dialog box opens, with the Name and Location tab displayed.

2. Type **Project** in the Named text box.

3. Select 3½ **Floppy (A)** in the Look in text box's drop-down list.

   You have instructed Windows to find any file that has **Project** as part of the file name and to search drive A for a match.

4. Click the **Find Now button**.

The files you created in Unit 3's projects should be listed in the bottom of the dialog box because they all have *Project* in the file name.

5. Click **Project 2** in the file list.

The document opens in WordPad (or in Microsoft Word, if that application is present on your system).

6. Close **WordPad** or **Word**, and then close **Find**.

TASK 7 | *Previewing Files*

What: View the contents of a file without opening the file.

How: Choose File | Quick View.

Why: Previewing a file is quicker than opening it and is handy if you are not sure it's the file you want.

Tip: Use this time-saving feature when you have a few files that have similar names.

We saw in Unit 2 that the View as Web Page option displays information about a file selected in a My Computer or Windows Explorer window. Windows 98 also includes the Quick View program that lets you preview certain types of documents without opening them. To use Quick View:

1. Select the file in My Computer or Windows Explorer.
2. Pull down the File menu and look for the Quick View option (or right-click the file name and look for it on the shortcut menu).
3. If the option is not present, this kind of document cannot be previewed with Quick View. If the option is present, choose it. The document is previewed in the Quick View window, as shown in Figure 4.14.

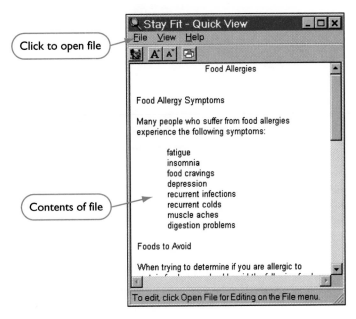

FIGURE 4.14 A Quick View of a Word Processing File

If the file in the Quick View window is the correct file, you can choose File | Open File for Editing. If it is not the correct file, you can click the window's Close button to return to My Computer or Windows Explorer.

POINTER

Previewing Graphics with the Web Page Option

If you choose the View as Web Page option in My Computer and then select a graphics file, Windows will display a preview of the file in the left side of the window.

EXERCISE 7 | *Previewing a Document*

1. Place the **Practice disk** in drive A, open **My Computer**, and open 3½ **Floppy (A)**.

2. Choose **View | as Web Page**.

   A new pane opens at the left of the window, displaying information about the disk in drive A.

3. Select **Project 2**.

   Information about the document is displayed in the left side of the window.

4. Choose **File | Quick View**.

   The Quick View window opens and displays a preview of the document. Note that only the text is shown, without special formatting.

5. Click the **Close button** in the title bar of the Quick View window.

6. Close **My Computer**.

TASK 8 | *Using the Classic Desktop*

What: Change the desktop to the Classic style.

How: Click the Start button and choose Settings | Folder Options | General tab | Classic style.

Why: You will want to know how to use computers that have earlier versions of Windows installed.

Tip: You have used the Web style in this book, but users of earlier versions of Windows don't need to change if they don't want to.

You have been learning to use Windows 98 by viewing the desktop in Web style. This has enabled you to become familiar with many new features, such as single-clicking the mouse on programs and folders, and using the Forward and Back buttons in My Computer. However, if you have used previous versions of Windows, you might want to work with the older or Classic Windows desktop.

To change to the Classic view:

1. Click the Start button.
2. Point to Settings.
3. Click Folder Options to open the Folder Options dialog box.
4. On the General tab, choose Classic style.

The screen will change to Classic style, as shown in Figure 4.15. Table 4.2 shows the differences in the way the mouse works in the two styles.

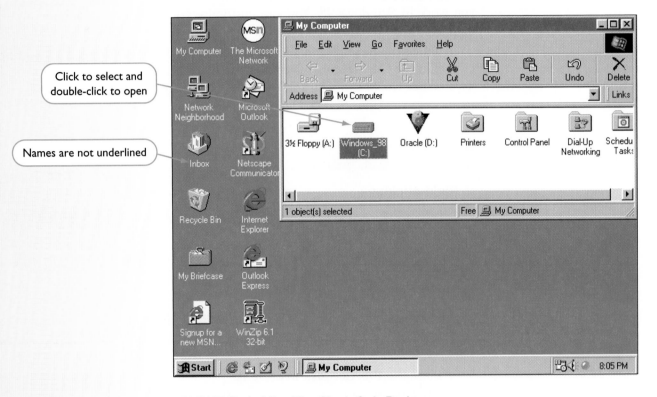

FIGURE 4.15   The Classic Style Desktop

Task	Web Style	Classic Style
Select a file or folder	Point to the item	Click the item
Open a file or start a program	Click the item	Double-click the item
Open a shortcut menu	Right-click the item	Right-click the item

TABLE 4.2   Pointing and Clicking in the Web and Classic Styles

One distinct difference between the Classic style and the Web style is the way folders open on the desktop. When you use the Web style and open folders using My Computer, each folder you click opens in the same window. In the Classic style, each folder you double-click opens in its own window on the desktop.

You don't actually have to choose only Web or only Classic style when you work in Windows 98. You can customize your desktop to combine elements of the two styles. To customize your desktop:

1. Click the Start button and choose Settings | Folder Options.
2. On the General tab, select Custom, based on settings you choose.
3. Click the Settings button to display the Custom Settings dialog box.
4. Select options that you want to customize.

EXERCISE 8 | *Using the Classic Desktop*

1. Place the **Practice disk** in **drive A**.
2. Click the **Start button** and choose **Settings | Folder Options**.

   The Folder Options dialog box opens.
3. Make sure the **General tab** is displayed and choose **Classic style**.
4. Click the **OK button**.

   The dialog box closes and the desktop changes to the Classic style.
5. Double-click the **My Computer icon** on the desktop.

   You must double-click an item to open it in the Classic style.
6. Double-click 3½ **Floppy (A)**.

   A second My Computer window opens displaying the contents of the 2 disk in drive A. In the Classic style, new folders are displayed in their own, separate My Computer window.

7. Single-click one of the **file names** in the disk in drive A.

In the Classic style, clicking a file name selects the file but does not open it.

8. Pause a second and single-click the **same file name** again.

The file is ready for you to rename it.

9. Type a **new name** for the file, and press **Enter**.

The file is renamed. You can also rename files using the shortcut menu in the Classic view.

10. Close both My Computer windows.

11. Return to Web style desktop.

TASK 9 | *Changing the Desktop Background*

What: Change the background on your Windows 98 desktop.

How: Choose My Computer | Control Panel | Display | Background tab

Why: The default display is fine, but variety adds interest.

Tip: You can use the Paint accessory to create your own background—see the Help files for details.

Windows 98 lets you customize the desktop background. Your choices range from the plain green background shown in the screens in this book, to the Windows 98 wallpaper shown in Figure 4.16a, to elaborate combinations of wallpapers and patterns. To start:

1. Right-click an empty area of the desktop to open a shortcut menu.
2. Choose Properties to open the Display Properties dialog box shown in Figure 4.16b.
3. If necessary, click the Background tab.

To choose a wallpaper:

1. Select a graphic file from the list in the Wallpaper section to see a preview on the monitor in the dialog box.
2. Choose a Display option from the drop-down list:
   - **Tile** to repeat the image to fill the desktop.
   - **Center** to center the image on the desktop.
   - **Stretch** to enlarge the image to fill the desktop.
3. Click the Apply button to display the wallpaper on the desktop.

If you choose the Center display, you can fill the remaining desktop space with a pattern. Or you can use a pattern instead of wallpaper.

To choose a pattern:

1. Click the Background tab's Pattern button to open the Pattern dialog box, shown in Figure 4.16c.

2. Select a file from the Pattern drop-down list to see a preview in the Preview section.
3. Click OK to close the Pattern dialog box and display the selected pattern on the monitor in the Display Properties dialog box.
4. Click the Apply button to display the pattern on the desktop.

When you have made all your selections, click the dialog box's OK button.

POINTER

Using a Web Page in the Background

You can make a Web page (an HTML document) your desktop wallpaper by right-clicking the desktop to display the shortcut menu. Choose Properties | Background tab. Click the Browse button and select the Web page you saved. It will appear with an *.html* or *.htm* extension. Use the settings described in this task to place the image on the desktop. (You will learn more about Web documents in Unit 8.)

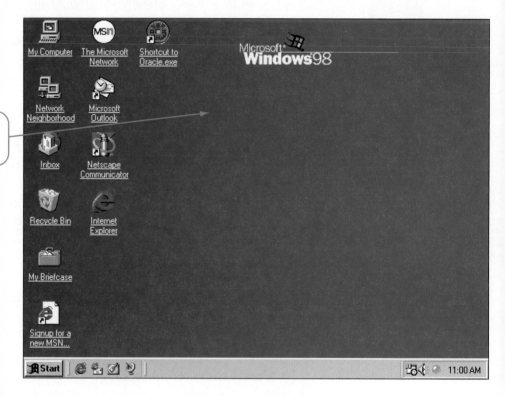

One of the desktop backgrounds you can choose

(a) The Windows 98 Wallpaper

FIGURE 4.16   Changing the Desktop Background

The selected background is previewed here

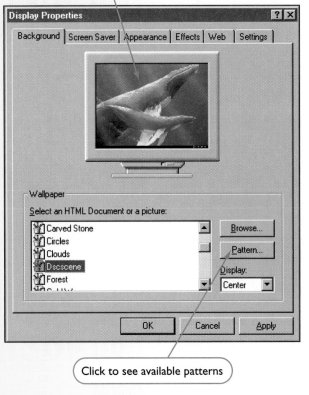

Click to see available patterns

The selected pattern is previewed here

(b) Choosing a Wallpaper   (c) Choosing a Pattern

FIGURE 4.16   Changing the Desktop Background *(continued)*

EXERCISE 9 | *Changing the Desktop Background*

1. Right-click an **empty area of the desktop**.

A shortcut menu opens.

2. Choose **Properties**.

The Display Properties dialog box opens.

3. If necessary, click the **Background tab**.

The current settings are shown. Make a note of them so you can return to them at the end of the exercise.

4. Select a **Wallpaper** image from the list.

The image appears on the small monitor in the dialog box.

5. Click the down arrow for the **Display option** and choose **Tile**, then **Stretch**, then **Center**.

The selected image changes on the monitor in the dialog box.

6. With the Center option selected, click the **Pattern button** in the dialog box.

The Pattern dialog box opens, displaying the current settings. Make a note of them so you can return to them at the end of the exercise.

7. Choose a **Pattern** from the list.

The pattern appears in the Preview section of the Pattern dialog box.

8. Click the **OK button** in the Pattern dialog box.

The Pattern dialog box closes, and the pattern appears on the monitor in the Display Properties dialog box.

9. Click the **Apply button**.

The selected wallpaper and pattern appear on the desktop. Drag the Display Properties dialog box to a different position so you can see the Wallpaper design in the center.

10. Click the down arrow for the **Display option**, and choose **Tile**, and then click the **Apply button**.

The selected wallpaper is tiled over the whole desktop, and the pattern disappears.

11. Experiment with other wallpapers, patterns, or both, and when you have found a selection you like, click the **OK button**.

The dialog box closes and the selection appears on the screen.

12. Repeat the steps to return the display to its former settings.

POINTER

Using Web Graphics

You can use individual images that you see on Web pages as your desktop wallpaper. Simply right-click the image while you are on line and choose Save as Wallpaper from the shortcut menu. Remember to check the copyright on images that you save from other people's Web documents.

S U M M A R Y

After completing this unit, you should
- be able to select files (page 82)
- have learned to copy and move files (page 84)
- be able to rename a file (page 92)
- be able to delete files (page 93)
- be able to restore files from the Recycle Bin (page 96)
- be able to find files (page 99)
- have learned to find out about a file before opening it (page 101)
- have learned to use the Classic desktop (page 102)
- be able to change the desktop background (page 105)

K E Y   T E R M S

contiguous files (page 82)   **Recycle Bin** (page 93)
noncontiguous files (page 82)

T E S T   Y O U R   S K I L L S

True/False

1. To select noncontiguous files, hold down the Ctrl key while clicking files.
2. You can search for files by the date that they were created.
3. You can have several files in the same folder with the same name.
4. Files deleted from the 3½ Floppy disk are not placed in the Recycle Bin.
5. You can store as many files as you like in the Recycle Bin.

Multiple Choice

1.   To copy files, you
     a. can hold the Ctrl key while clicking and dragging
     b. must select the files first
     c. can choose Edit | Undo Copy if you place the files in the wrong folder
     d. all of these answers

2. Deleting
   a. does not place files deleted from the hard disk in the Recycle Bin
   b. does place files deleted from the 3½ Floppy (A) drive in the Recycle Bin
   c. deletes all of a folder's files if you delete the folder
   d. all of these answers

3. Using the Windows Find utility, you can narrow the search for files by
   a. specifying the time of day when they were created
   b. specifying the file type
   c. specifying the name of the person who created the file
   d. all of these answers

4. To change the name of a file, you would use which option?
   a. Rename
   b. Restore
   c. Copy
   d. Find

5. The Recycle Bin
   a. can't be cleared
   b. is sized at approximately 10 percent of the hard drive
   c. never clears files unless you select File | Empty Recycle Bin
   d. all of these answers

Short Answer

1. If you choose Quick View in My Computer, Windows will display a _____ of the document.
2. To work with files, you must first _____ them.
3. The _____ _____ is the folder that holds deleted files.
4. If you _____ a file, the original will remain intact in its original location.
5. Hold down the _____ key to select contiguous files.

PROJECTS

1. a. Preview the contents of a file. Copy the display of the preview screen.
   b. Place the screen display in a WordPad document with your name and the title **Unit 4 Project 1**. Print the document.
   c. Delete the screen display and then save the file on the *Practice* disk as **Unit 4 Project 1**.

2. a. Create a new folder on the *Practice* disk and name the folder **Reports**. Copy the project files from Unit 3, along with the *Unit 4 Project 1* file, to the *Reports* folder. Copy the display of the *Reports* folder with the files displayed.
   b. Place the screen display in a WordPad document with your name and the title **Unit 4 Project 2**. Print the document.
   c. Delete the screen display and then save the file on the *Practice* disk as **Unit 4 Project 2**.

3. a. Delete all the files from the *Reports* folder except *Unit 4 Project 1*. Copy the display of the *Reports* folder with the file displayed.
   b. Place the screen display in a WordPad document with your name and the title **Unit 4 Project 3**. Print the document.
   c. Delete the screen display and then save the file on the *Practice* disk as **Unit 4 Project 3**.

4. a. Delete the *Reports* folder. Copy the display of the *Practice* disk with its files displayed.
   b. Place the screen display in a WordPad document with your name and the title **Unit 4 Project 4**. Print the document.
   c. Delete the screen display and then save the file on the *Practice* disk as **Unit 4 Project 4**.

Getting Started

UNIT OBJECTIVES

- Start Microsoft Word 2000
- Become familiar with the Word interface
- Use the Word Help system
- Create a document using a Word wizard
- Save a document
- Print a document
- Exit from Word

Microsoft Word is the word processing component of Microsoft Office 2000. **Word processing** includes creating, editing, formatting, saving, and printing documents. In this book you will learn how to perform all of those tasks and more. Unit 1 will get you started, showing you how to start Word, create a document, save it, and exit from the software. You'll also learn how to use the built-in Help system. If you already know another Windows program, you'll have a head start, but all you really need to know are basic Windows skills such as using your mouse. (If you need help with Windows 98, refer to *Quick, Simple Microsoft Windows 98* in this series.)

What: Start Word.

How: Click the Start button and choose Programs | Microsoft Word.

Why: You must know how to start an application in order to use it.

Tip: If you are working in a computer lab, you may be given instructions for another way to start Word.

Microsoft Word 2000 is **word processing software**—a program used primarily to create text documents such as letters, memos, and reports. To start Word:

1. Click the Start button on the Windows taskbar.
2. Point to Programs.
3. Click Microsoft Word, as shown in Figure 1.1.

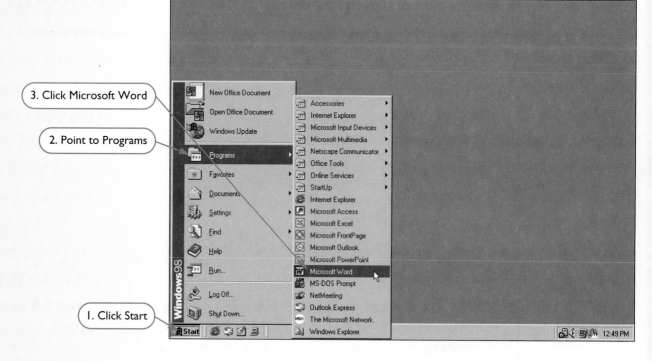

FIGURE 1.1   Starting Microsoft Word 2000

EXERCISE 1 | *Starting Word*

1. Click the **Start button** on the Windows taskbar.
   The Start menu opens.

2. Point to **Programs**.
The Programs menu opens.

3. Click **Microsoft Word**.
Word starts and displays a blank document, like that in Figure 1.2.

4. Keep Word open on your screen for use in the next exercise.

TASK 2 | *Becoming Familiar with the Word Interface*

What: Learn to use the various parts of the Word interface.

How: Use the mouse to explore.

Why: To use Word effectively, you need to be familiar with its elements.

Tip: Word uses a **graphical user interface**, or **GUI** (pronounced "goo-ey"), letting you communicate with the computer by selecting icons and other graphical screen elements rather than by typing commands.

When you start Word, a new blank document opens inside the program window. Figure 1.2 shows the opening screen before you type anything into the text-editing area.

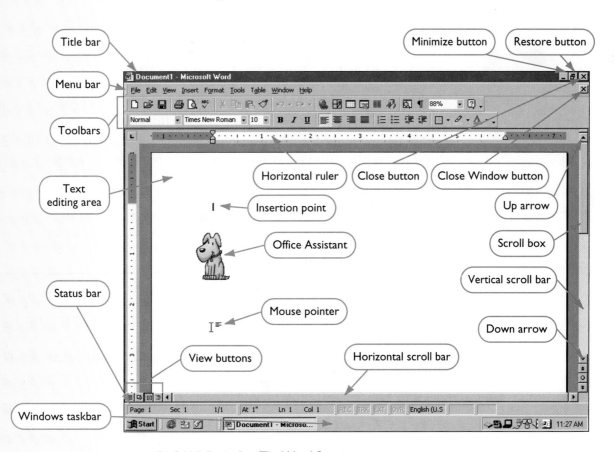

FIGURE 1.2   The Word Screen

My Screen Doesn't Match the Figure

Word can be customized in many ways, and your screen may not match the book's. For instance, Word lets you keep several documents open at the same time, each in its own window. Parts of the screen look slightly different when you have two or more documents open. You will see how this works in Unit 2.

TITLE BAR

Like all windows, the Word window has a **title bar** across the top. The title bar names the program and the document contained in the window. At its right edge it contains the buttons described in Table 1.1.

Button	Name	Description
▬	Minimize	Shrinks the window to a button on the taskbar
☐	Maximize	Enlarges the window to fill the desktop
▣	Restore	In a maximized window, replaces the Maximize button; returns the window to its previous size
✖	Close	Closes the window

TABLE 1.1   Buttons That Close and Size a Window

- Clicking the **Close button** closes the window. If no other document is open, clicking this button also exits you from the program.
- Clicking the **Maximize button** expands the window to fill the desktop. When the window is maximized, the Maximize button changes to a **Restore button**. Clicking the Restore button shrinks a window back to its previous size.
- The **Minimize button** reduces the window to a button on the taskbar without closing it. You can display the window again by clicking the taskbar button.

MENU BAR

Word's **menu bar**, which is located below its title bar, displays the names of menus, as seen in Figure 1.2. When you click a menu name, a pull-down menu appears from which you select a command or other option, as shown in Figure 1.3.

When you click a menu name, a set of basic menu options appears; in a few seconds the menu expands to show the complete list. As you work, Word

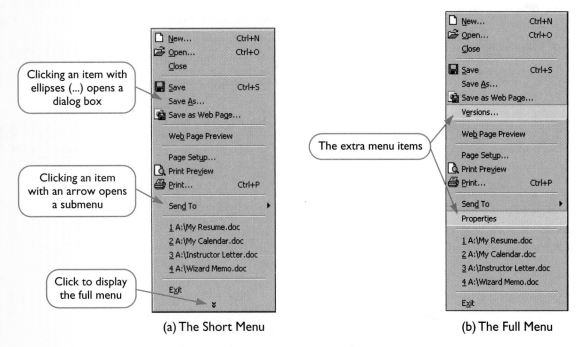

Clicking an item with ellipses (...) opens a dialog box

Clicking an item with an arrow opens a submenu

Click to display the full menu

The extra menu items

(a) The Short Menu

(b) The Full Menu

FIGURE 1.3   The File Menu

POINTER

Display the Full Menu

Word lets you customize many of its features, and the menu display is one of them. You can choose to see the full menus immediately instead of after a pause. You'll see how to do this in Exercise 2.

keeps track of which menu options you use, and adds those options to the short menu. At any time you can click the down arrows at the bottom of the menu to display the full menu.

Instructions in this text to choose menu commands are shown as **Menu Name | Menu Command**. For example, "choose File | Open" means to choose File from the menu bar and Open from the drop-down menu.

POINTER

Use the Keyboard to Open a Menu

Notice that each menu choice in Figures 1.2 and 1.3 has an underlined character. Pressing this character on the keyboard (often while holding down the Alt key) has the same effect as clicking the choice with the mouse. For example, to open the File menu, you can click its name on the menu bar or hold down the Alt key and press the letter F. Once a menu is open, you can choose an item by clicking it or by typing the underlined letter.

To close a menu without choosing a command, either click the mouse outside the menu or press the Esc key on the keyboard.

A menu choice on a pull-down menu can appear:

- with a check mark (✓) in front of it—to indicate an option that is turned on in a group where more than one choice is permitted
- without a check mark (✓)—to indicate that the option is turned off
- with a dot (•) in front of it—to indicate the option that is turned on in a group where only one choice is permitted
- grayed-out—to indicate it is not available at the present time
- followed by a right-pointing arrow (➤)—to indicate that clicking it will open a submenu
- followed by an ellipsis (…)—to indicate that clicking it will open a dialog box like the one shown in Figure 1.4.

POINTER

The Menu Bar's Close Window Button

When only one document is open, the menu bar has a Close Window button for that document at its right edge. Clicking this button closes the document but doesn't exit you from Word.

DIALOG BOXES

Dialog boxes are windows in which you provide Word with information needed to perform a task. Some dialog boxes, like the one in Figure 1.4, are **tabbed,** with each tab containing a group of similar options.

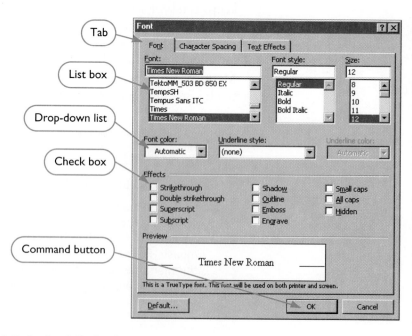

FIGURE 1.4 A Dialog Box

Dialog boxes contain **command buttons** that allow you to issue commands. Two common command buttons are the OK button and the Cancel button. When you have made your selections in a dialog box, you click the OK button. If you simply want to close the dialog box, you click the Close button or the Cancel button.

When a dialog box contains a **text box**, you can type your response in it. Other ways of selecting options in a dialog box include clicking a **radio button** (also called an **option button**) or **check box** or selecting items from a **list box**. Table 1.2 shows some of the buttons that appear in dialog boxes.

Button	Description
OK	Closes the dialog box and accepts input
Cancel	Closes the dialog box, rejecting input
?	Provides help on an object in a dialog box
Apply	Applies the settings without closing the dialog box
	Allows user to enter text
Center ▼	Provides choices on a drop-down list
☑ Strikeout ☑ Underline	Allows user to check more than one option in the group
⊙ Quick (erase) ○ Full	Allows user to select only one option in the group
14 ▲▼	Allows user to increment the number with the up arrow, decrement the number with the down arrow, or type the option in the text box
Slow ·····/····· Fast	Allows user to increase or decrease option
Yes	Implements the changes
No	Does not implement the changes
Next >	Proceeds to the next step of a wizard
< Back	Returns to the previous step of a wizard
Finish	Completes a wizard and closes it

TABLE 1.2 Dialog Box Buttons

> ## POINTER
>
> ### Moving a Dialog Box
> When a dialog box opens on the screen and you need to see the text that it has covered, click and drag the title bar of the dialog box to move it on the screen.

TOOLBARS AND RULER

Word has more than a dozen **toolbars** with buttons you can click to perform actions. Some toolbars are displayed by default; others appear only when needed; and some can be displayed manually by choosing View | Toolbars. Toolbars save you time.

Clicking a toolbar button has the same effect as choosing a command from the menu bar but is quicker. Besides buttons, toolbars can contain list boxes. Clicking the downward-pointing arrow at the right edge of the box (▼) opens a list from which you can make a choice.

The **Standard** and **Formatting toolbars** are displayed by default. The Standard toolbar contains buttons for commands from the File and Edit menus and other buttons that start some of Word's special features. The Formatting toolbar contains buttons for commands from the Format menu. These toolbars normally appear below the menu bar, but you can move them, as explained in the pointer box "Moving a Toolbar." The two toolbars can share a single row or can be displayed on separate rows. When the toolbars are separate, each displays its complete set of buttons. When the toolbars share a row, Word keeps track of which buttons have been used recently and displays those buttons, displacing buttons that haven't been used. To display the missing buttons, you click the More Buttons button at one end of the toolbar. Figure 1.5 shows the Standard and Formatting toolbars.

POINTER

Moving a Toolbar

You can move a toolbar to its own row or other location on the screen by dragging its move handle. If you double-click a toolbar that is docked at an edge of the screen, it floats freely on the screen and displays a title bar. Double-click it again to redock it.

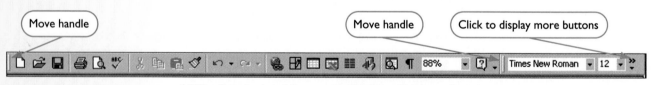

Move handle   Move handle   Click to display more buttons

(a) The Standard and Formatting Toolbars Sharing a Row

Click the arrow to display a list

(b) The Standard Toolbar

FIGURE 1.5   Toolbars

(c) The Formatting Toolbar

FIGURE 1.5 Toolbars *(continued)*

Microsoft Word Help

POINTER

ScreenTips

If you hold the pointer over any button without moving it for a few seconds, a **ScreenTip** appears to tell you what task that button initiates.

The **horizontal ruler**, which shows indents, margins, and tab settings, appears below the toolbars. You will use the ruler to set tabs in Unit 4. To display or hide the ruler, choose View | Ruler. You can display the ruler temporarily by pointing the mouse below the toolbar.

TEXT-EDITING WINDOW

The **text-editing window** is the area that displays the text you type. The **insertion point** (a blinking vertical line) marks your current location in the document. The **pointer** (or *cursor*) moves on the screen as you move the mouse on the desktop. In the text area it is shaped like an I-beam; elsewhere it is usually shaped like an arrow.

The **Office Assistant** can be displayed in the text-editing window, providing you with help. You will learn to use Word Help in the next task.

Scroll bars appear at the right edge and bottom of the text-editing window, allowing you to move through a document using the mouse.

- Click the up and down arrow on the vertical scroll bar to move the display up or down one line.
- Click below the up arrow to move the display up one screen.
- Click above the down arrow to move the display down one screen.
- Click and drag the **scroll box** down or up to quickly scroll down or back up a window.

The horizontal scroll bar contains buttons that allow you to change the view of your document. The Normal, Web Layout, Print Layout, and Outline views are useful for different tasks. You'll see how to use them in Unit 3, Task 7.

STATUS BAR

At the bottom of the window is the **status bar**. The left end of the status bar displays information about the location of the insertion point in the document. (The 1/1 indicator in Figure 1.2, for instance, tells you that you are on page 1 of a one-page document.) The right end contains a series of buttons and mode indicators. Point to a button and a ScreenTip displays its name. Some of these indicators are grayed out when they are not in use. Double-click them to toggle them on and off. You will learn to use some of these buttons as you go through this book.

TASKBAR

The Windows 98 **taskbar**, which appears along the bottom of the screen, contains the Start button and buttons for all open programs and files. When you have two or more documents open in Word, the taskbar displays a button for each of them. You will use these buttons to switch from one document to another.

SHORTCUT MENU

Like other Windows programs, Word provides quick access to often-used tasks by means of **shortcut menus**. To open a shortcut menu, point to an object and click the right mouse button. The content of the menu varies with the object you click. Figure 1.6 shows a shortcut menu that opens if you right-click selected text in a Word document.

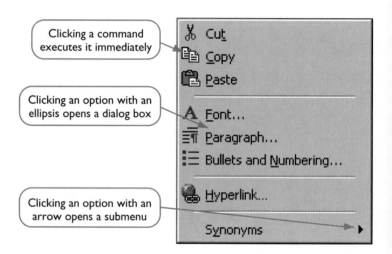

FIGURE 1.6   A Shortcut Menu

EXERCISE 2 | *Becoming Familiar with the Word Interface*

---

1. Choose **Tools | Customize**.
   Click the Tools menu name on the menu bar, and when a pull-down menu opens, click the Customize command. The Customize dialog box opens on the screen.

2. Click the **Options tab**.
The Options tab moves to the front and becomes active. It displays the current settings for the toolbars as well as other interface options you can customize. You could click a box to select it or clear it, and then click the Close button to change the option. Examine the options before you go to the next step.

3. Click the **Close button**.
The dialog box closes.

4. Choose **View | Ruler**.
If the ruler was displayed, it is no longer displayed. If the ruler was not displayed, it now appears.

5. Move the mouse pointer over any **toolbar button** and hold it there.
A ScreenTip shows the name of the button.

6. Click the **Minimize button** on the title bar.
Word is reduced to a button on the taskbar.

7. Click the **Document 1 button** on the taskbar.
The Word window is restored to its former size.

8. Keep Word running for use in the next exercise.

TASK 3 | *Getting Help*

What: Use Word's online Help.
How: Click the Office Assistant or choose Help | Microsoft Word Help.
Why: Word provides extensive online documentation that is easy to use.
Tip: Press the F1 key on the keyboard to launch Word Help.

When the Office Assistant is visible on the screen, Help is just a click away. Click the cartoon character to open the Help bubble shown in Figure 1.7a.

To get help:

1. Type a question into the text box. For example, if you want help on saving a document, type "How do I save a document?"
2. Click the Search button. Word will provide a list of Help topics to choose from, as shown in Figure 1.7b.
3. Select a topic from the list to display the Help document, as shown in Figure 1.7c.

4. To display the entire Help window, click the Show button. The window expands to include the Contents, Answer Wizard, and Index tabs, along with the Help buttons shown in Figure 1.7d and described in Table 1.3.

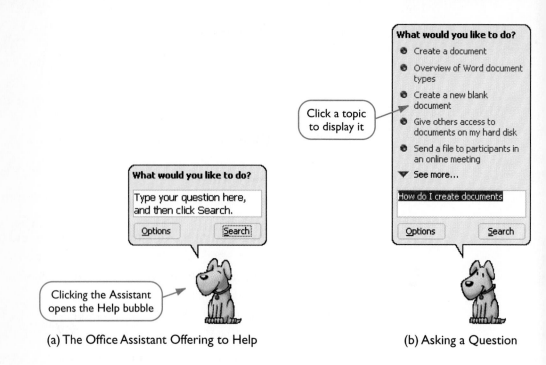

(a) The Office Assistant Offering to Help

(b) Asking a Question

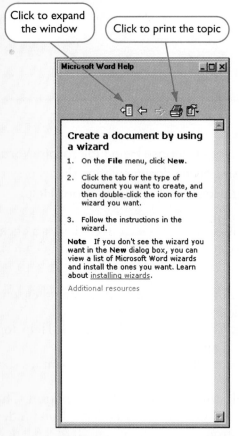

(c) The Help Document Displayed

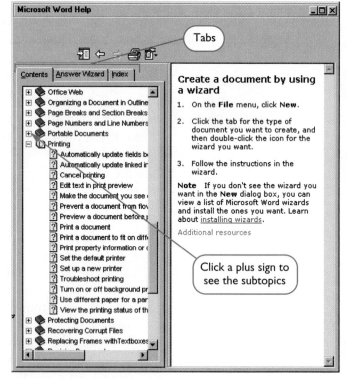

(d) The Complete Help Window Displaying the Contents Tab

FIGURE 1.7   Using Word's Help

Button	Description
	Reduces the Help window to hide the tabs
	Returns to the previous help topic
	If you have used the Back button, you can click the Forward button to return to the previous topic
	Prints the current Help topic
	Provides options on a drop-down list

TABLE 1.3   Buttons in the Microsoft Word Help Window

- To use Help Contents, click the Contents tab. Click the plus sign before the topic to display the list of subtopics. Click a topic to display the Help document.

- To use the Answer Wizard, click the Answer Wizard tab. Type a question in the text box and click the Search button. Word will display a list of Help topics.

- To use the Help Index, click the Index tab. Type a topic in the Keywords text box and click the Search button. Word will display a list of topics.

POINTER

Displaying, Hiding, and Changing Assistants

The Office Assistant character, Rocky, says, "If you fall into a ravine, call Lassie. If you need help in Office, call Rocky."

- If the Office Assistant isn't displayed on the screen, choose Help | Show the Office Assistant, press the F1 key on the keyboard, or click the Microsoft Word Help button on the Standard toolbar.

- If Rocky gets in the way, drag him to another part of the screen or choose Help | Hide the Office Assistant. If you would prefer a different Assistant, right-click Rocky and choose Choose Assistant from the shortcut menu.

- To stop using the Assistant, right-click Rocky, choose Options from the shortcut menu, and clear the *Use Office Assistant* check box in the Options tab of the Office Assistant dialog box.

To use other Help features:

- To get help on screen features, choose Help | What's This? The mouse pointer changes to the Help pointer, with a question mark. Click any part of the screen to get help on that feature.

- To link to up-to-date help, choose Help | Office on the Web. Word will open your browser and connect you to Microsoft's Web site.

Connecting to Microsoft on the Web

You must have a modem and an Internet Service Provider to successfully log on to the Web from your home, or be attached to a network with a gateway to the Internet at work or in a computer lab.

- To get help in a dialog box, click the **?** in the dialog box title bar. The pointer changes to the Help pointer, with a question mark. Click the option in the dialog box that you want explained. Word will display an explanation, as shown in Figure 1.8.

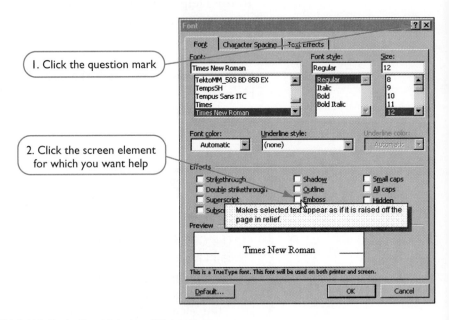

FIGURE 1.8   Help in a Dialog Box

EXERCISE 3 | *Getting Help*

1. If the Office Assistant is not already displayed, choose **Help | Show the Office Assistant**.
   The Assistant appears on the screen. Click it and a Help bubble appears.

2. If the Assistant is already on the screen, click the **Office Assistant**.
   The Help bubble appears.

3. Type **How do I create documents?** and click the **Search button**.
   A list of topics is displayed in the Help bubble.

4. Click **Create a document**.
   The Microsoft Word Help window opens and displays the page you selected.

5. If necessary, scroll the Help window and then click **Create a document by using a wizard**.

The Help window displays this document.

6. After reading the contents, click the **Close button** in the Help window.

The Help window closes. Keep Word running for use in the next exercise.

TASK 4 | *Using a Wizard*

What: Use a wizard to help create a document.

How: Choose File | New.

Why: While you are learning to use Word, you can create nicely formatted documents using the built-in wizards.

Tip: Make use of wizards, but learn as much about Word as you can, because you will also need to create documents on your own.

Word provides assistance creating documents with a feature called **wizards**. This handy feature provides a series of dialog boxes in which you give Word information about your document. When you finish filling in the dialog boxes, Word displays your document.

To create a document using a wizard:

1. Choose File | New to display the New dialog box, shown in Figure 1.9a.
2. Click the tab for the kind of document you want to create.
3. Select a wizard.
4. Click OK to display the wizard's Start panel, like the one shown in Figure 1.9b.
5. Click the Next button to move from panel to panel, providing the necessary information. You can skip a panel at any time, and can jump to a different panel by clicking its name in the map at the left side of any panel.
6. Click the Finish button at any step to complete the wizard and display the document.

EXERCISE 4 | *Using a Wizard to Create a Memo*

1. Choose **File | New**.
The New dialog box opens.

2. Click the **Memos tab**.
Available memos are listed, as shown in Figure 1.9a.

3. Click the **Memo Wizard**.
The Memo Wizard is selected.

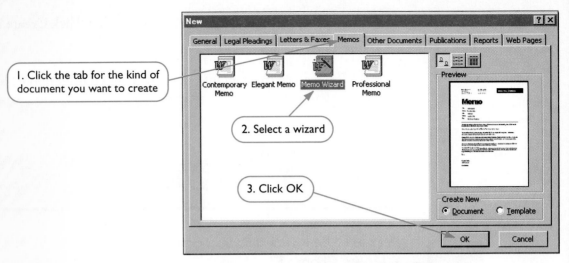

1. Click the tab for the kind of document you want to create

2. Select a wizard

3. Click OK

(a) The New Dialog Box

Click a panel name to jump to it

Click the Next button to move from panel to panel

(b) The Memo Wizard's Start Panel

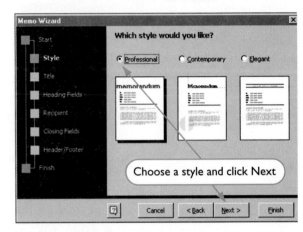

Choose a style and click Next

(c) The Wizard's Style Panel

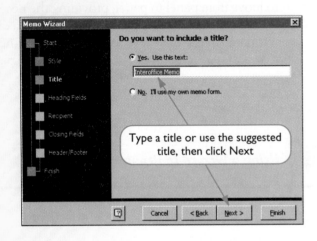

Type a title or use the suggested title, then click Next

(d) The Title Panel

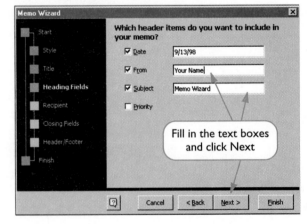

Fill in the text boxes and click Next

(e) The Heading Fields Panel

FIGURE 1.9 Using the Memo Wizard

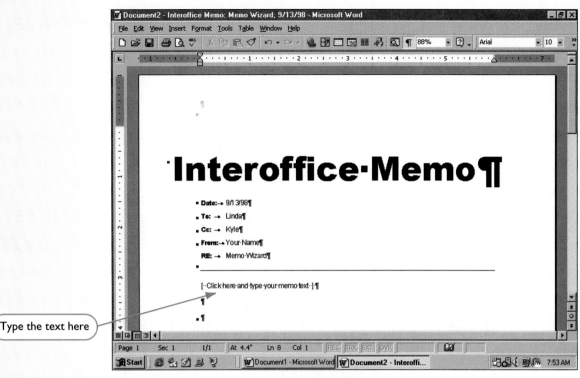

(f) The Memo on the Screen

FIGURE 1.9   Using the Memo Wizard (continued)

4. Click **OK**.
   The dialog box closes, and the Start panel of the wizard is displayed, as shown in Figure 1.9b.

5. Click **Next**.
   The Style panel is displayed, as shown in Figure 1.9c.

6. Make sure **Professional** is selected and click **Next**.
   The Title panel is displayed, as shown in Figure 1.9d.

7. Make sure the **Yes** option is selected, to accept the suggested title, and click **Next**.
   The Heading Fields panel is displayed, as shown in Figure 1.9e.

8. Make sure **Date**, **From**, and **Subject** are selected; type **your name** and a **subject** in the appropriate text boxes; and click **Next**.
   The Recipient panel is displayed.

9. Click in the **To text box** and type the name of **your instructor**. If you like, enter a name in the **Cc text box**.
   You won't need a separate page for this short distribution list. We will also skip over the next two panels of the wizard.

10. Click **Finish**.
    The memo opens on your screen, as shown in Figure 1.9f.

11. If the Office Assistant asks whether you want to do more with the memo, click **Cancel**.

12. Click the text **Click here and type your memo text**.
The text is selected.

13. Type **Creating a memorandum is easy to do using a Word wizard**.
When you start to type, your text replaces the selected text.

14. Keep the memo on your screen for use in the next exercise.

TASK 5 | *Saving a Document*

What: Save a document on a disk.

How: Choose File | Save As.

Why: When the computer is turned off, the document will be lost unless you have saved it.

Tip: It's a good idea to save your documents every 10 to 15 minutes to avoid losing a lot of work if the system shuts down unexpectedly.

To save a document you have created:

1. Choose File | Save As. The Save As dialog box opens, as shown in Figure 1.10.
2. Type a name for the document in the File name text box.
3. Specify the drive and folder to store the document in the Save in list box.
4. Click the Save button.

FIGURE 1.10   The Save As Dialog Box

CHOOSING A FILE NAME

Keep these points in mind when choosing names for your files:

- Word suggests a name for the document in the File name text box, composed of the first few words of the document you created.

- Word automatically adds **.doc** on the end of document names. This **three-letter extension** to the file name is used by the software to display and open files. The *.doc* extension designates the file as a Microsoft Word document.

- Documents can be given names of up to 255 characters. You should give your documents meaningful names that represent their content, so that finding them later will be easy.

- The following characters can't be used in document names:

    / \ > < * ? | : ;

    You don't have to memorize these characters, because if you try to save a document using one of them, a message box prompts you to choose a different name.

POINTER

Erasing the File Name in the Name Text Box

Because the suggested file name is selected (highlighted) when you open the Save As dialog box, you don't need to erase the suggested name before giving the file a different name. Simply start typing, and the name you type will replace the suggested name.

CHOOSING A DRIVE AND FOLDER

When you save a document, you must specify the drive (and optional folder) in which it will be stored. When you open the Save As dialog box, the Save in list box shows the default drive and folder for saving Word documents, or the most recently used folder if that is different.

- Make sure the Save in list box shows the disk drive in which you want to save the document.

- If it does not, click the down arrow in the list box to display a list of the drives on your system.

- Click a different drive to select it and move it into the Save in list box. For instance, to save the document on a floppy disk in drive A, you would click 3 1/2 Floppy (A), as shown in Figure 1.11.

- The folders and files in the selected drive are shown in the list in the dialog box. To save a document in one of the folders, double-click the folder name to select it and move it into the Save in list box.

- The Save As dialog box includes the **Places bar** along the left edge to help you organize your files into folders. Table 1.4 describes the buttons on the Places bar. When you click a button on the bar, that folder name appears in the Save in list box. This is a quick way to select the folder.

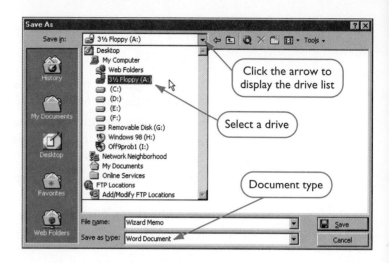

FIGURE 1.11   Choosing a Drive in Which to Save a File

Button	Folder Description
History	List of documents that were used recently; you can't save a file here, but can find a recently used file here to open it
My Documents	The default folder for storing Microsoft Office files
Desktop	Saves the file to the desktop for quick access
Favorites	Folder where you can store files you use often
Web Folders	Storage locations for Web documents

TABLE 1.4   Folders on the Places Bar

POINTER

Using File | Save

After you have saved a file and given it a name using the File | Save As option, save it again by choosing File | Save, by clicking the Save button on the toolbar, or by pressing Ctrl+S. All three of these options perform the same task—that is, saving the current file under the name you gave it without opening the Save As dialog box.

POINTER

Formatted Disk Needed

You will need a formatted $3^1/_2''$ disk in order to save files on the $3^1/_2$ floppy (A) drive.

EXERCISE 5 | *Saving the Memo*

1. With the memo from Exercise 4 open on the screen, choose **File | Save As**.
The Save As dialog box opens, with the suggested name *Interoffice Memo* selected.

2. Type **Wizard Memo**.
The name replaces the suggested name.

3. Click the down arrow in the **Save in list box**.
A list of drives drops down, as shown in Figure 1.11.

4. Insert a formatted disk into drive A on the computer, and then choose **3¹/₂ Floppy (A)**.
The Save in list box reflects the change.

5. Click the dialog box's **Save button**.
The file will be saved on the disk in drive A. The title bar shows the new name.

6. Keep the document on the screen for use in the next exercise.

TASK 6 | *Printing a Document*

What: Produce a hard copy of a document.

How: Choose File | Print.

Why: You will want to have paper copies of your documents.

Tip: To send the document to the attached printer without changing any options, click the Print button on the Standard toolbar or press Ctrl+P.

When you choose File | Print, the Print dialog box opens, as shown in Figure 1.12.

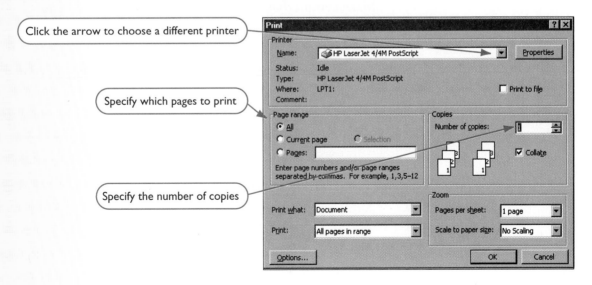

FIGURE 1.12 The Print Dialog Box

To print a document:

1. Check the Printer name to see which printer will actually print the document. To change printers, click the down arrow in the Name list box and select a different printer from the list.
2. Change the Page range option if necessary, by clicking an option button, as shown in Table 1.5.
3. Change the Copies option to change the number of copies that will be printed.

Page Range	Description
All	Prints the entire document (the default)
Current page	Prints the page containing the insertion point
Pages	Prints specified pages: use a hyphen for a range of pages—for example, 3-10; separate single pages with commas—for example, 2,4,12
Selection	Prints the selected text

TABLE 1.5   Page Range Options in the Print Dialog Box

EXERCISE 6 | *Printing the Memo*

1. Choose **File | Print**.
   The Print dialog box opens.
2. In the Printer section, check the printer shown in the **Name** list box to be sure you will print to the correct printer.
3. Check that **All** is selected in the Page range and that Number of copies is set to **1**.
4. Make certain that your printer is turned on and has paper loaded.
5. Click the **OK button**.
   The document will print.
6. Keep the document on the screen to use in the next exercise.

TASK 7 | *Exiting from Word*

What: Exit from Word.

How: Choose **File | Exit**.

Why: You should exit from the software correctly and close Windows before turning off the computer.

Tip: Never turn off the computer while you have programs running.

You should always exit from Microsoft Word when you have finished working with the application. You do so by choosing File | Exit. If you have not saved the file you were working on, Word will prompt you to do so. When you exit from Word, you are returned to the Windows desktop.

EXERCISE 7 | *Exiting from Word*

1. Choose **File | Exit**.
2. If you are asked whether you want to save the changes to your document, select **No**.

REVIEW

SUMMARY

After completing this unit, you should
- know how to start Microsoft Word 2000 (page 2)
- be familiar with the Word interface (page 3)
- be able to use Help (page 11)
- be able to create a document using a Word wizard (page 15)
- be able to save a document (page 18)
- be able to print a document (page 21)
- know the proper way to exit from Word (page 23)

KEY TERMS

check box (page 7)

Close button (page 4)

command button (page 7)

dialog box (page 6)

Formatting toolbar (page 8)

graphical user interface (GUI)
(page 3)

horizontal ruler (page 9)

insertion point (page 9)

list box (page 7)

maximize (page 4)

menu bar (page 4)

minimize (page 4)

Office Assistant (page 9)

option button (radio button)
(page 7)

Places bar (page 19)

pointer (page 9)

radio button (page 7)

restore (page 4)

ScreenTip (page 9)

scroll bar (page 9)

scroll box (page 9)

shortcut menu (page 10)

Standard toolbar (page 8)

status bar (page 9)

tabbed dialog box (page 6)

taskbar (page 10)

text box (page 7)

text-editing window (page 9)

title bar (page 4)

three-letter extension (page 19)

toolbar (page 8)

word processing (page 1)

word processing software (page 2)

wizard (page 15)

TEST YOUR SKILLS

True/False

1. The status bar is located at the top of the screen and contains the name of the current application.
2. ScreenTips provide help on the functions of buttons.
3. You should never turn off the computer before you have correctly exited Word.
4. Word is used primarily for text documents.
5. Word is an application that is part of Office 2000.

Multiple Choice

1. The Office Assistant
   a. can't be turned off
   b. allows you to type questions to ask for help
   c. is the only way to access help in Microsoft Word
   d. all of these answers

2. When you are using a dialog box and need help, you
   a. must cancel the operation and use the Office Assistant
   b. must cancel the operation and use the Help menu
   c. click the [?] in the dialog box and then click on the option you want help for
   d. exit the dialog box and initiate a help search

3. The status bar
   a. contains information about the location of the insertion point
   b. contains menu choices
   c. contains the Windows Start button
   d. contains the Minimize and Maximize buttons

4. The scroll bars
   a. let you view other locations in your document
   b. contain View buttons
   c. are both horizontal and vertical
   d. all of these answers

5. To change the number of copies that the printer will print, you use which option?
   a. all   b. current page
   c. copies   d. print what

Short Answer

Match the letter of the correct word with the correct location in Figure 1.13:

___ a. Ruler   ___ b. Menu bar
___ c. Title bar   ___ d. Status bar
___ e. Office Assistant   ___ f. Help menu

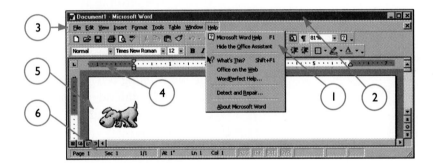

FIGURE 1.13

What Does This Do?

Write a brief description of the function of the following:

1. **?**	2. Cancel	3. Finish	4. ▬	5. Start
6. I	7. ?	8. ⇗	9. OK	10.

On Your Own

1. Use the Memo wizard to create a memo. Address the memo to yourself. In the body of the memo, create a To Do list as a reminder of what you need to accomplish in the next week. Save the memo as **ToDo**. Print the memo.
2. Use Help to find information on a topic you are unsure about. Print the resulting Help screen.

3. If you have access to the World Wide Web, choose Help | Microsoft on the Web. Find information that is of interest.
4. Choose a different Office Assistant.
5. Use the Help Index to look up **documents**, then **naming**. Print the resulting Help screen.

PROJECTS

1. a. Ask the Office Assistant the question **Wizards?** Select the option **Create a Letter**.
   b. Print the Create a Letter Help topic.

2. a. Use the Letter Wizard located on the Letters & Faxes tab of the New dialog box to create a letter. Address the letter to your instructor, using your school address, and sign your name to the letter. Leave the body of the letter as is.
   b. Save the document as **Instructor Letter**.
   c. Print the letter.

3. a. Use the Calendar Wizard located on the Other Documents tab of the New dialog box. Create a calendar for the current month.
   b. Save the calendar as **My Calendar**.
   c. Print the document.

4. a. Use the Resume Wizard located on the Other Documents tab of the New dialog box to create a résumé. Include headings that apply to you.
   b. Save the résumé as **My Resume**. You will add information to the résumé in the next unit. You will learn how to insert the *é* with an acute accent in Unit 5.
   c. Print the résumé.

Creating and Editing Documents

UNIT OBJECTIVES

- Create a document from a blank document
- Move around a document
- Delete characters
- Insert text and type over text
- Undo a task
- Check spelling and grammar
- Open and close documents
- Switch between open documents
- Preview a document before printing it

In the following tasks, you will learn to use Word to create documents for a small home-based dog kennel that raises and sells purebred Jack Russell terriers. The owner recently acquired a computer and Microsoft Word 2000, and wants to use them to help run the business more efficiently. In this unit you will learn to create documents without the help of wizards. You will also learn to use important editing features such as deleting characters, checking spelling, checking grammar, and inserting or typing over text.

TASK 1 | Creating a Document from a Blank Document

What: Create a document.

How: Choose File | New or click the New Blank Document button on the Standard toolbar.

Why: Creating your own documents is a basic word processing task.

Tip: Word's AutoComplete feature helps you type certain common phrases and the current date. Start typing the date and the current date will appear in a yellow box. Press Enter to accept the text, or continue typing to ignore it.

When you start Microsoft Word, a blank document is displayed on the screen. When you want to start another new document, click the New Blank Document button on the Standard toolbar or:

1. Choose File | New to open the New dialog box.
2. Click the General tab in the New dialog box.
3. Select Blank Document.
4. Click OK.

Word displays a blank document, and you can just start typing. As you type, the Office Assistant may appear, offering you assistance based on what you type.

POINTER

Customizing the Office Assistant

When you begin to type a letter, the Office Assistant offers to help. If you choose to get help with the letter, the Letter Wizard will start. To type your own document without using the wizard, click "Just type the letter without help" in the Office Assistant bubble. To keep the Assistant from offering help every time you start a letter, right-click the cartoon figure, choose Options, and clear the box *Show tips about using features more efficiently*.

With a word processor, you don't need to press Enter at the end of a line, because the program automatically carries the text over to the next line, in a feature called **word wrap**. Pressing Enter begins a new paragraph. Therefore, you press Enter only at the end of a paragraph or when you want to end a short line such as a title.

1. Start Word.
   A new blank document opens, with the temporary name *Document1*.

2. Choose **File | New**.
   The New dialog box opens.

3. Click the **General tab** if it is not already selected.
   The General tab moves to the front and becomes active.

4. Select **Blank Document** and click **OK**.
   A new blank document appears on the screen, with the temporary name *Document2*.

5. Type the business name and address shown below, pressing **Enter** *once* at the end of the first two lines and *twice* at the end of the third. If the Office Assistant bubble appears, click **Just type the letter without help**.

JRT Purebreds
2000 Friendly Street
Eugene, OR 97405

   Pressing Enter twice leaves a blank line after the address.

6. Type **the current date**. If Word's AutoComplete feature displays the date in a yellow box as you type, accept it by pressing **Enter**. When the date is complete, press **Enter** *twice*.
   The AutoComplete feature is enabled by default, but another user may have turned it off. You will learn more about this feature in Unit 5.

7. Type the inside address shown below, pressing **Enter** *once* at the end of the first two lines and *twice* at the end of the third.

Greg Jones
900 River View Way
Depot Bay, OR 97874

   A line of space is left below the address.

8. Type **Dear Mr. Jones:** (including the colon) and press **Enter** *twice*.

9. Type the body of the letter shown on page 30, pressing **Enter** *twice* at the end of each paragraph and nowhere else.

The following information is provided as a full description of the Jack Russell terrier breed. I hope this answers your questions.

The Jack Russell terrier was developed in the south of England in the 1800's to work European red fox both above and below ground. The terrier was named for the Reverend John Russell, whose terriers trailed hounds and chased foxes from dens.

Jack Russell terriers range in size between 12″ and 14″. A well-bred Jack Russell terrier has a strong head that is in good proportion to the rest of the body. These dogs are full of life and intelligence. They have dark, almond-shaped eyes; small, V-shaped drop ears; and a white or white with black or tan coat.

Jack Russell terriers are friendly and clever. They are bold killers. As pets they are playful and highly affectionate, wanting quite a bit of attention.

If you have any other specific questions, please contact me.

10. Type **Yours truly,** (including the comma) and press **Enter** *four times.*

11. Type **your name** and press **Enter**.
Your document should look like Figure 2.1.

12. Save the letter as **JRT History**.

13. Print the letter.
If you don't remember how, review Task 6 in Unit 1.

14. Keep the document on the screen for use in the next exercise.

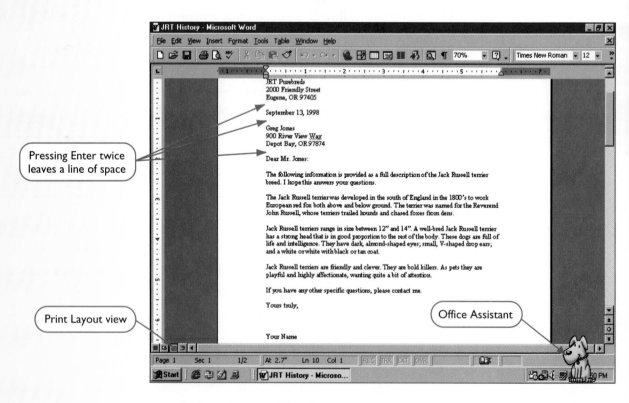

FIGURE 2.1 The Completed Letter

TASK 2 | *Moving Around a Document*

What: Move the insertion point in a document.

How: Use the keyboard or the mouse.

Why: Knowing shortcuts for moving the insertion point will save you time.

Tip: Word keeps track of the last three locations where you edited or typed new text. Press Shift+F5 to move back to these locations one at a time.

The first step in editing a document is placing the insertion point where you want to make a change.

To move around a document with the mouse:

- Point to the new location and click.
- Use the scroll bars to view other parts of the document and then point to the new location and click.

You can also use the keyboard to move through the document. Table 2.1 shows the keystrokes for using the keyboard to move the insertion point.

Keys	Result
left arrow, right arrow	Moves one character left or right
up arrow, down arrow	Moves one line up or down
End	Moves to the end of the current line
Home	Moves to the beginning of the current line
Ctrl+End	Moves to the end of the document
Ctrl+Home	Moves to the beginning of the document
Page Up, Page Down	Moves up or down one screen

TABLE 2.1   Keys That Move the Insertion Point

POINTER

Ctrl+End, Ctrl+Home

In this text, the instruction "press Ctrl+Home" means that you should press and hold down the Ctrl key while you press the Home key, and then release both keys.

POINTER

Select Browse Object

The three buttons at the bottom of the vertical scroll bar allow you to scroll through a document by page or by another element, such as footnote or heading. Click the Select Browse Object button to see the list of objects; select one of them; then click a double arrow to jump to the previous or next example of that object in the document. If you choose Page, clicking the double arrows will scroll through the document a page at a time.

EXERCISE 2 | *Moving Around a Document*

1. With the *JRT History* document on the screen, point to the **beginning of the first paragraph** and click the mouse.
   The insertion point moves to the first paragraph.

2. Point to the **date** and click the mouse.
   The insertion point moves to the date line.

3. Hold down the **Ctrl key** and press the **End key**, and then release both keys.
   The insertion point moves to the end of the document.

4. Press **Ctrl+Home**.
   The insertion point moves to the beginning of the document.

5. Press the **down, right, left,** and **up arrow keys**.
   The insertion point moves one character or one line at a time.

6. Keep the document on the screen for use in the next exercise.

TASK 3 | *Deleting Characters*

What: Erase unwanted characters and correct errors.

How: Use the Backspace and Delete keys on the keyboard.

Why: Using the keyboard to erase errors while you type is fast and simple.

Tip: To delete text after you type, select it and press the Delete key. You will learn shortcuts for selecting text in Unit 3.

When you are typing and notice that your text has errors, you can use either of two keys on the keyboard to delete characters.

- Use the Backspace key to erase characters to the left of the insertion point.
- Use the Delete key to erase characters to the right of the insertion point.

Each time you press either the Delete or Backspace key and release it, Word will delete one character. If you hold either key down, Word will continue to delete characters until you release the key.

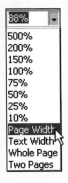

EXERCISE 3 | *Deleting Text*

1. With the *JRT History* document on the screen, press **Ctrl+Home**.
The insertion point moves to the top of the document.

2. Press the **Delete key**.
The character to the right of the insertion point is erased.

3. Press **Delete** several times.
Several characters are deleted.

4. Click at the end of the **last paragraph of text** in the body of the letter.
Use the vertical scroll bar if necessary to see the last paragraph.

5. Press the **Backspace key**.
A character to the left of the insertion point is erased.

6. Leave the document open on the screen for the next exercise.
Don't worry about the errors you have introduced. You will see how to close a document without saving changes in Task 7.

What: Insert text or type over existing text.

How: Double-click the OVR button on the status bar to switch between Insert and Overtype mode.

Why: Sometimes Word's Overtype mode is quicker to use than Insert mode.

Tip: Instead of switching to Overtype mode to replace a word, you can double-click it to select it and then just start typing. The text you type will replace the selected text.

When you click in a document and type, existing text moves to the right, making room for the new text as you type. This is Word's default editing mode, called Insert mode.

To insert text into a document in Insert mode:

1. Move the insertion point to the desired location.
2. Type the additional text, including spaces.

Word has another editing mode, called Overtype, where each character you type in existing text *replaces* the character to its right. You may sometimes find this mode useful.

To type over existing text using Overtype mode:

1. Move the insertion point to the beginning of the location where you want to replace text.
2. Double-click the OVR mode indicator on the status bar.
3. Type text to replace the existing text, character for character
4. Delete any remaining, unwanted characters.

POINTER

The OVR Mode Indicator

The OVR mode indicator on the status bar is a toggle. When it is black, it is turned on and you are in **Overtype mode**. Double-click it to turn it off. It is grayed out, and you are back in **Insert mode**.

EXERCISE 4 | *Inserting and Typing Over Text*

I. With the *JRT History* document on the screen, click after the letter **d** in the word **breed** in the first paragraph of the body.
   Be sure to click before the space.

2. Press the **Spacebar**.
A space is inserted.

3. Type **of dogs**
The existing text automatically moves to the right to make room for the inserted text.

4. Double-click the **OVR mode indicator** on the status bar.
The indicator changes from gray to black, and you are now in Overtype mode.

5. Move the insertion point to the beginning of the word **killers** in the last paragraph.

6. Type **hunters**
The word *killers* is replaced by the word *hunters*. Because both words have seven characters, no other editing is necessary.

7. Double-click the **OVR mode indicator** on the status bar.
The indicator is grayed out, and you are back in Insert mode. Your letter should look like the one in Figure 2.2.

8. Print the document.

9. Leave the document open on the screen for the next exercise.

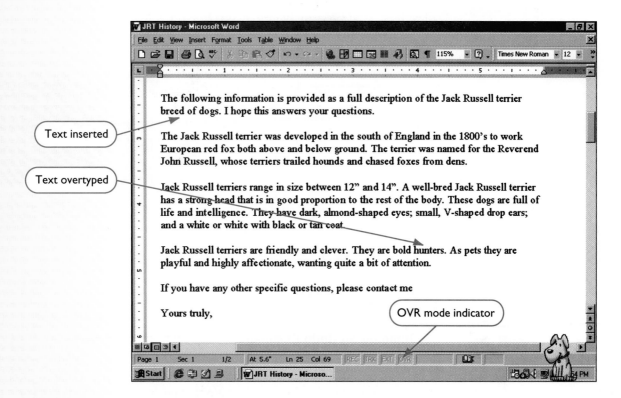

FIGURE **2.2** The Updated Letter

What: Undo one or more actions.

How: Choose Edit | Undo or click the Undo button on the Standard toolbar.

Why: People make mistakes.

Tip: You can try new things without being afraid of ruining your document if you get in the habit of using Undo.

You will erase text by mistake, try a new function that doesn't work as you thought it would, or just change your mind when you are using Word. You can easily undo the last action you took by choosing Edit | Undo. The Undo menu option is worded to let you know what action will be undone. If your last action was to enter text, the command will read "Undo Typing." If you have just deleted a word, it will read "Undo Clear." (Word refers to a delete operation as *clearing text.*)

If you want to undo more than one action, click the down arrow next to the Undo button on the Standard toolbar, and a list of actions will be displayed as shown in Figure 2.3. Clicking the fifth action on the list will undo the last five actions.

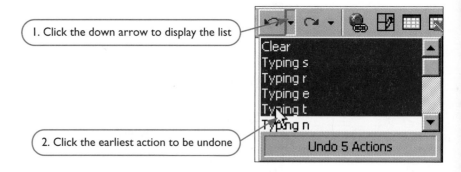

1. Click the down arrow to display the list

2. Click the earliest action to be undone

FIGURE 2.3 Undoing Several Actions at Once

POINTER

Undoing an Undo Command

If you click Undo and then change your mind, you can click the Redo button on the Standard toolbar to reverse the process. Click the Redo button's down arrow to see a list of actions you can redo all at once.

EXERCISE 5 | *Undoing an Action*

1. With the *JRT History* document on the screen, click the mouse before the word **clever** in the last paragraph.
Be sure to click *after* the space.

2. Type **very** and press the **Spacebar**.
The word *very* is inserted before *clever*.

3. Choose **Edit | Undo Typing**.
The word *very* is deleted.

4. Leave the document open on the screen for the next exercise.

TASK 6 | *Checking Spelling and Grammar*

What: Check for spelling and grammar errors as you type or when you finish typing.

How: Choose Tools | Spelling and Grammar or click the Spelling and Grammar button on the Standard toolbar.

Why: You can produce grammatical documents with perfect spelling using Microsoft Word, but you will still need to proofread your documents because you may type the wrong word (such as *from* for *form*) but spell it correctly.

Tip: To turn on the automatic spell checker, choose Tools | Options | Spelling and Grammar tab. Make sure the *Check Spelling as you Type* check box is selected.

As you type, Word marks words with red and green wavy underlines to alert you to errors in your document.

- Red wavy underlines indicate words not spelled like those in Word's dictionary. These may be misspelled words, but they may also be correctly spelled words such as proper names, technical terms, or foreign words.

- Green wavy underlines indicate constructions that don't follow Word's rules of grammar and writing style (look up Help for *Grammar and writing style options* to see how Word checks grammar).

You can fix either type of error while you type or edit it when you finish typing.

To fix spelling and grammar errors while you type:

1. Right-click the marked word to open a shortcut menu.
2. Choose a correction from the menu, as shown in Figure 2.4. The shortcut menu will close and the correction will be made.

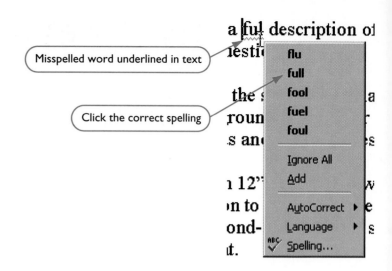

a ful description of

Misspelled word underlined in text

lestic

flu

full

the

fool

roun

fuel

foul

s and

Ignore All

Add

12"

n to

AutoCorrect ▶

ond-

Language ▶

t.

Spelling...

Click the correct spelling

FIGURE 2.4   The Spelling Shortcut Menu

POINTER

The Spelling and Grammar Status Button

An open book button on the status bar tells you whether the open document contains anything the spelling or grammar checker considers an error. If the button has a check mark, there are no errors; if it has an X, there are errors. If you double-click the button, the insertion point will jump to the next error in the document, and a shortcut menu will open suggesting a correction.

To run the spell checker and grammar checker after you have finished typing:

1. Choose Tools | Spelling and Grammar, or click the Spelling and Grammar button on the Standard toolbar, to open the Spelling and Grammar dialog box shown in Figure 2.5.
2. Spelling errors are shown in red, and grammar errors are shown in green. You can choose from the options described in Table 2.2.

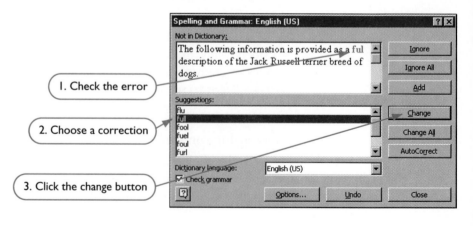

1. Check the error

2. Choose a correction

3. Click the change button

FIGURE 2.5   The Spelling and Grammar Dialog Box

Button	Description
Ignore	Ignores the error for one time
Ignore All	Ignores the error throughout the entire document
Add	Adds the word to the dictionary so it will not be flagged again
Change	Changes the current error
Change All	Corrects the error throughout the document
AutoCorrect	Adds the correction to the AutoCorrect feature, explained in Unit 5

TABLE 2.2   The Spelling and Grammar Dialog Box's Command Buttons

Sometimes Word spots an error but misdiagnoses it. To correct the error yourself, edit the text in the dialog box and click the Change button.

POINTER

Where Does the Spelling and Grammar Check Begin?

The spelling and grammar checker starts from the insertion point, checks to the bottom of the document, and then asks whether you want to continue checking. If you start the check with text already selected, Word checks just the selected text and then asks whether you want to continue. It's a good idea to move the insertion point to the top of the document before starting the check.

EXERCISE 6 | *Checking Spelling and Grammar*

1. With the *JRT History* document on the screen, move the insertion point to the end of the word **full** in the first paragraph. Backspace over the second **l**.
   Full is misspelled.

2. Move the insertion point after the first word (*The*) in the second paragraph. Press the Spacebar and type the word **The**.
   The text now reads *The The*.

3. Move the insertion point to the word **ground** in the second paragraph. Delete the letter **o** from the word.
   Ground is misspelled.

4. Move the insertion point after the word **intelligence**. Delete the **period** and type a **comma**.

The sentence is incorrect. Your document should look like the one in Figure 2.6.

5. Point the mouse to the misspelled word **ful** and click the right mouse button.

A shortcut menu opens offering choices.

6. Click **full**.

The word is corrected in the letter.

7. Point to the word **The** with the wavy red underlines and click the right mouse button.

8. Click the option **Delete Repeated Word**.

The duplicate will be deleted.

9. Press **Ctrl+Home**.

The insertion point moves to the top of the document.

10. Choose **Tools | Spelling and Grammar**.

The Spelling and Grammar dialog box opens.

11. Complete the spelling and grammar check for the letter by changing or ignoring all errors.

12. Keep the document open on the screen for use in the next exercise.

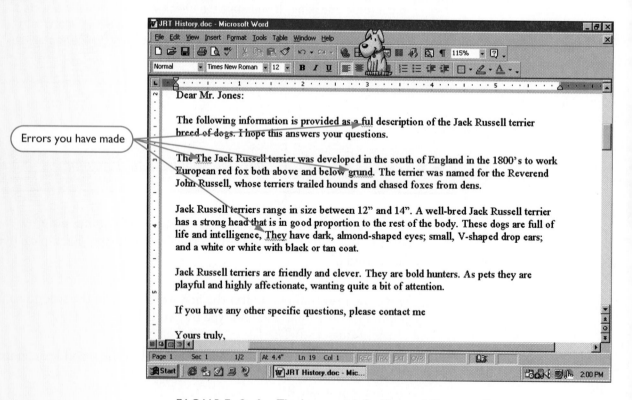

FIGURE **2.6** The Letter with Spelling and Grammar Errors

What: Open and close documents you have saved on disk.

How: Choose File | Open and File | Close.

Why: You can't use Word without acquiring this skill.

Tip: The Open dialog box works the same way as the Save As dialog box. You can find a recently used document by clicking the History button on its Places bar.

When you want to return to a document you have saved on a disk, you can do so by choosing File | Open. The Open dialog box opens, as shown in Figure 2.7. To open a document:

1. In the Look in list box, select the drive where the document is stored. This will display the drive's folders and documents in the dialog box.
2. If the document is stored in a folder, double-click the folder in the list. This will move the folder into the Look in box and display its documents in the dialog box.
3. Select the document from the list in the dialog box.
4. Click the Open button, and the document will open in the text-editing window.

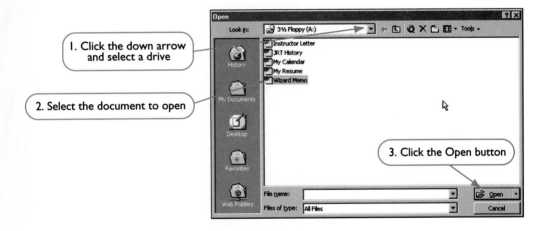

FIGURE 2.7 The Open Dialog Box

POINTER

Document versus File

You will find all kinds of documents referred to as files in Office 2000 dialog boxes. A **file** is simply a document you have given a name and saved on disk.

Sometimes you will want to close open files and continue working in Microsoft Word. Close a file by choosing File | Close. If you have made changes to the document that you have not saved, Word will display the message box shown in Figure 2.8.

POINTER

Closing a File Using the Close Button

If only one document is open, you can close it but stay in Word by clicking the Close button on the menu bar. If more than one document is open, you can close the document but stay in Word by clicking the Close button on the title bar.

You can:

- Save the file and close it
- Close the file without saving it
- Cancel the operation

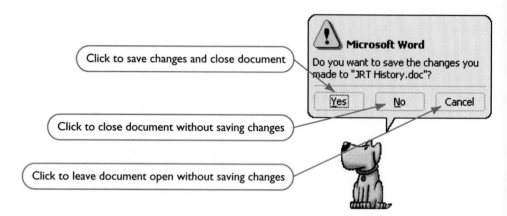

FIGURE 2.8   The Save Changes Message Box

EXERCISE 7   *Opening and Closing Documents*

1. With the *JRT History* document on the screen, choose **File | Open**.
The Open dialog box opens.

2. Select the drive and folder that contains the projects you saved in Unit 1.
The documents are listed in the dialog box.

3. Select **Wizard Memo** and click the **Open button**.
The document is displayed on the screen. There are now two open documents: *JRT History* and *Wizard Memo*. Each has a button on the taskbar.

4. Choose **File | Open**.
The Open dialog box opens.

5. Select **My Resume** and click the **Open button**.
The document is displayed on the screen. There are now three open documents, each with a button on the taskbar.

6. Choose **File | Close**.
The *My Resume* document closes and the *Wizard Memo* document is displayed on the screen. The *JRT History* document is still open but not displayed.

7. Leave the *JRT History* and *Memo Wizard* documents open for use in the next exercise.

TASK 8 | *Switching Between Documents*

What: Move between open documents.

How: Click the document's button on the taskbar.

Why: Keeping more than one document open and switching between them makes it easy to perform such operations as cutting and pasting text from one to the other.

Tip: If you want to see more than one open document at a time, choose Window | Arrange All. Word will **tile** the windows horizontally on the screen.

Every open document has a button on the taskbar. To display a different open document, click its taskbar button. The first document is still open, but is not displayed. Figure 2.9 shows buttons on the taskbar for the two documents you left open at the end of the last exercise.

FIGURE 2.9 The Taskbar with Two Open Documents

EXERCISE 8 | *Switching Between Open Documents*

1. Click the **JRT History button** on the taskbar.
The *JRT History* document is displayed on the screen.

2. Click the **Wizard Memo button** on the taskbar.
The memo replaces the *JRT History* document on the screen.

3. Close the **Wizard Memo** document.

Choose File | Close or click the Close button on the title bar. The *JRT History* document is displayed.

4. Keep the *JRT History* document open for use in the next exercise.

| **TASK 9** | *Previewing a Document* |

What: See how the document will look on paper without printing it.

How: Choose File | Print Preview or click the Print Preview button on the Standard toolbar.

Why: It is a waste of paper to print documents and then decide that you don't like how they look.

Tip: The Shrink to Fit button on the Print Preview toolbar is a handy option when you see that only a line or two will print on the final page. Search Help to find out how to use this option.

When you choose File | Print Preview, the document is displayed in Print Preview, as shown in Figure 2.10.

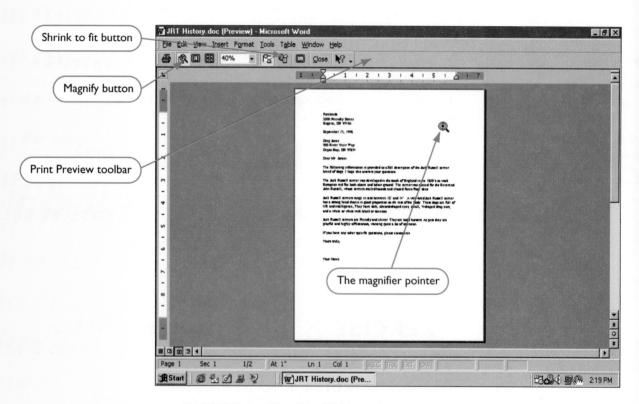

FIGURE 2.10   The *JRT History* Document in Print Preview

Table 2.3 describes the buttons available on the Print Preview toolbar and their functions.

Button	Description
🖨	Sends the document to the printer without opening the Print dialog box
🔍	Toggles between magnifier and editing views; when the magnifier view is selected, the pointer changes to a magnifying glass and the text cannot be edited
▤	Displays one page of a multipage document
▦	Displays multiple pages in a multipage document; click the button and then drag the mouse over the thumbnail pages to choose a layout
100% ▾	Changes the magnification of the document
🔲	Toggles the ruler on and off
📑	Reduces the type size of the document to make it fit on fewer pages
▣	Displays the document full screen, without the toolbars
Close	Closes the Print Preview window
▶?	Provides What's This? help for items on the screen

TABLE 2.3 Print Preview Toolbar Buttons

POINTER

The Magnifier Button

The pointer changes to a magnifying glass when the Magnifier button is activated. A plus sign inside the glass indicates that clicking the document will magnify it. A minus sign indicates that the document has already been magnified.

EXERCISE 9 | *Previewing a Document*

1. Choose **File | Print Preview**.
   The display changes to Print Preview.

2. Move the pointer over the document. If the pointer changes to a magnifying glass with a plus sign, click the **document**. If the pointer is an I-beam, click the **Magnifier button** on the toolbar and then click the **document**.

The document is magnified, and the pointer's plus sign changes to a minus sign.

3. Click the **document** a second time.

The document returns to the original display, and the pointer's minus sign changes to a plus sign.

4. Click the toolbar's **Close button**.

The Print Preview window closes.

5. Close the document. When asked whether to save changes, click **No**.

REVIEW

SUMMARY

After completing this unit, you should
- know how to create a document from a blank document (page 29)
- be able to move around a document (page 31)
- know how to delete characters (page 32)
- be able to insert text (page 34)
- be able to type over text (page 34)
- know how to undo (page 36)
- be able to check spelling (page 37)
- be able to check grammar (page 37   )
- know how to open files (page 41)
- know how to close documents (page 41)
- be able to switch between open documents (page 43)
- be able to preview a document before printing it (page 44)

KEY TERMS

file (page 41)

Insert mode (page 34)

Overtype mode (page 34)

tiled windows (page 43)

word wrap (page 28)

TEST YOUR SKILLS

True/False

1. You do not need to proofread your documents if you use Word's Spelling and Grammar checker.
2. You can switch to any open document by clicking its button on the taskbar.
3. It is a prudent idea to preview your documents before printing them.
4. The Backspace key deletes characters to the left of the insertion point.
5. To overtype text, you double-click the OVR indicator on the status bar.

Multiple Choice

1. To move to the top of a document, you would choose
   a. Shift+F5
   b. Ctrl+Home
   c. Ctrl+End
   d. OVR

2. The Delete key deletes a character
   a. to the right of the insertion point
   b. above the insertion point
   c. to the left of the insertion point
   d. below the insertion point

3. Text is automatically moved to the right to make room for what you are typing when you are
   a. deleting text
   b. overtyping text
   c. saving text
   d. inserting text

4. If you want to see alternative spellings for a word underlined with a red wavy line, you would
   a. point to the word and click the right mouse button
   b. point to the word and click the left mouse button
   c. click the OVR mode indicator on the status bar
   d. all of these answers

5. Documents that you type can be
   a. saved
   b. closed without saving
   c. opened if they have been saved
   d. all of these answers

Short Answer

Match the letter of the correct word with the correct location in Figure 2.11:

___ a. indicates that the preview can be enlarged
___ b. Overtype mode indicator
___ c. indicates an open document
___ d. returns to the text-editing window
___ e. prints the current document

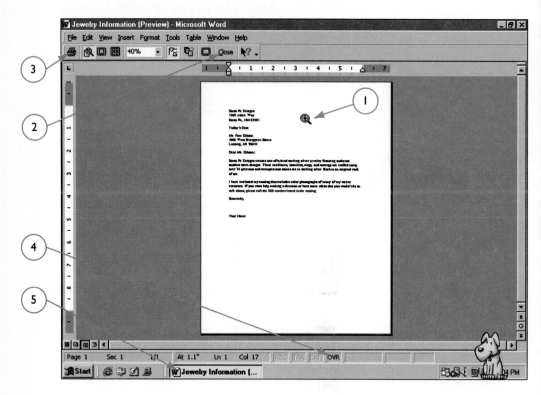

FIGURE 2.11

What Does This Do?

Write a brief description of the function of the following:

1.	Ctrl+Home	6.	Ignore All
2.	⬛	7.	Delete key
3.	OVR	8.	↺ ▼
4.	red wavy underline	9.	↻ ▼
5.	Backspace key	10.	Ctrl+End

On Your Own

1. Open a new blank document. Type three paragraphs from a magazine article that interests you. Check the document's spelling, proofread it, and correct errors. Save the document, preview it, and print it.
2. Open the **Instructor Letter** you created in Unit 1 using the wizard. Compose the body of the letter describing what you have learned so far about Microsoft Word 2000. Check the document's spelling, proofread it, and correct errors. Save the document, preview it, and print it.
3. Open a new blank document. Write a letter to a friend or family member to whom you've been meaning to write. Check the document's spelling, proofread it, and correct errors. Save the document, preview it, and print it.
4. Open a new blank document. Create a list of things you need to do or purchase. Check the document's spelling, proofread it, and correct errors. Save the document, preview it, and print it.
5. Open a new blank document. Create a document of your own choosing. Check the document's spelling, proofread it, and correct errors. Save the document, preview it, and print it.

PROJECTS

1. a. Open the document **My Resume** that you created using the Resume Wizard. Fill in the résumé with your real, accurate information.
   b. Check the document's spelling, proofread it, and correct errors by deleting unwanted text, inserting text, or typing over text.
   c. Save the document again with the same name. (Remember to save documents that have already been saved by choosing File | Save.)
   d. Preview and then print the document.

2. a. Create the document shown below.
   b. Check the document's spelling, proofread it, and correct errors by deleting unwanted text, inserting text, or typing over text.
   c. Save the document as **Internet Information**.
   d. Preview and then print the document.

Welcome to the World Wide Web

The World Wide Web was the brainchild of scientists who wanted a better way to link research documents that resided on computers all over the world. The result was creation of hypertext links.

Hypertext generally appears in the body of a document underlined and in a color such as blue. The idea behind hypertext is that the user clicks the underlined blue text and is transferred to another document stored on a computer located anywhere in the world. The hypertext link has the address of the document embedded in it, so that when the user clicks the text, the address is accessed and the document is downloaded to the user. This address is called a URL, for Uniform Resource Locator.

(continued)

URL's are becoming as common as e-mail addresses and phone numbers for businesses, government agencies, as well as individuals. You can go to a URL to check your favorite sports team, book a flight on an airline, check out a college, or look up information on almost any subject you can think of.

3. a. Create a new blank document. Type in at least four paragraphs on a topic of interest to you. Then save the document using any name you like.
b. Check the document's spelling, proofread it, and correct errors by deleting unwanted text, inserting text, or typing over text.
c. Save the document again with the same name.
d. Preview and then print the document.

4. You have been making and selling jewelry at craft fairs for several years, and now you are trying to organize your business, Santa Fe Designs, with the help of a computer and Microsoft Word.

a. Create the letter shown below.
b. Check the document's spelling, proofread it, and correct errors by deleting unwanted text, inserting text, or typing over text.
c. Save the document as **Jewelry Information**.
d. Preview and then print the document.

Santa Fe Designs
1569 Aztec Way
Santa Fe, NM 87501

Today's Date

Pam Gibson
1008 West Evergreen Street
Lansing, MI 76540

Dear Ms. Gibson:

Santa Fe Designs creates one-of-a-kind sterling silver jewelry featuring authentic Southwestern designs. These necklaces, bracelets, rings, and earrings are crafted using over 35 precious and semiprecious stones set in sterling silver. Each is an original work of art.

I have enclosed my catalog, which includes color photographs of many of my recent creations. If you want help making a decision or have some ideas that you would like to talk about, please call the 800 number listed in the catalog.

Sincerely yours,

Your Name

PROJECTS

1. a. Use the Letter Wizard to compose a cover letter to accompany your résumé. Use an actual employer, and address it to the actual person.
   b. Check the document's spelling, proofread it, and correct errors by deleting unwanted text, inserting text, or typing over text.
   c. Save the document as **Cover Letter**.
   d. Preview and then print the document.

2. a. Create the following document from scratch.
   b. Check the document's spelling, proofread it, and correct errors by deleting unwanted text, inserting text, or typing over text.
   c. Save the document as **Accessibility**.
   d. Preview and then print the document.

Accessibility for People with Disabilities

Microsoft Word contains features that make it easier for people who have low vision to read and for those with limited dexterity to write. People with disabilities can take advantage of the following features:

You can change the magnification of your document.

You can use shortcuts to insert frequently used text and graphics.

You can use the AutoComplete feature to insert entire items, such as today's date, the days of the week or month, your name, or AutoText entries, when you type a few identifying characters.

You can create a toolbar that contains only the buttons and menus you use most often.

You can also make the toolbar buttons larger and group the related ones together.

If you have the Microsoft IntelliMouse pointing device, you can scroll and zoom directly from the mouse. For example, you can automatically scroll to the end of the document with just one mouse click without using keys.

More Creating
and Editing Documents

UNIT OBJECTIVES

- Create an envelope
- Create mailing labels
- Create a document using a template
- Select text and delete selected text
- Cut, copy, and paste text
- Use Find and Replace
- Change the document view

So far you have created documents with the help of Word's wizards and using a blank document. In this unit, you'll learn how to create envelopes and mailing labels and use Word's templates—yet another way to create documents. You will also learn more ways to edit your documents. You'll find out how to select text, cut or copy text to other places in a document, and use Word's Find and Replace feature.

What: Create an envelope to go with a letter.

How: Choose Tools | Envelopes and Labels.

Why: A professional-looking mailing includes a printed envelope.

Tip: Purchasing standard-sized envelopes will make creating envelopes easier.

After creating a letter using Word, you will probably want to mail it. If your printer supports the printing of envelopes, you can easily create an envelope using Word.

1. Choose Tools | Envelopes and Labels to open the Envelopes and Labels dialog box.
2. Make sure the Envelope tab is selected, as shown in Figure 3.1a.
3. Type the delivery address in the Delivery address text box or edit the one that Word places there. (See the pointer box "Delivery and Return Addresses" for details.)
4. Type the return address in the Return address text box, edit the one that Word places there, or choose to omit a return address by selecting the Omit check box. (See the pointer box "Delivery and Return Addresses" for details.)
5. If you are not using a standard business-size envelope, click the Options button and select a different size from the drop-down list.
6. Do one of the following:
   - Click the dialog box's Print button to print the envelope immediately.
   - Click the Add to Document button to place the envelope in the current document for later printing.

POINTER

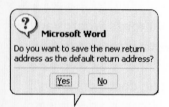

Delivery and Return Addresses

- When you open the Envelopes and Labels dialog box, Word looks from the insertion point forward in the open document for the first paragraphs that look like an address. If it finds such paragraphs, it automatically inserts them into the dialog box's *Delivery address* text box. If you select an address or place the insertion point at the beginning of an address before opening the dialog box, Word will insert that address in the *Delivery address* text box.

- When working on your own computer, Word lets you set a default return address (in Tools | Options | User Information). If an incorrect return address is displayed in the Envelopes and Labels dialog box, just select it and type a different address. In a computer lab, if Word asks you whether you want to save the new return address as the default return address, click No.

If you click the Options button in the Envelopes dialog box, the Envelope Options dialog box opens, as shown in Figure 3.1b. You can:

- change the size of the envelope
- have Word convert the Zip code into a machine-readable bar code that prints above the delivery name
- include the FIM-A mark that marks the front of the envelope for sorting courtesy reply envelopes
- change the font for the delivery and return addresses (you will learn about fonts in Unit 4)

If you click the Printing Options tab, you can change the way the envelope is fed into your printer. Word usually chooses the correct option for your printer on its own.

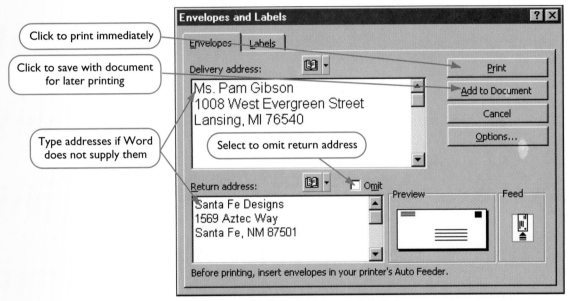

(a) The Envelopes and Labels Dialog Box's Envelopes Tab

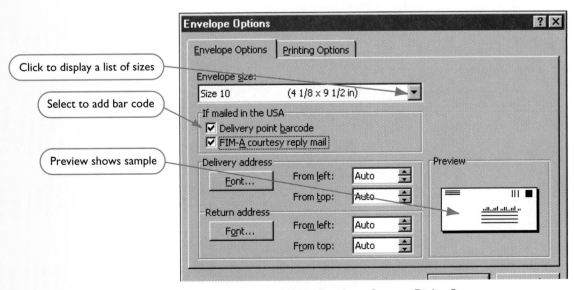

(b) The Envelope Options Dialog Box

FIGURE 3.1   Creating an Envelope

Printing Envelopes in the Computer Lab

You might not be able to print an envelope in the computer lab. Check with your lab administrator or instructor for instructions on printing envelopes on your specific printer.

EXERCISE 1 | *Creating an Envelope*

1. Open the **Jewelry Information** document you created in Project 4 at the end of Unit 2.
The insertion point is automatically placed at the beginning of the document.

2. Click at the beginning of the inside address (before the **P** in **Pam Gibson**).
Clicking before the delivery address, or selecting the address, ensures that Word will choose the correct address when it creates the envelope.

3. Choose **Tools | Envelopes and Labels**.
The Envelopes and Labels dialog box opens.

4. Make sure the **Envelopes tab** is selected, and check the Delivery Address text box to be sure the inside address from the letter appears there. If it does not, type it there.

5. Type the following address in the Return Address text box:

> Santa Fe Designs
> 1569 Aztec Way
> Santa Fe, NM 87501

The Envelopes and Labels dialog box should look like the one in Figure 3.1a.

6. Click the **Add to Document button** in the dialog box.
The envelope is placed at the top of the *Jewelry Information* document.

7. If Word asks whether you want to save the new return address as the default return address, click **No**.

8. Choose **File | Print Preview**.
The Print Preview shows the envelope you have created.

9. Click the **Close button** on the Print Preview toolbar.
The Print Preview screen closes.

10. If you aren't sure you can print envelopes on the printer attached to your computer, skip to step 14.

11. If you have been instructed in printing envelopes on the printer attached to your computer, make sure the printer is turned on, and place a business-size (#10) envelope in it.

12. Choose **File | Print**.
The Print dialog box will open.

13. Click **OK**.
The envelope will print, and then the letter. Depending on your printer, you may have to feed the envelope manually.

14. Close the document without saving it.

TASK 2 | *Creating Mailing Labels*

What: Create mailing labels.
How: Choose Tools | Envelopes and Labels.
Why: For some mailings, you may need labels rather than envelopes.
Tip: Using labels that Word supports (a type listed in the Label Options dialog box) makes it easier to print labels.

If you need to print labels, you can create them easily in Word. You can create a whole sheet of return-address labels for yourself, or print a single label from a sheet to use on a large package.

> **POINTER**
>
> **Address Labels for a Mass Mailing**
> In Unit 7, you will learn to create form letters and mailing labels with addresses you have saved in an address file. This is a handy feature for almost every type of business.

1. Choose Tools | Envelopes and Labels and click the Labels tab to display the dialog box shown in Figure 3.2a.
2. Type the correct address or edit the one that Word displays in the Address box.
3. Select the *Use return address* check box if you want to include the default return address on the label.
4. To print an entire page of the labels, all with the address that appears in the Address box, select the *Full page of the same label* option button.
5. To print just one label, select the *Single label* option button and specify the row and column to print (see "Printing a Single Label from a Sheet," below).
6. To send the label directly to the printer, click the Print button.
7. To place the labels in a new document, click the New Document button.

PRINTING A SINGLE LABEL
FROM A SHEET

If you select *Single label* to print one label at a time, you must specify the column and row where you want the label to print. For example, if the sheet of labels has 3 columns and 8 rows, the first time you use the sheet you would specify the label in column 1, row 1. The next time you use the sheet, you would specify column 2, row 1.

SELECTING A LABEL TYPE

Word provides the capability to print many types of labels. To select a label, click the Options button on the Labels tab to open the Label Options dialog box, shown in Figure 3.2b.

1. Choose a brand of labels in the *Label products* drop-down list.
2. Choose a specific label in the *Product number* drop-down list. The *Label information* area displays the specifications of this label.
3. Click OK to return to the Labels dialog box. Word previews the label and lists its name and dimensions.

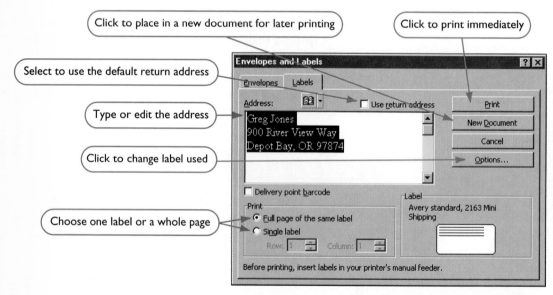

(a) The Envelopes and Labels Dialog Box's Labels Tab

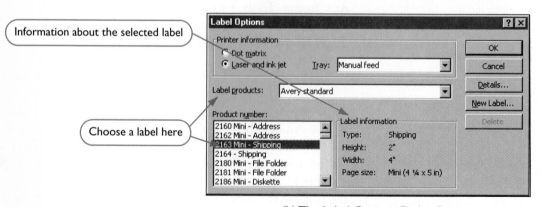

(b) The Label Options Dialog Box

FIGURE **3.2** Creating a Label

Printing Labels in the Computer Lab

Most inkjet printers will print labels on regular paper just like any other document. However, most laser printers expect the sheet of labels, like individual envelopes, to be manually fed. Check with your lab administrator or instructor before printing.

EXERCISE 2 | *Creating Mailing Labels*

1. Open the **JRT History** document and click at the beginning of the inside address (before the **G** in **Greg Jones**).
   Clicking before the delivery address, or selecting the address, ensures that Word will choose the correct address when it creates the label.

2. Choose **Tools | Envelopes and Labels**.
   The Envelopes and Labels dialog box opens.

3. Click the **Labels tab**.
   The Labels tab is set to the most recently used label.

4. Make sure the inside (delivery) address of the letter appears in the Address box. If it does not, type it there.

5. Click the **Full Page of the same label option**.
   You will save a page of labels in a new document.

6. Click the **Options button**.
   The Label Options dialog box opens.

7. Click the down arrow in the Label products list box and choose **Avery standard**.
   The complete list of supported Avery labels is placed in the *Product number* list.

8. In the Product number list, select **2163 Mini – Shipping**.
   This is a sheet of two shipping labels.

9. Click **OK**.
   The Label Options dialog box closes, and the Envelopes and Labels dialog box now shows a preview of the selected label.

10. Click the **New Document button**.
    The label will appear in a new document, as shown in Figure 3.3.

11. Close the documents without saving them.
    On your own computer, you could print the labels immediately or save the document for later printing.

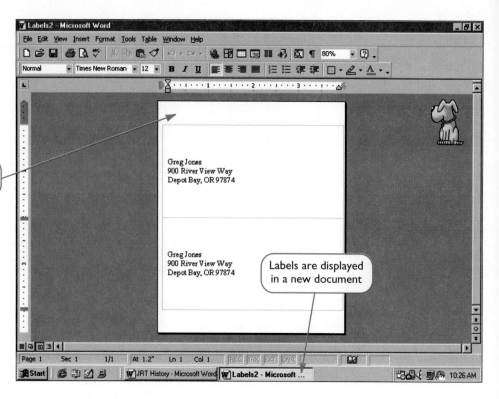

Word displays a whole sheet of the label you selected

Greg Jones
900 River View Way
Depot Bay, OR 97874

Greg Jones
900 River View Way
Depot Bay, OR 97874

Labels are displayed in a new document

FIGURE 3.3 The Labels in a New Document

TASK 3 | *Creating a Document Using a Word Template*

What: Use a template to create a document.

How: Choose File | New.

Why: Many documents follow standard formatting, and Word helps by setting them up for you as templates.

Tip: Before creating a complicated document, always look to see if a built-in Word template already exists.

You have used a wizard to create a document, and you have created a document from scratch. Between those two options lies a very helpful feature—the template. **Templates** are document models that include formatting and sometimes some sample text. You open them, edit them to suit your needs, type in your own text, and then save them. Word's templates appear in the New dialog box. (Anything shown there without the word "wizard" is a template.)

POINTER

The Blank Document Template

The blank document that greets you when you start Word is itself based on a template, the Normal template. The documents you create with it have a standard page size, standard margins, standard paragraph spacing, a standard font and font size, and so on. You will learn more about these formatting features in Unit 4.

Quick, Simple Microsoft Word 2000

To create a document using a Word template:

1. Choose File | New and click the tab for the type of document you want to create. Each tab displays at least one template. (The Letters and Faxes tab is shown in Figure 3.4.)
2. Select the template you want to use.
3. Click OK to display a new document based on the template.
4. Edit the document as you would any other document.

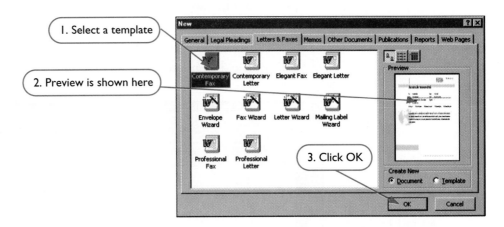

FIGURE 3.4 The New Dialog Box Displaying Word's Built-in Letter & Fax Templates

---

EXERCISE 3 | *Creating a Document Using a Word Template*

---

1. Choose **File | New**.
The New dialog box opens.

2. Click the **Letters & Faxes tab**.
Word's letter and fax wizards and templates are shown here (see Figure 3.4).

3. Select **Contemporary Fax** and click **OK**.
A new document based on the Contemporary Fax template opens, as shown in Figure 3.5. Note its temporary name, *Document2—Fax Coversheet*.

4. Click the bracketed text block **Click here and type address**.
The whole text block is selected when you click it.

5. Type the following text:

```
JRT Purebreds
2000 Friendly Street
Eugene, OR 97405
```

6. Click the text block after **To:** and type **Jane Smith**.

7. Click the text block after **From:** and type **your name**.

8. Click the text block after **Fax:** and type **954-988-3452**.

9. Click the text block after **Re:** and type **Jack Russell Terrier**.

10. Click the text block after **Pages:** and type **2**.

11. Click the text block after **CC:** and type **Greg Brown**.

12. Double-click the check box before **Please Comment**.
    A check mark is placed in the check box.

13. Double-click in the margin by **Notes:** to select it, and press the **Delete key**.

14. Save the document as **Fax Cover Sheet**.

15. Print the document and then close it.

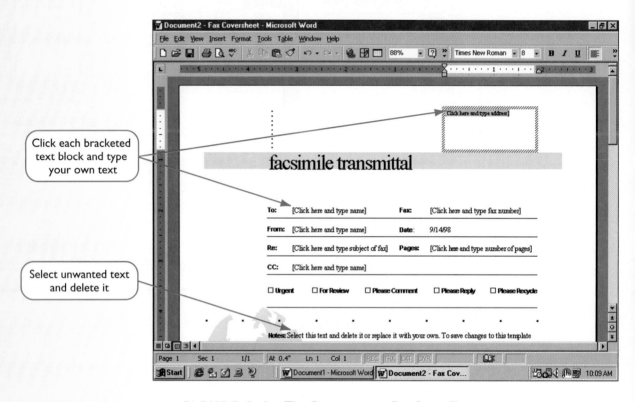

FIGURE 3.5 The Contemporary Fax Cover Sheet

TASK 4 | *Selecting Text and Deleting Selected Text*

What: Select text in a document.

How: Use the mouse or the keyboard.

Why: To perform many operations on text, you first select the text.

Tip: To deselect text, click outside the selection or press an arrow key.

In order to delete blocks of text, format them, and perform many other tasks, you must first select the text you want to work with. **Selected text** appears highlighted, as shown in Figure 3.6.

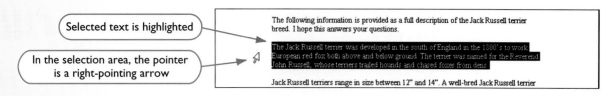

Selected text is highlighted

In the selection area, the pointer is a right-pointing arrow

FIGURE 3.6 Selected Text

You can use the mouse to select text by clicking in the text or in the **selection area** in the left margin. When you move the pointer into the selection area, it changes to a right-pointing arrow, and you can click it to select text. Table 3.1 describes the ways in which you can select text using the mouse.

Text to Select	Action
Any amount of adjacent text	Click and drag over the text
A single word	Double-click the word
A line	Click in the selection area next to the line
A sentence	Hold down Ctrl and click in the sentence
A paragraph	Triple-click in the paragraph, or double-click in the selection area next to the paragraph
A block of text	Click at the beginning of the text you want to select, then hold down Shift while you click at the end of the text
An entire document	Triple-click in the selection area

TABLE 3.1 Selecting Text Using the Mouse

You can also use the keyboard to select text. Table 3.2 describes some of the keyboard shortcuts. Search Help for "Select text" to see the complete list.

Text to Select	Action
A single character	Shift+right or left arrow key
A word	Shift+Ctrl+right or left arrow key
From the insertion point to the beginning or end of the line	Shift+Home or Shift+End
From the insertion point up or down a line	Shift+up or down arrow key
From the insertion point to the end of the document	Shift+Ctrl+End
From the insertion point to the beginning of the document	Shift+Ctrl+Home
An entire document	Ctrl+A

TABLE 3.2 Selecting Text Using the Keyboard

Once you have selected text, you can perform numerous operations on it. In this task, you will delete selected text by pressing the Backspace or the Delete key.

POINTER

Extend Selection Mode

Click at the beginning of a block of text you want to select and then double-click the EXT mode indicator on the status bar. Now you are in Extend Selection mode. Use the arrow keys to extend the selection, or click at the end of the text you want to select. To turn off Extend Selection mode, press Esc or double-click the mode indicator.

EXERCISE 4 | *Selecting and Deleting Text*

1. Open the **JRT History** document.
2. Click and drag with the mouse over any **three or four words** in the body of the letter.
   The text is selected.
3. Click **outside the selection**.
   The text is deselected.
4. Double-click any **word**.
   The word is selected.
5. Click **outside the word**.
   The word is deselected.
6. Hold down the **Shift key** and press the **right arrow key** repeatedly.
   One character at a time is selected.
7. Click **outside the selection**.
   The characters are deselected.
8. Hold down **Ctrl** and click the mouse anywhere in the **first sentence** of the letter.
   The sentence is selected.
9. Press **Delete**.
   The sentence is removed from the document.
10. Choose **Edit | Undo Clear**.
    The sentence is replaced in the document.
11. Leave the document open to use in the next exercise.

What: Cut or copy and paste text from one location to another.

How: Choose Edit | Cut or Edit | Copy and then Edit | Paste, or click the Cut or Copy and then the Paste buttons on the Standard toolbar.

Why: Moving text by cutting and pasting saves time in editing, and copying and pasting is much quicker than retyping.

Tip: Right-click selected text to open a shortcut menu with Cut and Copy commands.

As you create documents, you will want to move text around or copy text from one location or document to another. To do so, you cut or copy the original text and place it in the new location. There are several ways to perform these operations.

To quickly move or copy text over a short distance:

1. Select the text to be cut or copied.
2. Click and drag with the right mouse button—the pointer has a small box attached to it, as shown in Figure 3.7a.
3. Click in the spot where you want to copy or move the selected text.
4. Release the mouse to display the shortcut menu shown in Figure 3.7b.
5. Choose Move Here or Copy Here.

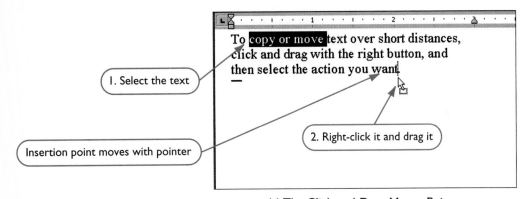

(a) The Click-and-Drag Mouse Pointer

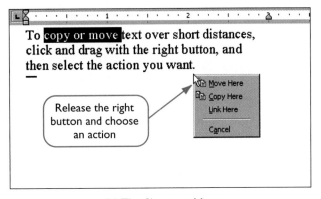

(b) The Shortcut Menu

FIGURE 3.7 Dragging Text a Short Distance

To move or copy text over a long distance:

1. Select the text to be cut or copied.
2. Do any of the following:
   - Choose Edit | Cut or Edit | Copy.
   - Click the Cut or Copy button on the Standard toolbar.
   - Right-click the selection and choose Cut or Copy from the shortcut menu.

Word places the selected text on the **Windows Clipboard**—a temporary memory location.

To paste text from the Clipboard:

1. Move the insertion point to the desired location.
2. Do any of the following:

   - Choose Edit | Paste.
   - Click the Paste button on the Standard toolbar.
   - Right-click and choose Paste from the shortcut menu.

You can paste the contents of the Windows Clipboard into the same document, another document, or even another application. Open the document or application, place the insertion point where the text is to go, and paste.

POINTER

Copy versus Cut

Cutting and copying text are basically the same operation; however, **cutting** takes the original from its current location, while **copying** leaves the original and places a duplicate in the new location.

THE OFFICE CLIPBOARD

The Windows Clipboard holds a single item—the last one you have copied or cut. However, Microsoft Office 2000 has its own clipboard, the **Office Clipboard**, which stores the last 12 items you have cut or copied from an Office document. The Office Clipboard is not emptied when you exit from Word, but holds its contents until you turn off the computer.

The Office Clipboard may open as a floating toolbar on your screen when you cut or copy more than one item in a session; but you can also open it manually, by choosing View | Toolbars | Clipboard.

To use the Office Clipboard:

1. If the Clipboard is not already displayed, choose View | Toolbars | Clipboard to display the Office Clipboard as a floating toolbar (see Figure 3.8). Like any other toolbar, you can drag it by its title bar if it gets in the way, or dock it at any edge of the screen, or let it share a row with another toolbar.

2. Cut or copy any items you like. As you do, each item is placed on the Office Clipboard, with an icon to indicate which Office application created it. Office Clipboard contents are added from left to right and top to bottom, so that the most recently cut or copied item (the one that is also stored on the Windows Clipboard) is displayed at the bottom right edge of the toolbar.

3. To view the contents of an individual item, point to it, and a ScreenTip will appear.

4. To paste an item at the insertion point in the document, click the item on the toolbar. You can paste it again and again.

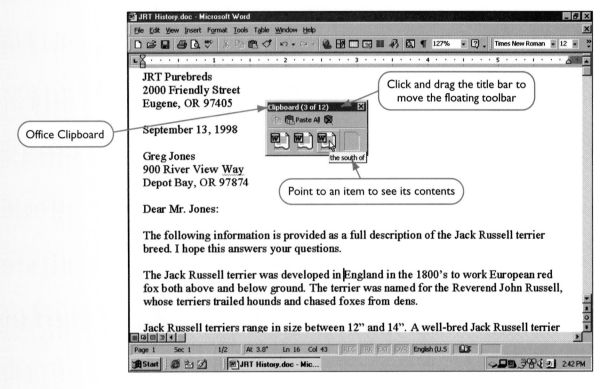

FIGURE 3.8   The Office Clipboard in a Document

Table 3.3 describes the buttons on the Clipboard toolbar.

Button	Description
📋	Copies the selected text to the Clipboard
📋	Pastes all of the Clipboard items at the position of the insertion point
📋	Clears the Clipboard

TABLE 3.3   Clipboard Toolbar Buttons

EXERCISE 5A | *Dragging Text*

1. With the *JRT History* document on the screen, select the last sentence of the first paragraph, **I hope this answers your questions**.
To select a sentence, hold down Ctrl while you click in it.

2. Right-click **the selected text** and hold down the mouse button.
The pointer has a box attached to it, and the insertion point turns gray.

3. Drag the text to the start of the final paragraph of the letter, before the sentence beginning **If you have any other specific questions**.
The insertion point moves with the pointer. If the end of the letter is not visible on the screen, hold the mouse near the bottom of the screen and the document will scroll.

4. When the gray insertion point is in front of the word **If**, release the mouse button.
A shortcut menu opens.

5. Choose **Move Here**.
The selected sentence is placed at the insertion point, and it remains selected.

6. Click the **right arrow key** to deselect the sentence, and press the **Spacebar** to add a space between the sentences.

7. Print the document.

8. Continue to the next exercise.

EXERCISE 5B | *Using Edit / Cut and Edit / Paste*

1. Select the entire **second paragraph** of the letter.
To select a paragraph, move the pointer to the left of the paragraph until it changes to a right-pointing arrow, and then double-click.

2. Choose **Edit | Cut**.
The text is removed from the document and placed on the Windows Clipboard.

3. Press **Ctrl+End**.
The insertion point moves to the end of the document.

4. Choose **Edit | Paste**.
The text is pasted at the insertion point.

5. Choose **Edit | Undo**.
The text disappears from the end of the document.

6. Click the **New Blank Document button** on the Standard toolbar.
A new blank document opens with its own button on the taskbar.

7. Click **Edit | Paste**.
The Clipboard contents are pasted into the new document.

8. Click the **JRT History button** on the taskbar.
   The letter becomes the active document.

9. Click the **down arrow** next to the **Undo button** and select **Cut**.
   The cut text is restored to the letter.

10. Continue to the next exercise.

EXERCISE 5C | *Using Edit / Copy and Edit / Paste*

1. Select the **first sentence of the third paragraph**.
   The sentence is highlighted.

2. Choose **Edit | Copy**.
   The sentence is copied to the Windows Clipboard.

3. Click the new document's **taskbar button** to display the document, and then choose **Edit | Paste**.
   The sentence is pasted into the new document.

4. Close the new document without saving it.

EXERCISE 5D | *Pasting More than One Item from the Office Clipboard*

1. With the *JRT History* document on the screen, choose **View | Toolbars | Clipboard**.
   The Office Clipboard toolbar opens on the screen. Drag it by the title bar to move it out of the way.

2. Select the **first paragraph** and click the **Copy button** on the Standard toolbar.
   The new item is placed on the Office Clipboard.

3. In the same manner, copy the **second paragraph** to the Office Clipboard.

4. Move the pointer over the Office Clipboard's items and read the **ScreenTips** that appear.

5. Press **Ctrl+End**.
   The insertion point moves to the end of the document.

6. Click the Clipboard icon for the **last item copied**.
   The last item is pasted into the document.

7. Click the Clipboard toolbar's **Paste All button**.
   All Clipboard contents are pasted into the document at the insertion point.

8. Close the document without saving it.

9. Click the Clipboard toolbar's **Close button**.

TASK 6 | *Using Find and Replace*

What: Find text in a document and replace text in a document.
How: Choose Edit | Find and Edit | Replace.
Why: There are dozens of uses for Find and Replace, including correcting a misspelled name in a document.
Tip: If you select the Replace dialog box's *Find all word forms* option and replace *come* with *go*, Word will also replace *came* with *went*.

Looking for specific text in a long document is tedious, but Word will do it for you. To find text:

1. Choose Edit | Find to open the Find and Replace dialog box, shown in Figure 3.9a.
2. Type the text that you want to find in the Find What text box.
3. Click the Find Next button to start the search.
   - If there is a match for the text you typed, the insertion point will move to the first instance of it. The Find and Replace dialog box will remain open, in case you want to find the next instance of the word or phrase.
   - If there is no match for the text you typed, Word will display a message box stating that the search item was not found, as shown in Figure 3.9b.

You can limit the search by choosing the options shown in Table 3.4. (To hide the options so the dialog box takes up less space on the screen, click the Less button. The Less button is then replaced by a More button.)

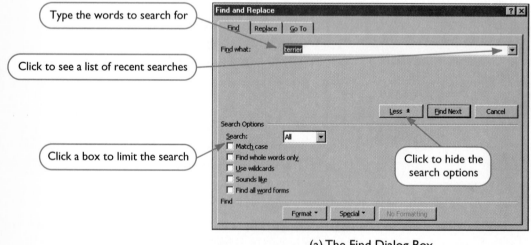

(a) The Find Dialog Box

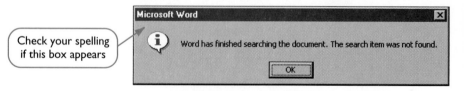

(b) The Item Not Found Message Box

FIGURE 3.9 The Find and Replace Operation

Option	Description
Match case	Finds only text with specified capitalization
Find whole words only	Finds only complete words
Use wildcards	Lets you use the **?** and ***** characters to find any single character or any group of characters
Sounds like	Finds words that may not be spelled exactly alike but sound the same
Find all word forms	Finds all forms of the word such as tenses for verbs
Format	Allows you to specify formatting in the search
No formatting	Removes the search formatting
Special	Finds special characters

TABLE 3.4   Find and Replace Options

POINTER

Word Doesn't Find Your Text

If Word doesn't find the text, you may not have typed it exactly as it appears in the document. Check your spelling and check other options such as the case, whole word, and formatting options.

Replacing text in a document is similar to finding text. To replace text:

1. Choose Edit | Replace.
2. Type the text you want to replace in the Find What text box, as shown in Figure 3.9c.

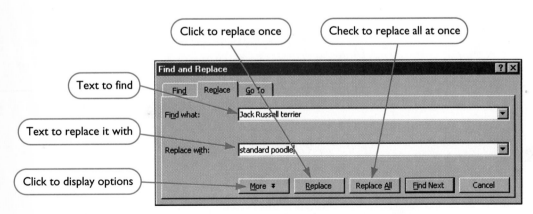

(c) The Replace Message Box

FIGURE 3.9   The Find and Replace Operation *(continued)*

3. Type the text you want to replace it with in the Replace with text box.
4. Click Find Next to move the insertion point to the matching text.
5. Do one of the following:
   - Click Replace to replace the text.
   - Click Find Next to move to the next instance without replacing the text.
   - Click Replace All to replace every instance of matches throughout the entire document.
   - Click the More button to set the options described in Table 3.4.

EXERCISE 6A | *Finding Text*

1. Open the **JRT History** document.

2. Choose **Edit | Find**.
The Find and Replace dialog box opens.

3. Type **terrier** in the Find What text box.

4. Click **Find Next**.
The insertion point moves to the first instance of the word *terrier*.

5. Click **Find Next** several times to see how it works.

6. Click the **Cancel button**.
The dialog box closes.

EXERCISE 6B | *Replacing Text*

1. Choose **Edit | Replace**.
The Find and Replace dialog box opens.

2. Type **Jack Russell terrier** in the Find What text box.

3. Type **standard poodle** in the Replace With text box.

4. Click **Find Next**.
The insertion point moves to the first match.

5. Click **Replace**.
Jack Russell terrier is replaced with *standard poodle*.

6. Click **Find Next**.
The insertion point moves to the next match.

7. Click **Find Next**.
The insertion point moves to the next match without changing the text.

8. Click **Replace All**.

All matching text is replaced.

9. Print the document.

10. Close the document without saving it.

TASK 7 | *Changing the View and the Zoom*

What: Change the document view and zoom.

How: Choose View | Normal (or View | Print Layout), View | Zoom.

Why: Different views will help you work more easily and see your results.

Tip: Use Print Preview to display multiple pages at one time.

Word can display documents in different views. Sometimes Word switches views automatically to enable you to use a particular feature, but you can also change views manually, and may want to do so to perform different tasks. To change views, choose the View menu or use the buttons on the horizontal scroll bar.

The view options are described in Table 3.5. The Normal and Print Layout views are useful for everyday tasks such as entering and editing text and changing the layout and format of pages. The other views have more specialized functions.

View	Button	Description
Normal	≡	Used to type and edit documents; doesn't display margins, headers and footers, or graphics (see Figure 3.10a)
Web Layout	▣	Shows how the document will look in a Web browser
Print Layout View	▤	Displays all document elements and is used to make adjustments to the page (see Figure 3.10b)
Outline View	▤	Shows the structure of the document and allows you to click and drag headings to reorganize the document

TABLE 3.5 View Options

Zoom box

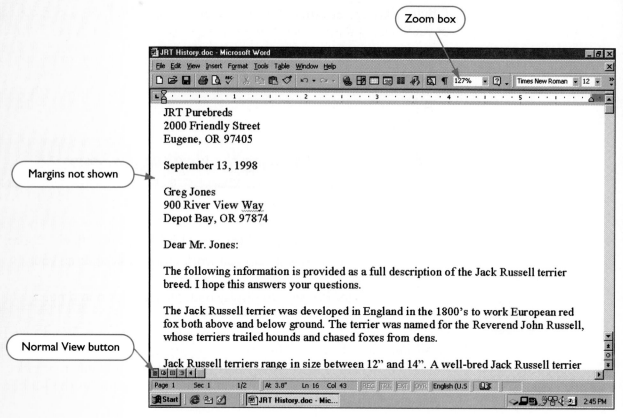

Margins not shown

Normal View button

(a) Normal View

Margins are displayed

Vertical ruler

Print layout View button

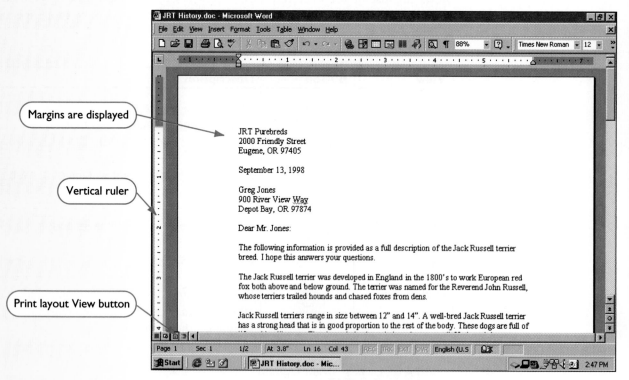

(b) Print Layout View

FIGURE 3.10   Two Document Views

Besides changing the view of a document, you can also zoom out to see more of your document or zoom in to get a closer look at a part of your document. To change the zoom, choose View | Zoom or click the down arrow in the Zoom box on the Standard toolbar.

- When you choose View | Zoom, the Zoom dialog box opens, where you can select a preset zoom or type a custom zoom in the Percent box. A Preview section lets you see the result. Click OK and the screen display changes.

- When you click the down arrow in the Zoom box, a list of preset zooms drops down; click a zoom and the screen display changes. You can also click in the zoom box and type a custom zoom.

POINTER

Microsoft IntelliMouse

If you are using the Microsoft IntelliMouse, you can zoom the screen in and out by holding the Ctrl key as you rotate the center wheel forward or backward.

EXERCISE 7 | *Changing the View and the Zoom*

1. Open the **JRT History** document.
2. Choose **View | Print Layout**.
   This view displays the document's margins.

3. Click the **Normal View button** on the horizontal scroll bar.
   This view doesn't show the margins.

4. Click the down arrow in the **Zoom box** on the Standard toolbar and select **50%**.
   The text may be too small to read, but you can see the whole document.
5. Click the down arrow in the **Zoom box** and select **Page Width**.
   Page Width is a useful zoom for editing.
6. Close the document.

REVIEW

SUMMARY

After completing this unit, you should
- be able to create an envelope (page 54)
- be able to create mailing labels (page 57)
- be able to create documents using templates (page 60)
- be able to select text (page 62)
- know how to delete selected text (page 62)
- be able to cut, copy, and paste text (page 65)
- know how to find text in a document (page 70)
- know how to replace text in a document (page 70)
- be able to change document views (page 73)
- know how to zoom in and zoom out of documents (page 73)

KEY TERMS

cut (page 66)

copy (page 66)

Office Clipboard (page 66)

selected text (page 62)

template (page 60)

Windows Clipboard (page 66)

TEST YOUR SKILLS

True/False

1. Normal view doesn't display margins.
2. You can have Word convert the Zip code into a machine-readable representation and place it on an envelope.
3. You can only print a full page of every label you create.
4. A template supplies you with some of the formatting for a document.
5. You can select text in a document using the mouse or the keyboard.

Multiple Choice

1. To select an entire document, you could
   a. press Ctrl+A
   b. move to the beginning of the document and press Ctrl+Shift+End
   c. select all of the text with the mouse
   d. all of these answers
2. You can paste the Clipboard contents
   a. in the same document   b. in another document
   c. in another application   d. all of these answers
3. To see your document without all screen elements, you would work in
   a. Print Preview   b. Print Layout view
   c. Normal view   d. all of these answers

4. Microsoft Word templates
   a. do everything for you including printing the document
   b. search for matches to text you type
   c. allow you to create nicely formatted documents even when you are just beginning to learn Word
   d. all of these answers
5. When you cut text from a document
   a. a copy of the original remains in the document
   b. the text can be pasted only into the same document it was cut from
   c. the original is removed from the document
   d. all of these answers

Short Answer

1. To select one word using the mouse, you would _____-_____ the word.
2. To copy or cut text, you must _____ it first.
3. To quickly check the spelling of a word with a wavy red underline, you can click the _____ _____ _____.
4. The _____ is the memory location of cut or copied text.
5. You must move the _____ _____ to the desired location before you paste text.

What Does This Do?

Write a brief description of the function of the following:

1.	Add to Document	6.	Find Next
2.		7.	
3.	Replace All	8.	Match case
4.	Single label Row: 1 Column: 1	9.	
5.		10.	Replace

On Your Own

1. If you are able to print envelopes on your printer, create and print an envelope.
2. If you are able to print mailing labels, create and print a single label.
3. Practice finding and replacing text in a document.
4. Practice moving text within a single document.
5. Practice copying text to a new document.

PROJECTS

1. a. Open the **Cover Letter** document that you created to accompany your résumé. Use the Replace command to change the company name to Acme Development.
   b. Create an envelope to send your cover letter and résumé to Acme Development.
   c. Print the letter, your résumé, and an envelope. Close the file without saving it.

2. a. Use the Avery #5668 label to create address labels for yourself. Create a full page of the same label and have Word place the labels in a new document.
   b. When you are satisfied with the labels, print the document. Close the file without saving it.

3. a. Use the Contemporary Letter template to create the following letter:

Company Name:	Santa Fe Designs
Return Address:	1569 Aztec Way
	Santa Fe, NM 87501
Recipient's address:	Kyle June
	1059 Oak Way
	Teaneck, NJ 00765

Body of Letter:

Thank you for your recent order of the turquoise and silver ring. We hope you will be pleased with our craftsmanship. We use only the highest quality gems and precious metals and craft them into unique fine jewelry.

If we can be of any assistance, please don't hesitate to call us.

   b. Check the document's spelling, proofread it, and correct errors by deleting unwanted text, inserting text, or typing over text.
   c. Save the document as **Ring**.
   d. Preview and then print the document.
   e. Create a second letter using the Elegant Letter template. Use the same company name and return address you used for the first letter, but send it to a different person.

Recipient's address:	Mary Smith
	P.O. Box 97
	Napavine, WA 94024

   f. Copy the body of the first letter into the second letter. Then use the Replace option to change **turquoise and silver ring** to **silver wolf pendant**.
   g. Check the document's spelling, proofread it, and correct errors by deleting unwanted text, inserting text, or typing over text.
   h. Save the document as **Pendant**.
   i. Preview and then print the document.

4. a. Use the Elegant Memo template to create the memo shown below.
   b. Check the document's spelling, proofread it, and correct errors by deleting unwanted text, inserting text, or typing over text.
   c. Save the document as **Computer Use**.
   d. Preview and then print the document.

TO: ALL EMPLOYEES

FROM: YOUR NAME

SUBJECT: PERSONAL USE OF COMPUTERS

Our current computer usage policy states that "personal use of computers on company time is not allowed." It has come to light that many employees are using the World Wide Web for personal business, such as booking flights and planning vacations.

You are welcome to continue such activities during nonwork hours, such as lunch, breaks, or after work. However, continued personal use during work hours will not be tolerated.

Formatting Documents

UNIT OBJECTIVES

- Use bold, italic, and underline
- Change the font, size, color, and other font attributes
- Change text alignment
- Change line spacing
- Indent paragraphs
- Set custom tab stops

Formatting is the structure and layout of a document and its individual parts. Documents can be formatted to call attention to important points, manage the space on the page, and make the documents more attractive. Formatting in Word takes place at four levels: the character, the paragraph, the page, and the section. In this unit you will learn character and paragraph formatting. Unit 6 explains page and section formatting. **Character formatting** applies to individual characters or selected text. You format characters to change the way the text looks on the page. **Paragraph formatting** applies to whole paragraphs. You format paragraphs to change how paragraphs line up and are spaced on the page.

What: Format characters using bold, italic, and underline.

How: Click the Bold, Italic, or Underline button on the Formatting toolbar.

Why: Bold, italic, and underlining have specific uses, but all three set text off from the surrounding text.

Tip: Toolbar buttons that are turned on look pushed into the toolbar and have a lighter color.

When you type text in a new document, Word formats it in the style known as Regular. You can change this style and other formatting features of text as you type it, or select existing text and change its formatting. Word's Formatting toolbar has buttons and boxes that act as shortcuts to many common formatting actions. This task shows you how to use the toolbar to change the style to bold or italic and to underline characters. You can also apply this technique to other formatting tasks.

To change the style of existing text using the toolbar:

1. Select the text to be formatted.
2. Click the Formatting toolbar's Bold, Italic, and/or Underline buttons to apply this formatting.
3. Click outside the selected text to deselect it and turn off the toolbar buttons.

To format text as you type:

1. Position the insertion point where you want to type new text (or at the beginning of a new document).
2. Click the Formatting toolbar's Bold, Italic, and/or Underline buttons to turn on this formatting.
3. Type the text; it will have the formatting you turned on.
4. Click the toolbar buttons again to turn off the formatting; new text you type from that point forward will not have the formatting.

To remove formatting from text:

1. Select the text with the formatting you want to remove, and the toolbar buttons for the formatting look pushed in.
2. Click the buttons for the formatting you want to remove.
3. Click outside the selection to see the result.

POINTER

Separate the Toolbars to Format Text

Word lets you display the Standard and Formatting toolbars on a single row or separately. Formatting using the toolbar is easier when the toolbars are separate. You can drag a toolbar to a separate row by its move handle, or you can choose Tools | Customize and clear the *Standard and Formatting toolbars share one row* check box. The screens in this unit show the toolbars on separate rows.

1. Open the **JRT History** document.
The letter appears on the screen.

2. Click and drag to select the text **Jack Russell terrier** in the first paragraph.
The text is highlighted.

3. Click the **Bold** and **Underline buttons** on the Formatting toolbar.
The buttons are turned on and look pushed in.

4. Click **outside the selected text**.
The text is bold and underlined and the Bold and Underline buttons are turned off.

5. Select **Reverend John Russell** in the second paragraph.

6. Click the **Italic button**.
The button is turned on and looks pushed in.

7. Click **outside the selected text**.
The text is italic and the Italic button is turned off.

8. Double-click the word **friendly** in the next-to-last paragraph.
The word is selected.

9. Click the **Bold button**.
The Bold button is turned on.

10. Click the **Italic button**.
The Italic button is turned on.

11. Click the **Underline button**.
The Underline button is turned on.

12. Click **outside the selected text**.
The text is bold, italic, and underlined, and all three buttons are turned off.

13. Select the text **Jack Russell terrier** in the first paragraph.
This text is bold, so the Bold button looks pushed in.

14. Click the **Bold button**.
The button is turned off and no longer looks pushed in.

15. Click **outside the selected text**.
The text is no longer bold. Your document should look like the one in Figure 4.1.

16. Save the document with the same name.

17. Print the document and leave it open for the next exercise.

 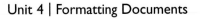

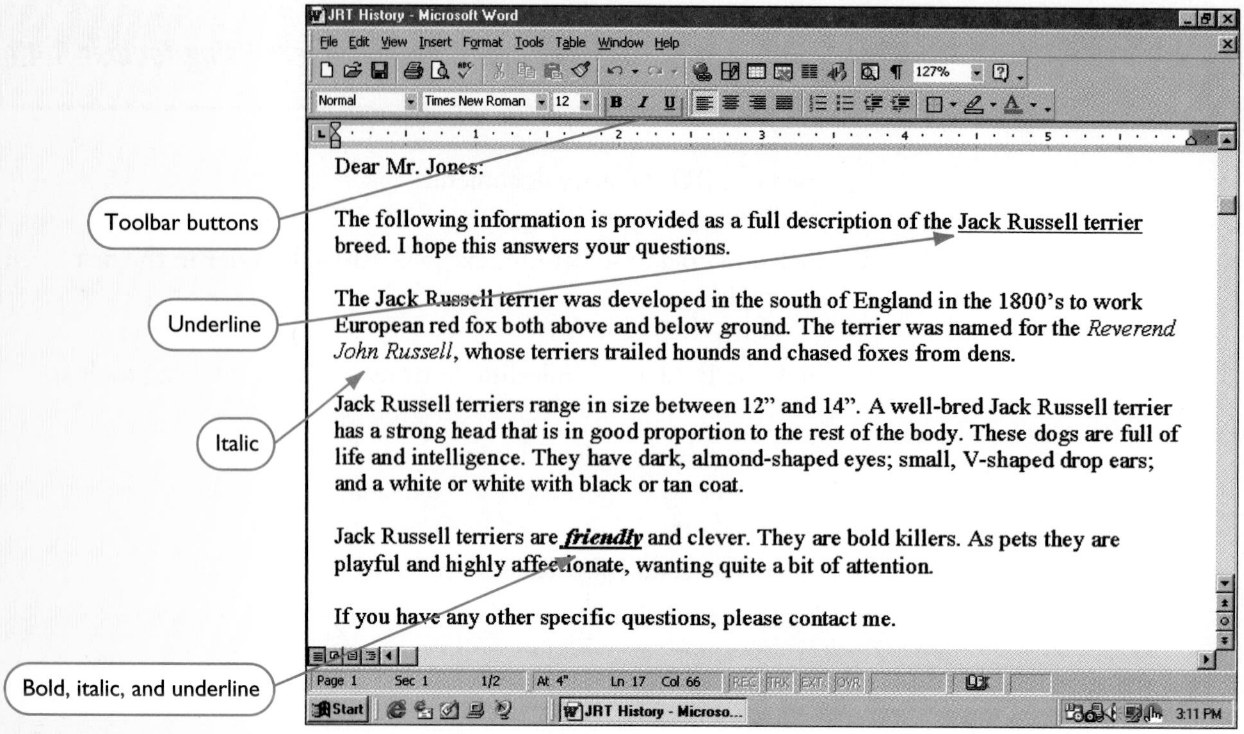
JRT History - Microsoft Word
File Edit View Insert Format Tools Table Window Help
Normal
Times New Roman
12
127%
Toolbar buttons
Underline
Italic
Bold, italic, and underline
Dear Mr. Jones:
The following information is provided as a full description of the Jack Russell terrier breed. I hope this answers your questions.
The Jack Russell terrier was developed in the south of England in the 1800's to work European red fox both above and below ground. The terrier was named for the Reverend John Russell, whose terriers trailed hounds and chased foxes from dens.
Jack Russell terriers range in size between 12" and 14". A well-bred Jack Russell terrier has a strong head that is in good proportion to the rest of the body. These dogs are full of life and intelligence. They have dark, almond-shaped eyes; small, V-shaped drop ears; and a white or white with black or tan coat.
Jack Russell terriers are friendly and clever. They are bold killers. As pets they are playful and highly affectionate, wanting quite a bit of attention.
If you have any other specific questions, please contact me.
Page 1 Sec 1 1/2 At 4" Ln 17 Col 66 REC TRK EXT OVR
Start
JRT History - Microso...
3:11 PM

FIGURE 4.1 The Document with Bold, Italic, and Underline

TASK 2 Formatting Characters Using the Font Dialog Box

What: Format text by changing the font, font size, color, and effects.
How: Choose Format | Font.
Why: You can add emphasis and readability to text by formatting it.
Tip: You can use the toolbar to change the font, font size, and font color, but the dialog box has the advantage of displaying a preview of the selected formatting.

When you type text in a new Word document, it is automatically formatted for you in a font called Times New Roman and in the size called 12 point. Times New Roman is one of several fonts, or typefaces, that come with Microsoft Windows. (A **font** is a complete set of characters with its own design and name.) Type sizes are measured in **points**, and 12 point is the default type size for text in a new Word document. (There are 72 points in an inch.) You can change font, font size, and font color and add other effects.

Overformatting Text

Use character formatting only to set off elements that you want to emphasize for the reader. Too much formatting makes text hard to read and may be confusing or distracting rather than helpful.

To format text that already exists:
1. Select the text.
2. Choose Format | Font | Font tab.
3. Make selections in the Font dialog box, as shown in Figure 4.2.
4. View the changes in the Preview section of the dialog box and, when you are satisfied, click OK.
5. Click outside the text to see the formatting.

To format text as you type:
1. Choose Format | Font | Font tab.
2. Make selections in the Font dialog box, as shown in Figure 4.2.
3. View a sample in the Preview section of the dialog box and, when you are satisfied, click OK.
4. Type the text.
5. Repeat Steps 1 through 3 to turn off the formatting or change it again.
6. Continue typing.

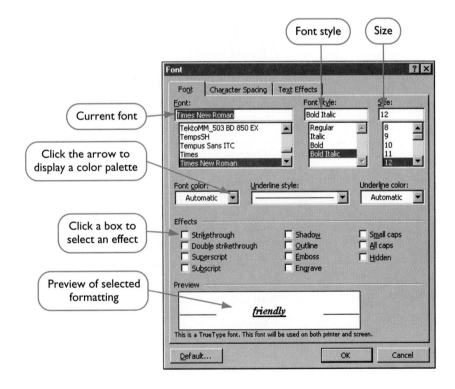

FIGURE **4.2**   The Font Dialog Box

Returning to the Default Character Format

Press Ctrl+Spacebar to cancel character formatting and return to the default format. In a blank document, default format is 12-point Times New Roman font, Regular style.

These options can be changed in the Font dialog box:

- **Font:** the name of the current font is displayed in the Font box, and a sample appears in the Preview box. You can preview another font by selecting it in the list.

- **Font Style:** Most fonts have four styles: Regular, Bold, Italic, and Bold Italic.

- **Size:** Choose a size from the list or type a size not displayed there.

- **Underline:** Word provides many underline styles in addition to the default single-line underline.

- **Font Color:** Choose a color from the palette that drops down when you click the arrow; the result in a printout depends on whether you are using a color printer.

- **Effects:** Uses one of the effects shown in Table 4.1.

Effect	Result
Strikethrough	Draws a single line through the text
Double strikethrough	Draws two lines through the text
Superscript	Raises text above the base line and reduces its size
Subscript	Lowers text below the base line and reduces its size
Shadow	Adds a shadow to text
Outline	Outlines characters
Emboss	Formats text to appear raised off the page
Engrave	Formats text to appear pressed into the page
Small caps	Formats lowercase characters as small capital letters (smaller than the surrounding caps)
All caps	Formats lowercase characters as capital letters
Hidden	Prevents text from displaying when printed

TABLE 4.1   Font Effects

POINTER

Text Size

For easy reading of ordinary text documents, keep the body text in the 10-point to 13-point range. Headings can range from 14-point to 16-point for emphasis. Reserve larger sizes for titles and special effects or for different kinds of documents (ads, flyers, newsletters, etc).

POINTER

Using the Toolbar to Change the Font

Click the down arrow in the Formatting toolbar's Font box to see a list of fonts installed on your system. By default, Word shows the font name in a sample of the font. Click a font to select it. Choose a font size in the same way. (You can type a font size in the Font size box or choose a size from the drop-down list.) There is also a toolbar button for Font Color. Clicking its arrow displays a palette of colors from which you can choose. The button shows the currently selected color; clicking the button sets that color.

EXERCISE 2 | *Formatting Characters Using the Font Dialog Box*

1. With the *JRT History* document on the screen, press **Ctrl+Home** to move to the top of the letter.

2. Select the **return address** at the top of the document:

JRT Purebreds
2000 Friendly St.
Eugene, OR 97405

The three lines are highlighted.

3. Choose **Format | Font** and, if necessary, click the **Font tab**.
The current settings for the selected text are displayed.

4. Scroll in the **Font list box** and select **Arial**.
The Preview section shows the sample text in the Arial font.

5. Scroll in the **Size list box** and select **16**.
The Preview sample changes to 16-point type.

6. Click the down arrow for **Font Color**.
A palette is displayed.

7. Click **Blue**.
A ScreenTip displays color names as you point to them. The Preview sample is formatted blue.

8. In the Effects section, select the **Emboss check box**.
Embossed text looks raised off the page.

9. Click **OK**.

   The dialog box closes, and the text is formatted as shown in Figure 4.3. (You must deselect the text to see the effect.)

10. Save the document with the same name.

11. Print the document and keep it open for the next exercise.

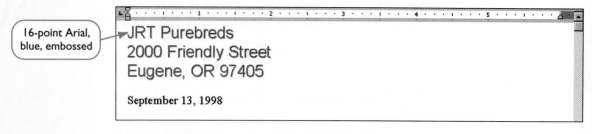

16-point Arial, blue, embossed

JRT Purebreds
2000 Friendly Street
Eugene, OR 97405

September 13, 1998

FIGURE 4.3 The Formatted Return Address

TASK 3 | *Aligning Paragraphs of Text*

What: Change the horizontal alignment of paragraphs of text.

How: Click the Align Left, Center, Align Right, or Justify button on the Formatting toolbar.

Why: Centering titles and justifying text can make a document look more professional.

Tip: You can also choose Format | Paragraph to change text alignment, but it is much faster to use the toolbar.

In Tasks 1 and 2 you learned to format characters. Starting with this task you will format paragraphs. You'll start by learning to change how paragraphs of text line up horizontally on the page.

To change the alignment of an existing paragraph or paragraphs:

1. Click anywhere in a single paragraph, or select several paragraphs.
2. Click an alignment button on the Formatting toolbar to create the effects described in Table 4.2.

Button	Name	Description
≣	Align Left	Text starts at the left margin, making a straight left edge and a ragged right edge; this is the default alignment
≣	Center	Each line of the paragraph is centered between the right and left margins
≣	Align Right	Text lines up at the right margin and has a ragged left edge
≣	Justify	Text lines up at both the left and right margins

TABLE 4.2 Paragraph Alignment Options

To set paragraph alignment before you type:
1. Click an alignment button on the Formatting toolbar.
2. Type the text.

POINTER

Click and Type

Have you noticed horizontal lines next to the pointer? They indicate that Word's click and type feature is in effect. (To turn it on, choose Tools | Options | Edit tab and select the *Enable click and type* check box.) In Print Layout view you can place text anywhere on a page by double-clicking. If you double click at the right margin, the text you type will be right aligned. (The lines next to the pointer are aligned right, just like those of the Align Right button on the toolbar.) Double-click in the center of the document and the lines you type will be centered.

EXERCISE 3 | *Aligning Paragraphs of Text*

1. With the *JRT History* document on the screen, choose **View | Print Layout**.
We will use the point and click feature in this exercise. This feature does not work in Normal view.

2. Click the down arrow in the **Zoom box** and select **Page Width**.
The left and right margins are shown.

3. Press **Ctrl+Home** and select the **return address** you formatted in Exercise 2.
Each of these lines is a paragraph.

4. Click the **Center button** on the Formatting toolbar.
The paragraphs are centered and now form a letterhead.

5. Click anywhere in the **date paragraph**.

6. Click the **Align Right button**.
The paragraph containing the date is aligned at the right margin.

7. Click anywhere in the **first paragraph** of text.

8. Click the **Justify button**.
The paragraph is aligned at both the left and right margins.

9. Select the block of paragraphs from the closing (**Yours truly** through **your name**).

10. Click the **Center button**.
The signature block is centered.

11. Click anywhere in the **first paragraph**.

12. Click the **Align Left button**.
The first paragraph is aligned left.

13. Double-click below your name **at the right margin,** when the pointer has right-aligned horizontal lines next to it.
The insertion point is set at the right margin.

14. Type your initials.
The text is right aligned. Your document should look like the one in Figure 4.4.

15. Save the document with the same name.

16. Print the document and leave it open for the next exercise.

Letterhead centered

Date aligned right

Signature block centered

Initials aligned right

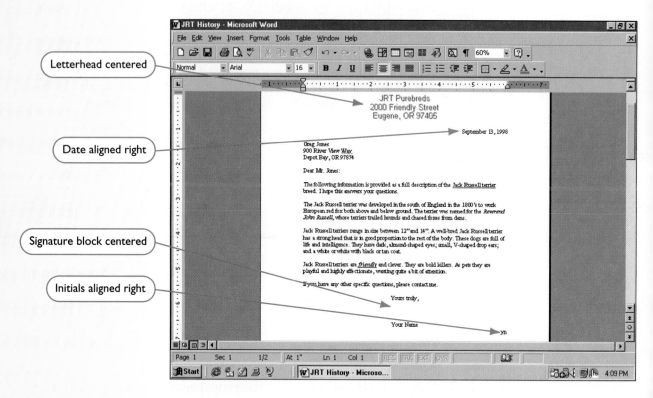

FIGURE 4.4   The Document with Paragraphs Realigned

TASK 4 | *Changing the Line Spacing of Paragraphs*

What: Change the spacing between the lines in a paragraph.
How: Choose Format | Paragraph | Indents and Spacing tab.
Why: Some documents need to be double spaced.
  Tip: Never press Enter at the end of every line to create double-spacing.

Word single-spaces your documents by default, but lets you choose a different spacing for a whole document or an individual paragraph.

To change the line spacing in existing paragraphs:

1. Place the insertion point in a paragraph or select multiple paragraphs for new line spacing.
2. Choose Format | Paragraph to open the Paragraph dialog box.
3. If necessary, click the Indents and Spacing tab shown in Figure 4.5.
4. Click the down arrow for *Line Spacing* to display a list.
5. Do one of the following:
   - Choose *Single*, *1.5*, or *Double*.
   - Choose *At Least*, *Exactly*, or *Multiple* and then type a number in the *At* box or use its increment or decrement arrow.
6. Click OK.

POINTER

Line Spacing for an Entire Document

To double-space an entire document, turn the option on before you begin typing. If you need to change the spacing of a whole document after you have typed it, remember the Ctrl+A shortcut for "Select All."

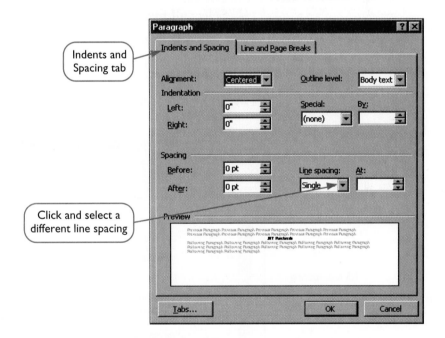

FIGURE 4.5   The Paragraph Dialog Box

1. With the *JRT History* document on the screen, click anywhere in the **first paragraph** of the letter.

2. Choose **Format | Paragraph**.
The Paragraph dialog box opens.

3. Make sure the **Indents and Spacing tab** is selected.

4. In the Paragraph dialog box, click the down arrow for **Line Spacing**.
A list drops down.

5. Select **1.5 lines** and click **OK**.
The dialog box closes, and the selected paragraph is respaced.

6. Select the **second paragraph** of the letter.

7. Choose **Format | Paragraph**.

8. In the Line Spacing list, select **Double** and click **OK**.
The dialog box closes, and the selected paragraph is double spaced, as shown in Figure 4.6.

9. Print the document.

10. Select **all five paragraphs** in the body of the letter.

11. Choose **Format | Paragraph**.

12. In the Line Spacing list, select **single**.
The body of the letter is single spaced, as it was at the start of the exercise.

13. Leave the document open for the next exercise.

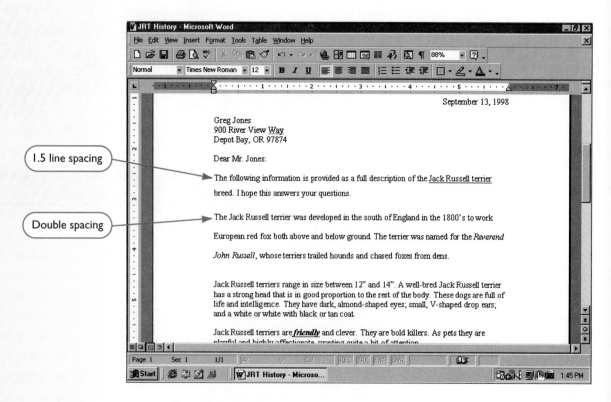

FIGURE 4.6   The Document After Step 8

What: Indent paragraphs from the left and/or right margins.
How: Choose Format | Paragraph | Indents and Spacing tab.
Why: You will want to set text off by indenting it from the margins.
Tip: Indent individual paragraphs or groups of paragraphs from the left and right margins; but to change the margins for the whole document, choose File | Page Setup, as explained in Unit 6.

Word provides several kinds of paragraph indents that are useful for different purposes. A first line indent automatically indents the first line of every paragraph. You can use a hanging indent to indent every line but the first in each paragraph of a reference list. In many research paper styles, you indent quoted material from both left and right margins. Word lets you set all of these options in the Paragraph dialog box.

The default paragraph style has no indent. When you indent a paragraph, the indentation is measured from the margin. To indent existing paragraphs:

1. Place the insertion point in a paragraph or select multiple paragraphs to be indented.
2. Choose Format | Paragraph to open the Paragraph dialog box.
3. Click the Indents and Spacing tab, shown in Figure 4.7.
4. Specify a left indent (in inches) by typing a number in the *Left* box of the Indentation section (or use the increment and decrement arrows in the text box).

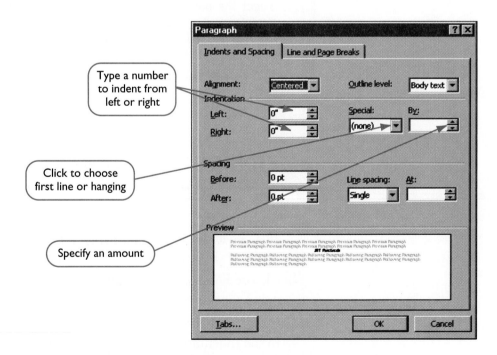

FIGURE 4.7 The Paragraph Dialog Box

5. Specify a right indent in the same way, using the *Right* box of the Indentation section.

6. Specify a first line or hanging indent by selecting it in the *Special* drop-down box, as explained in Table 4.3.

Option	Result
First line indent	Indents only the first line of the paragraph by the amount you type in the *By* box
Hanging	Indents all lines except the first line of the paragraph by the amount you type in the *By* box

TABLE 4.3   Special Indentation Options

- You can specify multiple indents before clicking OK: for example, type a 1 in both the *Left* and *Right* boxes to indent the selected paragraphs one inch from both left and right margins.

- If you change your mind after indenting text, change the left or right indentation back to 0 or change the *Special* indent to *None*, and the text will again line up at the margin.

POINTER

Restoring the Default Paragraph Format

Select the paragraphs and press Ctrl+Q to remove special paragraph formatting. For regular text paragraphs using the blank document (Normal) template, this is single spacing, left alignment, and no paragraph indent.

EXERCISE 5 | *Indenting Paragraphs*

1. With the *JRT History* document on the screen in Print Layout view, click anywhere in the **first paragraph** of the letter.
   You don't have to select the whole paragraph to format it.

2. Choose **Format | Paragraph**.
   The Paragraph dialog box opens.

3. Make sure the **Indents and Spacing tab** is selected.

4. In the Indentation section, set both the **Left** and **Right** indents to **1″**.
   You can type the number or click the increment arrows.

5. Click **OK**.

The dialog box closes, and the first paragraph is indented 1″ from both margins.

6. Move the insertion point to the **second paragraph**.

7. Choose **Format | Paragraph**.

The Paragraph dialog box opens.

8. Click the down arrow for **Special**.

A list drops down.

9. Choose **Hanging**, and click **OK**.

The second paragraph is formatted with a hanging indent.

10. Move the insertion point to the **third paragraph**.

11. Choose **Format | Paragraph**.

12. Click the down arrow for **Special**.

13. Choose **First line**.

14. In the **By box** type 1″ and click **OK**.

The first line of the third paragraph is indented by 1″. Your letter should look like the one in Figure 4.8.

15. Print the document and close it without saving it.

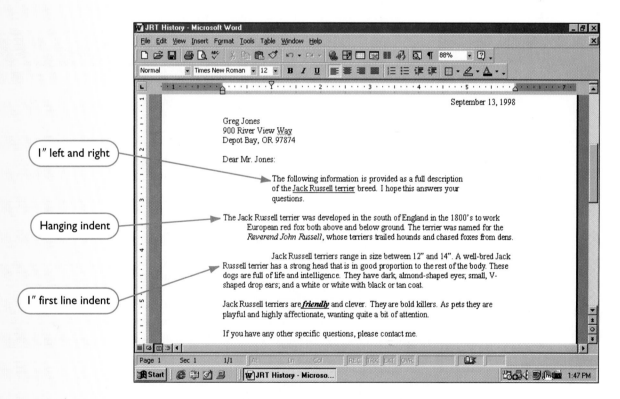

FIGURE 4.8 The Letter with Indented Paragraphs

TASK 6 | *Setting Tabs*

What: Set custom tabs.
How: Choose Format | Tabs.
Why: You can line up text on tabs to create better-looking documents.
Tip: Never use the Spacebar to line up text; it will align on the screen, but not when you print it out. Always use the Tab key.

A **tab stop** is a horizontal position within a paragraph that you can set for placing and aligning text. When you press the Tab key, the insertion point moves to the next tab stop. By default, Word sets left tab stops every half-inch. You can use these preset tab stops for many purposes. However, if you want text to line up differently, you need to set your own tabs.

Word includes five types of tabs. Table 4.4 describes the types, and Figure 4.9 illustrates their use.

As paragraph formats, tab settings apply to selected paragraphs or to new text from the insertion point forward. To have custom tabs apply to a whole document, set them before you type it.

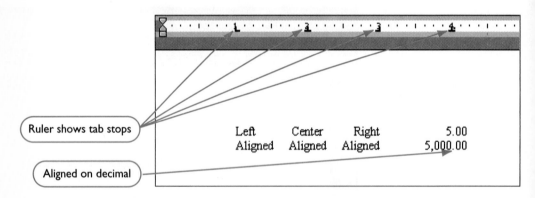

Ruler shows tab stops

Aligned on decimal

| Left | Center | Right | 5.00 |
| Aligned | Aligned | Aligned | 5,000.00 |

FIGURE 4.9   Four Tab Types

Tab	Button on the Ruler	Description
Left	**L**	Text lines up to the right of the tab
Center	**⊥**	Text is centered around the tab point
Right	**⌐**	Text lines up to the left of the tab
Decimal	**⊥·**	Lines up data on a decimal point (period)
Bar	**I**	Places a vertical bar at the tab stop

TABLE 4.4   Types of Tabs

The easiest way to set and delete tabs is to use the horizontal ruler. To set a tab with the ruler:

1. If the ruler is not displayed, choose View | Ruler to display it.
2. Click the ruler's Tab Alignment button as many times as needed to select the tab type to be set. The Tab Alignment button cycles through the five tab types as you click it, displaying the images shown in Table 4.4. Figure 4.10 shows the ruler with the Tab Alignment button displaying a Left tab.

POINTER

Indenting Paragraphs Using the Ruler

In Task 5, you learned to indent paragraphs using the Paragraph dialog box. The Tab Alignment button also shows the First Line Indent and Hanging Indent marks, allowing you to change these settings on the ruler as well.

3. When the tab type is set, move the pointer to the spot on the ruler where the tab is to go, and click. The tab stop is set, and a tab mark is displayed on the ruler.

To remove a tab stop using the ruler, drag the tab mark off the ruler down into the document and release the mouse button. The tab stop is deleted, and its mark is removed from the ruler.

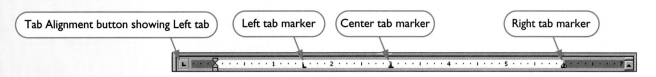

Tab Alignment button showing Left tab   Left tab marker   Center tab marker   Right tab marker

FIGURE 4.10   The Ruler Displaying Tabs

POINTER

Display Nonprinting Characters

Click the Show/Hide ¶ button on the Standard toolbar to toggle the display of nonprinting characters in your document on and off. A paragraph sign (¶) shows you the position of each paragraph break in the document, a centered dot represents each space, and a right-pointing arrow represents each tab character. Displaying these nonprinting characters makes editing easier.

Some advanced tab settings are available in the Tabs dialog box. To display the box, shown in Figure 4.11, choose Format | Tabs.

To set tabs individually in the dialog box:

1. Type the location where you want the tab in the *Tab stop position* text box.
2. Select the type of tab in the *Alignment* section.
3. Select a leader if you want to use one. (A **leader** is a line of dots or dashes in the blank space before a tab stop, leading the reader's eye across the page.)
4. Click the Set button.
5. Repeat Steps 1–4 to set more tabs and, when all are set, click OK.

To delete a tab using the dialog box:

1. Select the tab in the list.
2. Click the Clear button.

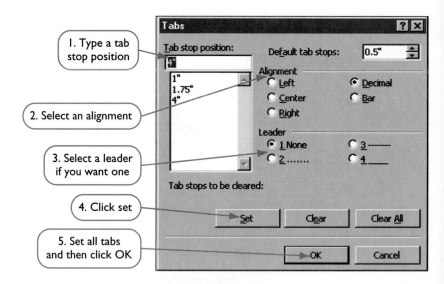

FIGURE 4.11   Setting Tabs Using the Tabs Dialog Box

EXERCISE 6 | *Setting Tabs*

1. Click the **New Blank Document button** on the Standard toolbar.
   A new blank document opens.

2. Click the **Show/Hide ¶ button** on the Standard toolbar to turn it on.
   Now, pressing the Tab key will display a nonprinting arrow on the screen.
3. Press **Tab** and type **1st**
4. Press **Tab** and type **Rent**
5. Press **Tab** and type **$650.00**
6. Press **Enter**.
7. Press **Tab** and type **15th**

8. Press **Tab** and type **Phone**

9. Press **Tab** and type **$75.00**

10. Press **Ctrl+A**.
The whole document is selected, and any tabs you set will apply to all paragraphs.

11. If the ruler is not displayed, choose **View | Ruler**.

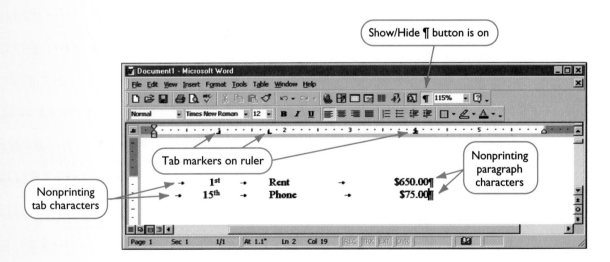

12. Click the **Tab Alignment button** on the ruler enough times to display the **Right Tab button**.
If you point to the button, a ScreenTip will display its name.

13. Point the mouse to the **1″ mark** on the ruler and click.
A right tab is set, and the dates move to the new alignment.

14. Click the **Tab Alignment button** enough times to display the **Left Tab button**.

15. Point the mouse to the **1¾″ mark** and click.
A left tab is set, and the text moves to the new alignment

16. Click the **Tab Alignment button** enough times to display the **Decimal Tab button**.

17. Point the mouse to the **4″ mark** and click.
A decimal tab is set, and the dollar amounts line up at the decimals.

18. Click and drag the **decimal tab** off the ruler.
When you release the mouse button, the custom tab is deleted, and the dollar amounts move back to a default tab stop.

19. Print the document and close it without saving it.

FIGURE 4.12   The Document with Custom Tabs

SUMMARY

After completing this unit, you should be able to

- format characters using bold, italic, and underline (page 82)
- change the font, font size, and font color of text (page 84)
- apply special effects to text (page 84)
- change the alignment of paragraphs (page 88)
- change the spacing of lines within paragraphs (page 90)
- indent paragraphs (page 93)
- set custom tab stops (page 96)

KEY TERMS

character formatting (page 81)   **paragraph formatting** (page 81)

font (page 84)   **point** (page 84)

formatting (page 81)   **subscript** (page 86)

hanging indent (page 94)   **superscript** (page 86)

justify (page 88)   **tab stop** (page 96)

leader (page 98)

TEST YOUR SKILLS

True/False

1. Justified text lines up at both the left and right margins.
2. You can only make text italic after you type it into the document.
3. Superscript places text below the base line.
4. You should keep body text in the 10–13 point range for easy reading.
5. With a hanging indent, the first line of the paragraph is not indented, but all subsequent lines of the paragraph are indented.

Multiple Choice

1. In Word 2000, you can format by
   a. character
   b. paragraph
   c. page or section
   d. all of these answers

2. To double-space an entire document so that it is formatted correctly, you could
   a. press Enter at the end of every line of text
   b. set tabs at intervals
   c. choose Format | Paragraph and select an option
   d. all of these answers

3. To increase the amount of space between lines of text, you change which feature?
   a. tabs
   b. line spacing
   c. margins
   d. indents

4. To increase the amount of white space on the left and right of a paragraph, you use which feature?
   a. tabs
   b. indents
   c. line spacing
   d. embossing

5. To have numbers line up on a decimal point, you use which feature?
   a. subscript
   b. strikethrough
   c. decimal tab
   d. number tab

Short Answer

1. If you want to format text you have already typed, you must _____ it first.
2. Never use the _____ to indent text because it will be a mess when you print.
3. _____ are a series of dots, dashes, or other marks that can precede a tab.
4. The alignment option that lines text up at both the right and left margins is _____.
5. _____ is a complete set of type characters with its own design and name.

What Does This Do?

Write a brief description of the function of the following:

1.	Single ▼	6.	⊥
2.	☰	7.	⊥
3.	Times New Roman ▼	8.	**B**
4.	*I*	9.	☰
5.	12 ▼	10.	☐ Superscript

On Your Own

1. Open a document, select the entire document, and change the spacing to double.
2. Open a document, select text using various methods, and try out various types of character formatting, including the Effects in the Font dialog box.

3. Open a document, select text using various methods, and try out numerous fonts, font sizes, and colors.

4. Open a new document and display the ruler. Set the different types of tabs at various locations on the ruler. Type text, pressing the tab key to test the results.

5. Open a document, indent paragraphs using various methods, and change the alignment of the paragraphs.

PROJECTS

1. a. Create a letterhead for Santa Fe Designs, using the text shown below. Use any of the formatting techniques you've learned so far to create the letterhead.

   b. Save the document as **Designs letterhead** and print it.

   c. Copy the text of the *Ring* document you created earlier (but not its letterhead) onto the *Designs* letterhead.

   d. Choose File | Save As and save the document as **Rings2**. Print the document.

Santa Fe Designs
1569 Aztec Way
Santa Fe, NM 87501

---

2. a. Create the document shown below, centering the title and changing the title font to Impact, size 16 or another font on your system. Use appropriate types of tabs to set up the columns as shown.

   b. Check the document's spelling, proofread it, and correct errors.

   c. Save the document as **Software Suites**.

   d. Preview and then print the document.

Software Productivity Suites

As the millennium approached, three companies shared the market for productivity software, with Microsoft's package the biggest seller. The companies, suites, and current versions were:

Maker	**Suite Name**	**Version**
Corel	Corel WordPerfect Suite	8
IBM	Lotus SmartSuite	Millennium
Microsoft	Microsoft Office	2000

Your Name

---

3. a. Create the document shown below, double-spacing the body, centering the title, changing the title font to 16-point Tremor or another font on your system, and formatting characters as shown.

   b. Check the document's spelling, proofread it, and correct errors.

   c. Save the document as **Y2K**.

   d. Preview and then print the document.

Y2K

Y2K stands for the Year 2000 problem. This problem is the result of the way computers have been programmed to deal with dates. Programmers have used a maximum of 2 digits to represent each segment of the date, for example, **8/3/98**. This system limits the input to numbers between 00 and 99 for each part of the date.

If you add 1 to the year portion of the above date, you will see the year 99 and translate that easily to **1999**. Further, if you add 2 to the above date, you will see 00 and translate that easily to **2000**. However, a computer doesn't make that jump with you. When a computer adds 2 to 98 it gets 00, but it reads the date as **1900** because that is the number that it has always substituted for the first two digits of the year. Computers have no idea about century changes.

The Year 2000 problem seems simple; however, implementing the program changes on **all computers** is the problem of the century.

POINTER

Capitalize First Letter of Sentences?

If Word is set to capitalize the first letter of sentences, you will have trouble typing the document in Project 4. To change this option, choose Tools | AutoCorrect | AutoCorrect tab, and clear the *Capitalize first letter of sentences* check box.

---

4. a. Create the document shown below, formatting it as shown.
   b. Check the document's spelling, proofread it, and correct errors.
   c. Save the document as **eCom**.
   d. Preview and then print the document.

---

eCommerce

eCommerce is the business trend that uses electronic communication to conduct business. As the World Wide Web becomes more generally available and as consumers become more familiar with it, commerce over the Web will grow.

Today, couch potatoes idly watch TV and channel-surf during commercials. This paradigm is shifting as the TV appliance is changing, enabling television access to the World Wide Web. Web access will turn TV from a passive pastime to an interactive experience.

Some of these changes are reflected in the following:

Large companies are already planning marketing strategies to entice consumers to their sites through multimedia extravaganzas.

As the Web becomes a global communication tool, new markets will open in other countries.

As digital signatures are implemented, secure transactions over the Web will be guaranteed.

Customers will value the immediate service, convenience, personal attention, and flexibility of electronic commerce.

PROJECTS

1. a. Create the press release shown below, formatting as it is shown.
   b. Check the document's spelling, proofread it, and correct errors.
   c. Save the document as **News**.
   d. Preview and then print the document.

PRESS RELEASE

Contact information: your name
JRT Kennels
2000 Friendly St.
Eugene, OR 97405

JRT Kennels announces the addition two new services: JRT Grooming and JRT Wash 'em Yourself.

JRT Purebred Kennels Expands Its High-Quality Services.

Eugene, Oregon, August 3, 1999: JRT Kennels, a quality breeder and operator of clean, friendly boarding kennels, is expanding its services with two new additions.

JRT Grooming will open August 15, 1999, providing full-service grooming for all breeds of dogs. JRT Grooming will use only natural products to help protect your animal. JRT Grooming is located next to the JRT Kennel at 2000 Friendly Street in Eugene. The grooming services will be available from 8 to 4 daily.

Wash 'em Yourself will open September 1, 1999. Wash 'em Yourself provides self-service grooming facilities for pets of all types. The facility includes waist-high tubs, hand showers with adjustable nozzles, and a full line of natural products. The facility will be open daily from 12 to 8 and is located at 2002 Friendly Street.

---

2. a. Create the cover letter shown at the top of next page, formatting it as shown (but designing the letterhead as you like).
   b. Check the document's spelling, proofread it, and correct errors.
   c. Save the document as **Cyber Business**.
   d. Preview and then print the document.

CYBER BUSINESS
6000 Waterside Ave.
San Diego, CA 98888

current date

Santa Fe Designs
1569 Aztec Way
Santa Fe, NM 87501

Dear Mr. Simms:

Enclosed you will find the result of the research conducted by our staff at *Cyber Business*. You will be interested to note that all businesses are benefiting from a Web presence, but <u>small businesses</u> such as yours are <u>benefiting the most</u>.

If our company can be of any service to you or if you have any further questions, please contact me personally.

Sincerely,

your name

encl.

---

e. Create the report shown below, changing the title font to one of your choosing and increasing the title size to 16. Use paragraph formatting to approximate the indents shown.
f. Check the document's spelling, proofread it, and correct errors.
g. Save the document as **Business Today**.
h. Preview and then print the document.

Business Today

Business in today's world is shifting from paper communications (letters, memos, catalogs, business cards, reports, etc.) and telephone conversations to electronic communications (e-mail, faxes, voice mail, shared documents, etc.). This communication shift is being enhanced by the presence of the *World Wide Web*.

> Today businesses have a **level playing ground on the Web**, that is, large businesses have no advantage over small businesses. An attractive Web presence that provides customer service and satisfaction can be created and operated by one person or a corporation. And a Web presence makes every business a player in the <u>global</u> market.

Marketing your business with a friendly, informative Web site will place your business at the forefront of your industry. **Consumers will be more educated in the future and will shop on line for the products that you are providing**.

If you are planning to create a presence for your business on the *World Wide Web*, start by conducting a thorough search of the Web for all your competition. Expand your search to find sites that you would personally trust or that you would avoid. Find out what works from the bottom up. Then you will be ready to develop a plan for your site.

Automating Tasks

UNIT OBJECTIVES

- Format text using built-in styles
- Use AutoCorrect
- Edit AutoCorrect entries
- Use AutoText
- Use AutoFormat
- Create bulleted and numbered lists
- Use borders and shading
- Include special symbols

Word includes many features that will save you time. Some of these features provide help with editing, some of them simplify the formatting of characters, and some provide easy ways to format paragraphs. You can use Word's built-in styles to format text, such as headings in longer documents. You can also have Word correct and place text in your document using the AutoCorrect and AutoText features. You can set text off from surrounding text by placing it in bulleted or numbered lists or placing a border around it. You can easily insert special symbols not available from the keyboard.

What: Assign standard formatting to paragraphs in your document.
How: Click the down arrow in the Formatting toolbar's Style box.
Why: Styles are a powerful way of automatically formatting text.
Tip: Don't edit Word's built-in styles. That way you will always have access to the styles that come with Microsoft Word 2000.

Styles are named formatting options built into Word. Using a named style allows you to quickly format text consistently throughout a document. For example, all text you format with the built-in Heading 1 style will look the same. Styles are extremely useful in long documents that contain headings and subheadings. You can keep all headings on the same level formatted identically without having to remember what formatting you used.

To use Word's built-in styles to format a heading or text paragraph:

1. Place the insertion point in the text you want to format.
2. Click the down arrow in the Style box on the Formatting toolbar. A drop-down list shows the available styles, such as those in Figure 5.1.
3. Click a style name, and the paragraph is formatted with that style.

The New Blank Document's built-in styles

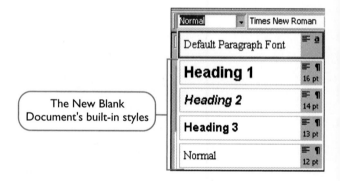

FIGURE 5.1 The Style List Box

POINTER

Selecting or Not Selecting Text

When you select a word and click the Bold button, you are applying a character style. The heading styles in the Style box, however, are paragraph styles—that is, they format an entire paragraph. To apply a paragraph format, you don't need to select the whole paragraph. Clicking anywhere in the paragraph will do the job.

EXERCISE 1 | *Formatting Text Using Built-in Styles*

1. Open a new blank document.

2. Type the following text, on three lines:

> This is heading 1
> This is heading 2
> This is heading 3

3. Place the insertion point in the first line you typed and click the down arrow in the Formatting toolbar's **Style box**.
A list of available styles drops down.

4. Click **Heading 1**.
The list closes, and the text is formatted using the Heading 1 style.

5. Place the insertion point in the second line and format it for **Heading 2**.
The text is formatted using the Heading 2 style.

6. Place the insertion point in the third line and format it for **Heading 3**.
The text is formatted using the Heading 3 style. Your document should look like the one in Figure 5.2.

7. Print the document and close it without saving it.

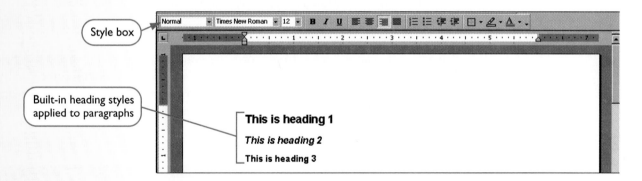

FIGURE 5.2 Heading Styles Applied to Paragraphs

What: Use Word's AutoCorrect feature to correct spelling errors and replace designated text as you type.

How: Type any error recognized by AutoCorrect and Word will automatically correct it.

Why: You probably make typing errors that AutoCorrect can correct for you.

Tip: AutoCorrect is not the same as AutoComplete. AutoCorrect automatically changes text, whereas AutoComplete suggests the complete text of dates and other items in a yellow box that appears as you type.

Word has a list of corrections for many common typing errors and a feature called **AutoCorrect** that can automatically correct these errors as you type. You may not even have noticed this occurring because it works so fast. For example, if you type *teh* instead of *the*, AutoCorrect will transpose the two mistyped letters as you press the Spacebar, so you might not even notice the correction.

POINTER

AutoCorrect Doesn't Seem to Work

To have AutoCorrect work automatically as you type, you must select the *Replace text as you type* check box in the AutoCorrect dialog box.

You can set AutoCorrect to perform several different kinds of corrections. To see the list, choose Tools | AutoCorrect to open the AutoCorrect dialog box, and select the AutoCorrect tab, shown in Figure 5.3. Checking or clearing the boxes at the top of the list sets the corrections that AutoCorrect will make automatically.

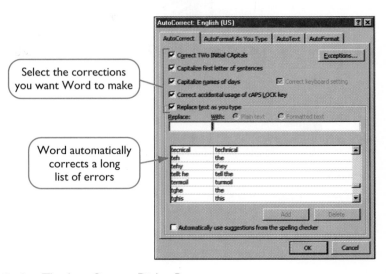

Select the corrections you want Word to make

Word automatically corrects a long list of errors

FIGURE **5.3**   The AutoCorrect Dialog Box

EXERCISE 2 | *Using AutoCorrect*

1. Open a new blank document.

2. Choose **Tools | AutoCorrect**.
   The AutoCorrect dialog box opens.

3. Select the **Replace text as you type** and **Capitalize first letter of sentences** check boxes if they aren't selected, and then click **OK**.
   The dialog box closes.

4. Type **teh** and press the **Spacebar**.
   Word changes the word to *The*.

5. Type **i** and press the **Spacebar**.
   Word changes the lowercase letter to a capital.

6. Type **wehn** and press the **Spacebar**.
   Word changes it to **when**.

7. Close the document without saving it.

TASK 3 | *Editing AutoCorrect Entries*

What: Add, delete, or change AutoCorrect entries.

How: Choose Tools | AutoCorrect.

Why: Customizing AutoCorrect can save you time.

Tip: To include paragraph formatting with an AutoCorrect entry, click the Show/Hide ¶ button to display nonprinting characters, and include the paragraph mark (¶) when you select text. The formatting is stored in the mark.

Word's AutoCorrect feature corrects hundreds of typographical errors automatically, and you can add to the list. To view the list, choose Tools | AutoCorrect to open the AutoCorrect dialog box, and select the AutoCorrect tab. You can scroll the list, or type the first letters of a word in the *Replace* text box to jump to that part of the alphabet. AutoCorrect entries appear in two columns. The left, or *Replace*, column contains the word to be replaced; the right, or *With*, column contains the correction. For example, when you typed *teh* in Exercise 2, Word changed it to *the* because *teh* is in the left column and *the* is in the right column of the list.

To add your own items to the list:

1. Type the word you want to replace in the *Replace* text box.
2. Type what you want it replaced with in the *With* text box.
3. Click the Add button to add it to the list. Figure 5.4 illustrates this procedure.

To remove an entry:

1. Select the entry.
2. Click the Delete button.

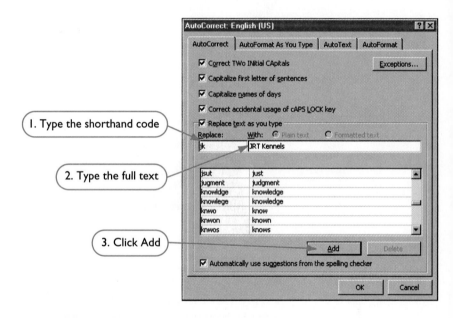

FIGURE 5.4   Adding an AutoCorrect Entry

EXERCISE 3 | *Adding Entries to AutoCorrect*

1. Open a new blank document.

2. Choose **Tools | AutoCorrect**.
The AutoCorrect dialog box opens with the AutoCorrect tab selected.

3. Make sure that the **Replace text as you type** check box is selected.

4. Type **jk** in the **Replace text box**.
This is what you will type in the document.

5. Type **JRT Kennels** in the **With text box**.
This is what Word will substitute when you type *jk* and press the Spacebar.

6. Click the **Add button**.
The entry is added to the list.

7. Click **OK**.
The dialog box closes.

8. In the blank document, type **jk** and press the **Spacebar**.
The two-character code is changed to the full name of the company.

9. Choose **Tools | AutoCorrect**.
The AutoCorrect dialog box opens.

10. Type **jk** in the **Replace text box**.
The list scrolls to this entry.

11. Click the **jk entry** in the list.
The whole entry is selected.

12. Press the **Delete button** in the dialog box.
The entry is deleted from the list and placed in the text boxes above it, so you can click the Add button if you change your mind.

13. Click the dialog box's **Close button**.
The dialog box closes and the entry is deleted.

14. Close the document without saving it.

TASK 4 | *Using AutoText*

What: Insert text automatically into a document.

How: Choose Insert | AutoText.

Why: You can save typing by inserting text into documents.

Tip: If you use AutoText often, you might find it faster to use the AutoText toolbar. Choose View | Toolbars | AutoText to display the toolbar.

If you type the same text again and again, you can save typing by storing it as AutoText. Later, you can use this **boilerplate text** (text that is used over and over, such as paragraphs in legal documents or form letters) to assemble documents without having to retype them.

To create your own AutoText entries:

1. Type the text or open the document that contains it.
2. Select the text.
3. Choose Insert | AutoText | New to display the Create AutoText dialog box, shown in Figure 5.5.
4. Type a name for the text entry in the text box or accept the name provided.

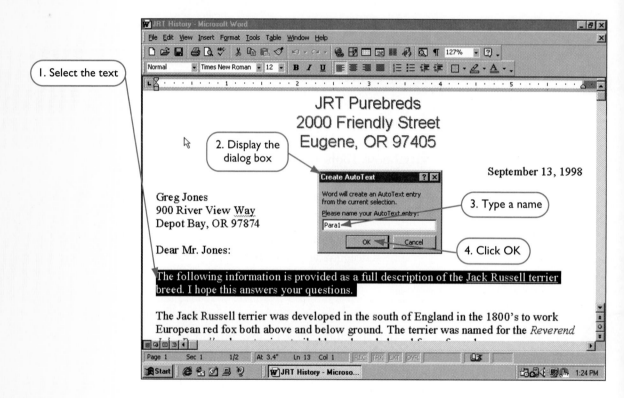

FIGURE 5.5   Creating an AutoText Entry

To insert a custom AutoText entry into a document:

1. Place the insertion point where you want the AutoText to appear.
2. Choose Insert | AutoText | AutoText to open the AutoCorrect dialog box with the AutoText tab displayed, as shown in Figure 5.6.
3. Select an AutoText entry in the list, and a preview is displayed below.
4. Click the Insert button.

The dialog box closes, and the AutoText entry appears in the document at the insertion point.

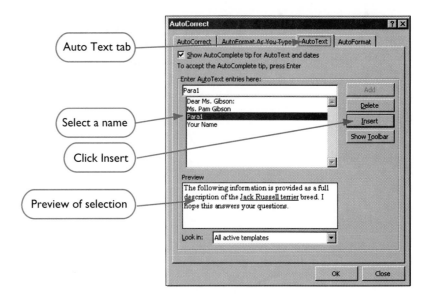

Auto Text tab

Select a name

Click Insert

Preview of selection

FIGURE 5.6 Selecting a Custom AutoText Entry

To delete AutoText items that you no longer need:

1. Choose Insert I AutoText I AutoText.
2. Select the AutoText item in the list (and look at the Preview section to check your choice).
3. Click the Delete button.

1. Open the **JRT History** document.
2. Select the **first paragraph** of the body of the letter.
   Figure 5.6 shows the letter open with the paragraph selected.
3. Choose **Insert | AutoText | New**.
   The Create AutoText dialog box opens.
4. Type **Para1** and click **OK**.
   The selected text is now an AutoText entry named Para1; the Create AutoText dialog box closes.
5. Select the **second paragraph** of the letter.
6. Choose **Insert | AutoText | New**.
   The Create AutoText dialog box opens again.
7. Type **Para2** and click **OK**.
   The selected text is now the AutoText entry named Para2.
8. Click the **New Blank Document button** on the Standard toolbar.
   A new document opens.
9. Choose **Insert | AutoText | AutoText**.
   The AutoCorrect dialog box opens with the AutoText tab displayed. It contains the two new entries you have just created.
10. Select **Para2** and click the **Insert button** as shown in Figure 5.7.
    The text is inserted into the document. Notice that you can insert AutoText entries in any order.
11. Choose **Insert | AutoText | AutoText**.
    The dialog box opens again.
12. Select **Para1** and click the **Insert button**.
    The text is inserted into the document.
13. Print the document.
14. Choose **Insert | AutoText | AutoText**.
    The AutoCorrect dialog box opens again with the AutoText tab displayed.
15. Select **Para1** and click the **Delete button**.
    The item is deleted from the list.
16. Select **Para2** and click the **Delete button**.
    The item is deleted from the list.
17. Close both documents without saving them.

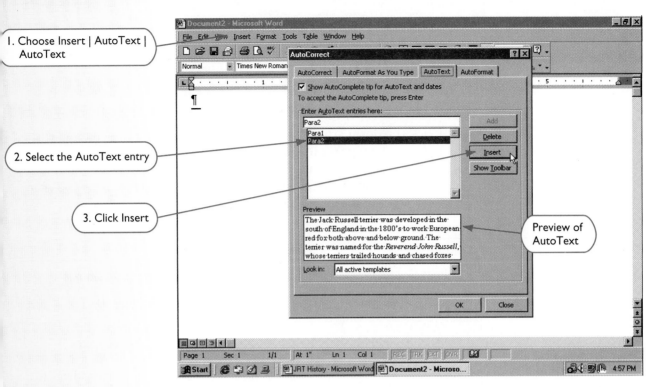

1. Choose Insert | AutoText | AutoText

2. Select the AutoText entry

3. Click Insert

Preview of AutoText

FIGURE 5.7 Inserting a Custom AutoText Entry into a Document

TASK 5 | *Using AutoFormat*

What: Have Word automatically format a document.

How: Choose Format | AutoFormat.

Why: Like most of the features in this unit, AutoFormatting can save you time.

Tip: AutoFormat formats documents when you choose the Format | AutoFormat command. The AutoFormat as You Type option (described in the pointer box) automatically formats text as you type it.

You can have Word format your documents automatically after you have typed them. To use this feature:

1. Choose Format | AutoFormat to open the AutoFormat dialog box, shown in Figure 5.8.

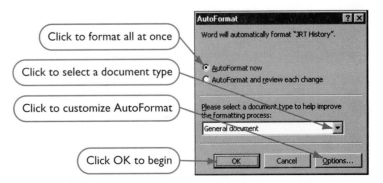

Click to format all at once

Click to select a document type

Click to customize AutoFormat

Click OK to begin

FIGURE 5.8 The AutoFormat Dialog Box

2. Click one of these option buttons:

- Select *AutoFormat Now* to have Word format the entire document automatically.
- Select *AutoFormat and Review Each Change* to have Word stop at each proposed change for confirmation.

3. Click the down arrow to choose a type of document, such as a *Letter*, or leave the type set to *General document*.

4. If you want to customize AutoFormat, click the Options button to display the AutoFormat tab of the AutoCorrect dialog box, where you can select or clear the check boxes. Table 5.1 describes these features.

Option	Result
Headings	Applies built-in heading styles to headings
Lists	Applies built-in list styles to lists
Automatic Bulleted Lists	Applies built-in bulleted list formatting
Paragraphs	Applies paragraph styles other than headings to paragraphs
Replaces	Automatically replaces characters with formatted characters, such as superscripting ordinals in 1st. Check the dialog box for other options.

TABLE 5.1 AutoFormat Options

POINTER

Formatting As You Type

When you type something and Word changes it and you don't know why and can't undo it no matter how many times you try, it is terribly frustrating. These formatting changes may occur as you type your documents because of options selected on the AutoCorrect dialog box's AutoFormat As You Type tab. To change the items that Word automatically formats as you type, choose Tools | AutoCorrect | AutoFormat As You Type tab. For example, if you type your e-mail address in a document and it keeps turning blue and is underlined, the *Replace Internet and network paths with hyperlinks* option is selected, automatically converting e-mail and Web addresses into hypertext as you type. Explore this dialog box, using the Help button to get information on each option.

EXERCISE 5 | *Using AutoFormat*

1. Create the following document, pressing the **Tab key** to indent the list of contents:

JRT Purebred
2000 Friendly St.
Eugene, OR 97405

New Product
The JRT Purebred Kennel has created a blend of dog food for the small, energetic dog. Our new brand, "1st Choice," is recommended by vets.

Contents
   - lamb
   - rice
   - garlic
   - extra vitamins and minerals

Your dog will need only 1/2 cup per serving for a complete balanced diet.

Information
For more information, check our new Web site at http://www.jrt.com/dogfood.html.

Depending on how the AutoFormat As You Type options are set on your computer (see the pointer box "Formatting As You Type"), Word may format some of this text as you type it.

2. Choose **Format | AutoFormat**.

3. Check the document type box to be sure it is set to **General document**.

4. Make sure the **AutoFormat now** option is selected.

5. Click **OK**.

Word will format your document. Sample results are shown in Figure 5.9, but your results may be different, depending on the AutoFormat options that are in effect.

6. Save the document as **Dog Food** and then close it.

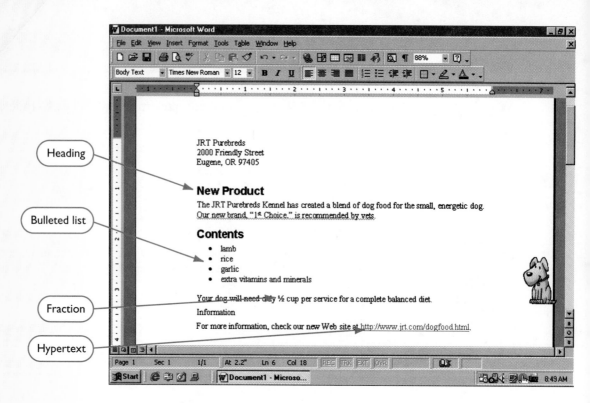

FIGURE 5.9 The AutoFormatted Document

TASK 6 | *Creating Bulleted and Numbered Lists*

What: Create lists with bullets and numbers.

How: Choose Format | Bullets and Numbering or click the Bullets or Numbering button on the Formatting toolbar.

Why: You can make information easier to read by placing it in a list.

Tip: To remove one bullet or number from a bulleted or numbered list, click between the bullet and the text or the number and the text, and then press the Backspace key. The bullet or number will disappear. A numbered list will renumber. To remove the indent, press Backspace again.

Any list in a Word document can easily be formatted automatically with numbers or **bullets**, small icons or other characters at the beginning of each line. You can use the feature either before or after you type, and the easiest method is to use the toolbar buttons.

To create a bulleted or numbered list as you type:

1. Click the Bullets or Numbering button on the Formatting toolbar.
2. Type the text, pressing Enter after each item in the list.

3. At the end of the list, click the toolbar button again to turn off the feature, and continue typing the document.

To place bullets or numbers in existing text:

1. Place each item in the list in a separate paragraph.
2. Select the list.
3. Click the Bullets or Numbering button.

To change a bulleted list to a numbered list or a numbered list to a bulleted list:

1. Select the list.
2. Click the button for the type of list you want.

To remove bullets or numbers from a list:

1. Select the list.
2. Click the button for the formatting you want to remove.

To change the bullet or number style (see figure 5.10):

1. Choose Format | Bullets and Numbering to open the Bullets and Numbering dialog box.
2. Select the appropriate tab, click the box that displays the style you want to use, and then click OK.

The style you choose is used thereafter for all lists you create using the toolbar buttons. To change the style again, you must use the dialog box. If you get un-expected results in a lab or on a shared computer, check the dialog box to change the bullet.

POINTER

Wrong Numbers?

If you are creating several numbered lists in a document, you may find that they start with the wrong number. That is, a list you want to start at 1 continues from the preceding list, or a list you want to continue from the preceding list starts with 1. To correct the error, select the incorrectly numbered list, choose Format | Bullets and Numbering | Numbered tab, and select the option button to *Restart numbering* or *Continue previous list*.

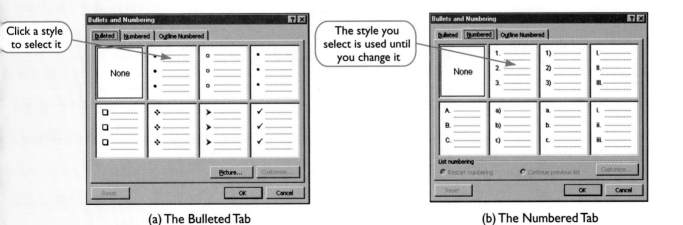

(a) The Bulleted Tab　　　　　　　　(b) The Numbered Tab

FIGURE 5.10　The Bullets and Numbering Dialog Box

Figure 5.11 shows a document containing a multilevel list with both bullets and numbers. To create a multilevel bulleted or numbered list:

1. Turn on bullets or numbers.
2. Type the list.
3. To indent a subtopic, press the Tab key or the Increase Indent button on the Formatting toolbar. Word will automatically use a different bullet or numbering style for the subtopic.
4. To return to the previous level of the list, press Shift+Tab or click the Decrease Indent button on the Formatting toolbar.

You can also use the Tab key or the toolbar buttons to change the level of an item in an existing list.

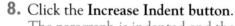

EXERCISE 6 | *Creating Bulleted and Numbered Lists*

1. Open a new blank document.

2. Type the following text:

> Jack Russell terrier pups ready to be sold:
> Eight-week-old females
> Black and white
> Brown and white
> Eight-week-old male, tan and black
> Twelve-week-old male, white
> Twelve-week-old female, brown, tan, and white
> We also have a litter that will be ready in about a month. It includes:
> Female, black and white
> Female, tan
> Three males, brown and white

3. Select the list of puppies, starting with **Eight-week-old females** and ending with **Twelve-week-old female**.

4. Click the **Numbering button**.
The list is formatted with numbers.

5. Place the insertion point at the beginning of the second line of the list (**Black and white**).

6. Press the **Tab key**.
The paragraph is indented and the numbering character changes.

7. Place the insertion point at the beginning of the third line of the list (**Brown and white**).

8. Click the **Increase Indent button**.
The paragraph is indented and the numbering character changes.

9. Select the **last three lines** of the document.

10. Choose **Format | Bullets and Numbering**.

11. Select the **Bulleted tab**.

12. Select a bullet style, and click **OK**.

The last three lines are formatted as a bulleted list. Your document should look like the one in Figure 5.11.

13. Print the document.

14. Close the document without saving it.

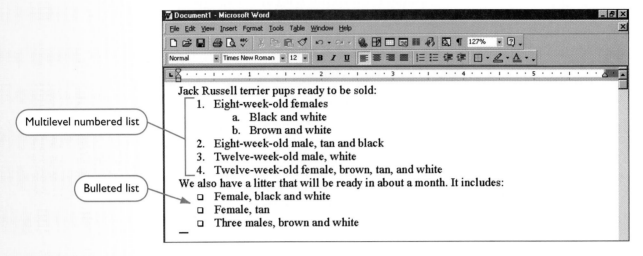

FIGURE **5.11**   The Document with Bulleted and Numbered Lists

---

TASK 7 | *Using Borders and Shading*

What: Emphasize text by placing a border around it and adding shading.

How: Choose Format | Borders and Shading or click the Borders button on the Formatting toolbar.

Why: You can create professional-looking documents by placing text in a shaded box.

Tip: Select a light color for shading over text so that it doesn't interfere with the readability of the document.

You can set off a word or group of words, a line of text, a paragraph or a group of paragraphs, or a whole page by placing it in a border. You can also apply shading to text or add shading to the area inside a border.

To place a border around a paragraph:

1. Place the insertion point any place in the paragraph or select multiple paragraphs.
2. Click the Borders button's down arrow to open the menu in Figure 5.12a.
3. Select a border.

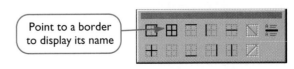

(a) The Drop-down Borders Menu

FIGURE **5.12**   Using Borders and Shading

The paragraph or selected paragraphs will be formatted with the selected border, and the menu will close.

To place a border around a word, a group of words, or a line of text:
1. Select the text.
2. Click the Borders button's down arrow and click the Outside Border button (or the button for any side, such as Left or Top).

The selected text will be surrounded by a border.

To customize a border, add a border to a page, or apply shading, use the Borders and Shading dialog box, which opens when you choose Format | Borders and Shading. Figure 5.12b shows the dialog box's Borders tab.

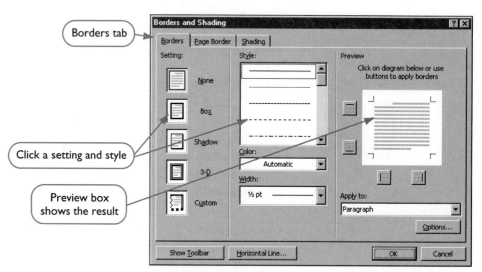

(b) The Borders and Shading Dialog Box's Borders Tab

FIGURE **5.12** Using Borders and Shading *(continued)*

To use the dialog box to place a border around text:
1. Place the insertion point in the paragraph or on the page or select the text.
2. Choose Format | Borders and Shading and then select the Borders tab to place a border around text, or the Page Borders tab to place a border around a page.
3. Change the style, color, width, and effects (such as 3-D or shadow), or create a custom border. Notice the preview section of the dialog box displays the options you select.

4. Click the borders in the Preview box or the buttons surrounding the box to turn the selected border on or off.

5. Click OK to apply the border to selected text or a paragraph. For a Page border, click the *Apply to* box's down arrow and choose one of the options: *Whole document*; *This section*; *This section - First page only*; and *This Section - All except first page*. (You will learn more about document sections in Unit 6.)

6. Click OK to apply the border and close the dialog box.

To place shading behind text:

1. Select the text or paragraphs to be shaded.

2. Choose Format | Borders and Shading to open the Borders and Shading dialog box, and select the Shading tab (shown in Figure 5.12c).

3. Select a Fill option from the palette. The box to the right of the palette will display the name of the selection and the preview section will display the results.

4. In the Pattern section (if you want a pattern), click the Style box's down arrow and select a style, then click the Color box's down arrow to select a color for the pattern.

5. Click the *Apply to* box's down arrow and make a selection.

6. Click OK.

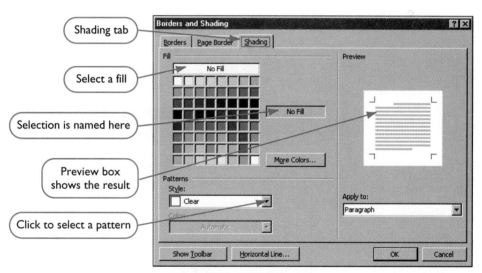

(c) The Borders and Shading Dialog Box's Shading Tab

FIGURE 5.12   Using Borders and Shading *(continued)*

EXERCISE 7 | *Using Borders and Shading*

1. Open the **JRT History** document.

2. Place the insertion point in the first paragraph and click the **Borders button's down arrow**.

   The Borders menu drops down, displaying buttons for the borders you can use. If you point to a button, a ScreenTip will show its name.

3. Click the **Outside Border button**.

The first paragraph is enclosed in a single outside border, and the menu closes. The Outside Border button is now displayed on the toolbar.

4. Place the insertion point in the second paragraph.

5. Click the **Borders button**.

A single outside border is applied to this paragraph.

6. Place the insertion point in the third paragraph.

7. Choose **Format | Borders and Shading**.

8. Make sure the **Borders tab** is selected.

9. Scroll in the **Style list box** and select one of the **dark three-line borders** that appear midway down the list.

10. In the **Setting section**, click **Shadow**.

11. Click the **Shading tab**.

12. In the **Fill section**, select the **Gray – 10% shading** (third from the left in the top row).

The name of the shading is shown in a box in the Fill section. The Preview section shows the result of the selections you have made.

13. Click **OK**.

The dialog box closes, and the paragraph has a fancy border, a shadow, and shading. Your document should look like the one in Figure 5.13.

14. Print the document.

15. Close the document without saving it.

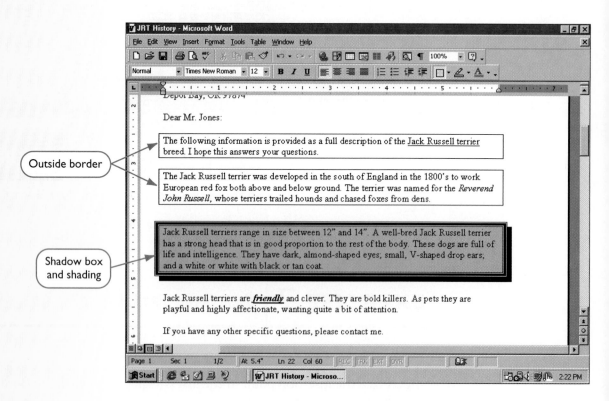

FIGURE 5.13 The Document with Borders and Shading

TASK 8 | *Including Special Symbols*

What: Use symbols that are not on the keyboard.

How: Choose Insert | Symbol.

Why: Not all characters that you may want to use are on the keyboard.

Tip: After you insert a symbol into your document, select it to use the toolbar's Font Size box to change its font size.

You may want to include such symbols as the trademark symbol ™, the copyright symbol ©, or the registered symbol ® in a document, and these are not available on your keyboard.

To include these and other symbols:

1. Place the insertion point where you want the symbol to appear.
2. Choose Insert | Symbol. The Symbols tab of the Symbol dialog box opens, as shown in Figure 5.14.
3. Click a symbol to select it and enlarge it for easier viewing.
4. Click the Insert button to place it in your document.
5. Click the Close button to close the dialog box.

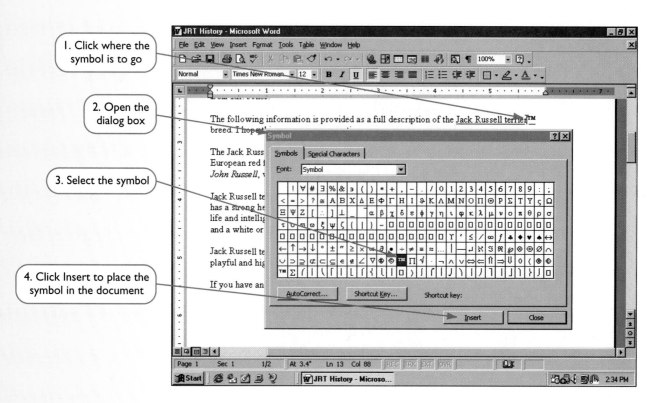

FIGURE 5.14 Inserting a Symbol in a Document

Once a symbol has been placed in your document, it can be edited like any other text; that is, you can delete it, copy it, cut it, change its color and size, and so forth.

Can't Find a Symbol

To display more symbols, choose a different font in the Symbol dialog box. Click the Font box's down arrow to display a list of fonts on your system. The Symbol, Wingdings, and Webdings fonts are good places to look. To find accented letters, such as the *é* in *résumé*, choose the font listed as *normal text*.

EXERCISE 8 | *Inserting Symbols*

1. Open the **JRT History** document.
2. Place the insertion point immediately after the word **terrier** in the first paragraph.
3. Choose **Insert | Symbol**.
   The Symbol dialog box opens.
4. Make sure the **Symbols tab** is selected.
5. If necessary, click the down arrow for the **Font box** and select the **Symbol** font.
6. Click the ™ **symbol**, as shown in Figure 5.14.
   The symbol is selected and enlarged.
7. Click the **Insert button**.
   The symbol is placed in the document.
8. Click the **Close button**.
   The dialog box closes.
9. Print the document.
10. Close the document without saving it.

SUMMARY

After completing this unit, you should
- be able to format text using built-in styles (page 108)
- know how to use AutoCorrect (page 110)
- be able to edit AutoCorrect entries (page 111)
- be able to use AutoText (page 113)
- know how to use AutoFormat (page 117)
- be able to create bulleted and numbered lists (page 120)
- be able to format with borders and shading (page 123)
- know how to include special symbols in documents (page 127)

KEY TERMS

AutoComplete (page 110)
AutoCorrect (page 110)
AutoText (page 113)

boilerplate text (page 114)
bullets (page 120)
style (page 108)

TEST YOUR SKILLS

True/False

1. Styles are built-in corrections to common typing errors.
2. Your document can include characters that are not on your keyboard.
3. AutoText stores boilerplate text.
4. You can place a border around paragraphs and pages.
5. You can add your own text to the AutoCorrect feature so that text will be automatically replaced as you type.

Multiple Choice

1. Styles
   a. appear on the File | New menu
   b. format text
   c. automatically correct common typing errors
   d. all of these answers

2. Borders and shading
   a. place numbers before a list
   b. place bullets before a list
   c. place lines and colors around paragraphs
   d. all of these answers

3. AutoCorrect
   a. corrects typing errors
   b. places a red wavy line under errors
   c. places alternatives in a yellow box
   d. can't be edited

4. To place a paragraph of often used text in a document, you would use
   a. AutoCorrect
   b. AutoText
   c. AutoPaste
   d. AutoImport

5. To insert the copyright symbol into a document, you would
   a. type it
   b. choose Insert | Symbol
   c. choose Insert | AutoText
   d. all of these answers

Short Answer

Fill in the menu choices necessary to complete the tasks:

1. Add a symbol: _____
2. Add a border: _____
3. Add a bulleted list: _____
4. Add selected text to the AutoText list: _____
5. Add a border around a page: _____

What Does This Do?

Write a brief description of the function of the following.

1.		6.	
2.	Normal	7.	AutoFormat now
3.	TM	8.	Gray - 10% shading
4.		9.	
5.		10.	Restart numbering

On Your Own

1. Open a document and apply the various built-in styles to text so that you are familiar with Word's styles.
2. Open a document and insert various characters not available from the keyboard.
3. Open a document and apply borders and shading to various parts of the document so that you are familiar with these options.
4. Open a document and insert AutoText and add your own text to Auto-Correct. Use these two features so that you understand the difference between them.
5. Open a document and use the AutoFormat feature to format the document. Check the AutoFormat As You Type dialog box so that you are familiar with this option also.

PROJECTS

1. a. Open the **Computer Sales** document and make the editing changes shown below.
   b. Save the document and print it.

Maker	Suite Name	Version
Corel	Corel® WordPerfect® Suite	8
IBM	Lotus® SmartSuite	Millennium
Microsoft	Microsoft® Office	2000
© Your Name		

2. a. Open the **Y2K** document and place a border around the document.
   b. Place the title in another border and shade the area within the border.
   c. Save the document and print it.

3. a. Open the **eCom** document. Remove the hanging indents from the last four paragraphs and make the four paragraphs a bulleted list.
   b. Save the document and print it.
   c. Change the bulleted list to a numbered list. Print the document.

4. a. Create the document shown on the following page, formatting it with styles as indicated.
   b. Save the document as **Computer Parts**. Print the document.

Personal Computers *<heading 1>*
Computer Systems *<heading 2>*
Computer systems are made up of several categories of hardware devices.
Input Devices *<heading 2>*
Input devices are the hardware devices used to get information into the computer. The most common types of input devices are:

- keyboard
- mouse
- joystick
- track ball
- microphone
- touch screen
- scanner

Output Devices *<heading 2>*
Output devices are hardware devices that display the computer information for the user. Some of the most common output devices are:

- monitor
- printer
- speakers

Storage *<heading 2>*
Storage devices permanently store files. These files are the programs or the data created using programs. The most common storage devices are:

- floppy disks
- hard disks
- CD-ROM
- tapes

System Unit *<heading 2>*
The unit or box that is the heart or brain of the system contains several parts.
Motherboard *<heading 3>*
The *motherboard* is the main system board inside the system unit. It contains the circuitry that connects everything in the system together.
Microprocessor *<heading 3>*
The *microprocessor* is the silicon chip that actually runs the system. *Pentium II* is the name of one of the most advanced microchips for the personal computer.
Random Access Memory—RAM *<heading 3>*
Random Access Memory, called **RAM**, is a memory location that stores programs and data while you are working on the computer. When the computer is shut down, the information in RAM is emptied.

Formatting Pages and Enhancing Documents

UNIT OBJECTIVES

- Insert breaks
- Change page margins
- Insert page numbers
- Insert headers and footers
- Insert footnotes
- Create a table
- Create a chart from table data
- Use WordArt
- Include a graphic

Word's page and section formatting features help you design and lay out multipage documents. You can change the page margins, create manual page breaks for title pages, add page numbers, headers, or footers on every page of the document to help the reader, and insert footnotes. You can also enhance the visual appeal and readability of your documents through the use of tables, charts, graphics, and WordArt. These elements set off and emphasize important information and can be used in documents of any length.

TASK 1 | *Inserting Breaks*

What: Manually insert a page or section break into a document.

How: Choose Insert | Break.

Why: Manual page breaks ensure that information will start on a new page, even if you cut or add text nearby.

Tip: Don't press Enter again and again to reach the bottom of a page; use the page break feature instead.

If you want text to start on a new page but the insertion point has not reached the bottom of the current page, you can insert a manual page break. Text you type after the page break will appear on a new page in a printout.

To insert a page break into a document:

1. Place the insertion point where you want the current page to end.
2. Choose Insert | Break. The Break dialog box opens, as shown in Figure 6.1a.
3. Make sure Page break is selected.
4. Click OK to insert a page break and close the dialog box.

When you print the document, the text after the break will begin on a new sheet of paper. On the screen, the manual break is shown by a *Page Break* mark, which can be selected like any text character. To delete the manual page break, select the mark and press Delete. Figure 6.1b shows a manual page break in Normal view.

POINTER

Ctrl+Enter

For quick insertion of a page break, you can use the key combination Ctrl+Enter to place a manual page break at the location of the insertion point.

Word allows you to create sections in your longer documents. Sections enable you to change headers, footers, margins, and page numbers for a group of pages such as a chapter, instead of using the same ones for the whole document. To create a section break:

1. Place the insertion point where you want the section break.
2. Choose Insert | Break. The Break dialog box opens, as shown in Figure 6.1a.
3. Select a section break type, as shown in the Microsoft Word Help screen shown in Figure 6.1c.
4. Click OK to insert the section break and close the dialog box.

The section break appears on the screen as a *Section Break* mark.

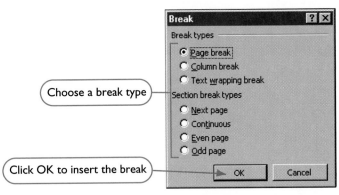

Choose a break type

Click OK to insert the break

(a) The Break Dialog Box

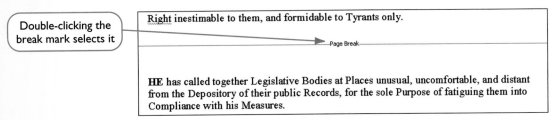

Double-clicking the break mark selects it

Right inestimable to them, and formidable to Tyrants only.

Page Break

HE has called together Legislative Bodies at Places unusual, uncomfortable, and distant from the Depository of their public Records, for the sole Purpose of fatiguing them into Compliance with his Measures.

(b) A Manual Page Break in Normal View

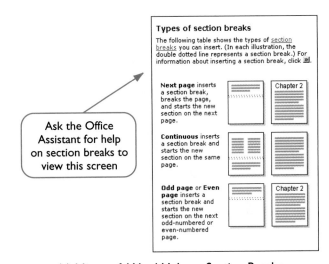

Ask the Office Assistant for help on section breaks to view this screen

(c) Microsoft Word Help on Section Breaks

FIGURE 6.1   Inserting Breaks

EXERCISE 1 | *Inserting a Break*

1. Open a new blank document in Print Layout view.
2. Type the following text, using **Center alignment** and pressing **Enter** *twice* after the last line.

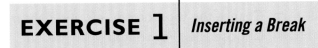

Jack Russell Terriers
Report on the Breed
Your Name

3. Choose **Insert | Break**.
The Break dialog box opens.

4. Make sure that **Page break** is selected and click **OK**.
A second page is created.

5. Save the document as **JRT Report**.

6. Click the down arrow in the **Zoom box** and select **Two Page**.
The document should look like Figure 6.2.

7. Close the document.

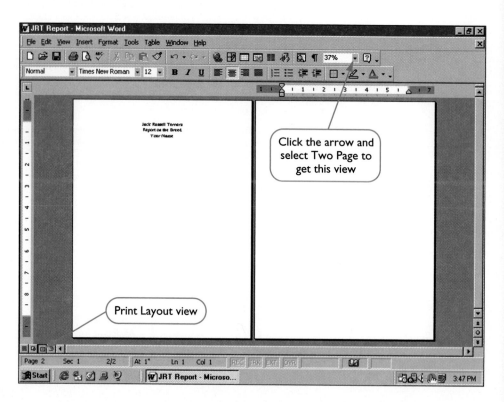

FIGURE 6.2 The *JRT Report* Document with a Manual Page Break

---

TASK 2 | *Changing the Page Margins*

What: Change the top, bottom, left, and right margins of the document.

How: Choose File | Page Setup | Margins tab.

Why: There are times when you will want to increase or decrease the amount of white space on the printed page.

Tip: Word won't let you set a margin smaller than your printer can use.

The **margins** are the white space around the edges of the text on the printed page. Word sets the top and bottom margins to 1″ and the left and right margins to 1.25″. These settings will work for many documents that you create,

but if you want more or less white space around the whole docu
change them. To change margins:

1. Choose File | Page Setup to display the Page Setup dial
2. Click the Margins tab to display it, as shown in Figure 6
3. Increase or decrease the number in the *Left, Rigl
   Bottom* boxes.
4. Choose to apply the new margins to the Whole Document or more
   Point Forward. If you select the This Point Forward option, a section
   break is placed in the document so that the new margins you set will
   not affect the margins up to the section break.
5. If you will be printing both sides of a page and binding the document,
   choose Gutter and define the amount of space to add to the binding
   edge of each page to leave room for a binding.

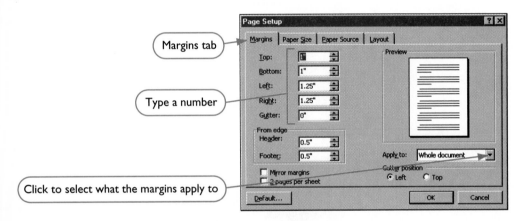

FIGURE 6.3 The Page Setup Dialog Box

POINTER

Change Margins or Indent Paragraphs?

If you need to change the left or right paragraph indents for some of
the text in a document but not all or even most of it, you should choose
Format | Paragraph and change the indents. But if you want to change
the indentation for the whole document, you should choose File | Page
Setup and change the margins.

POINTER

The Page Setup Dialog Box

Investigate the options on the tabs of the Page Setup dialog box. The
Paper Size tab lets you switch between **Portrait** and **Landscape
orientation**. (In Landscape orientation, the long edge of the paper is at
the top.)

1. Open the **JRT History** document.

For this exercise, you'll use the *JRT History* document, not the *JRT Report* document you created in Exercise 1.

2. Choose **File | Page Setup**.

The Page Setup dialog box opens.

3. Make sure the **Margins tab** is selected, and then type the following settings:

- Top: 2
- Bottom: 1.5
- Left: 2
- Right: 2

4. Click **OK**.

The dialog box closes, and the margins are changed.

5. Click the **Print Preview button** on the Standard toolbar.

Your document should look like the one in Figure 6.4.

6. Print the document and close it without saving it.

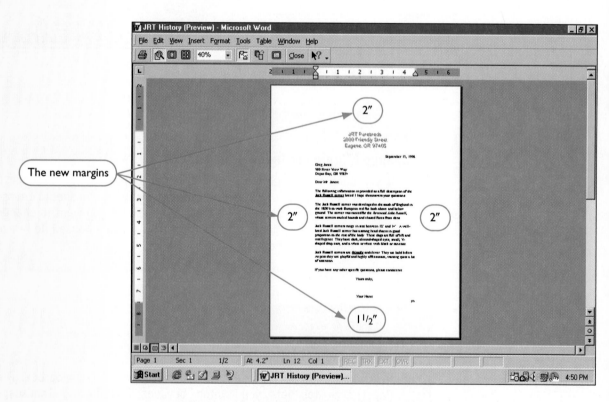

FIGURE 6.4 The *JRT History* Document with New Margins

TASK 3 | *Inserting Page Numbers*

What: Have Word automatically include page numbers on multipage documents.

How: Choose Insert | Page Numbers.

Why: Readers expect multipage documents to include page numbers for easy reference.

Tip: Don't type page numbers manually, because if you insert or delete text, the page numbers will be wrong.

You can have Word insert page numbers automatically on each page of a document. If you delete, insert, or move text, Word will automatically update the page numbering.

To add page numbers to a document:

1. Choose Insert | Page Numbers. The Page Numbers dialog box opens, as shown in Figure 6.5.
2. Choose a Position—the top or the bottom of the page.
3. Choose an Alignment—left, right, center, inside, or outside.
4. Select or clear the check box to *Show number on first page*. (You won't want a page number on the first page if it is a title page, for instance.)

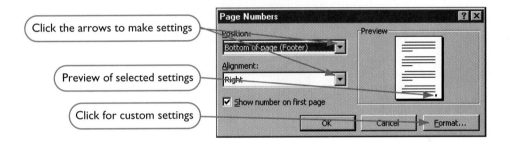

FIGURE 6.5 The Page Numbers Dialog Box

POINTER

Wrong Number?

- To change the starting number or the format of the number that is placed on the page, click the Format button on the Page Numbers dialog box. The Page Number Format dialog box opens and gives you the choice of numbering with lowercase Roman numerals, for instance.

- To number chapters or sections individually rather than consecutively, insert a section break and reset the starting number for each section.

1. Open the **JRT Report** document in **Normal view**.
In this exercise you'll use the *JRT Report* document you created in Exercise 1.

2. Choose **Insert | Page Numbers**.
The Page Numbers dialog box opens.

3. Select **Top of page (Header)** in the Position section.

4. Select **Right** in the Alignment section.

5. Check the box to **Show number on first page**.

6. Click **OK**.
The dialog box closes, and the document changes to Print Layout view, where you can see the page numbers.

7. Click the **Print Preview button** on the Standard toolbar, and switch to Multiple Pages view if necessary. The document should look like Figure 6.6.

8. Print the document, and close the document without saving it.

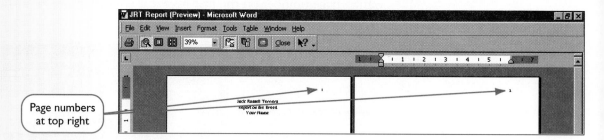

Page numbers at top right

FIGURE 6.6 The *JRT Report* Document with Page Numbers

TASK 4 | *Including Headers and Footers*

What: Place headers at the top of every page and footers at the bottom of every page of a multipage document.

How: Choose View | Header and Footer.

Why: Professional-looking reports and other long documents include headers or footers.

Tip: Placing the name of the document in the footer is a handy way to remember the file name if you have a printout. To have Word do it automatically, use the Insert AutoText button on the Header and Footer toolbar.

You can have Word automatically insert text at the top or the bottom of every page of a multipage document. Text at the top of each page is a **header**, and text at the bottom of each page is a **footer**. You can place page numbers, the date, or any other text you want in a header or footer.

To insert headers and footers into a document:

1. Choose View | Header and Footer. The document view changes to Print Layout view, the Header and Footer toolbar is displayed, a header section is displayed in the document, and the insertion point moves into it, as shown in Figure 6.7.
2. Type the text you want in the header and format it using buttons on the Formatting toolbar or the Format menu's dialog boxes.
3. Insert other items by clicking the buttons on the Header and Footer toolbar. Table 6.1 describes these buttons.
4. Click the Close button on the Header and Footer toolbar. The resulting header and footer can be viewed in Print Layout view or in Print Preview.

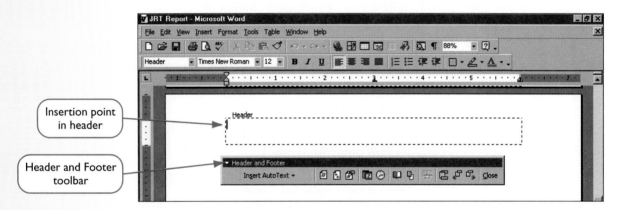

FIGURE 6.7 Viewing the Header in a Document

Button	Description
Insert AutoText ▾	Inserts predefined text; click the down arrow and select it
#	Inserts the page number
⊞	Inserts the total number of pages in a document
⊞	Opens the Page Number Format dialog box
🗓	Inserts the current date
⊘	Inserts the current time
📖	Opens the Page Setup dialog box, where you can assign different headers to odd and even pages or the first page

TABLE 6.1 Header and Footer Toolbar Buttons

🗐	Shows or hides the text in the document
📇	Uses the header or footer from the previous section of the document
🖳	Switches between the header and footer area
🗐	Shows the header or footer from the previous section
🗐	Shows the header or footer from the next section of the document
Close	Closes the Header and Footer toolbar and window

TABLE 6.1   Header and Footer Toolbar Buttons *(continued)*

- To edit a header or footer, double-click it in Print Layout view or choose View | Header and Footer, then make your changes.
- To set different headers and footers in different parts of a document, insert section breaks. You can set different headers and footers for each section.

POINTER

Header/Footer Alignment

To move header or footer text from the left margin to the center or the right margin, press the Tab key. The first time you press Tab, text will be centered, and the second time you press Tab, text will be right aligned.

EXERCISE 4 | *Inserting Headers and Footers*

1. Open the **JRT Report** document and move the insertion point to the second page.

2. Choose **View | Header and Footer**.
   The document switches to Print Layout view; the Header and Footer toolbar is displayed; a header section is displayed; and the insertion moves into it.

3. Press the **Tab key** *twice*, and type your **last name**.
   The text you type aligns with the right margin. (You can see a Right tab in the horizontal ruler.)

4. Click the **Switch between Header and Footer button** on the Header and Footer toolbar.
   The footer section is displayed, and the insertion point moves into it.

5. Type **Page** and press the **Spacebar**.

 6. Click the **Insert page number button** on the Header and Footer toolbar.
A code is inserted that will print the correct page number on each page, even if text is added or deleted.

7. Press the **Spacebar**, type **of**, and press the **Spacebar**.

 8. Press the **Insert number of pages button** on the Header and Footer toolbar.
A code is inserted that will print the number of the last page of the document.

9. Press the **Tab key** *twice*.

 10. Click the **Insert date button** on the Header and Footer toolbar.
A code is inserted that will print the current date, which is taken from the computer's clock.

11. Click the **Close button** on the Header and Footer toolbar.

12. Preview the document.
Your document should look like the one in Figure 6.8.

13. Click the document with the **magnifying pointer** so that you can read the header and footer.

14. Save the document and print it.

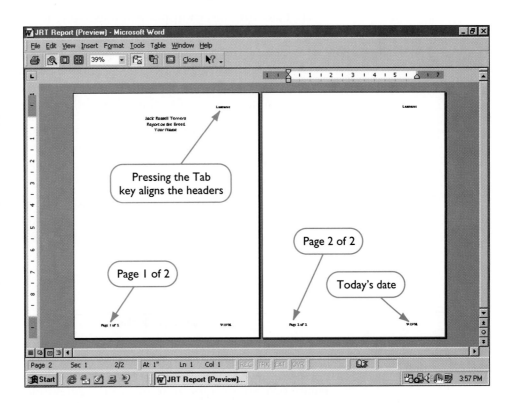

FIGURE 6.8 The *JRT Report* Document with Headers and Footers

TASK 5 | *Including Footnotes*

What: Credit the source of quotations at the bottom of the page by creating a footnote.

How: Choose Insert | Footnote.

Why: When you use material that someone else created, you need to give proper credit, and a footnote is a standard way to do it.

Tip: Footnotes and footers are two completely different features even though they both appear at the bottom of the page.

When you include a quotation in a document or when you want to supply the reader with extra information, you can easily create a **footnote**. Footnotes are used extensively in research to cite sources. The footnote feature performs two tasks:

1. It places a superscript reference number at the location of the insertion point in the document.
2. It places the reference number a second time at the foot of the page, followed by text you type.

To create a footnote:

1. Place the insertion point immediately following the text you want to reference.
2. Choose Insert | Footnote to open the Footnote and Endnote dialog box.
3. Check that the Footnote and AutoNumber option buttons are selected, and click OK. A superscript reference number is placed at the insertion point and the display changes as follows:

   - In Normal view, a footnote window opens at the bottom of the screen, where the reference number is repeated. The insertion point moves to this line, ready for you to type the footnote's contents, as seen in Figure 6.9a.

   - In Print Layout view, a separator line is placed at the foot of the page, the reference number is repeated there, and the insertion point moves just after the number, ready for you to type the footnote's contents.

4. Type the text for the footnote.
5. To return to the document:

   - In Normal view, click the Close button in the Footnote window.
   - In Print Layout view, double-click the footnote reference number, or just click back in the text.

Figure 6.9b shows a footnote in Print Preview. Note the separator line above the footnote.

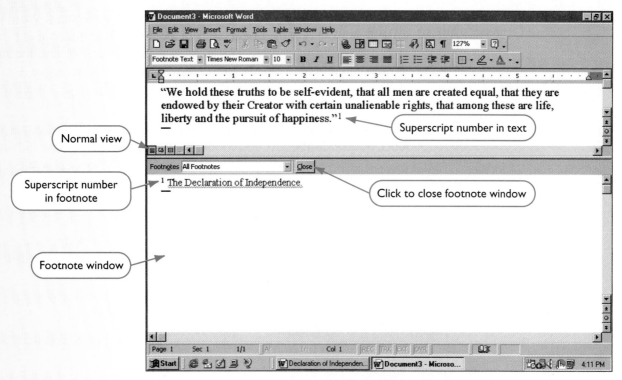

Normal view

Superscript number in text

Superscript number in footnote

Click to close footnote window

Footnote window

(a) Inserting a Footnote in Normal View

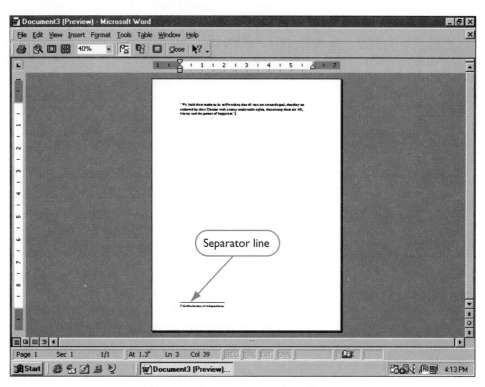

Separator line

(b) Viewing the Footnote in Print Preview

FIGURE **6.9**   Inserting a Footnote

To create other footnotes in the same document, repeat these steps. Word will number the new footnotes in the proper order, whether they precede or follow earlier footnotes. Because Word automatically keeps track of the footnote numbers, you can add or delete footnotes as necessary without renumbering.

Once you have created a footnote, it's easy to edit, view, or delete it:

- To edit a footnote, choose View | Footnotes, or double-click the footnote reference number in the text. In Normal view the footnote window will open; in Print Layout view the insertion point will jump to the foot of the page.
- To quickly view a footnote's contents while in the text, point to the footnote reference number and a ScreenTip will display the footnote text, but without character formatting.
- To delete a footnote, select the superscript number in the body of the document and press Delete. Both the reference and the footnote will be deleted. (Selecting the footnote doesn't work.)

POINTER

Endnotes

Some research paper styles call for endnotes instead of footnotes. **Endnotes** are notes that appear at the end of the document instead of at the foot of the page. If you know how to insert footnotes, you will have no trouble inserting endnotes: just select Endnotes instead of Footnotes in the Footnote and Endnote dialog box. Most style manuals specify that endnotes begin on a new page. To accomplish this, insert a manual page break before the first note.

EXERCISE 5 | *Inserting a Footnote*

1. Open a new blank document in Normal view.
2. Type the following text, including the quotation marks:

"Work consists of whatever a body is obliged to do. Play consists of whatever a body is not obliged to do."

3. Place the insertion point after the last quotation mark.
4. Choose **Insert | Footnote**.
   The Footnote and Endnote dialog box opens.
5. Check that the **Footnote** and **AutoNumber option buttons** are selected in the dialog box, and then click **OK**.
   The dialog box closes; a superscript number 1 is placed at the position of the insertion point; a footnote window opens at the bottom of the screen; a superscript number 1 is placed there; and the insertion point moves after the number, ready for you to type.

6. In the Footnote window, following the superscript number, type **Mark Twain, *The Adventures of Tom Sawyer* (1876), Chapter 2**.

7. Press the footnote window's **Close button**.

8. Click the **Print Layout View button** on the horizontal scroll bar.
   In Print Layout view, the footnote is visible at the foot of the page.

9. Click the **Print Preview button** on the Standard toolbar.
   This view shows the footnote in place, too. Notice that Word automatically inserts a short horizontal line to separate the body text from the footnote.

10. Print the document, and close it without saving it.

TASK 6 | *Inserting a Table*

What: Place information in a table.

How: Choose Table | Insert | Table or use the Insert Table button on the Standard toolbar.

Why: Word's table feature helps you organize rows and columns of text, numbers, and even graphic images.

Tip: Use tables instead of setting tab stops for most information that will appear in columns and rows. Tables are easier to set up and easier to use.

Word's tables feature lets you set up tables in a document and then type text or numbers or insert images into the cells. You can format the table yourself or use one of several built-in formats. Tables are made up of **columns** and **rows**, and the intersection of a column and row is called a **cell**. Tables look like an electronic spreadsheet with the columns running vertically and the rows running horizontally.

To create a table:

1. Place the insertion point in the document where you want the table to appear.

2. Choose Table | Insert | Table. The Insert Table dialog box opens, as shown in Figure 6.10a.

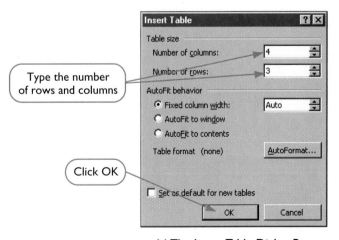

(a) The Insert Table Dialog Box

FIGURE **6.10**   Creating a Table

3. Type the number of columns and rows.
4. Click OK. The dialog box closes, and the blank table is placed in the document, as shown in Figure 6.10b.

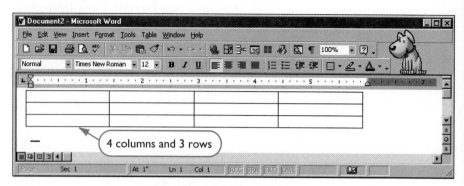

(b) The Blank Table in the Document

FIGURE **6.10**   Creating a Table *(continued)*

To enter information in a table, click in a cell and type. If the text you type is longer than the cell, the row will automatically expand to accommodate it, and the text will wrap to the next line.

To move the insertion point to another cell:

• Click in a cell.
• Press the Tab key to move forward one cell.
• Press Shift+Tab to move backward one cell.

To add a row at the bottom of the table:

1. Place the insertion point in the cell at the bottom right of the table.
2. Press the Tab key.

To have Word automatically format the table:

1. Place the insertion point in the table.
2. Choose Table | Table AutoFormat to open the Table AutoFormat dialog box, shown in Figure 6.10c.
3. Select a format from the list.
4. View the format in the Preview section of the dialog box.
5. Click OK, and the table will be formatted.

To delete the entire table from the document, choose Table | Delete | Table, and both the table and the contents w\ill be deleted.

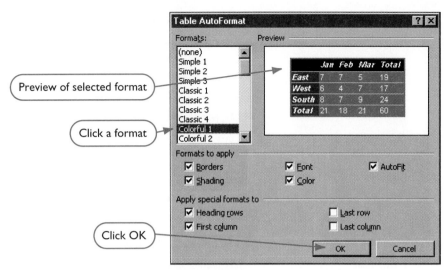

Preview of selected format

Click a format

Click OK

(c) The Table AutoFormat Dialog Box

FIGURE **6.10**   Creating a Table *(continued)*

POINTER

Editing Tables

You can merge cells, split cells apart, add and delete columns and rows, and perform many other actions. With the Tables and Borders toolbar, you can draw elaborate tables and format them in numerous ways. Search Help for advanced Table features.

EXERCISE 6 | *Inserting a Table*

1. Open a new blank document.

2. Type **Number of Dogs Sold in the First Quarter** and press **Enter** *twice.*
This paragraph will be the table title.

3. Choose **Table | Insert | Table**.
The Insert Table dialog box opens.

4. In the Table size section, set the **Number of columns** to **4** and the **Number of rows** to **3**, and then click **OK**.
Type the numbers or use the increment arrows. When you click OK, the dialog box closes, and the table appears in the document.

5. Choose **Table | AutoFormat Table**. The Table AutoFormat dialog box opens.

6. In the **Formats list**, choose **Colorful 1**, and click **OK**.
The table is formatted. The insertion point is blinking in the top left cell.

7. Press the **Tab key** to move to column 2.

8. Type **Jan**, press **Tab**; type **Feb**, press **Tab**; type **Mar**, press **Tab**.
   Pressing Tab in the last cell of a row moves the insertion point to the next row.

9. Type **Females**, press **Tab**; type **12**, press **Tab**; type **16**, press **Tab**; type **18**, press **Tab**.

10. Type **Males**, press **Tab**; type **14**, press **Tab**; type **10**, press **Tab**; type **12**.
    The completed table should look like Figure 6.11.

11. Save the document as **Sales**, print it, and leave it open to use in the next exercise.

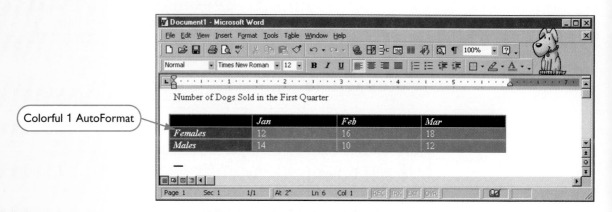

FIGURE 6.11 The Completed Table

TASK 7 | *Creating a Chart from Table Data*

What: Create a chart from information in a table.

How: Insert | Picture | Chart.

Why: Word's charts are simple, attractive, and easy to understand.

Tip: Make sure the data you type in the table is correct, so that the chart will be a picture of accurate data.

To create a chart from a Word table, use the built-in application named Microsoft Graph. Using this application is easy, but you must create the table so that Word knows what is text, what is numbers, and where to put each of them in a chart. You do this by following some simple rules, which you already used to create the table in the previous exercise:

- Place text labels in the top row and left column.
- Place only numbers in the remaining cells of the table.

Word uses the text in the first row as labels under the chart on its **x axis**. Word uses the text in the first column as the **legend** explaining what the data in a chart represent.

To create a chart from a table:

1. Select the table.
2. Choose Insert | Picture | Chart. The screen changes to show the Graph menu bar and toolbar within the Word window; the chart is created and displayed in the Word document; and a separate Datasheet window opens. You can click in a cell of the Datasheet window and add or change the chart data. This is shown in Figure 6.12.

   - While the chart is activated, you can edit it, format it, and change the chart type by using buttons on the Graph toolbar.

   - If you open Help while the chart is activated, the help displayed will be for the Microsoft Graph program. Use this help for more information on the program, including the use of the toolbar buttons.

3. To accept the chart, deactivate it, and return to the document window with the Word toolbars, click outside the chart.

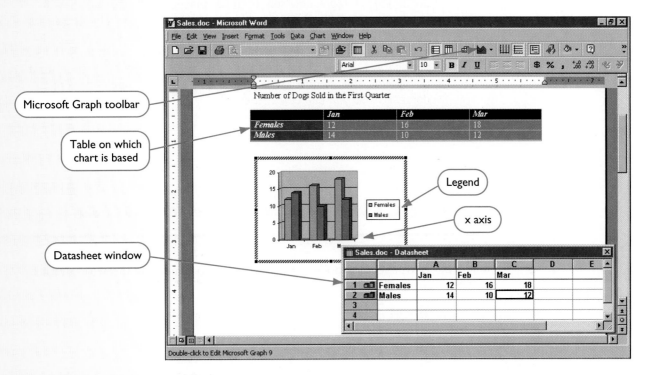

FIGURE 6.12 Creating a Chart with Microsoft Graph

POINTER

Moving and Sizing a Chart

To select a chart but not activate it for editing, click it. When a chart is selected, it has small boxes around its outer edge, called **sizing handles**. Point to a sizing handle and the pointer changes to a two-headed arrow; click and drag to resize the chart in the direction you drag. You can also delete a chart that is selected, by pressing the Delete key.

To move a chart, right-click it and choose Format Object from the shortcut menu. The Format Object dialog box opens. Click the Layout tab, select the Square wrapping style, and click OK to close the dialog box. Now when you point to the chart, the pointer changes to a four-headed arrow. Click and drag the chart to move it.

Linked and Embedded Objects

You can include objects in your Word documents that are created in other applications. This is known as Object Linking and Embedding, or **OLE** (pronounced "oh-lay"). When you use Microsoft Graph to create a chart from Word data, you are actually embedding a Microsoft Graph object in the Word document. When you double-click the chart to activate it, the Word toolbar changes to show the Microsoft Graph commands, and you are able to edit the object from within Word. The Graph chart is **embedded** in the Word document and becomes a part of it.

Suppose you had created the same sales graph in Microsoft Excel and wanted to include it in your Word document. You could embed it there, or you could choose instead to link it to the Word document (using the Insert | Object | Create from File tab). When you link an object to a Word document, a representation of it is placed in Word, along with a shortcut, or link, to its original location. Now if the original object is updated, the linked image in the Word document will be updated automatically. **Linked objects** must be edited in their original software application. If you double-click the linked object in the Word document, the source application will start and open the original document, so you can edit it there.

EXERCISE 7 | *Creating a Chart from Table Data*

1. With the *Sales* document on the screen, place the insertion point in **any cell** of the table.

2. Choose **Table | Select | Table**.
   The entire table is selected.

3. Choose **Insert | Picture | Chart**.
   The chart is created and inserted in the document; a Datasheet window opens where you can add to or change the chart data; and the menu bar and toolbar change to those for Microsoft Graph.

4. Click **outside the chart**.
   The chart is deactivated; the Datasheet window closes (see Figure 6.13); and the toolbars now show Word buttons.

5. Click **in the chart** to select it.
   The chart is surrounded by handles. You could point to it and drag it to move it, or click and drag a handle to resize the chart.

6. Save the document under the same name, and then print it and close it.

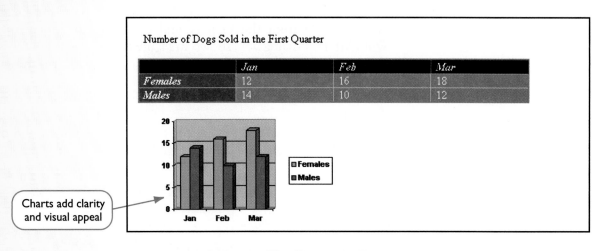

Charts add clarity and visual appeal

FIGURE 6.13 The Chart in the Document

TASK 8 | *Inserting WordArt Objects*

What: Insert a WordArt drawing object into a document.

How: Choose Insert | Picture | WordArt.

Why: You can create highly formatted text to use in titles or for special purposes with WordArt.

Tip: Don't overuse WordArt and make your documents look too busy.

If you want to create a title or heading with fancy lettering, you can use the Microsoft Office feature named WordArt.

1. To start WordArt, use one of the following methods, both of which open the WordArt Gallery shown in Figure 6.14a:

   • Choose Insert | Picture | WordArt.
   • Display the Drawing toolbar and click the Insert WordArt button.

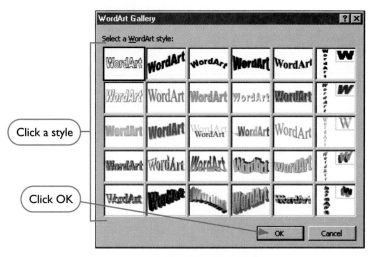

Click a style

Click OK

(a) The WordArt Gallery

FIGURE 6.14 Using WordArt

2. Select a style from the Gallery and click OK to display the Edit WordArt Text dialog box, shown in Figure 6.14b.
3. Type your text in the Text box. The text you type replaces the sample, *Your Text Here.*
4. Use the boxes and buttons on the dialog box's toolbar to format the font.
5. Click OK to insert the formatted text into the document and display the WordArt toolbar, as shown in Figure 6.14c.

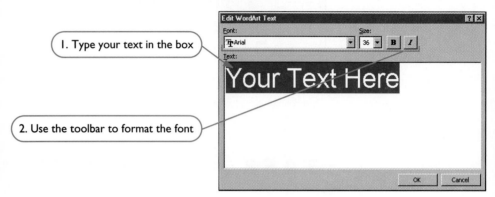

(b) The Edit WordArt Text Dialog Box

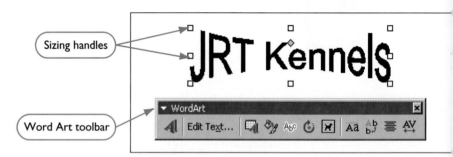

(c) The WordArt Object Selected and the WordArt Toolbar

FIGURE 6.14 Using WordArt *(continued)*

6. Fine-tune the WordArt object using the buttons on the WordArt toolbar, described in Table 6.2.
7. When the object is selected:

- Size it by clicking and dragging a sizing handle when the pointer is a two-headed arrow.
- Move it by pointing to it and dragging when the pointer is a four-headed arrow.
- Delete it by pressing Delete.

Button	Description
◢▌	Starts WordArt
Edit Text...	Opens the Edit WordArt Text dialog box
▣◢	Opens the WordArt Gallery
✎	Opens the Format WordArt dialog box
Abc	Opens the WordArt Shape dialog box
↺	Rotates the WordArt object
▦	Selects a style for wrapping text around the WordArt object
Aa	Makes all text the same height
A b b ↲	Changes the text from horizontal to vertical
≡	Changes the alignment of the WordArt object
AV ↔	Changes the spacing of characters

TABLE 6.2 WordArt Toolbar Buttons

EXERCISE 8 | *Inserting a WordArt Object*

1. Open the **Dog Food** document, which you created in Unit 5.
2. Delete the text **JRT Purebred** at the top of the document.
3. Choose **Insert | Picture | WordArt**.
   The WordArt Gallery opens.
4. Choose a **style** and click **OK**.
   The Edit WordArt Text dialog box opens with sample text selected.
5. In the Edit WordArt Text dialog box, type **JRT Kennels** in the Text box, click the down arrow in the Size box and change the font size to **16**, then click **OK**.
   The text appears in the document with sizing handles around it, and the WordArt toolbar is displayed, as shown in Figure 6.14c.
6. Move the WordArt to the **top of the document** above the address.
   Point to the WordArt; when the pointer is a four-sided arrow, click and drag it to a new position.

7. Size the WordArt as appropriate.
Point to a sizing handle; when the pointer is a two-sided arrow, click and drag the handle to resize the art.

8. Click the **Format WordArt button** on the WordArt toolbar.
The Format WordArt dialog box opens.

9. Click the **Color and Lines tab** of the dialog box.
The current settings are shown.

10. In the **Fill section**, click the down arrow for the **Color box**.
A palette of color opens.

11. Select **Red**.

12. In the **Line section**, click the down arrow for the **Color box** and select **Black**.

13. Click **OK**.
The dialog box closes and the formatting is applied.

14. Click **outside the WordArt object**.
The WordArt object is deselected, and the WordArt toolbar closes. Your document should look similar to Figure 6.15.

15. Save the document under the same name, print it, and leave it open to use in the next exercise.

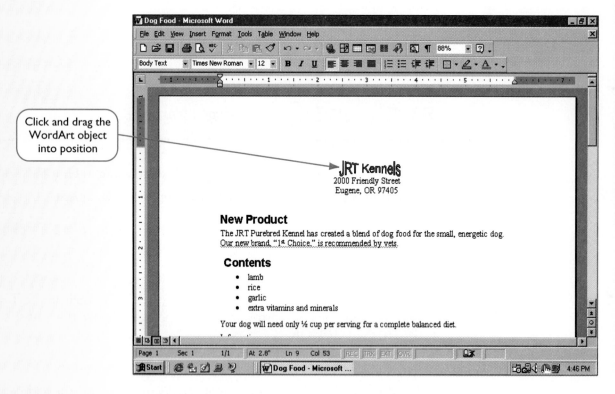

Click and drag the WordArt object into position

FIGURE 6.15   The *Dog Food* Document with a WordArt Object

TASK 9 | *Inserting a Graphic*

What: Insert a graphic image into a document.
How: Choose Insert | Picture | Clip Art.
Why: You can add interest to your documents by including graphics.
Tip: If you want additional clipart images free from Microsoft, you can click the Clips Online button in the ClipArt dialog box. You will be connected to http://www.microsoft.com/clipartgallerylive.

Images can add impact to your documents. Where can you find images to use? You can

- use images that come bundled with Microsoft Office
- create your own images in a drawing program
- scan images on a scanner
- buy collections of images on compact disks
- take digital photographs for use in a document
- find libraries of images on the World Wide Web (see the tip above)

To insert an image into a document:

1. Move the insertion point to the location where you want a clipart image to appear.
2. Choose Insert | Picture | ClipArt to display the Insert ClipArt dialog box shown in Figure 6.16a.
3. Choose a category.
4. Select an image in that category.
5. Click the Insert clip button (as shown in Figure 6.16b) and then close the dialog box. The image will be placed in the document.

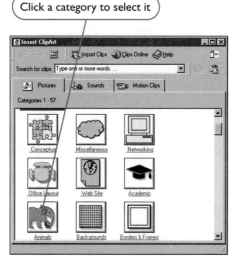

(a) Choosing a Category   (b) Inserting a Selected Image

FIGURE 6.16 The Insert ClipArt Dialog Box

To move, size, or delete the object, click it to select it and then:

- Click inside it and drag to move it.
- Click and drag a sizing handle to resize it.
- Press the Delete key to delete it.
- Click outside it to deselect it.

When a picture is selected, the Picture toolbar is displayed. You can use the Picture toolbar to make certain changes in the image. Point to any button on the toolbar and a ScreenTip tells you its name.

POINTER

Images in Tables

You can include images in tables, such as photographs of employees or pictures of inventory items in a catalog. Place the insertion point in the desired cell before inserting the picture.

EXERCISE 9 | *Inserting Clip Art*

1. With the *Dog Food* document open on the screen, press **Ctrl+Home**.
   The insertion point moves to the top of the document.

2. Choose **Insert | Picture | Clip Art**.
   The ClipArt dialog box opens.

3. Make sure the **Pictures tab** is selected, and then click **Animals** in the category list.
   The list changes to show the clipart images available in this category.

4. Click any **clipart image**.
   A toolbar opens.

5. Click the **Insert clip button** and then close the Insert ClipArt dialog box.
   The image is inserted into your document.

6. Click the **clipart image**.
   The image is selected and surrounded by sizing handles.

7. Point to the **bottom right handle** and drag the two-headed pointer.
   The image is resized.

8. If the Picture toolbar is not displayed, right-click the document and select **Show Picture Toolbar**.

9. Click the toolbar's **Text Wrapping button**, and select **Square**.
   Experiment with different wrapping styles if you like. They specify how text will surround the image.

10. Click and drag to move the image above the text **New Product**. Your document should look similar to the one in Figure 6.17 (you probably have a different image).

11. Save the document under the same name and print it.

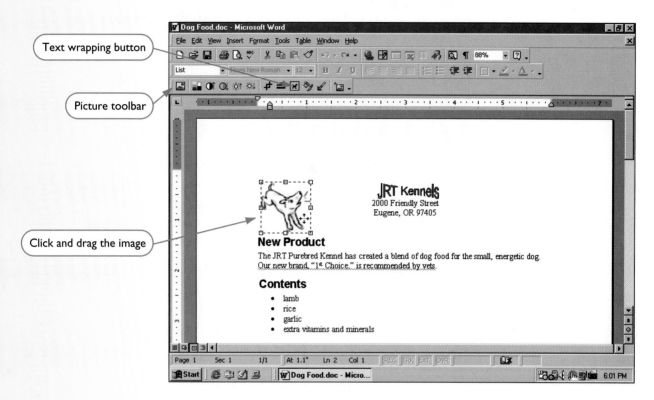

Text wrapping button

Picture toolbar

Click and drag the image

FIGURE 6.17 Dragging the Clip Art into Position

REVIEW

SUMMARY

After completing this unit, you should

- be able to insert breaks (page 134)
- be able to change page margins (page 136)
- know how to insert page numbers (page 139)
- be able to include headers and footers (page 140)
- know how to footnote references (page 144)
- know how to include tables (page 147)
- be able to create charts from tables (page 150)
- be able to use WordArt (page 153)
- be able to include graphics (page 157)

KEY TERMS

cell (page 147)

column (page 147)

embedded object (page 152)

endnote (page 146)

footer (page 141)

footnote (page 144)

header (page 141)

legend (page 150)

landscape orientation (page 137)

linked object (page 152)

margin (page 136)

OLE (object linking and
  embedding) (page 152)

portrait orientation (page 137)

row (page 147)

sizing handles (page 151)

x axis (page 150)

TEST YOUR SKILLS

True/False

1. A header is text that appears at the top of the page.
2. The footer feature places a superscript number in the text.
3. You should always number your own pages because Word doesn't keep track of them.
4. Word automatically renumbers footnotes when you insert or delete them.
5. Graphics can't be moved but they can be sized.

Multiple Choice

1. To start a new page, you would
   a. press the Enter key numerous times
   b. press Ctrl+Insert
   c. choose Insert | Break
   d. choose Insert | New Blank

2. Footnotes
   a. appear at the top or bottom of the page
   b. cite references or provide extra information for the reader
   c. are never numbered
   d. can't be deleted because of automatic numbering

3. A footer
   a. appears at the bottom of the page
   b. can contain the page number
   c. can contain the current date
   d. all of these answers

4. Sizing handles
   a. appear around ClipArt images
   b. appear around WordArt objects
   c. appear around charts
   d. all of these answers

5. Charts
   a. use the labels to plot data
   b. use numbers to plot data
   c. use numbers in the legend
   d. all of these answers

Short Answers

1. The footnote reference number appears formatted as _____.
2. The _____ describes the data in the chart.
3. _____ make numbers in tables more understandable.
4. You probably don't want a page number on the first page of a document if it is a _____ page.
5. If you want to start typing on a new page in a document, you can insert a _____ _____.

What Does This Do?

Write a brief description of the function of the following:

1.	◢		6.	Ctrl+Enter
2.	⊞		7.	⊞ Insert Table.
3.	▣		8.	▣
4.	▣		9.	▣
5.	▣ Clip Art.		10.	⋯Section Break (Next Page)⋯

On Your Own

1. Create a table that includes labels across the top and down the first column. Place numbers in the rest of the table. Format the table.
2. Use the table you created in #1 and create a chart. Use Word Help to learn more about Microsoft Graph, and experiment with different chart types and formats.
3. Open a document, change the margins, and insert page breaks. Place a header and a footer that includes the page numbers in the multipage document.

4. Open a document and insert a piece of clip art. Move it to the desired position and size it. If you have access to the World Wide Web, use the Clips Online button to link to Microsoft's Clipart Gallery. Download a new graphic.
5. Use WordArt to create an invitation, announcement, or some other document that you would use personally.

PROJECTS

1. a. Open the **Computer Parts** document. Insert a page break before each heading formatted with Heading 2 style.
   b. Create a header on every page containing your last name at the left margin, the current date in the center, and the page number at the right margin.

c. After the line of text on the first page, create the footnote shown below, using italics as shown.

d. Save the document under the same name and then print it.

[1] *Computer Information Systems*, Vol. 1, p. 112.

2. a. Open the **Computer Parts** document and insert at the end of the document the table shown below. (If Word capitalizes the first letter of the i486 and i386 cells, choose Tools | AutoCorrect and change the option.)

b. Create a chart from the table data like the one shown below the table.

c. Save the document under the same name and print it.

Original Cost and Speed of Four Generations of Computer Chips

Chip	Speed in MHz	Cost in Dollars
Pentium II	400	900
Pentium	300	1200
i486	166	2000
i386	100	3000

3. a. Open the **Computer Parts** document and place a graphic image of your choosing on the first page to create a title page. Center the image on the page.

b. Delete the text on the title page. Use WordArt to create the text on the title page.

c. Save the document under the same name and print it out.

4. a. Using Word's labels feature, select a business card label type. Create a full page of your personal business cards.

b. After placing the cards in a new document, format and align the text and include a graphic. Save the document as **Business Cards**.

c. If your printer will print cards, print a page of them. Use real card stock if you have it.

PROJECTS

1. Create the research paper shown below, following these instructions:
   a. Create a title page using the following text, centering the text on the line. Then add an appropriate piece of clip art, and place a border around the title page (but not the other pages in the paper). (Tip: Before you start, choose Tools | AutoCorrect | AutoFormat As You Type tab and clear the check box to *Define styles based on your formatting.*)

> Linking to the Internet
>   Your name
>   The current date

   b. Place the Abstract in a border and place light shading in the box.
   c. In the document text:

   - Use the built-in style Heading 1 for the title.
   - Use the built-in style Heading 2 for the other headings.
   - Insert a bulleted list as shown.
   - Format bold and italic as shown.

   d. Place the data in a table as shown, and create a chart from the table data.
   e. In the list at the end, insert symbols as shown and change their size to 18 point. (Look in the Wingdings and Webdings fonts for these symbols.) You can use tabs or a table. Hint: If you use a table, you can select it and then use the Format | Borders and Shading dialog box to remove the borders.
   f. Place page breaks as indicated.
   g. Place page numbers on all pages except the title page.
   h. Double-space the document.
   i. Set the margins at 1.5″ left and right and 1.25″ top and bottom.
   j. Save the document as **Internet Research** and print it.

Linking to the Internet

Abstract: To link to the Internet, you need to connect your computer to the phone line, using a **modem**. Moreover, you must subscribe to a commercial service, **Internet Service Provider (ISP)**, or **freenet** in order to make the link active. Choosing the provider that meets your needs can require time and research.

<insert a page break>

Commercial Services

Commercial online services are some of the oldest services available for connecting to the Internet. Some of the most well known include:

- America Online®
- CompuServe®
- Microsoft® Network
- Prodigy Internet™

Commercial services are the best option for users who are new to the Internet.[1] They provide not only Internet access but also many utilities, extensive help, and easy-to-install software. Commercial services are accustomed to first-time users, and they make it easy to open an account and learn to access information on line.

<insert footnote 1> Linda Ericksen and Emily Kim, *Projects for the Internet* (Boston: Addison-Wesley, 1998) p. 25.

<insert a page break>

Internet Service Providers (ISPs)

Internet Service Providers are springing up all over. ISPs allow you to use your own software, known as a **browser**, to surf the Web. These services make high-speed connections a priority. You may need to get help elsewhere because not all of these services are meant for the novice.

Many ISPs are located in your community, making it easy to check them out.

<insert a page break>

Freenets

Freenets are local, nonprofit ISPs. These services are usually run by volunteers and are often associated with libraries or community centers.[2] These services provide free access to low-income users who would not otherwise have an Internet account, and charge moderate fees for all users who can afford to pay.

<insert footnote 2> http://detroit.freenet.org/

<insert a page break>

Costs

The prices vary by location, level of service, and competition. Table 1.1 shows the monthly average for each type of service over the last three years.

	First Year	Second Year	Third Year
Commercial	35	33	38
ISP	19	25	20
Freenet	7	10	12

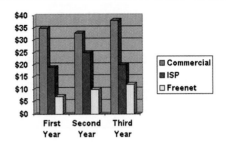

Choosing a Service

Before signing up with any service, you should research available providers. After narrowing your options, contact the services and ask the following questions.

- What are <u>all</u> the monthly costs?
- Are there time limits to online sessions?
- Are busy signals common during peak hours?
- Is technical support provided and when is it available?
- Does the service host Web pages?
- Is there an extra charge for e-mail accounts?

2. Create the business plan shown below for the small business known as Spread the Light Candles.

a. Create a title page using the following text, centering the text on the line. Then add an appropriate piece of clip art, and place a border around the title page (but not the other pages of the document).

> Spread the Light Candles
> Your name
> The current date

b. Place the Executive Summary in a border and place light shading in the box.

c. In the document text:
- Use the built-in style Heading 1 for the title.
- Use the built-in style Heading 2 for the numbered headings.
- Format the Objectives section as a bulleted list.

d. Place the data in a table as shown, and create a chart from the table data.

e. Place page breaks as indicated.

f. Place page numbers on all pages except the title page.

g. Double-space the document.

h. Set the margins at 1.5" all around.

i. Save the document as Candle **Plan** and print it.

Business Plan: Spread the Light Candles

1. 0 Executive Summary

Spread the Light Candles sells candles, incense, and other aromatherapy products. This business plan is part of our regular business planning process. We revise this plan every year.

<insert a page break>

1. 1 Objectives

- Increase sales to more than $50,000 by our sixth year.
- Improve inventory turnover through special promotions.

1. 2 Mission

Our goal is to sell candles and incense, as well as other high-quality aromatherapy products. We believe in complete customer satisfaction. We offer the best available products at very competitive prices.

<insert a page break>

2. 0 Company Summary

Spread the Light Candles is a 4-year-old candle and incense reseller with sales of $10,000 to $20,000 per year. We have an excellent reputation.

2. 1 Company Ownership

Spread the Light Candles is owned and managed by a single proprietor.

2. 2 Company History

With the rise in popularity of aromatherapy, Spread the Light Candles has experienced a steady growth in sales, as shown by the figures below.

	Second Year	Third Year	Fourth Year
Sales	10,000	14,500	15,000
Gross	2,000	2,500	2,600
Net	1,800	1,900	2,000

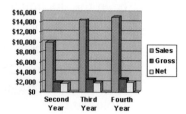

2. 3 Company Facilities

We have one location—a 1,000-square-foot warehouse located close to the major shipping facilities in our area.

Merging Documents

UNIT OBJECTIVES

- Use Mail Merge Helper
- Create the data source
- Edit the main document
- Merge the documents
- Create merged labels

Most businesses today use personalized form letters for the bulk of their correspondence; that is, they merge customer lists into form letters. Using form letters not only saves the time it would take to type individual letters; it also prevents errors. This feature is called a mail merge. **Mail merge** allows you to merge an address file with letters, envelopes, and labels. In order to perform a mail merge, you need to have an address file and a form letter document. Word 2000 makes creating the two files and merging them together easy, but you have to follow a process that has numerous steps. The Mail Merge Helper walks you through these steps.

What: Start Word's built-in feature for creating a mail merge.

How: Choose Tools | Mail Merge.

Why: If you follow the steps in the helper, you will easily create successful merges.

Tip: Before you create mail merge documents, plan them so that you include all the data you will need.

Most businesses need to send the same letter to many different people. It would be possible to open a master letter and edit the inside address and salutation for each individual to whom the letter was going, but a mail merge automates this process. Word 2000 includes the Mail Merge Helper that guides you through the process step by step. You will start the Mail Merge Helper in this task and use it throughout this unit. The name *mail merge* comes from the actual merging of two different types of documents.

You need to create two types of documents before you run the merge:

- **Data Source**: a list of names and addresses. You may have different data sources for different purposes, but you will probably use the same data source again and again. A list of customers can be used to mail catalogs, notices of sales or events, or holiday wishes, for instance.

- **Main Document**: a form letter, envelope, or label containing the text that will go to everyone in the mailing, plus codes that tell Word what information from the data source to use in specific locations in the document.

When you run the merge, Word combines, or merges, the data source and the main document, producing a copy of the main document addressed to each individual in the data source.

To start the mail merge process:

1. Choose Tools | Mail Merge to open the Mail Merge Helper dialog box, shown in Figure 7.1.
2. Click the Create button in the *Main document* section to display a list of document types you can create:

    - Form Letters
    - Mailing Labels
    - Envelopes
    - Catalogs

3. Select a document type, and a message box gives you the option of creating a new main document or using the open document, as shown in Figure 7.2.
4. Select a source for the main document.

Word redisplays the Mail Merge Helper, which you will continue to use in the next task.

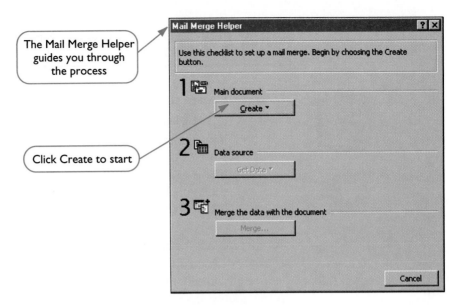

The Mail Merge Helper guides you through the process

Click Create to start

FIGURE 7.1 The Mail Merge Helper Dialog Box

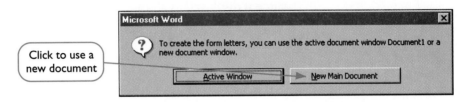

Click to use a new document

FIGURE 7.2 Choosing a Source for the Main Document

EXERCISE 1 | *Starting the Mail Merge Helper*

1. With Word open, choose **Tools | Mail Merge**.
The Mail Merge Helper dialog box opens.

2. Click the **Create button** in the *Main document* section.
A list of document types drops down.

3. Click **Form Letters**.
A message box opens, giving you a choice of creating a new main document or using the document in the active window.

4. Click **New Main Document**.
The message box closes; a new document opens (temporarily named Document2) that you will use as the main document; and the Mail Merge Helper displays the new document's name.

5. Leave the Mail Merge Helper open while you continue to the next task.

What: Create the data source to be used in a mail merge.

How: In the Mail Merge Helper, choose Get Data | Create Data Source.

Why: If you create a document containing the names and addresses you want to use in the merge, you can use it again and again.

Tip: If you can't find a Zip code for an address and you have access to the Web, look it up at the U.S. Postal Service Web site at http://www.usps.com.

Word provides help, through the Mail Merge Helper, in creating the **data source**—the electronic address book. You must have names and addresses stored electronically to perform a merge. The data source document, like a paper address book, is made up of records. Each record contains all of the information about a single addressee. The individual elements of each record—title, first name, last name, street address, city, etc.—are called **fields**. When the data source is displayed as a table, these fields form its first row, or **header row**.

To create or use a data source:

1. Click the Get Data button in the Mail Merge Helper's *Data source* section to display a list of data sources you can use:

    * Create Data Source
    * Open Data Source
    * Use Address Book
    * Header Options

2. To use an already created data source, select Open Data Source, and the Open dialog box opens to let you specify the file location and name.

3. To create a new data source with the Mail Merge Helper, select Create Data, and the Create Data Source dialog box opens, as shown in Figure 7.3.

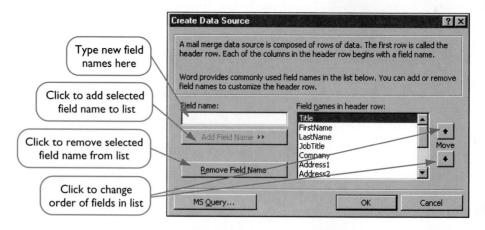

FIGURE 7.3 The Create Data Source Dialog Box

CREATING THE DATA SOURCE

The Create Data Source dialog box lets you specify the fields for the data source. Word provides field names commonly used in mail merge applications. Any field name you do not remove from the sample list will appear in the header row of the data source.

To remove a field name that you will not need:
1. Select the field in the *Field names in header row* list.
2. Click the Remove Field Name button.

To add a field name not in the list:
1. Type the new name in the *Field name* text box.
2. Click the Add Field Name button.

To change the order in which field names appear in the header row:
1. Select the field name to be moved.
2. Click the up or down Move buttons enough times to place the field name where you want it.

When you have tailored the list of field names to your needs, click OK. The Save As dialog box opens so that you can save the data source document. Name the document and specify a location in which to store it. The Save As dialog box closes, and the data source document is stored.

Let's review what you have done so far. You have chosen to create a new main document and a new data source; you have specified the fields that will be used in the data source; and you have saved the data source. But the main document has not yet been created, and the data source contains no names and addresses. The Mail Merge Helper now lets you choose the next step. A message box, shown in Figure 7.4, gives you these options:

- Edit Data Source
- Edit Main Document

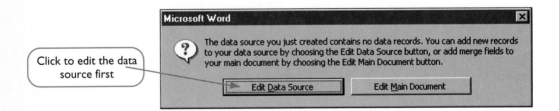

FIGURE 7.4 Choosing the Next Step

EDITING THE DATA SOURCE

You'll choose to edit the data source by entering new records. To edit the data source:

1. Click the Edit Data Source button to display the Data Form dialog box, shown in Figure 7.5.
2. Enter the data for the first record.
3. Click the Add New button or press Enter in the last field to create a new blank record, and continue entering records until the list is complete.

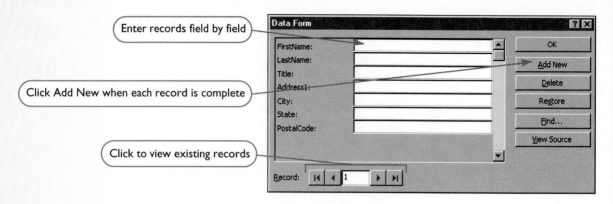

Enter records field by field

Click Add New when each record is complete

Click to view existing records

FIGURE 7.5   The Data Form Dialog Box

- To enter data, click in the text box for a field, type the data, and press Enter or Tab to move to the next field. Each record is numbered, and the number of the currently displayed record appears in the dialog box.

- Navigation buttons for the First, Last, Previous, and Next records enable you to move from record to record in the data source. Command buttons in the Data Form dialog box perform other actions, listed in Table 7.1.

POINTER

Where Did the Data Form Come From?

Word creates the data form based on the information supplied in the Create Data Source dialog box; that is, it contains the field names you included.

Button	Description
◄	Moves to the first record in the file
◄	Moves to the previous record
►	Moves to the next record
►►	Moves to the last record
OK	Closes the dialog box and displays the main document
Add New	Adds the current record to the data source and creates a new blank record
Delete	Deletes the current record
Restore	Restores the current record to its unedited state
Find...	Finds records based on criteria; see Figure 7.6
View Source	Displays the data source as a table; see Figure 7.7

TABLE 7.1   Data Form Dialog Box Buttons

To edit data in the data source:

1. Display the record to be edited.
2. Edit the field contents.
3. Move to the next record to be edited, and when finished editing, click OK.

To delete a record:

1. Display the record to be deleted.
2. Click the Delete button.

POINTER

Deleting Records

Deleting records is permanent. The Restore button in the Data Form dialog box doesn't restore deleted records.

To find a record that matches criteria:

1. Click the Find button to open the Find in Field dialog box, shown in Figure 7.6.
2. Type the text you want to find.
3. Select the field that it occurs in.
4. Click Find First.

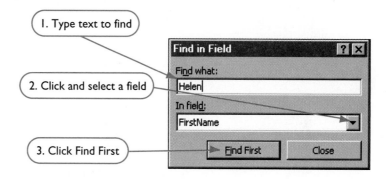

FIGURE 7.6 The Find in Field Dialog Box

To display the data source as a table and print the table:

1. Click the View Source button to close the dialog box and display the data source document, as shown in Figure 7.7. on page 176.
2. Edit the source as you would any Word table. You can use the buttons on the Database toolbar to sort the records in alphabetical order, to find a specific record, or to perform other operations. (Point to a button to display its name in a ScreenTip.)
3. Choose File | Print to print the table.

Dividing Up Data

Notice that the default field names separate the data into small parts. For example, instead of a Name field, there are three fields: Title, FirstName, and LastName. Separating data into small parts enables you to use the individual parts in many ways. With a single field for the whole name, for instance, you wouldn't be able to use the salutation "Dear Linda" or "Dear Ms. Ericksen"; you'd be limited to "Dear Ms. Linda Ericksen."

EXERCISE 2 | *Creating and Editing the Data Source*

1. If the Mail Merge Helper isn't displayed on your screen, choose **Tools | Mail Merge**.

2. Click the **Get Data button**.
A list of data sources drops down.

3. Select **Create Data Source**.
The Create Data Source dialog box opens.

4. Remove the following field names by selecting each of them and clicking the **Remove Field Name button**:

- JobTitle
- Company
- Address2
- Country
- HomePhone
- WorkPhone

5. Select the **Title field**, and click the **Move down arrow** *twice* to move it after last name.

6. Click **OK**.
The Save As dialog box opens.

7. Choose a drive and folder for the document, type **Addresses** in the File name text box, and click **Save**.
The Save As dialog box closes, and the blank main document is displayed. The Mail Merge toolbar is displayed on the screen. A message box opens, giving you the option of editing the main document or the data source.

8. Click the **Edit Data Source button**.
The Data Form dialog box opens.

9. Click in the **FirstName text box** and type **Marge**, then press **Enter** or the **Tab key**.
The insertion point moves to the LastName field.

10. In the same way, enter the other fields for the first record:

```
Wentworth
Ms.
P.O. Box 19853
Sedona
AZ
87656
```

11. Click the **Add New button** or simply press **Enter** to display the form for the second record. Continue adding all the following records, just as you did record 1.

Record 2:
Larry
Adams
Mr.
34982 W. Dixie Highway
Louisville
KY
40596

Record 3:
Shelly
Montgomery
Ms.
7612 University Ave.
Golden
CO
78965

Record 4:
Bobby
Gordon
Mr.
5672 Stone Mountain Way
Atlanta
GA
67854

Record 5:
Helen
Jones
Mrs.
987 Lake View Ave.
Burlington
VT
12392

12. Click the **View Source button**.
The data source document opens, as shown in Figure 7.7 on page 176. The Database toolbar is displayed.

13. Choose **File | Print** and then click **OK**.
The table is printed.

14. Leave the data source open while you continue to the next task.

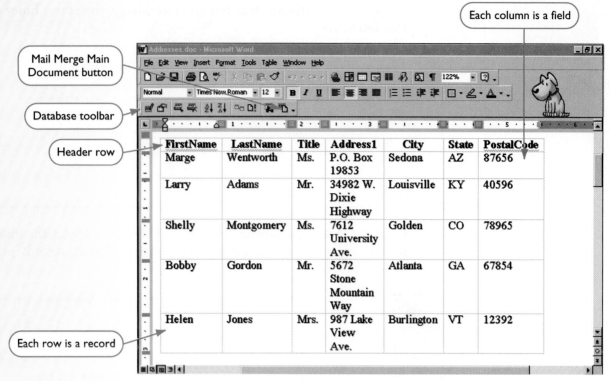

Each column is a field

Mail Merge Main
Document button

Database toolbar

Header row

Each row is a record

FIGURE 7.7   The Data Source Document

TASK 3 | *Editing the Main Document*

What: Type the contents of the main document and add the field names to prepare to run the merge.

How: In the main document, choose the Insert Merge Field button on the Mail Merge toolbar.

Why: For Word to insert the correct data from the data source into the main document, you have to specify the field names and their location.

Tip: Include punctuation, such as the comma after a city name, in the main document, not in each individual address in the data source.

When you started the Mail Merge Helper, you chose to create a new main document for the mail merge. That document is still blank, and it has not yet been saved. The next step in the mail merge is to edit this document.

- If the main document is a mailing label, it may consist only of fields from the data source.

- If it is a form letter, it will have two parts: the text that will go to everyone in the mailing, plus the field names that tell Word what information from the data source to use in specific locations in the document.

You create the parts of the letter that will remain constant by typing as you would any other document.

To place the contents of the data source into the letter, you use the Mail Merge toolbar, which is automatically displayed in the main document:

1. Click in the main document where the first field is to appear.
2. Click the Insert Merge Field button on the Mail Merge toolbar. A list of the fields in the data source drops down, as shown in Figure 7.8.

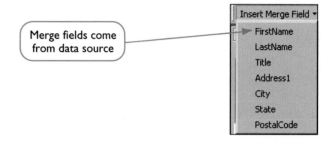

Merge fields come from data source

FIGURE 7.8 The Insert Merge Field List

3. Click a field name to insert it in the document at the insertion point and close the drop-down list.
4. Continue to insert field names where they are to go in the document.
5. Save the document. If you want a hard copy, you can print it as you would any other Word document.

Figure 7.9 on page 179 shows an example of a finished form letter document, containing text and merge fields. You will create this document in the following exercise.

POINTER

Inserting Merge Fields

When you insert the merge field name, you are inserting a field code. You can't type the same words and have the merge work. The code is displayed within chevrons, and if you click it in the document, you will see that it is a single character with a gray background. (For more information, search for Help on merge fields.)

EXERCISE 3 | *Editing the Main Document*

1. With the screen still displaying the data source in table view, click the **Mail Merge Main Document button** on the Database toolbar.
   If your screen is not displaying the data source, choose Tools | Merge and click the Edit button in the Main document section of the Mail Merge Helper. The main document is displayed. It is still blank, and the insertion point is at the top. Use Figure 7.9 as a model as you follow through the balance of this exercise.

2. Click the **Insert Merge Field button** on the Mail Merge toolbar.
The field names in the data source are displayed.

3. Click **Title**.
The list closes, and the Title merge field is inserted in the document at the insertion point within chevrons.

4. Press the **Spacebar**.
You will insert spaces and punctuation in the address by typing them in the ordinary way.

5. Click the **Insert Merge Field button**, click **FirstName**, and press the **Spacebar**.

6. Click the **Insert Merge Field button**, click **LastName**, and press **Enter**.

7. Click the **Insert Merge Field button**, click **Address1**, and press **Enter**.

8. Click the **Insert Merge Field button**, click **City**, type a **comma**, and press the **Spacebar**.

9. Click the **Insert Merge Field button**, click **State**, and press the **Spacebar**.

10. Click the **Insert Merge Field button**, click **PostalCode**, and press **Enter** *twice*.

11. Type the **current date** or begin to type it and press **Enter** if the Auto-Complete date is displayed, then press **Enter** *twice*.

12. Type **Dear** and press the **Spacebar**.

13. Click the **Insert Merge Field button**, click **Title**, and press the **Spacebar**.

14. Click the **Insert Merge Field button**, click **LastName**, type a **colon**, and press **Enter** *twice*.

15. Type the body for the letter shown below.

Thank you for your interest in our product line. We make all our dog food here at the kennels. All the foods have been tried on various breeds of working dogs, and we have noticed a loss of extra body fat and an increase of energy after the dogs have been eating the food for several weeks.

I would like to offer you a special introductory sampler of all the flavors so that your dog can try them out. There is a money-back guarantee—your dog will look, feel, and act better.

Sincerely,

Your name

---

16. Place the insertion point in front of **I** at the beginning of the second paragraph.

17. Click the **Insert Merge Field button**, click **FirstName**, type a **comma**, and press the **Spacebar**.
Your document should look like the one in Figure 7.9.

18. Save the document as **Sales Letter**.
It's a good idea to save the document in the same folder as the data source.

19. Print the letter, and leave it open on the screen while you continue with the next task.

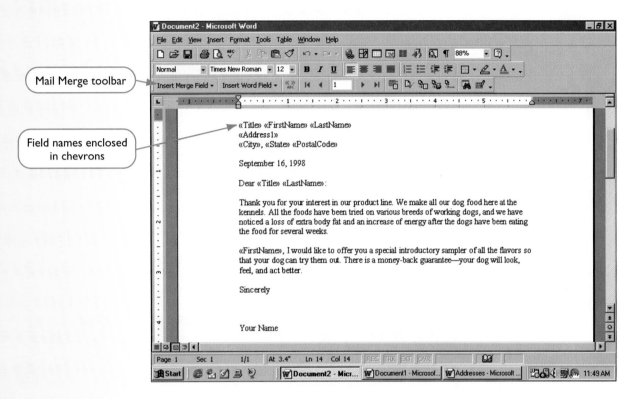

FIGURE 7.9 The Completed Main Document

TASK 4 | *Merging the Documents*

What: Merge the main document and the data source.

How: Choose Tools | Mail Merge | Merge.

Why: To create an individual copy of the letter addressed to each person in the address file, you merge the main document and the data source.

Tip: Sometimes merges create unexpected results, so it's a good idea to merge to a document before sending a large merge to the printer.

When both documents—the data source and the main document—have been created, you are ready to run the merge. To merge the documents:

1. Display the Mail Merge Helper by clicking its button on the Mail Merge toolbar.
2. Click the Merge button in the Mail Merge Helper dialog box. The Merge dialog box opens, as shown in Figure 7.10.

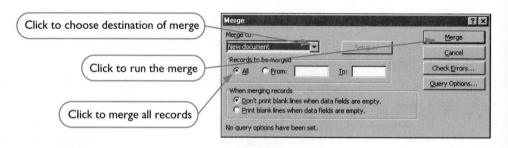

FIGURE **7.10**   The Merge Dialog Box

3. Click the down arrow for the *Merge To* box to choose whether to merge the documents to a new document, the printer, or electronic mail.
4. In the *Records to be merged* section, choose whether to merge all of the records or to specify the records by record number in the data source. (This option is handy if you want to test a sampling of a merge on a large data source.)
5. Click the Merge button to run the merge. Word will create a new document, *Form Letters*, containing all of the letters, each starting on a new page, as shown in Figure 7.11.

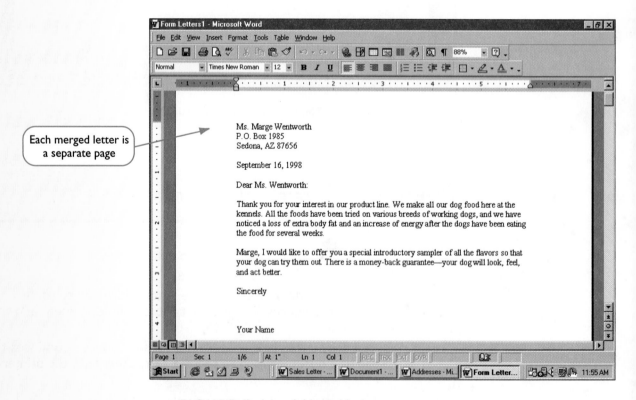

FIGURE **7.11**   A Merged Letter

6. Check the letters.

7. Print the document, or rerun the merge, changing the *Merge to* option to Printer.

POINTER

Query Options

To send the merged document only to certain people in the data source, you set query options by clicking the Query Options button in the Merge dialog box. For example, you can send the letter to people who live in a certain city or state or are in a certain range of Zip codes.

EXERCISE 4 | *Merging the Documents*

1. Choose **Tools | Mail Merge**.
   The Mail Merge Helper dialog box opens.

2. Click the **Merge button**.
   The Merge dialog box opens.

3. Make sure the *Merge to* option is set to **New Document** and the *Records to Merge* is set to **All**.

4. Click the **Merge button**.
   A new document opens, containing the letters.

5. Close the letters without saving them.

TASK 5 | *Creating Merged Labels*

What: Create mailing labels to go with the merged letters

How: Tools | Mail Merge

Why: Many people prefer to print sheets of labels and then place them onto envelopes.

Tip: If you are going to print a large data source to mailing labels, merge the first 20 or so first to make sure the printout is correct.

To create mailing labels to go with the letters, use the same data source. You use the Mail Merge Helper to help you create mailing labels.

To create mailing labels:

1. Choose Tools | Mail Merge to open the Mail Merge Helper dialog box.

2. Click the Create button in the *Main document* section.

3. Choose Mailing Labels from the drop-down list.
4. When a message box asks for the source of the main document, click the New Main Document button.
5. Click the Get Data button in the *Data source* section.
6. When a message box asks for the source, click the Open Data Source button.
7. When the Open dialog box opens, specify the drive and folder of the data file and click Open.
8. When a message box appears, click the Set Up Main Document button to open the Label Options dialog box, shown in Figure 7.12a.
9. Choose a manufacturer in the *Label products* section.
10. In the *Product number* list, select the label you want to use.
11. Click OK and the Create Labels dialog box opens, as shown in Figure 7.12b.
12. Use the Insert Merge Field button to create the label just as you did to create the form letter.
13. Run the merge just as you did for the letter.

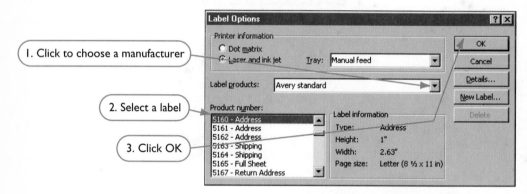

(a) The Label Options Dialog Box

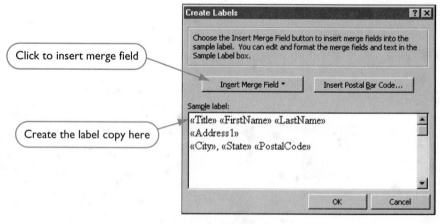

(b) The Create Labels Dialog Box

FIGURE 7.12   Creating Merged Labels

Merging to Envelopes

Follow the same basic steps outlined in this task to merge the data source to envelopes by choosing Envelopes as your main document and then selecting the envelope type.

EXERCISE 5 | *Merging Mailing Labels*

1. Choose **Tools | Mail Merge**.
   The Mail Merge Helper dialog box opens.

2. Click the **Create button** in the Main Document section.

3. Choose **Mailing Labels**.
   A message box asks for the source of the main document.

4. Click **New Main Document**.

5. In the Mail Merge Helper dialog box, click the **Get Data button**.
   A message box asks for the source.

6. Click **Open Data Source**.
   The Open dialog box opens.

7. Select the **Addresses** document you created earlier in this unit, and click the **Open button**.
   A message box appears.

8. Click **Set Up Main Document**.
   The Label Options dialog box opens.

9. Choose **Avery standard** and **#5160 - Address**, and then click **OK**.
   The Create Labels dialog box opens.

10. Use the **Insert Merge Field button** and the keyboard to create a data main document matching Figure 7.12b.

11. When the fields are complete, click the **OK button**.
    The dialog box closes, and you return to the Mail Merge Helper dialog box.

12. In the Mail Merge Helper dialog box, click **Merge**.
    The Merge dialog box opens.

13. Make sure the Merge To option is set to **New document,** and click the **Merge button.**

The mailing labels will appear on the screen, as shown in Figure 7.13.

14. Print the document and close it without saving it.

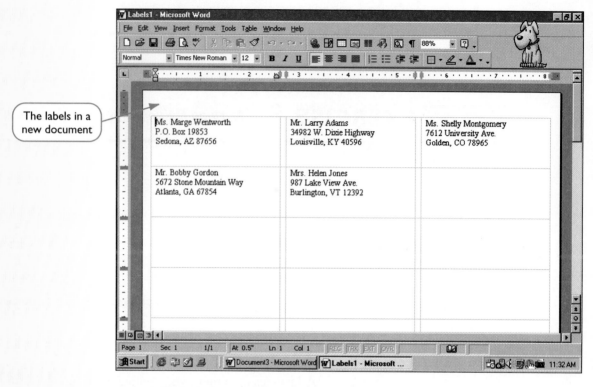

The labels in a new document

FIGURE **7.13** The Mailing Labels in a New Document

REVIEW

SUMMARY

After completing this unit, you should
- be able to use Mail Merge Helper (page 169)
- know how to create the data source (page 170)
- know how to edit the main document (page 176)
- be able to merge the documents (page 179)
- be able to create merged labels (page 181)

KEY TERMS

data source (page 168)
field (page 170)
header row (page 170)

mail merge (page 167)
main document (page 168)

TEST YOUR SKILLS

True/False

1. A mail merge document looks like a personal letter typed to each recipient.
2. Merges save businesses time and money.
3. The data source contains the letter you plan to send.
4. A record is the information about one person.
5. A field is an individual data category.

Multiple Choice

1. You can merge names and addresses to
   a. letters
   b. the Web
   c. graphic images
   d. all of these answers

2. The form letter contains
   a. the names and addresses of people to send the letters to
   b. the data source
   c. the text that you want all recipients of the letter to receive
   d. the records

3. The data source
   a. can be viewed as a form
   b. can be viewed as a table
   c. can be used with any number of form documents
   d. all of these answers

4. A record
   a. is made up of fields
   b. is all the information about one person
   c. can be searched for matching data
   d. all of these answers

5. You can send the form letter to some of the people in the data source by
   a. specifying a range of record numbers to merge
   b. querying the data source
   c. creating a new file
   d. answers a and b

Short Answer

1. Codes in the main document drawn from the field names in the data source are called _____ _____.
2. A _____ is the individual pieces of information in a data source.
3. The _____ _____ is the first row of cells in the data table, containing the field names.
4. The _____ _____ can be letters, mailing labels, or envelopes.
5. You can view the data source as a form or a _____.

What Does This Do?

Write a brief description of the function of the following:

1.	View Source	6.	🗒️
2.	Restore	7.	▶️
3.	Insert Merge Field ▾	8.	1
4.	◀️	9.	Delete
5.	Add New	10.	Get Data ▾

On Your Own

1. Add three more people to the **Addresses** data source.
2. Create a second form letter from scratch.
3. Merge the edited data source and the second form letter.
4. Create envelopes for everyone in the data source.
5. Create mailing labels for everyone in the data source.

PROJECTS

1. a. Create a data source document for a form letter using the four following records.
   b. Save the document as **Customers** and then print it.

Ms.	Mr.
Jess	Peter
Gray	Gold
145 W. Moon St.	P. O. Box 45678
Haverhill	Grand Rapids
MA	MI
01836	67854

(continued)

Mrs.	Mr.
Jean	John
White	Cruz
987 Upper River Rd.	345 Rio Grande Ave.
Tahoe City	Bisbee
CA	AZ
87651	78974

c. Create a main document following the instructions below.

- Create a letterhead for the main document that includes the following address and a clipart image.

Spread the Light Candles
P.O. Box 1700
Miami, FL 33301

- Insert today's date and merge codes for the inside address and salutation, and then type the body of the letter:

As the owner of Spread the Light Candles, I want to thank you for your past orders. We are contacting our valued customers to inform them of a very special sale. Our candles will be offered at discount prices below even our everyday low prices. Check out the enclosed catalog and order today, as supplies are limited to stock on hand.
Yours truly,

Your Name

d. Save the letter as **Candle Sales** and then print the letter.
e. Merge the letter and the data source. Print the form letters.
f. Create mailing labels to use with the letters. Print the labels.

2. a. Add the following records to the Customers data source file, and then print the file:

Mr.	Ms.
Larry	Kim
Alexander	Kieko
397 Union Street	200 Ocean View
Phoenix	Florence
AZ	OR
78900	97532

b. Create the following main document:

- Use the letterhead you created in Project 1.
- Insert merge codes for the inside address and salutation.
- Type the body of the letter as shown below.

Thank you for your recent order. We want to offer you a special promotion. If you provide us with the names and addresses of three of your friends so that we can send them our catalog, we will send you a $10 gift certificate. This gift certificate is good on future orders and cannot be used to pay existing bills.

Thanks,

Your name

---

c. Save the letter and **Gift Offer**. Print the form letter.
d. Merge the *Gift Offer* document and the *Customers* data source. Print the letters.

3. a. Create a data source using five of your family or friends, or use addresses of local businesses, drawn from the classified phone directory. Print the data source.
b. Create a main document that is a letter to people in the data source. It can be informing people of your progress in school, about your family, a holiday letter, or any information of your choosing. Include merge codes for the inside address and salutation. Save the letter and print it.
c. Merge the letter and the data source. Print the letters.

4. a. Add four more people to the data source you created in Project 3. Print the data source.
b. Create a second letter with different content from what you used in Project 3. Save the letter and print it.
c. Merge the letter with the data source. Print the letters.

Using Word with the World Wide Web

UNIT OBJECTIVES

- Create hyperlinks
- Create Web documents using the Web Page Wizard
- Create a Web page using a template
- Create a Web page from an existing Word document

The World Wide Web is changing how we do business, learn, communicate, and have fun. It is the most remarkable change agent since the invention of the printing press. Knowing how to use the Web to find information, do research, and conduct business is becoming an essential skill.

You have already learned how to use the Web to get help in Word and acquire new clipart. You have seen how to find a Zip code for a mail merge at the U.S. Postal Service's Web site and how to include a Web address in documents. In this unit you'll learn to link your documents to others on the Web and to use Word to create Web documents.

TASK 1 | *Creating Hyperlinks*

What: Create links from documents on your computer to documents located anywhere in the world.

How: Choose Insert | Hyperlink.

Why: Hyperlinks let you provide online users with up-to-date information.

Tip: You can use hyperlinks to jump to multimedia files, such as sounds and videos.

A **hyperlink** is text or a graphic that contains a pointer to another object. It's like a super shortcut. When you click the link, you are transferred to the linked object, which will open in a **browser** (software for viewing documents on the Web) or in the software that created the object. The destination the hyperlink jumps to can be another file located on your hard disk, a file on your company's intranet, or a document on the World Wide Web.

A hyperlink is represented by a "hot" image or text which includes the address or **URL, Uniform Resource Locator**, of the document. Hot text is usually formatted as blue and underlined: for example, http://www.prenhall.com. You can tell when you are pointing to a link because the mouse pointer changes to a hand with a pointing finger.

Let's see how hyperlinks work. Suppose you are writing a paper about the risks of heart disease in women. After searching the Web for up-to-date information, you decide to include a hyperlink to the American Heart Association Web site located at http://www.women.americanheart.org. Word formats the hyperlink (blue text and underlined) in your document. When your Word document is read electronically, the reader can click the blue text and be connected to the American Heart Association site, as shown in Figure 8.1. When the Word document is printed, the hyperlink appears formatted—underlined and, if a color printer is used, blue.

You can create hyperlinks to existing documents, to other parts of the same document, to a new document, and to an e-mail address.

POINTER

Web Addresses

In the Web address http://www.prenhall.com, *http* stands for **HyperText Transfer Protocol**, the communication standard used for Web documents; and *www.prenhall.com* is the **domain name**, the address of the server that holds the documents. You must type a URL precisely in order to display the Web page. Note that the forward slash character is used instead of the backslash character. If the address uses a lowercase letter, you can't type a capital.

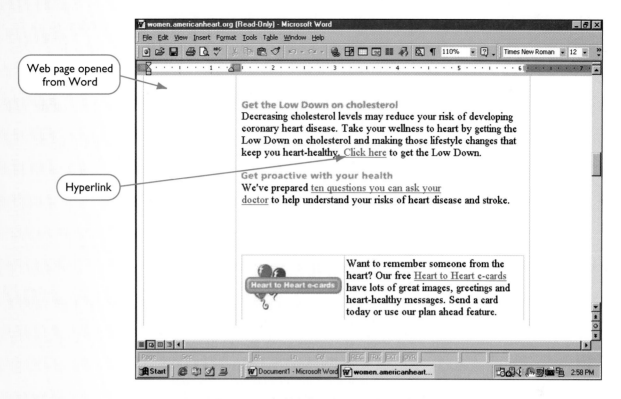

FIGURE 8.1   A Web Page Viewed from Within Word

LINKING TO AN EXISTING DOCUMENT

To create a hyperlink to an existing document:

1. Select the text to format.
2. Choose Insert | Hyperlink. The Insert Hyperlink dialog box opens, as shown in Figure 8.2.
3. In the *Link to* section, click the Existing File or Web Page button.
4. If you know the address, type it in the *Type the file or Web page name* text box.

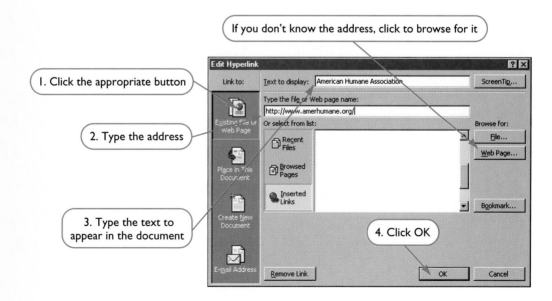

FIGURE 8.2   Inserting a Hyperlink to an Existing Document

Unit 8 | Using Word with the World Wide Web   191

5. If you don't know the address, use the *Browse for* section to locate it:
   - Click the File button to open the Link to File dialog box, where you can select the file.
   - Click the Web Page button to start your browser and connect you to the World Wide Web, where you can use a search engine to locate the file.
6. Type the text that will be formatted as a hyperlink in the Text to display text box.
7. Click OK.

POINTER

Custom ScreenTips

When the reader points to a hyperlink in a Word document, a ScreenTip is displayed. By default, the ScreenTip is the address of the link. To create a custom ScreenTip:

1. Click the ScreenTip button in the Insert Hyperlink dialog box to open the Set Hyperlink ScreenTip dialog box.
2. Type the tip in the *ScreenTip* text box and click OK.

LINKING WITHIN THE SAME DOCUMENT

Sometimes you will want to link to locations within the same document so that the reader can find more information on a certain subject. To do so:

1. Select the text.
2. Choose Insert | Hyperlink.
3. In the *Link to* section, click the Place in This Document button.
4. Select an appropriate location.
5. Click OK.

LINKING TO A NEW DOCUMENT

While in one Word document, you can create a link to a new document, and Word will create the document and the link for you. To link to a new document:

1. Select the text to be formatted.
2. Choose Insert | Hyperlink.
3. In the *Link to* section, click the Create New Document button.
4. Type a name and location for the new document.
5. Click an option button to specify whether to open the file now.
6. Click OK, and Word creates the new document.

LINK TO AN E-MAIL ADDRESS

You may want people to respond to your electronic documents by e-mailing you. You could just include your e-mail address for the reader, but Word lets you make your e-mail address a hyperlink. People respond to your document by clicking your hot e-mail address in the document. A new e-mail message opens on their computer with your e-mail address in the To line of the message. To create a hyperlink to an e-mail address:

1. Click in the spot where you want the address to appear.
2. Choose Insert | Hyperlink.
3. In the *Link to* section click the E-mail Address button.
4. Type the e-mail address in the E-Mail address box.
5. Type the address as you want it to appear in the document in the *Text to display* text box.
6. If you like, type a subject in the *Subject* box.
7. Click OK, and Word places the e-mail address as a hyperlink in the document.

POINTER

Paste as Hyperlink

From any saved file, copy text to the Windows Clipboard. Move the insertion point to the desired location and choose Edit | Paste as Hyperlink. Word will paste the text as a hyperlink to the original document.

EDITING AND REMOVING LINKS

You may end up with a **dead link**, one that is no longer available, and want to edit or remove it from a document. You can't select it and press the Delete button, because clicking it opens it. Instead, you use the right mouse button.

To edit a hyperlink:

1. Right-click the hyperlink to open a shortcut menu.
2. Point to Hyperlink, to open submenu.
3. Click Edit Hyperlink to open the Edit Hyperlink dialog box.
4. Edit the link and click OK.

To remove a hyperlink:

1. Right-click the hyperlink to open a shortcut menu.
2. Point to Hyperlink to open submenu.
3. Click Remove Hyperlink, and the hyperlink is removed.

POINTER

AutoFormatting Hyperlinks

Word's AutoFormat As You Type feature will recognize Internet and network addresses you type and format them for you. To turn on automatic formatting, choose Tools | AutoCorrect | AutoFormat As You Type tab. In the *Replace as you type* section, select the *Internet and network paths with hyperlinks* check box.

1. Open the **JRT History** document.

2. Place the insertion point after the period following the word **me** at the end of the letter and press **Backspace**.

3. Type a **comma** and press the **Spacebar**.

4. Type **jim@jrt.com** and press the **Spacebar**.

5. If AutoFormat As You Type automatically formats the address, press **Backspace** and type a **period**, then proceed to step 10. Otherwise, proceed to step 6.

6. Select the **e-mail address** you just typed, and then choose **Insert | Hyperlink**.
   The Insert Hyperlink dialog box opens.

7. Click the **E-mail Address button** in the *Link to* section.
   The e-mail tab is displayed.

8. If necessary, type **jim@jrt.com** in the E-mail address text box, and then click **OK**.
   The dialog box closes and the text is formatted as a hyperlink in the letter.

9. Type a **period** following the hyperlink to end the sentence.

10. Press **Enter** *twice* and then type the following text:

We want to point all of our valued customers to an organization that has been protecting children and animals for well over 100 years. Visit the American Humane Association and find out how you can help.

---

11. Select the text the **American Humane Association**.

12. Choose **Insert | Hyperlink**.
    The Insert Hyperlink dialog box opens.

13. Click the **Existing File or Web Page button** in the Link to section.

14. Type the following URL in the **Type the file or Web page name text box**:

---

http://www.americanhumane.org/

---

15. Click **OK**.
    The dialog box closes, and the text is formatted as a hyperlink, as shown in Figure 8.3. When the user clicks the hyperlink, the American Humane Association Web page opens, as shown in Figure 8.4.

16. Print the document and close it without saving it.

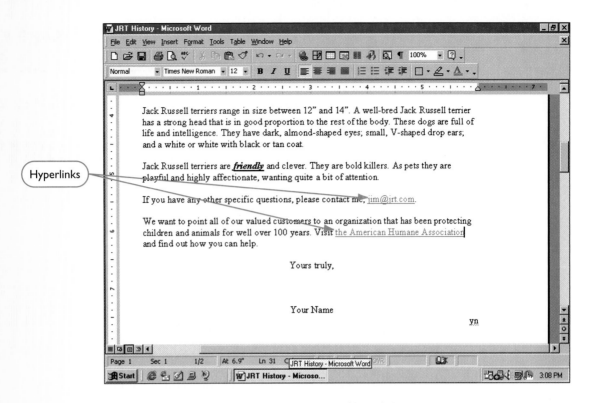

Hyperlinks

Jack Russell terriers range in size between 12" and 14". A well-bred Jack Russell terrier has a strong head that is in good proportion to the rest of the body. These dogs are full of life and intelligence. They have dark, almond-shaped eyes; small, V-shaped drop ears; and a white or white with black or tan coat.

Jack Russell terriers are **_friendly_** and clever. They are bold killers. As pets they are playful and highly affectionate, wanting quite a bit of attention.

If you have any other specific questions, please contact me, jim@jrt.com.

We want to point all of our valued customers to an organization that has been protecting children and animals for well over 100 years. Visit the American Humane Association and find out how you can help.

Yours truly,

Your Name

yn

FIGURE 8.3 The Document with Hyperlinks

When the reader clicks the link, the document opens

FIGURE 8.4 The Linked Document

TASK 2 | *Creating Web Documents Using the Web Page Wizard*

What: Create documents for publication on the World Wide Web.

How: Choose File | New | Web Page tab.

Why: Many small businesses are able to compete in a world market at very little expense by maintaining a presence on the World Wide Web.

Tip: To learn more about creating Web pages, you can search the Web itself for tips and tutorials.

Word's Web Page Wizard offers help in creating Web pages. You can create all types of Web documents, from simple pages to complete sites, using the built-in wizard.

To use the Web Page Wizard:

1. Choose File | New | Web Pages tab.
2. Select the Web Page Wizard and click OK to display the wizard's Start panel.
3. Click Next to display the Title and Location panel, shown in Figure 8.5a.

   • Type the site title, which will appear in the browser's title bar.

   • Type the location where the Web document will be saved, such as on your floppy disk. After you have completed your Web site, you will need to transfer it to the Web server that will host your site.

4. Click Next to display the Navigation panel, shown in Figure 8.5b, and choose a layout for the page.
5. Click Next to display the Add Pages panel, shown in Figure 8.5c, and choose the type of pages to add.
6. Click Next to display the Organize Pages panel.

   • Select a page and click the Move Up or Move Down button to change the position of a page.

   • Click the Rename button to rename the selected page.

7. Click Next to display the Visual Theme panel.

   • Select the *Add a visual theme* option to change fonts, bullets, and the background.

   • Click the Browse Themes button to display the Theme dialog box.

   • Click a theme and a sample is displayed in the right side of the dialog box; when you have selected the theme you want, click OK.

8. Click the Finish button to close the wizard, create the document, and display it in a Word window, as shown in Figure 8.5d.
9. Delete and insert text to customize the Web page.
10. Save changes by choosing File | Save; print the document by choosing File | Print.

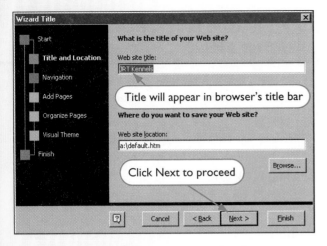

(a) The Title and Location Panel

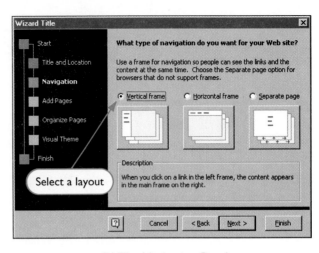

(b) The Navigation Panel

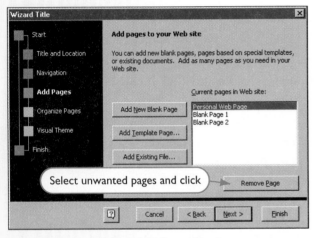

(c) The Add Pages Panel

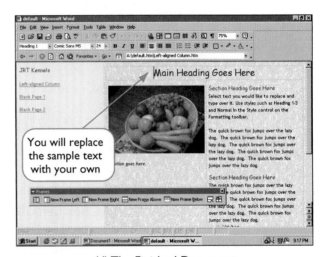

(d) The Finished Document

FIGURE 8.5   Using the Web Page Wizard

POINTER

Install Themes

If you select a theme that hasn't been installed on your hard drive, a message box lets you know. Click the Install button to install the theme and then display it.

POINTER

The Web Page Wizard Creates Folders

When you create a Web page using the Web Page wizard, it may contain many files, including graphics. The wizard creates folders for the files on the drive you select. To publish your document on the Web, you must send all of these files to the Internet Service Provider.

EXERCISE 2 | *Creating a Web Document Using the Web Page Wizard*

1. With a formatted disk in the 3 1/2 Floppy (A) drive, choose **File | New**.
The New dialog box opens.

2. Click the **Web Pages tab**.
The tab lists Word's built-in templates and wizards for the Web.

3. Select **Web Page Wizard** and click **OK**.
The dialog box closes; a new document window opens; and the Web Page Wizard's Start panel is displayed.

4. Click the Wizard's **Next button**.
The wizard's Title and Location panel is displayed.

5. Click in the **Web site title text box** and type **JRT Kennels**.

6. Click in the **Web site location text box** and type **a:\default.htm**.

7. Click **Next**.
The Navigation panel is displayed.

8. Make sure **Vertical frame** is selected and click **Next**.
The Add Pages panel is displayed.

9. In the **Current pages in Web site list** do the following:
- Remove **Personal Web page** if it is in the list.
- Click the **Add Template Page button**, and a new window opens to show samples of the templates.
- Click **Left-aligned Column** and click **OK**, and the sample window closes.
- If **Blank Page 1** and **Blank Page 2** are shown in the list, leave them; if they are not in the list, click the **Add New Blank Page button** *twice*.

10. Click **Next**.
The Organize Pages panel is displayed.

11. In the text box listing the hyperlinks, select **Left-aligned Column** and then click the **Move Up button** *twice* to place it at the top of the list.

12. Click **Next**.
The Visual Theme panel is displayed.

13. Click the **Browse Themes button**.
The Theme dialog box opens.

14. In the **Choose a Theme list**, click **Cactus**.
A sample is shown.

15. Click **OK**.
The Theme dialog box closes. The Finish panel is displayed.

16. Click **Next**.

17. Click **Finish**.

Be patient while Word creates your Web document. Because it is being saved on a floppy disk, this will take a while. When the process is complete, the document is displayed on the screen in Web Layout View.

18. Click the **Print button**.

The document is printed.

19. Choose **File | Close**.

TASK 3 | *Creating a Web Page Using a Template*

What: Create a Web page using a Word template.

How: Choose File | New | Web Pages tab.

Why: Word can provide help organizing your site with a template.

Tip: If you want your company logo on your Web site, scan it and use it as you would any graphic image.

If you want more freedom creating your Web site than the Web Page Wizard gives you, you can use one of several templates that come with Word. You can add a theme to the page to provide consistent formatting.

To create a Web page using a template:

1. Choose File | New | Web Pages tab.
2. Choose a template and click OK.
3. Insert and delete text to customize the Web page.
4. Choose Format | Theme.
5. Select a theme and click OK.
6. Choose File | Save as Web Page to save the file in the correct format.
7. Choose File | Web Page Preview to view the page in your browser.
8. Click the Print button to print the page.

POINTER

When Not All Formats Will Convert

When you choose File | Save as Web Page, Word may caution you that some features aren't supported by browsers. If this happens, you can click the Continue button to ignore any problems.

---

1. With a formatted disk in the 3 1/2 Floppy (A) drive, choose **File | New | Web Pages tab**.
   The available templates and wizards are listed.

2. Choose **Right-aligned Column** and click **OK**.
   The dialog box closes, and a document based on the template is displayed, as shown in Figure 8.6.

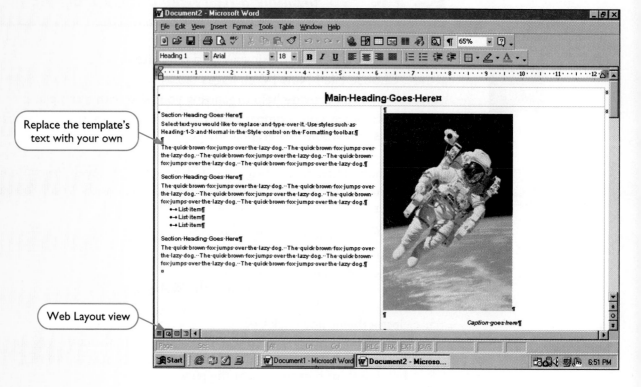

Replace the template's text with your own

Web Layout view

FIGURE 8.6 The Right-aligned Column Template

3. Select the **Main Heading** and type **your name**.

4. Choose **Format | Theme**.

5. Select **In Motion** in the Theme dialog box and click **OK**.
   The page is reformatted.

6. Choose **File | Save as Web Page**.
   The Save As dialog box opens.

7. Save the document as **Test Page** on the 3 1/2 Floppy (A) drive.
   The dialog box closes and Word saves the document. Be patient, because it will take a while.

8. Choose **File | Web Page Preview**.
   The document opens in your browser.

9. Click the **Print button** to print the page.

10. Close the browser.

TASK 4 | *Creating a Web Page from an Existing Word Document*

What: Create a Web Page using an existing document.
How: Choose File | Save As Web Page.
Why: You can use existing documents as part of a Web site.
Tip: Test your Web page in more than one browser because different browsers will display Web documents differently.

Web documents use a file format called **HyperText Markup Language,** or **HTML.** HTML is the computer language that is understood by all browser software—or almost so. Because HTML has been added to by various browser developers, not every formatting feature is understood by every browser. However, the newer browsers display most of the current formatting.

Word will save any open document in HTML format. To save a Word document file as a Web document:

1. Open or create a normal Word document.
2. Choose File | Save as Web Page.
3. Type a file name in the File name text box.
4. Make sure the *Save as type* box is set to Web Page.
5. Choose a drive and folder in which to save the document, and click OK.

The document is ready to be posted to the World Wide Web or to a server on your company intranet.

POINTER

Publishing Your Web Page

After creating a Web page, you will want to make it available to other people. To publish to the World Wide Web, contact an Internet Service Provider to host your page and get instructions.

EXERCISE 4 | *Saving an Existing Document as a Web Page*

1. Open the **eCom** document.
2. Choose **Format | Theme**.
3. Choose **Global Marketing** in the Theme dialog box and click **OK**.
   The document is displayed in Web Layout view with new formatting.
4. Choose **File | Save as Web Page**.
   The Save As dialog box opens.
5. Save the document as **Global**.
   The Save As dialog box closes, and Word saves the document. Be patient, because it takes a while.

6. Choose **File | Web Page Preview**.
The document is displayed in your browser.

7. Exit from the browser.

REVIEW

SUMMARY

After completing this unit, you should
* know how to create hyperlinks (page 190)
* be able to create Web documents using the Web Page Wizard (page 196)
* be able to create a Web page using a template (page 200)
* be able to create a Web page from an existing Word document (page 201)

KEY TERMS

browser (page 190)
dead link (page 193)
domain name (page 190)
HyperText Markup Language (HTML) (page 201)

HyperText Transfer Protocol (page 190)
Uniform Resource Locator (URL) (page 190)

TEST YOUR SKILLS

True/False

1. The URL is the address of a Web document.
2. All browsers display a particular HTML document exactly the same.
3. Links usually appear formatted—blue and underlined by default.
4. When you save a document as a Web document, Word converts it to HTML.
5. Hyperlinks can link to video and audio files.

Multiple Choice

1. A hyperlink
   a. links to documents located on the World Wide Web
   b. links to documents located on the company intranet
   c. links to documents on the hard drive
   d. all of these answers

2. When you save a document as a Web page, it is saved as what kind of document?
   a. a template   b. a theme
   c. an HTML document d. a hyperlink

3. To link to other Web pages, you would use
   a. templates   b. themes
   c. HTML   d. hyperlinks

4. When you save your file as a Web page, it can be viewed by a
   a. HTML   b. URL
   c. browser   d. template

5. The address of a Web document is the
   a. HTML   b. URL
   c. browser   d. all of these answers

Short Answer

Match the letter of the correct word with the correct location in Figure 8.7:

___ a. the HTML document   ___ b. title of Web page
___ c. hyperlink   ___ d. URL
___ e. menu bar

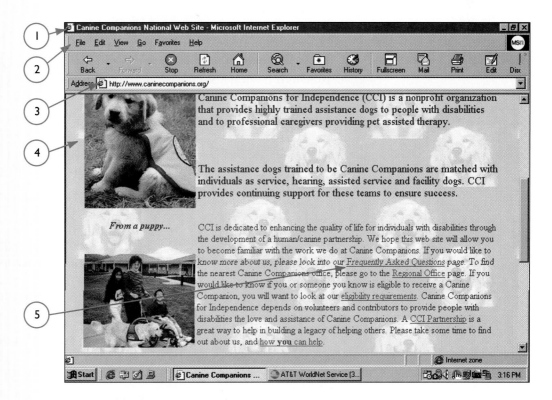

FIGURE 8.7

What Does This Do?

Write a brief description of the function of the following:

1.	For more information	6.	**Web Page Wizard**
2.		7.	◯ Horizontal frame
3.	◉ Vertical frame	8.	Save as Web Page...
4.	**Choose a Theme:**	9.	lindae@prenhall.com
5.	**Web site title:**	10.	http://www.irs.gov

On Your Own

1. Create a hyperlink from your document to a document located on the World Wide Web.
2. Save an existing document as a Web page.
3. Use the Web Page Wizard to create a Web page.
4. Use a Word template to create a Web page.
5. Research having a Web page hosted by an ISP in your area.

PROJECTS

1. a. Use the Personal Web Page template to create your own Web page. Use information about yourself or about an imaginary person. Format the page using an appropriate theme.
   b. Save the document as **Personal Web Page**, and then print the Web page.

2. a. Use the Web Page Wizard to create a home page for an organization such as one on your campus or one that you belong to. Format it appropriately.
   b. Save the document as **Organization Home Page** and then print the Web page.

3. a. Use the Table of Contents template to create a table of contents for your school's Web site.
   b. Save the document as **Table of Contents**. Print the Web page.

4. a. Open the **Y2K** document. Add hyperlinks to two documents on the Web.
   b. Save the document using the same name, and then print it.

PROJECTS

I. a. Create the data source shown below.
   b. Save it as **Tax** and then print it.

John Smith 234 Emerald St. Eugene, OR 97403	Sandra James 30355 Bay Ridge Pkwy. Ft. Lauderdale, FL 33308
Mary Jones 1925 Friendly St. Eugene, OR 97405	Sam O'Hara 456 Main St. New York, NY 09867

   c. Create a form letter as follows:

   • Create a letterhead for Reliable Tax and Accounting, 800 City View Parkway, Teaneck, New Jersey 00210.

   • Use fields from the *Tax* data source for the inside address and salutation.

   • Type the text shown below as the body of the letter.

> What is the last thing you want to spend your free time doing?
> That's right—your taxes.
> Take the frustration and worry out of doing your taxes this year by trusting the experts at Reliable Tax and Accounting. Each of us has over 10 years of experience and we are all certified Tax Preparation Professionals.
> For information on our competitive rates, call us today at 1-800-555-5555 or e-mail us at reliable@taxes.com.
> Sincerely,
>
> Your name

d. Save the form letter as **Reliable** and then print it.
e. Merge the form letters with the *Tax* data source. Print the letters.
f. Create mailing labels to accompany the letters. Print the labels.

2. Create a Web site for the Reliable Tax and Accounting Service. Use an appropriate visual theme. Make up information for the site. Print the site.

WRAP-UP

You are starting a travel service called Barefoot Adventures, which will take small groups of visitors to out-of-the-way places. To get the business started, you need to do the following:

- Create a letterhead (make up your own address information) including a graphic and print it.
- Use the letterhead to create a promotional letter; print the letter.
- Create business cards and print them.
- Run the Brochure Wizard, located on the Publications tab, and create a brochure that highlights locations to which you will be taking people on your trips. Print the brochure.

- Create a Web site for Barefoot Adventures. Print the Web site.
- Create a data source of five students in your class. Print the data source.
- Create a form letter using the letterhead, telling students about Barefoot Adventures. Print the form letter.
- Merge the form letter and data source. Print the resulting letters.
- Create mailing labels using the data source. Print the labels.

Getting Started

UNIT OBJECTIVES

- Start Microsoft Excel 2000
- Become familiar with the Excel interface
- Use Microsoft Excel Help
- Create a worksheet
- Save a workbook
- Print a worksheet
- Exit from Excel
- Open and close workbooks

In this book, you will learn to use the electronic spreadsheet application Microsoft Excel 2000. A **spreadsheet** is a grid of rows and columns into which you can enter text, numbers, and formulas for purposes of calculation and data analysis. Spreadsheets are used to create budgets, analyze costs, produce financial plans, and perform a host of other simple and complex numerical applications. What makes electronic spreadsheets so useful is that when one value changes, all related values are automatically updated. Thus you can use a spreadsheet to perform "what-if?" analysis, changing a value in a formula and immediately seeing the result as it ripples through the whole spreadsheet, or **worksheet**, to use Excel's term. In Unit 1, you learn how to start Excel and create, save, and print a simple worksheet.

What: Start Microsoft Excel 2000.

How: Click the Start button and choose Programs | Microsoft Excel.

Why: You must know how to start an application in order to use it.

Tip: If you are working in a computer lab, you may be given instructions for another way to start Excel.

Microsoft Excel 2000 is part of the Microsoft Office 2000 suite of applications for Windows 98 or Windows 95. You start it just as you start any other Windows program. To start Excel:

1. Click the Start button.
2. Point to Programs.
3. Click Microsoft Excel, as shown in Figure 1.1.

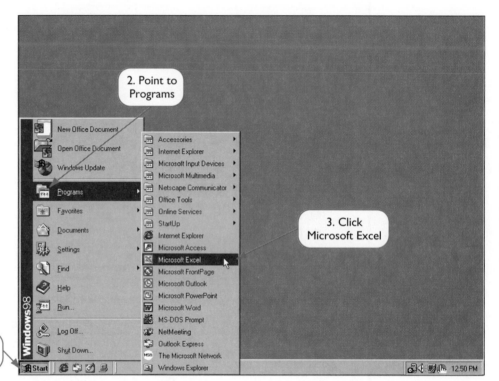

FIGURE 1.1 Starting Excel

EXERCISE 1 | *Starting Microsoft Excel 2000*

1. Click the **Start button** on the Windows taskbar.
   The Start menu opens.

2. Point to **Programs**.
   The Programs menu opens.

3. Click **Microsoft Excel.**
Excel starts and opens a new workbook, as shown in Figure 1.2.

4. Keep Excel on your screen for use in the next exercise.

TASK 2	*Becoming Familiar with the Excel Interface*

What: Learn to use the various parts of the Excel interface.
How: Use the mouse to explore.
Why: To use Excel effectively, you need to be familiar with its elements.
Tip: If you know Word, PowerPoint, or another Microsoft Office program, you already know a lot about Excel.

Figure 1.2 shows the Microsoft Excel screen that greets you when you start the program. Excel uses a **graphical user interface**, or **GUI** (pronounced "goo-ey").

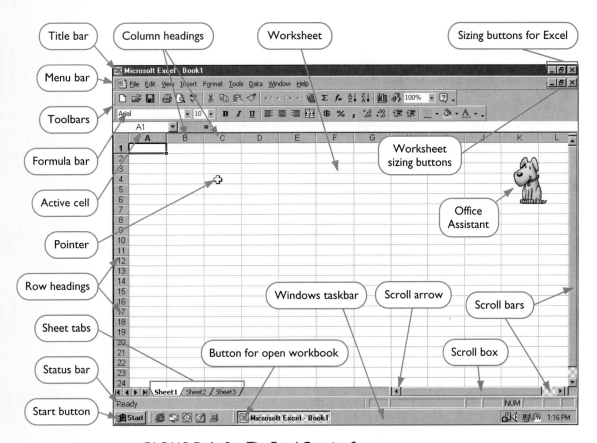

FIGURE 1.2   The Excel Opening Screen

That is, you communicate with the computer by selecting icons and other graphical elements on the screen rather than by typing commands. The opening Excel screen displays a worksheet (Excel's term for a spreadsheet) ready for you to enter text, numbers, and formulas. The window contains elements common to all Microsoft Office (and most Microsoft Windows) applications and some elements that are unique to Excel.

WORKSHEETS AND WORKBOOKS

Excel stores worksheets in files called **workbooks**, and a single workbook can contain many worksheets. When you start Excel, a new workbook is open on the screen, temporarily named Book 1. This workbook contains three worksheets, temporarily named Sheet 1, Sheet 2, and Sheet 3. Sheet 1 is displayed on the opening screen. Storing multiple worksheets in a single workbook file enables you to group related data. You will see how this works in Unit 7. Until then, you'll be working with a single worksheet stored in a workbook.

TITLE BAR

Like all windows, the Excel window has a **title bar** across the top. The title bar names the program and the workbook contained in the window. At its right edge, it displays the buttons described in Table 1.1.

Button	Name	Description
▬	Minimize	Shrinks the open window to a button on the taskbar
▢	Maximize	Enlarges the window to fill the desktop
▣	Restore	In a maximized window, replaces the Maximize button, returning the window to its previous size
✖	Close	Closes the window

TABLE 1.1   Buttons That Close and Size a Window

MENU BAR

Excel's **menu bar**, which is located below its title bar, displays the names of menus, as seen in Figure 1.2. When you click a menu name, a pull-down menu appears from which you select a command or other option, as shown in Figure 1.3.

When you click a menu name, a set of basic menu options appears; in a few seconds, the menu expands to show the complete list. As you work, Excel keeps track of which menu options you use and adds those options to the short menu. At any time, you can click the down arrows at the bottom of the menu to display the full menu.

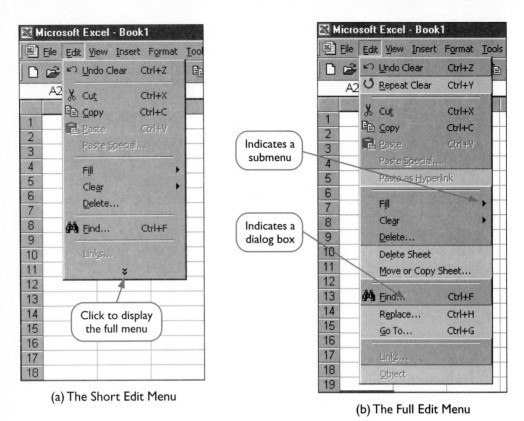

(a) The Short Edit Menu

(b) The Full Edit Menu

FIGURE 1.3 Menus

POINTER

Display the Full Menu

Excel lets you customize many of its features, and the menu display is one of them. You can choose to see the full menus immediately instead of after a pause. You'll see how to do this in Exercise 2.

Instructions in this text to choose menu commands are shown as **Menu Name | Menu Command**. For example, "choose File | Open" means to choose File from the menu bar and Open from the pull-down menu.

POINTER

Use the Keyboard to Open a Menu

Notice that each menu name in Figures 1.2 and 1.3 has an underlined letter. You can press and hold the Alt key and then press the underlined letter in the menu name to open the menu. For example, to open the File menu, you can click its name on the menu bar or hold down the Alt key and press the letter F. Once a menu is open, you can choose a command by clicking it or by pressing the underlined letter in the command name.

To close a menu without choosing a command, either click the mouse outside the menu or press the Esc key on the keyboard.

At the right edge of the menu bar are sizing buttons for the open worksheet. Clicking the Close Window button on the menu bar closes the worksheet window but leaves Excel open.

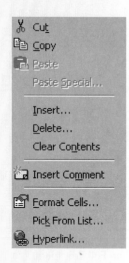

POINTER

Shortcut Menus

Like other Windows programs, Excel provides quick access to often-used tasks on **shortcut menus**. Point to the worksheet and click the right mouse button to display the shortcut menu. Select options from the menu.

A menu choice on pull-down menus can appear:

- with a check mark (✓) in front of it—to indicate an option that is turned on in a group where more than one choice is permitted
- without a check mark (✓)—to indicate that the option is turned off
- with a dot (●) in front of it—to indicate the option that is turned on in a group where only one choice is permitted
- grayed-out—to indicate it is not available at the present time
- followed by a right-pointing arrow (▶)— to indicate that clicking it will open a submenu
- followed by an ellipsis (…)—to indicate that clicking it will open a dialog box like the one shown in Figure 1.4. A **dialog box** is a window in which you provide Excel with information needed to perform a task. You will use the Save As and Print dialog boxes later in this unit.

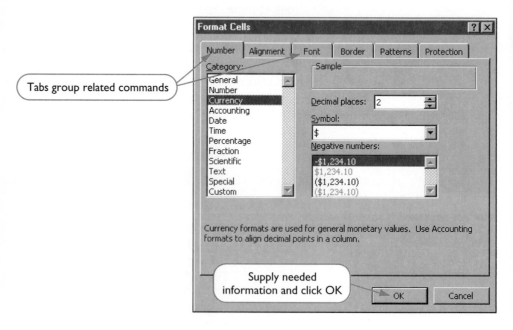

FIGURE 1.4   A Dialog Box

Moving Dialog Boxes

When a dialog box opens on the screen and you need to see the area of the worksheet that it has covered, click and drag the title bar of the dialog box to move it on the screen.

TOOLBARS

Excel has more than a dozen toolbars with buttons you can click to perform actions. Some toolbars are displayed by default; others appear only when needed; and some can be displayed manually by choosing View | Toolbars. Toolbars save you time.

Clicking a toolbar button has the same effect as choosing a command from the menu bar but is quicker. Besides buttons, toolbars can contain list boxes. Clicking the drop-down list arrow at the right edge of the box (▼) opens a list from which you can make a choice.

The **Standard** and **Formatting toolbars** are displayed by default. The Standard toolbar contains buttons for commands from the File and Edit menus and other buttons that start some of Excel's special features. The Formatting toolbar contains buttons for commands from the Format menu. These toolbars normally appear below the menu bar, but you can move them, as explained in the pointer box "Moving a Toolbar." The two toolbars can share a single row or can be displayed on separate rows. When the toolbars are separate, each displays its complete set of buttons. When the toolbars share a row, Excel personalizes them for you. It keeps track of which buttons you have used recently and displays those buttons, displacing buttons that haven't been used. To display the missing buttons, you click the More Buttons button at one end of the toolbar. Figure 1.5 shows the Standard and Formatting toolbars.

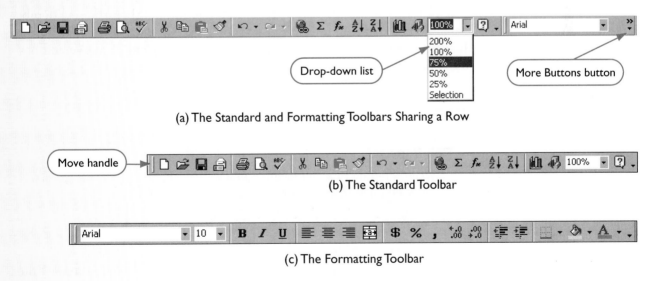

(a) The Standard and Formatting Toolbars Sharing a Row

(b) The Standard Toolbar

(c) The Formatting Toolbar

FIGURE 1.5   Toolbars

WORKSHEET

The worksheet is a grid of vertical **columns** and horizontal **rows**. The letters across the top of the worksheet are the column names, and the numbers down the side are the row numbers. The intersection of a column and row is a **cell**. Cell locations are designated by the column letter and then the row number. Thus the cell at the intersection of column B and row 8 is cell B8. This is the **cell address** or the **cell reference**. Notice the current or **active cell** has a heavy border.

- To make a cell active, you click it.
- To enter text and numbers into the active cell, type them and press Enter.

Scroll bars at the right edge and bottom of the worksheet window allow you to move through a document using the mouse. Click the arrows, drag the scroll box, or click the space on either side of the scroll box to view different parts of the worksheet.

The horizontal scroll bar contains **sheet tabs** you click to move from one worksheet to another within a workbook. (You will learn to use multiple worksheets in Unit 7.)

FORMULA BAR

Above the worksheet, below the toolbars, is the **formula bar**, shown in Figure 1.6. At its left is the **name box**, which identifies the cell location of the current or active cell. The large text box at its right displays the contents of the active cell. You can place contents in the active cell by typing it in the cell or in this box. Once you begin to type, two buttons appear on the formula bar. The Cancel button cancels the current typing operation; the Enter button enters the currently typed contents into the active cell, completing the entry.

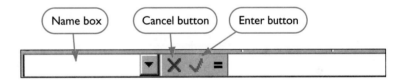

FIGURE 1.6 The Formula Bar

STATUS BAR

At the bottom of the window is the **status bar**, which displays information about the selected command or operation that you are performing. The left edge of the status bar displays information about the action being taken. For instance, when Excel is ready for you to enter information in the current cell, the status bar displays "Ready." While you are entering data, it displays "Enter." The right side of the status bar contains indicators to inform you that you have the Num Lock, Caps Lock, or other keys turned on.

WINDOWS TASKBAR

The Windows **taskbar**, which appears along the bottom of the screen, contains the Start button and buttons for all open programs and files. When you have two or more workbooks open in Excel, the taskbar displays a button for each of them.

1. With Excel open on your screen, choose **Tools | Customize**.
Click the Tools menu name on the menu bar, and when a pull-down menu opens, click the Customize command. The Customize dialog box opens on the screen.

2. Click the **Options tab**.
The Options tab moves to the front and becomes active. It displays the current settings for the toolbars as well as other interface options you can customize. You could click a box to select it or clear it, and then click the Close button to change the option. Examine the options before you go to the next step.

3. Click the **Close button**.
The dialog box closes.

4. Move the mouse pointer over any **toolbar button** and hold it there.
A ScreenTip shows the name of the button.

5. Click the **Minimize button** on the title bar.
Excel is reduced to a button on the taskbar.

6. Click the **Microsoft Excel button** on the taskbar.
The Excel window is restored to its former size.

7. Keep Excel running for use in the next exercise.

TASK 3 | *Getting Help*

What: Use Excel's online Help.
How: Click the Office Assistant or choose Help | Microsoft Excel Help.
Why: Excel provides extensive online documentation that is easy to use.
Tip: Press the F1 key on the keyboard to launch Excel Help.

When the **Office Assistant** is visible on the screen, Help is just a click away. Click the cartoon character to open the Help bubble shown in Figure 1.7a.

To get help:

1. Type a question into the text box. For instance, if you can't remember which is the workbook and which is the worksheet, you could type "What's the difference between workbooks and worksheets?"
2. Click the Search button. Excel will provide a list of Help topics to choose from, as shown in Figure 1.7b.
3. Select a topic from the list to display the Help document, as shown in Figure 1.7c.
4. To display the entire Help window, click the Show button. The window expands to include the Contents, Answer Wizard, and Index tabs, along with the Help buttons shown in Figure 1.7d and described in Table 1.2.

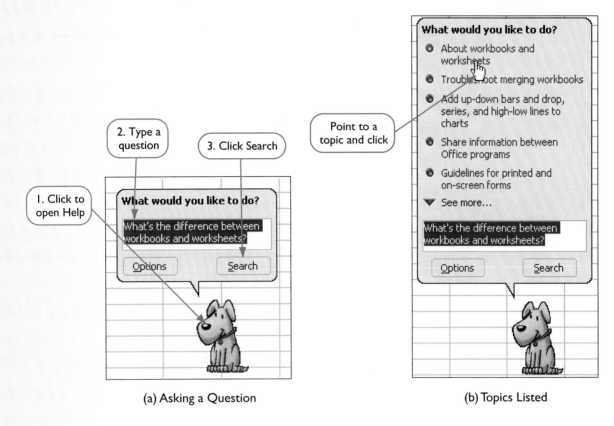

(a) Asking a Question

(b) Topics Listed

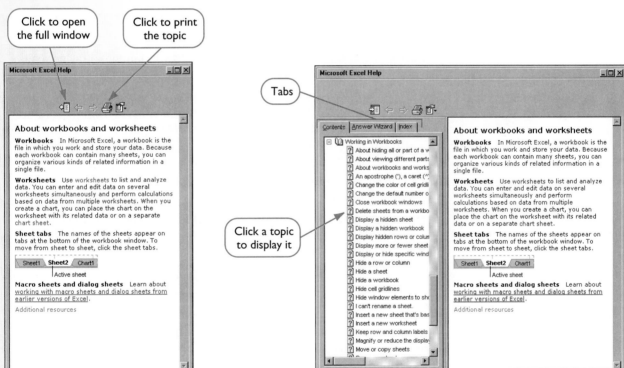

(c) The Help Topic Displayed

(d) The Full Help Window

FIGURE 1.7   Using Excel's Help

Button	Description
	Reduces the Help window to hide the tabs
	Returns to the previous Help topic
	If you have used the Back button, you can click the Forward button to return to the previous topic
	Prints the current Help topic
	Provides options on a drop-down list

TABLE 1.2 Buttons in the Microsoft Excel Help Window

- To use Help Contents, click the Contents tab. Click the plus sign before the topic to display the list of subtopics. (The plus sign then changes to a minus sign.) Click a topic to display the Help document.

- To use the Answer Wizard, click the Answer Wizard tab. Type a question in the text box and click the Search button. Excel will display a list of Help topics.

- To use the Help Index, click the Index tab. Type a topic in the Keywords text box and click the Search button. Excel will display a list of topics.

POINTER

Displaying, Hiding, and Changing Assistants

Rocky, one of the Office Assistants, says, "If you fall into a ravine, call Lassie. If you need help in Office, call Rocky."

- If the Office Assistant isn't displayed on the screen, choose Help | Microsoft Excel Help, press the F1 key on the keyboard, or click the Microsoft Excel Help button on the Standard toolbar.

- If Rocky gets in the way, drag him to another part of the screen or choose Help | Hide the Office Assistant. If you would prefer a different Assistant, right-click Rocky and select Choose Assistant from the shortcut menu.

- To stop using the Assistant, right-click Rocky, choose Options from the shortcut menu, and clear the *Use the Office Assistant* check box in the Options tab of the Office Assistant dialog box.

To use other Help features:

- To get Help on screen features, choose Help | What's This? The mouse pointer changes to the Help pointer, with a question mark. Click any part of the screen to get Help on that feature.

- To link to up-to-date help, choose Help | Office on the Web. Excel will open your browser and connect you to Microsoft's Web site.

- To get Help in a dialog box, click the question mark button in the dialog box title bar. The pointer changes to the Help pointer, with a question mark. Click the option in the dialog box that you want explained. Excel will display an explanation, as shown in Figure 1.8.

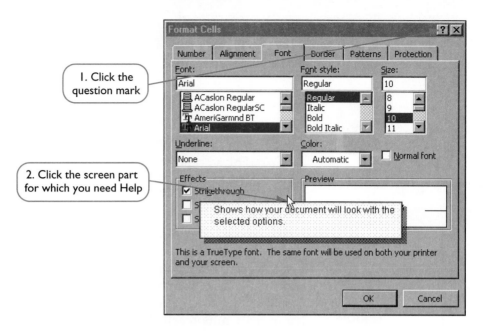

1. Click the question mark

2. Click the screen part for which you need Help

FIGURE 1.8 Help in a Dialog Box

POINTER

Connecting to Microsoft on the Web

You must have a **modem** and an **Internet Service Provider** to successfully log on to the Web from your home or be attached to a network with a gateway to the Internet at work or in a computer lab.

EXERCISE 3 | *Getting Help*

1. If the Office Assistant is not already displayed, choose **Help | Microsoft Excel Help**.

The Assistant appears on the screen, and the Help bubble appears.

2. If the Office Assistant is already on the screen, click the **Office Assistant**.

The Help bubble appears.

3. Type **What's the difference between workbooks and worksheets?** and click the **Search button**.

A list of topics is displayed in the Help bubble.

4. Click **About workbooks and worksheets**.

The Microsoft Excel Help window opens and displays the page you selected.

5. Read the contents of the Help window and then click the **Show button**.

The window expands to display the tabs.

6. Click the **Close button** in the Help window.

The Help window closes. Keep Excel running for use in the next exercise.

What: Move around the worksheet.

How: Use the scroll bars, the mouse, or the arrow keys.

Why: Many worksheets are too large to be displayed on the screen.

Tip: For a complete list of keys for moving around a worksheet, search for help on keyboard shortcuts.

IU	IV
	65533
	65534
	65535
	65536

When you start Excel, a new worksheet opens. But what you see on your screen is only a small part of the whole sheet. If you use the scroll bars to move to the right, you discover that the column headings don't end with Z. Column Z is followed by columns AA, column AB, and so forth, all the way through column IV. In fact, a worksheet has 256 columns. If you scroll down to the bottom of the sheet, you will see that there are 65,536 rows. Each worksheet has over 16 million cells.

POINTER

Cells, Cells, Cells

Each new workbook you open contains three worksheets, each with 256 columns and 65,536 rows, or 16,777,216 individual cells. If you multiply the number of cells in a single worksheet by the default three sheets, the result is more than 50 million cells in a workbook. And you can add new worksheets to a workbook, each with 16,777,216 cells of its own. You are not likely to run out of room for your data in Excel.

To move to a cell location that you can see on the screen, click in it. That cell will become the active cell.

To move to areas that you can't see on the screen:

- Use the keys described in Table 1.3.
- Use the scroll bars, or the **scroll box**. If you drag the scroll box, a **ScrollTip** will tell you the exact row number you are scrolling past vertically and the exact column letter you are scrolling past horizontally.
- Choose Edit | Go To to open the Go To dialog box, shown in Figure 1.9a, where you can type a cell location.
- Type a cell location in the name box on the formula bar (see Figure 1.9b) and press Enter.

Keystroke	Result
Arrow key	Moves one cell in the direction of the arrow
Ctrl + arrow key	Moves in the direction of the arrow to the last cell before a blank cell or to the edge of the worksheet if all cells are blank
Page Up	Moves up one screen
Page Down	Moves down one screen
Home	Moves to the beginning of the row
Ctrl + Home	Moves to cell A1
Crtl + End	Moves to the last cell containing data (in the bottom right of the worksheet)

TABLE 1.3 Keys for Moving Around a Worksheet

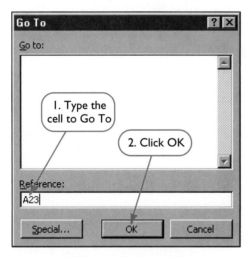

(a) The Go To Dialog Box   (b) The Name Box on the Formula Bar

FIGURE 1.9 Going to a Specific Cell

`100%` ▼

POINTER

Changing the Zoom

If you want to change the size of the display to enlarge it or to see more information on the screen, click the down arrow for the Zoom box on the Standard toolbar. A list drops down from which you can click a selection. To set a custom zoom, type a number in the Zoom box and press Enter.

1. With Excel running and a worksheet open on the screen, hold down the **Ctrl key** and press the **Home key**.
The active cell should be A1.

2. Hold down **Ctrl** and press the **right arrow key**.
The active cell should be IV1. Column IV is the right-most column in the worksheet.

3. Hold down **Ctrl** and press the **down arrow key**.
The active cell should be IV65536. This is the bottom right cell in the worksheet.

4. Hold down **Ctrl** and press **Home**.
The active cell should be A1.

5. Choose **Edit | Go To**.
The Go To dialog box opens.

6. Type **Z200** in the Reference text box and click **OK**.
The active cell should be Z200.

7. Click in the name box on the formula bar, type **A10**, and press **Enter**.
The active cell should be A10.

8. Use the arrow keys and scroll bars to move around the worksheet; then leave the worksheet open for use in the next exercise.

TASK 5 | *Creating a Worksheet Using Text, Numbers, and the AutoSum Function*

What: Place text and numbers in cells.

How: Type data in the active cell.

Why: Creating a worksheet of your own is the best way to start learning Excel.

Tip: Use different methods to complete a cell entry, depending on the location of the next cell you want to select.

To create a worksheet, you type constants and formulas into cells.

• A **constant** is a cell value that does not change. It can be either text or numbers. Text in worksheets is also referred to as **labels**, because it is used to identify the numeric data. When you type text in a cell, Excel aligns it at the left. When you type numbers, Excel aligns them at the right.

• A **formula** specifies the steps used to make a calculation. It can contain numbers, cell references, and mathematical operators such as multiplication and division signs. It can also contain built-in **functions**, which are predefined calculations. All formulas and functions in Excel start with an equal sign.

When you have finished typing the contents of a cell, you complete the entry using any of the following methods:

- Click the Enter button on the formula bar to complete the entry and leave the current cell selected.
- Press the Enter key on the keyboard to complete the entry and select the cell below.
- Press the Tab key to complete the entry and select the cell to the right.
- Press an arrow key to complete the entry and select the next cell in the direction of the arrow.
- Click in another cell to complete the entry and select the clicked cell.

Cancel or edit an entry as follows:

- To cancel typing before completing an entry, click the Cancel button on the formula bar or press the Esc key on the keyboard.
- To edit an entry before completing it, press the Backspace key and type the correct characters.
- To edit an entry after completing it, double-click the cell to place the insertion point in it, and use the arrow keys, the Backspace key, and the Delete key to correct the errors.

In the following exercise, you will enter text and numbers into a worksheet. You will also have Excel use one of its built-in functions to perform calculations. In later units, you will learn to create your own formulas and use more powerful functions.

> ### POINTER
>
> **AutoSum**
>
> Because the addition operation is used so often when creating spreadsheets, Excel has created a shortcut for adding cells. The AutoSum button on the toolbar uses the SUM function to add a **range** or group of cells. AutoSum can add a row of adjacent numbers or a column of numbers. Because Excel has to guess what cells you want to add, it outlines them for you in a blinking box. You will learn to change the selected cells in the next unit. To perform the calculation, click the Enter button on the formula bar.

> ### POINTER
>
> **A Physical Workout Log**
>
> Working out has become a common activity, and many people want to see their progress, so you will create a workout log for walking. To keep it simple, you'll record just three days and a total. When you become more familiar with Excel, you can expand and modify the log to match your personal exercise program.

1. With Excel running and a worksheet open on the screen, click in cell A1 and type **Workout Log**.
   The text appears in the formula bar and in cell A1. As you complete the following steps, check your progress against Figure 1.10.

2. Press **Enter**.
   The entry is completed, and A2 becomes the active cell. Notice that the text aligns at the left of the cell.

3. Type **your name** in cell A2 and press **Enter**.
   As you type, your name appears in the cell and in the formula bar. When you press Enter, the entry is completed, and A3 becomes the active cell.

4. Click in **B4**.
   B4 becomes the active cell.

5. Type **Mon**.
   The text appears in the formula bar and in cell B4.

6. Press the **Tab key**.
   The entry is completed, and C4 becomes the active cell.

7. Type **Tue** and press the **right arrow key**.
   The text is entered in cell C4, and D4 becomes the active cell.

8. Type **Wed** and click the **Enter button** on the formula bar.
   The entry is completed, and D4 remains selected.

9. Click in **E4** and type **Total**.
   The text appears in the formula bar and in cell E4.

10. Click in **A5**.
    The entry in E4 is completed, and A5 becomes the active cell.

11. Type **Miles** and press **Enter**.
    The text appears in A5, and A6 becomes active.

12. Type **Minutes** and press **Enter**.
    The text appears in A6, and A7 becomes active.

13. Type **Heart rate** and press **Enter**.
    The text appears in A7, and A8 becomes the active cell. Your screen should look like Figure 1.10.

14. Keep the workout log on the screen and proceed to the next exercise.

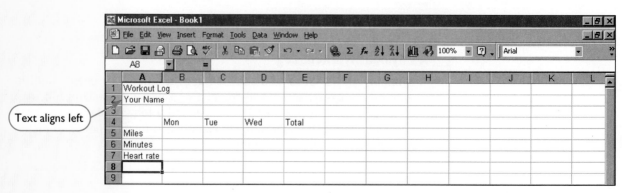

FIGURE 1.10   The Workout Log with Text

1. With the worksheet open from Exercise 5A, click in **B5**, type **4.5**, and press the **right arrow key**.

The number is placed in B5, and C5 becomes the active cell. Note that the number aligns at the right of the cell. As you complete the following steps, check your progress against Figure 1.11. If you are comfortable with entering data, skip the steps and use the figure as a model.

2. Type **6** and press the **right arrow key**.

The number is placed in C5, and D5 becomes the active cell.

3. Type **5.3** and press **Enter**.

The number is placed in D5, and D6 becomes the active cell.

4. Click in **B6**, type **35**, and click the **right arrow key**.

The number is placed in B6, and C6 becomes the active cell.

5. Type **55** and click the **right arrow key**.

The number is placed in C6, and D6 becomes the active cell.

6. Type **45** and press **Enter**.

The number is placed in D6, and D7 becomes the active cell.

7. Click in **B7**, type **120**, and press the **right arrow key**.

The number is placed in B7, and C7 becomes the active cell.

8. Type **180** and press the **right arrow key**.

The number is placed in C7, and D7 becomes the active cell.

9. Type **160** and press **Enter**.

The number is placed in D7 and D8 becomes the active cell. Your screen should look like Figure 1.11.

10. Keep the workout log on the screen and proceed to the next exercise.

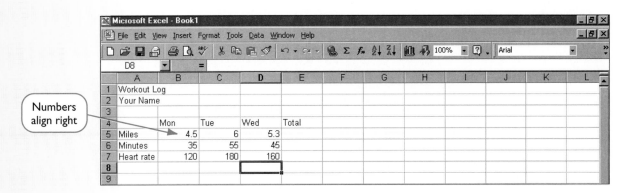

FIGURE 1.11   The Workout Log with Numbers

I. With the worksheet open from Exercise 5B, click in **E5**.
E5 becomes the active cell.

2. Click the **AutoSum button** on the Standard toolbar.
Excel displays the SUM function and outlines the cells used in the function, as shown in Figure 1.12.

3. Click the **Enter button** on the formula bar.
The result of the addition appears in the cell.

4. Click in **E6**.
E6 becomes the active cell.

5. Click the **AutoSum button**.
Excel displays the SUM function and outlines the cells used in the function.

6. Click the **Enter button** on the formula bar.
The result of the addition appears in the cell.

7. Keep the workout log on the screen and proceed to the next task.

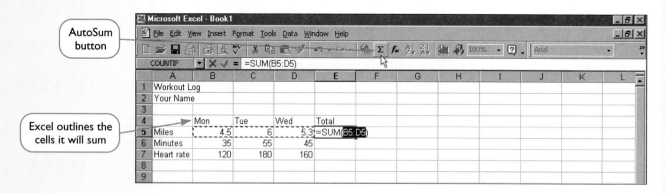

FIGURE 1.12 Using the AutoSum Button to Calculate Totals

TASK 6 | *Saving a Workbook*

What: Save a workbook on a disk.

How: Choose File | Save As.

Why: When the computer is turned off, the workbook will be lost unless you have saved it.

Tip: It's a good idea to save your work every 10 to 15 minutes to avoid losing a lot of work if the system shuts down unexpectedly.

To save a workbook you have created:

1. Choose File | Save As. The Save As dialog box opens, as shown in Figure 1.13a.
2. Type a name for the workbook in the File name text box.
3. Specify the drive and folder to store the document in the Save in list box, as shown in Figure 1.13b.
4. Click the Save button.

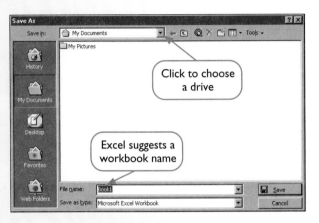

(a) The Default File Name and Location   (b) Naming the Workbook and Selecting a Drive

FIGURE 1.13   The Save As Dialog Box

CHOOSING A FILE NAME

Keep these points in mind when choosing names for your files:

- Excel suggests a name for the workbook in the File name text box, such as Book1.
- Excel automatically adds **.xls** on the end of document names. This **three-letter extension** to the file name is used by the software to display and open files. The .xls extension designates the file as a Microsoft Excel workbook.
- Workbooks can be given names of up to 255 characters. You should give your workbooks meaningful names that represent their content, so that finding them later will be easy.
- The following characters can't be used in file names: / \ > < * ? | : ; You don't have to memorize these characters, because if you try to save a workbook using one of them, a message box prompts you to choose a different name.

POINTER

Erasing the Name in the File Name Text Box

Because the suggested file name is selected (highlighted) when you open the Save As dialog box, you don't need to erase the suggested name before giving the file a different name. Simply start typing, and the name you type will replace the suggested name.

CHOOSING A DRIVE AND FOLDER

When you save a workbook, you must specify the drive (and optional folder) in which it will be stored. When you open the Save As dialog box, the Save in **list box** shows the default drive and folder for saving Excel workbooks, or the most recently used folder if that is different.

- Make sure the Save in list box shows the disk drive in which you want to save the workbook.
- If it does not, click the down arrow in the list box to display a list of the drives on your system.
- Click a different drive to select it and move it into the Save in list box. For instance, to save the document on a floppy disk in drive A, you would click 3½ Floppy (A), as shown in Figure 1.13b.
- The folders and files in the selected drive are shown in the list in the dialog box. To save a document in one of the folders, double-click the folder name to select it and move it into the Save in list box.

POINTER

Using File | Save

After you have saved a file and given it a name using the File | Save As option, save it again by choosing File | Save, by clicking the Save button on the toolbar, or by pressing Ctrl+S. All three of these options perform the same task—that is, saving the current file under the name you gave it without opening the Save As dialog box.

POINTER

Choosing a File Type

The *Save as type* list box lets you choose a file type for your documents. (Click the down arrow in the box to see the types available.) Ordinarily you want to use the default format, *Microsoft Excel Workbook*, but you can choose another type if you need to send the document to someone who doesn't have Microsoft Excel 2000 or if you want to post it on the Web.

EXERCISE 6 | *Saving the Workbook*

1. With the workout log open on the screen, choose **File | Save As**.
   The Save As dialog box opens, with the suggested name *Book1* selected.

2. Type **Workout Log**
   The name replaces the suggested name.

3. Click the down arrow in the **Save in list box**.
   A list of drives drops down, as shown in Figure 1.13b.

4. Insert a formatted disk into drive A on the computer, and then choose **3½ Floppy (A)**.
   The Save in list box reflects the change.

5. Click the dialog box's **Save button**.
   The file will be saved on the disk in drive A. The title bar shows the new name.

6. Keep the worksheet on the screen for use in the next exercise.

TASK 7 | *Printing a Worksheet*

What: Produce a hard copy of a worksheet.

How: Choose File | Print.

Why: You will want to have paper copies of your worksheets.

Tip: To send the worksheet to the attached printer without changing any options, click the Print button on the Standard toolbar or press Ctrl+P.

When you choose File | Print, the Print dialog box opens, as shown in Figure 1.14.

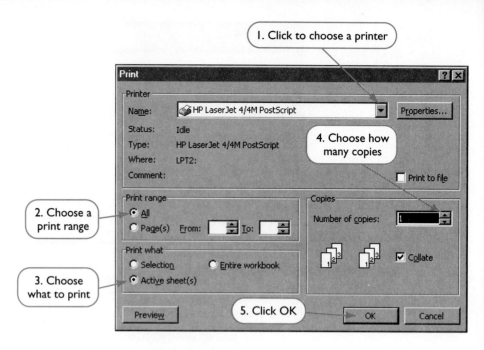

FIGURE 1.14 The Print Dialog Box

To print a worksheet:

1. Check the Printer name to see which printer will actually print the document. To change printers, click the down arrow in the Name list box and select a different printer from the list.
2. Change the print range if necessary, using the options shown in Table 1.4.

Page Range	Description
All	All is the default selection, which will print the entire worksheet
Pages	Prints specified pages

TABLE 1.4 Print Range Options

3. Change Print What if necessary, using the options in Table 1.5.

Print What	Description
Selection	Prints only the cells that are selected
Active Sheets	Prints every selected worksheet
Entire Workbook	Prints all worksheets that contain any data

TABLE 1.5 Print What Options

4. Change the Copies option to change the number of copies that will be printed.
5. Click OK to print the worksheet.

EXERCISE 7 | *Printing the Worksheet*

1. Choose **File | Print**.
   The Print dialog box opens.

2. In the Printer section, check the printer shown in the **Name** list box to be sure you will print to the correct printer.

3. Check that **All** is selected in the Page range and that Number of copies is set to **1**.

4. Make certain that your printer is turned on and has paper loaded.

5. Click the **OK button**.
   The worksheet will print.

6. Leave the workbook open for use in the next exercise.

TASK 8 | *Exiting from Excel*

What: Exit from Excel.

How: Choose File | Exit.

Why: You must exit from the software correctly and close Windows before turning off the computer.

Tip: You can also exit by clicking the Close button on the title bar.

You should always exit from Microsoft Excel when you are finished working with the application. You do so by choosing File | Exit. If you have not saved the file you were working on, Excel will prompt you to do so. When you exit from Excel, you are returned to the Windows opening screen.

EXERCISE 8 | *Exiting from Excel*

1. Choose **File | Exit**.

2. If you are asked to save your file, select **No**.

TASK 9 | *Opening and Closing Workbooks*

What: Open and close workbooks you have saved on disk.

How: Choose File | Open and File | Close.

Why: You will want to open files saved on your disk, and you will also want to close files that you are finished working with.

Tip: The Open dialog box works the same way as the Save As dialog box.

When you start Excel, a new workbook opens on the screen. To use a previously saved workbook, you must open it. To open a workbook:

1. Choose File | Open to display the Open dialog box, shown in Figure 1.15.
2. In the Look in list box, select the drive where the workbook is stored. This will display the drive's folders and documents in the dialog box.
3. If the workbook is stored in a folder, double-click the folder in the list. This will move the folder into the Look in box and display its workbooks in the dialog box.
4. Select the workbook from the list in the dialog box.
5. Click the Open button, and the workbook will open.

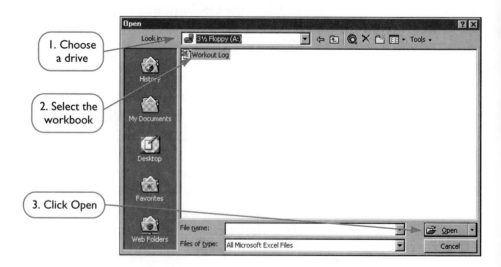

FIGURE 1.15   The Open Dialog Box

Sometimes you will want to close open workbooks and continue working in Excel. Close a workbook by choosing File | Close. If you have made changes to the workbook that you have not saved, Excel will display the message box shown in Figure 1.16.

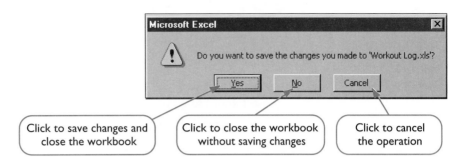

FIGURE 1.16 The Save Changes Message Box

You can:

- Save the file and close it
- Close the file without saving it
- Cancel the operation

POINTER

Opening and Closing Workbooks with Buttons

You can open a workbook using the Open button on the Standard toolbar instead of by choosing File | Open, and you can close a workbook but stay in Excel by clicking the Close Window button on the menu bar.

EXERCISE 9 | *Opening and Closing Workbooks*

1. Start Excel.
   A new workbook opens in the workbook window.

2. Choose **File | Open**.
   The Open dialog box opens.

3. Select the drive and folder that contains the **Workout Log** workbook.
   The file is listed in the dialog box.

4. If necessary, click the file name **Workout Log** to select it, and then click the **Open button**.
   The *Workout Log* workbook is displayed on the screen.

5. Choose **File | Close**.
   The workbook closes but you remain in Excel.

6. Click the **Close button** on the title bar.

REVIEW

SUMMARY

After completing this unit, you should be able to
- start Microsoft Excel 2000 (page 2)
- identify the parts of the Excel window (page 3)
- use Excel Help (page 10)
- create a worksheet (page 16)
- save a workbook (page 20)
- print a worksheet (page 23)
- exit from Excel (page 25)
- open saved workbooks (page 27)
- close workbooks (page 27)

KEY TERMS

active cell (page 8)
cell (page 8)
cell address (page 8)
cell reference (page 8)
column (page 8)
constant (page 16)
dialog box (page 6)
Formatting toolbar (page 7)
formula (page 16)
formula bar (page 9)
function (page 16)
graphical user interface
 (GUI) (page 3)
Internet Service Provider
 (ISP) (page 13)
labels (page 16)
list box (page 22)
maximize (page 4)
menu bar (page 4)
minimize (page 4)

modem (page 13)
name box (page 9)
Office Assistant (page 10)
range (page 17)
row (page 8)
ScreenTip (page 8)
ScrollTip (page 14)
scroll bar (page 9)
scroll box (page 14)
sheet tabs (page 9)
shortcut menu (page 6)
spreadsheet (page 1)
Standard toolbar (page 7)
status bar (page 9)
taskbar (page 9)
three-letter extension (page 21)
title bar (page 4)
workbook (page 4)
worksheet (page 1)

TEST YOUR SKILLS

True/False

1. The status bar is located at the top of the screen and contains the name of the current application.
2. Cells are the intersection of columns and rows.
3. You should never turn off the computer before you have correctly exited Excel.
4. Excel is used primarily for text documents.
5. One worksheet contains approximately 16 million cells.

Multiple Choice

1. The Office Assistant
   a. can't be turned off
   b. allows you to type questions to ask for help
   c. is the only way to access help in Microsoft Excel
   d. all of these answers

2. If A1 is the active cell and you want to make cell IV6 the current cell, you could
   a. scroll to the location
   b. choose Edit | Go To and type IV6
   c. press Ctrl + → and then press the ↓ five times
   d. all of these answers

3. When you are using a dialog box and need help, you
   a. must cancel the operation and use the Office Assistant
   b. must cancel the operation and use the Help menu
   c. click the question mark button in the dialog box and then click on the option you want help for
   d. exit the dialog box and initiate a help search

4. The status bar
   a. contains the READY indicator
   b. contains menu choices
   c. contains the Windows Start button
   d. contains the minimize and maximize buttons

5. Excel columns
   a. run horizontally across the screen
   b. run vertically on the screen
   c. intersect with rows to form cells
   d. both b and c

Short Answer

Match the letter with the correct location in Figure 1.17:

___ a. Enter button	___ b. Column heading
___ c. Title bar	___ d. Row heading
___ e. Formula bar	___ f. Active cell

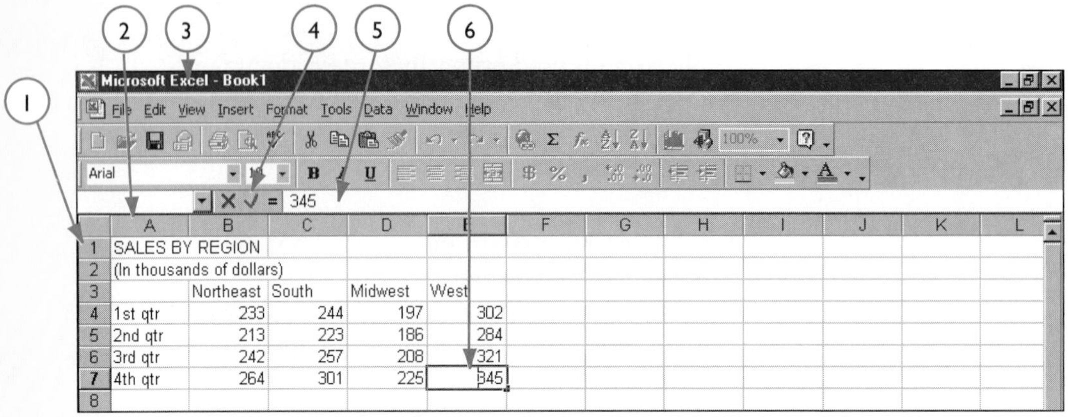

FIGURE 1.17

What Does This Do?

Write a description of the function of the following:

1.	Σ	6.	Ready
2.	?	7.	✓
3.	B	8.	X
4.	Start	9.	—
5.	3	10.	✛

On Your Own

1. Using the Excel Help feature, look up a topic that is unclear to you. Print the Help topic.
2. Open the **Workout Log** workbook and type different numbers in the cells that contain numbers. Print the worksheet and close it without saving it.
3. Open a new workbook. Type the recipient of your last five checks in column A. Type the amount of the checks in column D, next to the correct recipient. Use AutoSum to add up the total. Print the worksheet. Close the workbook without saving it.
4. Open a new workbook. Input both text and numbers into cells. Practice moving around the entire worksheet, using the methods described in this unit. Close the workbook without saving it.
5. Open Excel Help. Choose the Contents tab and click *Getting Help*. Choose the topic *Ways to get Assistance while You Work*. Read the topic and then print it.

PROJECTS

1. a. Create the following personal budget. Don't be concerned when Excel changes the form of the date when you type it. You'll learn about formatting dates in Unit 3.
    b. Use the AutoSum button to calculate the total.
    c. Save the workbook as **Budget**, and print the worksheet.

	A	B	C	D
1	your name			
2	today's date			
3				
4	Rent		500	
5	Utilities		120	
6	Car Payment		300	
7	Gas and Upkeep		75	
8	Insurance		100	
9	Food		200	
10	Entertainment		50	
11	Miscellaneous		50	
12	Total			
13				

2. a. Create the following accounts payable worksheet.
    b. Use the AutoSum button to calculate the total amount due in C12.
    c. Save the workbook as **Accounts Payable**, and print the worksheet.

	A	B	C	D
1	your name			
2	today's date			
3				
4	Mercury Athletics			
5	Date	Invoice #	Amt Due	
6	8/3/99	201	109.99	
7	8/5/99	202	350.01	
8	8/9/99	203	119.99	
9	8/11/99	204	499.99	
10	8/19/99	205	200.15	
11	8/20/99	206	379.95	
12	Total			
13				

3. a. Create the following list of courses.
   b. Use the AutoSum button to calculate the total number of credits in cell C14.
   c. Save the workbook as **Credits**, and print the worksheet.

	A	B	C	D	E
2	your name				
3	today's date				
4					
5	Course Name		Credits	Grade	
6					
7	English 101		3	B	
8	Intro to Computers		4	A	
9	Health and Wellness		2	A	
10	College Algebra		3	B	
11	Computer Apps		4	A	
12	U.S. History		3	C	
13	Philosophy		3	A	
14	Total				
15					

4. a. Create the following bowling game worksheet.
   b. Use the AutoSum button to calculate the totals for Bill and Sylvia only.
   c. Save the workbook as **Scores**, and print the worksheet.

	A	B	C	D	E	F
1	your name					
2	today's date					
3						
4	Tuesday Bowling League					
5		Game 1	Game 2	Game 3	Total	
6	Bill	200	210	185		
7	Sylvia	190	220	200		
8	Howard	175	190	185		
9						

Working with Workbooks

UNIT OBJECTIVES

- Create a new workbook and enter data in a series
- Create formulas
- Specify ranges with AutoSum
- Edit a worksheet
- Check the spelling in a worksheet
- Change the Page Setup options
- Display and print the worksheet formulas
- Copy and move text and numbers in a worksheet

In Unit 1, you learned to create, save, and print a worksheet. In Unit 2, you'll calculate data with your own formulas and learn more about using AutoSum for calculations. You'll fill a series of data automatically using the fill handle, copy and move data on the worksheet, and add and delete rows and columns. You'll check the spelling of text in the worksheet, control the way Excel prints worksheets, and produce a printout of your formulas.

In the following tasks, you will learn to use Excel to create workbooks for a small home-based dog kennel that raises and sells purebred Jack Russell terriers. The owner recently acquired a computer and Microsoft Excel 2000 and wants to use them to help run the business more efficiently.

TASK 1 | *Creating a New Workbook and Entering Data in a Series*

What: Open a new blank workbook and enter data in a series.

How: Choose File | New to open a new workbook; use the fill handle to fill a series of data.

Why: Many worksheets contain series of data, and the fill handle simplifies data entry.

Tip: You can also open a new workbook by clicking the Standard toolbar's New button.

When you start Excel, a blank workbook opens on the screen. When you want to start another new workbook:

1. Choose File | New to display the New dialog box, shown in Figure 2.1.
2. With the General tab displayed and Workbook selected, click OK.

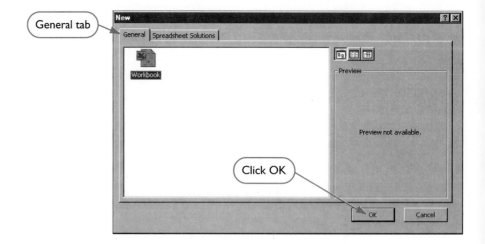

FIGURE 2.1   The New Dialog Box

A new workbook opens, ready for you to enter data. In Unit 1, you entered text and numbers in the *Workout Log* workbook. You typed data in the active cell and completed the entry by pressing Enter or an arrow key or by clicking the Enter button on the formula bar. In the exercise that follows, you will create a new workbook and enter data the same way, but you'll also use the fill handle to enter a series of numbers and dates.

The **fill handle** is the small square at the bottom right corner of the selected cell (see Figure 2.2). When you point to the fill handle, the pointer changes to a narrow black cross. If you drag the mouse while the pointer is this shape, Excel will copy the number in the active cell to the adjacent cells, or it will increment a series of numbers or dates.

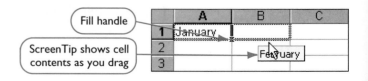

FIGURE 2.2   The Fill Handle

To use the fill handle to fill a series of months or days of the week, or to fill a series of numbered items in increments of 1:

1. Enter the first series item in a cell.
2. With the same cell selected, point to the fill handle and, when the pointer changes to a cross, drag in the direction in which you want the series to continue. As you drag, a ScreenTip will display the contents of the cells you pass over.

You will use the fill handle throughout this book, and will learn other ways to use it as you need them. The fill handle is one of Excel's best shortcuts.

EXERCISE 1 — Creating a New Workbook and Entering Data in a Series

1. Start Excel.
   A new workbook opens, with the temporary name *Book1*.

2. Choose **File | New**.
   The New dialog box opens.

3. With the General tab displayed and **Workbook** selected, click **OK**.
   A new workbook opens, with the temporary name *Book2*.

4. Click in **B3**.
   B3 becomes the active cell and has a heavy border. The small square at the bottom right of the border is the fill handle.

5. Type **January** and click the **Enter button** on the formula bar.
   January appears both in the formula bar and in cell B3.

6. Point to the **fill handle** at the bottom right of the selection border.
   The pointer changes to a narrow black cross.

7. Click and drag the fill handle 5 columns to the right, to **G3**.
   As you drag, a ScreenTip displays the months February through June.

8. Release the mouse button.
   The months are entered in the cells, and the cells remain selected.

9. Click in **A4**.
   Cells B3 through G3 are deselected, and A4 becomes the active cell.

10. Type **Year 1** and click the **Enter button** on the formula bar.
    The text is entered into A4, and A4 remains the active cell.

11. Point to the **fill handle**.
    The pointer changes to a narrow black cross.

12. Click and drag the fill handle down 4 rows, to **A8**, then release the mouse button.
    The series increments down the column.

13. Press **Ctrl+Home**.
    The selection moves to A1.

14. Type **Comparison of Dog Sales for the Last Five Years** and press **Enter**.

The text is entered in A1 but extends across several more cells. Because those cells are empty, the text is displayed across them. If the cells had contents, the text displayed in A1 would stop at the edge of the cell, though the complete text would be displayed in the formula bar. (You will learn to adjust cell widths in Unit 3.)

15. Click in **B4**, type **3000**, and press **Enter**.

The number is entered in B4, and B5 becomes active. Remember that numbers align right in the cell.

16. Using Figure 2.3 as your model, enter the numbers in cells **B5 through B8** and then in **C4 through G8**.

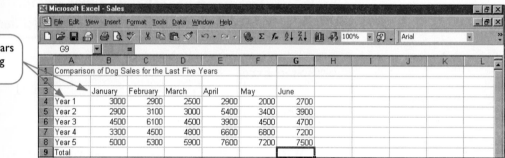

Months and years entered using fill handle

	A	B	C	D	E	F	G
1	Comparison of Dog Sales for the Last Five Years						
2							
3		January	February	March	April	May	June
4	Year 1	3000	2900	2500	2900	2000	2700
5	Year 2	2900	3100	3000	5400	3400	3900
6	Year 3	4500	6100	4500	3900	4500	4700
7	Year 4	3300	4500	4800	6600	6800	7200
8	Year 5	5000	5300	5900	7600	7200	7500
9	Total						

FIGURE 2.3 The *Sales* Workbook after Exercise 1

17. Save the workbook as **Sales**.

You will use this workbook in the balance of this unit and in Units 3 and 4.

18. Print the worksheet.

19. Keep your worksheet on the screen for use in the next exercise.

TASK 2 | *Creating Formulas*

What: Calculate numbers in the worksheet by creating formulas.

How: Type the formulas from scratch or select cells.

Why: The power of Excel is in its ability to calculate formulas.

Tip: If you use cell references instead of numbers in formulas, you can change the numbers in the cells referred to and the formulas will automatically show the new result.

You can calculate numbers in Excel with formulas and with built-in functions. In Unit 1, you used the built-in AutoSum function to add a row or column of numbers. In this task, you will write formulas from scratch.

Remember from Unit 1 that a **formula** specifies the steps used to make a calculation. It can contain numbers, cell references, and mathematical operators such as multiplication and division signs (see Table 2.1); and it starts with an equal sign.

Performing calculations with worksheet formulas is different from doing them with a calculator. For example, if you wanted to use a calculator to add the first row of numbers in the *Sales* workbook to see a total for January through June of Year 1, you would enter 3000, 2900, 2500, 2900, 2000, and 2700, pressing the + button after each number.

When you are doing a calculation in a worksheet, you use **cell location math**. That is, you tell Excel to add the contents of B4 to the contents of C4 to the contents of D4 to the contents of E4 to the contents of F4 to the contents of G4 to get a total of January through June of Year 1.

When you use cell location math in this way, you are telling Excel to add the contents of the cells whose addresses you list in the formula. The formula is independent of the cell contents; if the cell contents change, the formula calculates them accurately without having to be rewritten.

You use arithmetic **operators** with cell addresses and numbers. For example, to subtract the contents of A31 from A30:

$$=A30-A31$$

To multiply the contents of J24 by M15:

$$=J24*M15$$

To divide the contents of G5 by G10:

$$=G5/G10$$

Formulas can also contain specific numbers. For example, to multiply the contents of A12 by 50:

$$=A12*50$$

Operation	Operator Key	Example
Addition	+	=**A2**+**B2** adds the contents of A2 and B2
Subtraction	–	=**A2**–**B1** subtracts the contents of B1 from the contents of A2
Multiplication	*	=**A4*****B5** multiplies the contents of A4 and B5
Division	/	=**B4**/**C2** divides the contents of B4 by the contents of C2

TABLE 2.1   Using Arithmetic Operators in Formulas

CREATING A FORMULA BY TYPING IT

To type a formula in Excel:
1. Select the cell where you want the results of the formula to appear.
2. Type an equal sign (=). This tells Excel that what follows is a calculation.
3. Type the address of the first cell to be used in the formula, such as A4.
4. Type the correct mathematical operator, such as +.
5. Continue to type cell addresses and operators to specify the steps in the calculation.
6. Click the Enter button on the formula bar to complete the formula and display the calculated result in the active cell. (The formula bar continues to display the formula rather than the calculation.)

CREATING A FORMULA BY SELECTING CELLS

Instead of typing the cell addresses, you can use the mouse to select them. To create a formula by selecting cells (also called *pointing*):

1. Select the cell where you want the results of the formula to appear.
2. Type an equal sign (=). The status bar displays the word *Enter*.
3. Click in the first cell to be used in the calculation. The status bar displays the word *Point*.
4. Type the desired arithmetic operator. The status bar displays *Enter*.
5. Continue to click in cells and type operators to specify the steps in the calculation.
6. Click the Enter button on the formula bar to complete the formula and display the calculated result in the active cell. (The formula bar continues to display the formula rather than the calculation.)

POINTER

Circular Reference

One common mistake new users make is to include in their formulas the cell that shows the formula's result. For instance, they might type the formula =A1+A2+A3 in cell A3. This is called a **circular reference**.

To avoid circular references, make a blank cell the active cell before you start to type your formula and never include the active cell in the formula. If you do include a circular reference in a formula, a help screen will open with offers of assistance.

THE ORDER OF OPERATIONS

When creating formulas, you need to be aware of the **order of operations**, that is, the order in which Excel performs calculations. Consider the following formula: =5+3*8. Do this calculation in your head or with a pocket calculator and you'll get the answer 64, because you perform the mathematical operations in the order in which they appear in the formula. Excel uses a different order of operations, shown in Table 2.2. Excel calculates this formula as 29, because it multiplies before it adds.

Order	Operation
First	multiplication (*) and division (/)
Second	addition (+) and subtraction (−)

TABLE **2.2** Order of Operations

To change the order of operations, enclose the part of the formula to be calculated first in parentheses. For example, = (5+3)*8 would calculate as 64.

The order of operations applies to cell locations as well as numbers, so that =B3−B7/G12 calculates differently than =(B3−B7)/G12. To have the subtraction performed before the division, you would enclose the first two cell addresses in parentheses. For more information on other operations and their order, use Excel Help.

EXERCISE 2A | *Creating Formulas*

1. With the *Sales* workbook open on your screen, make **H3** the active cell.
2. Type **Total** and press **Enter**.
   H4 becomes the active cell.
3. In H4, type the following formula:

   =B4+C4+D4+E4+F4+G4

4. Click the **Enter button** on the formula bar.
   The calculated result appears in the cell, but the formula bar shows the formula.
5. Make **H5** the active cell and type =
   You will use the cell selection or pointing method to create a formula in this cell. An equal sign appears in the formula, and the status bar displays the word *Enter*.
6. Click **B5**.
   The formula now reads =B5, and the status bar displays the word *Point*. A moving border surrounds cell B5.
7. Type +.
   The formula now reads =B5+, and the status bar displays *Enter* again.
8. Enter the rest of the steps in the formula as follows:

   Click **C5**, type + and click **D5**, type + and click **E5**, type + and click **F5**, type + and click **G5**.

   As you build the formula by typing and pointing, the formula bar displays it.
9. Click the **Enter button** on the formula bar.
   The calculated result appears in the cell, but the formula bar continues to display the formula.
10. Click in **A9**, type **Total**, and press **Tab**.
11. Type the following formula in B9:

   =B4+B5+B6+B7+B8

12. Press **Tab** to move to C9, and then use the pointing method to create the formula:

   Type = and click **C4**, type + and click **C5**, type + and click **C6**, type + and click **C7**, type + and click **C8**

13. Click the **Enter button** on the formula bar.
Your worksheet should look similar to Figure 2.4.

14. If your worksheet has any errors, make the erroneous cell the active cell and retype the formula before going on.

15. Save the workbook and print the worksheet.

16. Close the workbook but leave Excel open for the next exercise.

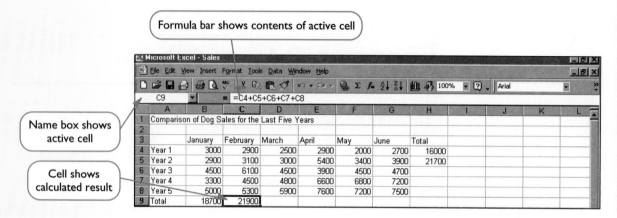

FIGURE 2.4 The *Sales* Workbook after Exercise 2A

EXERCISE 2B | *Using Formulas to Create an Invoice*

1. With Excel open, click the **New button** on the Standard toolbar.
A new workbook opens.

2. Using Figure 2.5 as your model, enter the text and numbers shown in columns A through D, rows 1 through 25.

3. Click in **D15**.
D15 becomes the active cell. You will create the formula by typing it in the next step.

4. Type **=A15*C15** and click the **Enter button** on the formula bar.
This formula multiplies the quantity by the unit price to calculate the total for the item. The formula appears in the formula bar, and the result appears in D15.

5. Click in **D16**.
D16 becomes the active cell. You will create the formula by pointing and clicking.

6. Type **=**, click in **A16**, type *****, click in **C16**, and then press the **Enter button** on the formula bar.
The result of the formula appears in the cell, but the formula bar displays the formula, =A16*C16.

7. Repeat steps 5 and 6 to type the formula in **D17**.
Remember to use the correct row number.

8. Repeat step 4 to create the formula in **D18**.
Remember to use the correct row number.

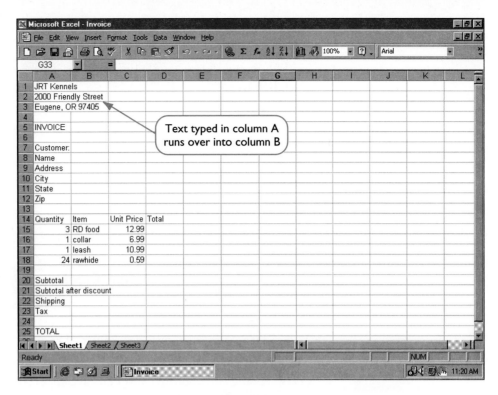

FIGURE 2.5 The *Invoice* Workbook for Exercise 2B

9. Click in **D20**.
Cell D20 becomes the active cell. You will use AutoSum to create the subtotal formula.

10. Click the **AutoSum button** on the Standard toolbar.
A moving border surrounds the cells Excel will sum, including blank cell D19. Blank cells are evaluated as a zero in a formula.

11. Click the **Enter button** on the formula bar.
The calculated sum (71.11) is displayed in D20, and the function is displayed on the formula bar.

12. Click in **D21**.
D21 becomes the active cell. This cell will contain a formula for the subtotal after a 10 percent discount (.10) is subtracted from it.

13. Type =**D20 – (D20∗.10)**
You use a cell reference (D20) for the subtotal, and figure the discount by multiplying the subtotal by 10 percent (D20∗.10). You don't have to use parentheses in this formula, because Excel multiplies before it subtracts, but parentheses make the operation easier to understand.

14. Press **Enter**.
The result appears in D21, and D22 becomes the active cell. Here you will enter the standard shipping charge of $10 on every order.

15. Type **10** and press **Enter**.
The result appears in D22, and D23 becomes the active cell. Tax is 7% of the merchandise before the discount is subtracted and before the shipping is included.

16. Type **=D20*.07** and press **Enter**.
The result appears in the cell. Notice that Excel includes extra decimal places. You will learn to control the appearance of numbers in the next unit.

17. Click in **D25**.

18. Type **=D21+D22+D23** and press **Enter**.
The total for the invoice appears in D25.

19. Type your name and address in the Customer section of the invoice.

20. Save the workbook as **Invoice**.

21. Print the worksheet and then close it.

TASK 3 | *Specifying Ranges with AutoSum*

What: Use AutoSum with different cell ranges.
How: Click the AutoSum button on the Standard toolbar.
Why: Using AutoSum to add cells avoids errors caused by mistyping cell references.
  Tip: You'll specify ranges for many operations in Excel, such as copying and moving.

In the previous task, you added cells by writing formulas. What if you had to add a column of 100 numbers? Typing every cell location for all 100 cells would be tedious and would very likely produce errors. To help automate the addition process, you could use the AutoSum feature that you used in Unit 1. However, to make AutoSum work correctly for you, you need to know more about how it works.

RANGES

The AutoSum feature uses the SUM function to add the numbers in a **range**, or group of two or more cells, for example, = SUM(B3:B12). Ranges can be made up of adjacent or nonadjacent cells, but the most common type of range is a rectangular group of contiguous cells. Ranges are used in calculations or operations. A range is defined by its first or top left corner cell and its last or bottom right corner cell. The range includes the opening cell reference, the closing cell reference, and all cells in between the two. When you specify a range, you separate the opening and closing cell address with a colon (:). The colon tells Excel that all the cells between the opening and closing addresses must be included with the opening and closing cells in the operation or calculation. The example = SUM(B3:B12) states the following: add the numbers in cells B3, B4, B5, B6, B7, B8, B9, B10, B11, and B12.

THE SYNTAX OF A FUNCTION

Looking at the example, we can see the following syntax for the SUM function:

- an equal sign (=) to indicate that the function begins a calculation
- a text name of two or more characters which designates what calculation the function will perform (for instance, the SUM function always adds)
- an opening parenthesis
- an opening cell location
- a colon (:)
- a closing cell location
- a closing parenthesis

The cell locations defined in the parentheses are called the function's **arguments**. Arguments are the constants, cell addresses including ranges, or operations that Excel uses to perform the predefined calculation designated by the function name. If a function calls for multiple arguments, the individual arguments are separated by commas. For example, = SUM(B3:B12,C8,D14) tells Excel to sum the numbers in the cells B3 through B12 and C8 and D14.

USING AUTOSUM

To use AutoSum and have Excel suggest the range of cells to sum:

1. Select the blank cell where you want the result to appear.
2. Click the AutoSum button on the Standard toolbar. Excel guesses at the range you want to sum, highlights the cells in the range, and lists the range as the argument in the SUM function.
3. Check the range shown as the function's argument.
   - If the cells are the ones you want to add, click the Enter button on the formula toolbar or click the AutoSum button again.
   - If Excel has selected the wrong cells for the calculation, cancel the operation by clicking the Cancel button on the formula bar, or edit the argument by clicking in it (either in the cell or in the formula bar) and typing the correct cell references.

> **POINTER**
>
> **Checking the Selected Range When Using AutoSum**
>
> When you click in a cell and then click the AutoSum button, Excel follows certain rules for selecting the range to sum. If you aren't aware of this, your worksheet may contain erroneous results. Always check the suggested range before completing the operation. For example, if the cell you click in has more numbers to its left than above it, Excel may sum the numbers to the left, though you wanted to sum those above. The SUM function is one of Excel's powerful and friendly features, but it automatically does what it is programmed to do, so you need to be an aware user.

To make sure that Excel adds the correct cells, use the following method:

1. Select the range you want to add.
2. Click the AutoSum button. Excel will place the SUM function in the adjacent cell.

When the cells you want to sum are not adjacent, you can select them manually by pointing. To use AutoSum to add nonadjacent cells:

1. Select the blank cell where you want the result to appear.
2. Click the AutoSum button.
3. Click the first cell. Excel will place the cell location in the argument's parentheses.
4. Hold down the Ctrl key and click each of the other cells. The cell addresses are added as arguments in the function, separated from each other by commas.
5. Release the Ctrl key.
6. Click the Enter button on the formula bar.

If you need to add several columns of numbers, you could use the SUM function individually on each column by using the methods described above. However, you can save time by selecting all of the cells to be added in all of the columns first.

To add more than one column of numbers at a time, use the following method:

1. Select all of the cells to be added.
2. Click the AutoSum button.

Excel places the SUM function in the blank cell below the selected cells in each column and completes the calculation.

POINTER

Use AutoSum or Create a Formula?

Using AutoSum can save typing errors so it is the recommended method for addition in a spreadsheet. However, don't assume Excel knows what you want to add—check every range as you use AutoSum so that you have correct results.

EXERCISE 3 | *Using AutoSum and Selecting Ranges*

1. Open the *Sales* workbook and click in **H6**.
   H6 becomes the active cell. You want to find the total sales for January through June of Year 3, contained in cells B6:G6.

2. Click the **AutoSum button**.
   Excel types the SUM function, highlights cells H4 and H5, and suggests the range H4:H5 in the cell and in the formula bar. This is not the range you want.

3. Edit the suggested range by clicking in the cell, backspacing over the wrong cells, and typing the correct ones.
The new range, B6:G6, is displayed in the cell and in the formula bar.

4. Click the **Enter button** on the formula bar.
The result, 28200, is displayed in the cell, while the formula bar continues to display the formula.

5. Repeat this procedure to place totals for years 4 and 5 in column H. If the wrong range is suggested, edit it before completing the operation.

6. Click in **D9**.
D9 becomes the active cell.

7. Click the **AutoSum button**.
Excel highlights the range to add.

8. If the correct location is highlighted, click the **AutoSum button** again.

9. Select the cells containing numbers in columns E, F, G, and H.
You will select the range E4:H8.

10. Click the **AutoSum button**.
All of the columns are added at once, and the sums are placed in row 9. Your worksheet should look like Figure 2.6.

11. Save the workbook and print the worksheet.

12. Keep the worksheet on the screen for use in the next exercise.

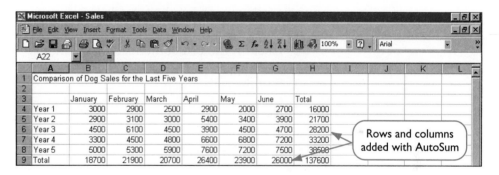

FIGURE 2.6 The *Sales* Workbook after Exercise 3

TASK 4 | *Editing Worksheets*

What: Correct mistakes and add new information to a worksheet.

How: Select cells and use Edit | Clear, Edit | Undo, Insert | Columns, Insert | Rows, Edit | Delete.

Why: You will want to make your worksheets error free and keep them up to date.

Tip: You can go to a cell quickly by pressing the F5 key. The Go To dialog box opens and you can type the cell address you want to go to, to edit its contents.

You will want to edit your worksheets to eliminate errors, to update information, or simply to place new information in them. You have already learned how to replace cell contents before completing an entry. (You can backspace and type the new information, click the Cancel button on the formula bar, or press Esc.) This task explains how to change an entry after it has been completed. You can edit or replace cell contents, delete cell contents, add and delete columns and rows, and undo these and other operations.

EDITING CELL CONTENTS

If you want to change the contents of a cell to something entirely different, it's easiest just to start again: select the cell, type the new information, and press Enter. If you want to edit the contents, you can do it either in the cell or in the formula bar.

To edit the contents in the cell:
1. Double-click the cell, and a flashing insertion point appears in the cell.
2. Do any of the following:

   • Use the arrow keys to move the insertion point.
   • Use the Backspace or Delete buttons to erase characters.
   • Type any new information.

3. Complete the entry using the same methods you are familiar with for placing new content in a cell.

To edit cell contents on the formula bar:
1. Make the cell the active cell to display its contents on the formula bar.
2. Click in the cell contents on the formula bar, and a flashing insertion point appears where you click.
3. Edit the cell contents.
4. Complete the entry by clicking the Enter box on the formula bar.

POINTER

The Range Finder

When you double-click a cell containing a formula, Excel color-codes the cell addresses used in the formula and surrounds the cells referred to with a border of the same color. This feature, the Range Finder, helps you locate cells used in a formula. For details, see Excel Help.

DELETING CELL CONTENTS

To delete the contents of a cell or range of cells, select the cells and press Delete. You can also use the Edit menu:
1. Select a cell or range of cells.
2. Choose Edit | Clear, and a submenu opens, as shown in Figure 2.7.

3. Choose from the following options:

- All—to clear both the contents (the data you have typed) and any formatting
- Contents—to delete only the data and leave any formatting
- Formatting—to delete only the cell formatting and leave the data

You will learn how to format cells in Unit 3.

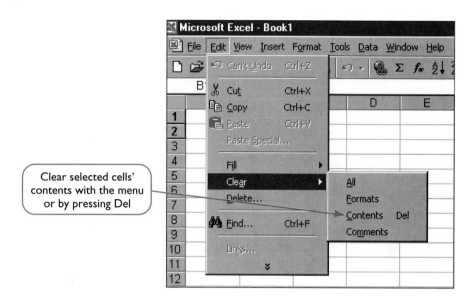

FIGURE 2.7 The Clear Menu

> **POINTER**
>
> **Selected Cells**
>
> When you select a range of cells, the top left corner of the selection appears white, while the rest of the selected range appears blue. Look in the Name box on the formula bar, and you will see that the top left cell in the range is the active cell. If you select a range and begin typing, what you type will be entered into this cell.

UNDOING AN ACTION

You will erase cells by mistake, try a new function that doesn't work as you thought it would, or just change your mind when you are using Excel. You can easily undo the last action you took by choosing Edit | Undo. The Undo menu option is worded to let you know what action will be undone. If your last action was to enter 6 into cell F14, the command will read *Undo typing "6" in F14*. If you have just deleted a word, it will read *Undo Clear*.

If you want to undo more than one action, click the down arrow next to the Undo button on the Standard toolbar, and a list of actions will be displayed as shown in Figure 2.8. Clicking the fifth action on the list will undo the last five actions.

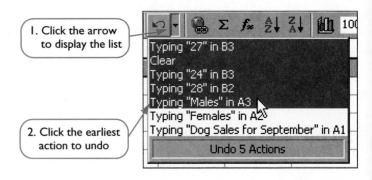

1. Click the arrow to display the list

2. Click the earliest action to undo

FIGURE 2.8 Undoing Several Actions at Once

POINTER

Redoing an Action

To redo one or more actions you have undone (that is, to reverse the undo), use the Redo button and list. They work the same way as the Undo button and list.

INSERTING AND DELETING ROWS AND COLUMNS

You can insert blank rows and columns in a worksheet.

- To insert a single column, click in the column to the right of the new one and choose Insert | Columns. (To insert a column to the left of column J, click a cell in column J.)

- To insert more than one column, start at the column just to the right of the new ones and select the same number of columns as you want to insert, then choose Insert | Columns. (To insert 4 columns to the left of column J, select columns J through M.)

- To insert a single row, click a cell in the row below the new one and choose Insert | Rows. To insert a blank row after row 7, click a cell in row 8.)

- To insert more than one row, start at the row below the new ones and select the same number of rows as you want to insert, then choose Insert | Rows. (To insert 4 rows below row 8, select rows 9 through 12.)

- To delete one or more rows or columns, select a cell in each row or column to be deleted and choose Edit | Delete to display the Delete dialog box in Figure 2.9. Make a choice in the dialog box and click the OK button.

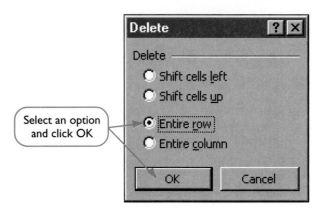

FIGURE 2.9   The Delete Dialog Box

POINTER

Selecting Rows, Columns, or the Whole Worksheet

- To select a row or a column, click the row or column heading.

- To select more than one adjacent row or column, click and drag over the headings.

- To select nonadjacent rows or columns, click the first heading, then hold down Ctrl while you click the others.

- To select the whole worksheet, click the Select All button, the gray rectangle at the top left corner of the worksheet, where the row and column headings meet.

POINTER

Deleting and Inserting Rows and Columns with the Shortcut Menu

You can use the shortcut menu to insert or delete rows or columns.

- To delete them, select them, click the right mouse button, and choose Delete from the shortcut menu.

- To insert them, select rows or columns at the spot where you want new ones to appear, click the right mouse button, and choose Insert from the shortcut menu.

Take Care When Inserting and Deleting Rows and Columns

Both deleting and inserting entire rows and columns should be used sparingly so that you don't create problems with the worksheet. Excel keeps formulas up to date by adjusting references to the shifted cells caused by inserting or deleting columns or row, with one exception: If the column or row is added to the edge of the range of cells, the formula is not adjusted. If one of your formulas displays **#REF**, the formula is trying to calculate a reference to a deleted cell. Planning a worksheet on paper before beginning to create it in Excel will help avoid problems.

EXERCISE 4 | *Editing Workbooks*

1. With the *Sales* workbook on the screen, make **D5** the active cell.

2. Choose **Edit | Clear | Contents**.
   The contents of D5 are deleted.

3. Choose **Edit | Undo Clear**.
   The contents of D5 are restored.

4. Choose **Insert | Columns**.
   A column to the left of column D is inserted.

5. Choose **Edit | Delete**.
   The Delete dialog box opens.

6. Choose **Entire Column** and click **OK**.
   The new column is deleted.

7. Click and drag to select from **D5** through **G5**.
   The cells are highlighted.

8. Press **Delete**.
   The cell contents are erased.

9. Choose **Edit | Undo Clear**.
   The cell contents are restored.

10. Double-click in **H4**.
    The cell is activated, so that you can edit it in place or on the formula bar. Notice that Excel color-codes the cell addresses used in the formula and surrounds those cells with a border of the same color.

11. Click at the end of the formula (after the G4), and backspace over **G4** and the + sign.
    You can edit the formula either in the cell or on the formula bar. It now reads =B4+C4+D4+E4+F4.

12. Click the **Enter button** on the formula bar.
    The formula recalculates, omitting the contents of G4.

13. Click the **Undo button**.

The worksheet should be back the way it was at the end of the previous exercise. If it is not, close the workbook without saving it and then reopen it.

TASK 5 | *Checking Spelling in the Worksheet*

What: Check the spelling of text in the worksheet.
How: Choose Tools | Spelling.
Why: People won't believe your calculations if they find spelling errors in your worksheet.
Tip: Always use the spelling checker before printing a worksheet.

The Microsoft Office 2000 applications share a dictionary that is used to check spelling in any of them. If you know how to use the spelling checker in Word, you already know how to use it in Excel.

To use the spelling checker:

1. Choose Tools | Spelling to display the Spelling dialog box shown in Figure 2.10.

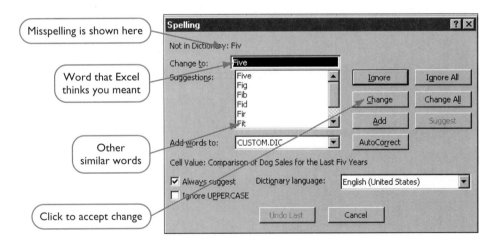

FIGURE 2.10   The Spelling Dialog Box

2. Spelling errors are indicated by Not in Dictionary. You can choose from the options described in Table 2.3.

3. If you are checking spelling and want to correct the error yourself, you can type and edit right in the dialog box. Then click the Change button to move to the next error.

Button	Description
Ignore	Ignores the error for one time
Ignore All	Ignores the error throughout the entire document
Add	Adds the word to the dictionary
Change	Changes the current error
Change All	Corrects the error throughout the document

TABLE 2.3   Spelling Options

POINTER

Using AutoCorrect

Excel automatically corrects many of your typing errors. You can control this feature by choosing Tools | AutoCorrect. Click the question mark button in the dialog box's title bar and then click any item for an explanation.

POINTER

Where Does the Spelling Checker Begin?

The spelling checker starts from the active cell, checks to the bottom of the worksheet, and then asks whether you want to continue checking. If you start the check with text already selected, Excel checks just the selected text and then asks whether you want to continue at the beginning of the sheet. It's a good idea to make A1 the active cell before starting the check.

POINTER

The Find and Replace Dialog Boxes

Excel, like Word, has another feature useful for finding data in a worksheet. You can find text, numbers, or even formulas in a worksheet, and you can have Excel replace them with other data. Use the Find and Replace dialog boxes to find and replace any data in a worksheet:

- To find data in a worksheet, choose Edit | Find. The Find dialog box opens. Enter the information to be found in the *Find what* text box and click the Find Next button.

- To replace data in a worksheet, choose Edit | Replace. The Replace dialog box opens. Enter the information to be replaced in the *Find what* text box and the replacement information in the *Replace with* text box. Click the Find Next button, and Excel highlights the information in the worksheet. Click the Replace button to replace it.

For more information, see Excel Help.

1. With the *Sales* workbook open, double-click in **A1**.

2. Delete the letter **e** from the word ***five***.
   The word *five* is incorrect.

3. Double-click in **C3** and delete the letter **u** from the word **February**.
   The word *February* is misspelled.

4. Double-click in **A6** and delete the letter **a** from **Year**.
   The word *Year* is incorrect.

5. Make A1 the active cell.

6. Choose **Tools | Spelling**.
   The Spelling dialog box opens, with the first spelling error listed next to *Not in Dictionary*, and suggested respellings are shown in the *Suggestions* list box. The change Excel thinks is the most likely is shown in the *Change to* text box. In this case, Excel has made the right guess.

7. Click the **Change button**.
   Excel makes the change in the worksheet and moves to the next error.

8. Make any changes necessary, selecting the correct spelling and clicking the **Change button** to make the worksheet text perfect.
   When the spelling check is complete, a message box lets you know.

9. Keep the worksheet open on the screen to use in the next exercise.

TASK 6 | *Using the Page Setup Dialog Box*

What: Change the look of the printout.

How: Choose File | Page Setup.

Why: Changing the page setup can make your worksheet more attractive and easier to understand.

Tip: You can also open the Page Setup dialog box from the Print Preview.

Small, simple worksheets print attractively enough using Excel's default page setup, but wide sheets or long ones need special treatment, and there are many ways to make even simple sheets more attractive. To make adjustments in the page setup, choose File | Page Setup to open the Page Setup dialog box. This dialog box has four tabs, each of which has useful settings.

PAGE TAB

The Page tab is shown in Figure 2.11a. Its Orientation section lets you choose whether to print the worksheet with the short or the long edge of the paper at the top:

- **Portrait** 8½ × 11 orientation
- **Landscape** 11 × 8½ orientation

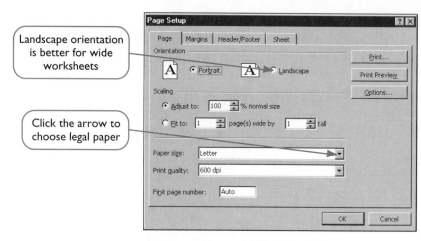

Landscape orientation is better for wide worksheets

Click the arrow to choose legal paper

(a) The Page Tab

FIGURE 2.11 The Page Setup Dialog Box

The Scaling section allows you to change the scale of the printout without changing the worksheet. You can choose to print:

- at more or less than 100%.
- to fit on a designated number of pages.

The Paper Size list box allows you to designate another paper size if your printer will support it. For example, you may want to print wide worksheets in landscape orientation on legal (8½ × 14) paper. To choose a different paper size, click the arrow in the list box to display the list of available sizes.

MARGINS TAB

The Margins tab, shown in Figure 2.11b, allows you to change the Top, Left, Right, and Bottom margins by typing a new number or clicking the increment or decrement arrow. You may want to use a smaller than normal margin to fit a worksheet onto a page.

The Center on Page section allows you to center a worksheet vertically and/or horizontally on the page. This is a useful option for small worksheets.

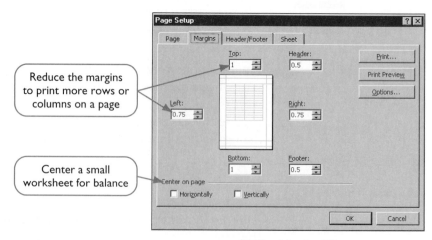

Reduce the margins to print more rows or columns on a page

Center a small worksheet for balance

(b) The Margins Tab

FIGURE 2.11 The Page Setup Dialog Box (continued)

HEADER/FOOTER TAB

A header is text that is printed at the top of every page of the printout. A footer is text that is printed at the bottom (foot) of every page. To include a standard header or footer on the printed page:

- Click the down arrow next to Header or Footer, as shown in Figure 2.11c.
- Select the information that you want to appear at the top or bottom of every page of the printout.

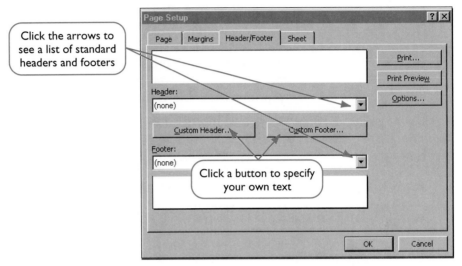

(c) Selecting a Standard Header

FIGURE 2.11   The Page Setup Dialog Box *(continued)*

To include your own information in the header or footer:

- Click the Custom Header or Custom Footer button.
- Type information, such as your name, in any of the three sections provided, as shown in Figure 2.11d.
- Click in a section and then click any of the buttons to insert the date, file name, page number, number of pages, etc. (To see a detailed explanation of the buttons, right-click any of them, and then click What's This?)

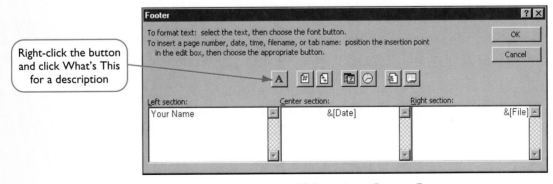

(d) Inserting a Custom Footer

FIGURE 2.11   The Page Setup Dialog Box *(continued)*

SHEET TAB

The Print Area text box shown in Figure 2.11e allows you to select a portion of the worksheet to print. This is a useful option only if you have a large worksheet and are always going to print just a portion of it. You can type the range to print or use the Collapse Dialog button (explained below) to select the range with the mouse.

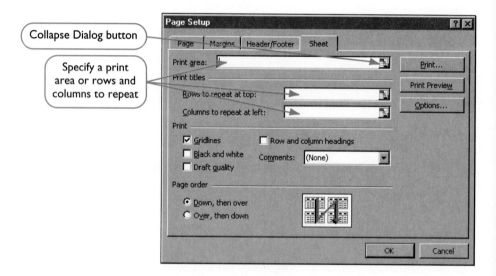

FIGURE 2.11 The Page Setup Dialog Box *(continued)*

The Print Titles section offers an important option for worksheets that will print out on more than one page. That is, it will repeat the titles you designate on every page of the printout. For example, if column A of a worksheet contains text that applies to the numbers in columns B through Z, but only columns A through H will print on the first page, it is useful to repeat column A as the first column on each succeeding page of the worksheet. That way, readers will not have to flip back and forth to read the printout. To choose the rows and columns to repeat, use the Collapse Dialog button as follows:

1. Click the Collapse Dialog button on the Rows to Repeat at Top options. The dialog box collapses to a single line and a title bar, as shown in Figure 2.11f.
2. If necessary, drag the collapsed dialog box by its title bar to move it out of the way.
3. Select the rows containing column headings that you want repeated at the top of every printed page.

4. Click the Collapse Dialog button again to restore the dialog box.

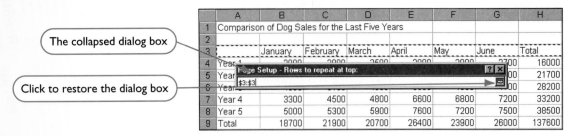

The collapsed dialog box

Click to restore the dialog box

(f) Using the Collapse Dialog Button to Select Columns to Repeat

FIGURE 2.11 The Page Setup Dialog Box *(continued)*

5. Repeat these steps, this time for the Columns to Repeat at Left option, this time selecting columns.

The Print section allows you to print **gridlines** (the lines between columns and rows), row numbers, and column letters along with the contents of the worksheet. Printing these elements makes it easier to troubleshoot a worksheet or discuss it with others.

EXERCISE 6 | *Using the Page Setup Dialog Box*

1. With the *Sales* workbook open, choose **File | Page Setup**.
   The Page Setup dialog box opens.

2. Click the **Page tab**.
   The current settings are shown.

3. Select **Landscape** in the *Orientation* section.
   The worksheet will now print across the long edge of the page.

4. Click the **Margins tab**.

5. Select **Horizontally** and **Vertically** in the *Center on Page* section.
   The worksheet will be centered on the printed page.

6. Click the **Header/Footer tab**.
   No header or footer is yet selected.

7. Click the down arrow for the **Header option**.
   A list of standard headers drops down.

8. Choose Page **1 of ?**.
   The page number along with the total number of pages will print in the header.

9. Click the **Custom Footer button**.
   The Footer dialog box opens.

10. Type **your name** in the left section.
    Your name will appear in the bottom left corner of every page.

11. Click in the Center section and then click the **Date button** in the dialog box.
    The current date will appear at the bottom center of every page.

12. Click in the Right section and then click the **File name button** in the dialog box.
    The file name will appear in the bottom right corner of every page.

13. Click **OK**.
The Custom Footer dialog box closes.

14. Click the **Sheet tab**.

15. Click the **Collapse Dialog button** on the Columns to Repeat at Left option.
The dialog box collapses to a single line and a title bar.

16. Click in any cell in column A.
Column A is surrounded by a moving border, and $A:$A is placed in the collapsed dialog box's text box. (You'll learn about the dollar signs in the next unit.)

17. Click the **Collapse Dialog button** in the collapsed dialog box.
The Sheet tab of the Page Setup dialog box is restored and now displays the address you selected. If your worksheet printed out on more than one page, all pages would contain the contents of column A at the left edge of the page.

18. If necessary, select **Gridlines**.
Now gridlines will print between the rows and columns of the worksheet.

19. Click **OK** to close the dialog box.

20. Save the workbook, print the worksheet, and leave it open for the next exercise.

TASK 7 | *Viewing and Printing Formulas*

What: Print the formulas rather than the results of formulas.

How: Choose Ctrl + ~.

Why: This procedure lets you check your formulas—and prove to your professor that you understood the assignment.

Tip: Print out the row and column headings to make the formula printout even more valuable.

It is easy to make mistakes in formulas. An easy way to proofread them is to print the worksheet with the formulas. To view formulas in their cells, press and hold the Ctrl key and while you press the **tilde (~) key**. (Figure 2.12 shows the *Sales* workbook with formulas displayed.) To toggle the display back to the regular view, press Ctrl+ ~ again.

Press Ctrl + ≈ to toggle formulas and calculated values

	A	B	C	D	E	F	G	H
1	Comparison of Dog S							
2								
3		January	February	March	April	May	June	Total
4	Year 1	3000	2900	2500	2900	2000	2700	=B4+C4+D4+E4+F4+G4
5	Year 2	2900	3100	3000	5400	3400	3900	=B5+C5+D5+E5+F5+G5
6	Year 3	4500	6100	4500	3900	4500	4700	=SUM(B6:G6)
7	Year 4	3300	4500	4800	6600	6800	7200	=SUM(B7:G7)
8	Year 5	5000	5300	5900	7600	7200	7500	=SUM(B8:G8)
9	Total	=B4+B5+B6+B7+B8	=C4+C5+C6+C7+C8	=SUM(D4:D8)	=SUM(E4:E8)	=SUM(F4:F8)	=SUM(G4:G8)	=SUM(H4:H8)

FIGURE 2.12 Displaying Formulas Instead of Calculated Values

1. With the *Sales* workbook open, press and hold the **Ctrl key** and press the ~ key.
All cells that showed the results of formulas (including the SUM function) now display the formulas.

2. Choose **File | Page Setup**.
The Page Setup dialog box opens.

3. On the Page tab, select **Fit to 1 page wide by 1 page tall**.
Now the whole worksheet will print on one page.

4. On the Sheet tab, select **Row and column headings** and click **OK**.
The dialog box closes. Now the row and column headings will print with the worksheet.

5. Print the worksheet.

6. After the worksheet prints, press **Ctrl + ~**.
The display returns to normal.

7. Choose **File | Page Setup**.

8. On the Page tab, clear the option to **Fit to 1 page wide by 1 page tall**.

9. On the Sheet tab, deselect **Row and column headings** and click **OK**.

10. Close the workbook without saving your changes.

TASK 8 | *Copying and Moving Data*

What: Cut and paste or copy and paste text and numbers from one location to another.

How: Edit | Cut or Edit | Copy and Edit | Paste, Edit | Fill

Why: Moving data on a worksheet is useful when editing, and copying cell contents saves typing time.

Tip: After you select the text to be moved or copied, you can click the right mouse button to open a shortcut menu with both Copy and Cut options.

Excel gives you a variety of methods for copying and moving data. Which one you choose may depend on whether you are copying or cutting to a position you can see on the worksheet or to a more distant spot. You'll learn about copying and moving formulas in a later unit.

COPYING BY FILLING

In Exercise 1 in this unit, you used the fill handle to fill a range with the months of the year. You can also use the fill handle to copy text or a number across columns or down rows.

1. Select the cell with the text or number you want to copy.
2. Point to the fill handle and the pointer changes to a thin black cross.
3. Drag the fill handle down or across the worksheet to copy the cell contents to the rows or columns you select, as shown in Figure 2.13a.

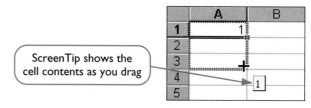

ScreenTip shows the cell contents as you drag

(a) Copying with the Fill Handle

FIGURE 2.13 Copying and Moving Data

POINTER

More Uses for the Fill Handle

- If you hold down Ctrl before dragging a number with the fill handle, the number will increment by 1 in each cell you drag it through. Release the mouse button before releasing the Ctrl key.

- If you select a range consisting of at least two numbers in a series and drag with the fill handle, the series will increment as you drag it.

- If you select a range that is a series, such as 1, 2, 3, and hold down Ctrl before dragging with the fill handle, the series will repeat instead of increment: you will get 1, 2, 3, 1, 2, 3, instead of 1, 2, 3, 4, 5, 6. Release the mouse button before releasing the Ctrl key.

You can also copy data to adjacent cells with the Fill command, as shown in Figure 2.13b:

1. Select the cell you want to copy and the cells to be filled.
2. Choose Edit | Fill to display a submenu.
3. Choose a direction to fill: Up, Down, Right, or Left.

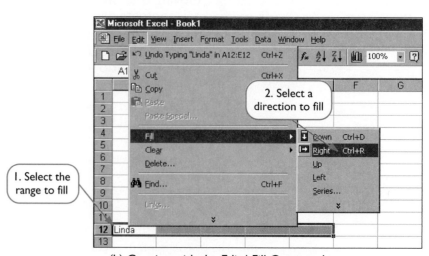

2. Select a direction to fill

1. Select the range to fill

(b) Copying with the Edit | Fill Command

FIGURE 2.13 Copying and Moving Data *(continued)*

MOVING BY DRAGGING

If you want to move cell contents to a nearby cell (one you can see on the worksheet), the easiest way is to use drag and drop.

1. Select the cell or range to be moved.
2. Point to the upper left corner of the top cell in the selection, and the pointer changes to an arrow.
3. Drag the cells to the new location and release the mouse button. As you drag, an outline shows the location, and a ScreenTip lists the address of the cells over which the pointer is moving. This is illustrated in Figure 2.13c.

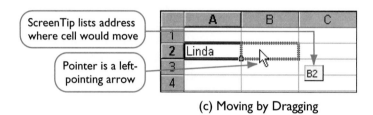

(c) Moving by Dragging

FIGURE 2.13   Copying and Moving Data *(continued)*

COPYING OR MOVING USING THE CLIPBOARD

To move or copy data using the **Windows Clipboard** (a memory location):

1. Select the cell or range to be cut or copied.
2. Choose Edit | Cut or Edit | Copy. Excel places the cell contents on the Windows Clipboard.
3. Select the cell or range (or the upper left corner of the range) where you want the cell contents to appear.
4. Click Edit | Paste.

You can paste cell contents in the same worksheet, into another worksheet, and into another application. Simply switch to the desired worksheet and cell location or application before initiating the paste step.

POINTER

Cutting versus Copying

Cutting and copying text are basically the same operation; however, cutting takes the original from its current location, while copying leaves the original and allows you to place a duplicate in the new location.

Pasting Cells

When you paste cells to a new location in the worksheet, be sure that the location doesn't contain valuable data because Excel pastes the new data over the old, replacing the cell contents. If you drag cells to a new location while holding down the Shift key, Excel will insert the cells where you drop them, moving existing cells aside to make room. Remember that you can undo the process if you need to.

The Windows Clipboard holds a single item—the last one you have copied or cut. However, Microsoft Office 2000 has its own clipboard, the **Office Clipboard**, which stores the last 12 items you have cut or copied from an Office document. The Office Clipboard is not emptied when you exit from Excel, but holds its contents until you turn off the computer.

The Office Clipboard may open as a floating toolbar on your screen when you cut or copy more than one item in a session; but you can also open it manually, by choosing View | Toolbars | Clipboard.

To use the Office Clipboard:

1. If the Clipboard is not already displayed, choose View | Toolbars | Clipboard to display the Office Clipboard as a floating toolbar (see Figure 2.14). Like any other toolbar, you can drag it by its title bar if it gets in the way, or dock it at any edge of the screen, or let it share a row with another toolbar.
2. Cut or paste any items you like. As you do, each item is placed on the Office Clipboard with an icon to indicate which Office application created it. Office Clipboard contents are added from left to right and top to bottom, so that the most recently cut or copied item (the one that is also stored on the Windows Clipboard) is displayed at the bottom right edge of the toolbar.
3. To view the contents of an individual item, point to it, and a ScreenTip will appear.
4. To paste an item at the insertion point in the document, click the item on the toolbar. You can paste it again and again.

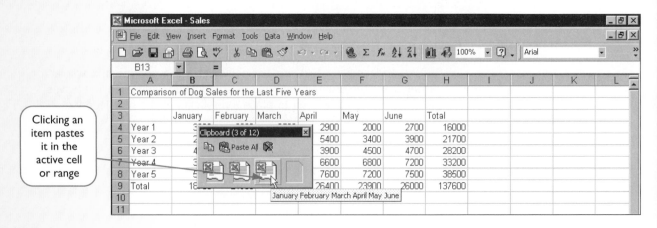

FIGURE 2.14 The Office Clipboard in a Worksheet

Table 2.4 describes the buttons on the Clipboard toolbar.

Button	Description
📋	Copies the selected text to the Clipboard
📋	Pastes all of the Clipboard items at the position of the insertion point
📋	Clears the Clipboard

TABLE 2.4   Clipboard Toolbar Buttons

EXERCISE 8 | *Cutting, Copying, and Pasting Data*

1. With the *Sales* workbook open on the screen, choose **View | Toolbars | Clipboard**.
The Office clipboard opens and floats on the screen.

2. If the Office clipboard hides the contents of any cell, click and drag its title bar to move it out of the way.

3. Select the range **B4:G8** and choose **Edit | Copy**.
The contents of the cells are copied to the Windows and Office clipboards, and the cells are surrounded by a moving border.

4. Click in **B12** and then choose **Edit | Paste**.
The cell contents are pasted into the range whose upper left cell is B12. The original cells are still surrounded by a moving border, to indicate that their contents can be pasted again.

5. Point to the **Excel item** on the Office clipboard.
A ScreenTip displays its contents. You can paste this item anywhere in the worksheet.

6. Click in **B19** and then click the **Paste button** on the Standard toolbar.
The cell contents are pasted again, and the original cells are still surrounded by a moving border.

7. Press **Esc**.
The cells are no longer surrounded by a moving border. The Windows clipboard has been cleared, but the Office clipboard still contains the item.

8. Click in **B26** and then click the **Excel item** on the Office clipboard.
The item is pasted in the range whose top left cell is B26.

9. Click in **G12** and then click and drag the fill handle to **H12**.
The contents of G12 are copied to H12.

10. Select the range **G13:G16** and then click and drag the fill handle to column H.

    The rest of the cells contents are copied from column G to column H.

11. Select **B12** and then point to the upper left corner of the cell until you get the left-pointing arrow.

12. Click and drag the contents from **B12** to **A12**.

    The contents of B12 are moved to A12.

13. Select the range **B13:B16** and then point to the upper left corner of the top cell in the range until you get the left-pointing arrow.

14. Click and drag the cells to **D20**.

    When you release the mouse button, a message asks whether you want to replace the contents of the destination cells.

15. Click **OK**.

    The cell contents are moved to the range whose upper left cell is D20, replacing the original cell contents.

16. Click and drag to select the range **B3:G3** (the cells containing the names of the months).

17. Choose **Edit | Cut**.

    The cell contents are placed on the Windows and Office clipboards, and the cells are surrounded by a moving border.

18. Use one of the methods you have learned in this exercise to paste the cell contents into the range whose upper left cell is B11.

    The cell contents disappear from B3:G3 and are pasted in B11:G11.

19. Choose **Edit | Undo Paste**.

    The text disappears from row 11 and is back in row 3.

20. Close the workbook without saving it.

R E V I E W

S U M M A R Y

After completing this unit, you should be able to

- create a new workbook (page 34)
- use the fill handle to fill a series (page 34)
- create formulas (page 36)
- specify ranges with AutoSum (page 43)
- edit a worksheet (page 45)
- use the built-in spelling checker (page 51)
- modify the page setup (page 53)
- print formulas (page 58)
- move and copy text and numbers in a worksheet (page 56)

KEY TERMS

argument (page 43)
cell location math (page 37)
circular reference (page 38)
fill handle (page 34)
formula (page 36)
gridlines (page 57)
hard copy (page 56)
landscape orientation (page 53)

Office Clipboard (page 62)
operators (page 37)
order of operations (page 38)
portrait orientation (page 53)
range (page 42)
tilde key (page 58)
Windows Clipboard (page 61)

TEST YOUR SKILLS

True/False

1. You are not able to undo deletions in Excel.
2. Formulas in Excel start with an =.
3. You can choose to print the spreadsheet with or without gridlines.
4. You can change the order that Excel uses to calculate formulas by placing parts of the formula in parentheses.
5. Formula printouts that also print the row and column headings make troubleshooting easier.

Multiple Choice

1. To view formulas in the spreadsheet, you use which key combination
   a. Shift+Prt Scr
   b. Ctrl+∧
   c. Ctrl+~
   d. Alt+Pg Dn

2. If you click the AutoSum button and the formula bar shows =SUM(A4:G4), Excel will
   a. add only cells A4 and G4
   b. add all cells in row 4 from column A through column G
   c. add all cells in row 4 from column B through column F
   d. need more information

3. If B10 contains the number 100, B11 contains the number 12, and B12 contains the number 5, the formula =B10–B11*B12 would calculate as
   a. 40
   b. 440
   c. 500
   d. 444

4. If B10 contains the number 100, B11 contains the number 12, and B12 contains the number 5, the formula =(B10–B11)*B12 would calculate as
   a. 40
   b. 440
   c. 500
   d. 444

5. If you wanted to add the contents of D9, E9, F9, G9 and place the result in H9, you would write the following formula:
   a. D9+E9+F9+G9+H9
   b. D9+E9+F9+G9
   c. =D9+E9+F9+G9
   d. =D9+E9+F9+G9+H9

Short Answer

Match the letter with the correct location in Figure 2.15:

___	a. Formula	___	b. File name
___	c. Result of formula	___	d. Name box
___	e. Fill handle	___	f. Changes the order of operations

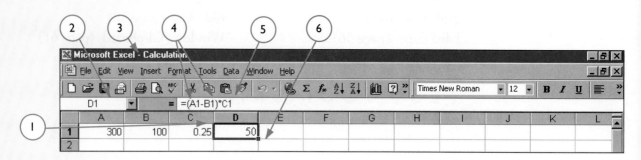

FIGURE 2.15

What Does This Do?

Write a brief description of the function of the following:

1.	✂	6.	📋
2.	┗━━━┿	7.	CTRL + ~
3.	/	8.	📑
4.	Σ	9.	—
5.	*	10.	📄

On Your Own

1. Open the **Scores** workbook. Use AutoSum to calculate the total for Howard. Edit the range that the function suggests.
2. Using **Scores**, show the formulas.
3. Using **Scores** with the formulas showing, print the worksheet.
4. Using **Scores** with the formulas showing, print the worksheet with the row and column headings.
5. Using **Scores** without the formulas showing, practice using all the copy and move functions explained in this unit.

> ### POINTER
>
> #### Creating or Opening a Workbook
>
> All projects are contained on the Instructor Resource Disk and on the World Wide Web at www.prenhall.com/ericksen. Check with your instructor to see if you should open the workbooks or create them from scratch.

PROJECTS

1. You are the owner of the home-based candle-making business named Spread the Light. You recently purchased a computer with Microsoft Excel and want to use it to create worksheets to track your income and expenses.
   a. Create the following worksheet or open **Light**.

	A	B	C	D	E	F	G	H
1	Spread the Light Candles							
2								
3	Budget January-June 1999							
4								
5	Revenue	January	February	March	April	May	June	Total
6	Mail Order	300	300	300	400	400	400	
7	Craft Fairs	0	0	0	900	1500	2000	
8	Wholesale	2000	2000	2000	3000	3000	3000	
9	Total							
10								
11	Expenses							
12	Supplies	800	800	500	400	200	200	
13	Postage	100	100	100	120	120	120	
14	Travel	0	0	0	10	100	100	
15	Total							
16								
17	Net Income							

   b. Add the totals in column H.
   c. Create formulas to add totals in rows 9 and 15.
   d. Create a formula to calculate net income in row 17. (Net income is total revenue less total expenses.) NOTE: You will find out how to widen cell A17 in the next unit. Don't worry for now if part of the text is hidden by the contents of cell B17.
   e. Create a header that contains your name on the left and **Project 2-1** on the right.
   f. Run the spelling checker.
   g. Save the workbook as **Light**.
   h. Print the worksheet in landscape orientation, centering the worksheet both horizontally and vertically on the page.
   i. Print the formulas with the row and column headings.

2. You are a dealer in kaleidoscopes. A new addition to your business, Rainbow Visions, is a computer with Microsoft Excel. You want to create worksheets for your small home-based business using Excel.
   a. Create the following first quarter income statement or open **Rainbow Visions**.
   b. Add the totals in column E.
   c. Total the expenses in row 12.
   d. Create the formulas to calculate net income (defined as revenue less expenses).
   e. Create a header that contains your name on the left and **Project 2-2** on the right.
   f. Run the spelling checker.
   g. Save the workbook as **Rainbow Visions**.
   h. Print the worksheet in landscape orientation.
   i. Print the formulas with the row and column headings.

	A	B	C	D	E
1	Rainbow Visions				
2	Income Statement				
3					
4		January	February	March	Total
5	REVENUE	5000	4500	6000	
6					
7	EXPENSES				
8	Publicity	500	450	600	
9	Postage	250	400	180	
10	Printing	6000			
11	Supplies	200	300	250	
12	Total				
13					
14	NET INCOME				

3. You work for your college while you are taking classes. You have to fill out a time card every month.
   a. Create the following worksheet or open **Time Card**.

	A	B	C	D	E	F	G	H	I
1	Your College Name								
2	Today's date								
3	Name:	Your Name							
4	Position:	Accounting Assistant							
5	Period:	Previous month							
6									
7	Hours	Mon	Tue	Wed	Thu	Fri	Sat	Sun	Total
8	Week 1	8	8	10	11	7			
9	Week 2	6	11	4	12	8	5	4	
10	Week 3	7		6	9	6	5	5	
11	Week 4	9	8	7	4	6	3	8	
12	Total								
13							Personal Leave		4
14							Subtotal		
15							Overtime		
16							Regular Hours		

   b. Add the total number of hours worked per week in column I.
   c. Total the hours for the month in I12.
   d. Write a formula for the subtotal in I14 that subtracts the personal leave time.
   e. Any hours over 160 for the pay period are considered overtime. Write a formula that shows the number of overtime hours in I15.
   f. Subtract the overtime hours to show the regular hours in I16.
   g. Run the spelling checker.
   h. Create a header that contains your name on the left and **Project 2-3** on the right.
   i. Save the workbook as **Time Card**.
   j. Print the worksheet in landscape orientation without gridlines.
   k. Print the formulas with the row and column headings.

4. You are thinking of traveling to Asia and want to track foreign exchange rates.
   a. Create the following foreign worksheet or open **Currency**.

	A	B	C	D
1	Your Name			
2	Foreign Exchange			
3	Foreign Currency in U.S. Dollars			
4	Country	Currency	Per $1	Per $100
5	China	Yuan	8.28	
6	Hong Kong	Dollar	7.748	
7	India	Rupee	42.525	
8	Japan	Yen	134.7	
9	Malaysia	Ringgit	3.8	
10	Philippines	Peso	43.35	
11	Singapore	Dollar	1.7389	
12	S. Korea	Won	1340.5	
13	Taiwan	Dollar	34.77	
14	Thailand	Baht	40.73	

b. Create a formula in column D that shows the value of each foreign currency for 100 U.S. dollars.

c. Run the spelling checker.

d. Create a header that contains your name on the left and **Project 2-4** on the right.

e. Save the workbook as **Currency**.

f. Print the worksheet in landscape orientation centered both horizontally and vertically.

g. Print the formulas with the row and column headings.

POINTER

Up-to-Date Currency Rates

If you are connected to the Internet, you can use actual figures for the day you complete this exercise by going to the following document on the World Wide Web: http://quote.yahoo.com/m3?u

PROJECTS

1. a. Create the following profit and loss statement for Spread the Light Candles or open **Profit-Loss**:

	A	B	C	D
1	Spread the Light			
2	Profit/Loss Statement			
3				
4			Year 1	Year 2
5	Sales		110,000	150,000
6	Cost of goods		45,000	62,000
7	Gross margin			
8				
9	Fixed costs		30,000	34,000
10				
11	Profit before taxes			
12				
13	Taxes		9,000	11,000
14				
15	Net profit			

   b. Create formulas in rows 7, 11, and 15.

   - Gross Margin is sales minus cost of goods.
   - Profit before taxes is gross margin minus fixed costs.
   - Net profit is profit before taxes minus taxes.

   c. Run the spelling checker.

   d. Create a header that contains your name on the left and **Check 1 Project 1** on the right.

   e. Save the workbook as **Profit-Loss**.

   f. Print the worksheet in landscape orientation without gridlines centered both horizontally and vertically on the page.

   g. Print the formulas with the row and column headings.

2. a. Create the following worksheet or open **Payroll**:

	A	B	C	D	E	F	G	H
1	JRT Kennels							
2	PT Payroll							
3	Today's date							
4					Deductions			
5	Name	Hours	Rate	Gross Pay	OASDI	HI	FIT	Net Pay
6	Black, B	20	6.75					
7	Brown, J	24	6.5					
8	Gold, J	36	6.75					
9	Hill, J	20	6.25					
10	Jones, S	25	6.25					
11	Smith, A	15	7					
12	Smith, J	36	7					
13	Stone, B	18	6.5					
14	Web, B	12	6.25					
15	White, M	19	7					

b. Write the following formulas:

Compute gross pay

Compute the deductions:

- OASDI is 6.2% of gross pay.
- HI is 1.45% of gross pay.
- FIT is 15% of gross pay.

Net pay—Gross pay minus all deductions.

c. Run the spelling checker.

d. Create a header that contains your name on the left and **Check 1 Project 2** on the right.

e. Save the workbook as **Payroll**.

f. Print the worksheet in landscape orientation.

g. Print the formulas with the row and column headings.

POINTER

Tax Rates

The rates used in this project are the 1998 rates. If you have access to the Internet, you can check the current rate for Social Security and Medicare by connecting to the Internal Revenue Service at the following address: http://www.irs.ustreas.gov/prod/tax_edu/teletax/tc751.html

Formatting the Worksheet

UNIT OBJECTIVES

- Use AutoFormat
- Use bold, italic, and underlining
- Change the font, size, color, and other font attributes
- Format numbers
- Adjust column widths
- Align data in cells
- Add a border and shading
- Add a graphic

Once you create and edit the worksheet, you will want to format it to make it as clear as possible. **Formatting** is the structure and layout of a worksheet and its individual parts. Excel's standard formatting is not meant to produce finished printouts. For instance, Excel formats all text at the left of the cell and all numbers at the right. If you enter *8.00*, Excel displays *8*. Excel has a host of formatting options you can choose to make text and numbers look the way you want them. In this unit, you will learn to format text to help your user understand the numeric data. You will also learn to make the numeric information as clear as possible by formatting the numbers, widening columns, and adding borders and shading.

TASK 1 | *Using AutoFormat*

What: Have Excel automatically format a worksheet.

How: Choose Format | AutoFormat.

Why: You can create attractive worksheets while you are learning to use Excel.

Tip: If you choose a format that you don't care for, simply choose Edit | Undo AutoFormat.

To have Excel automatically format a worksheet:

1. Select the range to be formatted.
2. Choose Format | AutoFormat to display the AutoFormat dialog box, as shown in Figure 3.1.
3. Select an AutoFormat from the illustrated list.
4. Click OK to apply the AutoFormat to the selection.

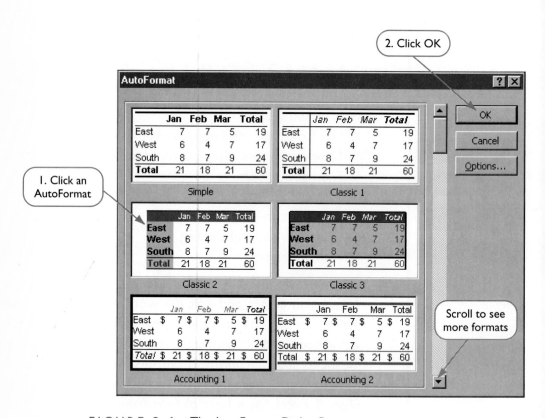

FIGURE 3.1 The AutoFormat Dialog Box

Formatting Guidelines

Formatting a worksheet should make the data clearer. Apply the following guidelines whenever you are creating and formatting a worksheet:

- Place a title at the top of the worksheet and center it over the columns.
- Use a header or footer that includes the current date and the name of the file.
- Format the numbers for easier understanding, for example, using comma style with large numbers and two decimal places for currency.
- Apply text formatting, graphics, and borders and shading sparingly so that you don't detract from the information.
- Place data in contiguous columns for better printouts.
- Print in landscape orientation.

EXERCISE 1 | *Using AutoFormat*

1. Open the *Sales* workbook.
2. Select the range **A1** through **H9**.
3. Choose **Format | AutoFormat**.
   The AutoFormat dialog box opens.
4. Scroll in the list of AutoFormats, click the **Colorful 2** style, and click **OK**.
   The dialog box closes, and the selected cells are formatted in the Colorful 2 style.
5. Click **outside the selection** to see the result.
   Your worksheet should look similar to Figure 3.2.
6. Print the worksheet.
7. Choose **Edit | Undo AutoFormat** so that the worksheet is ready for the next exercise.

The Colorful 2 AutoFormat

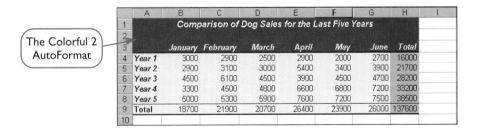

	A	B	C	D	E	F	G	H	I
1				Comparison of Dog Sales for the Last Five Years					
2									
3		January	February	March	April	May	June	Total	
4	Year 1	3000	2900	2500	2900	2000	2700	16000	
5	Year 2	2900	3100	3000	5400	3400	3900	21700	
6	Year 3	4500	6100	4500	3900	4500	4700	28200	
7	Year 4	3300	4500	4800	6600	6800	7200	33200	
8	Year 5	5000	5300	5900	7600	7200	7500	38500	
9	Total	18700	21900	20700	26400	23900	26000	137600	
10									

FIGURE 3.2 The AutoFormatted *Sales* Workbook

TASK 2 | *Using Bold, Italic, and Underline*

What: Format cell contents using bold, italic, and underline.

How: Click the Bold, Italic, or Underline button on the Formatting toolbar.

Why: Bold, italic, and underlining set cell contents off from the surrounding cells.

Tip: Toolbar buttons that are turned on look pushed into the toolbar and have a lighter color.

When you enter data in a new worksheet, Excel formats it in the font style known as Regular. You can change this style and other formatting features of data as you enter it, or select existing cells and change their formatting. Excel's Formatting toolbar has buttons and boxes that act as shortcuts to many common formatting actions. This task shows you how to use the toolbar to change the style to bold or italic and to underline characters. You can also apply this technique to other formatting tasks.

> ## POINTER
>
> ### Indenting Text in Cells
>
> The Increase Indent and Decrease Indent buttons on the Formatting toolbar let you indent text in a cell. You can click the button either before you type or after the text is entered.

To change the style of existing data using the toolbar:

1. Select the characters or cells to be formatted.
2. Click the Formatting toolbar's Bold, Italic, and/or Underline buttons to apply this formatting.
3. Click outside the selection to deselect it and turn off the toolbar buttons.

To format as you type:

1. Position the insertion point where you want to enter data.
2. Click the Formatting toolbar's Bold, Italic, and/or Underline buttons to turn on this formatting.
3. Enter the data in the cell; it will have the formatting you turned on.
4. Complete the entry in any of the methods you have learned. The formatting is turned off automatically.

To remove formatting from text:

1. Select the cells or characters with the formatting you want to remove, and the toolbar buttons for the formatting look pushed in.
2. Click the buttons for the formatting you want to remove to turn it off.

EXERCISE 2 | *Using Bold, Italics, and Underline*

1. With the *Sales* workbook open on the screen, select **A1** (*"Comparison of Dog Sales for the Last Five Years"*).

2. Click the **Bold** and **Underline buttons** on the Formatting toolbar.
   The text is formatted as bold and with a single underline. All of the text is formatted, even though it extends past the border of column A.

3. Select the range **B3: H3**.

4. Click the **Italic button**.
   The text is formatted as italic. Your worksheet should look like the one in Figure 3.3.

5. Close the workbook without saving it.

Buttons look pushed in

Active cell

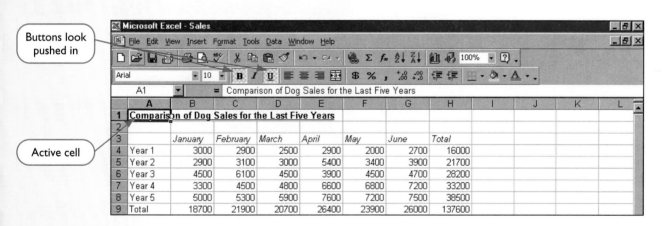

FIGURE 3.3 The *Sales* Workbook after Exercise 2

TASK 3 | *Formatting Text Using the Font Dialog Box*

What: Format text by changing the font, font size, color, and effects.

How: Choose Format | Cells | Font tab.

Why: You can add emphasis and readability to text by formatting it.

Tip: You can use the toolbar to change the font, font size, and font color, but the dialog box has the advantage of displaying a preview of the selected formatting.

When you enter data in a new workbook, it is automatically formatted for you in a font called Arial and in the size called 10 point. Arial is one of several fonts, or typefaces, that come with Microsoft Windows. (A **font** is a complete set of characters with its own design and name.) Type sizes are measured in **points**, and 10 point is the default type size for data in a new Excel workbook. (There are 72 points in an inch.) You can change the font, the font size, and the font color and add other effects.

To format the font:

1. Select the cells.
2. Choose Format | Cells | Font tab. The Format Cells dialog box opens with the Font tab displayed, as shown in Figure 3.4. The name of the current font is displayed in the Font box at the top of the dialog box, and a sample appears in the Preview box.

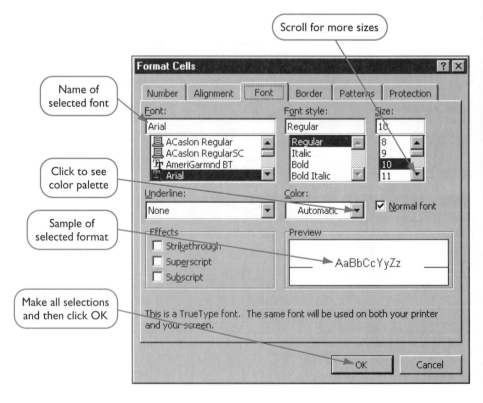

FIGURE 3.4 The Font Tab of the Format Cells Dialog Box

3. Make selections from the following options:
   - Change the font by selecting a name from the Font list.
   - Change the style of the font in the Font Style section.
   - Change the size of the font in the Size box.
   - Choose an underline style (Single, Double, Single Accounting, or Double Accounting) by clicking the arrow in the Underline box.
   - Change the color of the font by clicking the arrow in the Color box and choosing a color from the palette that drops down.
   - Add effects (Superscript [2^2], Subscript [H_2O], or Strikethrough [~~450~~]) by clicking a check box in the Effects section.

4. The selected formatting is previewed in the Preview section. When you are satisfied, click the OK button.

EXERCISE 3 | *Formatting Text Using the Font Dialog Box*

1. With the *Sales* workbook open, click in **A1**.

2. Choose **Format | Cells | Font tab**.
   The Format Cells dialog box opens with the Font tab displayed.

3. Make the following settings:
   - In the *Font style* box, click **Bold**.
   - Scroll in the *Size* box and click **12**.
   - Click the *Color* option's down arrow and, when a palette opens, click **Dark Blue**.

   When you point to the colors in the palette, a ScreenTip displays their name. As you make the selections, the Preview box shows a sample.

4. Click **OK**.
   The dialog box closes, and the cell is formatted in 12 point Arial bold, dark blue. Look at the toolbar and you will see the font and font size listed, and the Bold button will look pushed in.

5. Select the range **B3: H3**.

6. Choose **Format | Cells | Font tab**.
   The Format Cells dialog box opens with the Font tab displayed.

7. In the Font list, choose the font **Comic Sans MS** (or any other available font) and click **OK**.
   The dialog box closes, and the text is formatted in the new font.

8. Click and drag to select the range **B8:H8**.

9. Choose **Format** | **Cells** | **Font tab**.
   The dialog box opens again.

10. Click the down arrow for the **Underline** option, click **Single Accounting**, and then click **OK**.
    A single underline is placed below just the numbers in the cells. Your worksheet should look similar to the one in Figure 3.5, though you may have a different font in row 3.

11. Save the workbook and print the worksheet. Leave it open for use in the next exercise.

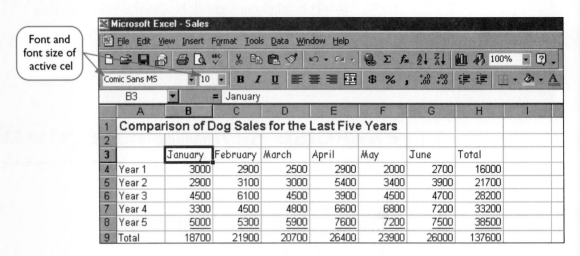

FIGURE 3.5   The *Sales* Workbook after Exercise 3

TASK 4 | *Formatting Numbers*

What: Format numbers so that they can be understood more easily.
How: Choose Format | Cells | Number tab.
Why: People expect consistency in formatting in worksheets.
Tip: Specify two decimal places when formatting currency.

How you format numbers depends in part on the audience for your work. But in general, you will want to use Comma style to put commas between thousands, Currency style to display dollar signs in totals, and two decimal places with currency. Although you can type dollar signs and commas as you input data, you will need to format the results of formulas.

To format numbers in a worksheet:

1. Select the cells to be formatted.
2. Choose Format | Cells | Number tab. The Format Cells dialog box opens with the Number tab displayed, as shown in Figure 3.6.

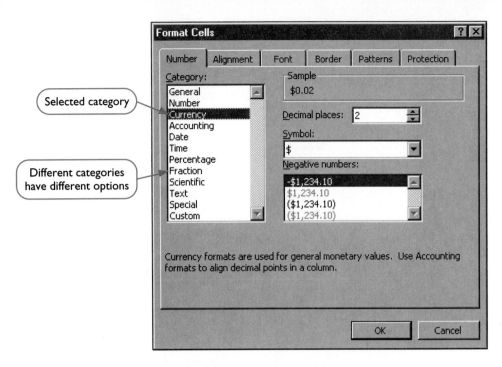

FIGURE 3.6   The Number Tab of the Format Cells Dialog Box

3. Select a type of formatting from the Category list.
4. Make selections from the resulting options, which differ with the category. For example, the Currency style, illustrated in Figure 3.6, lets you choose the number of decimal places to display, the currency symbol, and the format for negative numbers.

Excel's Formatting toolbar also contains buttons for often-used formats. Table 3.1 describes the function of these buttons.

Button	Name	Description
$	currency	Formats the selection with a dollar sign, a decimal point, and two decimal places
%	percent	Multiplies the cell contents by 100 and places a percent sign after the number
,	comma	Places a comma between thousands
.00 .0	idecimal	Increases the number of decimal places in the cell or selected cells one place every time you click it
.00 .0	ddecimal	Decreases the number of decimal places in the cell or selected cells one decimal place every time you click it

TABLE 3.1   Number Formatting Buttons

EXERCISE 4 | *Formatting Numbers*

1. With the *Sales* workbook open on the screen, select the range **B4:H4**. The cells are highlighted.

2. Hold down **Ctrl** and select the range **B9:H9**.
   This range is selected as well. To select a range of noncontiguous cells, select the first cells and then hold down Ctrl while you select the rest.

3. Choose **Format | Cells | Number tab**.
   The Format Cells dialog box opens with the Number tab displayed.

4. Select the **Accounting category**.
   The dialog box displays the options for the Accounting style.

5. Make the following settings:
   - Click in the **Decimal places box** and type **0** (zero).
   - Click the down arrow for the **Symbol option** and click **$** (the dollar sign).

6. Click **OK**.
   The dialog box closes, and the cells in rows 4 and 9 are formatted with the Accounting style, a dollar sign, and no decimal places.

7. Select the range **B5:H8** and click the **Comma Style button** on the Formatting toolbar.
   The cells are formatted with a comma between thousands and with two decimal places.

8. With the cells still selected, click the **Decrease Decimal button** *twice*.

9. Click outside the selection to see the result. Your worksheet should look like Figure 3.7.

10. Save the workbook and print the worksheet. Leave it open for use in the next exercise.

	A	B	C	D	E	F	G	H
1	**Comparison of Dog Sales for the Last Five Years**							
2								
3		January	February	March	April	May	June	Total
4	Year 1	$ 3,000	$ 2,900	$ 2,500	$ 2,900	$ 2,000	$ 2,700	$ 16,000
5	Year 2	2,900	3,100	3,000	5,400	3,400	3,900	21,700
6	Year 3	4,500	6,100	4,500	3,900	4,500	4,700	28,200
7	Year 4	3,300	4,500	4,800	6,600	6,800	7,200	33,200
8	Year 5	5,000	5,300	5,900	7,600	7,200	7,500	38,500
9	Total	$ 18,700	$ 21,900	$ 20,700	$ 26,400	$ 23,900	$ 26,000	$ 137,600

Accounting style

Comma style

FIGURE 3.7 The *Sales* Workbook after Exercise 4

TASK 5 | *Changing Column Widths*

What: Make columns wider or narrower.

How: Choose Format | Column | Width.

Why: The default column width isn't wide enough to display the contents of many cells.

Tip: Size your columns wider than their contents to make the numbers easy to read.

Excel sets the width of every column in the worksheet at 8.43 characters. When you type text that is longer than 8.43 characters, it will fall over into the next column. You will be able to read the text as long as the cell to the right is empty. If data is placed in the cell to the right, then the text is cut off (though it is not lost: you can still see it on the formula bar).

If numbers that are longer than the 8.43 characters are supposed to appear in a cell, Excel will automatically expand the column unless you have already changed the width of the column. If you have changed the column width and Excel can't fit a number in the cell, it does not cut off the number as it does text. Instead, it places the symbols ### in the cell.

POINTER

and E

Whenever you see ### in any cell of the worksheet, all you have to do is widen the column to see the number. You may also see a number expressed in scientific notation, such as 2.34E+08. Search Excel Help for "Tips on entering numbers" for more information.

USING THE MENUS

To specify column widths using the Column Width dialog box:

1. Make any cell in the column the active cell or select cells in several columns.
2. Choose Format | Column | Width. The Column Width dialog box opens, as shown in Figure 3.8.
3. Type the desired width in characters for the columns and click OK.

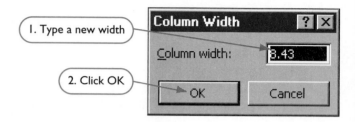

FIGURE 3.8 The Column Width Dialog Box

To change column widths using AutoFit Selection:

1. Make the cell you want to adjust the active cell or select cells to be adjusted in several columns.
2. Choose Format | Column | AutoFit Selection. Excel automatically adjusts the width of each column individually to fit the widest text in the selection.

USING THE MOUSE

You can also use the mouse to change the width of one or more columns, either manually or using AutoFit.

To change column width manually:

- Point the mouse to the right boundary of the column heading until you see the two-headed sizing arrow, shown in Figure 3.9; then click and drag the boundary. If you select more than one column before dragging, Excel will adjust all of them at the same time. As you drag, a ScreenTip will display the current column width.
- Drag the right boundary to the right to make the column wider.
- Drag the right boundary to the left to make the column narrower.

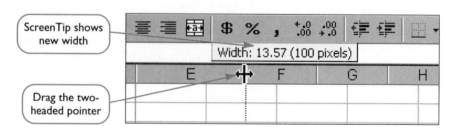

FIGURE 3.9 Resizing Column Width with the Mouse

To AutoFit a column's width using the mouse, double-click the column boundary rather than dragging it to the right. If you want to AutoFit several columns using the double-clicking method, select them first and then double-click any one of the column boundaries.

EXERCISE 5 | *Changing Column Widths*

1. With the *Sales* workbook open on the screen, point to the right boundary of the heading of **column B**.
2. When the two-headed sizing arrow appears, drag the boundary to the right.
   The column width increases.

3. Point to the right boundary of the heading of **column D**.

4. When the two-headed sizing arrow appears, drag the boundary to the left.
The column width decreases.

5. Select **columns F, G, and H**.

6. Choose **Format | Column | Width**.

7. Type **12** in the Column Width dialog box, and click **OK**.
The three columns expand to 12 characters.

8. With the three columns still selected, point to the right boundary of the heading of any of them.

9. When the two-headed sizing arrow appears, double-click.
The three columns are individually resized.

10. Close the workbook without saving it.

TASK 6 | *Aligning Data in Cells*

What: Change the alignment of cell contents.

How: Choose Format | Cells | Alignment tab.

Why: Realigning cell contents can make data easier to read and printouts more attractive.

Tip: It is best not to change the alignment of numbers, which appear at the right edge of the column by default, because this alignment makes for easy reading.

At times you will want to change the way data is aligned in cells. For example, labels can be centered over a column or right-aligned to appear over the numbers. For full control over alignment, use the menu options. For quick alignment, use the toolbar buttons.

USING THE MENUS

Choose Format | Cells | Alignment tab. The Format Cells dialog box opens with the Alignment tab displayed, as shown in Figure 3.10. The Text Control section has horizontal and vertical boxes.

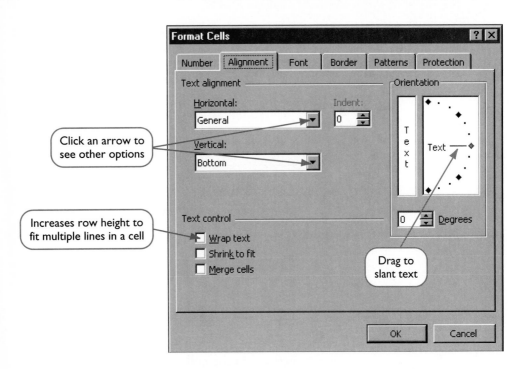

Click an arrow to see other options

Increases row height to fit multiple lines in a cell

Drag to slant text

FIGURE 3.10 The Alignment Tab of the Format Cells Dialog Box

- **Horizontal**: Click the down arrow for the Horizontal option and make a selection from the list described in Table 3.2.

- **Vertical**: Click the down arrow for the Vertical option and select *Bottom* (the default), *Top*, *Center*, or *Justify*.

Option	Result
General	Aligns text at the left of the cell and numbers at the right
Left	Aligns text at the left. If you type a number in the Indent box, data will be indented from the left edge of the cell by the amount you specify
Center	Centers the cell contents within the cell
Right	Aligns the data at the right of the cell
Fill	Fills selected cells with the character contained in them; fills any empty cells in the selection with the character in the nearest occupied cell to the left
Justify	Makes all cell contents as wide as the cell
Center Across Selection	Centers the contents of the left cell over the selected cells

TABLE 3.2 Horizontal Alignment Options

The Text Control section has check boxes that:

- **Wrap Text**: wraps multiple lines within a cell, increasing the row's depth to fit
- **Shrink to Fit**: reduces the font size to fit the text in the cell
- **Merge Cells**: combine two or more cells

POINTER

Wrapping Text

A quick way to wrap text in a cell is to insert a manual line break by pressing Alt+Enter. The cell will expand one row each time you press Alt+Enter.

The Orientation section of the dialog box allows you to rotate the text within the cell. Drag the indicator to the desired rotation or type in the desired result in the Degrees box. For example, if you choose 45 degrees, the text will be slanted in the cell, and if you choose 90 degrees, the text will appear vertical in the cell.

USING THE TOOLBAR

You can change many of the common alignment options from the toolbar. Table 3.3 describes the alignment buttons.

Button	Description
≣	Aligns text at the left of the cell
≣	Centers data within the cell
≣	Aligns text at the right edge of the cell
▦	Merges selected cells and centers the text in the merged cell

TABLE 3.3   Alignment Buttons

EXERCISE 6 | *Aligning Data in Cells*

---

1. Open the *Sales* workbook.

2. Select the range **B3: H3**.

3. Choose **Format | Cells | Alignment tab**.
The Format Cells dialog box opens with the Alignment tab displayed.

4. In the Horizontal drop-down box, select **Center** and then click **OK**.
The dialog box closes and the data is centered in each cell.

5. Select the range **A1: H1**.

6. Click the **Merge and Center button**.
The title is centered in the merged cells.

7. Select the range **B3:H3**.

8. Choose **Format | Cells | Alignment tab**.
The Format Cells dialog box opens with the Alignment tab displayed.

9. Drag the Orientation indicator upward to **45 degrees** and then click **OK**.
The dialog box closes, and the labels appear slanted, as shown in Figure 3.11.

10. Save the workbook and print the worksheet.

	A	B	C	D	E	F	G	H
1		Comparison of Dog Sales for the Last Five Years						
2								
3		January	February	March	April	May	June	Total
4	Year 1	$ 3,000	$ 2,900	$ 2,500	$ 2,900	$ 2,000	$ 2,700	$ 16,000
5	Year 2	2,900	3,100	3,000	5,400	3,400	3,900	21,700
6	Year 3	4,500	6,100	4,500	3,900	4,500	4,700	28,200
7	Year 4	3,300	4,500	4,800	6,600	6,800	7,200	33,200
8	Year 5	5,000	5,300	5,900	7,600	7,200	7,500	38,500
9	Total	$ 18,700	$ 21,900	$ 20,700	$ 26,400	$ 23,900	$ 26,000	$ 137,600

Title merged and centered

Labels slanted 45°

FIGURE 3.11 The *Sales* Workbook after Exercise 6

TASK 7 | *Adding a Border and Shading*

What: Placing a border around cells and shading cells.

How: Choose Format | Cells | Border and Format | Cells | Patterns.

Why: Borders and shading are effective ways to highlight data.

Tip: When you choose a shading, keep the printout in mind. If you don't have a color printer, the effect of a shading will be different from what you see on screen.

You can add a border around the worksheet or around an individual cell or range. You can also add a light shading to cells to provide emphasis. Use the toolbar to place a simple border around cells, or use the menus to do something more elaborate.

ADDING A BORDER USING THE MENU

To add a border using the menu:

1. Select the cells to be bordered.
2. Choose Format | Cells | Border. The Format Cells dialog box opens with the Border tab displayed, as shown in Figure 3.12.

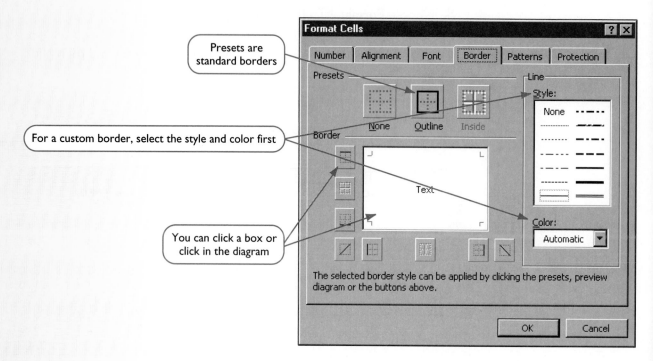

FIGURE 3.12   The Border Tab of the Format Cells Dialog Box

3. To choose a line style for the border, click one of the samples in the Style box.
4. To choose a color, click the down arrow for the Color option and click a color in the palette that drops down.
5. For a standard border, use the Presets section and choose:

   - Outline to place a border around the cells
   - Inside to place a border between cells
   - Both Outline and Inside to place a border both around the outside and between all the cells

6. For a custom border, use the individual buttons in the Borders section. Notice that you can even include diagonal lines.

ADDING A BORDER USING THE TOOLBAR

You can also use the Borders button on the Formatting toolbar to place a border around a cell or range.

1. Select the cells to be bordered.

2. Click the Borders button's down arrow to open the menu in Figure 3.13.
3. Select a border. The cells will be formatted with the selected border, and the menu will close.

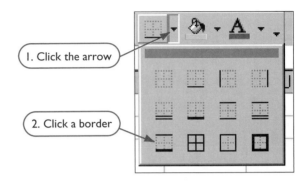

1. Click the arrow

2. Click a border

FIGURE 3.13 The Drop-Down Borders Menu

ADDING SHADING AND PATTERNS

To include shading and patterns in a worksheet:
1. Select the cells to have shading or a pattern.
2. Choose Format | Cells | Patterns. The Format Cells dialog box opens, with the Patterns tab displayed, as shown in Figure 3.14.
3. Select a color for the shading in the Color section.
4. Select a pattern from the Pattern section.

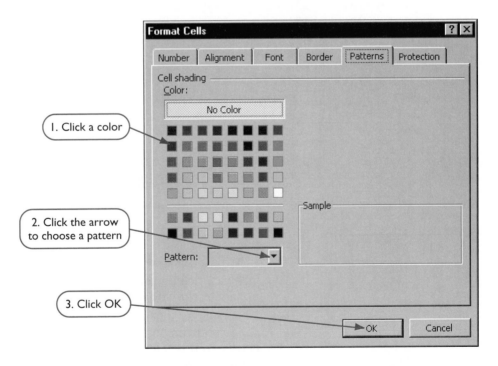

1. Click a color

2. Click the arrow to choose a pattern

3. Click OK

FIGURE 3.14 The Patterns Tab of the Format Cells Dialog Box

You can also use the Fill Color button on the Formatting toolbar to add shading to selected cells. Click the button's down arrow to open a palette of fill colors. Click a color to apply it to the selected cells and close the palette.

EXERCISE 7 | Adding a Border and Shading

1. With the *Sales* workbook open on the screen, select the range **B3: H3**.
2. Choose **Format | Cells | Border tab**.
   The Format Cells dialog box opens with the Border tab displayed.
3. Choose **Outline** and click **OK**.
   The dialog box closes, and the selected cells are formatted with a border.
4. With B3:H3 still selected, choose **Format | Cells | Patterns tab**.
   The Format Cells dialog box opens with the Patterns tab displayed.
5. Select a **light gray** and click **OK**.
   The dialog box closes, and the pattern is applied.
6. Click outside the selection to clear the highlight. Your worksheet should look like the one in Figure 3.15.
7. Save the workbook and print the worksheet.

Standard preset outline border

Choose a light pattern so the text will show

	A	B	C	D	E	F	G	H	I
1	Comparison of Dog Sales for the Last Five Years								
2									
3		January	February	March	April	May	June	Total	
4	Year 1	$ 3,000	$ 2,900	$ 2,500	$ 2,900	$ 2,000	$ 2,700	$ 16,000	
5	Year 2	2,900	3,100	3,000	5,400	3,400	3,900	21,700	
6	Year 3	4,500	6,100	4,500	3,900	4,500	4,700	28,200	
7	Year 4	3,300	4,500	4,800	6,600	6,800	7,200	33,200	
8	Year 5	5,000	5,300	5,900	7,600	7,200	7,500	38,500	
9	Total	$ 18,700	$ 21,900	$ 20,700	$ 26,400	$ 23,900	$ 26,000	$ 137,600	

FIGURE 3.15 The *Sales* Workbook after Exercise 7

TASK 8 | Adding a Graphic

What: Add a graphic image to the worksheet.

How: Choose Insert | Picture | Clip Art.

Why: You can include the company logo or other graphic that enhances the information in a worksheet.

Tip: If you want to include a graphic in the background of the worksheet, you can choose Format | Sheet | Background. The graphic is repeated to fill the sheet. This would work best with a light version of the company logo.

Inserting images related to your worksheet makes it look more professional. There are many sources of images. You can use the images bundled with Microsoft Office, create your own images in a drawing program, scan images on a scanner, buy CD's of images, or take digital photographs for use in a worksheet. (And not only can you insert clip art, but you can also insert pictures, sounds, and videos into an Excel worksheet. To find out more, use Excel Help.)

To insert an image into a worksheet:

1. Move to the area of the worksheet where you want a clipart image to appear.
2. Choose Insert | Picture | ClipArt to display the Insert ClipArt dialog box shown in Figure 3.16a.
3. Choose a category.
4. Select an image in that category.
5. Click the Insert clip button (as shown in Figure 3.16b) and then close the dialog box. The image will be placed in the worksheet.

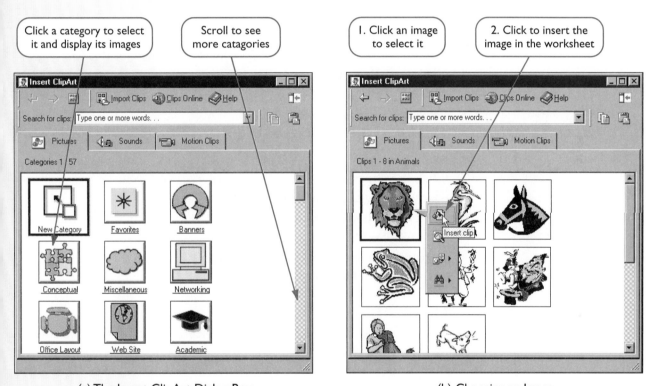

(a) The Insert ClipArt Dialog Box   (b) Choosing an Image

FIGURE 3.16   Inserting ClipArt

POINTER

Moving, Sizing, and Deleting an Image

To select an image, click it. When it is selected, it has small boxes around its outer edge, called **sizing handles**. Point to the image and the pointer changes to a four-headed arrow; click and drag it to move it. Point to a sizing handle and the pointer changes to a two-headed arrow; click and drag to resize the image in the direction you drag. You can also delete an image that is selected by pressing the Delete key.

When an image is selected, the Picture toolbar is displayed. You can use the Picture toolbar to make certain changes in the image. For example, use the Crop button to cut off some of the image. Point to any button on the toolbar and a ScreenTip tells you its name. To deselect the image, click outside it.

EXERCISE 8 | *Inserting Clip Art*

1. With the *Sales* workbook on the screen, click **A2**.

2. Choose **Insert | Picture | Clip Art**.
The ClipArt dialog box opens.

3. Make sure the **Pictures tab** is selected, and then click **Animals** in the category list.
The list changes to show the clipart images available in this category.

4. Click any **clipart image**.
A toolbar opens.

5. Click the **Insert clip button**.
The image is inserted into the worksheet.

6. Close the Insert ClipArt dialog box.

7. Click the **clipart image**.
The image is selected and surrounded by sizing handles.

8. Point to the **bottom right handle** and drag the two-headed pointer.
The image is resized.

9. Point to the center of the document. Click and drag the four-headed arrow to move the image if necessary.
Your worksheet should look similar to the one in Figure 3.17 (you probably have a different image).

10. Save the workbook and print the worksheet, then close the worksheet and exit from Excel.

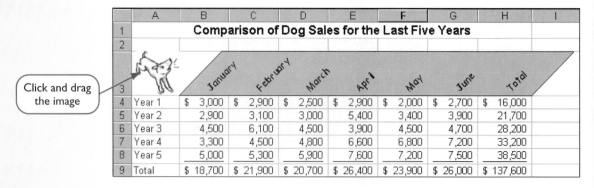

Click and drag the image

	A	B	C	D	E	F	G	H	I
1	**Comparison of Dog Sales for the Last Five Years**								
2									
3		January	February	March	April	May	June	Total	
4	Year 1	$ 3,000	$ 2,900	$ 2,500	$ 2,900	$ 2,000	$ 2,700	$ 16,000	
5	Year 2	2,900	3,100	3,000	5,400	3,400	3,900	21,700	
6	Year 3	4,500	6,100	4,500	3,900	4,500	4,700	28,200	
7	Year 4	3,300	4,500	4,800	6,600	6,800	7,200	33,200	
8	Year 5	5,000	5,300	5,900	7,600	7,200	7,500	38,500	
9	Total	$ 18,700	$ 21,900	$ 20,700	$ 26,400	$ 23,900	$ 26,000	$ 137,600	

FIGURE 3.17   The *Sales* Workbook after Exercise 8

S U M M A R Y

After completing this unit, you should be able to

- format using the AutoFormat option (page 74)
- apply bold, italic, and underline formatting to cell contents (page 76)
- format fonts using the Format Cells dialog box (page 78)
- format numbers (page 80)
- adjust column widths (page 83)
- align data in cells (page 86)
- add a border and shading (page 89)
- add a graphic (page 92)

K E Y   T E R M S

font (page 78)   **sizing handles** (page 93)

formatting (page 73)   **points** (page 78)

T E S T   Y O U R   S K I L L S

True/False

1. You can widen a column by double-clicking the boundary of the column heading.
2. You can rotate text in a cell.
3. You can change the size of the font but not the font in Microsoft Excel.
4. You should leave numbers aligned at the right of the column.
5. You can merge cells together in Excel.

Multiple Choice

1. If you want cells of numbers to appear with a $, you would
   a. choose Format | Cells | Number | Accounting
   b. choose Format | Cells | Number | Currency
   c. click the Currency Style button
   d. all of these answers

2. To expand a row so that it will display multiple lines you would:
   a. choose Wrap Text in the Format Cells dialog box
   b. choose Merge Cells in the Format Cells dialog box
   c. press Alt+Enter
   d. answers a and c

3. To center cell contents across the selected area, you would choose
   a. Format | Cells | Alignment tab | Center
   b. Format | Cells | Alignment tab | Right
   c. the Merge and Center button
   d. the Center button

4. If a column has been made too narrow to display a number, Excel will
   a. let it fall over into the cell to the right
   b. cut it off
   c. display $$$
   d. display ###

5. You can add color to a worksheet by
   a. changing the text color
   b. applying shading in a color
   c. adding a color border
   d. all of these answers

Short Answer

Match the letter with the correct location in Figure 3.18:

___ a. Double-click to widen column   ___ b. Currency format
___ c. Column isn't wide enough   ___ d. Center alignment
___ e. Accounting format   ___ f. Click and drag to size column

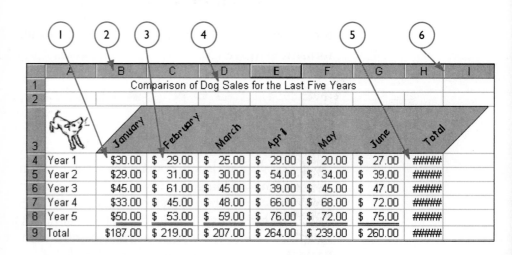

FIGURE 3.18

What Does This Do?

Write a description of the function of the following:

1.	**B**	6.	**,**
2.	🖼	7.	☰
3.	☰	8.	**U**
4.	▫	9.	**%**
5.	**$**	10.	**I**

On Your Own

1. Open a worksheet and place a border around it. Shade rows of data.
2. Open a worksheet and place a graphic in the worksheet.
3. Open a worksheet and format the text.
4. Open a worksheet and format the numbers.
5. Open a worksheet and use the AutoFormat feature. Try out various types of formatting.

PROJECTS

1. Open the **Light** workbook created in Project 1 Unit 2.
   a. Use AutoFormat to format the entire worksheet.
   b. Center the worksheet horizontally on the page.
   c. Print the worksheet in landscape orientation.
   d. Save the workbook.

2. Open the **Rainbow Visions** workbook created in Project 2 Unit 2.
   a. Format text by:
   - adjusting column widths to display all of the text
   - changing the font
   - rotating the labels for the months and total
   - centering the worksheet title over the worksheet and changing the font to bold in a larger size
   b. Format the numbers for Currency style, with two decimal places.
   c. Add a graphic to the worksheet that looks like a company logo.
   d. Change the header from Project 2-2 to **Project 3-2**.
   e. Center the worksheet horizontally on the page.
   f. Change the orientation to landscape, then preview and print the worksheet.
   g. Save the workbook.

3. Create the worksheet shown below, formatting as shown, or open **Sales by Category**.

	A	B	C	D	E	F
1		**Sales by Category** **Spread the Light Candles**				
2						
3		Candles	Incense	Oils	Total	
4	Retail	17,000.00	26,000.00	12,000.00		
5	Wholesale	30,000.00	40,000.00	20,000.00		
6	Mail Order	6,000.00	9,000.00	13,000.00		
7	Total					
8						

   a. Total the categories.
   b. Use the spelling checker.
   c. Center the title above the worksheet. (Hint: Wrap the text by inserting a manual line break with Alt+Enter. Then you can use the Merge and Center button on the toolbar.)

d. Change the title font.

e. Change the title size to 12.

f. Include a graphic.(Choose any graphic that you want.)

g. Center the labels in row 2 and format them as bold.

h. Shade row 2 blue.

i. Format the Total column and row for Accounting style, two decimal places.

j. Format the rest of the numbers for Comma style, two decimal places.

k. Insert a bottom border in cells B6:E6.

l. Place a blue outline border around the worksheet.

m. Create a header that contains your name on the left and **Project 3-3** on the right.

n. Change the orientation to landscape, then preview and print the worksheet.

o. Save the workbook as **Sales by Category**.

p. Print the formulas with the row and column headings.

4. Create the worksheet shown below or open Checkbook.

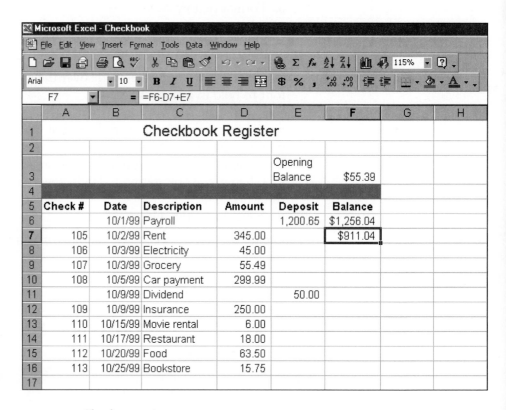

a. Shade row 4 green.

b. Center the title above the worksheet.

c. Make the title blue.

d. Make the title font size 14.

e. Use the spelling checker.

f. Format the Opening Balance in F3 for Currency style, two decimal places.

g. Format all other numbers in Comma style, two decimal places.

h. Write a formula in F6 that adds the deposit in E6 to the Opening Balance.

i.   Write a formula in F7 that starts with the balance in F6, adds any deposits, and subtracts any checks. (Hint: Remember that Excel evaluates blank cells as zero.)

j.   Click in cell F7 and drag the fill handle down to row 16. The formula is copied down the column, and automatically adjusted. You will learn this procedure in Unit 4 but are getting an advance look at it here.

k.   Create a header that contains your name on the left and **Project 3-4** on the right.

l.   Save the workbook as **Checkbook**.

m. Print the worksheet.

n.   Print the formulas with the row and column headings.

Using Functions and Other Calculations

UNIT OBJECTIVES

- Use the MIN function
- Use the MAX function
- Use the AVERAGE function
- Use AutoCalculate
- Use the PRODUCT function
- Use Fill to copy formulas
- Use absolute cell references
- Perform what-if analysis

You have seen how Excel's AutoSum feature uses the built-in SUM function to add a row or column of numbers. You've been introduced to the syntax of functions, with arguments separated by commas. In fact, you know a lot about functions already. This unit shows you some useful statistical and math functions and uses them to teach you more about formulas in general. You'll learn how to copy formulas from one part of a worksheet to another to avoid retyping them, and the use of absolute and relative cell references. The functions you'll learn in this unit all work in exactly the same way. The detailed explanation comes in Task 1 with the MIN function. Once you've learned to use MIN, you'll find it easy to use the other functions in this unit.

What: Use Excel's built-in MIN function.

How: Choose Insert | Function or click the Paste Function button on the toolbar.

Why: MIN finds the smallest value in a range of cells.

Tip: MIN is short for "minimum." You might use this function to find the lowest airline fare from a list on the Web.

Excel provides excellent help in constructing functions so you don't have to memorize their arguments and type them from scratch.

THE PASTE FUNCTION DIALOG BOX

When you choose Insert | Function or click the Paste Function button on the Standard toolbar, the Paste Function dialog box opens, showing you all of the functions that are available. Click any function and the dialog box describes what it does.

To use one of Excel's built-in functions:

1. Click in the cell where you want the results to appear.
2. Click the Paste Function button on the Standard toolbar. The Paste Function dialog box opens, as shown in Figure 4.1.

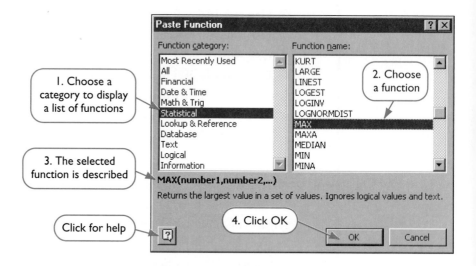

FIGURE 4.1   The Paste Function Dialog Box

3. Select a category in the *Function category* list and all of the functions in that category are listed in the *Function name* list.
4. Select a function in the *Function name* list.

   • The selected function is described at the bottom of the dialog box.
   • For more information about the function, click the Office Assistant button at the bottom left of the dialog box. Click the button for *Help with this feature* and then for *Help on selected function.* A Help window opens with details of the function's syntax and examples of its use.

5. Click OK to close the dialog box and open the Formula Palette.

THE FORMULA PALETTE

The Formula Palette, shown in Figure 4.2, helps you create a function by listing the required (and optional) arguments in editing boxes. In some cases, Excel can guess what the argument should be and will enter it into the editing boxes. When that's not possible, you can enter the arguments in the boxes by typing them, or click the Collapse Dialog button (which you used in Exercise 6 in Unit 2) and point to them in the worksheet. The Formula Palette contains explanations of the function and of each argument, and as you enter the arguments, it displays them and tells you the result. When you've entered the required information, you click OK, and the function is entered in the active cell.

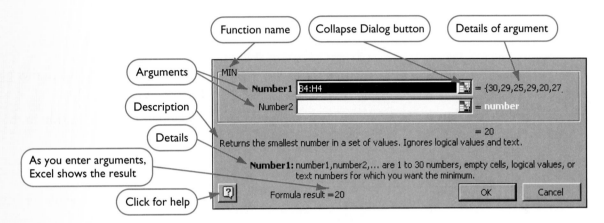

FIGURE 4.2 The Formula Palette for the MIN function

CONSTRUCTING THE MIN FUNCTION

Exercise 1 gives you hands-on experience using the MIN function, which finds the lowest value in a range of cells. You can use this function to analyze data, such as determining the lowest sales, the lowest score, or the smallest amount earned.

EXERCISE 1 | *Using the MIN Function*

---

1. Open the *Sales* workbook and click in I3.
   I3 becomes the active cell.

2. Type **Lowest** and press **Enter**.
   The label appears in I3, and I4 becomes the active cell. Notice that Excel remembers the formatting of the cells to the left and automatically continues it.

3. Click the **Paste Function button** on the Standard toolbar.
   The Paste Function dialog box opens.

4. In the *Function category* box, click **Statistical**.
The Statistical functions are listed in the *Function name* box.

5. Scroll to **MIN** and click it.
The selected function is described at the bottom of the dialog box, as shown in Figure 4.1.

6. Click **OK**.
- The Paste Function dialog box closes and the Formula Palette opens.
- In the *Number1* edit box, Excel enters its guess at the range you intend to use as the function's argument. (Note that the *Number1* label is bold, indicating this is a required argument.)
- The contents of each cell in the range are listed to the right of the edit box.
- The result of the function is shown at the bottom.
- The function is entered in the formula bar.

7. If the Formula Palette is in the way, click and drag it to another position.

8. If the cells to be evaluated are **B4:G4**, skip to step 12.

9. If the range is incorrect, click the **Collapse Dialog button** in the edit box.
The dialog box collapses to a single line and a title bar.

10. Select the range **B4:G4**.

11. Click the **Collapse Dialog button** again to restore the dialog box.

12. Click **OK**.
The Formula Palette closes, and the function is entered in I4. Your worksheet should look like the one in Figure 4.3.

13. Save the workbook and print the worksheet. Leave the rest of the column empty because you will learn about copying formulas and functions later in this unit.

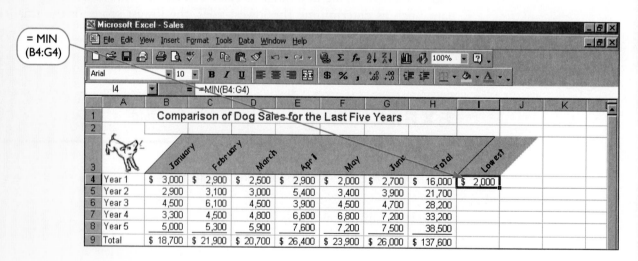

FIGURE 4.3 The *Sales* Workbook after Exercise 1

TASK 2 | *Using the MAX Function*

What: Use Excel's built-in MAX function.

How: Choose Insert | Function or click the Paste Function button on the toolbar.

Why: MAX finds the largest value in range of cells.

Tip: MAX is short for "maximum." A function like this is useful in a large worksheet where eyeballing a range of data for the highest number is impractical.

The MAX function finds the largest value in a range of cells. You can use this function to analyze data, such as determining the largest sales, the highest score, or the highest amount earned. The MAX function is another statistical function. It is entered exactly the same way as the MIN function in Task 1. Figure 4.4 shows the Formula Palette for this function.

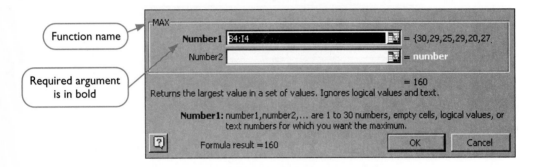

FIGURE 4.4 The Formula Palette for the MAX Function

EXERCISE 2 | *Using the MAX Function*

1. With the *Sales* workbook open on the screen, click in **J3**.
   J3 becomes the active cell.

2. Type **Highest** and press **Enter**.
   The label appears in J3, and J4 becomes the active cell. Notice that Excel remembers the formatting of the cells to the left and automatically continues it.

3. Click the **Paste Function button**.
   The Paste Function dialog box opens.

4. In the *Function category* box, click **Statistical**.
   The Statistical functions are listed in the *Function name* box.

5. Scroll to **MAX** and click it.
   The selected function is described at the bottom of the dialog box.

6. Click **OK**.
- The Paste Function dialog box closes and the Formula Palette opens.
- In the *Number1* edit box, Excel enters its guess at the range you intend to use as the function's argument.

7. If the cells to be evaluated are **B4:G4**, click **OK**.

8. If the range is not correct, click the **Collapse Dialog button**, select **B4:G4**, click the **Collapse Dialog button** again, and then click **OK**. The Formula Palette closes, and the function is entered in I4. Your worksheet should look like the one in Figure 4.5.

9. Save the workbook and print the worksheet. Leave the rest of the column empty, because you will learn about copying formulas and functions later in this unit.

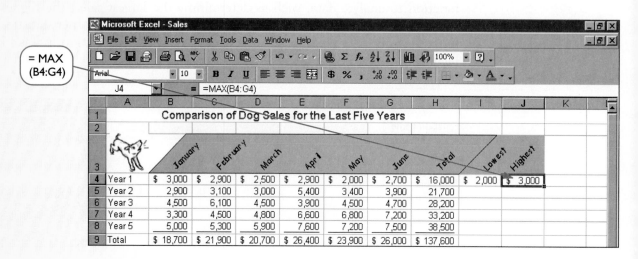

FIGURE 4.5 The *Sales* Workbook after Exercise 2

TASK 3 | *Using the AVERAGE Function*

What: Use the built-in AVERAGE function.

How: Choose Insert | Function or click the Paste Function button on the toolbar.

Why: AVERAGE finds the average value of a range of data.

Tip: If you include an empty cell in the range, Excel ignores it, but a cell containing a zero will change the average.

If you wanted to analyze data by showing the average grades in a class, the average sales, or the average amount earned, you could write a formula that adds up the range of cells and then divides the total by the number of cells. The AVERAGE function does this work for you. The AVERAGE function is another statistical function. It is entered exactly the same way as the MIN function in Task 1. Figure 4.6 shows the Formula Palette for this function.

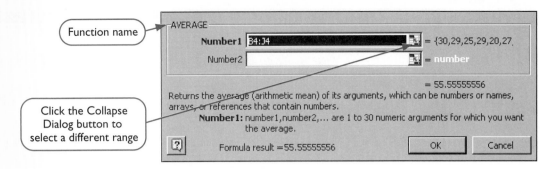

Function name

Click the Collapse Dialog button to select a different range

FIGURE 4.6 The Formula Palette for the AVERAGE Function

EXERCISE 3 | *Using the AVERAGE Function*

1. With the *Sales* workbook open on the screen, click in **K3**.
K3 becomes the active cell.

2. Type **Average** and press **Enter**.
The label appears in K3, and K4 becomes the active cell. Notice that Excel remembers the formatting of the cells to the left and automatically continues it.

3. Click the **Paste Function button**.
The Paste Function dialog box opens.

4. In the *Function category* box, click **Statistical**.
The Statistical functions are listed in the *Function name* box.

5. Scroll to **AVERAGE** and click it.
The selected function is described at the bottom of the dialog box.

6. Click **OK**.
  • The Paste Function dialog box closes and the Formula Palette opens.
  • In the *Number1* edit box, Excel enters its guess at the range you intend to use as the function's argument.

7. If the cells to be evaluated are **B4:G4**, click **OK**.

8. If the range is not correct, click the **Collapse Dialog button**, select **B4:G4**, click the **Collapse Dialog button** again, and then click **OK**.
The Formula Palette closes, and the function is entered in K4. Your worksheet should look like the one in Figure 4.7.

9. Save the workbook and print the worksheet. Leave the rest of the column empty, because you will learn about copying formulas and functions later in this unit.

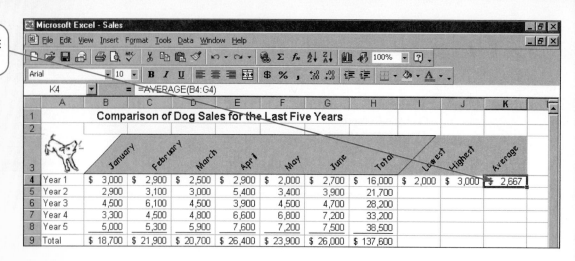

= AVERAGE
(B4:G4)

	A	B	C	D	E	F	G	H	I	J	K	
1			Comparison of Dog Sales for the Last Five Years									
2												
3		January	February	March	April	May	June	Total	Lowest	Highest	Average	
4	Year 1	$ 3,000	$ 2,900	$ 2,500	$ 2,900	$ 2,000	$ 2,700	$ 16,000	$ 2,000	$ 3,000	$ 2,667	
5	Year 2	2,900	3,100	3,000	5,400	3,400	3,900	21,700				
6	Year 3	4,500	6,100	4,500	3,900	4,500	4,700	28,200				
7	Year 4	3,300	4,500	4,800	6,600	6,800	7,200	33,200				
8	Year 5	5,000	5,300	5,900	7,600	7,200	7,500	38,500				
9	Total	$ 18,700	$ 21,900	$ 20,700	$ 26,400	$ 23,900	$ 26,000	$ 137,600				

FIGURE 4.7   The *Sales* Workbook after Exercise 3

TASK 4 | *Using AutoCalculate*

What: Make quick calculations for a range without entering a function.
How: Select the range.
Why: AutoCalculate helps you to avoid errors.
Tip: If the status bar is not displayed, choose View | Status Bar.

When you are creating a worksheet, there is always the possibility that you will make errors in data entry. In the past, many people would use a calculator to quickly check out some of their worksheet calculations. Excel's AutoCalculate feature offers a quick way to check your work as you go. Whenever you select a range, AutoCalculate performs one of several calculations and places the result on the status bar. You can choose from several functions for Excel to perform:

- average
- count
- number count
- maximum
- minimum
- sum

The function you choose remains in force until you change it.

To have AutoCalculate display the result of the currently selected function on the status bar, select a range.

To display the result of a different function:

1. Select a range.
2. Right-click the AutoCalculate area of the status bar to display a short-cut menu, shown in Figure 4.8.
3. Click a function to select it. The shortcut menu closes, and the calculated result of the selected function is displayed on the status bar.

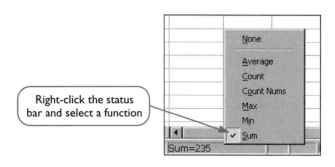

Right-click the status bar and select a function

FIGURE 4.8 The AutoCalculate Shortcut Menu

EXERCISE 4 | *Using AutoCalculate*

1. With the *Sales* workbook open on the screen, select **B4:G4**.
   The result of the most recently selected AutoCalculate function is displayed on the status bar.

2. Right-click the **AutoCalculate area of the status bar**.
   A shortcut menu opens.

3. Select **SUM** and compare the result with the Total in column H.

4. Select **MIN** and compare the result with the Lowest value in column I.

5. Select **MAX** and compare the result with the Highest value in column J.

6. Select **AVERAGE** and compare the result with the Average value in column K.

7. Close the workbook.

TASK 5 | *Using the PRODUCT Function*

What: Use Excel's built-in PRODUCT function.

How: Choose Insert | Function or click the Paste Function button on the toolbar.

Why: PRODUCT offers a quick way to multiply a range of numbers.

Tip: Like AutoSum, the PRODUCT function helps eliminate typing errors.

To multiply a group of numbers, you can write a formula that lists all the cells to be multiplied. However, the built-in PRODUCT function in the Math & Trig category can save you time and help to eliminate typing errors. The PRODUCT function is entered exactly the same way as the MIN function in Task 1. Figure 4.9 shows the Formula Palette for this function.

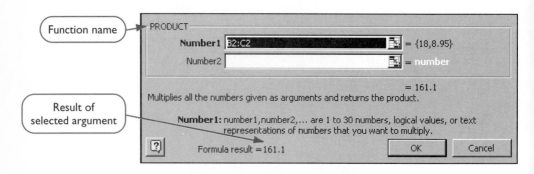

FIGURE **4.9** The Formula Palette for the PRODUCT Function

POINTER

Entering Arguments by Selecting Cells

When selecting noncontiguous cells as arguments using the Formula Palette, remember to select the first and then hold down Ctrl while you select the others.

EXERCISE 5 | *Using the PRODUCT Function*

1. Open a new workbook and enter the text and numbers shown in Figure 4.10.
2. Click in **D2** and then click the **Paste Function button**.
   The Paste Function dialog box opens.
3. Choose **Math & Trig** in the *Function category* list and **PRODUCT** in the *Function name* list, and click **OK**.
   The Formula Palette opens.

	A	B	C	D
1	Item	Quantity	Price	Total
2	Leash	18	$8.95	
3	Collar	27	$5.95	

FIGURE **4.10** The *Product* Workbook

4. If the range is correct (B2:C2), click **OK**. If the range is not correct, click the **Collapse Dialog button**, select the correct cells, click the **Collapse Dialog Button** again, and then click **OK**.
The Formula Palette closes, and the calculated result (161.1) is placed in D2.

5. Save the workbook as **Product** and then print the worksheet with formulas.
In the next task, you will learn to copy a function down a column.

TASK 6 | *Copying Functions and Formulas*

What: Copy formulas and functions down a column or across a row.

How: Choose Edit | Fill or use the fill handle.

Why: Many worksheets use the same formula repeatedly, and copying a correct formula saves time and avoids errors.

Tip: You can also copy formulas and functions using Edit | Copy and Edit | Paste.

In Task 8 of Unit 2, you saw how to copy text and numbers from one location to another in a workbook. You can use the same methods to copy functions and formulas, but to avoid mistakes, you need to be aware of how Excel treats cell references in functions and formulas. You'll learn that in this task and the next one.

USING EDIT | FILL

Once you have placed the correct function in a cell, you can use the Edit | Fill command to copy it down a column or across a row into adjacent cells. *Excel will automatically adjust the formula for the new location.*

To copy a formula across a row:
1. Select the cell with the formula and the adjacent cells where you want the formula to appear.
2. Choose Edit | Fill | Right.

To copy a formula down a column:
1. Select the cell with the formula and the adjacent cells where you want the formula to appear.
2. Choose Edit | Fill | Down.

USING THE FILL HANDLE

You can use the mouse to fill a range of cells with a formula or function. Point to the fill handle in the bottom right corner of the original cell that contains the formula, and drag it to adjacent cells. *Excel will automatically adjust the formula for the new location.*

POINTER

Using a Formula to Copy Cell Contents

If you want to repeat a cell's contents in a different location, you can use a formula to do so. For example, to repeat the contents of cell B12 in cell E100, click in E100 and type the formula =B12.

RELATIVE CELL REFERENCES

Look at Figure 4.11a. The formula in D3 adds the contents of B3 and C3. When you type this formula in cell D3, Excel reads it as: "Add the contents of the cell two columns to the left and the cell one column to the left." When you copy the formula down the column to row 4, as in Figure 4.11b, Excel reads it the same way: "Add the contents of the cell two columns to the left and the cell one column to the left." But now these cells are B4 and C4. The formula adjusts because Excel uses **relative cell references**. That is to say, Excel remembers the cell references in the formula in terms of their position *relative to* the cell in which the formula appears.

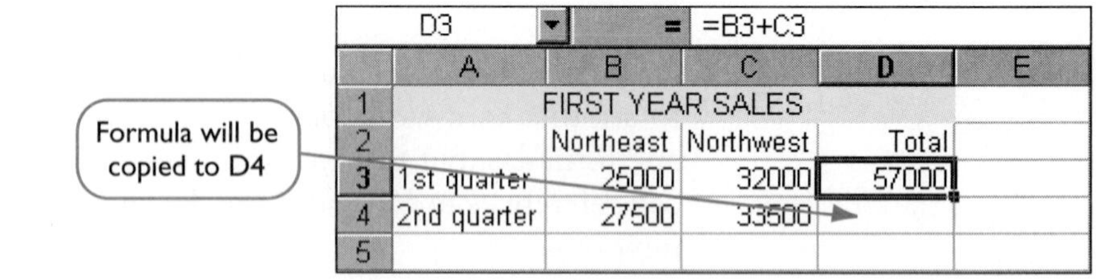

(a) A Formula Entered in Cell D3

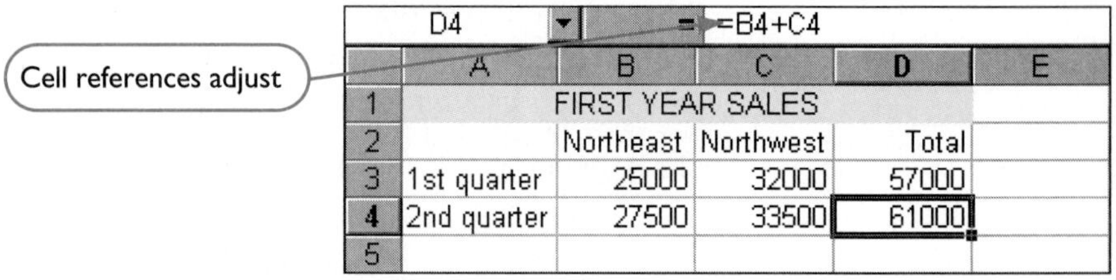

(b) The Same Formula Copied to Cell D4

FIGURE 4.11 Copying a Formula Using Relative Cell References

POINTER

Copying to Nonadjacent Locations

The Fill command and fill handle can be used only to copy formulas to adjacent cells—that is, either across a row or down a column. To copy formulas to other locations, you can use Edit | Copy and Edit | Paste, or drag and drop while holding down the Ctrl key.

Moving Formulas

If you move a formula, cell references within the formula don't change, because the cells referred to haven't moved.

EXERCISE 6 | *Copying Functions and Formulas*

1. Open the *Sales* workbook and select the range **I4:I8**.
Cell I4, containing the MIN function, is the active cell. (You can tell this because it is white, and because its address is shown in the Name box on the formula bar.)

2. Choose **Edit | Fill | Down**.
The formula is copied down the column to the adjacent selected cells, and the calculated result is placed in the cells.

3. Click in cells **I5, I6, I7,** and **I8,** and look at the cell contents on the formula bar.
You can see that the cell references have adjusted down the column.

4. Select the range **J4:K4**.
Cell J4, containing the MAX function, is the active cell, and K4, containing the AVERAGE function, is also selected.

5. Drag the fill handle in the bottom right corner of K4 down through **K8**.
The formula is copied down the two columns to the adjacent selected cells, and the calculated result is placed in the cells. Your worksheet should look like the one in shown in Figure 4.12.

6. Save the workbook and print the worksheet.

7. Print the formulas.

All cell references adjust

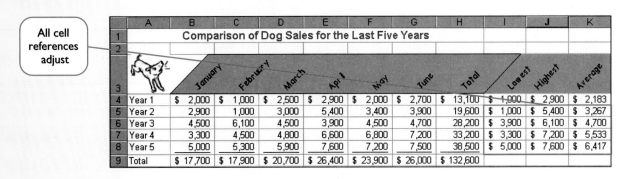

	A	B	C	D	E	F	G	H	I	J	K
1		Comparison of Dog Sales for the Last Five Years									
2											
3		January	February	March	April	May	June	Total	Lowest	Highest	Average
4	Year 1	$ 2,000	$ 1,000	$ 2,500	$ 2,900	$ 2,000	$ 2,700	13,100	$ 1,900	$ 2,900	$ 2,183
5	Year 2	2,900	1,000	3,000	5,400	3,400	3,900	19,600	$ 1,000	$ 5,400	$ 3,267
6	Year 3	4,500	6,100	4,500	3,900	4,500	4,700	28,200	$ 3,900	$ 6,100	$ 4,700
7	Year 4	3,300	4,500	4,800	6,600	6,800	7,200	33,200	$ 3,300	$ 7,200	$ 5,533
8	Year 5	5,000	5,300	5,900	7,600	7,200	7,500	38,500	$ 5,000	$ 7,600	$ 6,417
9	Total	$ 17,700	$ 17,900	$ 20,700	$ 26,400	$ 23,900	$ 26,000	$ 132,600			

FIGURE 4.12 The *Sales* Workbook after Exercise 6

What: Use relative and absolute cell references.

How: Place a dollar sign before the column letter or row number of a cell reference to make it absolute.

Why: Absolute cell references are used when you copy formulas that must refer to a specific cell without being adjusted when they are moved.

Tip: If you are uncertain about making cells absolute, simply type the formula using the correct locations rather than using the Fill command.

In the previous task, you copied functions down a column and saw the cells in the argument adjust to the new location automatically. You learned that the adjustment took place because the cell references were *relative*. But sometimes you may want to copy a formula and have part of it refer to the same cell, without adjusting the reference.

An example from the *Sales* workbook can make this clear. Figure 4.13 shows this workbook with some of the rows hidden. Suppose you have a formula to calculate the percentage of total sales that took place in January.

* Total sales of $137,600 are contained in cell H9.
* Total January sales of $18,700 are contained in B9.
* The formula =B9/H9 will make the calculation, as shown in Figure 4.13a.

But if you copy this formula to column C, as shown in Figure 4.13b, Excel displays an error message, #DIV/0! (The formula is instructing Excel to divide by zero.) Look at the formula bar. The formula, adjusted for the new position, is =C9/I9. But cell I9 is empty. The correct formula would be =C9/H9.

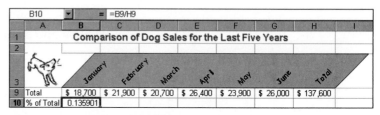

(a) A Relative Cell Reference Is Used ...

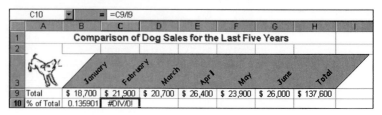

(b) ...When an Absolute Reference Is Needed

FIGURE **4.13** Copying a Formula

Excel's Error Messages

When you enter a formula that Excel doesn't understand, it often displays an error message in the cell. Use Excel Help to correct the error.

- The #NAME? error message occurs in a cell when Excel doesn't recognize the text in a formula.

- The #DIV/O! error message occurs in a cell when a formula divides by zero.

- The #NUM error message indicates that there is a problem with one of the numbers in the formula.

- The #REF error message occurs when a cell reference in a formula or function is not valid.

To keep a cell reference in a formula or function from adjusting, make the reference absolute. An **absolute cell reference** will not adjust to a new location when you copy or move the cell it is contained in.

To make a cell reference absolute, type a dollar sign before the part of the address that you don't want Excel to adjust: the column letter or row number or both. Table 4.1 shows the format used. In the example from the *Sales* workbook, the correct formula would be:

$$=B9/\$H\$9$$

The part of the formula referring to the month (B9) is relative, and changes when the formula is copied across the row. But the total sales are in a specific location (H9) that does not change, so that cell reference is absolute. You will know if a cell should be absolute if you want part of the formula to refer to a specific location.

Type	What It Looks Like	Result
Relative	A10	Both row and column adjust to a new location when copied
Absolute	$A$10	Neither row nor column adjusts to a new location when copied
Mixed	$A10	The column doesn't adjust but the row does when copied to a new location
Mixed	A$10	The column adjusts but the row doesn't when copied to a new location

TABLE 4.1 Relative and Absolute Cell References

Here is another example of absolute and relative references, using the Fill command to copy a formula down a column. The formula

$$=B15*\$C\$3$$

has one relative reference and one absolute reference. When that formula is copied to the cell below the current position using Edit | Fill | Down, it would read

$$=B16*\$C\$3$$

If you continue to use Edit | Fill | Down command, the C3 location would continue to be constant because of the dollar signs that make the cell reference absolute.

EXERCISE 7 | *Using Absolute Cell References*

1. With the *Sales* workbook on the screen, click in **A10**, type **% of Total**, and press **Tab**.
   B10 becomes the active cell.

2. In cell B10, type the following formula, which calculates the percentage of total dog sales that is represented by the total January sales:
   $$=B9/\$H\$9$$

3. Click the **Enter button** on the formula bar.
   The formula is placed in the cell and B10 remains the active cell.

4. Click the **Percent Style button** on the Formatting toolbar.
   The cell contents are formatted as a percentage.

5. With B10 as the active cell, select the cells through **G10**.

6. Choose **Edit | Fill | Right**.

The formula is copied across the row, and the absolute cell reference $H$9 does not adjust. Excel copies the formatting along with the cell contents, so that the cells are formatted in Percent style. Your worksheet should look like the one in Figure 4.14.

7. Save the workbook and print the worksheet, and then print the formulas.

Result when absolute reference is used for $H$9

	A	B	C	D	E	F	G	H	I	J	K
1	Comparison of Dog Sales for the Last Five Years										
2											
3		January	February	March	April	May	June	Total	Lowest	Highest	Average
4	Year 1	$ 3,000	$ 2,900	$ 2,500	$ 2,900	$ 2,000	$ 2,700	$ 16,000	$ 2,000	$ 3,000	$ 2,667
5	Year 2	2,900	3,100	3,000	5,400	3,400	3,900	21,700	$ 2,900	$ 5,400	$ 3,617
6	Year 3	4,500	6,100	4,500	3,900	4,500	4,700	28,200	$ 3,900	$ 6,100	$ 4,700
7	Year 4	3,300	4,500	4,800	6,600	6,800	7,200	33,200	$ 3,300	$ 7,200	$ 5,533
8	Year 5	5,000	5,300	5,900	7,600	7,200	7,500	38,500	$ 5,000	$ 7,600	$ 6,417
9	Total	$ 18,700	$ 21,900	$ 20,700	$ 26,400	$ 23,900	$ 26,000	$ 137,600			
10	% of total	14%	16%	15%	19%	17%	19%				

FIGURE 4.14 The *Sales* Workbook after Exercise 7

TASK 8 | *Performing What-If Analysis*

What: Change numbers referred to in formulas.

How: Change data in the worksheet.

Why: Excel instantly recalculates the formulas, allowing you to try out different options.

Tip: Any data that will be used several times in a worksheet, such as the tax rate, should be stored in a cell and then referenced in formulas. That way if the tax rate changes, you can change it in one cell, and all the formulas will recompute.

One of the most frequent uses of electronic spreadsheets is what-if analysis, where different assumptions are entered into a worksheet and the result is recalculated instantly. You might test the result of a reduction in the cost of supplies or a rise in rent or an increase in advertising. When you replace a number that is linked to other numbers in the worksheet, Excel recalculates the result. Every formula that references the cell that is changed will automatically be updated, allowing you to try out new ways of looking at your expenses or investments.

POINTER

Playing What-If

If you save the workbook after you have changed the numbers, you will lose the original information. To prevent this, save the workbook with the new numbers under a new file name or close the file without saving it.

EXERCISE 8 | *Performing What-If Analysis*

1. With the *Sales* workbook open, click in **B4**.

2. Type **10000** and press **Enter**.
All of the formulas in row 3 are recalculated. The January total changes, and so do the Percent of total and the total in H9.

3. Move to **C4** and type **1000**, and press **Enter**.
Further changes occur.

4. Click the **Undo button**.
Watch the changes.

5. Close the workbook without saving it.

REVIEW

SUMMARY

After completing this unit, you should be able to
- use the MIN function (page 102)
- use the MAX function (page 105)
- use the AVERAGE function (page 106)
- use AutoCalculate (page 108)
- use the PRODUCT function (page 109)
- copy formulas to adjacent cells (page 111)
- use relative and absolute cell references (page 114)
- perform what-if analysis (page 117)

KEY TERMS

absolute cell reference (page 115)
relative cell reference (page 112)

TEST YOUR SKILLS

True/False

1. Absolute formulas adjust to the location relative to their position.
2. You can use an Excel function to find the smallest number in a range of cells.
3. If you want to multiply cells, you could use the PRODUCT function.
4. AutoSum and AutoCalculate both place totals in the worksheet.
5. Relative cell addresses adjust to the new location they are copied to.

Multiple Choice

1. Which formula is relative?
   a. =$B12–B20
   b. =B$12–B20
   c. =B12–B20
   d. =$B$12–B20

2. Which formula has an absolute reference?
   a. =F7–G21
   b. =$F$7–G21
   c. =#F#7–G21
   d. =/F/7–G21

3. If you wanted to average the cells K5, K6, K7, K8, which of the following would be correct?
   a. =AVERAGE(K5:K8)
   b. =K5:K8
   c. =PRODUCT(K5+K6+K7+K8)
   d. all of these answers

4. The AutoCalculate feature
   a. doesn't place the result in the cell
   b. is used for checking your formulas as you work
   c. shows the results of your formulas in the status bar
   d. all of these answers

5. The easiest way to find the average of a group of cells is to
   a. use the AutoSum button
   b. add the cells up and divide by the number of cells
   c. use the AVERAGE function
   d. all of these answers

Short Answer

Match the letter with the correct location in Figure 4.15.

____ a. relative address   ____ b. absolute address

____ c. AutoCalculate feature   ____ d. active cell

____ e. Paste Function button

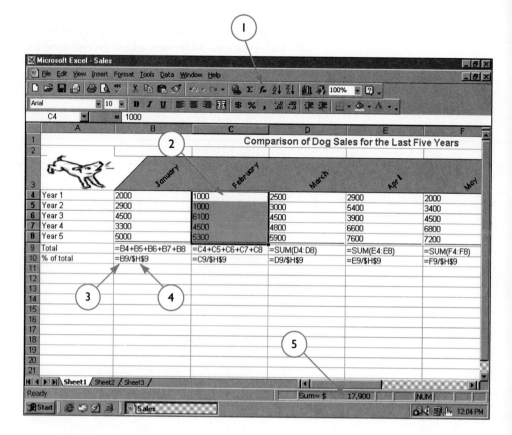

FIGURE 4.15

What Does This Do?

Write a description of the function of the following:

1.	f_x	6.	MAX
2.	5	7.	MIN
3.	$B$4	8.	PRODUCT
4.	Σ	9.	AVERAGE
5.	AutoCalculate	10.	F4 key

On Your Own

1. Open a worksheet and select cells that contain numbers. Check the results of AutoCalculate in the status bar.
2. Open a worksheet and find the highest value in a range of cells.
3. Open a worksheet and find the lowest value in a range of cells.
4. Open a worksheet and find the average value in a range of cells.
5. Open the Paste Function dialog box and check out other functions.

PROJECTS

1. Open the **Sales by Category** workbook you used in Project 3 of Unit 3.
   a. Place the label **Lowest** in F3.
   b. Use a function to show the sales of the lowest-selling product category.
   c. Use the Fill command to copy the formula down the column.
   d. Place the label **Highest** in G3.
   e. Use a function to show the sales of the highest-selling product category.
   f. Use the fill handle to copy the formula down the column.
   g. Reformat the worksheet to incorporate the two new columns.
   h. Change the header from Project 3-3 to **Project 4-1**.
   i. Save the workbook.
   j. Print the worksheet in landscape orientation.
   k. Print the formulas.

2. Open the **Light** workbook you used in Project 3-1.
   a. Extend this worksheet to 12 months, making up data for July through December. Hint: There are several ways in which you can do this. You could insert columns before the Total column, or move the Total column right, or delete the Total column and then create it again. Experiment with different ways and watch how Excel adjusts the result in the Total column as you enter data.
   b. Total the 12 months of sales in the column to the right of the December column.
   c. Format the worksheet.
   d. Save the workbook.
   e. Preview the worksheet before printing it. Make adjustments to print it on a single page or to repeat rows and columns if it prints on more than one page.
   f. Print the worksheet in landscape orientation.
   g. Print the formulas.

3. Create the following workbook or open **GPA**:

	A	B	C	D	E	F
1	Your Name					
2						
3	Transcript					
4						
5	Course	Credits	Grade	Points Total Points		
6	Intro to U.S. History	4	B	3		
7	Computer Concepts	4	A	4		
8	Business Communications	3	C	2		
9	Business Writing	3	B	3		
10	Intro to Psychology	4	A	4		
11	Intro to Sociology	4	A	4		
12	Physical Education	2	A	4		
13	College Algebra	4	C	2		
14	Intro to Biology	4	B	3		
15						
16	Total Credits			Total Points		
17						
18	Grade Point Average					
19						

a. Write a formula to compute total points for each course.
b. Copy the formula down the column.
c. Sum up the Total Credits.
d. Sum up the Total Points.
e. Write a formula to calculate the Grade Point Average.
f. Use the spelling checker.
g. Create a header that contains **Transcript** at the left, the date in the center, and **Project 4-3** on the right.
h. Preview the worksheet and make adjustments to fit it attractively on the page; then print it.
i. Save the workbook as **GPA**.
j. Print the formulas with the row and column headings.

4. Create the following workbook or open **Inventory**:

	A	B	C	D	E	F	G
1			Spread the Light				
2			Inventory				
3							
4	Item	Cost	Quantity	Invested	Selling Price	% Markup	
5	Candles, boxed	4.15	120		6.95		
6	Incense, cones	0.04	300		0.06		
7	Incense, stick	0.03	750		0.05		
8	Incense, bottled	0.99	100		1.25		
9	Tapers, thin	0.29	850		0.42		
10	Tapers, wide	0.49	400		0.95		
11	Votive	0.09	500		0.2		
12							
13			Average percentage markup:				
14							

a. In cell D5, use a function to show the amount invested in boxed candles.
b. Copy the formula down column D.
c. In cell F5, write a formula to calculate the percentage markup on boxed candles. (Hint: Find the result of the selling price minus the cost, and then divide the result by the cost. Don't forget to format the result as a percent.)
d. Copy the formula down column F.
e. Use a function to show the average markup on all the products.
f. Format rows 1 through 4 and 13 to resemble those in the figure.
g. Format the numbers.
h. Use the spelling checker.
i. Create a header that contains your name on the left and **Project 4-4** on the right.
j. Preview the worksheet and make adjustments to fit it attractively on the page; then print it.
k. Save the workbook as **Inventory**.
l. Print the formulas with the row and column headings.

CHECK POINT

FOR UNITS 3-4

PROJECTS

1. You decide to redo the *Payroll* workbook you made in the Check Point for Units 1 and 2 now that you know more about Excel. Create the following workbook or open **Payroll2**:

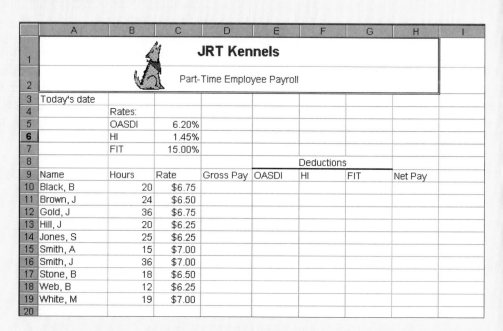

	A	B	C	D	E	F	G	H	I
1					JRT Kennels				
2					Part-Time Employee Payroll				
3	Today's date								
4		Rates:							
5		OASDI	6.20%						
6		HI	1.45%						
7		FIT	15.00%						
8							Deductions		
9	Name	Hours	Rate	Gross Pay	OASDI	HI	FIT	Net Pay	
10	Black, B	20	$6.75						
11	Brown, J	24	$6.50						
12	Gold, J	36	$6.75						
13	Hill, J	20	$6.25						
14	Jones, S	25	$6.25						
15	Smith, A	15	$7.00						
16	Smith, J	36	$7.00						
17	Stone, B	18	$6.50						
18	Web, B	12	$6.25						
19	White, M	19	$7.00						
20									

   a. Use a function to calculate Gross Pay.

   b. Write a formula that calculates each deduction using an absolute address to refer to the rates in C5, C6, and C7.

   c. Write a formula that calculates the Net Pay.

   d. Use the Fill command to copy formulas rather than typing all of them.

   e. Include a graphic.

   f. Use the spelling checker.

   g. Create a header that contains your name on the left and **Check 2 Project 1** on the right.

   h. Preview the worksheet and make adjustments to fit it attractively on the page; then print it.

   i. Save the workbook as **Payroll2**.

   j. Print the formulas with the row and column headings.

k. Change C5 to 6.1%.

l. Change C6 to 1.62%.

m. Change C7 to 18%.

n. Print the worksheet again.

o. Don't save this version of the workbook.

2. Create the following workbook or open **Budget Analysis**:

	A	B	C	D	E
1		JRT Kennels			
		January Budget Analysis			
2					
3					
4		Actual	Budget	Deviation	% Deviation
5	Sales	2000	2500		
6					
7	Variable Expenses				
8	Advertising	200	225		
9	Utilities	250	200		
10	Food	900	800		
11	Total				
12					
13	Fixed Expenses				
14	Insurance	400	400		
15	Taxes	250	250		
16	Kennel Fees	250	250		
17	Total				
18					
19	Total Expenses				
20	Net Profit				

a. Create formulas to calculate the data. Hints:

- Deviation equals Budget minus Actual.
- Percent of Deviation equals Deviation divided by Budget.
- Net Profit equals Sales minus Total Expenses.

b. Format the numbers.

c. Format the title and center it above the spreadsheet.

d. Include a graphic.

e. Use the spelling checker.

f. Create a header that contains your name on the left and **Check 2 Project 2** on the right.

g. Preview the worksheet and make adjustments to fit it attractively on the page; then print it.

h. Save the workbook as **Budget Analysis**.

i. Print the formulas with the row and column headings.

Using Financial Functions

UNIT OBJECTIVES

- Use the PMT function
- Use the PPMT function
- Use the IPMT function
- Use the FV function
- Use the SLN function

Everyone has to deal with financial issues—deciding if you can afford the car you want, saving money for a vacation or for college, deciding whether to refinance your home. In this unit, you'll see how Excel's built-in functions can help you make decisions. You'll learn how to figure out the monthly payment on a loan and see the tax implications in terms of interest payments. You'll learn to calculate how much money you must put aside every month to reach a financial goal. You'll see how to depreciate an asset.

The functions you have learned so far have required only one argument, usually a range of cells. The financial functions in this unit require several arguments. After you see the details with the PMT function in Task 1, you will be able to construct the other functions with ease.

TASK 1 | *Using the PMT Function*

What: Use Excel's built-in PMT function.

How: Choose Insert | Function or click the Paste Function button on the toolbar.

Why: PMT finds the payment on a loan.

Tip: The PMT function works like any formula in Excel, allowing you to copy it to adjacent columns or rows. You can analyze various interest rates and loan periods to help you figure out the best payment plan.

The Excel function PMT calculates the **payment** for a loan based on constant payments and a fixed interest rate. You supply Excel with three pieces of information (arguments) so that it can perform the calculation:

- **Pv:** the present value, or the amount of the loan
- **Rate:** the annual interest rate
- **Nper:** the number of periods (in years) over which the loan will be paid off

To use PMT to calculate the payment, you should first set up the worksheet. Use a separate cell for each argument so that you can easily compare different terms and loan amounts. A sample worksheet is shown in Figure 5.1.

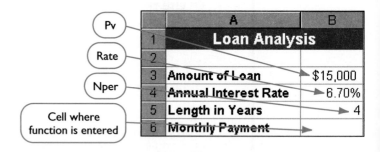

FIGURE 5.1 Setting Up a Worksheet to Calculate a Loan Payment

POINTER

Getting the Right Results

When you talk to a loan officer about a loan, both of you will refer to the loan as a 5-year or 30-year loan at 10% or 6%, and both of you know that you will make monthly payments and the interest rate will be a monthly rate, but Excel's financial functions use annual rates. To have them display monthly results, you must convert the arguments.

- To convert the Nper (number of annual periods) argument to months, multiply it by 12.

- To convert the Rate (fixed annual rate) argument to months, divide it by 12.

You will make these conversions in the Formula Palette, as shown in Exercise 1.

The Formula Palette Helps You Enter Arguments

Remember that the Formula Palette gives you a lot of help in entering the arguments.

- It lists mandatory arguments in bold type.
- When you click in the edit box for an argument, it explains what is required there.
- When you enter an argument, it displays the calculated result to the right of the edit box.
- It displays the result of the formula so you can troubleshoot before clicking OK.
- It has an Office Assistant button you can click to get more detailed information on the function.

CONSTRUCTING THE FUNCTION

Once you have set up the worksheet to contain the arguments, you are ready to construct the function. Click the Paste Function button and choose the function (remember that PMT is in the Financial category). When you click OK, the Formula Palette opens, as shown in Figure 5.2.

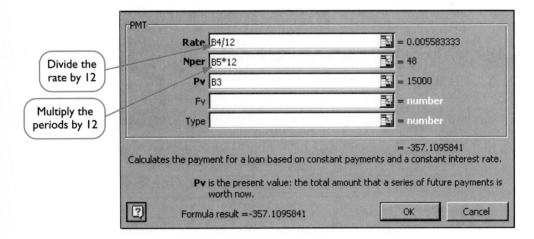

FIGURE 5.2   The Formula Palette for the PMT Function

1. Enter the mandatory arguments:

- **Rate:** Click in the Rate edit box and enter the cell address of the interest rate—B4 in Figure 5.1. Because the argument is based on an annual rate and you want to get a monthly payment, you must divide the annual rate by 12. In the example, you would enter B4/12.

- **Nper:** Click in the Nper edit box and enter the cell address of the length of the loan in years (the number of annual periods)—B5 in Figure 5.1. Because you have converted the annual rate to a monthly rate, you must also convert the number of periods from years to months. To do this, you multiply by 12. In the example, you would type B5*12 into the Nper edit box.

- **Pv:** Click in the Pv edit box and enter the cell address of the amount of the loan—B3 in Figure 5.1.

2. Click OK to close the Formula Palette and display the result as a negative amount.
3. Change the result from negative to positive. (See the pointer box "Changing the Payment from Negative to Positive.")

POINTER

Changing the Payment from Negative to Positive

The payment is considered a debit by Excel and therefore appears as a negative number. To make the result positive, edit the function by placing a minus sign between the equal sign and the function name—for example:

=–PMT(B4/12,B5∗12,B3)

If you prefer to change the sign as you construct the function, you can place a minus sign in front of the Pv (loan amount) argument.

In the next exercise, you will help the Jack Russell terrier breeders figure their payment on a loan for a truck. The truck costs $15,000. They could finance it for four, five, or six years. The interest rate goes up from 6.7% for four years to 7.2% for five years to 7.8% for six years.

EXERCISE 1 | *Using the PMT Function*

1. Open a new worksheet and enter the text and numbers shown in cells A1 through B6 in Figure 5.1 on page 128.
   Use what you have learned to format the cells, widening column A to display the complete text.

2. Click in **B6** and then click the **Paste Function button**.
   The Paste Function dialog box opens.

3. Choose **Financial** in the *Function category* list and **PMT** in the *Function name* list and then click OK.
   The Paste Function dialog box closes and the Formula Palette opens. Because the Formula Palette covers the cells containing the arguments, you will use the Collapse Dialog button to enter the arguments.

4. Click the **Collapse Dialog button** in the Rate edit box.
   The dialog box collapses to an edit box.

5. Click cell **B4** (the cell containing the annual interest rate of 6.70%), type **/12**, and click the **Collapse Dialog button** again.
   The argument B4/12 is entered in the Rate edit box. This is the annual rate divided by 12 to convert it to a monthly rate.

6. In the Nper edit box, enter the argument **B5*12**.

You can use the Collapse Dialog button or type the argument directly in the edit box. This is the length of the loan in years, multiplied by 12 to convert it to months.

7. In the Pv edit box, enter **B3**.

This is the present value, or amount of the loan.

8. Click **OK**.

The calculated monthly loan payment is displayed in B6 as a negative amount. The function is displayed on the formula bar.

9. Click in the formula bar just after the equal sign (before **PMT**) and type a **minus sign**.

The function now reads =−PMT(B4/12, B5*12,B3).

10. Click the **Enter button** on the formula bar.

The payment is displayed as a positive amount ($357.11).

11. Copy the amount in B3 to C3 and D3.

You will vary the rate and period of the loan to calculate other payment options.

12. Enter **7.2%** in C4 and **5** in C5.

13. Enter **7.8%** in D4 and **6** in D5.

14. Copy the function in B6 to C6 and D6.

Use the Edit | Fill command or the fill handle. The payments for the three terms and interest rates are displayed. Your worksheet should look like Figure 5.3.

15. Save the workbook as **Truck Loan**.

16. Print the worksheet and then print the formulas. Leave the workbook open for use in the next exercise.

	A	B	C	D
1	Loan Analysis			
2				
3	Amount of Loan	$15,000	$15,000	$15,000
4	Annual Interest Rate	6.70%	7.20%	7.80%
5	Length in Years	4	5	6
6	Monthly Payment	$357.11	$298.44	$261.54

FIGURE 5.3   The *Truck Loan* Workbook after Exercise 1

What: Use Excel's built-in PPMT function.

How: Choose Insert | Function or click the Paste Function button on the toolbar.

Why: PPMT calculates how much of each loan payment goes to the principal.

Tip: To fill a range with numbers that increment, hold down the Ctrl key while dragging the fill handle. This is a handy way to make a list of loan payments, as in Exercise 2.

When you begin to pay off a loan, most of the payment goes toward the interest. Later in the life of the loan, more of the payment goes toward the **principal**, or loan amount. Excel's PPMT function calculates how much of any particular payment goes to the principal. The function has four arguments, three of which are the same as those required for the PMT function:

- **Pv:** the loan amount
- **Rate:** the interest rate
- **Nper:** the total number of payments

Because the amount of the payment applied to the principal varies from payment to payment, a fourth argument is needed:

- **Per:** the payment number (a number between 1 and *Nper*)

Let's say that you decided on the four-year 6.7% loan on the $15,000 truck. You will build a worksheet to show the amount of each payment that is applied to the principal, using PPMT. Figure 5.4 shows the result.

EXERCISE 2 | *Using the PPMT Function*

1. With the *Truck Loan* workbook open on the screen, click in **A8**, enter **Payment Number**, and press **Tab**.

2. Enter **Amount Toward Principal** in **B8**, and format the text to wrap in the cell.
   To wrap text, choose Format | Cells | Alignment tab and select the *Wrap text* check box.

3. Enter the number **1** in **A9**, and click the **Enter button** on the formula bar.
   The number is placed in the cell and A9 remains the active cell.

4. Hold down **Ctrl** and drag the fill handle from **A9** down the column to **A56**.
   The numbers 1 to 48 will be placed down column A, representing the 48 payments for the four-year loan.

5. Click in **B9** and click the **Paste Function button**.
   The Paste Function dialog box opens.

6. Choose the **Financial** category and the **PPMT** function, and click **OK**.
   The Formula Palette opens.

7. Enter the Rate argument **$B$4/12**.
   The Rate is located in B4. Since the function will be copied down the column, the cell reference needs to be made absolute so that it is locked into B4.

8. Enter the Per argument **A9**.
   Per, the specific period or payment number, is listed in column A. The first period is in A9.

9. Enter the Nper argument **$B$5*12**.
   Nper is the total number of payments, located in B5. Since the function will be copied down the column, the cell reference needs to be made absolute so that it is locked into B5.

10. Enter the Pv argument **$B$3**.
    Pv, the amount of the loan, is located in B3. This cell reference also needs to be absolute.

11. Click **OK**.
    The calculated value is placed in B9 as a negative amount.

12. Click in the formula bar just after the equal sign (before **PMT**), type a **minus sign**, and then click the **Enter button** on the formula bar.
    The function now reads =−PPMT($B$4/12,A9,$B$5*12,$B$3).

13. Click and drag the fill handle to copy the formula down to **B56**.
    Notice that the payment to the principal increases during the life of the loan. Figure 5.4 shows the beginning of the payment series.

14. Save the workbook.

15. Print the worksheet and then print the formulas. Leave the workbook open for use in the next exercise.

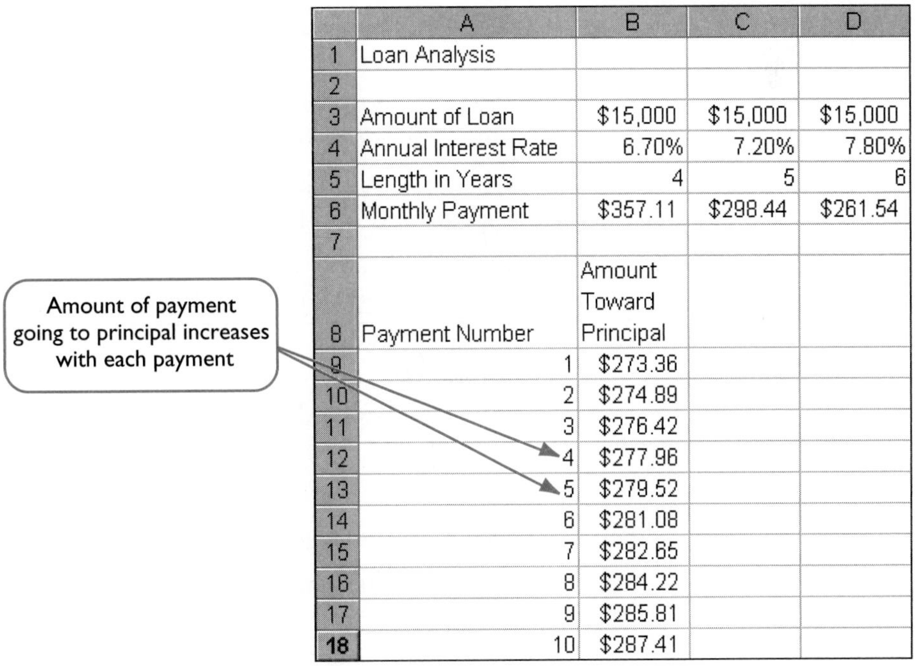

	A	B	C	D
1	Loan Analysis			
2				
3	Amount of Loan	$15,000	$15,000	$15,000
4	Annual Interest Rate	6.70%	7.20%	7.80%
5	Length in Years	4	5	6
6	Monthly Payment	$357.11	$298.44	$261.54
7				
8	Payment Number	Amount Toward Principal		
9	1	$273.36		
10	2	$274.89		
11	3	$276.42		
12	4	$277.96		
13	5	$279.52		
14	6	$281.08		
15	7	$282.65		
16	8	$284.22		
17	9	$285.81		
18	10	$287.41		

Amount of payment going to principal increases with each payment

FIGURE 5.4 The *Truck Loan* Workbook after Exercise 2

What: Use Excel's built-in IPMT function.

How: Choose Insert | Function or click the Paste Function button on the toolbar.

Why: IPMT calculates how much of each loan payment goes to interest.

Tip: Interest payments on mortgages are usually tax deductible.

The PPMT function calculates the amount of each payment that is applied toward the principal. The companion IPMT function calculates the amount that goes toward paying the **interest**, or what the lending institution charges for the use of its money. The arguments are the same as those for PPMT. Exercise 3 shows this function for the *Truck Loan* workbook.

> ### POINTER
>
> **Find the Total Principal and Interest**
>
> At the end of Exercise 3, your worksheet will show the amount of each loan payment that goes to principal and interest. Use AutoSum or AutoCalculate in cells B57 and C57 to check your work and to see how much interest you would pay over the life of the loan.

EXERCISE 3 | *Using the IPMT Function*

1. With the *Truck Loan* workbook open on the screen, click in **C8** and enter **Amount Toward Interest**, then format the cell to match B8.

2. Click in **C9**, click the **Paste Function button**, choose the Financial category's **IPMT** function, and click **OK**.
   The Formula Palette opens.

3. Enter the arguments as follows:
   - Rate: $B$4/12
   - Per: A9
   - Nper: $B$5*12
   - Pv: $B$3

4. Click **OK**.

5. Change the displayed result from a negative to a positive value.

6. Click and drag the fill handle to copy the formula down to **C56**.
   Notice that the payment to interest decreases during the life of the loan. Figure 5.5 shows the beginning of the payment series.

7. Save the workbook.

8. Print the worksheet, print the formulas, and then close the workbook.

	A	B	C	D
1	Loan Analysis			
2				
3	Amount of Loan	$15,000	$15,000	$15,000
4	Annual Interest Rate	6.70%	7.20%	7.80%
5	Length in Years	4	5	6
6	Monthly Payment	$357.11	$298.44	$261.54
7				
8	Payment Number	Amount Toward Principal	Amount Toward Interest	
9	1	$273.36	$83.75	
10	2	$274.89	$82.22	
11	3	$276.42	$80.69	
12	4	$277.96	$79.15	
13	5	$279.52	$77.59	
14	6	$281.08	$76.03	
15	7	$282.65	$74.46	
16	8	$284.22	$72.89	
17	9	$285.81	$71.30	
18	10	$287.41	$69.70	

> Payments continue to cell C56, with decreasing amounts going to interest

FIGURE 5.5 The *Truck Loan* Workbook after Exercise 3

TASK 4 | *Using the FV Function*

What: Use Excel's built-in FV function.

How: Choose Insert | Function or click the Paste Function button on the toolbar.

Why: FV calculates the future value of an investment.

Tip: If you make a cell with a function the active cell and then click the Paste Function button, the Formula Palette will open and will contain the data used to calculate the function.

Suppose the JRT Kennels wants to show dogs in Scotland in five years. The owner plans to put aside $100 a month in a savings account that pays 5.2% annual interest. How much money will there be in the account in five years? Will it be enough to transport the dogs to Scotland and enter them in the show? Excel's FV function calculates the future value of a constant investment at a constant interest rate. From what you already know about functions, you can guess that its arguments are:

- **Rate:** the annual interest rate
- **Nper:** the number of periods (in years) over which the deposits (payments to the bank) will be made
- **Pmt:** the amount of each deposit (payment)

With this function as with the other financial functions, you will convert years to months and negative to positive values.

EXERCISE 4 | *Using the FV Function*

1. Open a new worksheet and enter the text and numbers shown in cells A1 through B6 in Figure 5.6.

2. Format the cells attractively, widening column A to display the complete text.

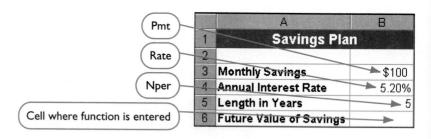

FIGURE 5.6   Setting Up a Worksheet to Calculate the Future Value of an Investment

3. Click in **B6**, click the **Paste Function button**, choose the Financial function **FV**, and click **OK**.
   The Formula Palette opens.

4. Enter the arguments as follows:
   - Rate: **B4/12**
   - Nper: **B5*12**
   - Pmt: **B3**

5. Click **OK**.
   The calculated result is displayed in B9 as a negative value.

6. Change the result from negative to positive.
   The result is $6,835.43.

7. Save the workbook as **Savings Plan**, print the worksheet, print the formulas, and then close the workbook.

TASK 5 | *Using the SLN Function*

What: Use Excel's built-in SLN function.

How: Choose Insert | Function or click the Paste Function button on the toolbar.

Why: SLN calculates the straight-line depreciation of an asset.

Tip: Excel contains several different functions for depreciating an asset, of which SLN is the simplest. Use Excel Help for more information.

When you purchase equipment for your business, such as a computer, its value will decrease over time. Since the **asset**, the computer, depreciates in value, this is known as depreciation.

Let's say you paid $3,500 for your computer. You know that in five years it will be worth only $150, and you want to figure the **depreciation** for each of the five years. **Straight-line depreciation** depreciates the asset the same amount each year for the life of the equipment. The arguments are:

- **Cost:** the cost of the equipment
- **Salvage:** the amount the equipment will be worth at the end of the period
- **Life:** the life of the equipment

Figure 5.7 shows a workbook set up for this function.

	A	B
1	**Straight-Line Depreciation**	
2		
3	**Cost of Computer**	$3,500
4	**Life of Computer**	5
5	**Salvage Value**	$150
6	**Annual Depreciation**	

FIGURE 5.7   Setting Up a Worksheet to Calculate Straight-Line Depreciation

POINTER

Depreciation and Taxes

The Internal Revenue Service provides useful tax information on the World Wide Web. The following is summarized from **IRS Tax Topic 704 Depreciation**, located at http://www.irs.ustreas.gov/prod/tax_edu/teletax/tc704.html.

If the item you purchase to produce income for your business or trade has a useful life of more than one year, then you depreciate, or spread the cost, over a number of years, deducting only a part of the cost each year.

The following guidelines must be adhered to:

1. The item must be used in business or other income-producing activity.
2. The item must be something that gets used up, wears out, or becomes obsolete.
3. The item must have a useful life that can be determined.

1. Open a new worksheet and enter the text and numbers shown in cells A1 through B6 in Figure 5.7 on page 137.

2. Widen column A to display the complete contents of the cells.

3. Click in **B6**, click the **Paste Function button**, choose the Financial function **SLN**, and click **OK**.
The Formula Palette opens.

4. Enter the arguments as follows:
  - Cost: **B3**
  - Salvage: **B5**
  - Life: **B4**

5. Click **OK**.
The calculated result is displayed in B6. The result is $670.00.

6. Click in D3 and type **Amount Depreciated**.

7. In D4, enter the formula =**B6∗5**.
The result will be the cost of the computer minus the salvage value, or $3,350.00.

8. Save the workbook as **Depreciation**, then print the workbook, print the formulas, and close the workbook.

R E V I E W

S U M M A R Y

After completing this unit, you should be able to
- calculate the payment on a loan using PMT (page 128)
- calculate how much of every payment goes to the principal using PPMT (page 132)
- calculate how much of every payment goes toward the interest using IPMT (page 134)
- calculate how much an investment will be worth using FV (page 135)
- figure straight-line depreciation using SLN (page 137)

K E Y   T E R M S

asset (page 137)　　　　　　　　principal (page 132)
depreciation (page 137)　　　　　salvage (page 137)
interest (page 134)　　　　　　　**straight-line depreciation**
payment (page 128)　　　　　　　　(page 137)

TEST YOUR SKILLS

True/False

1. Salvage is the life of the equipment.
2. Interest is usually expressed as a yearly rate and must be divided by 12 to get the monthly rate, if you make monthly payments.
3. The amount of payment that applies toward the principal increases with the life of the loan.
4. The amount of the payment that applies toward the interest increases with the life of the loan.
5. The term is the length of the loan.

Multiple Choice

1. To calculate the amount of your payment that applies to the interest, you would use
    a. PMT   b. PPMT
    c. FV   d. IPMT
2. To calculate the amount of your payment on a loan, you would use
    a. PMT   b. PPMT
    c. IPMT   d. PAY
3. To calculate the depreciation of a asset, you would use
    a. DEP   b. SLN
    c. PMT   d. FV
4. To calculate the amount of your payment that applies to the principal, you would use
    a. PMT   b. PPMT
    c. IPMT   d. FV
5. To calculate how much an investment will be worth in a given period of time, you would use
    a. IPMT   b. PPMT
    c. SLN   d. FV

Short Answer

Match the definition in the right column with the term in the left.

____	1. Nper	a. interest per period
____	2. Salvage	b. present value
____	3. Rate	c. number of periods over which the asset is depreciated
____	4. Life	d. total number of payments for the loan
____	5. Pv	e. value at the end of the life of the asset

What Does This Do?

Write a brief description of the function of the following:

1.	PMT	6.	6%/12
2.	PPMT	7.	4*12
3.	IPMT	8.	Nper
4.	FV	9.	Pv
5.	SLN	10.	−PMT

On Your Own

1. If you are making payments on a car, create a worksheet to calculate the monthly payments.
2. If you are paying off a loan or a credit-card balance, create a worksheet to calculate the amount of each payment that is applied to the principal and the amount to the interest.
3. Create a worksheet to calculate the amount you need to place in a savings account in order to have a desired amount when you finish college.
4. Create a worksheet to determine the annual depreciation on your computer, assuming you use it for business purposes.
5. Open one of the worksheets you have created and use what-if analysis by placing different values in the loan amounts.

PROJECTS

1. As the owner of Spread the Light Candles, you want to purchase a computer to keep track of inventory, customer lists, and budgets, and to create your own advertising. You can get a small business loan for $5,000 at 3.8% interest for four years or at 4.2% for five years.
   a. Create a worksheet that calculates the payment of this loan.
   b. Format the text and numbers, centering the title at the top of the worksheet.
   c. Use the spelling checker.
   d. Create a header that contains your name on the left and **Project 5-1** on the right.
   e. Save the workbook as **Candle Loan**.
   f. Print the worksheet.
   g. Print the formulas.

2. Open the **Candle Loan** workbook created in Project 1 and use the figures for the four-year 3.8% loan.

 a. Expand the worksheet to show how much of each payment goes toward the principal and how much toward the interest for every payment for the life of the loan.

 b. Edit the header so that it reads **Project 5-2**.

 c. Save the workbook.

 d. Print the worksheet.

 e. Print the formulas.

3. As the owner of Santa Fe Jewelry, you purchased silversmith equipment that cost $3,800. In six years, you figure that the equipment will be worth $750.

 a. Create a worksheet to calculate the depreciation.

 b. Format the text and numbers, centering the title at the top of the worksheet.

 c. Use the spelling checker.

 d. Create a header that contains your name on the left and **Project 5-3** on the right.

 e. Save the workbook as **Jewelry Depreciation**.

 f. Print the worksheet.

 g. Print the formulas.

4. Create a worksheet for a real loan—one that you already have or may need in the future—such as for a new car.

 a. Use three actual up-to-date rates and terms and compare the payments for each making sure that you present the information clearly. To find the current interest rate for the day you create this project, use the World Wide Web. HSH Associates Financial Publishers provides daily updates at http://www.hsh.com/today.html, or you can search for other resources using www.yahoo.com.

 b. Format the worksheet.

 c. Create a header that contains your name on the left and **Project 5-4** on the right.

 d. Save the workbook as **My Loan**.

 e. Print the worksheet.

 f. Print the formulas.

Using Date, Count, and IF Functions

UNIT OBJECTIVES

- Use the TODAY function
- Use the IF function
- Use the SUMIF function
- Use the COUNT, COUNTA, and COUNTBLANK functions
- Use the COUNTIF function

You first learned about functions using the AutoSum button in Unit 1. You learned more about the SUM function in Unit 2, and learned to use the Paste Function dialog box and the Formula Palette in Unit 4. You know how to use several of Excel's statistical functions (MIN, MAX, and AVERAGE) and two math functions (SUM and PRODUCT). In this unit, you will learn to use a date function to perform mathematical operations; you'll learn to use the IF function, which returns different results based on whether a condition is true or false; and you'll learn some handy functions for counting cells.

What: Use Excel's built-in TODAY function.

How: Choose Insert | Function or click the Paste Function button on the toolbar.

Why: The TODAY function returns today's date.

Tip: If you want to change the format of a date, choose Format | Cells | Number tab and click the Date option.

You have seen how to print the current date in the header of a worksheet. This is just one way in which you can use Excel's date functions. You can also use dates to perform mathematical calculations, such as how long a bill has been outstanding or when a movie rental is due.

In order to use dates and times for calculations, Excel regards them as numbers. If you type a date into a cell in a standard format, for example 12/24/99, Excel will format it as a date. Internally, however, Excel converts the formatted date to a **serial number**. In this numbering system, January 1, 1900 is designated as day one, and each day since then has had the number 1 added to it. Thus January 1, 1999 is day 36161, and January 1, 2000 is day 36526. You can see how this system makes date calculations easy. For example, in a worksheet that lists your customers, the amount they owe, and the date of their last payment, you can create a formula that subtracts the current date from the last-payment date to determine whether their bills are overdue.

> ### POINTER
>
> **36526 Is a Date?**
>
> If you type a date and it appears as a long number, it is probably formatted in the General number format. Click in the cell and choose Format I Cells. The Format Cells dialog box will open and display the format of the active cell. To change the format to a date format, click the Date category on the Number tab and make a selection.

There are several built-in functions that display or work with dates. The TODAY function places a formatted version of the current system date in the active cell.

To use TODAY:

1. Click in the cell where you want the date to appear.
2. Click the Paste Function button.
3. Choose Date & Time from the *Function category* list.
4. Choose TODAY from the *Function name* list.
5. Click OK. The Function Palette opens.
6. Click OK. (The TODAY function requires no arguments.) The Function Palette closes, and the current date appears in the cell.

Using TODAY

Since the TODAY function doesn't take any arguments, the quickest way to enter it is by typing it. Click in the cell and type =**TODAY**(). (Although there are no arguments, you still must type the parentheses.) The contents of the cell that contains the TODAY function will always update to the current system date. In other words, if you open the worksheet next week, the new current date will appear in the cell.

In the exercise that follows, you will use the TODAY function to determine whether your customers' bills are overdue. Using the TODAY function means that the current date will automatically be updated whenever you open the workbook.

EXERCISE 1 | *Using the TODAY Function*

1. Open a new workbook and duplicate the worksheet shown in Figure 6.1.

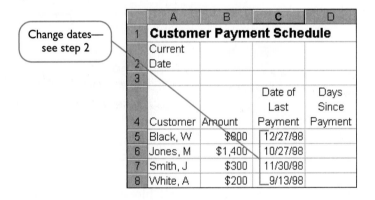

Change dates— see step 2

FIGURE 6.1   The Worksheet for Exercise 1

2. Change the dates shown in column C to make two of them less than 60 days in the past and two of them more than 60 days in the past.
The dates shown in the figure will all be more than 60 days in the past by the time you read this book.

3. In **B2**, type =**TODAY**().
The current date is placed B2.

4. In **D5**, type =$B$2–C5.
You are using an absolute cell reference to the cell with the TODAY function.

5. Format **D5** by choosing **Format** | **Cells** | **Number tab** | **General**.

6. Use the fill handle to copy the formula down to **D8**.
Your worksheet should look like the one in Figure 6.2, except that the dates will be different.

7. Save the workbook as **Overdue Bills**.

8. Print the worksheet and print the formulas, and keep the worksheet open for use in the next exercise.

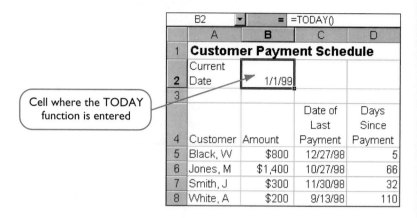

FIGURE 6.2   The *Overdue Bills* Workbook after Exercise 1

TASK 2 | *Using the IF Function*

What: Use Excel's built-in IF function.

How: Choose Insert | Function or click the Paste Function button on the toolbar.

Why: The IF function evaluates the condition you specify and returns different results depending on whether it is true or false.

Tip: Use the IF function with the comparison operators to determine the truth or falsity of the condition.

The IF function brings a great deal of power and flexibility to a worksheet. You can create worksheets that

- flag inventory items for reorder if they fall below a certain number
- pay commissions based on how much your salespeople sell
- determine taxes based on income levels
- look at students' final grade averages and determine whether they pass or fail

You use the IF function to evaluate a **condition** and determine if it is true or false. If the condition evaluates as true, Excel places one value in the cell or performs one operation. If the condition evaluates as false, Excel places another value in the cell or performs a different operation. The IF function has three arguments:

- **Logical test:** the value or expression that is to be evaluated as true or false
- **Value if true:** the value you want Excel to return if the logical test argument evaluates as true

- **Value if false:** the value you want Excel to return if the logical test argument evaluates as false

In the worksheet in Figure 6.3a, an IF function displays text showing whether a student passes or fails a course. The formula bar shows the IF function in C4. (Remember that arguments are separated by commas.) For the student in row 4:

- Logical test is whether the final average in B4 is greater than or equal to 70; this is written as (B4>=70)
- Value if true is **Pass**
- Value if false is **Fail**

Figure 6.3b shows the Formula Palette for this function. Look at it in detail to be sure you understand how it works.

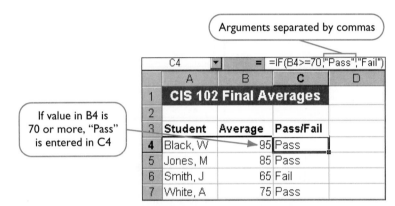

(a) The Function in the Worksheet

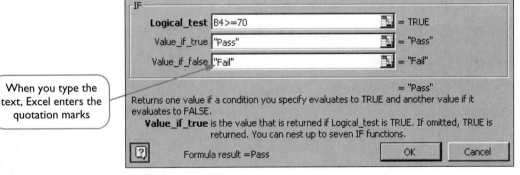

(b) The Formula Palette for the Function

FIGURE 6.3   An IF Function Used to Display Text Showing Whether Students Pass or Fail

The IF function is entered in C4 as:

$$=IF(B4>70, \text{"Pass," "Fail"})$$

This formula says if the content of B4 is greater than or equal to 70, put *Pass* in C4; otherwise put *Fail* in C4. The formula evaluates the condition B4>=70 as true or false; then it performs the first action if the condition is true and the second action if it is false.

The logical test argument uses the comparison operator >=, "greater than or equal to." Table 6.1 shows the comparison operators, which you will use again and again as you construct IF functions.

Operator	Meaning	Example
=	Equal to	A1=D1
>	Greater than	A1>D1
<	Less than	A1<D1
>=	Greater than or equal to	A1>=D1
<=	Less than or equal to	A1<=D1
<>	Not equal to	A1<>D

TABLE 6.1 Comparison Operators

You could also have Excel perform a mathematical operation based on whether a condition evaluates as true or false, for example, looking at sales for each salesperson to determine the commission. Figure 6.4 shows this function for the salesperson in row 4. If you look at the formula bar, you will see that the function tells Excel to evaluate the content of cell B4; if it is greater than or equal to 2000, then multiply B4 by .05; otherwise multiply B4 by .03.

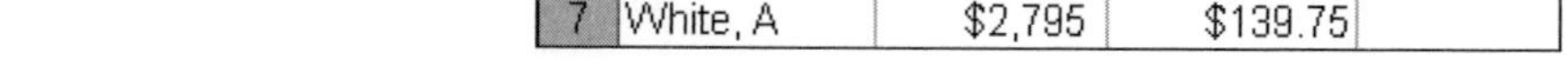

FIGURE 6.4 An IF Function Used to Perform a Mathematical Operation

The IF function is one of the Logical functions. You construct it using the Paste Function dialog box and the Formula Palette just as you have done with other functions. In the next exercise, you use an IF function with the *Overdue Bills* workbook to display the text "Overdue" if payments have not been made in the past 60 days.

1. With the *Overdue Bills* workbook on the screen, enter **Overdue?** in E4 and format it to match the other cells in row 4.

2. Click in **E5**, click the **Paste Function button** on the toolbar, choose the **IF function** in the Logical category, and then click **OK**.
   The Formula Palette opens.

3. In the Logical test edit box, type **D5>60**.
   The function will evaluate the contents of D5 to determine whether it is greater than 60.

4. In the Value_if_true edit box, type **OVERDUE**.

5. In the Value_if_false box, press the **Spacebar**.
   This will create a blank cell if the bill is not overdue.

6. Click **OK**.
   The cell will display the word OVERDUE if no payment has been made in more than 60 days (B5>60); otherwise it will be blank.

7. Use the fill handle to copy the formula down to E8.
   Your worksheet should look like the one in Figure 6.5. (You can reformat column E to match the figure if you like.) Remember that your results will be different because you have different dates.

8. Save the workbook.

9. Print the worksheet and print the formulas; keep the workbook open for use in the next exercise.

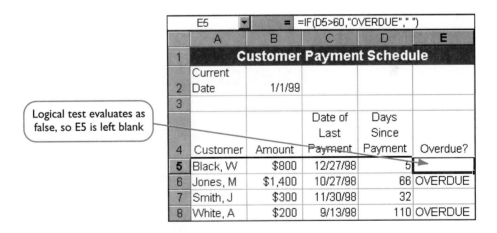

Logical test evaluates as false, so E5 is left blank

E5		=	=IF(D5>60,"OVERDUE"," ")	
	A	B	C	D	E

	A	B	C	D	E
1	**Customer Payment Schedule**				
2	Current Date	1/1/99			
3					
4	Customer	Amount	Date of Last Payment	Days Since Payment	Overdue?
5	Black, W	$800	12/27/98	5	
6	Jones, M	$1,400	10/27/98	66	OVERDUE
7	Smith, J	$300	11/30/98	32	
8	White, A	$200	9/13/98	110	OVERDUE

FIGURE 6.5 The *Overdue Bills* Workbook after Exercise 2

What: Use Excel's built-in SUMIF function.

How: Choose Insert | Function or click the Paste Function button on the toolbar.

Why: The SUMIF function adds the contents of a range of cells only if they meet a condition.

Tip: SUMIF gives you flexibility in the use of the SUM function.

The SUM function adds the contents of a range of cells. The IF function evaluates a condition and returns different results depending on whether the condition is true or false. The SUMIF function combines the SUM and IF functions, adding the contents of a range of cells only if the condition you set forth evaluates as true.

The SUMIF function is in the Math & Trig category. It has two required arguments and one optional argument:

- **Range:** the cell range to evaluate
- **Criteria:** the condition that defines which cells to sum (like the Logical test argument of the IF function, this argument uses comparison operators)
- **Sum range:** the range to sum (if different from the Range argument)

In the following exercise, you will use this function in the *Overdue Bills* workbook to calculate the total of the overdue bills. You will write a formula that will tell Excel to add only those bills that are listed as overdue in column E. This formula will tell you how much money you have outstanding in overdue bills that may become bad debts.

EXERCISE 3 | *Using the SUMIF Function*

1. With the *Overdue Bills* workbook open on the screen, enter **Total Overdue Bills** in **F4** and format it to match the other cells in row 4.

2. Click in **F5**, click the **Paste Function button**, choose the **SUMIF function** in the Math & Trig category, and then click **OK**.
   The Formula Palette opens.

3. In the Range edit box, type **E5:E8**.

4. In the Criteria edit box, type **OVERDUE**.

5. In the Sum_range edit box, type **B5:B8**.

6. Click **OK** and then format the cell for Currency.
   Your worksheet should look like the one in Figure 6.6.

7. Save the workbook.

8. Print the worksheet and print the formulas; keep the workbook open for use in the next exercise.

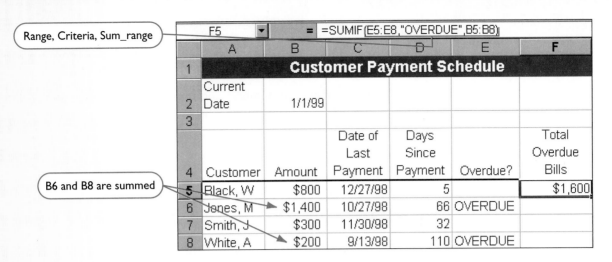

Range, Criteria, Sum_range

F5 | = =SUMIF(E5:E8,"OVERDUE",B5:B8)

B6 and B8 are summed

	A	B	C	D	E	F
1	**Customer Payment Schedule**					
2	Current Date	1/1/99				
3						
4	Customer	Amount	Date of Last Payment	Days Since Payment	Overdue?	Total Overdue Bills
5	Black, W	$800	12/27/98	5		$1,600
6	Jones, M	$1,400	10/27/98	66	OVERDUE	
7	Smith, J	$300	11/30/98	32		
8	White, A	$200	9/13/98	110	OVERDUE	

FIGURE 6.6   The *Overdue Bills* Workbook after Exercise 3

TASK 4 | Using the COUNT, COUNTA, and COUNTBLANK Functions

What: Use Excel's built-in counting functions.

How: Choose Insert | Function or click the Paste Function button on the toolbar.

Why: COUNT, COUNTA, and COUNTBLANK count cells in a range.

Tip: Zeroes are counted but blank cells are not with COUNT and COUNTA; only blank cells are counted with COUNTBLANK.

You can use the three variations of the COUNT function to count cells:

- Use COUNT to show you how many cells in a range contain numbers.
- Use COUNTA to show you how many cells in a range are not empty.
- Use COUNTBLANK to show how many cells in a range are empty.

Each function contains only one argument, the range of cells to be counted. You can use the Paste Function button and the Formula Palette or simply type the functions. Sometimes typing is quicker.

Figure 6.7 illustrates the use of the three functions. In the figure, the functions are entered in column B, but they are typed as text in column A for purposes of illustration.

Functions are entered in column B

	A	B	C	D	E	F	G	H	I	J
1		0	1			2	3		T	F
2	=COUNT(C1:J1):	4								
3	=COUNTA(C1:J1):	6								
4	=COUNTBLANK(C1:J1):	2								

FIGURE 6.7   Three Functions That Count Cells

EXERCISE 4 | *Using COUNT*

1. With the *Overdue Bills* workbook on the screen, enter **Active Customers** in G4 and format it like the other cells in row 4.

2. Click in **G5**, click the **Paste Function button**, choose the **COUNT** function in the Statistical category, and click **OK**.
   The Formula Palette opens.

3. In the Value1 edit box, type or select **B5:B8**.
   This range contains the amount owed by each active customer.

4. Click **OK**.
   Your worksheet should look like the one in Figure 6.8.

5. Save the workbook.

6. Print the worksheet and print the formulas; keep the workbook open for use in the next exercise.

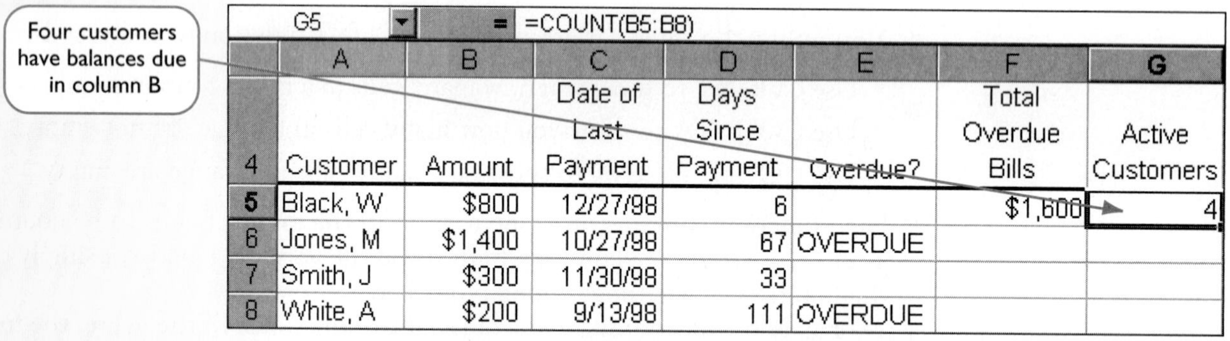

Four customers have balances due in column B

G5		=	=COUNT(B5:B8)				
	A	B	C	D	E	F	G
4	Customer	Amount	Date of Last Payment	Days Since Payment	Overdue?	Total Overdue Bills	Active Customers
5	Black, W	$800	12/27/98	6		$1,600	4
6	Jones, M	$1,400	10/27/98	67	OVERDUE		
7	Smith, J	$300	11/30/98	33			
8	White, A	$200	9/13/98	111	OVERDUE		

FIGURE **6.8**   The *Overdue Bills* Workbook after Exercise 4

TASK 5 | *Using the COUNTIF Function*

What: Use Excel's built-in COUNTIF function.

How: Choose Insert | Function or click the Paste Function button on the toolbar.

Why: The COUNTIF function counts the cells in a range only if they meet a condition.

Tip: COUNTIF gives you flexibility in the use of the COUNT function.

COUNTIF works like SUMIF; that is, cells are evaluated as true or false based on a condition. Excel counts only cells that evaluate as true. In the next exercise, you use this function to determine how many people have overdue bills.

EXERCISE 5 | *Using the COUNTIF Function*

1. With the *Overdue Bills* workbook on the screen, enter **Number Overdue** in H4 and format the cell like the others in row 4.

2. Click in **H5**, click the **Paste Function button**, choose **COUNTIF** in the Statistical category, and click **OK**.
   The Formula Palette opens.

3. In the Range box, type or select **E5:E8**.

4. In the Criteria box, type **OVERDUE**.

5. Click **OK**.
   Your worksheet should look like the one in Figure 6.9.

6. Save the workbook.

7. Print the worksheet and print the formulas; close the workbook and exit from Excel.

H5		= =COUNTIF(E5:E8,"OVERDUE")					
	A	B	C	D	E	F	G	H
			Date of Last Payment	Days Since Payment		Total Overdue Bills	Active Customers	Number Overdue
4	Customer	Amount			Overdue?			
5	Black, W	$800	12/27/98	5		$1,600	4	2
6	Jones, M	$1,400	10/27/98	66	OVERDUE			
7	Smith, J	$300	11/30/98	32				
8	White, A	$200	9/13/98	110	OVERDUE			

Cells E6 and E8 evaluate as "True" and are counted

FIGURE 6.9 The *Overdue Bills* Workbook after Exercise 5

Unit 6 | Using Date, Count, and IF Functions   153

S U M M A R Y

After completing this unit, you should be able to
- use the TODAY function (page 144)
- use the IF function (page 146)
- use the SUMIF function (page 150)
- use the COUNT function (page 151)
- use the COUNTA function (page 151)
- use the COUNTBLANK function (page 151)
- use the COUNTIF function (page 153)

K E Y   T E R M S

condition (page 146)
serial number (page 144)

T E S T   Y O U R   S K I L L S

True/False

1. You can do calculations with dates in Excel because all dates are converted to their serial numbers.
2. COUNTA counts only cells that contain numbers.
3. TODAY places the time in the active cell.
4. A condition must evaluate to either true or false.
5. The SUMIF adds cells only if the condition evaluates to true.

Multiple Choice

1. To count cells that meet a condition, you would use
    a. COUNT   b. COUNTA
    c. COUNTIF   d. COUNTBLANK

2. To add all the cells in a range, you would use
    a. SUM   b. SUMIF
    c. IF   d. ADDIF

3. To add only cells that meet a condition, you would use
    a. SUM   b. SUMIF
    c. IF   d. ADDIF

4. To find out how many days since a billing date until the present, you would
   a. subtract the current date from the billing date
   b. subtract the billing date from the current date
   c. use COUNT
   d. all of these answers

5. If you want to count only cells that contain numbers, you would use
   a. COUNTNUM
   b. COUNT
   c. COUNTA
   d. COUNTIF

Short Answer

1. The _____ _____ button helps you with functions.
2. The _____ function places the system date in the active cell.
3. The _____ _____ will update when you open the spreadsheet on another day.
4. The _____ of the function are enclosed in parentheses.
5. The _____ must evaluate to either true or false.

What Does This Do?

Write a description of the function of the following.

1.	SUMIF	6.	COUNTBLANK
2.		7.	COUNTA
3.	COUNT	8.	
4.	TODAY	9.	
5.	COUNTIF	10.	IF

On Your Own

1. Explore Microsoft Help for other functions that might be of use to you.
2. Create a checkbook register for the current month. Count the number of checks and the number of deposits.
3. Create a summary worksheet of your courses and grades earned. Count the number of courses in which you have received an A, B, C, etc.
4. On a blank worksheet, insert the current date. Use the date in computations subtracting or adding other dates.
5. Open an existing worksheet. Replace the SUM function in the worksheet with the SUMIF function, setting up a condition based on the data in the worksheet.

PROJECTS

1. Create the following workbook or open **Inventory Analysis**:

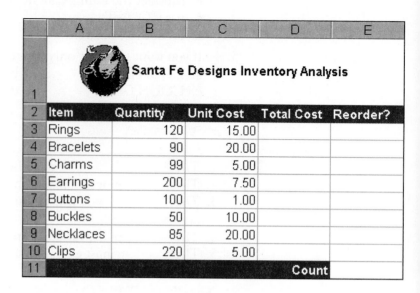

	Item	Quantity	Unit Cost	Total Cost	Reorder?
3	Rings	120	15.00		
4	Bracelets	90	20.00		
5	Charms	99	5.00		
6	Earrings	200	7.50		
7	Buttons	100	1.00		
8	Buckles	50	10.00		
9	Necklaces	85	20.00		
10	Clips	220	5.00		
11				Count	

  a. Use a function to calculate the total cost of inventory of each product.
  b. Write a formula that places the word REORDER in column E for any inventory item that has fallen below 100.
  c. Write a formula that counts only the items that need to be reordered.
  d. Format the worksheet as shown.
  e. Include a graphic.
  f. Use the spelling checker.
  g. Create a header that contains your name on the left and **Project 6-1** on the right.
  h. Save the workbook as **Inventory Analysis**.
  i. Print the worksheet in landscape orientation.
  j. Print the formulas.

2. Create the following spreadsheet or open **Video**:

	Item	Date Due	No. Days Overdue	Fine
2	Today's date:			
3				
5	Mediterranean			
6	Hawaii			
7	Inside Passage			
8	Dolphin Adventure			
9	Barrier Reef			
10	Bahamas			

a. Use a function to place the current system date in B2.
b. Type dates in the Date Due column. Make all dates in the past.
c. Write a formula to calculate the Number of days overdue in column C.
d. Write a formula in column D that multiplies the days overdue by 2.5. Format the result as currency, two decimal places, to levy a $2.50-per-day overdue fine.
e. Format the worksheet as shown.
f. Use the spelling checker.
g. Include a graphic.
h. Create a header that contains your name on the left and **Project 6-2** on the right.
i. Save the workbook as **Video**.
j. Print the worksheet in landscape orientation.
k. Print the formulas.

3. Create the following spreadsheet or open **Grades**:

	A	B	C	D	E	F	G
1			Computer Course				
2							
3	**Student**	**Test 1**	**Test 2**	**Test 3**	**Test 4**	**Average**	**Grade**
4	Adams, J	80	86	90	85		
5	Boyd, S	90	88	75	85		
6	Carr, J	65	0	75	77		
7	Davis, M	77	82	0	80		
8	Evans, B	98	90	92	100		
9	Farris, W	67	76	75	76		
10	Grant, S	86	80	0	79		
11	Hill, J	87	60	65	60		
12	Lake, P	90	92	90	98		
13	Stills, C	79		78	77		
14							
15							
16	Number Taking Test						
17						Number Passed	

a. In column F, write a formula to get the average for each student on each test. A missed test counts as a 0 grade.
b. In column G, use a function to give each student a Pass or Fail. Everyone whose test average is 70 or more passes; the others fail.
c. In row 16, count how many students took each test.
d. In G17, count the number of students who passed the course.
e. Create a header that contains your name on the left and **Project 6-3** on the right.
f. Use the spelling checker.
g. Save the workbook as **Grades**.
h. Print the worksheet in landscape orientation.
i. Print the formulas.

4. Create the following spreadsheet or open **Mileage**.

a. Write a formula to compute the amount the employee should be re-imbursed for mileage. When the number of miles is more than 20, the employee is reimbursed at the rate in cell B6. Fewer than 20 miles are reimbursed at the rate in B7.

b. Total the miles and reimbursement.

c. Create a header that contains your name on the left and **Project 6-4** on the right.

d. Use the spelling checker.

e. Save the workbook as **Mileage**.

f. Print the worksheet in landscape orientation.

g. Print the formulas.

	A	B	C
1		**Monthly Mileage Report**	
2	Your Name		
3	Current Date		
4			
5	Reimbursement per mile:		
6	> 20 miles	0.28	
7	< 20 miles	0.35	
8			
9	**Date**	**No. Miles**	**Amount**
10	10/3	19	
11	10/6	30	
12	10/9	12	
13	10/15	40	
14	10/18	21	
15	10/20	14	
16	10/25	35	
17	10/30	150	
18	**TOTAL**		

PROJECTS

1. Create the following Commissioned Employee Payroll workbook or open **Bonus**:

	A	B	C	D	E	F	G	H	I
1				**JRT Kennels** *Commissioned Employee Payroll*					
2									
3	Current date:								
4	**Bonus:**	**<=2,000**	**>2,000**		Rates:	**<=3,000**	**>3,000**		
5		8%	10%		OASDI	6.20%	6.20%		
6					HI	1.45%	1.45%		
7					FIT	21%	28%		
8							**Deductions**		
9	**Name**	**Base Pay**	**Total Sales**	**Bonus**	**Gross Pay**	**OASDI**	**HI**	**FIT**	**Net Pay**
10	Jones, L	3,000	2,000						
11	Smith, A	2,600	3,600						
12	Gold, M	3,600	3,600						
13	Hill, J	1,900	2,000						
14	Green, M	1,800	1,900						
15	Brown, B	2,300	2,800						
16	Savage, J	2,800	1,800						
17	Smith, J	1,700	1,500						
18									
19	**Total**								

a. Write a formula to compute the bonus, using the percentages shown in rows 4 and 5.

b. Write a formula to compute gross pay.

c. Use the deductions schedule in column F for employees with gross pay of less than $3,000 and the one in column G for those whose gross was more than $3,000.

d. Write a formula to compute net pay.

e. In C19, write a formula to total sales for the month.

f. In D19, write a formula to total the bonus column for the month.

g. Create a header that contains your name on the left and **Check Point 3-1** on the right.

h. Use the spelling checker.

i. Save the workbook as **Bonus**.

j. Print the worksheet in landscape orientation.

k. Print the formulas.

2. Create the following worksheet to help determine the best investment, or open **Investment**:

	A	B	C	D	E
1					
2			Market Trends		
3					
4	Monthly Investment	Interest Rate	Time in Years	Result	Meets Goal?
5	200	3.5%	2		
6	175	4.0%	3		
7	150	3.8%	3		
8	125	3.9%	3		
9	225	5.0%	4		
10	225	4.0%	3		
11	100	3.0%	5		
12	150	3.5%	2		
13	175	4.0%	3		
14				Count	

a. In D5, calculate the total amount that will be invested at the end of
the investment period.

b. In E5, write a formula to show whether the investment meets your
goals of $4,500. If the result is more than $4,500, place the word *Yes* in
column E. If the investment results in less than $4,500, leave the cell in
column E blank.

c. In E13, count how many cells in column E are blank to show how
many investments don't meet your goals.

d. Create a header that contains your name on the left and **Check
Point 3-2** on the right.

e. Use the spelling checker.

f. Save the workbook as **Investment**.

g. Print the worksheet in landscape orientation.

h. Print the formulas.

Working with Multiple Worksheets

UNIT OBJECTIVES

- Insert, delete, and select worksheets
- Rename worksheets
- Copy and move worksheets
- Calculate between sheets
- Create consolidated reports

In the previous units, you have used only one worksheet at a time. When you open a workbook, it contains three worksheets, and you can add more. Using more than one sheet in a workbook allows you to keep related data together for ease of use and to calculate easily between sheets. In this unit, you will use more than one sheet at a time, and you will create a consolidated worksheet that calculates across multiple sheets.

| *Inserting, Deleting, and Selecting Worksheets*

What: Add or delete worksheets.

How: Choose Insert | Worksheet or Edit | Delete Sheet.

Why: A single huge worksheet can be unwieldy; it is more difficult to navigate and slower to access than several smaller ones.

Tip: Right-click a worksheet tab to display a shortcut menu with options for inserting, deleting, renaming, moving, selecting, and copying worksheets.

Three sheet tabs on the horizontal scroll bar, labeled Sheet1, Sheet2, and Sheet3, give access to the three worksheets Excel provides with each new workbook. Most of the time, three sheets will be more than enough. But if you use Excel to create monthly reports, for instance, you might want to have a sheet for each month.

- To add a worksheet, choose Insert | Worksheet. The new worksheet is added immediately before the active sheet. This is illustrated in Figure 7.1a, where Sheet4 is placed before Sheet1 because Sheet1 was active when the command was issued.

- To delete a sheet, click the sheet tab and choose Edit | Delete Sheet, or right-click the sheet tab and choose Delete from the shortcut menu (see Figure 7.1b). Because you cannot undo the deletion, a warning message gives you the chance to change your mind. Figure 7.1c shows the message.

- To select a single worksheet, click its tab.

- To select more than one sheet, click tabs using the commands shown in Table 7.1. When you select more than one sheet, the sheets are grouped, and you can perform actions on all of them at once.

Result Wanted	Action Required
Select a sheet	Click a sheet tab
Select several adjacent sheets (see Figure 7.1d)	Select the first, then hold down Shift and click the last
Select nonadjacent sheets (see Figure 7.1e)	Select the first, then hold down Ctrl and click the tab for each other sheet
Select all sheets	Right-click any tab and click the short-cut menu's Select All Sheets command
Deselect a selected sheet	Click a tab for another sheet
Deselect one selected sheet in a group	Hold down Ctrl and click the tab for the sheet that is to be deselected
Ungroup grouped sheets	Right-click any grouped sheet and click the shortcut menu's Ungroup Sheets command

TABLE 7.1 Selecting and Deselecting Worksheets

> Sheet1 was active when this sheet was added

Sheet4 / Sheet1 / Sheet2 / Sheet3 /

(a) Adding a New Worksheet Before Sheet1

> Right-click the tab to open this menu

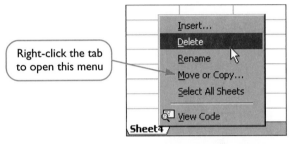

(b) Using the Shortcut Menu to Delete a Worksheet

> Sheet deletions cannot be undone

(c) The Warning Message for Deleting a Worksheet

> Select the first tab, hold down Shift, and click the last tab

Sheet1 / Sheet2 \ **Sheet3** /

(d) Selecting Adjacent Worksheets with the Shift Key

> Select the first tab, hold down Ctrl, and click the other tabs

Sheet1 / Sheet2 / Sheet3 /

(e) Selecting Nonadjacent Worksheets with the Ctrl Key

FIGURE 7.1   Adding and Selecting Worksheets

POINTER

Using the Tab-Scrolling Buttons

When not all of a workbook's sheet tabs are visible at once, you can scroll the tabs using the tab-scrolling buttons. In left to right order, they scroll to the first, previous, next, and last sheet tabs. For more information, press Shift+F1 and click one of the buttons.

EXERCISE 1 | *Inserting a Worksheet*

1. Open a new workbook.
   Sheet1 is the active sheet.

2. Choose **Insert | Worksheet**.
   Sheet4 is inserted before Sheet1.

3. Right-click the tab for **Sheet3**.
   A shortcut menu opens.

4. Click **Insert**.
   The Insert dialog box opens with the General tab displayed.

5. If necessary, click the **Worksheet icon**; click **OK**.
   Sheet5 is inserted before Sheet3.

6. Keep the workbook open for use in the next exercise.

TASK 2 | *Renaming Worksheets*

What: Rename a worksheet.

How: Double-click the tab and type a new name.

Why: Giving worksheets names that reflect their content makes them easier to use.

Tip: Keep names short so that all of the tabs are visible without scrolling.

If you have inserted several new worksheets, it is hard to keep track of which sheet contains what information. You can make using multiple sheets easier by renaming the sheets. For example, if you are creating monthly reports, you can name each sheet for the month it represents, or if you have several department budgets, you can name a worksheet for each department.

To rename a sheet:

1. Double-click the tab.
2. Type a new name.

You can also right-click the tab and choose Rename from the shortcut menu.

EXERCISE 2 | Renaming Worksheets

1. With the workbook from Exercise 1 open on the screen, double-click **Sheet1** and type **January**.
   The sheet is renamed.

2. Right-click **Sheet2**, choose **Rename**, and type **February**.

3. Click the sheet tab for **Sheet3**, choose **Edit | Delete Sheet**, and, when a message box warns you that the sheet will be permanently deleted, click **OK**.
   Sheet3 is deleted. Your sheet tabs should look like the ones in Figure 7.2.

4. Close the workbook without saving it.

Two sheets renamed and one deleted

| ◄ ◄ ► ► | Sheet4 / January / February \ **Sheet5** / |

FIGURE 7.2   The Worksheet Tabs after Exercise 2

TASK 3 | Moving and Copying Worksheets

What: Move or copy worksheets.

How: Choose Edit | Move or Copy Sheet.

Why: Copying a sheet to use it as the basis for a new one can save time; and changing the order of sheets can be a useful house-keeping procedure.

Tip: If you always need more than three sheets in a workbook, you can change the default number by choosing Tools | Options | General tab and typing a new number in the *Sheets in new workbook* box.

Excel makes it easy to move or copy worksheets in a workbook. You may not need to move worksheets often, but you'll find many occasions to copy sheets, as you'll see in the following tasks.

USING THE MENUS

To move or copy a sheet using the menus:

1. Make the sheet you want to move or copy the active sheet.

2. Choose Edit | Move or Copy Sheet, or right-click the sheet tab and choose Move or Copy from the shortcut menu. The Move or Copy dialog box opens as shown in Figure 7.3.

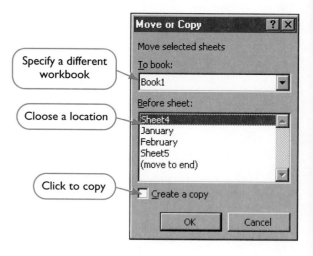

FIGURE 7.3   The Move or Copy Dialog Box

3. Make a selection in the *To book* box:

   - To move or copy the sheet within the same workbook, leave the current file name unchanged.

   - To move or copy the sheet to another workbook, specify the name of the file. (Click the arrow in the box to see a list of all open workbooks; if you open the destination workbook in advance, you can select its name.)

4. In the *Before sheet* box, select the sheet you want the moved or copied sheet to appear before.
5. Select the *Create a copy* check box to copy the sheet but leave it unselected to move the sheet.
6. Click OK. The current sheet will be moved or copied to the location you specified.

If you copy a sheet within the same workbook, the copy will have the same name as the original followed by a parenthetical number. The copy is number 2, as shown in Figure 7.4.

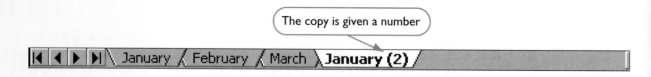

FIGURE 7.4   A Worksheet Copied to the Same Workbook

USING THE MOUSE

The fastest way to move a sheet within the same workbook is to use the mouse.

- To move a sheet, drag its sheet tab to the new location (see Figure 7.5a). The pointer has a workbook icon attached while you drag, and a downward pointing arrow shows where the sheet would be dropped.

- To copy a sheet within the same workbook, hold down Ctrl while you drag, and release the mouse button before the Ctrl key (see Figure 7.5b). When you drag holding down the Ctrl key, the drag-and-drop mouse pointer has a plus sign.

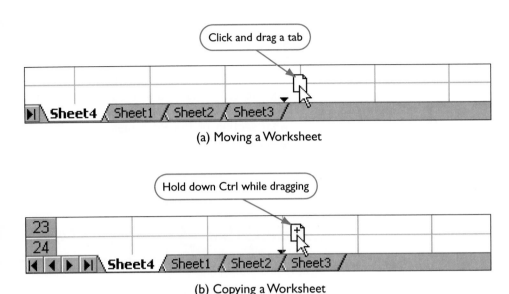

(a) Moving a Worksheet

(b) Copying a Worksheet

FIGURE 7.5 Moving and Copying Worksheets by Dragging and Dropping

WHY COPY?

A major reason for copying sheets is to make it easy to compare data. For example, if you were creating monthly reports, you would want to input data into the same blank worksheet at the end of each month. If you had a master worksheet that contained the labels, formatting, and formulas you needed for the monthly report, you could copy it and input new data into it each month. This would be much quicker than starting from scratch.

> ### POINTER
>
> **Templates**
>
> A workbook that contains labels, formatting, and formulas but not any specific data is called a **template**. Excel comes with several built-in templates, and you can create your own by saving a workbook as a template, using the *.xlt* extension. You can also purchase templates on disk or over the World Wide Web. Many large companies and government agencies develop templates for their employees, such as for electronic time cards, mileage reports, and many other types of reporting. If everyone uses the same template, then data can easily be compared and compiled. If you find that you use the same worksheet over and over, consider creating a template. See Excel Help for creating workbook templates.

In the following exercise, you will create a master worksheet and then copy it to other sheets, rename the copy sheets, and fill in the data.

EXERCISE 3 | *Moving and Copying Worksheets*

1. Open a new workbook and create the worksheet shown here on Sheet1, placing the formulas in the cells.
   Don't worry when you get an error message.

	A	B	C	D	E	F
1			Motor Vehicle Report			
2	Month Ending:					
3	Current Price:					
4						
5	Vehicle ID	Miles Traveled	Gas in Gallons	Miles per Gallon	Fuel Cost	Service Now?
6				=B6/C6	=C6*$B$3	=IF(B6>1000,"Yes","No")

2. Copy the sheet to a new worksheet.
3. Rename the new worksheet **Jan**.
4. In B2, type **1/31**.
5. In B3, enter the current price for a gallon of gasoline.
   If you don't know what gas costs in your area, ask a friend or enter $1.00.
6. Type the following data on the Jan worksheet:

	A	B	C
6	Sedan 1	645	20
7	Truck 1	1,400	45
8	Truck 2	2,300	90
9	Van 1	500	18

7. Copy the formulas in columns D, E, and F down the column.
8. Copy Sheet1 a second time and rename the copy **Feb**.

9. Enter **2/28** or **2/29** in B2 and a different price for a gallon of gas in B3.

10. Type the following data on the Feb worksheet:

	A	B	C
6	Sedan 1	950	31
7	Truck 1	1,200	40
8	Truck 2	400	15
9	Van 1	700	25

11. Copy the formulas in columns D, E, and F down the column.

12. Copy Sheet1 a third time and rename the copy **Mar**.

13. Enter **3/31** in B2 and a different price for a gallon of gas in B3.

14. Type the following data on the Mar worksheet:

	A	B	C
6	Sedan 1	600	20
7	Truck 1	1,900	65
8	Truck 2	300	12
9	Van 1	2,100	70

15. Copy the formulas in columns D, E, and F down the column.

16. Rename Sheet1 **Master** and move it to the last position in the workbook.

17. Save the workbook as **Vehicle Report**.

18. Print the entire workbook and then print the formulas for the entire workbook. Leave the workbook open for use in the next exercise.

TASK 4 | *Calculating Between Sheets*

What: Make calculations using cells in multiple worksheets.

How: Specify the sheet name as well as the cell address in a formula.

Why: If you store related records in a series of worksheets, you need to be able to access all of them in your calculations.

Tip: You can also use cells contained in other workbooks in a formula. Include the file name, the sheet name, and cell address in the formula. See Excel Help for details.

To perform calculations using cells on different sheets, you must include the sheet name with the cell address. Separate the sheet name from the cell address with an exclamation mark, and do not use spaces in the formula.

For example, to add the contents of cell F10 on Sheet1 and the contents of G15 on Sheet2, you would type:

=Sheet1!F10+Sheet2!G15

If the sheets were named Sept and Oct, you would type:

=Sept!F10+Oct!G15

POINTER

Pointing to Cells

To avoid typing errors in formulas, use the cell-selection or pointing method to create your formulas. Click the sheet tab and then click the cell you want to use. Excel will place the sheet name and cell address in the formula.

If the cells you want to include in the formula are in the same cell location on the different sheets, you can enter the addresses as a range:

1. Place the insertion point where you want the results to appear.
2. Type an = followed by the name of the function, such as SUM.
3. Type an opening parenthesis: =SUM(
4. Click the sheet tab for the first sheet that contains the data you want to add, such as Jan.
5. Click in the appropriate cell, such as G20.
6. Hold down the Shift key and click the tab of the last sheet you want to include in the range, such as Dec.
7. Click the Enter button on the formula bar.

The formula will add the contents of cell G20 on every sheet from Jan through Dec. The formula should look like:

=SUM(Jan:Dec!G20)

EXERCISE 4 | *Calculating Between Sheets*

1. With the *Vehicle Report* workbook open on the screen, make the **Jan** sheet active.
2. Use AutoSum to calculate totals for the **Miles Traveled** and **Fuel Cost** columns (columns B and E).
3. Repeat step 2 for the **Feb** and **Mar** worksheets.
4. Make the **Mar** worksheet active.

5. In A12, enter **Total Miles for Qtr 1**.

6. In A13, enter **Total Cost for Qtr 1**.

7. Enter a formula in B12 to sum the total miles in each month, as follows:
- Type =
- Click the **Jan sheet**
- Click **B10** (the cell that contains the total miles)
- Type +
- Click the **Feb sheet**
- Click **B10** (the cell that contains the total miles)
- Type +
- Click the **Mar sheet**
- Click **B10** (the cell that contains the total miles)
- Click the **Enter button** on the formula bar

Because the same cell on all three sheets (B10) was used in the formula, you could also have entered the formula as a range:

$$=SUM(Jan:Mar!B10)$$

8. Enter a formula in B13 to sum the total fuel cost in each month, this time using a range address:
- Type **=SUM(**
- Click the **Jan sheet**
- Click **E10** (the cell that contains the total fuel cost)
- Hold down **Shift** and click the **Mar sheet**
- Click the **Enter button** on the formula bar

9. Save the workbook; the Mar worksheet should look like Figure 7.6. Your costs will be different.

10. Print the **Mar** worksheet and then print its formulas. Leave the workbook open to use in the next exercise.

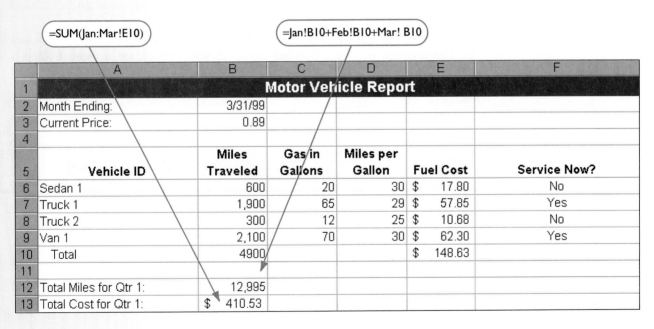

=SUM(Jan:Mar!E10)

=Jan!B10+Feb!B10+Mar! B10

	A	B	C	D	E	F
1			**Motor Vehicle Report**			
2	Month Ending:	3/31/99				
3	Current Price:	0.89				
4						
5	**Vehicle ID**	**Miles Traveled**	**Gas in Gallons**	**Miles per Gallon**	**Fuel Cost**	**Service Now?**
6	Sedan 1	600	20	30	$ 17.80	No
7	Truck 1	1,900	65	29	$ 57.85	Yes
8	Truck 2	300	12	25	$ 10.68	No
9	Van 1	2,100	70	30	$ 62.30	Yes
10	Total	4900			$ 148.63	
11						
12	Total Miles for Qtr 1:	12,995				
13	Total Cost for Qtr 1:	$ 410.53				

FIGURE 7.6 The *Mar* Worksheet after Exercise 4

What: Consolidate data from multiple worksheets.

How: Calculate using 3-D references.

Why: Most businesses need to create monthly, quarterly, and yearly reports.

Tip: Use master worksheets or templates so that consolidated reports are easy to compile.

Whether you are doing personal financial analysis or business reporting, compiling data into reports is a common practice. **Consolidated reports** compile individual reports into meaningful large reports, such as annual reports.

To create a consolidation worksheet:

1. Move to or create a blank worksheet.
2. Type labels that describe the consolidated data.
3. Click in a cell that will contain the data.
4. Write a formula that computes the consolidated data to provide meaningful information.

POINTER

3-D References

References to cells in other worksheets or workbooks are referred to as 3-D references. In Excel Help files, you can find help on consolidation reports by searching for "3-D references."

In the last exercise, you totaled the number of miles and the cost of fuel for the quarter. In the following exercise, you will create a more in-depth consolidated report.

EXERCISE 5 | *Creating a Consolidation Worksheet*

1. With the *Vehicle Report* workbook open on the screen, move to a blank sheet or insert one.

2. Name the worksheet **Consolidation**.

3. Type the following text:

	A	B
1	**Vehicle Use Quarterly Report**	
2	Current date:	
3		
4	Average Price of Gas	
5	Total Miles	
6	Average Miles	
7	Average Miles per Gallon	
8	Total Cost	

4. In **B4**, type **=AVERAGE(**

5. Click the **Jan** worksheet to make it the active sheet.

6. Click in cell **B3**.

7. Hold down the **Shift key** and click the **Mar sheet tab**.
You are telling Excel to average B3 in the range Jan through Mar.

8. Click the **Enter key** on the formula bar.
The average price of gasoline is placed in the cell.

9. Follow the method used in Exercise 4 to compute the **Total Miles** and **Total Cost**.

10. Write formulas to average the **miles** and **miles per gallon** for all three months.

11. Save the workbook. Print the **Consolidation** worksheet and then print its formulas.

12. Exit from Excel.

R E V I E W

SUMMARY

After completing this unit, you should be able to
- insert, delete, and select multiple worksheets (page 162)
- rename worksheets (page 164)
- move and copy worksheets (page 165)
- calculate between sheets (page 169)
- create consolidation worksheets (page 172)

KEY TERMS

consolidated report (page 172)
template (page 167)

TEST YOUR SKILLS

True/False

1. You can rename a worksheet.
2. You can copy but not move worksheets.
3. You can perform calculations between worksheets.
4. You can change the default number of sheets that Excel displays in a new workbook.
5. You can perform calculations between workbooks.

Multiple Choice

1. To separate the sheet name from the cell address, you use
   a. #   b. *
   c. !   d. $

2. You cannot include which one of the following in a formula?
   a. numbers   b. spaces
   c. cell locations   d. all of these answers

3. To multiply the contents of B15 on Sheet2 times J27 on Sheet4, your formula would look like:
   a. =J27!Sheet4*B15!Sheet2   b. =Sheet 2 B15*Sheet 4 J27
   c. =Sheet2!B15*Sheet4!J27   d. all of these answers

4. To subtract F10 on April from G20 on May, your formula would look like:
   a. =April!F10–May!G20   b. =May!G20–April!F10
   c. =G20–F10   d. all of these answers

5. To divide A21 on Sheet1 by G21 on Sheet2, your formula would look like:
   a. =A21!Sheet1/G21!Sheet2   b. =Sheet1!A21/Sheet2!G21
   c. =Sheet2!G21/Sheet1!A21   d. all of these answers

Short Answer

1. Write a formula to add G14 on January to G14 on February to G14 on March.
2. Write a formula to subtract A29 on Sheet1 from B17 on Sheet2.
3. Write a formula to multiply H9 on June by B14 on June.
4. Write a formula to divide C30 on Sheet1 by J12 on Sheet2.
5. Write a formula to multiply T3 on Sheet3 by T3 on Sheet2.

What Does This Do?

Write a description of the function of the following:

1.	Click a sheet tab	6.	=Sheet1!F10+Sheet2!G15
2.	Shift+left-click sheet tabs	7.	=SUM(Jan:Dec!G20)
3.	Right-click a sheet tab	8.	:
4.	Double-click a sheet tab	9.	!
5.	Ctrl+left-click sheet tabs	10.	Consolidation sheet

On Your Own

1. Open a worksheet and rename the three sheets.
2. Open a workbook and create formulas that use information located on different worksheets.
3. Open a workbook and create a consolidation worksheet.
4. Open a workbook and move and copy sheets in the workbook.
5. Create a multisheet workbook that calculates cells located on different sheets.

PROJECTS

1. Create the following worksheet or open **Rainbow Visions Financials**:

	A	B	C	D	E
1			Rainbow Visions		
2	Current date				
3	INCOME				
4		January	February	March	Total
5	Retail	1,000	1,250	1,500	
6	Wholesale	3,000	5,000	4,000	
7	Craft fairs	900	1,000	6,000	
8	Total				

a. Rename Sheet1 as **Qtr1**.
b. Format the worksheet and include a graphic.
c. Create the formulas to total the income by month and by category.
d. Save the workbook as **Rainbow Visions Financials**.
e. Copy the sheet three times.
f. Rename the first copy **Qtr2** and:
   - Change the months to April, May, June
   - Change Wholesale to: 1,800, 2,500, 6,000

g. Rename the second copy **Qtr3** and:
   - Change the months to July, August, September
   - Change Retail to 1,400, 1,800, 1,300
h. Rename the third copy **Qtr4** and:
   - Change the months to October, November, December
   - Change craft fairs to 200, 500, 1,900
i. Move to a blank sheet and create the consolidation worksheet shown below:

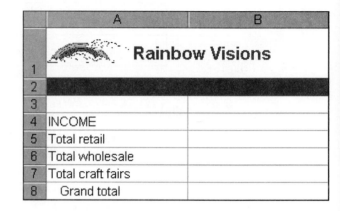

	A	B
1	Rainbow Visions	
2		
3		
4	INCOME	
5	Total retail	
6	Total wholesale	
7	Total craft fairs	
8	Grand total	

j. Rename the sheet **Consolidation**.
k. Create formulas to total the categories for all four quarters by pointing to or typing the cell locations.
l. Use the spelling checker.
m. Create a header that contains your name on the left and the text **Project 7-1** on the right.
n. Save the workbook.
o. Print the worksheets.
p. Print the formulas.

2. Using the *Rainbow Visions Financials* workbook created in Project 1, add the following data to the **Qtr1** tab:

	A	B	C	D
10	EXPENSES			
11	Cost of goods	400	300	400
12	Advertising	75		100
13	Catalog	1,500		
14	Travel	300	350	100
15	Insurance	100	100	100
16	Taxes	400	400	400
17	Rent	600	600	600
18	Utilities	100	120	90
19	Total			

a. Use AutoSum to total each month and total by category.
b. Copy the expense data to the other three sheets.
c. Make **Qtr2** the active sheet and:
   - Change the catalog expense for April to 100
   - Change travel to 500, 200, and 600

d. Make **Qtr3** the active sheet and:

- Change the catalog expense for July to 300
- Change the cost of goods to 500, 750, 300

e. Make **Qtr4** the active sheet and:

- Change the catalog expense for October to 0
- Change insurance to 50, 65, and 75

f. Add the following text to the **Consolidation** sheet:

	A	B
10	EXPENSES	
11	Total cost of goods	
12	Total advertising	
13	Total catalog	
14	Total travel	
15	Total insurance	
16	Total taxes	
17	Total rent	
18	Total utilities	
19	Grand total	
20		
21	Profit or loss	

g. Total the data from the quarterly sheets for the expenses in column A.

h. In B21, write a formula to compute the profit or loss.

i. Change the header to **Project 7-2**.

j. Save the workbook.

k. Print the worksheets.

l. Print the formulas.

3. Create the worksheet shown here or open **Barefoot**:

	A	B	C
1	**Barefoot Travel** **Assets**		
2			
3		This Year	Last Year
4	Accounts receivable	100,000	90,000
5	Cash on hand	18,000	12,000
6	Inventory	450,000	200,000
7	Total current assets		
8			
9	Fixed assets		
10	Buildings	1,000,000	900,000
11	Computers	250,000	300,000
12	Office equipment	50,000	50,000
13	Total		
14	Depreciation	25,000	25,000
15	Total fixed assets		
16			
17	Total assets		

a. Rename the sheet **Assets**.
b. Use AutoSum to total the current and fixed assets for this year and last year.
c. Subtract the depreciation from the total fixed assets.
d. Write a formula to compute the total assets.
e. Create the following worksheet on Sheet2:

	A	B	C
1	**Barefoot Travel Liabilities**		
2			
3		This Year	Last Year
4	Accounts payable	167,000	120,000
5	Taxes	90,000	85,000
6	Interest	10,000	9,000
7	Total		
8			
9	Long-term liability		
10	Office building mortgage	600,000	650,000
11	Garage mortgage	100,000	125,000
12	Total		
13			
14	Total liabilities		

f. Name Sheet2 **Liabilities**.
g. Create a formula to compute the total liabilities for this year and last year.
h. Rename Sheet3 **Equity**.
i. Place the labels **Total assets, Total liabilities**, and **Owners' equity** in A2:A4.
j. Create a formula to place the totals for total assets and total liabilities in B2 and B3.
k. Write a formula to compute owners' equity (assets less liabilities) in B4.
l. Create a header that has your name on the left and the text **Project 7-3** on the right.
m. Use the spelling checker.
n. Format the worksheet and include a graphic.
o. Save the workbook as **Barefoot**.
p. Print both worksheets.
q. Print the formulas.

4. Create the worksheet shown here or open **Motel**:

	A	B	C	D	E	F	G	H
1	**Dog and Cat Motel Weekly Payroll**							
2								
3	Current date							
4								
5	OASDI	6.20%						
6	HI	1.45%						
7	FIT	15%						
8								
9	**Name**	**Hourly Rate**	**Hours Worked**	**Regular Hours**	**Overtime Hours**	**Regular Pay**	**Overtime Pay**	**Gross Pay**
10	Black, B	6.75						
11	Gold, J	6.75						
12	Green, J	6.95						
13	Hill, J	6.25						
14	James, J	7.00						
15	Jones, S	6.25						
16	Smith, A	7.00						
17	Smith, J	6.95						
18	Stone, B	6.50						
19	White, M	7.00						

a. Use an IF function to determine regular hours. Any hours over 40 are considered overtime.

b. Use a function to determine overtime hours.

c. Write a formula to compute regular pay, which equals regular hours times hourly rate.

d. Write a formula to compute overtime pay, for which workers are paid time and a half (1.5 times regular pay).

e. Type the text shown here. (If you opened **Motel**, you can skip this step.)

	I	J	K	L	M
8	**Deductions**				
9	**OASDI**	**HI**	**FIT**	**Total Deductions**	**Net Pay**

f. Write a formula to compute gross pay.

g. Write a formula to compute OASDI. (The rate is located in B5.)

h. Write a formula to compute HI. (The rate is located in B6.)

i. Write a formula to compute FIT. (The rate is located in B7.)

j. Write a formula to total the deductions.

k. Write a formula to compute net pay.

l. Copy the worksheet four times, and name the copies **Week1**, **Week2**, **Week3**, and **Week4**.

m. Enter the hours worked for the employees for each week in the appropriate worksheet:

9	Name	Week1	Week2	Week3	Week4
10	Black, B	30	29	25	29
11	Gold, J	42	44	40	45
12	Green, J	48	40	18	39
13	Hill, J	39	39	29	45
14	James, J	45	20	45	60
15	Jones, S	20	39	19	35
16	Smith, A	29	48	23	45
17	Smith, J	30	30	40	41
18	Stone, B	46	42	40	49
19	White, M	25	19	39	49

n. Create a consolidation sheet that shows the following for each employee:

- Total hours worked
- Total overtime hours
- Total regular earnings
- Total overtime earnings
- Total net pay

o. Create a header that contains your name on the left and the text **Project 7-4** on the right.

p. Save the workbook as **Motel**.

q. Print all of the worksheets in landscape orientation.

r. Print the formulas.

Using Excel with Charts, Word, and the Web

UNIT OBJECTIVES

- Create charts
- Enhance charts
- Copy worksheet data to Microsoft Word
- Link worksheet data to Microsoft Word
- Link to the World Wide Web
- Save a workbook as a Web document

Charts can help to make your worksheet data easier to understand. Excel's chart feature creates charts of your data and lets you place them on their own sheet or in an existing sheet. You will learn to create and enhance charts in this unit. You'll also see how to copy and link charts and worksheet data to other applications, such as Microsoft Word. In order to keep numeric data up to date in a world that measures time in nanoseconds, many people use the World Wide Web with their worksheets. You will learn to link to the Web from Excel worksheets and turn your Excel workbooks into Web documents.

TASK 1 | *Creating Charts*

What: Create charts of worksheet data.

How: Choose Insert | Chart or click the Chart Wizard button on the Standard toolbar.

Why: A graphic image of data can help others understand the data better.

Tip: The wrong chart type can misrepresent information. Use Excel Help on "examples of chart types" to find the right type of chart for your data.

Charts can emphasize important points in your data and make them easier to understand. Excel's Chart Wizard helps you create charts from data that you select in your worksheets. If you change the data, the chart changes automatically. Figure 8.1a shows a column chart of the data in Figure 8.1b. Figure 8.1c shows the one-to-one correspondence between the data in the worksheet and the chart.

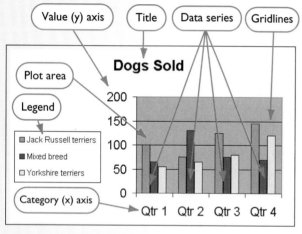

(a) An Excel Column Chart

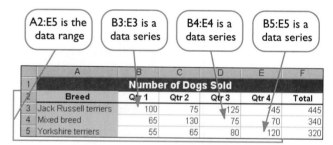

(b) The Data That Was Charted

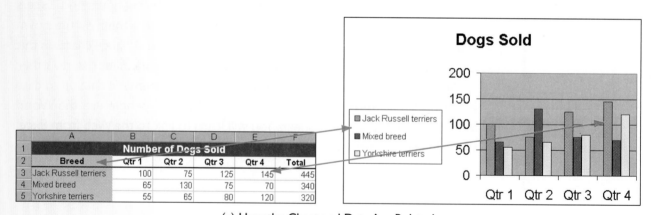

(c) How the Chart and Data Are Related

FIGURE 8.1 Excel's Charts

CHART ELEMENTS AND TYPES

A chart contains some or all the following elements:

- **x axis (category axis)**—horizontal axis at the bottom of the chart—contains labels
- **y axis (value axis)**—vertical axis along the left edge of the chart—contains numeric values
- **title**—text centered at the top of the chart that describes the overall chart; or text describing the x or y axis
- **plot area**—the central area of the chart, where values are represented as lines, bars, columns, slices of the pie, etc.
- **data series**—a group of data points in the row or column of the worksheet that is plotted in the chart
- **legend**—a box that identifies the colors used for the data series or categories in the chart
- **gridlines**—lines that run vertically and horizontally through the plot area from points (tick marks) on the x and y axes

Excel provides over a dozen chart types, as can be seen in Table 8.1. Which chart type to use depends on the type of data you are charting and the purpose of the chart. Excel Help shows uses for the most common types of charts. Figure 8.2 shows the Help screen for column charts.

Chart Type	Name	Description of Use
	Column	Compares values across categories
	Bar	Compares values across categories
	Line	Displays a trend over time
	Pie	Displays parts of the whole
	XY (Scatter)	Compares two values
	Area	Shows the trend of values over time
	Doughnut	Displays parts of the whole for multiple series of data
	Radar	Displays changes relative to the center point
	Surface	Displays trends in a continuous curve across two dimensions
	Bubble	Compares three sets of values
	Stock	Charts the high, low, and closing values for a stock
	Cylinder	Compares values across categories
	Cone	Compares values across categories
	Pyramid	Compares values across categories

TABLE 8.1 Types of Excel Charts

Choosing the type of chart to use is dependent on the type of data in the worksheet and the goal of the chart. Two main guidelines help you decide how the data should be charted.

- If the chart should illustrate comparisons among individual items, use a column, bar, or pie chart. For example, to compare the sales of several products, you would use the column or bar chart. The resulting chart would visually show the comparison by the size of the bars. To show the proportional size of items that make up the whole, such as what portion of the entire sales each item represents, use a pie chart. The size of the slices of the pie will show the percentage each represents.

- If the chart should illustrate trends over a period of time, use a line or area chart. For example, to show sales figures over a period of time, you would sample the data at equal intervals such as quarterly. The resulting chart would plot the change over time and draw lines to show the trend.

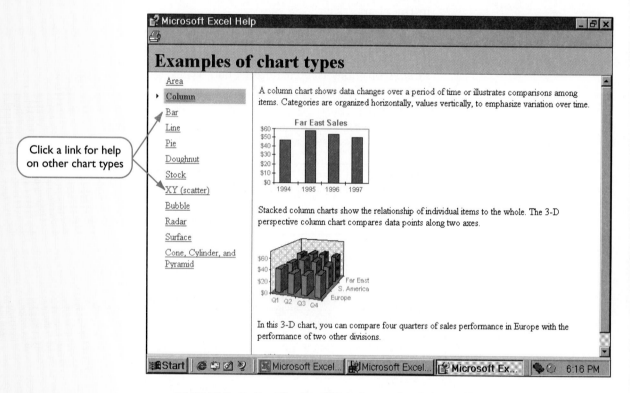

FIGURE 8.2   The Excel Help Screen for Column Charts

CREATING A CHART

Since charts are based on worksheet data, you must enter the data in a worksheet before you can chart it. The following guidelines will help in obtaining accurate, pleasing charts:

- Place labels in the column to the left of the data that indicate the categories.
- Place labels across the row above the data that indicate the type of data or the time over which the data will be analyzed.
- Place data in contiguous columns where possible.
- Format all of the data the same way.

To create a chart of Excel worksheet data:

1. Determine the type of chart that will display the data most effectively.
2. Select the cells that contain the data that you want charted—the **data range**.

POINTER

Selecting Data in Noncontiguous Columns

To include noncontiguous ranges in the chart, select the first group of cells, then hold down the Ctrl key while you select the other groups.

3. Click the Chart Wizard button on the Standard toolbar. The Chart Wizard opens, displaying the Step 1 of 4 – Chart Type page shown in Figure 8.3a.
   - Select a type of chart from the *Chart type* list.
   - Select a chart subtype.
   - Use the Press and Hold to View Sample button to see what your data will look like when charted.
   - Click the Next button.
4. The Step 2 of 4 – Chart Source Data page opens, as shown in Figure 8.3b. The chart you have specified is shown at the top, and options buttons below let you choose whether to plot the data series in rows or columns. Make a selection and then click the Next button.

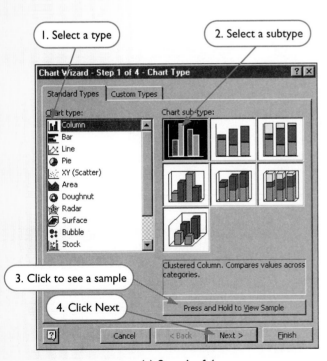

(a) Step 1 of 4

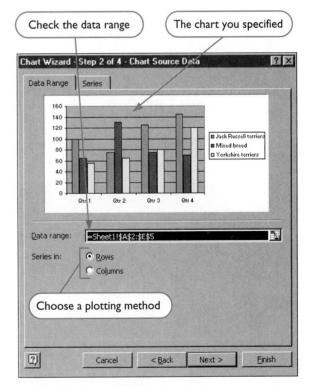

(b) Step 2 of 4

FIGURE 8.3   Using the Chart Wizard

- If you choose to chart by column, Excel uses the labels in the column at the left edge of the data range on the category axis (along the bottom of the chart). It uses the labels in the row across the top of the data range in the legend.
- If you choose to chart by row, Excel uses the labels in the column at the left edge of the data range in the legend. It uses the labels in the row across the top of the data range in the category axis (along the bottom of the chart).

5. When you click the Next button, the Step 3 of 4 – Chart Options page opens. Make selections on any or all of the six tabs and then click the Next button. Here are some examples:

- Titles tab, shown in Figure 8.3c, is where you can type titles for the chart and the category and value axes.
- Gridlines tab, shown in Figure 8.3d, is where you can select a variety of gridlines or none.
- Legend tab, shown in Figure 8.3e, is where you choose whether to show a legend and where to place it.

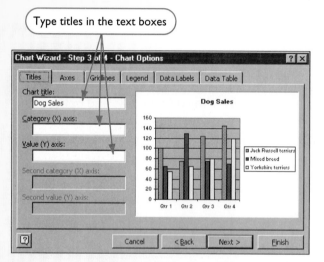

(c) Step 3 of 4: The Titles Tab

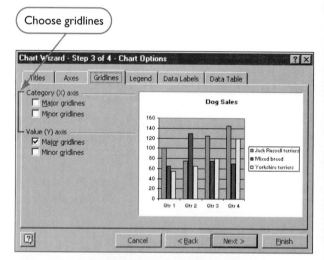

(d) Step 3 of 4: The Gridlines Tab

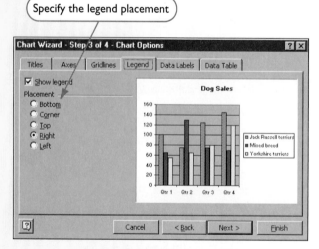

(e) Step 3 of 4: The Legend Tab

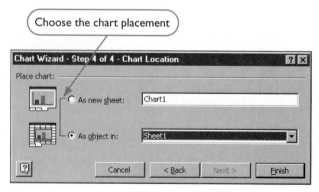

(f) Step 4 of 4

FIGURE **8.3** Using the Chart Wizard *(continued)*

6. When you click the Next button, the Step 4 of 4 – Chart Location page opens, as shown in Figure 8.3f. Select whether the chart will be an object in a worksheet or appear on its own sheet.
7. Click the Finish button to close the wizard and display the chart and the Chart toolbar, as shown in Figure 8.4.

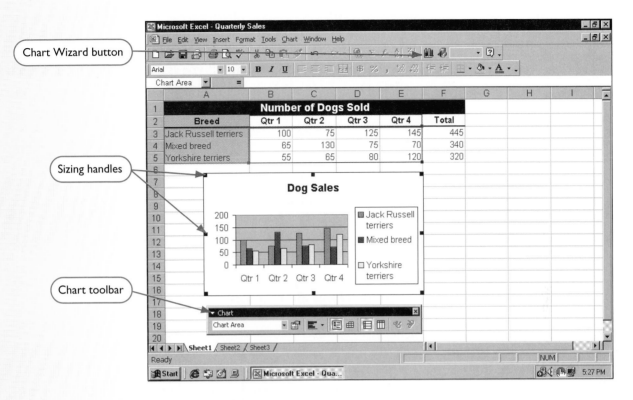

FIGURE 8.4 An Excel Column Chart in a Worksheet

EXERCISE 1 | *Creating Charts*

1. Create the worksheet shown here.

	A	B	C	D	E	F
1	**Number of Dogs Sold**					
2	**Breed**	**Qtr 1**	**Qtr 2**	**Qtr 3**	**Qtr 4**	**Total**
3	Jack Russell terriers	100	75	125	145	445
4	Mixed breed	65	130	75	70	340
5	Yorkshire terriers	55	65	80	120	320

2. Select **A2:E5**.
   This defines the data range.

3. Click the **Chart Wizard button** on the Standard toolbar.
   The Chart Wizard opens on the screen, displaying the Step 1 of 4 – Chart Type page.

4. Choose **Column** from the *Chart type* list, and select the **Clustered Column** subtype.

5. Click and hold the **Press and Hold to View Sample button**.
A sample of the chart is displayed in the window.

6. Click the other chart subtypes in turn and look at sample.
See the difference between a cluster column, a stacked column, and a 100% stacked column. Which type you use depends on what you want to emphasize with the data.

7. Select the **Clustered Column** subtype again and click the **Next button**.
The Step 2 of 4 – Chart Source Data page opens, with the Rows option button selected.

8. Examine the sample chart, then select **Columns** and examine the new sample.
Watch what happens when you switch between a data series in rows and one in columns.

9. Select **Rows** again and click **Next**.
The Step 3 of 4 – Chart Options page opens, with the Titles tab displayed.

10. Type **Dogs Sold** in the *Chart title* text box; wait until the preview is updated to display the title, and then click **Next**.
The Step 4 of 4 – Chart Location page opens.

11. Select **As object in Sheet 1** and click **Finish**.
The Chart Wizard closes, the chart appears in Sheet 1, and the Chart toolbar is displayed. The chart has small squares called sizing handles around its edges, showing that it is selected. Your screen should look something like Figure 8.4 on page 187.

12. Click **the white background area inside the chart**, hold down the mouse button, and drag the chart off to one side of the worksheet, then click **outside the chart** to deselect it.
The Chart toolbar closes.

13. To create a second chart, select cells **A3:A5**.

14. Hold the **Ctrl key** and select **F3:F5**.
Both groups of cells are selected. This is a noncontiguous range.

15. Click the **Chart Wizard button**.

16. In Step 1 of the Chart Wizard, choose **Pie** from the *Chart type* list and **Pie with a 3-D visual effect** as the subtype, then click **Next**.

17. In Step 2, make sure **Columns** is selected and click **Next**.

18. In Step 3, type **Total by Breed** in the *Chart title* text box and click **Next**.

19. In Step 4, select **As new sheet** and click **Finish**.
The Chart Wizard closes, and the chart appears on a new sheet, named Chart1. It will resemble Figure 8.5.

20. Click the **Print Preview button** on the Standard toolbar to view the chart sheet as it will print, then click the Print Preview toolbar's **Close button**.

21. Save the workbook as **Quarterly Sales**.

22. Print the entire workbook. Keep the workbook open for use in the next exercise.

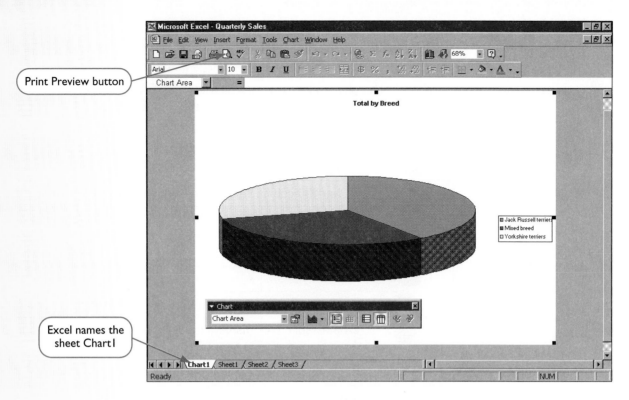

Print Preview button

Excel names the
sheet Chart1

FIGURE **8.5**   The Chart Sheet Created in Exercise 1

TASK 2 | *Enhancing a Chart*

What: Enhance a chart.

How: Use buttons on the Chart toolbar.

Why: You can change the size, position, and formatting of a chart to make it clearer and more appealing.

Tip: Data in the chart will automatically update when you change data in the worksheet.

In Exercise 1, you moved a chart that was covering the worksheet data. To move a chart:

1. Click it to select it and display sizing handles around its outer edge.
2. Click and drag the white background of the chart area.
3. Release the mouse button when the chart is where you want it.

To size a chart:

1. Click it to select it and display sizing handles around its outer edge.
2. Point to a handle (the pointer changes to a two-headed arrow).
3. Click and drag to resize the chart. If you click a corner handle, the width and height will be resized proportionately. As you drag, an outline shows the new size of the chart.

To delete a chart:

1. Click it to select it and display sizing handles around its outer edge.
2. Press the Delete key.

To edit the chart, click it to select it and display the Chart toolbar. Then use the toolbar buttons to change the chart type or format. Table 8.2 describes the toolbar buttons.

Button	Name	Description
`Chart Area ▾`	Chart Objects	Selects individual areas of the chart
	Format Chart Object	Displays the Format Chart Object dialog box, which allows you to change patterns, colors, fonts, etc.
	Chart Type	Allows you to change the type of chart
	Legend	Toggles the display of the legend on or off
	Data Table	Displays the chart along with the chart range in a table
	By Row	Plots the data by row
	By Column	Plots the data by column
	Angle Text Downward	Angles selected text downward
	Angle Text Upward	Angles selected text upward

TABLE 8.2   Chart Toolbar Buttons

EXERCISE 2 | *Modifying the Chart*

1. With the *Quarterly Sales* workbook open on the screen, select the **column chart** on Sheet1.

2. Move the chart so that it is directly under the data.

3. Size the chart so that it is the same width as the occupied columns above it.

4. Click the **By Column button**.
   The data is charted by column.

5. Click the **By Row button**.
   The data is charted by row.

6. Click the **Chart Type button's down arrow**.
   A menu of chart types drops down.

7. Choose **Line**.

The chart data is plotted in a line chart.

8. Click the **Chart Type button's down arrow**.

9. Choose **Bar**.

The chart changes to a bar chart.

10. Click **outside the chart** to deselect it and then print the worksheet.

11. Click the **Chart Type button's down arrow** and choose **Column**.

12. Click the **Chart1 tab** to display the pie chart.

13. Click the title, **Total by Breed**.

The title is selected and has move handles around it. Notice that the Chart Objects box on the Chart toolbar now reads "Chart Title," showing that this is the object selected.

14. Click the Chart toolbar's **Format Chart Object button**.

Because the title is selected, the ScreenTip will read *Format Chart Title*. The Format Chart Title dialog box opens.

15. Click the **Font tab**.

The current font and font size are shown.

16. Change the Size to **24** and click **OK**.

The dialog box closes, and the title font size is changed.

17. Click the **white background area** of the chart.

The whole chart is selected, and the Chart Objects box now reads "Chart Area."

18. Press the **Delete key**.

The pie chart is deleted.

19. Click the **Undo button**.

The chart is restored.

20. Save the workbook.

21. Right-click different areas of the chart on the chart sheet and on Sheet1, choose any available option, and experiment with different formatting effects. Remember that you can click the Undo button whenever you make a change you don't like. Close the workbook without saving it when you have finished.

TASK 3 | *Copying Worksheet Data to a Microsoft Word Document*

What: Copy worksheet data to a Microsoft Word document.

How: Choose Edit | Copy and Edit | Paste.

Why: You may want to include worksheet data in a text document.

Tip: You can create and copy a worksheet containing a map of geographic regions if you use Excel's Map feature. Use Help to find out about this feature.

You have learned to copy data from one part of a sheet to another part of the same sheet. You also have copied from one sheet to another sheet in a workbook. Copying from Excel to a Microsoft Word document is done in the same way. To copy worksheet data:

1. Select the information that you want to copy.
2. Choose Edit | Copy.
3. Start Word, open the document into which you want to paste the data, and place the insertion point where you want the data to appear.
4. Choose Edit | Paste.

EXERCISE 3 | Copying Worksheet Data to a Microsoft Word Document

1. Open the **Quarterly Sales** workbook to Sheet1 and select **A1:F5**.
2. Choose **Edit | Copy**.
   The worksheet data is placed on the Windows Clipboard.
3. Click the **Start button** on the Windows taskbar.
4. Choose **Programs**, and then **Microsoft Word**.
   Word starts, with a new blank document on the screen. The insertion point is at the beginning of the document, ready for you to begin typing.
5. Create the following document in Word.

Yearly Sales

JRT Kennels had a good year last year. We sold more purebred Jack Russell terriers than ever before. We also sold small, mixed-breed dogs and Yorkshire terriers. The following table shows the sales of each breed by quarter.

If you are not familiar with Word, don't worry. Just type the text as shown. Press the Enter key *twice* after the heading and at the end of the text paragraph, but nowhere else. To format the heading, click and drag to select it, then use toolbar buttons (they are the same ones you know from Excel).

6. Choose **Edit | Paste**.
   The worksheet data is pasted into the document. Your document should look like Figure 8.6. If you are familiar with Word, you can click in the pasted data and see that it is a Word table.
7. Save the document as **Yearly Sales** following the same procedure used to save an Excel document.
8. Choose **File | Print** to print the Word document.
9. Keep the Word document open for use in the next exercise.

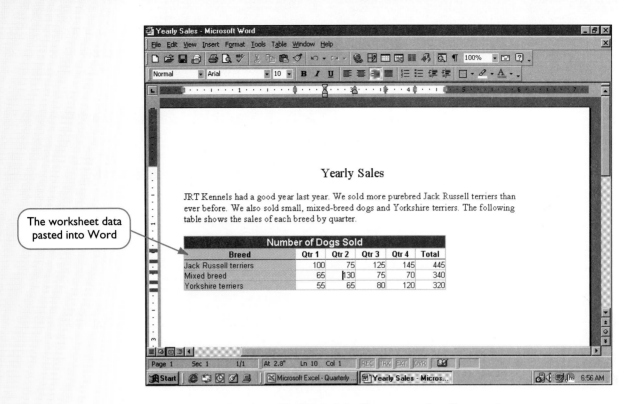

FIGURE **8.6** The *Yearly Sales* Document after Exercise 3

TASK 4 | Linking Worksheet Data to a Microsoft Word Document

What: Create a link from worksheet data to a Word document.

How: Choose Edit | Copy and Edit | Paste Special.

Why: When the original object is updated, the linked image will update too.

Tip: Always save your worksheet before linking between programs; the linking operation requires a large amount of your system resources, with the increased possibility of a system crash.

Copying data from Excel to Word is useful, but it is limited in that it creates static information in the Word document. If the data in the Excel worksheet changes, you have to remember to copy it into the Word document again, and delete or overwrite the old copy. To keep the Word document automatically updated if the Excel worksheet information changes, you need to create a link between the worksheet and the Word document.

To create a link:

1. Copy the data.
2. Open Microsoft Word.
3. Choose Edit | Paste Special. The Paste Special dialog box opens, as shown in Figure 8.7.
4. Select the Paste Link option button.
5. In the *As* box, choose Microsoft Excel Worksheet (or Chart) Object.
6. Click OK.

Word places a representation of the Excel data in the Word document along with a link to the Excel workbook. When you return to Excel and make changes in the worksheet, the data will be changed in the Word document also.

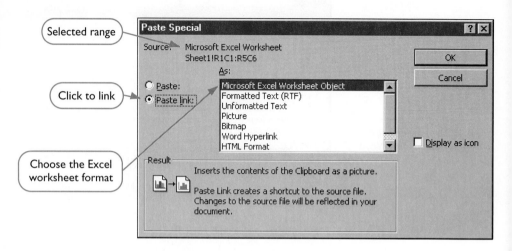

FIGURE 8.7 The Paste Special Dialog Box

POINTER

Copying, Linking, and Embedding

There are three ways to include an Excel object in a Word document: copy it, link it, or embed it. Copying was used in Task 3, and linking is used in Task 4. Embedding isn't used in this unit, but is explained here to complete the list. All three methods start with copying the Excel data.

- You can paste the Excel data from the Windows Clipboard directly into the Word document, as described in Task 3. This is quick and simple but limited.

- Using the Paste Special command in Word and choosing the Paste Link option, you can **link** the Excel object to the Word document, as described in Task 4. When you do this, a representation of the Excel object is placed in Word, along with a link to its original location (the Excel workbook). Now if the workbook is updated, the linked image in the Word document will be updated automatically. Linked objects must be edited in their original software application. If you double-click the linked Excel chart in the Word document, Excel will start and open the original workbook, so you can edit it there.

- You can use the Paste Special command in Word to **embed** the Excel object in the Word document. (Choose Paste instead of Paste Link in the Paste Special dialog box.) When you embed the object, an actual copy of the original, not just an image of it, is placed in the Word document, but it is independent of the original. Changes in the original are not carried over to the embedded object. When you double-click the embedded object in Word, the Word toolbar changes to show the Microsoft Excel commands, and you are able to edit the object from within Word.

Linking and embedding are the two elements of the technology known as Object Linking and Embedding, or **OLE** (pronounced "oh-lay").

EXERCISE 4 | Linking Worksheet Data to a Microsoft Word Document

1. If the *Yearly Sales* document and *Quarterly Sales* workbook are not both open, start Word and Excel and open them.

2. Click the Windows taskbar button for the **Quarterly Sales** workbook to display it and, with Sheet1 active, select **A1:F5**.

3. Choose **Edit | Copy**.
   The worksheet data is placed on the Windows Clipboard.

4. Click the **Yearly Sales button** on the Windows taskbar.
   The Word document is displayed on your screen.

5. Hold down **Ctrl** and press **End**.
   The insertion point moves to the bottom of the document, below the copy of the Excel data you made in Exercise 3.

6. Press **Enter** a few times.

7. Choose **Edit | Paste Special**.
   The Paste Special dialog box opens.

8. Select the **Paste Link option button**.

9. In the *As* box, choose **Microsoft Excel Worksheet Object** and click **OK**.
   An image of the Excel data is pasted into the Word document, along with a link to the original.

10. Save the document and then close it.
    Close the document by clicking the Close button on the menu bar. Word will remain open, but with no document on the screen.

11. Click the **Microsoft Excel button** on the Windows taskbar.
    Excel becomes active.

12. Change the number in **B3** to **200**.
    The formulas recompute and the chart redraws.

13. Save the workbook and exit from Excel.

14. Click the **Microsoft Word button** on the Windows taskbar.
    The Word window opens on the screen, but no document is open. If you exited from Word by mistake in step 10 just start Word again.

15. Click the **File** menu name and click the **Yearly Sales** file name at the bottom of the file menu.
    The document opens.

16. Compare the two versions of the Excel data in the document.
    The copied data has not changed, but the linked data shows 200 Jack Russell terriers sold in the first quarter. The document should look like Figure 8.8.

17. Double-click the linked data.
    Excel starts and opens the workbook.

18. Exit from both Excel and Word.

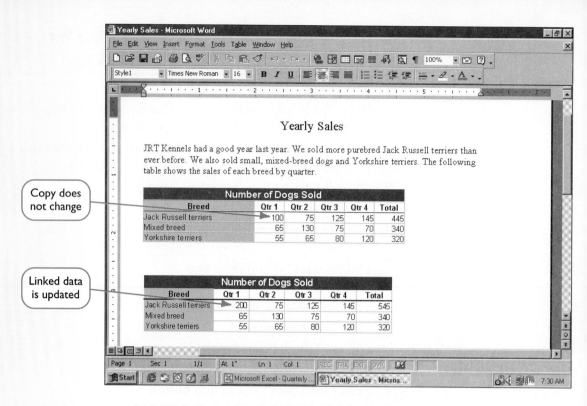

Copy does not change

Linked data is updated

FIGURE 8.8   The *Yearly Sales* Document after Exercise 4

TASK 5 | *Linking to the World Wide Web*

What: Create a link from an Excel worksheet to the World Wide Web.

How: Insert | Hyperlink.

Why: The World Wide Web is changing how we do business, learn, communicate, and have fun.

Tip: To learn more about the World Wide Web, you can search the Web itself for tips and tutorials.

You can link a cell in an Excel worksheet to a document located on the World Wide Web. That document can be anyplace in the world. If, for example, you wanted to link your worksheet to a government agency or organization that provides information on personal savings, you would format the text in your worksheet as a hyperlink. This link is called a **hyperlink** because it is hot; that is, when you click the hot text, you are transferred to the linked document.

To create a hyperlink in a worksheet:

1. Move to the cell where you want the hyperlink to appear and type the text you want your readers to see.
2. Choose Insert | Hyperlink. The Insert Hyperlink dialog box opens, as shown in Figure 8.9a.
3. If you know the Web address (called the **URL**, for **Uniform Resource Locator**), type it in the *Type the file or Web page name* text box.

4. If you do not know the address, click the Web page button to browse for the page on the Web.
5. Click OK to create the hyperlink. The text in the cell is formatted as a hyperlink (blue and underlined), as shown in Figure 8.9b. Now when you or another user opens the worksheet and clicks the link, the Web document will open in the computer's Web browser, as shown in Figure 8.9c.

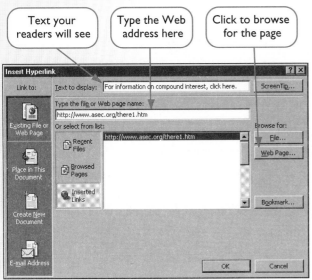

(a) The Insert Hyperlink Dialog Box

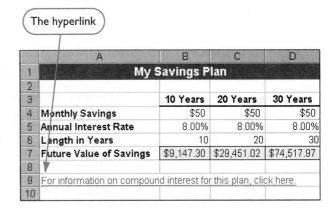

(b) The Hyperlink in the Workbook

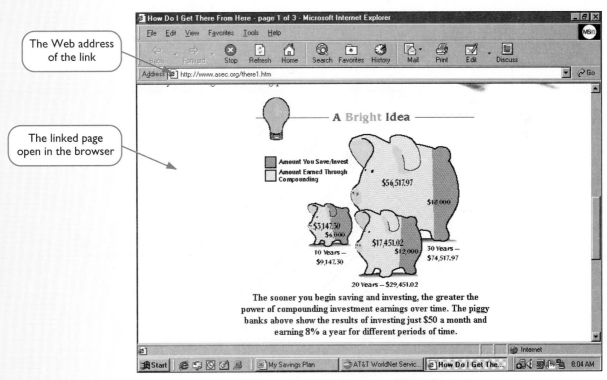

(c) The Linked Web Document Open in the Browser

FIGURE **8.9**   Inserting a Hyperlink in a Workbook

Linking to the World Wide Web

In order to link to a Web site successfully, you must have a network connection in the computer lab or a modem and an account with an Internet Service Provider.

EXERCISE 5 | *Linking to the World Wide Web*

1. Open the **Quarterly Sales** workbook.
2. Move to a blank cell below the worksheet data.
3. Type **Financial Net** and click the **Enter button** on the formula bar.
4. Choose **Insert | Hyperlink**.
   The Hyperlink dialog box opens, showing the contents of the active cell ("Financial Net") in the *Text to display* text box.
5. In the *Type the file or Web page name* text box type the following URL:
   http://www.financenet.gov
6. Click **OK**.
   The text is formatted as a hyperlink (blue with a single underline).
7. If you have a link to the Internet either in a lab through the network or at home with a modem and an account with an Internet Service Provider, click the **hypertext**.

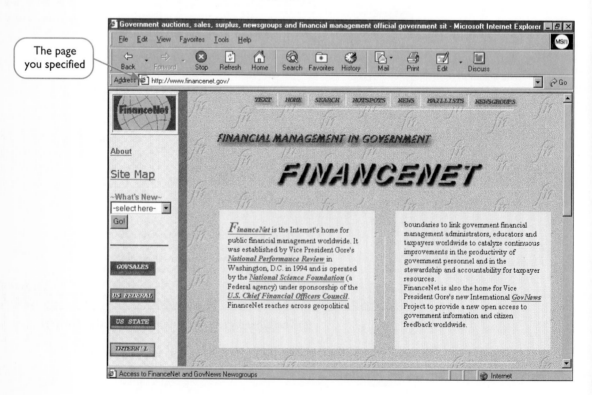

FIGURE **8.10**   The Exercise 5 Hyperlink Open in a Browser

The Financial Network Web site opens in your browser, as shown in Figure 8.10.

8. Close the browser and close the workbook without saving it.

TASK 6 | *Saving a Workbook as a Web Document*

What: Save a workbook in HTML format.

How: Choose File | Save As Web Page.

Why: You can include a worksheet on your Web site.

Tip: Make sure all the data and formulas in your worksheet are correct before posting it for others to see.

Web documents are saved as a different type of file from regular Excel worksheets. Web documents are saved in the universal Web language **HTML**, or **HyperText Markup Language**—the computer language that is understood by all browser software.

You can save any workbook as a Web document using Excel 2000, and it will be converted into HTML for you.

To save a workbook as a Web document:

1. Open or create a normal Excel workbook.
2. Choose File | Save as Web Page.
3. Type a file name in the File name text box.
4. Make sure the *Save as type* is set to Web Page.
5. Check the Save in location, changing it as necessary.
6. Click Save.

> ### POINTER
>
> **Formatting Conversion**
>
> Excel may caution you that some features aren't supported by browsers. It's safe to click the Continue button.

The document is ready to be posted to the World Wide Web or to a server on your company or school intranet.

> ### POINTER
>
> **Publishing Your Web Page**
>
> After creating a Web page, you will want to make it available to other people. To publish to the World Wide Web, contact an Internet Service Provider to host your page. Find out how to structure your files for the ISP's server. Then copy all files, including all graphics, to the ISP.

EXERCISE 6 | *Saving a Workbook as a Web Document*

1. Open the **Quarterly Sales** workbook.
2. Choose **File | Save as Web Page**.
3. In the File name text box, type **Quarter**, check that the *Save as type* text box is set to *Web page*, choose a drive on which to store the file, and click **Save**.

   The workbook is saved as a Web page in the location you chose.
4. Exit from Excel.
5. Use My Computer to display the contents of the drive or folder where you saved the workbook.

   You will find a folder named *Quarter files* and a document named *Quarter*.
6. Double-click the **Quarter** document.

   Your browser will start and will display the document. Notice that because you saved the whole workbook, you can click the Chart1 tab at the bottom of the page and view the pie chart too. Your screen will look similar to Figure 8.11.
7. View the document and then exit from the browser.

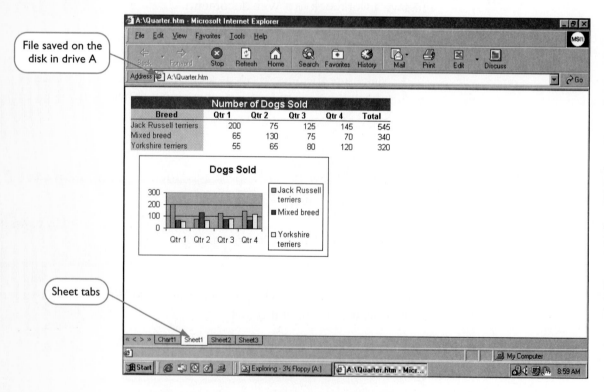

FIGURE 8.11   The *Quarter* Document Viewed with Internet Explorer

REVIEW

SUMMARY

After completing this unit, you should be able to

- create charts (page 182)
- enhance charts (page 189)
- copy worksheet data to Microsoft Word (page 191)
- link worksheet data to Microsoft Word (page 193)
- link to the Word Wide Web (page 196)
- save a workbook as a Web document (page 199)

KEY TERMS

data range (page 185)
data series (page 183)
embed (page 194)
gridlines (page 183)
hyperlink (page 196)
HTML—HyperText Markup Language (page 199)
legend (page 183)

link (page 194)
OLE (page 194)
plot area (page 183)
URL—Uniform Resource Locator (page 196)
x axis (page 183)
y axis (page 183)

TEST YOUR SKILLS

True/False

1. You can link Excel worksheets to documents on the World Wide Web.
2. You cannot create an active link from Excel to Word.
3. If you copy information from Excel to Word, the information is static.
4. Charts help others understand numeric data.
5. Excel includes a map feature for geographical data.

Multiple Choice

1. To chart data that changes over time, you would use a
   a. pie chart
   b. line chart
   c. radar chart
   d. all of these answers

2. To chart one body of data, you would use a
   a. pie chart
   b. line chart
   c. radar chart
   d. all of these answers

3. A chart legend
   a. is used only in column charts
   b. replaces a chart title
   c. describes what the bars represent
   d. all of these answers

4. Microsoft Excel allows you to copy
   a. worksheet data
   b. charts
   c. active links
   d. of these answers
5. To link to a document on the World Wide Web, you create
   a. a hyperlink
   b. a hypercell
   c. a hypersheet
   d. all of these answers

Short Answer

1. The address of a Web document is called its _____.
2. You can create an _____ link between worksheet data and a Word document.
3. Excel charts are easy to create using the _____ _____.
4. In order to link to documents on the World Wide Web, your computer needs to have a network link in the computer lab or a _____ and a link to an Internet Service Provider.
5. You can select noncontiguous cells by holding down the _____ key while using the mouse.

What Does This Do?

Write a description of the function of the following:

1.		6.	
2.		7.	
3.		8.	http://www.irs.gov
4.		9.	
5.		10.	

On Your Own

1. Open a worksheet and create a chart of data.
2. Using the chart in #1, change the chart type and format numerous times to experiment.
3. Open a workbook and save the document as a Web document.
4. Open a workbook and copy a chart to Microsoft Word. Type text to accompany the worksheet chart and print the Word document.

5. Open a worksheet and link it to the following Web address: http://library.advanced.org/10326/investment_basics/index.html. Click the hyperlink to connect to the Web site shown in Figure 8.12.

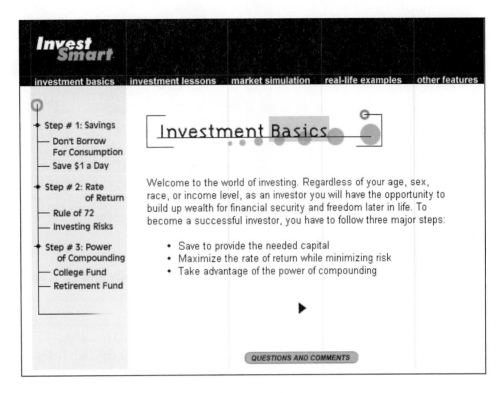

FIGURE 8.12

PROJECTS

1. Create the following worksheet or open **Candle Analysis**:

	A	B	C	D	E	F
1	**Spread the Light Candles**					
2	**Sales Analysis**					
3		January	February	March	Total	Average
4	Votive	175	200	150		
5	Tapers	400	300	350		
6	Tea	450	475	400		

   a. Create the formulas for Total and Average.
   b. Chart the three-month's data in a column chart.
   c. Include a title and legend on the chart.
   d. Create a pie chart of the total sales for three types of candles.
   e. Include a title and legend on the chart.
   f. Print the worksheet with the chart.
   g. Save the workbook as **Candle Analysis**.

2. Using the *Candle Analysis* worksheet, copy the two charts to Microsoft Word. Write an explanation in Word to accompany the charts. Print the Word document.

3. Create the following worksheet or open **Net Worth**:

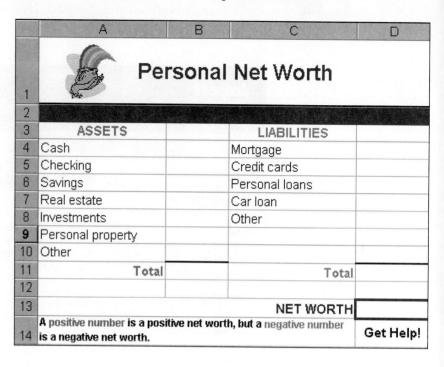

	A	B	C	D
1			Personal Net Worth	
2				
3	ASSETS		LIABILITIES	
4	Cash		Mortgage	
5	Checking		Credit cards	
6	Savings		Personal loans	
7	Real estate		Car loan	
8	Investments		Other	
9	Personal property			
10	Other			
11	Total		Total	
12				
13			NET WORTH	
14	A positive number is a positive net worth, but a negative number is a negative net worth.			Get Help!

a. Write a formula to total the assets.
b. Write a formula to total the liabilities.
c. Write a formula to subtract liabilities from assets.
d. Using the text in D14, create a hyperlink to the following URL:
   http://www.sec.gov/consumer/cosra/brochure.htm
e. Copy the worksheet to a second sheet.
f. Enter numbers in the cells on the second sheet.
g. Save the file as **Net Worth**.
h. Print the worksheet.
i. Print the formulas.
j. Print the consumer brochure that you linked to.
k. Save the workbook as a Web document.
l. Open the Web version in your browser.
m. Print the Web page.

4. Open the Currency workbook you created at the end of Unit 2.
   a. Move to A16 and type **Yahoo Currency Calculator**.
   b. Select the text and link it to the following URL:
      http://quote.yahoo.com/m3?u
   c. Test the link.
   d. Print the Currency Exchange Calculator.
   e. Print the worksheet.

PROJECTS

1. Create the following worksheet or open **Toys**:

	A	B	C	D	E	F
1			JRT Dog and Cat Toys Sales by Location			
2		Valley Mall	Downtown	Garden Way	Capital Center	Total
3	Catnip mice					
4	Fake bones					
5	Rawhide Chews					
6	Feather Friends					
7	Total					

   a. Write formulas to compute the totals.

   b. Insert a graphic.

   c. Format the worksheet.

   d. Copy the worksheet to Sheet2.

   e. Rename Sheet2 **Qtr1**.

   f. Enter the data shown here:

	A	B	C	D	E	F
2		Valley Mall	Downtown	Garden Way	Capital Center	Total
3	Catnip mice	350.50	125.00	225.75	400.00	
4	Fake bones	400.00	300.00	450.50	300.00	
5	Rawhide Chews	200.00	200.00	200.00	250.00	
6	Feather Friends	500.00	400.00	300.00	500.00	
7	Total					

   g. Create a column chart of four toys by location.

   h. Print the worksheet and the chart.

   i. Print the formulas.

   j. Create a bar chart of the four locations by toys.

   k. Print the worksheet and the two charts.

   l. Create a pie chart of the total sales by location.

   m. Create a pie chart of total sales by category.

   n. Include a header that has your name at the left margin and the text **Check Point 4-1** at the right margin.

o. Print the worksheet and all four charts.

p. Save the workbook as **Toys**.

q. Copy the worksheet to Microsoft Word.

r. Write a two-sentence report in Word.

s. Print the report, including the worksheet.

2. Use the **Toys** workbook you created in Project 1.

a. Copy Sheet1 to a blank sheet.

b. Rename the sheet **Qtr2**.

c. Enter the data shown here:

	A	B	C	D	E	F
2		Valley Mall	Downtown	Garden Way	Capital Center	Total
3	Catnip mice	550.50	425.00	425.75	300.00	
4	Fake bones	300.00	350.00	350.50	300.00	
5	Rawhide Chews	400.00	280.00	500.00	350.00	
6	Feather Friends	200.00	200.00	400.00	300.00	
7	Total					

d. Copy Sheet1 to another blank sheet.

e. Rename the sheet **Qtr3**.

f. Enter the data shown here:

	A	B	C	D	E	F
2		Valley Mall	Downtown	Garden Way	Capital Center	Total
3	Catnip mice	250.50	525.00	200.75	600.00	
4	Fake bones	300.00	400.00	250.50	500.00	
5	Rawhide Chews	500.00	500.00	400.00	550.00	
6	Feather Friends	200.00	200.00	500.00	400.00	
7	Total					

g. Copy Sheet1 to another blank sheet.

h. Name the sheet Qtr4.

i. Enter the data shown here:

	A	B	C	D	E	F
2		Valley Mall	Downtown	Garden Way	Capital Center	Total
3	Catnip mice	650.50	400.00	600.00	400.00	
4	Fake bones	600.00	400.00	550.00	700.00	
5	Rawhide Chews	700.00	700.00	500.00	450.00	
6	Feather Friends	400.00	600.00	300.00	600.00	
7	Total					

j. On a new blank sheet, create a consolidation sheet.
  • Total all four quarters by location and category.
  • Find the average sales at each location.
  • Create a chart of the totals data.

k. Save the workbook.

l. Print the consolidation worksheet.

m. Print the formulas.

WRAP-UP

You can use Excel to take control of your personal finances. To do so create the following worksheets, formatting them as appropriate:

- Create a three-month budget. Keep track of actual expenses and show the difference between budgeted and actual.

- Create a personal net worth statement.

- Modify or create a personal checkbook register.

- Create a savings sheet for a personal goal. Compare different amounts or different rates.

- Analyze the actual data for a loan that you might get.

- Create a depreciation worksheet for your computer.

- Create a worksheet that analyzes your tax data. Show earnings and taxes. Link the sheet to the following URL:

    http://www.irs.gov/plain/forms_pubs/pubs/p402.htm

- Format all sheets as appropriate.

Save and print the workbooks and the formulas.

NOTE: If you are asked to complete this wrap-up as an assignment, you can change the figures in any or all of the worksheets so that you are not revealing personal information.

Getting Started

UNIT OBJECTIVES

- Start Microsoft Access 2000
- Become familiar with the Access interface
- Become familiar with Access tables
- Become familiar with forms and reports
- Save objects in Access
- Close objects and exit Access
- Become familiar with database design

Microsoft Access 2000 is **database management system** software. In this book, you will learn how to create a database, organize and update the data, ask questions called **queries** to find the information that you need, and choose attractive and functional methods for viewing the information on screen and in printed reports.

Unit 1 gets you started learning about databases and the main components of Access. The unit assumes you know basic computer and Windows skills, such as how to use a mouse and the keyboard to enter data, as well as how menus and buttons work. If you need help with these skills, begin with *Quick, Simple Microsoft Windows 98* in this series.

What: Start Microsoft Access 2000.

How: Click the Start button and choose Programs | Microsoft Access.

Why: You must know how to start an application in order to use it.

Tip: If you are working in a computer lab, you may be given instructions for another way to start Access.

You are probably like most people in that you collect information and even organize it for easier access. In that sense, you are already familiar with databases. A database can be as simple as an address book containing the names, addresses, and telephone numbers of family and friends; as large as the Social Security Administration's collection of names, numbers, earnings, and benefits; or as complex as WalMart's lists of inventory, suppliers, employees, sales, and prices.

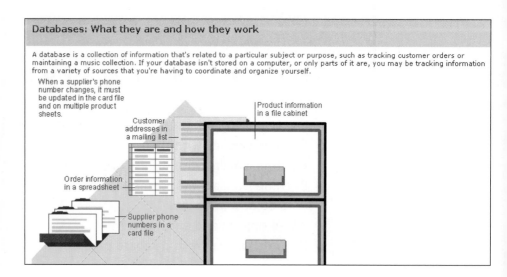

All these lists have certain components in common. The most basic element of a database is data. For example, a telephone number such as (201) 555-7382 represents a single item of **data**. One data element may be a social security number, a part number, a quantity of products available, the amount of a sale, or a date. Data alone are merely numbers or letters. When you collect and organize data, you get **information**. Data serves as the raw material, whereas information helps us to make decisions. For example, a list of all employees of a company can be viewed as data. Information results when the employee list is used to provide reports that show employees by department, alphabetized lists of employees with their telephone extensions and e-mail addresses, or lists of employees that fit certain categories such as those that have received training or those that belong to a certain group.

A set of data in the list is referred to as a **record**. For example, a record in your address book is the row that contains a person's name, address, and phone number. A record in an employee database is all of the personal information about one employee. Each record contains the same **fields** or catagories located in columns, such as name, street address, city, postal code, and telephone number.

A collection of similar records is commonly called a database, but Access uses the term **table**. Within a table, you typically have some specific type of organization. For example, most address books alphabetize entries, called records, by last name so that you have a page or two for the As, for the Bs, and so on. Similarly, an Access address table can list entries alphabetically or numerically, as shown in Figure 1.1.

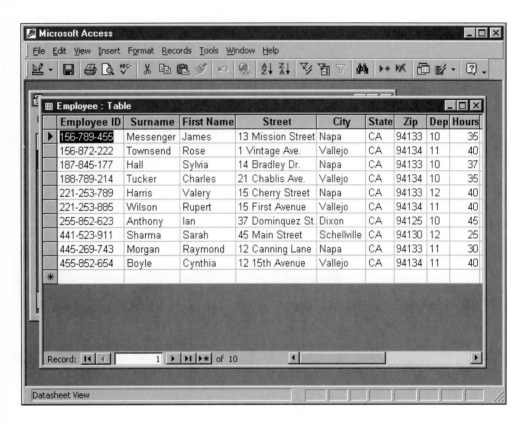

FIGURE 1.1   An Electronic Address Book

RELATIONAL DATABASES

Access, like most **database management systems (DBMS)** available today, is a **relational database management system**. A relational DBMS is more powerful than paper-based systems, such as an address book, because it contains many tables that are linked together. For example, your paper address book may contain other information besides addresses and phone numbers for your friends, business associates, and relatives. It may contain a calendar where you write down appointments, birthdays, and anniversaries. While the same cover holds both "tables," the calendar table and the address table, they are not connected or linked as they can be when input electronically using a DBMS.

When you collect together one or more tables of related data in Access, you have a **database**. This database is a single file stored on your disk that contains all of the related data for a business application. An Access database may contain other objects, such as reports or queries, which allow you to retrieve and view data stored in tables in meaningful ways.

STARTING ACCESS 2000

If you want to create a database yourself or to use an existing database, you need to start Access. To start Access, follow these steps:

1. Click the Start button on the Windows taskbar.
2. Point to Programs.
3. Click Microsoft Access, as shown in Figure 1.2.

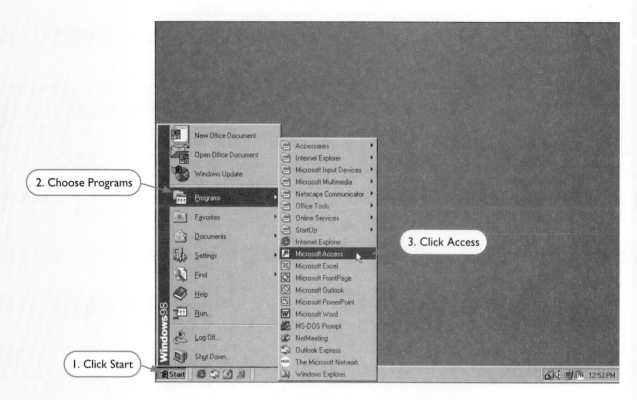

FIGURE 1.2   Starting Microsoft Access

Access starts and displays the Microsoft Access dialog box, as shown in Figure 1.3. This dialog box asks if you want to create a new database or open an existing one.

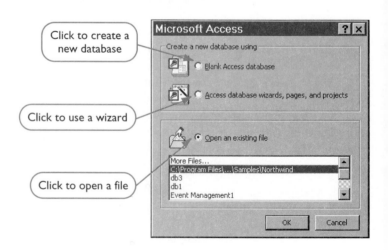

FIGURE 1.3   The Microsoft Access Opening Dialog Box

Unlike Word or Excel, which allow you to open blank documents or worksheets, you must open an existing database or create a new one in order to view the database screen. Access 2000 includes a sample database named Northwind that you will use in the following exercises to help become familiar with Access.

1. Click Northwind in the dialog box.
2. Click OK.

The Northwind: Database window opens, as shown in Figure 1.4.

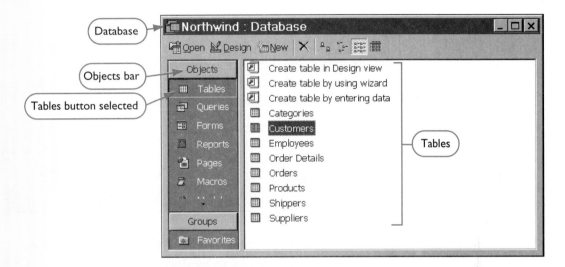

FIGURE 1.4   Northwind Database

POINTER

Getting Help

Microsoft provides on-line Help for Access 2000, just as it does for all applications. Use Help to find answers to your questions, as you would for Word or Excel. Remember that you can print help documents by clicking the Print button. When the Print dialog box displays, click OK.

POINTER

Opening an Existing Database

If you see the name of an Access database file in the initial Access dialog box, you can double-click it to start Access and open the file automatically. If the file you want is not listed in the dialog box, choose the More Files option to display the Open dialog box.

EXERCISE 1 | *Starting Access*

1. Click the **Start button** on the Windows taskbar.
The Start menu opens.

2. Point to **Programs**.
The Programs menu opens.

3. Click **Microsoft Access**.
The opening Access dialog box displays.

4. Select Northwind and click **OK**.
The Northwind: Database window displays.

5. Keep the window open for use in the next exercise.

TASK 2 | *Becoming Familiar with the Access Interface*

What: Learn the various parts of the Database window.
How: Use the mouse to explore.
Why: Much of your activity in Access will begin with choices made in the Database window.
Tip: When you pause the mouse pointer over many areas of the screen, a ScreenTip appears, giving the name of the element to which the mouse pointer is pointing.

Unlike Word or Excel, Access does not begin with a blank area for you to begin typing. Instead, it shows the Database window with objects in the Objects bar, which is located along the left edge of the window. These **objects** are the elements that make up an Access database. Notice that Tables is one type of object in an Access database. Table 1.1 describes the objects listed on the Objects bar.

Object	Description
Tables	Tables are the basic components upon which all other database objects work. Tables store the data about one specific topic. Databases in Access usually contain more than one table.
Queries	Queries turn the raw data of a table into information by allowing you to ask questions about the data. When you run the query, Access displays the data that matches or answers the question you asked.
Forms	Forms, which make data entry easier and more accurate, are used to type a new record or edit existing table data.

(continued)

TABLE 1.1   Access Objects

▣ Reports	Reports specify how you want information to appear when it is printed.
▤ Pages	A data access page interacts with live data via the Internet. The data exists in a separate database file, outside of the Access database that holds the data access page. You also can use data access pages to distribute data from Access via e-mail or to create and edit Web information.
▤ Macros	A macro stores a series of actions or commands that happen in sequence. You can give the macro a name and attach it to a command button.
▥ Modules	Modules automate and customize Access databases.

TABLE 1.1 Access Objects *(continued)*

To display a list showing the contents of each type of object, click the button with the object type name on the **Objects bar**. For example, to see the tables contained in a database, click the Tables button on the Objects bar. The list of tables in the database is displayed in the right pane of the Database window, as shown in Figure 1.4.

TABLES

To work with the data in a table, you must open the table. For example, to open the Customers table in the Northwind database, follow these steps:

1. Click the Table button on the Objects bar.
2. Click the Customers table.
3. Click the Open button on the Database toolbar.

The Customers table displays, as shown in Figure 1.5.

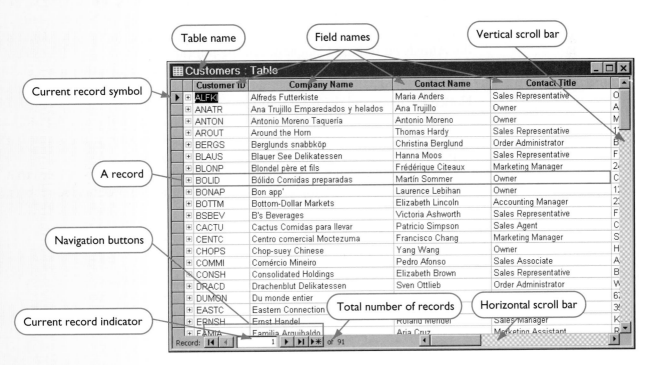

FIGURE 1.5 Customers Table Window

EXERCISE 2 | *Opening a Table*

1. Click the **Tables button** in Northwind Database window.
  The list of tables displays in the right pane of the Database window.

2. Click the **Customers** table in the table listing.
  The Customers table is selected.

3. Click the **Open button** on the Database toolbar.
  The Customers table displays.

4. Keep the table open for use in the next exercise.

TASK 3 | *Becoming Familiar with Access Tables*

What: Navigate, edit, and print a table.

How: Use navigation and toolbar buttons to display and print data in a table.

Why: Tables can contain hundreds or even thousands of records, so you must be able to locate a particular record.

Tip: Use the Maximize button on the title bar to display as much data on the screen as possible.

Access tables display the data that has been entered into the database. The data is divided into elements called fields, and all the fields associated with one entry in the table make up a record. For example, the Customers table includes the fields: Customer ID, Company Name, Contact Name, Contact Title, and so on. The first record in the Customers table displays the data for the Alfreds Futterkiste Company. All the information about the Alfreds Futterkiste Company appears under the correct field heading. Furthermore, each record in the database contains the same type of data under the same fields. Notice the fields and the records displayed in Figure 1.5.

The **current record symbol** that appears to the left of the first field indicates the current record, and the **current record indicator** in the status bar displays the current record number, as shown in Figure 1.5.

You can view records that appear below the current display and fields that appear to the right of the display by using the horizontal and vertical scroll bars.

You can move to records in the table using the navigation buttons located on the status bar. Table 1.2 describes the navigation buttons.

Button	Description
◄	Makes the first record in the table the current record.
◄	Makes the record previous to the current record in the table the active record.
►	Makes the record immediately after the current record in the table the active record.
►|	Makes the last record in the table the current record.
►✳	Creates a new blank record at the end of the table.

TABLE 1.2   Table Navigation Buttons

To edit an existing record, follow these steps:
1. Make the record to be edited the current record using one of the navigation tools.
2. Click in the field to be edited.
3. Use the Backspace or Delete keys to delete unwanted characters or select the field information and press the Delete key to clear the field.
4. Type new data.
5. Input the data into the field, using one of the following methods:

- Press Enter to move to the right one field in the same record and continue editing the record. A pencil icon appears in the place of the current record indicator to indicate that the record is being edited.

- Click the mouse in another record. The current record indicator moves to the new record.

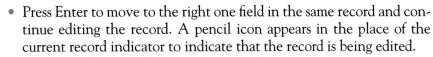

POINTER

Undoing the Last Change

You can use the Undo button to restore an edited record to its original condition. However, Access allows you to undo only the last action performed. For example, if you edit two records and change your mind, you will only be able to undo the edit you made to the last record. The previous edit can't be undone.

To add a new record to the table, click the New Record button. Access automatically adds a blank record at the bottom of the table and marks it with an *(asterisk). Type the new information in the appropriate fields.

Closing a Table

To close an open table, click the Close button on the Table window's title bar. The Table window closes and the Database window displays.

To see what the table will look like when printed, choose File | Print Preview. The table displays as shown in Figure 1.6.

Print button

Close button

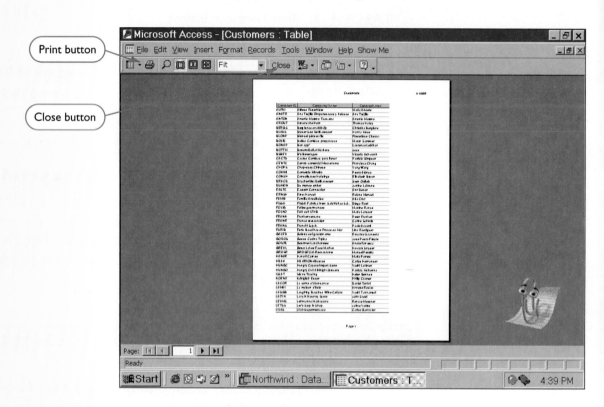

FIGURE 1.6   Print Preview

You use the Access print preview just as you do any other Office 2000 preview screen. If you are satisfied with the print format used by Access, click the Print button on the Preview toolbar, or you can return to the database table by clicking the Close button on the Preview toolbar.

To change the look of the table printout, choose File | Page Setup. The Page Setup dialog box displays, as shown in Figures 1.7a and 1.7b.

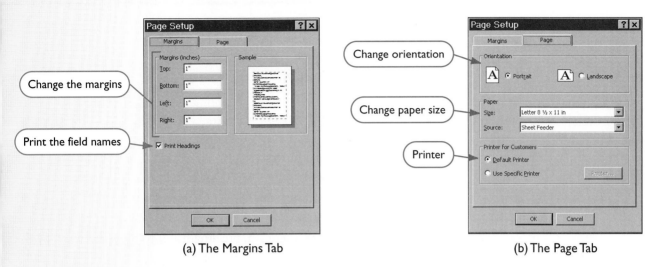

Change the margins

Print the field names

Change orientation

Change paper size

Printer

(a) The Margins Tab

(b) The Page Tab

FIGURE 1.7   The Page Setup Dialog Box

- Use the Margins tab, shown in Figure 1.7a, to change the margins on the printed page. You can also omit printing the field names by removing the check from the Print Headings check box; however, printing the field names helps clarify the data.

- Use the Page tab of the Page Setup dialog box, shown in Figure 1.7b, to change the orientation of the paper from portrait to landscape, the paper size, and the printer that will print the table.

To print a table, use one of the following methods:

- Click the Print button to send the table directly to the designated printer.

- Choose File | Print to display the Print dialog box, as shown in Figure 1.8. Use the Print dialog box just as you would for all other Office software, with one exception: to print only a range of records, select the range before opening the dialog box and choose Selected Records in the Print Range.

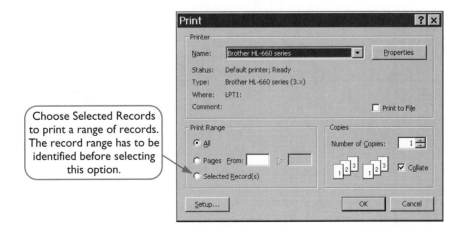

Choose Selected Records to print a range of records. The record range has to be identified before selecting this option.

FIGURE 1.8   The Print Dialog Box

1. Using the Customers table, click the **Next button**.
   Record two becomes the active record.
2. Click the **Previous button**.
   Record one becomes the active record.
3. Click the **Last Record button**.
   The last record becomes the active record.
4. Click the **First Record button**.
   Record one becomes the active record.
5. Click the **New Record button**.
   A new blank record is added to the end of the table.
6. Enter the data shown in Table 1.3, pressing **Enter** to move between fields.

Field Name	Field Data
Customer ID	ZZZWI
Company Name	Western Sun Imports
Contact Name	Natalie Ericksen
Contact Title	Buyer
Address	1300 University Ave.
City	Eugene
Region	OR
Postal Code	97406
Country	USA
Phone	(541) 678-0987
Fax	(541) 656-4567

TABLE 1.3   New Customer Record

7. Click the **First Record button**.
   Record one becomes the active record.
8. Click in the **Contact Name** field for Record 1.
   Contact Name is the active field.
9. Delete **Maria Anders** and type **Sue Smith**.
   Sue Smith replaces Maria Anders as the Contact Name for the first record.

10. Click the **Undo button**.
    Marie Anders is restored to the Contact Name field for the first record.
11. Choose **File | Print**.
    The Print dialog box displays.

12. Click **OK**.

The table prints on the selected printer.

13. Click the **Close button** on the Customers table title bar.

The table is closed and the Database window displays.

| TASK 4 | *Becoming Familiar with Forms and Reports* |

What: Use other database objects to view and print data.

How: Choose Forms or Reports in the Database dialog box.

Why: You use forms to input data and reports to create attractive printouts.

Tip: Access 2000 provides a report option that allows you to create mailing labels from the address data stored in a database. Search Help for more information.

Forms and Reports are Access objects used to work with the data stored in tables, allowing you to view and print formatted data.

FORMS

Access **forms** are database objects that simplify data entry. To open a form, follow these steps:

1. Click the Forms button in the Database dialog box.
2. Select the desired form.
3. Click the Open button on the Database toolbar.

The form displays, as shown in Figure 1.9.

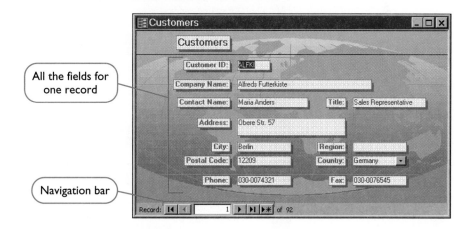

FIGURE 1.9   The Customers Form

All fields for one record are displayed on the form so that you can add and edit records more easily than you can working in table view. The data being viewed is the same data that is saved in the table; forms are just a different way to view it. Notice that forms use the same navigation buttons to move between records that a table uses.

One advantage of forms over tables is their ability to display graphic images, such as the photograph of a Northwind employee displayed in the Employee form in Figure 1.10. A table can display only a reference to the actual photograph.

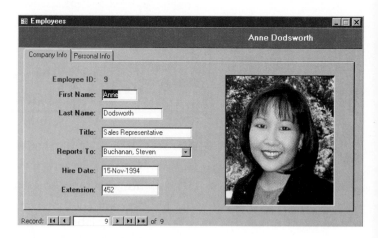

FIGURE 1.10   Photo Displays on a Form

REPORTS

Reports are formatting instructions that Access follows to print the information contained in a table so that it is clear and attractive. To view a report, follow these steps:

1. Click the Reports button in the Database dialog box.
2. Select the report from the list.
3. Click the Preview button.

The report displays, as shown in Figure 1.11.

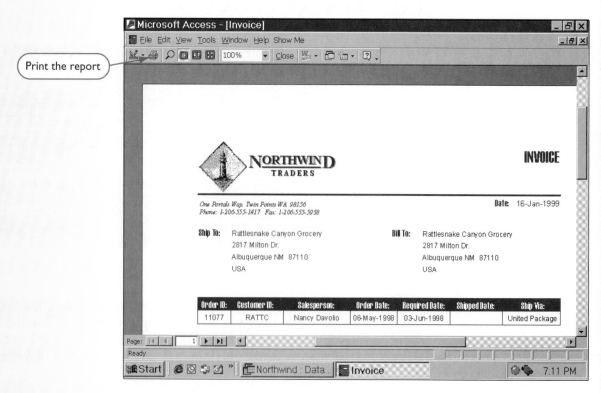

FIGURE 1.11   A Sample Report

If the report meets your approval, click the Print button on the Preview toolbar. The report is printed on the default printer.

POINTER

Switching Between Open Windows

You may wish to switch to a different window when you have more than one object open at once, because each object opens in its own window. For example, you may have both a table and a form or two tables open at the same time. Open the Window menu, then choose the object name to switch to the window for the selected object.

EXERCISE 4 | *Using Forms and Reports*

1. Click the **Forms button** in the Database dialog box.
  The list of forms displays.

2. Click the **Suppliers form** and click the **Open button**.
  The Suppliers form displays.

3. Use the navigational buttons to display various records.
  Click the Close button on the Suppliers title bar.

4. Click the **Reports button** in the Database dialog box.
  The list of reports displays.

5. Click the **Summary of Sales by Quarter** report.
  The report is selected.

6. Click the **Preview button**.
  The report displays.

7. Click the **Print button** on the Print Preview window toolbar.
  A copy of the report is printed.

8. Leave the report on the screen for use in the next exercise.

TASK 5 | *Saving Database Objects and Closing a Database*

What: Save changes you made to a database object.

How: Click the Save button or choose File | Save.

Why: Whenever you make changes to an object in the database, you must save the object before you close its window and continue working with the database.

Tip: Because you save changes to the database objects as you go, you do not have to save the whole database file when you close it.

The process of saving an Access database file doesn't resemble the saving process in any other Windows application you've ever used. Unlike Word, Excel, and PowerPoint, you cannot create a file in Access, type information, and print it without saving. In fact, Access requires you to name and save the database design *first*, before you even begin to create objects or enter records. Furthermore, every time you make changes to a table design, query, form, or report, you must save that object before closing it.

Because Access requires you to save any changes before continuing, it prompts you to save an object you're closing, even if you have forgotten to click the Save button. Tables represent one significant exception. Access automatically saves changes, additions, and deletions to table data, so you never need to remember to save your table.

You generally close database objects before you close the database itself. As each object is closed, Access reminds you to save it if you have made changes to its design. When you close the database, Access closes any open objects first, and if there were changes to those objects, Access reminds you to save them before closing the database. So if you're paying attention to the prompts, it is difficult to lose your work in Access.

EXERCISE 5 | *Saving an Object and Closing a Database*

1. With the Summary of Sales by Quarter report on the screen, click the **Close button**.
   Because you made no changes, you do not need to save it before you close it.

2. Click the **Close button** on the Database window to close the database file.
   The window closes with no reminder, and you don't have to save the database file itself.

3. Exit Access by clicking the **Close button** for the Access window or by choosing **File | Exit** from the menu.

TASK 6 | *Designing Databases*

What: Before you create a database, you need to be familiar with how to design one.

How: Analyze data before you sit down at the computer.

Why: A poorly designed database can keep you from accessing the desired information.

Tip: Gather all output needed from the database, such as reports, invoices, phone lists, and so on, before you begin to design the structure of the tables.

This unit teaches you about Access 2000 by using a built-in database named Northwind. In the next unit, you learn to create a database from scratch using Access. However, before you sit down at your computer with Access running to create a database, you need to design the database on paper. Unlike creating a document in word processing software, creating the structure of a database requires careful planning. You must determine the fields that tables should contain, the tables that the database should contain, and the relationships between the tables.

Step 1 | Determine All Fields

To help you determine what fields are needed in tables, you should gather all the data that the application will use and study how output, such as reports, will use the data. For example, if you need to compile statistics about minority employees, you must have a field in a table in the personnel database that contains that information. Analyze all paper reports and forms to help you determine the necessary data and break down all fields into their smallest element. For example, instead of a Name field, divide the data into first name, middle initial, and last name so that later you can use the fields separately.

Step 2 | Group Related Fields

Although this step sounds easy, many people have trouble with it when applying it to fields. Think about entering the data to help you define the grouping. For example, if you will be inputting data from a paper form, make sure that all the data on the form is grouped together for easy data entry.

Step 3 | Create Tables

Once you have related fields grouped together, create and name the tables that will contain the fields. Doing this ahead of time on paper will be a valuable aid when you sit down at your computer.

Step 4 | Normalize the Data

Normalizing the data means to eliminate redundancy. For example, if your instructor wants to keep student information such as the home address and phone number along with courses the student has taken and grades for the courses in one table, she would have duplicate data. She could place the information for a student along with the course and the grade. However, when the student takes a second or third course from her, she would have to enter the student's personal information a second and third time, along with the course and grade information. Redundancy leads to errors. Inputting the same data over and over is a waste of time, but even worse, what happens when the student moves? If your instructor doesn't get all the redundant data updated, then the database is corrupt.

The solution is to break the data into tables and link the tables. Your instructor could have a student table that contains personal information, a course table, and a grade table. A relationship would exist between these tables to associate grades and courses with specific students.

Step 5 | Define the Primary Key

A **primary key** is a field that uniquely identifies each record in the table. For example, last names don't work in the Student table because we might have more than one Smith or Jones in the table. To the IRS or even a college, we are uniquely identified by our social security number, so that could function as a primary key in a student or personnel table. If no field exists that uniquely identifies each record, Access provides the AutoNumber data type or you can create your own.

The primary key links tables together by adding one field's unique identification field (primary key) to another table to create a relationship. For example, if your instructor created a student table, a course table, and a grade table, she would need to link them together. She would use the Student ID to uniquely identify each record in the student table and the course Registration Number to uniquely identify each course in the course table. She would relate the information from both tables, using the grade table. The grade table would include only the Student ID to identify the student, the Registration Number to identify the course, and the final grade each student earns in each course. When you take a second course from her, she would use the grade table again and your Student ID to identify you. The Registration Number would still identify the second course in the course table, and the grade for that course would be input. Table 1.4 shows the Grade table.

StudentID	RegNum	Grade
456-89-1111	8765	A
345-87-3456	9876	B
980-76-8765	8765	C
456-89-1111	9876	A

TABLE 1.4   The Grade Table

Notice that the first student took two courses from this instructor and that more than one student took each course. When a student moves, the data in the student table is updated. There is no duplicate data because the student table has one record for each student.

In Unit 2, you learn the steps to follow in Access to define the primary key and link tables.

EXERCISE 6 | *Analyzing Data*

1. Use your collection of music CDs as sample data to analyze on paper.
2. Write down information on seven CDs, making sure that you have more than one CD from the same music company.
3. Notice that you have redundant data.
4. Divide the information into two tables. Create one table for the CD information such as artist, title, and so on. Create a second table for music company information such as address, phone, and so on.
5. Create a primary key for the records in the music company table, such as CompanyID.
6. Include the CompanyID field in the CD table. This will link the tables together.

You will learn more about relationships in the next unit.

REVIEW

SUMMARY

After completing this unit, you should be
- able to start Microsoft Access 2000 (page 2)
- familiar with the Access interface (page 6)
- familiar with Access tables (page 8)
- familiar with forms and reports (page 13)
- able to save objects in Access (page 15)
- able to close objects and exit Access (page 15)
- able to design a database (page 16)

KEY TERMS

current record indicator (page 8)
current record symbol (page 8)
data (page 2)
database (page 3)
database management system (DBMS) (page 3)
field (page 3)
form (page 13)
information (page 2)
normalizing (page 17)

objects (page 6)
Objects bar (page 7)
primary key (page 18)
query (page 1)
record (page 2)
relational database management system (page 3)
report (page 14)
table (page 3)

TEST YOUR SKILLS

True/False

1. Access is an example of a database management system.
2. "Information" means the same thing as "data."
3. An Access database usually contains one table, one query, and one form.
4. When you start Access, the first thing you see is a blank document.
5. Reports are formatting instructions to Access for printing the data.

Multiple Choice

1. An example of a database is
   a. a card catalog in a library
   b. an address book
   c. a telephone book
   d. all of these answers

2. The information concerning a single item in a database is called a
   a. field
   b. query
   c. record
   d. table

3. The categories that every record contains are called
   a. fields
   b. forms
   c. queries
   d. records

4. The category of software to which Access 2000 belongs is
   a. field
   b. report
   c. DBMS
   d. table

5. In Access, you normally save changes
   a. before you print
   b. before you close an object's window
   c. when you finish using Access
   d. all of these answers

Short Answer

Match the item with the screen element:

_____ a. Table name
_____ b. Field name
_____ c. A record
_____ d. Current record symbol
_____ e. Adds a new record to the bottom of the table

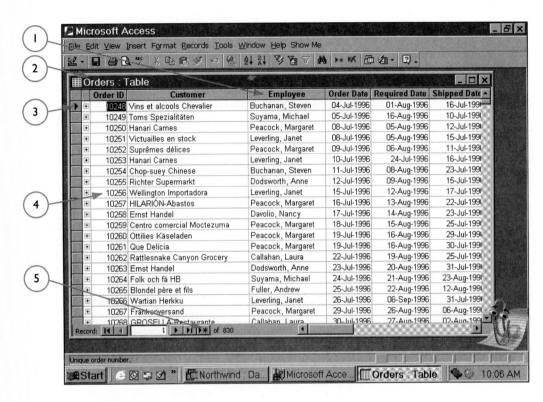

FIGURE 1.12

What Does This Do?

Write a summary of the function of the following:

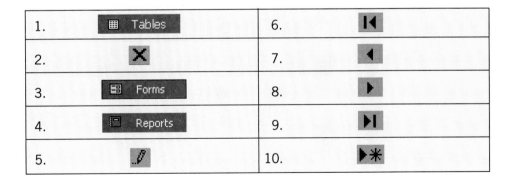

1.	Tables	6.	⏮
2.	✕	7.	◀
3.	Forms	8.	▶
4.	Reports	9.	⏭
5.	✎	10.	▶✳

On Your Own

1. Search Help for information on a topic that isn't clear to you.
2. Open Northwind and display a table that the exercises didn't use. Edit the table and undo your edits.
3. Open a Northwind table and print the data.
4. Open a report in the Northwind database and print the report.
5. Open a form in the Northwind database and compare working with data in a form to working with data in a table.

PROJECTS

1. Choose Help | Microsoft Access Help or click the Office Assistant if it is displayed on the screen. Type *database* in the text box and click the Search button. Select the topic *Databases: What they are and how they work*. The eight-page topic displays as shown in Figure 1.13. Read the information on each page of the eight-page topic to become more familiar with database concepts.

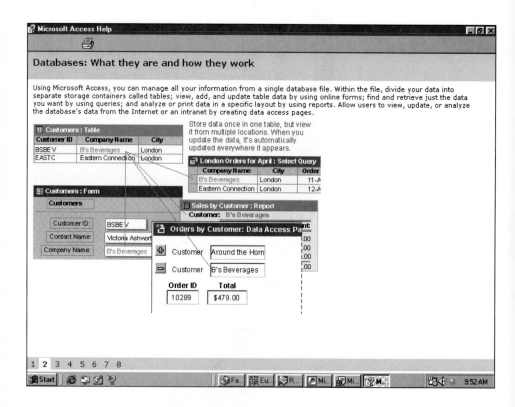

FIGURE 1.13   Microsoft Access Help Defines Databases

2. Open the Northwind database. Open the Shippers table. Add a new shipper to the table.

Press Enter in the first field to have Access automatically number the new record.

Type the data shown in Table 1.5.

Print the table.

Field Name	Field Data
Company Name	AirPlane Express
Phone	(800) 123-4567

TABLE 1.5 New Shippers Record

3. Using the Northwind database, open the Products form. Add a new product using the data shown in Table 1.6. (Use the drop-down box located on the Suppliers and Category fields to select the field entry.)

Close the Products form.

Open the Products table. The new record is added to the bottom of the table.

Print the table.

Field Name	Field Data
Product Name	Karen's Nettle Tea
Supplier	Grandma Kelly's Homestead
Category	Beverages
Quantity Per Unit	10 boxes x 20 bags
Unit Price	$25.00
Units In Stock	17
Units On Order	25
Reorder Level	10
Discontinued	leave blank

TABLE 1.6 New Products Record

4. Using the Northwind database, display the Alphabetical List of Products report. After viewing the report, print it out.

Display the Summary of Sales by Year report and print it out.

Creating a Database

UNIT OBJECTIVES

- Create a new database in Access
- Create a table using Datasheet view
- Create a table in Design view
- Define a primary key
- Switch between Design and Datasheet views
- Set table field properties
- Change the table design
- Use a Table Wizard to create a table
- Document the table

You learned in Unit 1 that a database uses tables to store data that can be related together. In this unit, you will create a database that contains information necessary to run a small Web-based mail order business called Spread the Light—Candles. The database for Spread the Light will contain employee, customer, and order information. To avoid redundancy, the database will require a table of employees, another table containing customer information, and a third table containing order information. You will use three different methods for creating these tables: the Datasheet view, the Design view, and the Table Wizard. You will also define property settings for the fields in the tables.

TASK 1 | *Creating a Database*

What: Create a new database.

How: Start Access and choose Blank Access database.

Why: To create tables in Access, you first need to create a database to contain them.

Tip: To help you start creating a database, create written lists of all data items and group them by subject.

Before you create the tables that you have designed on paper, you need to create a container to hold them. A database acts as the container holding all the database objects together. To create a new database, follow these steps:

1. When Access starts, the Microsoft Access dialog box shown in Figure 2.1 displays.

2. Choose the Blank Access database option.

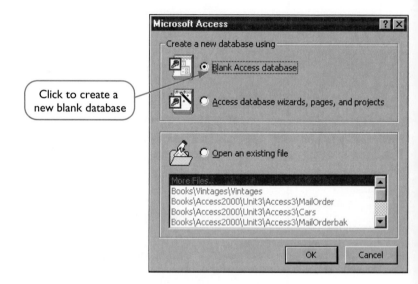

Click to create a new blank database

FIGURE 2.1 The Microsoft Access Dialog Box

3. Choose the drive and/or folder where you want to store your database and give the database a name.

Remember that Access uses a single file to store all the elements of a database. In Figure 2.2, drive A is selected to store the database and the name MailOrder is typed in the File name list box.

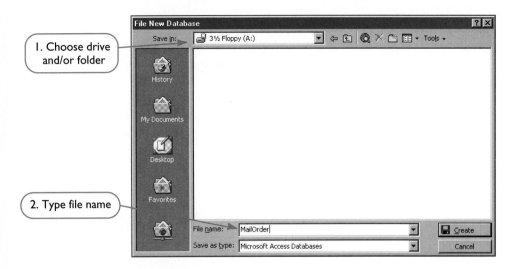

1. Choose drive and/or folder

2. Type file name

FIGURE 2.2   Choosing a Drive and File Name

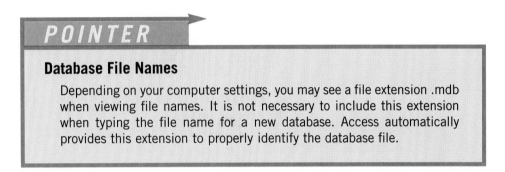

Database File Names

Depending on your computer settings, you may see a file extension .mdb when viewing file names. It is not necessary to include this extension when typing the file name for a new database. Access automatically provides this extension to properly identify the database file.

4. Click the Create button and Access creates the database and opens it in the **Database window**, as shown in Figure 2.3.

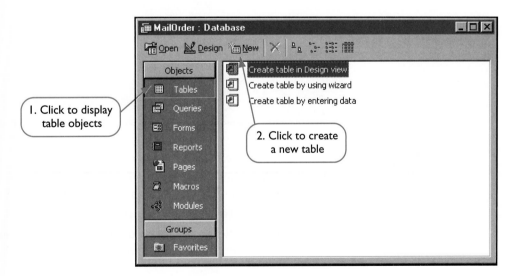

1. Click to display table objects

2. Click to create a new table

FIGURE 2.3   The MailOrder Database Window

POINTER

Creating a New Database from Within Access

If you inadvertently close the Microsoft Access dialog box when starting Access, you can create a new database by clicking the New Database button on the Access toolbar. The New dialog box opens and you choose Database. Then, proceed as described in Task 1 to create the database.

EXERCISE 1 | *Creating a Database*

1. Start Microsoft Access.

The Access program opens and displays the Microsoft Access dialog box, as shown in Figure 2.1.

2. Under **Create a new database using**, select the **Blank Access database** option and click **OK**.

The File New Database dialog box opens, as shown in Figure 2.2.

3. In the **Save in** list box, choose the drive and folder where you want to store the database.

This book uses drive **A:** for the examples. You may be using a different location for your files.

4. In the **File name** text box, type **MailOrder** without using a space between the words.

5. Click the **Create button**.

Access creates a new blank database called MailOrder on your disk, and the MailOrder Database window opens, as shown in Figure 2.3. The MailOrder database will be used in the exercises that follow.

TASK 2 | *Creating a Table Using Datasheet View*

What: Create a table.

How: Click the Tables choice in the Objects bar on the Database window. Click New and choose Datasheet View.

Why: To create a table to store data.

Tip: Keep field names brief to display as many fields as possible on the screen or when printing tables.

Creating tables in a database is a five-step process:

1. Use one of the methods this unit describes to create the table.
2. Enter each field name and select the field type.
3. Identify the primary key.
4. Enter field properties.
5. Save the table design.

Tables can be created in Datasheet view, in Design view, or by using a wizard. Each of these methods has certain benefits and limitations. For example, in the **Datasheet view** that this task uses, you can see the results of the table as it is constructed. But, by using Datasheet, Access makes certain assumptions about the size of fields and the type of data that you are using. By using Design view later in this unit, you will see that you can be more specific about the data.

To create a new table in Datasheet view, complete the following steps:

1. Click the Tables choice in the Objects bar located in the Database window.
2. Click the New button in the Database window.
3. Select Datasheet View in the New Table dialog box, as shown in Figure 2.4, and click OK.

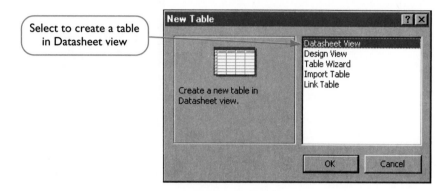

FIGURE 2.4 Choosing Datasheet View

A Datasheet for a new table that is temporarily called Table1 opens, as shown in Figure 2.5.

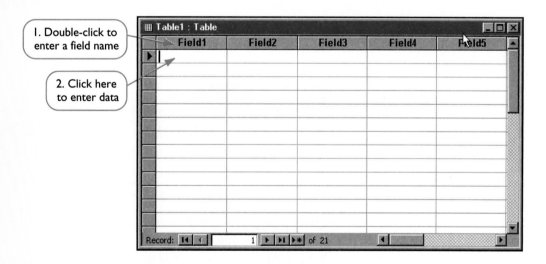

FIGURE 2.5 A New Table in Datasheet View

Access organizes the Datasheet into rows (records) and columns (fields). At the top of each column is a field name, such as Field1 and Field2. To replace the field names with more descriptive names, follow these steps:

1. Double-click on a field name.
2. Type a new name for the field.

To enter data in the table, click in the space below the field name and type the data. Figure 2.6 shows the Datasheet for the Employees table with field names changed to reflect the type of data. Records for eight employees have also been entered into the table. Access removes the extra columns that were not used for this table when you save the table design.

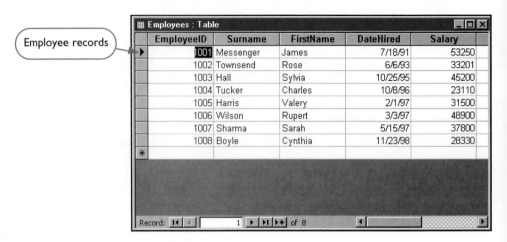

FIGURE 2.6   The Employees Table

 Save the table by clicking the Save button or choosing File | Save. The Save As dialog box opens where you should type the table name, as shown in Figure 2.7.

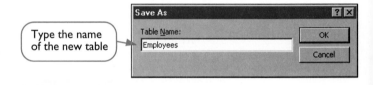

FIGURE 2.7   Giving the Table a Name

POINTER

Data Alignment in the Datasheet

By default, text fields align left in the column, and numeric and date fields align to the right.

Access prompts you to give the table a primary key, as shown in Figure 2.8. Although most tables should have a primary key, you will learn to set it in a later task. If you select *Yes*, Access adds a key field to your table. Selecting *No* avoids setting a key, but you can return to the table later in Design view and specify a key.

After completing a table and entering its data, you can close it by clicking the Close button on the table window. The name of the new table appears in the Database window, as shown in Figure 2.9.

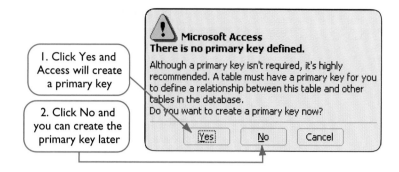

1. Click Yes and Access will create a primary key

2. Click No and you can create the primary key later

Microsoft Access
There is no primary key defined.

Although a primary key isn't required, it's highly recommended. A table must have a primary key for you to define a relationship between this table and other tables in the database.
Do you want to create a primary key now?

Yes   No   Cancel

FIGURE 2.8   The Primary Key Request

The Employees table appears as a table object

FIGURE 2.9   The Employees Table Appears in the Tables Objects Window

You will create the employee table for the Spread the Light—Candles company in the MailOrder database in the next exercise.

EXERCISE 2   *Creating a Table Using Datasheet View*

1. If necessary, click **Tables** in the **Objects** bar in the Database window.

2. Click the **New button** on the Database window toolbar.
The New Table dialog box opens, as shown in Figure 2.4.

3. Click **Datasheet View** in the New Table dialog box to select it, then click **OK**.
A Datasheet for Table1 opens, and you define the fields for the Employee table and enter its data.

4. Double-click the name **Field1** in the first column header to select it.
Only the field name should be selected and not the entire column. If you accidentally select the column, double-click again in the Field1 header to select it.

5. Type **EmployeeID**, without spaces, in the header to replace the name Field1.

If any characters remain from the original name, use the backspace or Delete keys to delete them. EmployeeID is the complete name of the first field in the table.

6. Similarly, follow steps 4 and 5 to replace Field2 with **Surname**, Field3 with **Firstname**, Field4 with **DateHired**, and Field5 with **Salary**.

A real Employee table would have much more information than used here. Additional fields might include the employee's address, the department where he or she works, a home address and phone number, and so on. But for the purpose of learning Access, we will limit the table to five fields, as defined above.

7. Click in the blank space in the first row under the EmployeeID column (field) and type **1001**.

8. In the same row, under Surname, type **Messenger**.
Under FirstName, type **James**.
Under DateHired, type **7/18/91**.
Under Salary, type **53250**.

These are the data for the first employee's record in the table.

9. Enter data for the other employees, as shown in Figure 2.6.

10. Click the **Save button** on the Access window toolbar to save the table design.

The Save As dialog box opens.

11. Type **Employees** in the Table Name text box of the Save As dialog box and click **OK**.

The prompt to create a primary key displays. Later in this unit, you will learn to define the employee number as the primary key for this table.

12. Click **No** and the table design is saved.

Records automatically save as they are typed, but the table design requires that you save it the first time or after any change has been made to it, such as deleting a field or inserting a new one.

13. Click the **Close button** to close the table window.

The table is closed, and you are returned to the Database window. The Tables Objects window lists the table name Employees, as shown in Figure 2.9.

TASK 3 | *Creating a Table in Design View*

What: Create a table.

How: In the Object bar, click Tables. Click the New button and choose Design View.

Why: To create a table to store data.

Tip: Design view is most effective for complex tables with many fields and different types of data. It is the preferred method of creating tables.

Use **Design view** to create or modify the design of a table, but not its record content. The design contains the table's fields, such as a customer number or name, and their properties, including the data type, format, and for some types, the field length. Other properties, such as defining the primary key and choices for data validation, are also included in the design.

To create a table in Design view, follow these steps:

1. Click Tables in the Objects bar of the Database window.
2. Click the New button in the Database window toolbar.
3. Choose Design View.

The Table window opens in Design view, as shown in Figure 2.10.

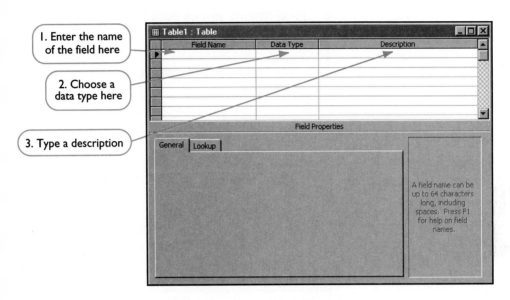

FIGURE 2.10 The Table Window in Design View

POINTER

Modifying Table Design

To modify the design of an existing table:

1. Click **Tables** in the Object bar of the Database window.
2. Click the name of the table you want to open in the Database window.
3. Click the **Design button** in the Database window.

FIELD NAMES

Each field in the table design must be given a name to identify it and the data that the field will eventually contain. The following rules apply to field names:

- Each field name must be unique; that is, each field must have a different name.
- A field name can be a maximum of 64 characters in length.
- A field name can include any combination of letters, numbers, spaces, and special characters except a period (.), an exclamation point (!), an accent grave (`), and brackets ([ ]).
- Don't begin a field name with leading spaces.

Although you can include spaces in a field name, it is best to avoid this as it can lead to conflicts in more complex applications that use Visual Basic. Instead of using Customer Name for a field, type it as CustomerName or include an underscore between the words, such as Customer_Name. You should also use a name that doesn't duplicate the name of a property or other element used by Microsoft Access; otherwise, your database can produce unexpected results in some situations. A field name such as Sum or Name could be confused with other Access elements and should be avoided.

POINTER

Field Names versus Data in the Field

The rule for avoiding spaces applies only to the field name and not to the data in the field. Thus, a field may be named AddressLine (no space), but the data it contains may be "123 North Street," which contains spaces.

DATA TYPES

After giving the field a name, you need to define a data type. The **data type** determines the type of data that a field can store. Fields containing data such as names, addresses, or phone numbers use the Text data type. An all-numeric field that might be used in a calculation, such as quantity or amount, uses the Number data type. Dollar amounts can use Currency. Table 2.1 shows a list of Access data types.

Data Type	Description
Text	Text and/or numbers. Works for numeric fields that don't require calculations, such as a phone number. Maximum of 255 characters.
Memo	Long text or combinations of text and numbers. Up to 65,535 characters.
Number	Numeric data used in mathematical calculations.
Date/Time	Date and time values for the years 100 through 9999.
Currency	Currency values used in mathematical calculations involving data with one to four decimal places.
AutoNumber	A sequential number incremented by 1. Can also be defined as a random number.
Yes/No	Yes and No fields contain only one of two values Yes/No, True/False, or On/Off.
OLE Object	An object, such as an Excel spreadsheet, a Word document, graphics, sounds, or other binary data linked to or embedded in an Access table.
Hyperlink	Text or combinations of text and numbers stored as text and used as a hyperlink address.
Lookup Wizard	Creates a field that allows you to choose a value from another table.

TABLE 2.1   Data Types

When the insertion point is in the Data Type column, a drop-down arrow appears. Click the arrow to view a selection of data types, as shown in Figure 2.11. If you know the data type you want to use, such as Currency, you can simply type the first letter of the data type to select it.

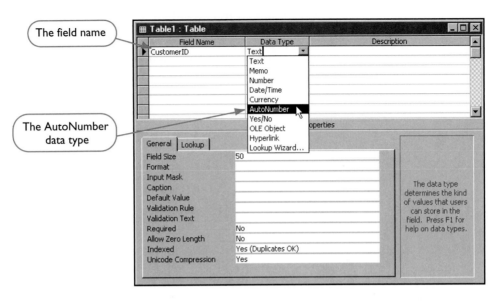

The field name

The AutoNumber data type

FIGURE 2.11   Data Type Choices

POINTER

Numeric Fields

Numbers, in numeric fields, can be represented in many different ways. Some choices that may be made in the Field Size property are Integer, Long Integer, or Decimal numbers. Search Help for more information.

A field may also include a description. This is useful for documenting the field so that others may understand its use, so it is a good habit to include a brief description.

After defining the fields in Design view, switch to Datasheet view to add records. The field names you designated in Design view will appear on the table.

You will create the customer table for the Spread the Light—Candles company in the next exercise.

EXERCISE 3 | *Creating a Table in Design View*

1. If the **MailOrder database** created in Exercise 1 is not already open, open it.

2. Click **Tables** in the Objects bar of the Database window and click the **New button** in the Database window.
   The New Table dialog box opens.

3. In the **New Table** dialog box, click **Design View** to select it.

4. Click **OK**.
The Table window opens in Design view, as shown in Figure 2.10.

5. In the first blank row under the **Field Name** heading, type **CustomerID**.

6. Click in the first blank row under **Data Type**.
A drop-down arrow appears in the box, as shown in Figure 2.11.

7. Click the **drop-down arrow** and choose **AutoNumber**.
This choice causes CustomerID to be an automatically sequentially numbered field, beginning with 1 and increasing in increments of 1 as new records are added.

8. Repeat steps 5 to 7 and enter the remaining fields into the design. Table 2.2 lists all of the fields for the table.
Notice that, although PhoneNumber contains numbers, it is defined as text to allow for parentheses, spaces, and hyphens in the number.

Field Name	Data Type
CustomerID	AutoNumber
CompanyName	Text
BillingAddress	Text
City	Text
State/Prov	Text
PostalCode	Text
Country	Text
PhoneNumber	Text

TABLE 2.2   Customer

9. Click the **Save button** on the Access window toolbar to save the table design.
The Save As dialog box opens.

10. In the **Table Name** text box of the Save As dialog box, type **Customers** and click **OK**.

11. When asked to create a primary key, click **No**.
Access saves the table design and returns to Design view. Leave the table in this state and proceed to the next task.

What: Specify a primary key.

How: Use the menu command Edit | Primary Key.

Why: To ensure that records in the table are unique and to link tables within a database.

Tip: Tables must have a primary key in order to create relationships for them.

The field that is designated as the primary key has unique contents for each record in the table, thus ensuring that you do not enter a duplicate record into the table. In the Customers table, this would require that each customer have a unique identification number, and in the Employees table that each employee have a unique employee number.

To create a primary key:

1. Open the table in Design view.
2. Place the insertion point in the field that is to be defined as the primary key.
3. Choose Edit | Primary Key from the Access menu bar.

As a result, a key symbol appears in the row selector for the primary key field, as shown in Figure 2.12.

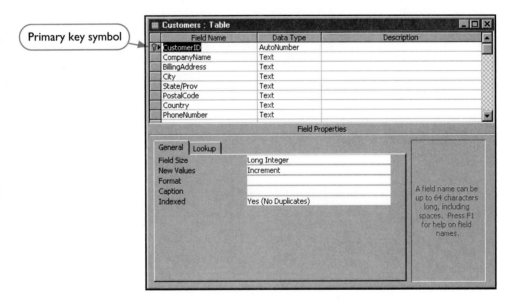

FIGURE 2.12 A Key Symbol Identifies the Primary Key

An alternate method for creating the primary key is to right-click the row and choose Primary Key from the shortcut menu, as shown in Figure 2.13.

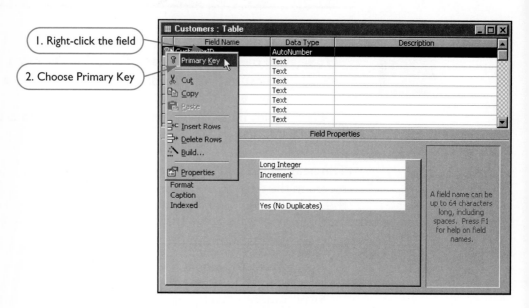

1. Right-click the field

2. Choose Primary Key

FIGURE 2.13   Primary Key Is Also an Option in the Shortcut Menu

POINTER

Table Row Selector

Each row in the table contains a button to the left of the row, called the **Row Selector**. If the table has a primary key, a key symbol appears in this button. Clicking the Row Selector selects the entire row. You will use this button when you want to select the entire record.

EXERCISE 4 | *Defining the Primary Key*

1. Using the Customers table, click in the **CustomerID** field name.
The exact position of the insertion point is not important, but it must be in the field that you will define as the primary key.

2. Choose **Edit | Primary Key** from the Access window menu bar.
CustomerID becomes the primary key field and a key symbol appears in the row selector beside the field, as shown in Figure 2.12.

3. Right-click the **Row Selector button** beside the CustomerID row.
A shortcut menu appears with the Primary Key choice appearing pressed in to indicate that it is currently selected.

4. Click outside of the shortcut menu to cancel the operation.
You return to the table design window.

5. Be sure the key symbol is showing beside the CustomerID field, as shown in Figure 2.12. If it is not, repeat step 2 to define the key.

6. Click the **Save button** on the Access window toolbar to save the design change.
Access saves the table with the CustomerID as the primary key.

7. Leave the table on the screen for use in the next exercise.

TASK 5 | *Switching Between Design and Datasheet View*

What: Use the View button.

How: Click the View button on the Access window toolbar to switch between Design and Datasheet View.

Why: To enter data into the table in Datasheet view or to return to Design view.

Tip: If you click the arrow beside the View button, you can see the current view selected and choose the view you need.

The View button on the toolbar switches Access from Design view to Datasheet view. When you are in Datasheet view, clicking the button changes back to Design view. After creating the table design, you will want to change to Datasheet view to enter the data. If the design was not correct, you may need to change back to Design view to change the design.

When you are in Datasheet view, you can enter the data for the table. Records are entered as shown in Figure 2.14, using the same techniques discussed in Task 2. The difference is that the Datasheet already contains the field names that were entered in the design.

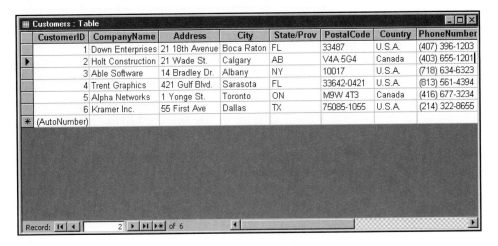

CustomerID	CompanyName	Address	City	State/Prov	PostalCode	Country	PhoneNumber
1	Down Enterprises	21 18th Avenue	Boca Raton	FL	33487	U.S.A.	(407) 396-1203
2	Holt Construction	21 Wade St.	Calgary	AB	V4A 5G4	Canada	(403) 655-1201
3	Able Software	14 Bradley Dr.	Albany	NY	10017	U.S.A.	(718) 634-6323
4	Trent Graphics	421 Gulf Blvd.	Sarasota	FL	33642-0421	U.S.A.	(813) 561-4394
5	Alpha Networks	1 Yonge St.	Toronto	ON	M9W 4T3	Canada	(416) 677-3234
6	Kramer Inc.	55 First Ave	Dallas	TX	75085-1055	U.S.A.	(214) 322-8655
(AutoNumber)							

Record: 2 of 6

FIGURE 2.14 Data in the Customers Table

1. With the Customers table in Design view, click the **View button** on the Access window toolbar.
   The Customer table displays in Datasheet view. Currently there are no records in the table.

2. Press **Enter** on the first field of the table to input the AutoNumber automatically.

3. Enter the records shown in Figure 2.14 into the Datasheet.

POINTER

Saving the Design versus the Data

Recall that Access automatically saves records as you enter the data. Therefore, you will not need to save the data that you type. Only if you change the table design will you need to save the revised design.

4. Click the **Close button** on the Datasheet view window to close the window.
   You return to the Database window, and the Customers table now appears in the Tables object window.

TASK 6 | *Set Field Properties*

What: Set the field property settings.

How: Select the field in Design view to display the Properties tab.

Why: To change a field's size, format, caption, default, or other settings.

Tip: The available property settings change depending on the data type of the selected field.

Field property settings can affect how a field displays in Datasheet view, control the size or content of the data, or help you to enter the data. Table 2.3 describes some of the common properties.

Property	Description
Field Size	The **field size** defines the maximum size of the data that you can enter into the field. Acceptable values vary depending on the data. For example, two characters are sufficient for state names, whereas phone numbers will require more.
Format	In numeric and currency fields, the **format** affects the display of decimal places, currency symbols ($), and thousands separator (,) in the field value. A number such as 12345.678 could also display as $12,345.68, 12,345.68 or 12345.678.
Input Mask	An **input mask** assists with entering data, such as a phone number, by automatically placing the first three digits in parentheses and placing the dash after the next three characters. Masks prevent typing characters over and over, and they also provide consistent formatting in records.
Caption	**Captions** provide a name to describe fields when displaying the data in Datasheet view and other Access objects. You might use a field name such as UnitOfMeasure, but a caption of Unit of Measure makes the display in the datasheet more readable.
Default Value	A value that is automatically entered in the field for a new record. Used when a common value, such as a state name, will be used often when entering data. The **default value** can be typed over to include other data.
Validation Rule	Sets a condition that the data entered in the field must meet. For example, you might not allow dates before 1900 in the employee start date.
Validation Text	The error message that displays if the data doesn't meet the Validation Rule.
Required	Data must be placed in the field when you create the record. For example, you might make the last name field a required field in the personnel table.

TABLE 2.3   Commonly Used Properties

To change a property setting:
1. In Design view, select the field whose property you want to change. Properties for the currently selected field display only one at a time.
2. If necessary, click the General tab in the Field Properties window to open it.
3. Choose the property you want to change.

Figure 2.15 shows the BillingAddress field with the text "Address" entered into the Caption property.

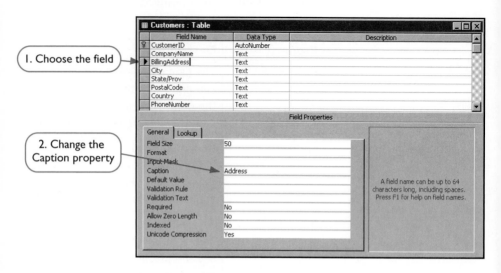

FIGURE 2.15   Changing the Caption Property

USING THE INPUT MASK FIELD PROPERTY

An input mask helps format data in fields without having to type all the special characters. For example, 567983455 is a Social Security number, and 8008765678 is a phone number, but they are hard to understand in their present form. It would require extra data entry to include the special characters between the appropriate numbers as they are input into tables, so Access supplies input masks. Input masks place the numbers in a standard format by including the special characters.

To use the Input Mask Wizard, follow these steps:

1. Click in the Input Mask field property to activate the property button.
2. Click the property button to start the Wizard.
3. Save the table as directed by Access, and the first screen of the Input Mask Wizard displays, as shown in Figure 2.16.
4. Follow the steps through the wizard by clicking the Next button, or click the Finish button at any point to use the selected mask.

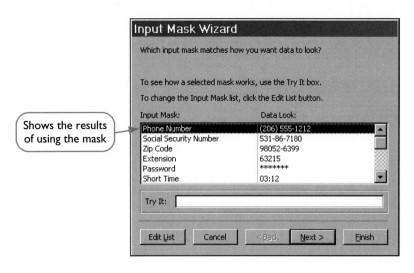

Input Mask Wizard

Which input mask matches how you want data to look?

To see how a selected mask works, use the Try It box.
To change the Input Mask list, click the Edit List button.

Input Mask:	Data Look:
Phone Number	(206) 555-1212
Social Security Number	531-86-7180
Zip Code	98052-6399
Extension	63215
Password	*******
Short Time	03:12

Shows the results of using the mask

Try It: [   ]

Edit List   Cancel   < Back   Next >   Finish

FIGURE 2.16   Enter Test Data in the Try It Textbox

USING THE VALIDATION RULE FIELD PROPERTY AND THE VALIDATION TEXT FIELD PROPERTY

Access provides the validation rule field property to help avoid errors in data by limiting the data that fields accept. The validation rule allows you to set up a test for the data entered into a field. For example, if Spread the Light—Candles started business in 1990, a simple validation rule would be to not allow hiring dates in the employee table before 1990. This rule would force the entries to conform to the dates the company has been in business. You can construct simple validation rules by using operators. Table 2.4 describes these operators.

Operator	Description	Example
<	Less than	<#1/1/99# The date entered must be before 1/1/99
>	Greater than	>#1/1/99# The date entered must be after 1/1/99
<= >=	Less than or equal to; Greater than or equal to	>=#1/1/99# and <=#12/31/99# The date entered must be between January 1, 1999 and December 31, 1999
<>	Not equal to	<>#2/29/99# The date entered cannot be equal to 2/29/99

TABLE 2.4   Validation Rule Operators

To create a validation rule, follow these steps:

1. Click in the Validation Rule field property to display the property button.
2. Click the property button to display the Expression Builder, as shown in Figure 2.17.
3. Construct a simple expression by clicking the operator buttons and typing the data. Dates are enclosed in number signs when typed into an expression, and text is enclosed in double quotes, while numbers require no special formatting. (Use the Help button in the dialog box to get specific help in constructing expressions.)
4. For more complex operators than those available from the buttons, click the Operators folder and then double-click the desired operator, as shown in Figure 2.17.

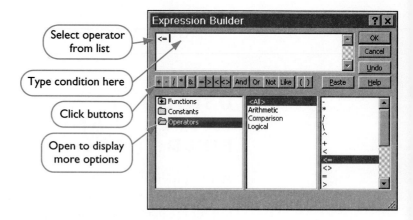

FIGURE 2.17 Use the Expression Builder to Create Validation Rules

Once you establish the condition for the field to match, it is a good idea to make use of the Validation Text property to provide specific help to the person doing data entry. For example, if the person doing data entry for Spread the Light—Candles tried to input a hire date of 1970, Access would supply a general error message that might not help identify the error. But by using the validation text field property, you can type the message "The hire date must be after January 1, 1990" for the user to see when the validation rule is not met.

EXERCISE 6 | *Changing Field Properties*

1. If necessary, click the **Tables** choice in the Objects bar of the Database window.
2. Click **Customers** in the Database window to select it.
3. Click the **Design button** in the Database window to open the table in Design view.

4. In the Design view window, click in the **BillingAddress** field name.
   The Properties Field window displays for the BillingAddress field.
5. If necessary, click the **General** tab in the Properties window to view it.

6. In the General tab of the Field Properties window, click in the text box beside **Caption**.

7. Type **Address** in the Caption text box, as shown in Figure 2.15.

8. In the Design view, click in the **City** field name.
   The Field Properties window for City displays.

9. Click in the **Field Size** text box and select the value 50.

10. Overtype the value 50 with **30**.
    The City field is now limited to a value no larger than 30 characters.

11. Click in the **PhoneNumber** field.

12. Click in the **Input Mask Field Property** text box to display the property button at the right edge of the text box.

13. Click the **Property button**.
    Access prompts you to save the table.

14. Click **Yes** to save the table.
    The Input Mask Wizard displays.

15. The Phone Number Input Mask should be selected, so click the **Next** button.

16. The Wizard displays the sample phone number with formatting; to accept it and stop the Input Mask Wizard, click **Finish**.

17. Move to the field named **Country**.

18. Click in the Default Value field and type **"U.S.A."** (including periods and quotation marks).
    Most of your customers are located in the U.S.A., so that value will automatically appear when you create a record. Simply type another country in the field to replace U.S.A. when entering data.

19. Click in the **Validation Rule** field property to activate the Property button.

20. Click the **Property button** to open the Expression Builder.

21. Click the **Not Equal to button** and type **"Zimbabwe"** (placing it in double quotes) and click **OK**.

22. Click in the Validation Text field property and type: **Orders cannot be sent to Zimbabwe**.

23. Click the **Save button** in the Access window toolbar to save the changes.

24. Switch to Datasheet view and input a new record.
    Notice the mask for phone and the default value U.S.A. in the record.

25. Type **Zimbabwe** in the Country field and attempt to move to another field.
    Notice the error message that displays.

26. Close the table.
    Access reminds you that a field has been changed to a shorter size. This is the result of changing City's Field Size from 50 to 30. If you have City data in the table that is longer than 30 characters, Access reduces it in size to 30 and some characters are lost. None of our cities are that long, so we will not have a problem.

27. Click **Yes** to proceed.
    Access saves the table design.

What: Change the table design.

How: Open the table in Design view.

Why: To add or delete a field and change the field's name or its property settings.

Tip: Changing the data type can result in loss of data in a field. Access will warn you if this is about to happen, but be sure that your data is appropriate for the new data type.

Changing the table design can affect data currently stored in the table. It's usually best to spend more time planning the design in order to minimize later changes. However, you may need to change the design of a table for a number of reasons, such as new field is needed to store an e-mail address. You might also want to change the name of a field or revise or enter property settings. Any of these changes require you to open the table in Design view.

To change a table's design from the Database window, complete the following steps:

1. If necessary, click the Tables choice in the Objects bar.
2. Click the table name to select it.
3. Click the Design button in the Database window toolbar.

POINTER

Changing Table Designs from the Datasheet View

If you are in Datasheet view and notice something that you want to change in the table's design, click the View button to switch from Datasheet view to Design view and make your changes.

INSERTING A FIELD

You can insert a new field in the table design using either of the following methods:

- Move to the empty row at the end of the last field in the table and enter the information for the new field.

- Right-click the row selector button of the row where you want to insert a new field. From the shortcut menu, choose Insert Rows, as shown in Figure 2.18. A row is inserted before the one you selected. Now enter the field information into the new row.

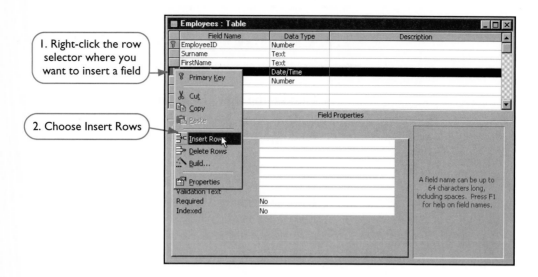

FIGURE 2.18 Inserting a Row Using the Shortcut Menu

DELETING A FIELD

You can delete a field from the table design using either of the following methods:

- Click the row selector of the field you want to delete and press the Delete key.
- Right-click the row selector of the field you want to delete and choose Delete Rows from the shortcut menu, as shown in Figure 2.19.

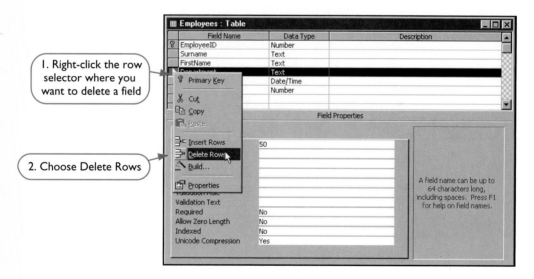

FIGURE 2.19 Using the Shortcut Menu to Delete a Row

1. Choose the **Employees** table in the **MailOrders** Database window.

2. Click the **Design** button in the Database window toolbar to open the table in Design view.

3. Right-click the **Row Selector button** at the left of the EmployeeID row. The shortcut menu opens.

4. Choose **Primary Key** from the shortcut menu.
   Access places a key symbol in the EmployeeID row selector to indicate that this is the primary key field.

5. Right-click the **Row Selector button** on the **DateHired** row to select the row.
   The shortcut menu opens.

6. Click **Insert Rows** in the shortcut menu.
   Access inserts a new row in the table design. At this point, it will still be selected.

7. Click in the **Field Name** column of the inserted row and type **Department**.

8. Choose **Text** for the Data Type.

9. Click the **View button** to change to Datasheet view.
   Access prompts you to save the table.

10. Click **Yes**.
    The table data displays in the Datasheet with a new column (Department) that is currently empty.

11. In the first row of the datasheet, type **100** in the Department column.
    The value 100 aligns left in the column because this is a text field.

12. Click the **View button** to return to Design view.

13. Click in the **Field Name** of the empty row following Salary.

14. Type a new field called **Fulltime**.

15. Choose a **Data Type** of **Yes/No**.
    The Yes/No data type creates a check box in the field in Datasheet view. A check mark may be entered in this box, where the check represents full time and no check mark represents not full time or part time.

16. Click the **Save button** in the Access window toolbar to save the table design.

17. Click the **View button** to return to Datasheet view.

18. Click in each **Fulltime** check box to enter a **check mark** for all employees except Charles Tucker and Sarah Sharma.

19. Click the **View button** to return to Design view.

20. Click the **Row Selector button** beside the Department row to select it.

21. Press the **Delete** key.
    Access asks if you want to permanently delete the selected field and lose the data.

22. Click **Yes** to delete the field and click the **Close button** on the Design view window.

Access asks if you want to save the changes to the table's design.

23. Click **Yes** to save the changes.

You are returned to the Database window.

TASK 8 | *Using the Table Wizard*

What: Create a new table using the Table Wizard.

How: With Tables open, click the New button and choose Table Wizard.

Why: The Table Wizard provides a number of sample tables on which you can base your table design.

Tip: You can choose fields for your table from several of the sample tables. If one table does not provide all the fields you need, choose the fields needed from one table; then switch to another and continue to select the fields you need.

The **Table Wizard** provides a variety of sample tables that you can use to create your table. You choose a table from a selection that includes a Mailing List, Customers, Products, Orders, Invoices, and so on. After choosing the table, you are presented with a list of possible fields to be used for the table. You then select the fields for your table from this list to create the new table.

To use the Table Wizard, complete the following steps:

1. Click the Tables choice in the Objects bar of the Database window.
2. Click the New button in the Database window toolbar.
3. Choose Table Wizard from the New Table dialog box.

The first dialog box of the Table Wizard appears, as shown in Figure 2.20.

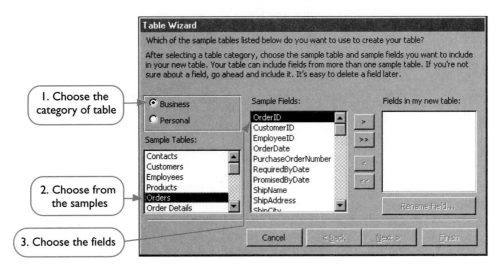

FIGURE 2.20 The First Step in the Table Wizard

ADDING FIELDS TO YOUR DESIGN

To add fields to the design of your table, complete the following steps:

1. Choose a sample table.

   In the left window under Sample Tables, choose the table that is most similar to the table you want to create. You can choose from a variety of Business and Personal types of tables. Figure 2.20 shows the Business option selected and the Orders table chosen.

2. Select the fields for the table.

   Sample Fields lists the fields that apply to the selected table. You build your table design by clicking to select a field that you want and then clicking the right-arrow button to place the field in your table under the heading Fields in my new table.

POINTER

Using the Add Fields Buttons

The double right arrow button will move all fields to your table. The single left arrow removes an unwanted field from your table. The double left arrow removes all fields from your table.

REMOVING A FIELD

If you happen to copy a field you don't want in your table, remove it as follows:

1. Select the field under **Fields in my new table**.
2. Click the single left-pointing arrow button to remove the field from your list.

RENAMING A FIELD

A field in your new table may be renamed if you simply prefer to use a different name for it. Another reason for renaming a field would be when the sample table does not contain a field that you need for your design.

To rename a field, complete the following steps:

1. Choose a field from the list that is similar to what you need.
2. Click the Rename Field button and type the new field name.

The example shows the field FreightCharge selected, but an InvoiceAmount is what is really needed. Because the selected field represents a dollar amount, renaming it to InvoiceAmount (see Figure 2.21) would provide the needed field.

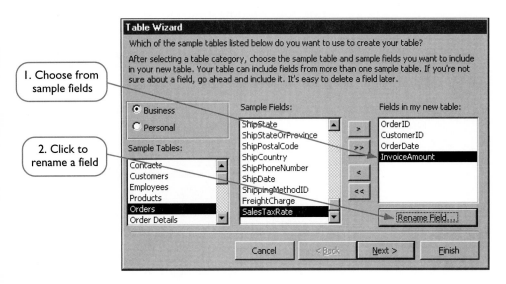

FIGURE 2.21   Changing the Field Name FreightCharge to InvoiceAmount

NAMING THE TABLE

Click the Next button, and the next step of the Table Wizard opens. Figure 2.22 shows the table name Orders used for the sample table. The option, Yes, set a primary key for me is selected so that the wizard will choose the field for the key.

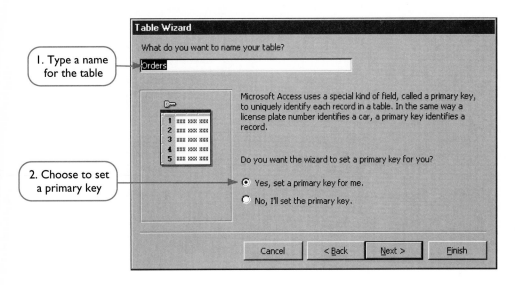

FIGURE 2.22   Naming the Table

RELATING THE TABLE

Click the Next button, and the relating tables step of the Table Wizard opens, as shown in Figure 2.23. Unit 3 discusses how to define table relationships, so we will not relate tables. Click the Relationships button to display the Relationships window shown in Figure 2.24.

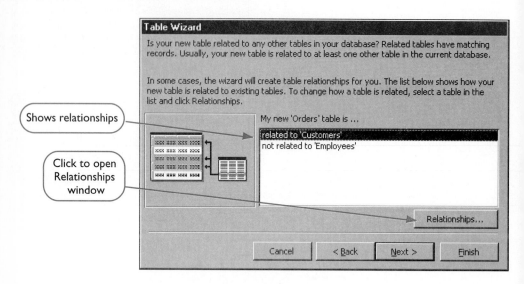

FIGURE 2.23 Table Relationships

Select the Tables aren't related option, and click OK. Click the Next button to display the last step of the Table Wizard. To enter data, select Enter data directly into the form and click the Finish button.

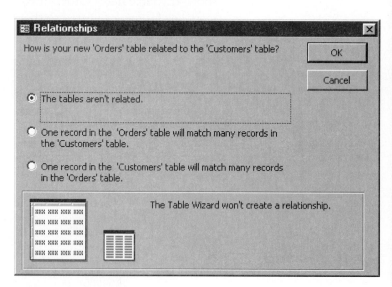

FIGURE 2.24 Defining Relationships

The table opens in Datasheet view to allow data entry. Figure 2.25 shows the completed Orders table.

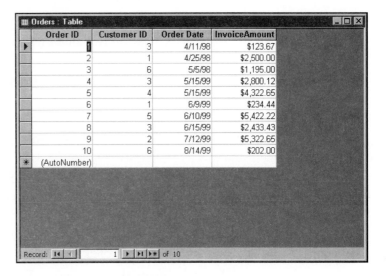

Order ID	Customer ID	Order Date	InvoiceAmount
1	3	4/11/98	$123.67
2	1	4/25/98	$2,500.00
3	6	5/5/98	$1,195.00
4	3	5/15/99	$2,800.12
5	4	5/15/99	$4,322.65
6	1	6/9/99	$234.44
7	5	6/10/99	$5,422.22
8	3	6/15/99	$2,433.43
9	2	7/12/99	$5,322.65
10	6	8/14/99	$202.00
(AutoNumber)			

FIGURE 2.25   Data in the Orders Table

POINTER

Datasheet View versus Design View

You would normally open the table to add the data. However, if the design requires some fine-tuning at this stage, opening it in Design View will let you make further changes to its design before you add the data.

EXERCISE 8 | *Using the Table Wizard*

1. If necessary, click the **Tables** choice in the Objects bar of the MailOrder Database window.
2. Click the **New button** in the Database window.
   The New Table dialog box opens.
3. Click **Table Wizard** to select it, then click **OK**.
   The first step of the Table Wizard opens.
4. Make sure the **Business** option is selected. Under Sample Tables, click **Orders**.
   A list of sample fields for the table displays in the center window.
5. Under Sample Fields, click **OrderID** to select it.
6. Click the single right-arrow button to copy the **OrderID** field to the list **Fields in my new table**.

7. Repeat steps 6 and 7 to copy the **CustomerID**, **OrderDate**, and **FreightCharge** fields to your new table. You will need to scroll the list to find FreightCharge.

8. Click the **FreightCharge** field in your list to select it.

9. Click the **Rename Field button** in the wizard.
   The Rename Field dialog box opens.

10. In the Rename Field dialog box, type **InvoiceAmount** as the new field name and click **OK**.
    The field name changes in your list of fields.

11. Click the **Next button**.
    The next step of the Table Wizard opens.

12. Accept the name **Orders** for the table and make sure **Yes, set a primary key for me** is selected. Then, click the **Next** button.
    The Related Tables step of the Table Wizard opens as shown in Figure 2.23.

13. Click the **Relationships button**, select **The Tables aren't related option**, and click **OK**. Click the **Next button**.

14. Verify that the option **Enter data directly into the table** is selected, and click the **Finish button**.
    The Orders table opens in Datasheet view.

15. Enter the data shown in Figure 2.25 into the Orders table.

16. Click the **Close button** on the Datasheet window to close the table and return to the Database window.

TASK 9 | *Documenting the Table*

What: Print the table design.
How: Choose Tools | Analyze | Documenter.
Why: To view and print the fields, properties, and other settings for a table's design.
Tip: Close any open tables before you begin documenting the database.

As you have seen in the table design view, it is necessary to move from field to field to see the properties of each field in the table. By using the Access **Documenter** tool, you can view and, if required, print all of the specifications for each field in the table. This tool is useful for creating a hard copy of your database design.

To view the table documentation, complete the following steps:

1. Choose Tools | Analyze | Documenter.
   The Documenter dialog box opens, as shown in Figure 2.26.

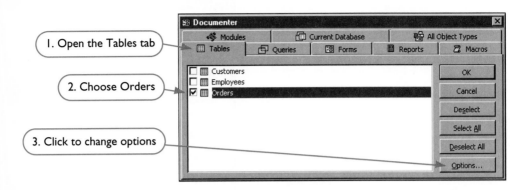

FIGURE 2.26 Choosing the Orders Table in the Documenter Dialog Box

2. Open the Tables tab and choose the table you want to document.
3. Click the Options button to open the Print Table Definition dialog box and choose the option settings you want for the documentation, as shown in Figure 2.27.

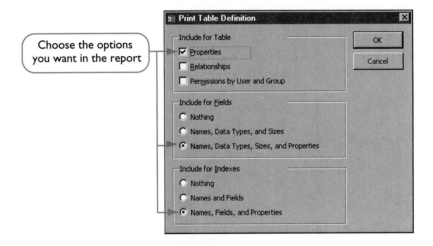

FIGURE 2.27 Options for the Documentation

4. Click OK to close the Options dialog box.
5. Click OK in the Documenter dialog box.

Figure 2.28 shows the generated Object Definition report. You can click the Print button on the Object Definition Report toolbar to print a copy of this report.

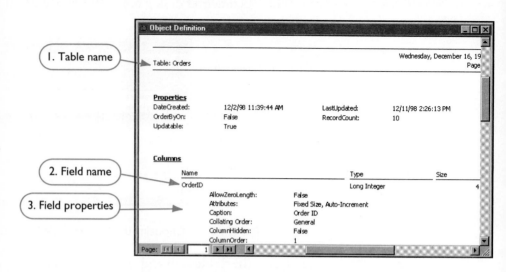

1. Table name

2. Field name

3. Field properties

FIGURE 2.28 The Object Definition Report for the Orders Table

---

EXERCISE 9 | *Documenting the Table*

1. Choose **Tools | Analyze | Documenter** from the Access window menu bar.
   The Documenter dialog box opens.

2. If necessary, click the **Tables** tab to open it and click the **Orders** check box to select the **Orders** table.

3. Click the **Options button** in the Documenter dialog box.
   The Print Table Definition dialog box opens.

4. Make sure only **Properties** is checked and the other options are unchecked in the Print Table Definition dialog box under **Include for table**.

5. Choose the option **Names, Data Types, Sizes,** and **Properties** under **Include for fields**.

6. Choose **Names, Fields,** and **Properties** under **Include for Indexes**.

7. Click **OK** twice.
   After a processing delay, Access creates the Object Definition report.

8. Click the **Print button** on the Object Definition Report toolbar to print the report.

9. Click the **Close button** on the Object Definition window.
   Access returns to the Database window.

S U M M A R Y

After completing this unit, you should be able to

- create a new database in Access (page 26)
- create a table in the database using Datasheet view (page 28)
- create a table in Design view (page 32)
- set a primary key (page 37)
- set the table properties (page 40)
- use the Table Wizard to create a table (page 49)
- use the Documenter to create an Object Definition report (page 54)

K E Y   T E R M S

caption (page 41)
data type (page 34)
Database window (page 27)
Datasheet view (page 29)
default value (page 41)
Design view (page 33)
Documenter (page 54)

field property (page 41)
field size (page 41)
format (page 41)
input mask (page 41)
Row Selector (page 38)
Table Wizard (page 49)

T E S T   Y O U R   S K I L L S

True/False

1. You need a separate database for each table in Access.
2. You need to specify the data type of a field in Datasheet view.
3. A primary key field controls the order in which records display.
4. The data type determines the type of data that a field accepts.
5. Input Masks limit the type of data that you can type into a field.

Multiple Choice

1. When creating a table in Datasheet view, a field is given a name by
   a. its validation rule
   b. changing the column heading
   c. changing the row heading
   d. defining the data type

2. When a table contains a primary key
   a. the records are displayed in ascending order based on the key value
   b. each record must contain a unique key value
   c. a key symbol appears beside the field in the Design window
   d. all of these answers

3. When you are naming a field, which character should be avoided in the name?
   a. letter
   b. number
   c. space
   d. slash (/)

4. Why might you need to click on the Table Row Selector in the design window?
   a. to insert a row
   b. to delete a row
   c. to set a primary key
   d. all of these answers

5. A Validation Rule
   a. formats the data in a field
   b. limits the data that can be entered into a field
   c. places text in an error message
   d. all of these answers

Short Answer

1. Using a _____ _____ requires that each field have a unique value.
2. To limit the number of characters that may be entered into a text field, you would change the _____ value.
3. The _____ _____ provides a number of sample tables that you can use to create your design.
4. Access organizes the _____ into rows and columns.
5. You use the _____ _____ property to create a message to the user about incorrect data typed into a field.

What Does This Do?

Write a description of the function of the following items:

1.	New	6.	Input Mask
2.	💾	7.	Design
3.	primary key	8.	caption
4.	row selector	9.	...
5.	X	10.	validation rule

1. Search Access Help for information about primary keys.
2. Create a table for which you can set field properties to try them out.
3. Create a new database of your own choosing to organize some of your own data.
4. Search Access Help for information on field properties.
5. Print the structure of one of the tables in the Northwind database.

PROJECTS

1. As the owner of JRT Kennels you want to organize all your records into a database using Access 2000. You have lists of dogs and the people who have purchased them both in file cabinets and binders. One problem you notice is that, over the years, customers have purchased several dogs from you, and you have not been able to keep up-to-date records. List the following information in Word 2000 and group data about each subject into tables: customer's name, customer's complete address, dog's name, breed, date of purchase. Print the grouped data.

2. Create a database called JRT Kennels. Create a customer table with the following fields:

Field Name	Data Type
CustomerID	text (set as primary key)
FirstName	text
LastName	text
Address	text
City	text
State/Prov.	text (size 2)
PostalCode	text
Country	text (default USA)
Phone	text (use an Input Mask)

Print the structure of the table, using an Object Definition report.

Input the following records:

111	John	Smith	123 Orchard Dr.	Walnut Creek	CA	98765	USA	(654)123-3245
112	Sue	Mason	18 View St.	Winooski	VT	05409	USA	(345)234-9876
113	Bob	Jones	567 Lake Dr.	Denville	NJ	09876	USA	(202)341-9456
114	Mary	Lawrence	987 Hill Dr.	Calgary	AL	87654	Canada	(345)345-9876

Print the table.

3. Using the JRT Kennel database created in Project 2, create a Dog table, using the following fields.

Field Name	Data Type
DogID	AutoNumber (set as primary key)
Name	text
Breed	text (default Jack Russell Terrier)
PurchaseDate	date (must be after 1/1/85)

Print the structure of the table, using an Object Definition report.

Input the following records:

1	Misty	Jack Russell Terrier	1/1/91
2	Jessie	mixed	2/9/92
3	Toto	Yorkshire Terrier	8/15/94
4	Mickey	Jack Russell Terrier	10/5/93
5	Hobo	Yorkshire Terrier	6/7/97
6	Prince	Yorkshire Terrier	5/15/99

Print the table.

So far you have created two independent tables in the JRT Kennel database. You will learn to relate the tables in the next unit. Relating the tables will pull together the information from the Customer and Dog tables so that you will know which person purchased which dog(s), using the following:

Dog	Purchased By
Misty	111—John Smith
Jessie	112—Sue Mason
Toto	113—Bob Jones
Mickey	111—John Smith
Hobo	114—Mary Lawrence
Prince	113—Bob Jones

PROJECTS

1. Seeds and Sprouts is a mail order company specializing in seeds for the home gardener. You will get started helping them set up an Access database in this project and continue working with the database in the following units. To simplify data, they sell all seeds in one-ounce packages.

   Create a Seeds and Sprouts database.

   Create a Plant table, using the fields that Table 2.5 lists.

Field Name	Data Type
ProdNum	text (set as primary key)
Name	text
Type	text (default vegetable)
Variety	text (default summer)
Per/Oz	number

TABLE 2.5   Plant Table Fields

Create a Customer table, using the fields that Table 2.6 lists.

Field Name	Data Type
CustID	text (set as primary key)
LastName	text
FirstName	text
Address	text
City	text
State/Prov.	text (size=2)
Postal Code	text (use an Input Mask)
Country	text (default USA)

TABLE 2.6   Customer Table Fields

Print the structure of both tables, using the Object Definition report.

2. Enter the data in Table 2.7 into the Plant table.

ProdNum	Name	Type	Variety	Per/Oz
101	Red cabbage	vegetable	summer	800
102	Oriental cabbage	vegetable	fall	700
103	Early Brussels Sprouts	vegetable	spring	800
104	Early Girl Tomato	vegetable	spring	100
105	Petunia	annual	summer	400
106	Begonia	annual	summer	300
107	Rock Geranium	perennial	summer	100
108	Pansy	annual	spring	400
109	Leek	vegetable	winter	800
110	Carrot	vegetable	fall	800
111	Beet	vegetable	summer	700
112	Iris	bulb	spring	3
113	Aster	perennial	summer	10
114	Poppy	perennial	summer	20
115	Sunflower	annual	summer	50
116	Forget-me-not	annual	spring	400
117	Sweet Pea	annual	spring	200
118	Cosmos	annual	summer	500
119	Pea	vegetable	spring	100
120	Radish	vegetable	summer	700

TABLE 2.7 Data for the Plant Table

Print the Plant table.

3. Enter the data in Table 2.8 into the Customer table.

CustID	LastName	FirstName	Address	City	State/Prov.	Postal Code	Country
1111	Jones	Sue	345 Onyx St.	Eugene	OR	97403	USA
1112	Collins	Grace	4404 Ocean View	Ft. Lauderdale	FL	00303	USA
1113	Bird	Georgia	45 Garden Loop	Lexington	KY	40608	USA
1114	Campbell	Jo	150 Oak St.	Cambridge	NH	20987	USA
1115	Park	Ann	P. O. Box 978	McGrath	AK	98765	USA
1116	Hanson	Pat	76 Capital St.	Frankfort	KY	48765	USA
1117	Nelson	Karen	34 Lake St.	Kalamazoo	MI	34567	USA
1118	Smith	Shirley	233 Mountain View	Glacier	BC	98765	Canada
1119	O'Hagan	Jean	678 Pine St	Bellingham	WA	97654	USA
1120	Bean	Jack	234 Border Dr.	Bisbee	AZ	67890	USA

TABLE 2.8   Data for the Customer Table

Print the Customer table.

4. Alphabets Children's Books would like you to create an inventory database. As you start analyzing the data, you notice that almost all of the books in the store come from three publishers and that including the publisher information with the book list will cause redundancy problems. You decide to divide the data into two tables—a book table and a publisher table. Create a database from scratch and name it Alphabets Inventory.

Create the Book table using the fields that Table 2.9 lists.

Print the structure of the table, using the Object Definition report.

Field Name	Data Type
BookID	text (set as primary key)
Title	text
Last	text
First	text time
Pubdate	date/time (must be after 12/31/49)
PubID	text

TABLE 2.9   Book Table Fields

Create the Publisher table using the fields that Table 2.10 lists.

Print the structure of the table, using the Object Definition report.

Field Name	Data Type
PubID	text (set as primary key)
Pub	text
Address	text
City	text
State/Prov.	text (change the size to 2 and use the default NY)
Postal Code	text (use an Input Mask for this field)

TABLE 2.10   Publisher Table Fields

Relating Tables and Working with Data

UNIT OBJECTIVES

- Create a relationship between tables
- Add records to a table
- Use the Lookup Wizard
- Edit records in a table
- Delete records from a table
- Find records and replace data
- Sort the records
- Move or copy records

In the last unit, you learned to create tables, specify the data that can be entered in a field, and set a primary key for the table. In this unit, you will learn to use the primary key to link two tables together to set up a relationship between the tables. You will also work with the actual data in the records of the table by inputting data, editing records, deleting records, finding and replacing data in a record, sorting records, and copying and moving records to different tables. You will also create a lookup table to limit data entry in certain fields of the table.

TASK 1	*Creating Relationships Between Tables in a Database*

What: Define relationships between tables in the database.

How: In the Database window, use Tools | Relationships.

Why: To combine related data from two or more tables.

Tip: To combine data from two separate tables, each table needs a matching field that provides the relationship between the tables.

RELATIONAL DESIGN

Relationships define how the data in separate tables is linked. For example, in the Spread the Light—Candles MailOrder database, the Customers and Orders tables have been created as two separate tables even though the orders in the Orders table are recorded for customers who are in the Customers table.

Suppose the database design was different. If a single table held the customer and order information, that table would be similar to the one shown in Figure 3.1. Notice the redundant data. Clearly, this is a poor design.

1. Redundant data

2. One record contains customer and order data

CustomerOrders : Table

CustomerID	CompanyName	Order ID	Order Date	InvoiceAmount
1	Down Enterprises	2	25-Apr-98	$2,500.00
1	Down Enterprises	6	09-Jun-99	$234.44
1	Down Enterprises	12	15-Aug-99	$2,345.10
2	Holt Construction	9	12-Jul-99	$5,322.65
2	Holt Construction	11	15-Aug-99	$123.45
3	Able Software	1	11-Apr-98	$123.67
3	Able Software	4	15-May-99	$2,800.12
3	Able Software	8	15-Jun-99	$2,433.43
3	Able Software	13	15-Aug-99	$675.44
4	Trent Graphics	5	15-May-99	$4,322.65
5	Alpha Networks	7	10-Jun-99	$5,422.22
6	Kramer Inc.	3	05-May-98	$1,195.00
6	Kramer Inc.	10	14-Aug-99	$202.00

Record: 1 of 13

FIGURE 3.1   A Table That Does Not Take Advantage of Relational Database Design

To create an effective relational design, place repetitive data into a separate table. Repetitive or redundant data only needs to be stored once when using a relational database. To avoid redundant data, place all customer information in one table and all order information in another, as shown in Figure 3.2. That way the customer information needs to be typed only once in the Customers table and not each time a new order is recorded.

It is not enough to simply pull out redundant data while creating a relational table because you would not know which orders belong to which customers. With relational design, there must be a matching field in each table that provides a link between the tables.

The main or **primary table** uniquely identifies each record with a primary key, such as CustomerID in the Customer table. Then, the primary key of the

66   Quick, Simple Microsoft Access 2000

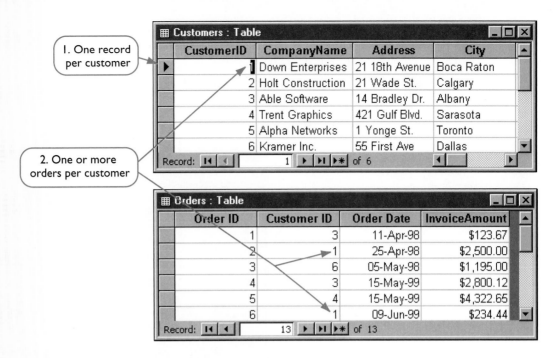

1. One record per customer

2. One or more orders per customer

FIGURE 3.2 Designing Relational Tables

Customer table repeats in the Order table to link an order to a customer. When the primary key of one table links the primary table to a **secondary table**, that field becomes a **foreign key** in the secondary table. For example, the CustomerID is the primary key in the Customers table and is a foreign key in the Orders table. The CustomerID provides the link between the records of the two tables and is the matching field that relates the tables together.

CREATING A RELATIONSHIP

To create a relationship between tables in a database, you need two or more tables that have the necessary ingredients in their design. In the Spread the Light—Candles MailOrder database, the Customers and Orders tables fulfill the requirements. The Customers table—the primary table—has a CustomerID field that can link to the CustomerID field in the Orders table—the secondary table—where the order information for the customer resides.

POINTER

Matching Field Types

You can run into problems linking tables if the data type of the primary key and the foreign key are a mismatch. So when you are getting started with Access, it is safest to make both the primary key and the foreign key text fields and input the data manually. For that reason, we have avoided using AutoNumber in the primary key fields in the projects even though AutoNumber would be faster for data entry.

To create a relationship between tables in Access, use the Relationships window. To open this window and create a relationship, follow these steps:

1. Close all tables.
2. Click the Relationships button on the Access toolbar, or choose Tools | Relationships.

The Relationships window opens, as shown in Figure 3.3.

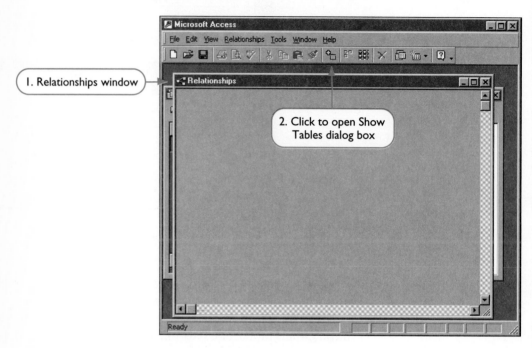

FIGURE 3.3 The Relationships Window

3. If the Show Table dialog box is not open, click the Show Table button to open it as shown in Figure 3.4.

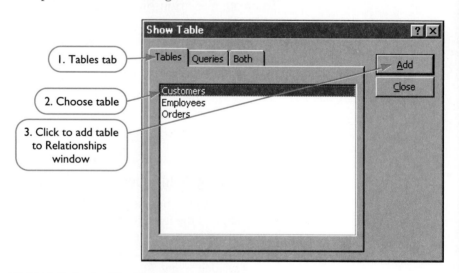

FIGURE 3.4 The Show Table Dialog Box

4. Choose the tables to include in the relationship. Either double-click the table name or select a table and click the Add button. An image of the table is added to the Relationships window.
5. Repeat the process as needed to add all the tables required in the relationship.

Relating Tables

Each individual relationship is between two tables. However, the Relationships window can be used to add more than one relationship to an Access database because each table can be related to several other tables if necessary.

6. After selecting the necessary tables, click the Close button in the Show Table dialog box. The Relationships window contains the selected tables, as shown in Figure 3.5. If necessary, you can drag or resize the window to view the tables.

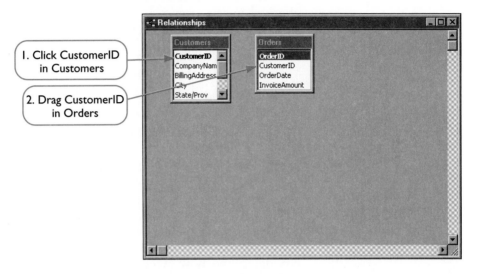

1. Click CustomerID in Customers

2. Drag CustomerID in Orders

FIGURE 3.5   The Relationships Window Containing Two Tables

7. Create a relationship by dragging the primary key field from the primary table to the matching field in the secondary table. The Edit Relationships dialog box displays, as shown in Figure 3.6. When this dialog box opens, check that the correct fields in each table have been selected for the relationship. If not, cancel the edit and repeat the process of dragging between the table fields, being careful to select the fields you need.

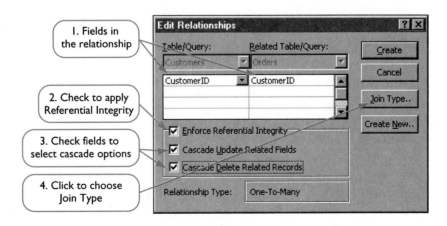

1. Fields in the relationship

2. Check to apply Referential Integrity

3. Check fields to select cascade options

4. Click to choose Join Type

FIGURE 3.6   The Edit Relationships Dialog Box

What to Do About Relationship Problems

If your relationship between two tables does not turn out as expected, there may be a way to repair the damage. Check out the following reasons why relationships sometimes don't work.

• The primary table should use a primary key field in the relationship.

• Both tables must have matching fields to relate.

• Both fields used in the relationship must be the same data type. For example, you can't link a text field to a numeric field.

The Edit Relationships dialog box has three check boxes that are shown checked in the example. We will deselect these options because they are beyond the scope of this introduction:

• **Enforce Referential Integrity** keeps you from accidentally deleting or changing data that might destroy the relationship.

• **Cascade Update Related Fields** lets you update (edit) a field in the primary table, and Access will then automatically update a related field in the secondary table. In the example, a change to CustomerID in the Customer table would cause the ID field in the Orders table to update automatically.

• **Cascade Delete Related Records** causes Access to delete all records in the secondary table (Orders) that have the same CustomerID if you delete a record in the primary table (Customers).

Click the **Join Type** button in the Edit Relationships dialog box to open the Join Properties dialog box shown in Figure 3.7. The options in this dialog box determine how Access will handle records from the primary and secondary tables when they are joined. In the figure, the second option determines that all records in the Customer table will be included in the relationship, but any records in the Orders table that do not have a matching CustomerID will not be included. With this option, it is possible that some customer records will not have any matching orders, but in that case we still want to keep the customer record in the relationship.

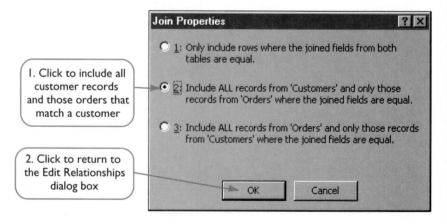

FIGURE 3.7 The Join Properties Dialog Box

After creating the relationship and making the necessary option choices, click the Create button. Access creates the relationship and shows the result in the Relationships window, as shown in Figure 3.8. If the Enforce Referential Integrity option is selected, the line drawn between the two table images contains a number 1 and an infinity symbol. The number 1 and the infinity symbol signify that this is a one-to-many relationship. One record in the Customers table can have many related records in the Orders table. That is, one customer can place many orders, but a specific order has only one customer.

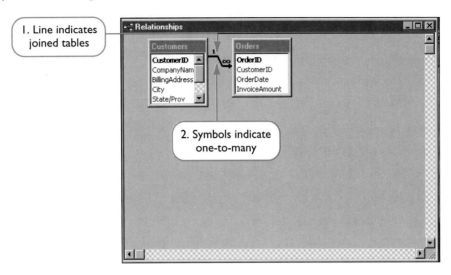

FIGURE 3.8 The Related Tables

POINTER

Printing a Hard Copy of the Relationships

With the Relationships window displayed, choose File | Print Relationships to send a copy of the relationship window to the Print Preview window. Click the Print button on the Print Preview toolbar to print the report.

POINTER

Deleting Relationships

If you have a relationship you no longer need, or you would like to change a relationship, it is easier to delete the relationship and start over. Complete the following steps to delete the relationship between tables.

1. Choose Tools | Relationships or click the Relationships button to open the Relationships window.
2. Click the Relationship line between the two tables. It will turn bold.
3. Press the Delete key to delete the relationship.

When the Relationships window closes, Access will ask if you want to save the changes to the layout of the Relationships. Click Yes to save the Relationships, and Access returns you to the Database window. As you work with these tables, the relationship settings that you define will operate on all updates to the tables.

EXERCISE 1 | *Creating Relationships*

1. If necessary, open the MailOrder database and close any tables that are open.
   To create a relationship, tables that are to be used in the relationship must be closed.

2. Choose **Tools | Relationships** from the Access menu bar or click the **Relationships button** on the Access toolbar.
   The Relationships window opens. Your window may also contain the Show Table dialog box.

3. If necessary, click the **Show Table button** on the Access toolbar.
   The Show Table dialog box opens in the Relationships window.

4. Click **Customers** in the **Tables** tab of the Show Table dialog box.

5. Click the **Add button** in the Show Table dialog box.
   Access adds the Customers table to the Relationships window.

6. Double-click **Orders** in the **Tables** tab of the Show Table dialog box.
   Access adds the Orders table to the Relationships window.

7. Click the **Close button** on the Show Tables dialog box.
   The tables you selected now appear in the Relationships window.

8. Click and drag from **CustomerID** in the Customers table to **CustomerID** in the Orders table.
   The Edit Relationships dialog box opens. If CustomerID is not shown under Customers and Orders in the dialog box, click Cancel and repeat step.

9. Deselect the following options by clicking the check box: **Cascade Update Related Fields, Enforce Referential Integrity, Cascade Delete Related Records**.

10. Click the **Join Type button** in the Edit Relationships dialog box.
    The Join Properties dialog box opens.

11. Click option number **2** in the Join Properties dialog box.
    Option 2 will cause all Customer records to be included in the relationship, but only those orders that have a matching CustomerID in a customer record will be included.

12. Click **OK** in the Join Properties dialog box.
    The dialog box closes, and Access returns you to the Edit Relationships dialog box.

13. Click the **Create button** in the Edit Relationships dialog box.
    Access creates the relationship and returns you to the Relationships dialog box.

14. Choose **File | Print Relationships**.
    Access displays the Relationships as a report in Print Preview with only a line between the tables. The number one and the infinity symbol will not appear because Referential Integrity was deselected.

Quick, Simple Microsoft Access 2000

15. Click the **Print button** on the Print Preview window.
Access prints the report on the attached printer.

16. Close the Print Preview window and if necessary close the Report window.
Save the changes to the report. The Relationship window displays.

17. Click the **Close button** on the Relationship window.
Access returns you to the Database window.

TASK 2 | *Adding Records to Tables*

What: Add a new record to a table.

How: Open the table and choose Insert | New Record.

Why: To add new employees to the Employee table or new customers to the Customer table.

Tip: Set default data for as many fields as possible to cut down on data entry.

You have already added some data to tables in the previous units, but we will look at three slightly different methods for adding a new record, so you can use the method that suits you. Tables in the database will need to have new data added to them. For example, as the company hires new employees, we will want to include them in the Employee table for future reference. Normally, Access provides a blank record at the end of the table identified by an asterisk (*) in the Row Selector button. You can click in that record and immediately begin typing new data. The following methods are more useful when the table contains enough records so that the end of the table is not normally in view.

To add records to an existing table, open the table in Datasheet view and then use one of the three following methods to insert the new record:

- Choose Insert | New Record from the menu bar.
- Click the New Record button on the toolbar or status bar.
- Right-click the Record selector button and choose New Record from the shortcut menu.

Following any one of these operations inserts a new blank record at the end of the table. Data may now be typed into the record, as shown in Figure 3.9.

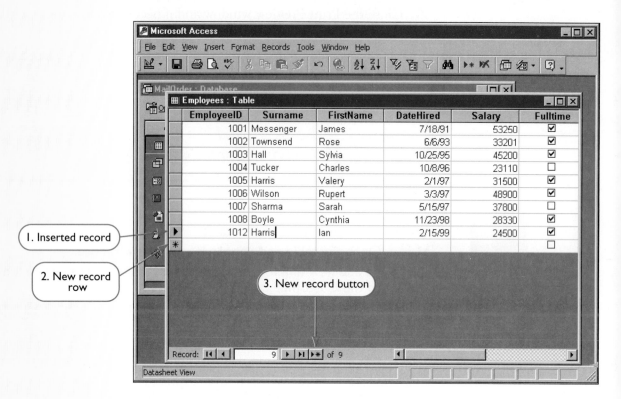

FIGURE 3.9 Inserting a New Record

EXERCISE 2 | *Inserting a New Record*

1. Choose the **Employees** table from the **Tables** choice in the Objects bar of the MailOrder database window.

2. Click the **Open button** on the Database window.
   The Employees table opens in Datasheet view.

3. Choose **Insert | New Record** from the Access menu bar.
   The insertion point moves to a new blank record at the end of the table.

4. Type the data for new employee Ian Harris, EmployeeID 1012, into the record, as shown in Figure 3.9.

POINTER

If the New Record Button Is Dimmed

If you are already in the new record at the end of the table, the New Record button will appear dimmed on the toolbar, indicating that it is not available.

5. Click the **New Record button** on the Access toolbar.

6. In the blank record, type the information for Raymond Morgan, EmployeeID 1009, as shown in Figure 3.10.
The record appears in the table, but it is not in order by the EmployeeID.

EmployeeID	Surname	FirstName	DateHired	Salary	Fulltime
1001	Messenger	James	7/18/91	53250	☑
1002	Townsend	Rose	6/6/93	33201	☑
1003	Hall	Sylvia	10/25/95	45200	☑
1004	Tucker	Charles	10/8/96	23110	☐
1005	Harris	Valery	2/1/97	31500	☑
1006	Wilson	Rupert	3/3/97	48900	☑
1007	Sharma	Sarah	5/15/97	37800	☐
1008	Boyle	Cynthia	11/23/98	28330	☑
1012	Harris	Ian	2/15/99	24500	☑
1009	Morgan	Raymond	1/29/99	22600	☑

2. Record out of order

1. Inserted record

FIGURE 3.10   Inserting a New Record with a Lower EmployeeID

7. Click the **View button** on the Access toolbar to switch to Design view.

8. Click the **View button** on the Access toolbar to return to Datasheet view.
The record for employee 1009 is now in order in the table. Closing the table and opening it again would also result in the data being ordered by the primary key.

TASK 3 | *Using the Lookup Wizard*

What: Modifying a field to use a lookup table.

How: Switch to Design view and choose Lookup Wizard under the Data Type.

Why: If the data in a field is limited to a certain body of choices, you can save data entry by placing the possible choices in a table.

Tip: Only use a lookup table for data that will not change or will change only rarely.

You may have noticed that some data in certain fields is limited to a body of data, such as the 50 states, certain breeds of dogs sold by a kennel, or specific plant types. You can use an option called the Lookup Wizard to place the possible choices in a table, so that instead of having to type the information, the user can select it from a list.

To create a lookup table, follow these steps:

1. Open the desired table in Design view.
2. Type the field name for the field and click in the Data Type text box.
3. Click the dropdown list and select Lookup Wizard.

Step one of the Lookup Wizard displays, as shown in Figure 3.11.

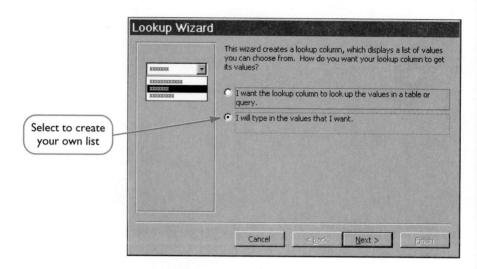

FIGURE 3.11   Choose Between Using a Table or a List That You Enter

4. Select the **I will type in the values that I want** option.
5. Click the Next button to display the second step of the wizard, as shown in Figure 3.12.

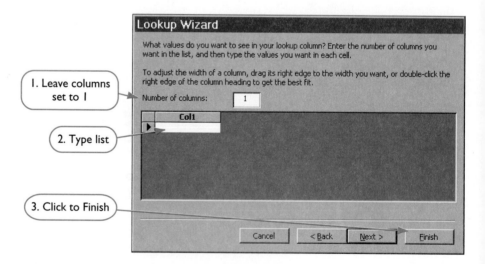

FIGURE 3.12   Enter the Possible Values

6. Type the list in the space provided in the dialog box. When the list is complete, click Next or the Finish button. If you click the Next button, the Finish dialog box displays and you should then click Finish.
7. Return to Datasheet view and add a record.
8. When you get to the field, click the dropdown box and choose one of the options you typed in the list using the wizard.

EXERCISE 3 | *Using the Lookup Wizard*

1. In Design view, create a new table called Test.

2. Type the field name Housing.
The field name is input into the table.

3. Click in the Data Type box.
The data type down arrow displays.

4. Click the down arrow and choose Lookup Wizard.
The Lookup Wizard launches.

5. Select the **I will type in the values that I want** option.

6. Click the **Next** button.
The second step of the Lookup Wizard displays.

7. Leave the number of columns set to 1 and click in the text box under the Col1 heading.

8. Type **rent** and press Tab; type **own** and press Tab; type **other** and press Tab.

9. Click the **Finish** button.

10. Save the design and return to Datasheet view.

11. Click in the Housing field to display the down arrow.

12. Click the down arrow to display the list and click on **own**.
The option **own** appears in the field.

13. Close the table.

TASK 4 | *Editing Record Contents*

What: Change the contents of a record in the table.

How: In Datasheet view, click in the field to be modified and insert or delete characters.

Why: This procedure is needed to change field contents, such as an address, phone number, amount, or other information.

Tip: If you make an incorrect change, you can use Undo, providing no other change has been made to the table.

Editing field contents is necessary when a customer or employee changes their address, phone number, or other information. Almost any table contains data that at some point in time may need to be changed. Sometimes the reason for the change is as simple as correcting a typographical error.

Editing the contents of a field in an Access Datasheet is similar to editing text in a Word document. Table 3.1 shows typical field editing actions.

To	Action
Select a word	Double-click
Select text	Drag over the text to be selected
Delete selected text	Press Delete
Place the insertion point	Click in the field
Delete characters to the left	Press the Backspace key
Delete characters to the right	Press the Delete key

TABLE 3.1   Editing Field Contents

EXERCISE 4 | Editing Record Contents

1. Open the **Employees** table in Datasheet view.
2. Place the insertion point in the FirstName field for Raymond Morgan, EmployeeID 1009.
3. Edit the name to change it from **Raymond** to **Ray**.
4. Click in the DateHired field and change the date from **1/29/99** to **12/9/99**.
5. Click in the EmployeeID field of Ian Harris's record. Change his EmployeeID from **1012** to **1010**.
   Your results should appear as shown in Figure 3.13.

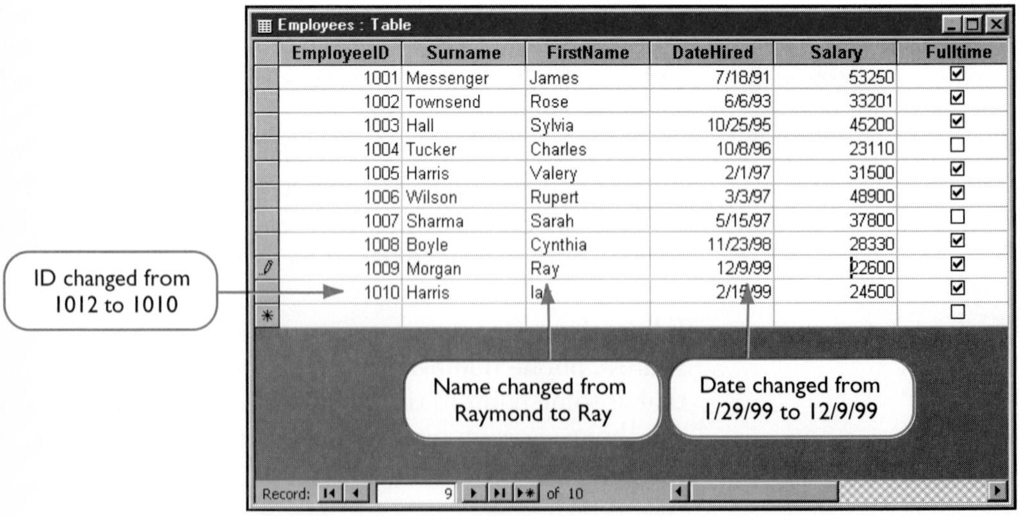

ID changed from 1012 to 1010

Name changed from Raymond to Ray

Date changed from 1/29/99 to 12/9/99

FIGURE 3.13   Changes to the Field Contents of the Employees Table

TASK 5 | Deleting a Record

What: Delete a record from the table.

How: Click the Delete button on the toolbar or choose Edit | Delete.

Why: To remove a record that is no longer required in the table.

Tip: It is advisable to backup your database often. You can do this in Windows Explorer by making a copy of the database file.

In the normal process of events, records in your table may no longer be required. You will occasionally want to **delete records**. However, you will want to do so sparingly because they will be gone forever.

POINTER

Deleting Records

Never delete records that you might have a use for in the future. For example, you would never delete the record for an employee who quits your company, because you would have no records for the IRS or for any other important record keeping. Create a table of former employees and move the record to that table. (You will learn to move and copy records later in this unit.)

To delete a record, complete the following steps:

1. Place the insertion point anywhere in the record to be deleted.
2. Either click the Delete Record button in the toolbar or choose Edit | Delete.

As shown in Figure 3.14, Access prompts you to ensure that you intend to delete the record. If you choose Yes, the record is permanently deleted from the table. After the record is deleted you will not be able to undo the operation and restore the record.

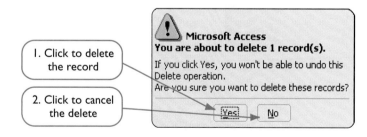

FIGURE 3.14 Access Makes Sure You Want to Delete the Record

To practice deleting a record, you will delete an employee from the Employee table. In reality, you would never delete an employee. (See Pointer: Deleting Records, page 79.)

(See Pointer: Deleting Records, page 79.)

POINTER

Can You Restore a Deleted Record?

Records you delete are permanently deleted, and the deletion can't be undone. The only way to restore deleted records is from a backup file you create of your data.

EXERCISE 5 | *Deleting a Record*

1. If necessary, open the **Employees** table in Datasheet view.
2. Click to place the insertion point in EmployeeID **1007**, which is the record for Sarah Sharma.
3. Click the **Delete Record button** in the Access toolbar.
   A prompt displays and advises you that the record is about to be permanently deleted, as shown in Figure 3.14.
4. Click **Yes** to delete the record.

TASK 6 | *Finding a Record*

What: Locate a record in the table.

How: Use Edit | Find to locate a record by providing a sample value.

Why: To quickly find a record without the need to manually scroll through the table.

Tip: The Find button on the toolbar is a quick method for opening the Find dialog box.

When you only have a few records in the table, it is easy to simply look down the rows to **find** the record you need. But in reality, there are often hundreds, or even thousands, of records, which makes it difficult to scroll through the table and find a record you need. This is where the Find command is especially useful. To locate a record in the table, first place the insertion point in the field you want to search and then choose Edit | Find or click the Find button to open the Find and Replace dialog box, as shown in Figure 3.15. Type the value and click the Find Next button to have Access look for the first record containing that value. Click Find Next again and the next record that matches the value will be found.

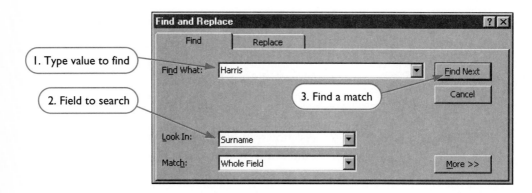

FIGURE 3.15   Using the Find Tab in the Find and Replace Dialog Box

FIND OPTIONS

Options in the Find and Replace dialog box can be used to make your searching more effective. You will not need to use these options often, but in the right situation they can make the difference between a successful search and one that does not get an accurate match. Table 3.2 describes the available options. You will need to click the More button to see them all.

Option	Choices	Purpose
Look in	Field or Table	Choose the field or the entire table for searching.
Match	Whole Field	Matches all characters in the field.
	Any Part of Field	Looks for the characters you type within any part of the field. For example, searching for "del" would be found within Costa del Sol.
	Start of Field	Matches only the beginning of the field. For example, "Costa" would be found in Costa del Sol.
Search	Up, Down, All	Determines the direction of the search. All is the default.
Match Case	When checked	Matches upper and lower case as typed. A search for "sarah" would match "sarah" but not "Sarah."
Search Fields as Formatted	When checked	Used for searching date fields to match the exact formatting used in the date.

TABLE 3.2   Find Options

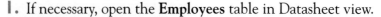

EXERCISE 6 | *Finding a Record*

1. If necessary, open the **Employees** table in Datasheet view.

2. Click to place the insertion point in the **Surname** field of the first record in the table.

3. Choose **Edit | Find** from the Access menu bar or click the **Find** button on the Access toolbar.
The Find and Replace dialog box is opened.

4. As shown in Figure 3.15, type **Harris** in the **Find What** text box of the Find and Replace dialog box.

5. Click the **Find Next button**.
Access locates the first record containing Harris and highlights the surname. You may need to move the Find What box out of the way to see the name.

6. Click the **Find Next button** again.
Access locates the next record containing Harris and highlights the surname.

7. Continue to click the **Find Next button**.
As no other records contain the name Harris, an Access message tells you that the item was not found.

8. Click **OK**.

9. Click **Cancel** to close the Find and Replace dialog box.

TASK 7 | *Replacing Field Contents*

What: Locate a field and replace its content.

How: Use Edit | Find and the Replace tab to locate a record and replace its field content.

Why: To automatically replace matching data in any number of records.

Tip: Select Match Whole Field to avoid replacing only partial matches in fields.

The **Replace** command is a powerful tool for replacing the contents of matching fields in the table. If all customers in a certain area code have their code changed, using Replace is a quick way of making the change. A commission rates table can be changed from a rate of 5% to 6.5% quickly and easily with this command. Replace works like the Find command, but in addition to typing the value you want to find, you also type its replacement value. To replace data, choose Edit | Replace. Then, provide the values needed, as shown in Figure 3.16.

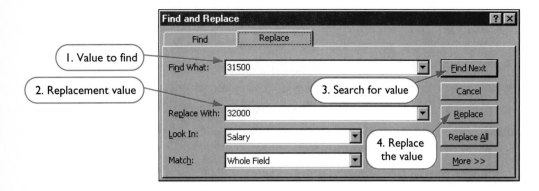

FIGURE 3.16 Using the Replace Tab in the Find and Replace Dialog Box

---

EXERCISE 7 | *Replacing Field Contents*

1. If necessary, open the Employees table in Datasheet view.
2. Click in the **Salary** field of the first record.
3. Choose **Edit | Replace** from the Access menu bar.
   The Find and Replace dialog box opens.
4. In the **Find What:** text box, type **31500**.
5. In the **Replace With:** text box, type **32000**.
   Be sure that **Look in** shows **Salary** and that **Match** shows **Whole Field**, as shown in Figure 3.16.
6. Click the **Find Next button**.
   The first record containing 31500 is found and highlighted.
7. Click the **Replace button**.
   Access replaces the value 31500 with 32000.
8. Click the **Find Next button**.
   As no other records contain the value 31500, Access tells you that the item was not found.
9. Click **OK**.
10. Click **Cancel** to close the Find and Replace dialog box.

TASK 8 | *Sorting the Table*

What: Sort the records in the table in a new order.

How: Choose Records | Sort from the menu bar.

Why: To view the records in the Datasheet ordered by a field that you choose.

Tip: You can view the table in either ascending or descending order.

Records in the table may be easier to read or understand if they are sorted on a field, such as a surname. In the Datasheet, you can **sort** the table's records on a specific field by completing the following steps:

1. Select the field in the view.
2. Choose Records | Sort.
3. Choose either Sort Ascending or Sort Descending.

The **ascending** option orders the records from lowest to highest (0 to 9 or A to Z) while the **descending** option orders from highest to lowest (9 to 0 or Z to A). For example, the table in Figure 3.17 shows the Employees table after it has been sorted in ascending order on the surname field.

Sorting does not affect the order of records in the table because the primary key controls the actual order of the records. Sorting only changes your view of the records in the Datasheet.

To sort a table using toolbar buttons, complete the following steps:

1. Click in the column you want to sort by.
2. Click either the Sort Ascending or Sort Descending button in the toolbar to create the desired order.

FIGURE 3.17 The Employee Table Sorted in Ascending Order from the Lowest to Highest Surname

---

EXERCISE 8 | *Sorting the Table*

1. In the Employees table datasheet, click in a **Surname**.
2. From the Access menu bar, choose **Records | Sort | Sort Ascending** or click the **Sort Ascending button** on the Access toolbar.

The records in the table are sorted from lowest to highest on the employee's surname field, as shown in Figure 3.17.

3. Click in the **Salary** field.

4. From the Access menu bar, choose **Records | Sort | Sort Descending** or click the **Sort Descending button** on the Access toolbar.
   The records in the table are sorted from highest to lowest on the salary. The highest salaries come first going down the column to the lowest salary.

5. Click in the **EmployeeID** field.

6. From the Access menu bar, choose **Records | Sort | Sort Ascending** or click the **Sort Ascending button** on the Access toolbar.
   Access sorts the records in the table by the EmployeeID, which is the primary key field.

7. Click the **Close button** on the Datasheet to close the Employees table.
   Access prompts you to save the changes to the table design.

8. Click **No** so that the changes to the design of the table are not saved.

TASK 9	***Moving and Copying Records to Another Table***

What: Moving or copying records from one table to another.

How: Use Cut and Copy as you would in your word processing software.

Why: You might want to remove out-of-date records from a table but keep them in another table.

Tip: Data must be pasted to the same field type as the original data. That is, you can't paste a text field into a numeric field.

As you administer your database, you may find that some records get out of date, such as employees who quit, products that are no longer available, or customers who haven't done business with you in years. To keep the database from becoming too large with data that you don't need, you will want to remove those records. However, if you simply delete the records, you will lose all the information associated with that record. Instead, you should move the records to another table in the database designated to contain the out-of-date records. For example, if you create a Former Employee table, you can move records for employees who quit to that table.

> **POINTER**
>
> **Moving or Copying Records**
>
> In order to successfully move or copy records from one table to another, both tables must contain like field names that appear in the same order and use the same data type. Otherwise, Access will not paste the data in the new table.

To move or copy records, follow these steps:

1. Open the table with the records to move or copy.
2. Select the record to move or copy.
3. Click the Cut button to move the record or click the Copy button to copy the record.
4. Open or switch to the table to receive the records.
5. Choose Edit | Paste Append.

Access adds the record to the bottom of the table.

You will create a table for former employees in the next exercise.

EXERCISE 9 | *Moving a Record*

1. Create a new table called Former Employees.
   The new table opens.

2. Place the same field names and data types contained in the Employees table.

3. Save the structure of the new table and close the table.

4. Open the Employees table and add a new record that contains your name and address information. Make up any data as necessary.

5. Select the new record.

6. Click the **Cut button**.
   Access removes the record from the table and places the data on the clipboard.

7. Switch to the Former Employees table.

8. Choose **Edit | Paste Append**.
   Access places the record in the new table.

9. Close both tables.

R E V I E W

SUMMARY

After completing this unit, you should be able to

- create a relationship between tables (page 66)
- add records to a table (page 73)
- use the Lookup Wizard (page 75)
- edit records in a table (page 77)
- delete records from a table (page 79)

- find records and replace data (page 80)
- sort the records (page 83)
- move or copy records (page 85)

KEY TERMS

ascending order (page 84)

cascade update (page 70)

cascade delete (page 70)

delete records (page 79)

descending order (page 84)

editing (page 77)

find (page 80)

foreign key (page 67)

Join Type (page 70)

primary table (page 66)

Referential Integrity (page 70)

Replace (page 82)

secondary table (page 67)

sort (page 84)

TEST YOUR SKILLS

True/False

1. Two tables must be related using the primary key.
2. The Lookup Wizard creates a list of data to choose from when entering records.
3. Once you have defined a relationship between two tables, you cannot delete it.
4. You would use the Replace operation to change a value, such as an area code, to a new value in all matching records.
5. Sorting a table on the salary field in descending order places the employee with the highest salary first.

Multiple Choice

1. The primary key and the foreign key must
   a. contain the same data
   b. be the same data type
   c. be the same size
   d. all of these answers

2. To move or copy a record from one table to another, you must have two tables
   a. with the same field structure
   b. with the same field types
   c. with the fields in the same order
   d. all of these answers

3. To create a link between two tables, you must have
   a. a primary key in the primary table
   b. a separate key in a separate table
   c. an open key in the secondary table
   d. all of these answers

4. Which procedure is the correct way to insert a new record?
   a. choose Insert | New Record
   b. click the New Record button on the toolbar
   c. right-click the Record selector button and choose New Record from the shortcut menu
   d. all of these answers

5. When you delete a record from the table
   a. you can undo the delete providing a new record has not been inserted
   b. it is stored in a temporary Deleted Records file
   c. it is permanently removed from the table
   d. the table must first be backed up before a delete is possible

Short Answer

Match the elements to their location on the screen in Figure 3.18.

____ a. indicates a one to many relationship
____ b. primary key
____ c. foreign key
____ d. primary table
____ e. secondary table

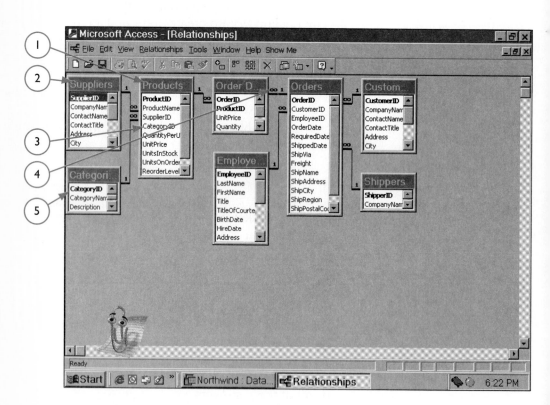

FIGURE 3.18

What Does This Do?

Write a description of the function for the following:

1.		6.		
2.		7.		
3.	an * in front of a record	8.		
4.		9.		
5.		10.		

On Your Own

1. Open a table and sort the data by ascending order and then descending order.
2. Open a table and find data in the table.
3. Open a table and replace data in the table using the Replace feature.
4. Open a table and add new records to the table.
5. Open a table in Design view and run the Lookup Wizard to create a list of data choices for a field.

PROJECTS

1. Open the JRT Kennel Database. So far, you have created two tables: the Customer table and the Dog table. You have included a primary key for each table, but the tables are not related.

   Open the Dog table and add a new field named *Purchased By*. Make the new field a text field. Using the data from Unit 2, Project 3, input the correct Customer Number into the *Purchased By* field. For example, you want the correct Customer Number for John Smith in the record for Misty since that is the customer who purchased that specific dog.

   Once you have input all the correct customer numbers in the new field in the Dog table, close all open tables, and create a link between the two tables by relating them together.

   Print the relationships, save the relationships, and close the database.

2. Open Alphabets Inventory and open the Publishers table.

   Input the data Table 3.3 lists into the Publisher table.

   Save the table.

   Print the table.

PubID	Pub	Address	City	State/Prov.	Postal Code
101	Prentice Hall	One Lake St.	Upper Saddle River	NJ	074589087
102	Addison-Wesley Longman	100 Main St.	New York	NY	009010987
103	Macmillan	400 Liberty St	Buffalo	NY	076540987

TABLE 3.3   Data for the Publisher Table

Open the Books table and input the data from Table 3.4.

Save the table.

Sort the table by book title.

Print the sorted table.

Save the table.

Close the database.

BookID	Title	Last	First	Pubdate	PubID
a3	My First Letters	Smith	Jean	1/1/90	101
a8	Alphabet Soup	Murry	Bob	1/1/87	101
a9	Animal Alphabet	Jones	Sue	3/15/91	102
b4	Computer Fun	Baxter	Hal	6/30/98	103
b9	My First Pet	Smith	Al	1/1/97	103
b10	My Garden	Jeanne	Karen	3/31/99	101
c3	Playing Music	Hill	Izzy	1/31/98	101
c12	Cartooning	Grenne	Jan	2/15/93	103
c4	Origami	Jones	Angela	12/15/90	102
d1	Drawing Animals	Brown	Sue	11/30/76	102

TABLE 3.4   Data for the Book Table

3. Open the Alphabets Inventory database. Link the tables by creating a relationship between the tables. Print the relationship report. Save the relationship and close the database.

4. Open the Alphabets Inventory database. Create a new table and call it Out of Print. Place the same field names and field types in the new table as there are in the Books table. Move the record d1 from the Book table to the Out of Print table.

Print both tables.

Close the database.

Querying the Database

UNIT OBJECTIVES

- Use Filter by Selection in a table
- Use Filter by Form in a table
- Use the Simple Query Wizard to create a query
- Edit the contents of a query
- Use Design view to create a query
- Use And and Or criteria in a query
- Use linked tables in a query

Companies often have large tables that contain hundreds or even thousands of records. From these tables of data, a company might want to list all of the customers who have ordered the same product, have an overdue bill, haven't placed an order in over six months, or any other information that will help their business. You could use the Find operation that the previous unit discusses; however, Find selects only one record at a time, making it difficult to view or print all of the records that are found. A more efficient way of working is to filter the data or to create a query. Filtering data is a quick method for creating a query with only simple requirements, such as to display all the records for customers who live in Dallas. For more complex needs, Access provides a Query option in the Objects bar where the Query Wizard, Design view, or other methods are available to create the query.

What: Use Filter by Selection.

How: Select a field in the table and click the Filter by Selection button.

Why: To create a datasheet containing records that match your selected value.

Tip: When you run water through a filter, all unwanted elements are left behind. When you filter data, you are restricting which records in the table should display.

Filter by Selection is a quick way to find like data in the table. For example, if you want to see all the vegetable seeds in your inventory, select the value "vegetable" and have Access filter out all the records that don't match that value. Access displays a datasheet containing records from your table that match the filter. For example, Access would create a temporary table displaying only vegetable seeds.

To filter the table, follow these steps:

1. Select a value in the table. Figure 4.1 shows the value "Canada" selected in the Country column of the Customers table.
2. Click the Filter by Selection button on the toolbar.

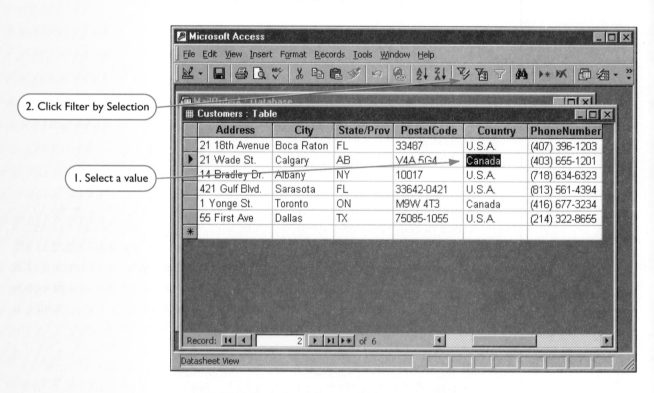

FIGURE 4.1 Selecting a Value for Filtering

Access filters the table based on the selected value and opens a datasheet containing the results, as shown in Figure 4.2.

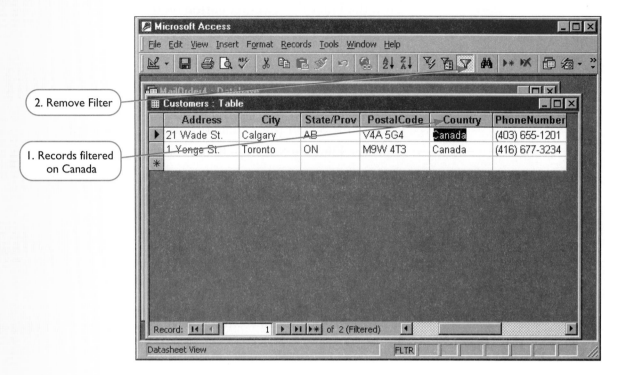

FIGURE 4.2 The Filtered Data

3. Click the **Remove Filter** button to remove the filter and display all data in the table.

To display all records for customers except for those in Canada, use the **Filtering Excluding Selection** option available from the Records menu. Complete the following steps to use this option:

1. Select the field containing the data that you want omitted in the output.
2. Choose Records | Filter | Filter Excluding Selection.

Access displays all records except those containing the data you selected.

Displaying filtered data is just another way of viewing the table. This data may be edited or printed like any other datasheet. If you want a printout of all vegetable seeds from the inventory table, filter the inventory table as described above and then print the resulting datasheet.

In the next exercise, you will filter for those customers of Spread the Light—Candles who live in Canada, those who live in Florida, and those who don't live in Canada.

EXERCISE 1 | *Using Filter by Selection*

1. Open the **MailOrder** database.
2. Open the **Customers** table in Datasheet view.
3. Select a record containing the value **Canada** in the **Country** column, as shown in Figure 4.1.

It is not strictly necessary to select the word Canada. Having the insertion point in the field will suffice.

4. Click the **Filter by Selection button** on the Access toolbar. Access filters the table and displays only records containing the country Canada in the datasheet, as shown in Figure 4.2.

5. Print the resulting table.

6. Click the **Remove Filter button** on the Access toolbar to return to the full display of the table data.

7. Click in the **State/Prov** column of a record containing **FL** as the state.

8. Click the **Filter by Selection button** on the Access toolbar. Access displays all customer records in Florida.

9. Print the resulting table.

10. Click the **Remove Filter button** on the Access toolbar.

11. Select a Country field containing Canada.

12. Choose **Records | Filter | Filter Excluding Selection**. Access displays all records except those containing Canada.

13. Print the resulting table.

14. **Close** the Customers table without saving changes to its design.

TASK 2 | *Using Filter by Form*

What: Filter table records using a form.

How: In Datasheet view, click the Filter by Form button.

Why: Using Filter by Form lets you select several fields to be used in the filtering process.

Tip: If you type the first few letters of a value in a field on the form, Access will supply the full name from existing data. For example, if you click in the CompanyName field and type "Al," the name Alpha Networks appears.

Filter by Form provides a form where you select the example values from the field or fields you want to filter. There are two advantages to using the form over the simple filter described in Task 1. First, the form allows you to set a filter on more than one field. Second, the form allows you to use conditions or **criteria** using relational operators to filter the data. For example, using the Filter by Selection described in Task 1, Access finds matches equal to the contents of another record in the table. Using the Filter by Form, you can filter multiple fields and filter for data that is not only equal to but that is also greater than or less than the contents of another record in the table.

To use Filter by Form, open the table you want to filter and follow these steps:

1. Click the Filter by Form button to open the Filter by Form window.

2. If necessary, click the Clear Grid button to remove any selected items from the form.

3. In the Filter by Form window, select the value(s) in the fields you want to filter. The example in Figure 4.3 shows the Fulltime field selected with a check mark to indicate filtering on full-time employees.

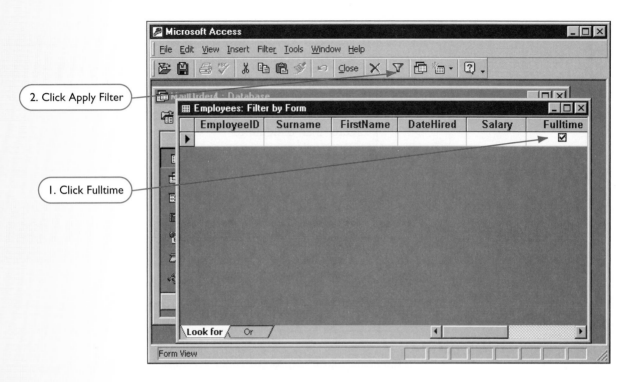

FIGURE 4.3 Fulltime Filtering Selected

4. Click the Apply Filter Button to filter the table. Figure 4.4 shows the result of filtering for full-time employees.

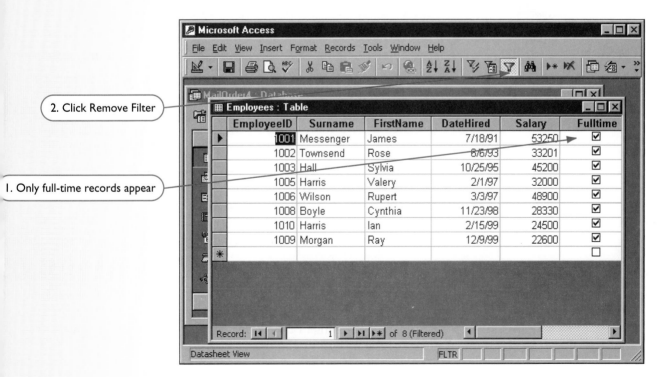

FIGURE 4.4 Filtered Results for Full-time Employees

5. Click the Remove Filter button to display all of the table contents. Using Filter by Form to set up a condition makes use of the **conditional operators**. Table 4.1 describes the operators.

Operator	Meaning	Example
<	Less than	<45000
>	Greater than	>21500
=	Equal to	=5
>=	Greater than or equal to	>=28000
<=	Less than or equal to	<=100
NOT	Not equal to	not 28330

TABLE 4.1   Conditional Operators

EXERCISE 2 | *Using Filter by Form*

1. If necessary, open the **MailOrder** database.
2. Open the **Employees** table in Datasheet view.
3. Click the **Filter by Form button** on the Access toolbar.
   The Filter by Form window opens, containing the fields from the datasheet.
4. Click the **Clear Grid button** on the Access toolbar.
   This step will remove any selected items from the form that might interfere with the filtering. Values could exist from previous filter operations.
5. In the Filter by Form window, click the checkbox in **Fulltime** so that it contains a check mark, as shown in Figure 4.3.
   Yes/No boxes are shown with shading to indicate they are not selected. A check mark indicates Yes and an empty box indicates No.
6. Click the **Apply Filter button** on the Access toolbar.
   Access filters the table and the results show only full-time employees, as shown in Figure 4.4
7. Click the **Remove Filter button** on the Access toolbar.
   The datasheet displays the complete contents of the table.
8. Click the **Filter by Form button** on the Access toolbar.
   The previous settings for the filter display in the form.
9. Without removing the setting for Fulltime, click in the Salary field.
   A drop-down arrow appears under Salary.
10. Click the arrow and choose **28330**.
11. Click at the beginning of the value 28330 so that the insertion point is in front of the 2.

12. Type the greater than symbol (>).

The Salary value now contains the expression >28330. See Table 4.1 for a list of operators.

13. Click the **Apply Filter button** on the Access toolbar.

Access displays records for full-time employees whose salary is greater than 28330, but not the employee whose salary is 28330.

14. Click the **Remove Filter button** on the Access toolbar.

15. **Close** the table without saving changes to the design.

TASK 3 | *Using the Simple Query Wizard*

What: Use Simple Query Wizard to create a query.

How: Click the New button in the Queries object window to open the New Query dialog box and then choose **Simple Query Wizard**.

Why: You can choose the table and fields to use in the query and then save the query settings for later use.

Tip: You can create either a detail or summary query with the wizard. A detail query shows records from the table that match the query, while a summary query summarizes the data found in the matching records.

One benefit of using a query over a filter is that you can save your settings and use the same query again. For example, if you often need to view records for customers in Florida and Texas, you could create the query and save it. The next time you need this same information, you can simply open the query and use it again. Queries also provide for more complex matches than are possible by simply filtering the data.

To create a query, follow these steps:

1. Open the Queries object in the Database window.
2. Click the New button, and the New Query dialog box opens, as shown in Figure 4.5.

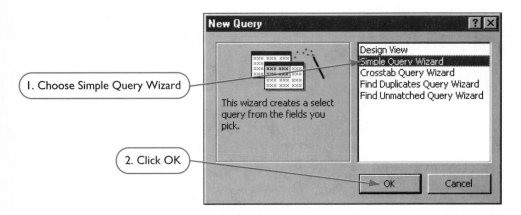

FIGURE 4.5 Choosing Simple Query Wizard from the New Query Dialog Box

3. In the first step of the Simple Query Wizard, choose the table and fields you want to query. Figure 4.6 shows the Employees table selected under Tables/Queries and all fields from the table, except the Salary field, moved under Selected Fields.

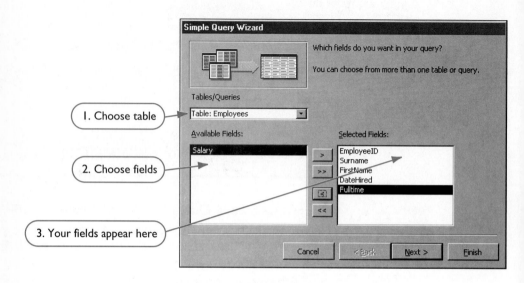

1. Choose table
2. Choose fields
3. Your fields appear here

FIGURE 4.6   Choosing the Table and Fields for the Query

4. Choose a **Detail** or **Summary** query. Figure 4.7 shows a Detail query selected. A Detail query displays all records that match the query.

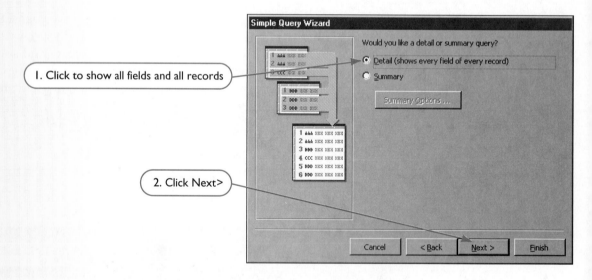

1. Click to show all fields and all records
2. Click Next>

FIGURE 4.7   Choosing a Detail Query

5. Choose a name for the query. You can either accept the name that Access provides, as shown in Figure 4.8, or you can type your own. Also choose whether to open the query in the view window or in design mode.

Figure 4.9 shows the View window for the query. It displays all records from the table in the datasheet. Notice that the datasheet does not include the Salary field because it was excluded in the query design.

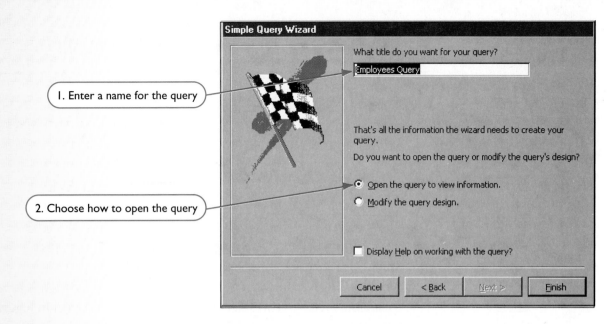

1. Enter a name for the query

2. Choose how to open the query

FIGURE 4.8 Name the Query and Choose to Open in the View Window

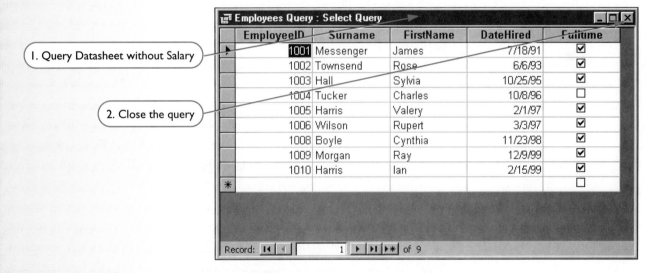

1. Query Datasheet without Salary

2. Close the query

FIGURE 4.9 Viewing the Query Results

POINTER

Saving the Query

The Simple Query Wizard automatically saves queries that it creates. When you close the Wizard, it saves the query in the Queries tab using the name that you supply.

In the following exercise, you will set up a simple query using only one table and simply excluding one field from the results. Running a query that has no criteria displays all the records in the resulting table. You will learn to add criteria in the next task and include multiple tables in the query later in this unit.

EXERCISE 3 | *Using the Simple Query Wizard*

1. Click the **Queries** choice in the Objects bar of the Database window to open it.

2. Click the **New button** in the Database window toolbar.
   The New Query dialog box opens.

3. Click **Simple Query Wizard** to select it, as shown in Figure 4.5.

4. Click **OK**.
   The Simple Query Wizard dialog box opens.

5. Under **Tables/Queries**, click the drop-down arrow and click **Table:Employees** to select it.

6. Using the arrow buttons, move all fields except **Salary** from the **Available Fields** to the **Selected Fields** column, as shown in Figure 4.6.

7. Click **Next**.
   The Simple Query Wizard opens the next step.

8. Make sure the **Detail** option is selected, as shown in Figure 4.7.

9. Click **Next**.
   The step to name the query in the Simple Query Wizard opens.

10. Select the **Open the query to view information** option, as shown in Figure 4.8.

11. Click **Finish** to accept the name **Employees Query**.
    The Employees Query: Select Query opens, showing all records in the view without the Salary field, as shown in Figure 4.9.

12. Close the **Employees Query: Select Query** window.
    The Employees Query now appears in the Queries objects window.

TASK 4 | *Editing a Query*

What: Edit the contents of a query.

How: Open the query in Design view.

Why: To add or remove fields, define sorting, or enter criteria.

Tip: You can test your query while developing it by switching between Design view and Datasheet view.

You can edit a query to add or remove fields or to change how it operates by supplying various requirements, such as sorting or criteria values. You can either edit the query by clicking the View button when viewing the query or by selecting the query and clicking the Design button.

ADDING A FIELD TO THE QUERY

To add a field from the table to the query, you can use any of the following methods:

• Double-click the field name in the table window.

- To add several fields at a time, first select the fields, using either of these methods:
  - Click on the first field. Then, hold down the Shift key and click on the last field in the group
  - Click on the first field. Then, hold down the Ctrl key and click on each field
- Drag individual fields or selected fields to the query.

Figure 4.10 shows a query after adding the Salary field to the query by double-clicking the salary field's name.

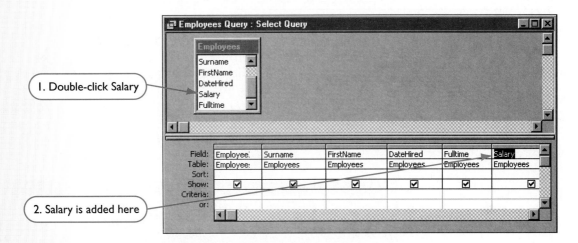

FIGURE 4.10   Adding the Salary Field to the Query

DELETING A FIELD FROM THE QUERY

You may delete a field from the query if it is no longer needed for the view. To delete a field, complete the following steps:

1. Point to the header above the column to be deleted until the mouse pointer becomes a dark arrow.
2. Click to select the column, as shown in Figure 4.11.
3. Press the Delete key.

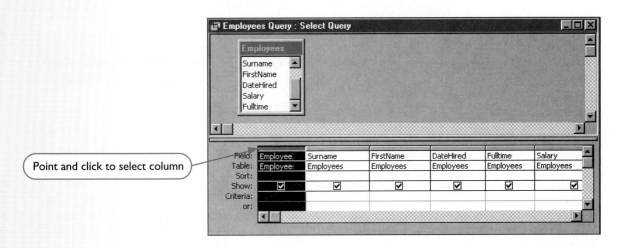

FIGURE 4.11   Selecting the EmployeeID Field for Deletion from the Query

Deleting a field from the query does not delete it from the table.

POINTER

Moving a Column

You can move a column in the query to a new location. For example, to move the FirstName field to the left of the Surname field, click in its header to select the FirstName column. Then, drag the column to its new position in the query.

SORTING QUERY RESULTS

The query results show the records in the same order that they appear in the table. To view the results in a different order, you can **sort** the data. To sort the output of a query, select the Sort order option. Figure 4.12 shows Ascending selected for the Sort order under the Surname. When viewing this query, the records will appear ordered alphabetically by the Surname contents.

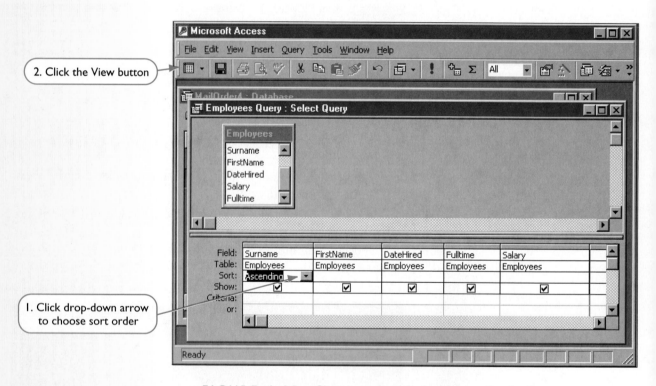

FIGURE 4.12 Choosing a Sort Order of Ascending for Surname

ADDING A CRITERIA

A criteria is a value or expression that determines which records are included in the query results. This is the most powerful aspect of querying a database. You can ask complex questions and get results by creating criteria. Access uses a **Query by Example (QBE)** method for defining the criteria. For example, to view all records in a personnel database of employees who make less than $25,000, you would enter <25000 under the Salary field. If you wanted to see all female employees in the Marketing department who make between $25,000 and $29,000 and have worked for the company less than five years, you would enter the following criteria:

Gender	Dept	Annual Salary	HireDate
F	Marketing	>=25000and<=29000	>=1/1/93

The HireDate in the example assumes the query is run in 1999.

If you want to see students in a Student table who have a 3.5 gpa or above, are computer majors, are not U.S. citizens, and are more than 25 years old, you would enter the following criteria:

GPA	Major	Country	DOB
>=3.5	Computer	NOT USA	<1/1/74

Figure 4.13 shows the simple criteria >=1/1/98 entered as the criteria for DateHired. The criteria will match all dates for January 1, 1998 or later in the query results. Use the operators that Table 4.1 lists to create criteria.

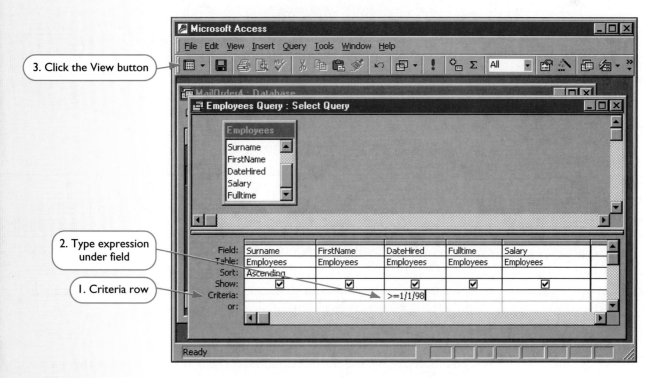

FIGURE 4.13   Creating Criteria for DateHired

Show Fields

The Show row in the Query Design table contains a check box by default, meaning that the field contents will be shown or displayed in the table when you view the Query results. If you want to set a condition on a field but not have the field display, you would click on the check to remove it. For example, if you set a criteria for all customers who live in the USA, you could eliminate the Country field from the resulting table and the printout by removing the check from the Show box.

SAVING THE CHANGES TO A QUERY

When you have made additions, deletions, or changes to an existing query, Access will ask if you want to save these changes before the query is closed. Select Yes to save these changes or No to abandon the changes.

Using Existing Query Settings

If you want to use an existing query to create a new query, open the query in Design view and make the changes you want. Then, use File | Save As to save the revised query under a different name from its original.

EXERCISE 4 | *Editing a Query*

1. If necessary, click the **Queries** choice in the Objects bar of the Database window to open it.

2. Click **Employees Query** to select it. Click the **Design button** on the Access toolbar.

3. In the table window of the query, scroll to see the Salary field and then double-click **Salary**.
   Access adds the Salary field to the end of the fields in the query, as shown in Figure 4.10.

4. If necessary, use the horizontal scroll bar at the bottom of the query window to view all the fields.

5. With the mouse, point to the header above the EmployeeID field until the pointer becomes a small dark arrow. Click the header.
   The entire EmployeeID column becomes selected, as shown in Figure 4.11.

6. Press the **Delete** key.
   Access removes the EmployeeID column from the query.

7. Click the **View button** on the Access toolbar to view the query results.
Observe that EmployeeID is no longer in the query and that Salary now appears in the datasheet.

8. Click the **View button** on the Access toolbar to return to the design window.

9. In the Query window, click in the **Sort** row under the **Surname** column.
A drop-down arrow appears in the Sort field.

10. Click the drop-down arrow and choose **Ascending** from the list.
Ascending appears as the sort order for the Surname field, as shown in Figure 4.12.

11. Click the **View button** on the Access toolbar to view the results.
Observe that Access sorts the results by the Surname.

12. Click the **View button** on the Access toolbar to return to the design window.

13. In the Criteria row under the DateHired column, type **>=1/1/98**, as shown in Figure 4.13.
This query will match only records that contain a DateHired that is greater than or equal to January 1, 1998.

14. Click the **View button** on the Access toolbar to view the results.
Observe that the results show only dates on or after January 1, 1998, and that they are sorted by Surname.

15. Click the **View button** on the Access toolbar to return to the design window.

16. Click the **Close button** on the Employees Query: Select Query design window.
Access asks if you want to save the changes to your query design.

17. Click **Yes** to save your changes.

TASK 5 | *Creating a Query in Design View*

What: Use Design view to create a query.

How: In the Queries objects, click New and choose Design view.

Why: Design view provides the most options and flexibility to create complex expressions in the query.

Tip: If you want to create a query to match some but not all of the field contents, you would use the Like operator and the * or ? wildcards. For example, to find customers who have the 514 area code, you would place the condition *Like "(514)*"* in the Phone field criteria.

So far in this unit, you have used the Simple Query Wizard to create and save a query. However, Access also allows you to design your own queries in the Query Design view. Once you have used the wizard to create even a simple query, it is easy to move on to designing your own.

To create a query using Design view, follow these steps:

1. Click the Queries choice on the Objects bar.
2. Click the New button.
3. Choose Design View in the New Query dialog box, as shown in Figure 4.14.

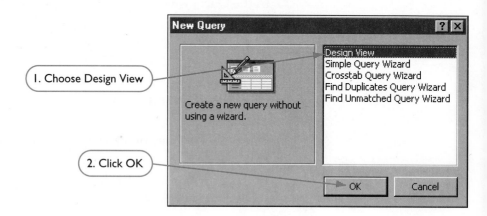

FIGURE 4.14   Choosing Design View

The Query Design window opens with a Show Table dialog box, as shown in Figure 4.15.

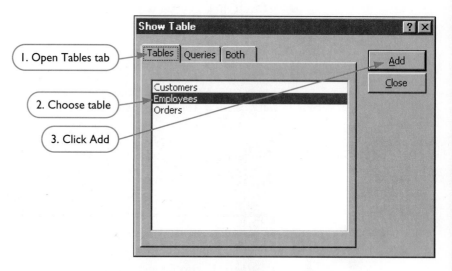

FIGURE 4.15   The Show Table Dialog Box

Select the desired tables and then close the Show Table dialog box.

After adding tables to the query, you can place fields in the query table from any of the tables, using the methods described earlier in the unit for adding the fields to the query. After adding fields, create the criteria.

MORE COMPLEX CRITERIA

The examples of criteria described so far in this unit all result in limiting the output by combining criteria with **And**. For example, running the following criteria on the Student table results in the students who have a 3.5 gpa or above And are computer majors And are not U.S. citizens And are more than 25 years old:

GPA	Major	Country	DOB
>=3.5	Computer	NOT USA	<1/1/74

Using these criteria, you would not see English majors who have a 3.5 gpa, are not U.S. citizens, and are less than 25 years old because all criteria must be matched. The And criteria means that all criteria entries must be matched. For example, Figure 4.16 shows a sample And criteria in the query window.

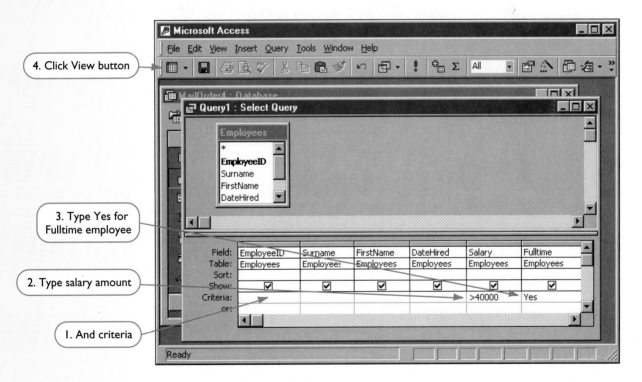

FIGURE 4.16   Criteria for Salary over $40,000 and a Full-time Employee

Without actually knowing it, we enter And criteria because the expressions entered all appear in the same row of the table. Figure 4.17 shows the results of this query.

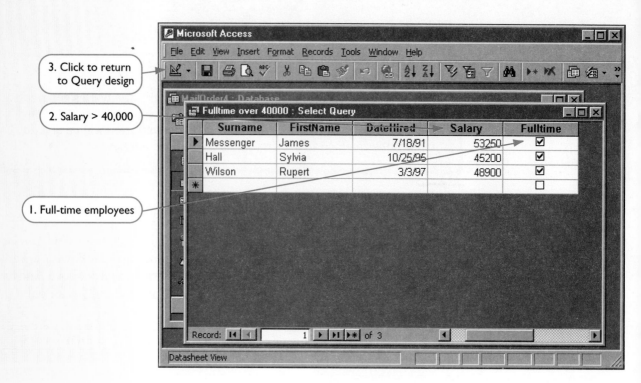

FIGURE 4.17   Full-time Employees with a Salary Greater than $40,000

When you want to have the query find one or more of several possibilities in a field, you should use an **Or** criteria. To place an Or criteria in the table, place it on a line below the first criteria line—designated by Or. For example, to see students who are computer or English majors, you would type the criteria on two separate criteria lines, as follows:

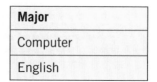

Major
Computer
English

To find customers in Florida or Texas, you would use two criteria rows in the query. In one you would type FL and below it, in a second row, type TX, as shown in Figure 4.18. Then, if either of the states gets a match in the record, the data from that record displays in the query results, as shown in Figure 4.19.

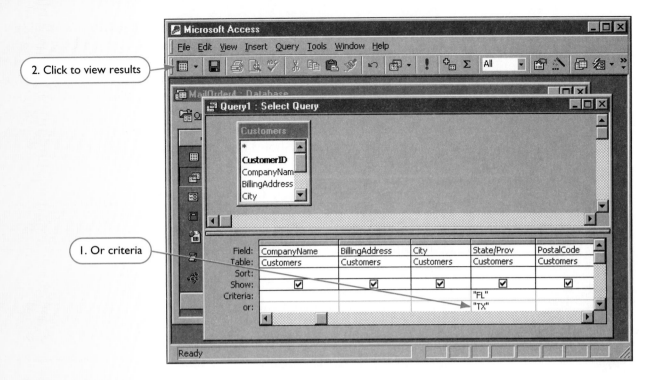

2. Click to view results

1. Or criteria

FIGURE 4.18 Defining an Or Criteria

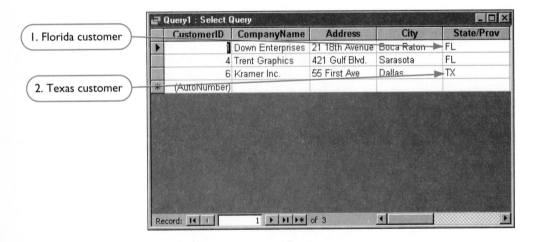

1. Florida customer

2. Texas customer

FIGURE 4.19 Customers from Florida or Texas

Access allows you to mix And and Or criteria together in the same query. However, you can end up with some unexpected results if you aren't careful. If you want to see students who have a 3.5 gpa or greater, are computer or English majors, are not U.S. citizens, and are over 25 years old, you might enter the criteria as follows:

GPA	Major	Country	DOB
>=3.5	Computer	NOT USA	<1/1/74
	English		

However, the above criteria would not produce the desired results. You would get students who have 3.5 gpa or greater, are computer majors, are not U.S. citizens, and are more than 25 years old, plus you would get English majors who have any gpa, are from any country, and are any age. The reason for these results is that the criteria is read as GPA greater than or equal to 3.5 And Major equal to Computer And Country not equal to USA And DOB less than 1/1/74 Or Major equal to English. You would need to complete the criteria for the second row in order to avoid this problem, as shown in the following:

GPA	Major	Country	DOB
>=3.5	Computer	NOT USA	<1/1/74
>=3.5	English	NOT USA	<1/1/74

EXERCISE 5A | *Creating an And Query in Design View*

1. If necessary, open the **Queries** choice in the Objects bar of the Database window.
2. Click the **New button** on the Database window.
   The New Query dialog box opens.
3. Choose **Design View** from the **New Query** dialog box, as shown in Figure 4.14.
4. Click **OK**.
   The Show Table dialog box opens.
5. In the **Show Table** dialog box, click **Employees** to select the table, as shown in Figure 4.15. Click **Add** to add the table to the query.

POINTER

Opening the Show Table Dialog Box
If the Show Table dialog box did not open, you can open it by choosing Query | Show Table.

6. Click **Close** to close the Show Table dialog box.
7. Select all fields except for EmployeeID.
8. Drag the selected fields to the query design.
9. If necessary, drag the header dividers between the fields so that all fields are visible.
10. In the **Criteria** row under **Salary**, type **>40000**.
11. In the **Criteria** row under **Fulltime**, type **Yes**.
    Your criteria entries should now appear as shown in Figure 4.16.

12. Click the **View button** on the Access toolbar to preview your results.
Your results should match those shown in Figure 4.17.

13. Click the **View button** on the Access toolbar to return to the design view.

14. Click the **Save button** on the Access toolbar.
Access prompts you to save your query design.

15. Type **Fulltime over 40000** for the file name.

16. Click **OK**.
Access saves the query, which now appears in the Query choice of the Database window.

EXERCISE 5B | *Creating an Or Query in Design View*

1. If necessary, open the **Queries** choice in the Objects bar of the Database window.

2. Click the **New button** on the Database window.
The New Query dialog box opens.

3. Choose **Design View** from the **New Query** dialog box, as shown in Figure 4.14.

4. Click **OK**.
The Show Table dialog box opens.

5. In the **Show Table** dialog box, click **Customers** to select the table.

6. Click **Add** to add the table to the query.

7. Click **Close** to close the Show Table dialog box.

8. Add all of the fields from the Customer table to the query design.

9. In the **Criteria** row under **State/Prov**, type **FL**.

10. In the second criteria row under **State/Prov**, type **TX**.
Access adds the quotation marks around the state when you leave the field. Your criteria entries should now appear as shown in Figure 4.18.

11. Click the **View button** on the Access toolbar to view your results.
Your results should match those shown in Figure 4.19.

12. Click the **View button** on the Access toolbar to return to the design view.

13. Click the **Close button** on the Select Query window.
Access prompts you to save your query design.

14. Type **FL or TX** for the file name and click **OK**.
Access saves the query, which now appears in the Query tab of the Database window.

What: Create a query to supply data from linked tables.

How: Click the Queries objects in the Database window, click the New button, and choose Simple Query Wizard.

Why: To provide data from two or more related tables in the query results.

Tip: Access provides some specialized query wizards, such as the Find Unmatched Query Wizard. The Find Unmatched Query Wizard helps you find records in one table that have no related records in a second table. This would allow you to find customers who do not have orders in the order table. Search Help for more information on other Query Wizards.

You have learned so far that most Access databases are made up of related tables. You will find that to create meaningful results from a query, you will need to include fields from related tables in a query. For example, if JRT Kennels wants to set up a query for one specific breed of dog, that is easy. But if they want the resulting table to include not just the customer number but also the customer name with the dog purchased, then the information will need to come from the two related tables.

Queries on single tables are useful when all of the data needed exists in one table. However, data will frequently be stored in relational tables resulting in more effective storage and ease of access, as we have seen in the Customers and Orders tables of the MailOrder database. In this situation, the query will need to have access to two or more tables to supply all of the data needed for the query results. One method to create a multitable query described in this task is selecting the tables and fields required for the query in the Simple Query Wizard and then entering the needed criteria into the query design.

To create a query using linked tables, complete the following steps:

1. Open the Queries object in the Database window.
2. Click the New button and the New Query dialog box opens.
3. Choose Simple Query Wizard.
4. Choose the tables and fields for the query in the Simple Query Wizard.

Figure 4.20 shows the first four fields selected from the Customers table, which is the primary table in the relationship. This figure also shows the last three fields selected from the Orders table, which is the secondary table in the relationship.

5. In the next step of the Simple Query Wizard, choose either Detail or Summary. Detail provides all of the records from the tables that match the query's requirements.
6. Enter a name for the query.
7. Open the query in Design view.

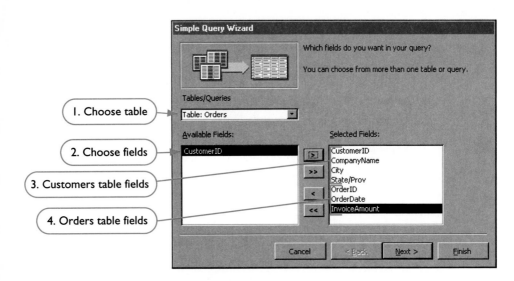

FIGURE 4.20   Choosing Fields from Linked Tables for the Query

The Query Design window in Figure 4.21 shows the tables and their relationship.

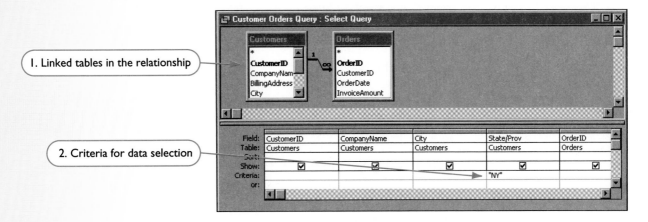

FIGURE 4.21   Entering the Criteria

8. Add any needed criteria for the query.

For this example, enter NY into the Criteria of the State/Prov column to view customer orders from that state.

9. View the query results, as shown in Figure 4.22.

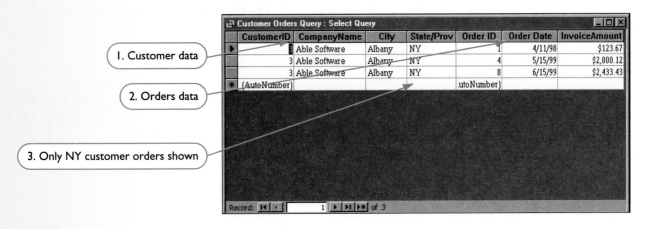

FIGURE 4.22   Viewing the Orders for Customers in NY

1. If necessary, click the **Queries** choice in the Objects bar of the Database window.

2. Click the **New button** on the Database window.
   The New Query dialog box opens.

3. Choose **Simple Query Wizard** in the New Query dialog box.

4. Click **OK**.
   The Simple Query Wizard dialog box opens.

5. Under Tables/Queries, click the drop-down arrow and choose **Table: Customers**.

6. Under Available Fields, choose **CustomerID**, **CompanyName**, **City**, and **State/Prov**, and move the fields to the Selected Fields window.

7. Under Tables/Queries, click the drop-down arrow and choose **Table: Orders**.

8. Under Available Fields, choose **OrderID**, **OrderDate**, and **InvoiceAmount** and move the fields to the Selected Fields window.
   Your results should match Figure 4.20.

9. Click the **Next button**.
   The step for choosing a detail or summary query of the Simple Query Wizard opens.

10. Click the **Detail** option.
    This option shows every field of every record.

11. Click the **Next button**.
    The step of the Simple Query Wizard to give the query a title opens.

12. Under What title do you want for your query?, type **Customer Orders Query**.

13. Click the option **Modify the query design**.
    The query opens in Design view.

14. Click the **Finish button**.
    The query opens in Design view, as shown in Figure 4.21.

15. In the State/Prov column in the Criteria row, type **NY**.

16. Click the **Datasheet View button** on the Access toolbar.
    Access applies the query specifications to the Customers and Orders tables and the results display in the Select Query window, as shown in Figure 4.22.

17. Click the **Close button** in the upper-right corner of the Customer Orders Query: Select Query window and save the changes.
    The query closes and Access returns you to the Database window.

S U M M A R Y

After completing this unit, you should be able to

- use Filter by Selection in a table (page 92)
- use Filter by Form in a table (page 94)
- use the Simple Query Wizard to create a query (page 97)
- edit the contents of a query (page 100)
- use Design view to create a query (page 105)
- use And and Or criteria in a query (page 107)
- use linked tables in a query (page 112)

K E Y   T E R M S

And (page 107)
conditional operators (page 96)
criteria (page 94)
Detail (page 98)
Filter by Form (page 94)
Filter by Selection (page 92)
Filtering Excluding Selection
  (page 93)

Or (page 108)
Remove Filter (page 93)
Show Fields (page 104)
Simple Query Wizard (page 97)
sort (page 102)
Summary (page 98)

T E S T   Y O U R   S K I L L S

True/False

1. A filter displays records from a table based on your field selection in the datasheet.
2. When using Filter by Form, you can use only one field in the filtering.
3. You use the Simple Query Wizard to select the fields from the table that you want to use for the query results.
4. To sort the results of a query, it is necessary to sort the datasheet before creating the query.
5. In a query, a criteria expression determines which records from the table display in the results.

Multiple Choice

1. When using Filter by Selection to find all customers located in Dallas you would
   a. sort the datasheet on the City field
   b. select a City field containing the name Dallas
   c. click a drop-down arrow on the City field and select the city you want
   d. use the Filter Excluding Selection menu command

2. When using Filter by Form to find all customers located in Lima, Peru, you would
   a. sort the datasheet on the Country and City fields
   b. select a City field containing the name Lima
   c. click a drop-down arrow on the City field and select Lima, and from the drop-down list on Country select Peru
   d. this filtering is not possible

3. In the Simple Query Wizard, you
   a. determine the tables used
   b. determine the fields that will display
   c. create criteria
   d. answers a and b

4. Using a criteria such as <12/31/98 would
   a. display all records containing a date
   b. display all records in 1998
   c. display all records before December 31, 1998
   d. display all records after December 31, 1998

5. The difference between a query with a criteria using two Or values and one using two And values is
   a. And entries are entered in the same criteria row
   b. Or entries are entered in two criteria rows
   c. And requires a match on all values while Or requires a match on only one value
   d. all of these answers

Short Answer

1. The letters QBE mean _____ _____ _____.
2. To view only records in the table for Canadian customers, you could use the Filter by _____ method.
3. When filtering records, you would click the _____ _____ button to display all records from the table.
4. You would need to open the Query _____ window to add or delete a field in the query.
5. The _____ determines which records from the table are included in the query results.

What Does This Do?

Write a description for the function of the following:

1.	▽↯	6.	✻ New
2.	<=	7.	And
3.	▤	8.	▽
4.	✕	9.	Or
5.	>=	10.	▼

On Your Own

1. Filter a table using the Filter by Selection method.
2. Filter a table using the Filter by Exception method.
3. Filter a table using Filter by Form.
4. Use the Simple Query Wizard to set up a query.
5. Use Design View to try various criteria.

PROJECTS

1. Using the JRT Kennel Database, perform the following operations:
   - Filter the Customer table to show all customers who live outside California. Print the resulting table.
   - Filter the Customer table to show all customers living in New Jersey. Print the results.
   - Filter the Dog table to show Yorkshire Terriers. Print the resulting table.
   - Filter the Dog table to show Yorkshire Terriers purchased after 1/1/95. Print the results.

2. Using the JRT Kennel Database, perform the following operations:
   - Use a query to show Customer Name and Dog Name for Yorkshire Terriers. Print the results of the query.
   - Use a query to show Customer Name and Dog Name for Yorkshire Terriers or Mixed-breed dogs for customers living in the USA. Print the results.
   - Use a query to show Yorkshire Terriers or Jack Russell Terriers purchased between 1/1/91 and 12/31/96. Print the results.

3. Using the Alphabets Inventory database, perform the following operations:
   - Use a query to produce an alphabetized listing of books with the name of the publisher. Print the results.
   - Use a query to produce a list alphabetized by author's last name and include book title and publisher name. Print the results.
   - Use a query to find books with the title *Cartooning* or *Origami*. Include the author's name and publisher name. Print the results.

4. Using the Alphabets Inventory database, perform the following operations:
   - Use a query to produce a list alphabetized by book name of books written after 1/1/93. Print the results.
   - Use a Query to produce a list sorted in chronological order of books written between 1/1/90 and 12/31/97.
   - Use a Query to produce a list alphabetized by publisher name of books written before 1/1/97.

1. In the Check Point for Units 1–2, you created the Seeds and Sprouts database and input records into two tables. Now you want to be able to link customers with the seeds they have ordered, but a simple link between the two tables will not provide the information necessary.

   To relate the two tables, create a third table in the database and call it Orders. Because Seeds and Sprouts fills each seed order on an individual basis, depending on season, climate, and seed type, each type of seed ordered is given a unique order number.

   Table 4.2 lists the fields for the Orders table.

Field Name	Data Type
OrderNum	Auto Number–set as a primary key
CustID	text
ProdNum	text

TABLE 4.2   Orders Table Fields

   After creating the table, create the link from the Customer table and the Plant table to the Orders table. Print the Relationship.

   Input the orders shown in Table 4.3.
   Print the Orders table.

OrderNum	CustID	ProdNum
1	1118	107
2	1111	103
3	1117	116
4	1112	101
5	1118	112
6	1113	102
7	1115	104
8	1114	105
9	1115	101
10	1116	101
11	1119	108
12	1120	109
13	1111	110
14	1119	111
15	1112	106
16	1118	101
17	1117	115
18	1114	114
19	1115	113
20	1120	101
21	1112	115

TABLE 4.3   Orders Table Data

2. Using the Seeds and Sprouts database, create queries for each of the following and print the results of each:
   - an alphabetized list of vegetables
   - an alphabetized list of spring vegetables
   - an alphabetized list of annuals
   - an alphabetized list of annuals or perennials
   - an alphabetized list of customers who live in the USA
   - an alphabetized list of customers who have ordered red cabbage (101)
   - a list of seeds that contain more than 100 seeds per ounce displayed from largest to smallest amount
   - a list of seeds that contain more than 100 and less than 700 seeds per ounce displayed from the smallest to the largest amount
   - a list of all orders sorted by order number that includes the name of the customer and the name of the seeds
   - a list of orders sorted by order number for annuals or perennials that includes the name of the customer and the name of the seeds

Getting Started

UNIT OBJECTIVES

- Start PowerPoint 2000
- Create a Presentation using the AutoContent Wizard
- Become familiar with the PowerPoint Interface
- Use Help
- Print the Slides and the Outline
- Exit from PowerPoint

Microsoft PowerPoint 2000 is presentation software that creates slide shows, which can either run continuously on a computer or move under the control of a speaker or viewer. PowerPoint also includes features to convert computer presentations into transparencies to present on an overhead projector, into 35mm slides to present on a slide projector, or into a Web document to present on the World Wide Web. PowerPoint provides many formatting options for helping you create an attractive presentation along with features that help you with the style and content of the presentation. In Unit 1, you learn how to start PowerPoint and create, save, and print a simple presentation.

What: Start Microsoft PowerPoint.

How: Click the Start button and choose Programs | Microsoft PowerPoint.

Why: You must know how to start an application in order to use it.

Tip: If you know the name of the file you want to use, click the Start button, click Open Office Document, and select the document.

Microsoft PowerPoint 2000 is **presentation software**—a program used primarily to create slide shows. Figure 1.1 shows the first slide of a presentation viewed on a computer screen.

FIGURE 1.1   Title Slide for a Presentation

To start PowerPoint, complete the following steps:

1. Click the **Start button** on the Windows taskbar.
2. Point to Programs.
3. Click Microsoft PowerPoint.

The PowerPoint dialog box displays when you start PowerPoint, as shown in Figure 1.2.

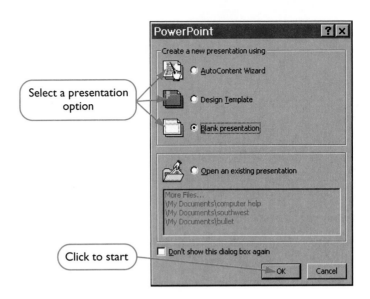

Select a presentation option

Click to start

FIGURE 1.2   PowerPoint Dialog Box

4. You can select from the following:

- AutoContent Wizard. PowerPoint asks you for information about the purpose, content, and other features of your presentation.
- Design Template. PowerPoint provides blank, styled templates to help you design your presentation.
- Blank presentation. Opens a blank presentation formatted using preset or default settings.
- Open an existing presentation. Opens a presentation that was created earlier.

5. Click OK to start the software.

EXERCISE 1 | *Starting Microsoft PowerPoint*

1. Click the **Start button** on the Windows taskbar.
   The Start menu opens.
2. Point to **Programs**.
   The Programs menu opens.
3. Click **Microsoft PowerPoint**.
   PowerPoint starts and displays the dialog box shown in Figure 1.2.
4. Click **AutoContent Wizard** and **OK**.
   The AutoContent Wizard dialog box displays.
5. Keep PowerPoint open to the dialog box for use in the next exercise.

TASK 2 | *Creating a Presentation Using the AutoContent Wizard*

What: Use the AutoContent Wizard to get started.

How: Follow the steps through the wizard to create a presentation.

Why: PowerPoint provides help with the formatting as well as the content when you use one of the built-in wizards.

Tip: It's a good idea to use the AutoContent Wizard when you are new to PowerPoint because it not only sets up your slide show, but it also places sample content on the slides.

After you select the AutoContent Wizard, follow the steps to create a presentation.

The wizard information dialog box displays in the first step, as shown in Figure 1.3.

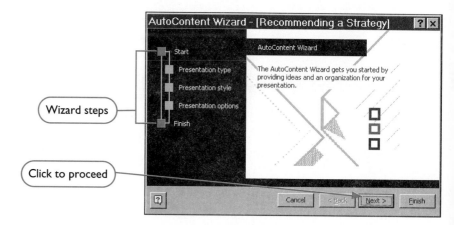

FIGURE 1.3 AutoContent Wizard Opening Screen

To create a presentation using the AutoContent Wizard, complete the following steps:

1. Click the Next button to start the wizard.

The Presentation Type dialog box displays, as shown in Figure 1.4.

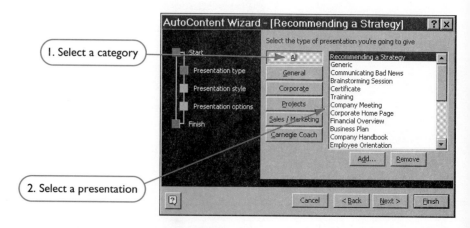

FIGURE 1.4 Select a Presentation Type

You must choose a type of presentation. PowerPoint provides the categories and presentations shown in Table 1.1.

AutoContent Categories	Presentations by Category
General	Generic Recommending a Strategy Communicating Bad News Training Brainstorming Session Certificate
Corporate	Business Plan Financial Overview Company Meeting Employee Orientation Group Home Page Company Handbook
Projects	Project Overview Reporting Progress or Status Project Post-Mortem
Sales / Marketing	Selling a Product or Service Marketing Plan Product / Services Overview
Carnegie Coach	Selling Your Ideas Motivating a Team Facilitating a Meeting Presenting a Technical Report Managing Organizational Change Introducing and Thanking a Speaker

TABLE 1.1   Built-in Presentations

2. Select a presentation category and then select a specific presentation from the resulting list.

3. Click the Next button to display the Presentation Style dialog box shown in Figure 1.5.

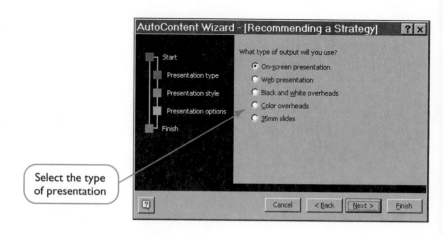

FIGURE 1.5 Select a Presentation Style

4. Select the type of output that you will use from the following choices:
   - on a computer
   - on the Web
   - as overheads
   - as 35mm slides

5. Click the Next button and the Presentation Options dialog box displays, as shown in Figure 1.6.

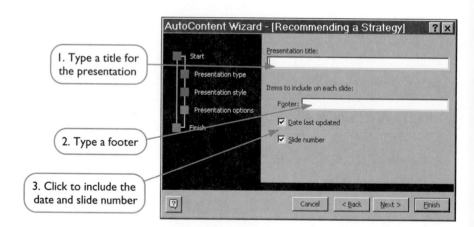

FIGURE 1.6 Select Presentation Options

6. Type the following information in the text boxes of the Presentation Options dialog box:
   - the title of the presentation
   - footer items that will appear at the bottom of every slide, such as footer text, date last updated, slide number

7. Click the Next button. The Finish dialog box displays, as shown in Figure 1.7.

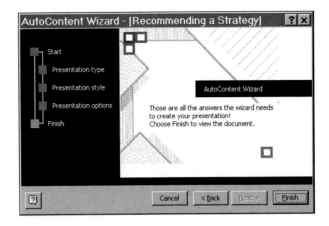

FIGURE 1.7 Wizard Finish Dialog Box

8. Click the Finish button to create the presentation.

The presentation generated by the wizard displays in two adjacent window panes, as shown in Figure 1.8.

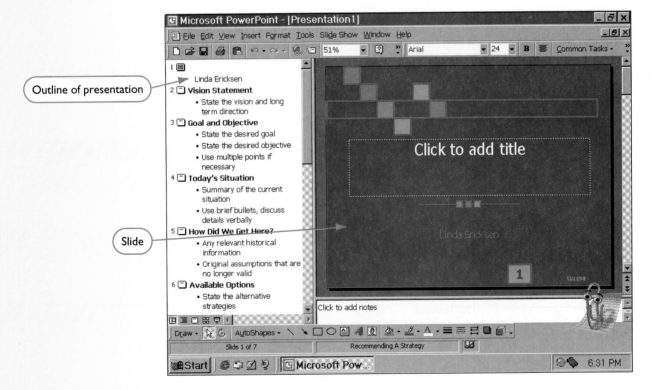

FIGURE 1.8 The Result of the Wizard

The left panel displays the outline of the presentation, and the right pane displays the slides that were generated.

1. Choose **AutoContent Wizard** from the opening PowerPoint dialog box.
2. Click **OK**.
   The AutoContent Wizard Start dialog box displays.
3. Click the **Next button** in the Start Wizard dialog box.
   The Presentation Type dialog box displays.
4. In the Type of Presentation dialog box, click the **Sales/Marketing button**.
   The list of presentations under that category displays.
5. Select **Marketing Plan** from the list of presentations.
6. Click the **Next button**.
   The Presentation Style dialog box displays.
7. Select **On-screen presentation** from *What type of output will you use?*
8. Click the **Next button**.
   The Presentation Options dialog box displays.
9. Type **Sample Presentation** in the Presentation Title text box.
10. Type your name in the Footer text box and leave the date last updated and slide number selected.
11. Click the **Next button**.
    The Finish dialog box displays.
12. Click the **Finish button**.
    Your screen should look like Figure 1.9.
13. Keep the presentation on the screen for use in the next exercise.

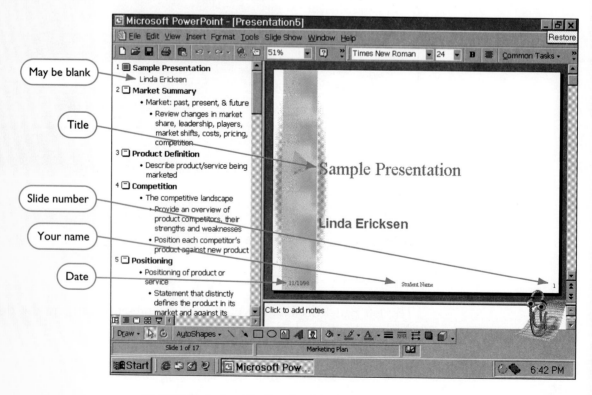

FIGURE 1.9   The Result of the Exercise

What: Become familiar with the PowerPoint interface.

How: Use the mouse to explore.

Why: To use PowerPoint effectively, you need to be familiar with its elements.

Tip: If you know Word, Excel, or another Microsoft Office program, you already know a lot about PowerPoint.

Figure 1.10 shows the Microsoft PowerPoint screen that greets you when you start working with the program. PowerPoint uses a **graphical user interface**, or **GUI** (pronounced "goo-ey"). That is, you communicate with the computer by selecting icons and other graphical elements on the screen rather than by typing commands.

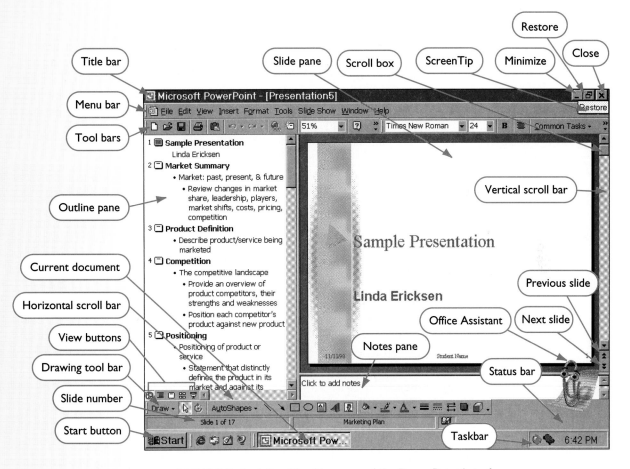

FIGURE 1.10 The Elements of the PowerPoint Interface

TITLE BAR

Like all windows, the PowerPoint window has a **title bar** across the top. The title bar names the program and the presentation the window contains. Table 1.2 describes the buttons that this window contains.

Button	Name	Description
▬	Minimize	Shrinks the window to a button on the taskbar
☐	Maximize	Enlarges the window to fill the desktop
⧉	Restore	In a maximized window, replaces the Maximize button; returns the window to its previous size
✖	Close	Closes the window

TABLE 1.2 Buttons That Close and Size a Window

MENU BAR

PowerPoint's **menu bar**, which is located below its title bar, displays the names of menus, as seen in Figure 1.10. When you click a menu name, a drop-down menu appears from which you select a command or other option, as shown in Figure 1.11.

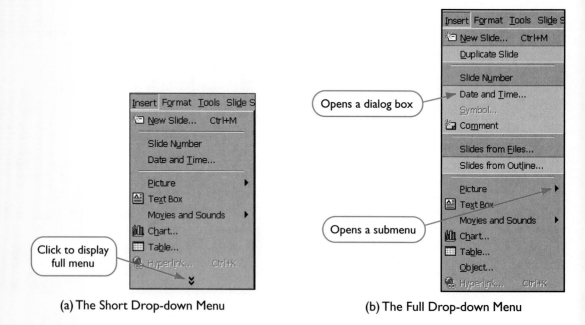

(a) The Short Drop-down Menu   (b) The Full Drop-down Menu

FIGURE 1.11   PowerPoint Drop-down Menu

When you click a menu name, a set of basic menu options appears. In a few seconds the menu expands to show the complete list. As you work, Power-Point keeps track of which menu options you use and adds those options to the short menu. At any time, you can click the down arrows at the bottom of the menu to display the full menu.

Instructions in this text to choose menu commands are shown as **Menu Name I Menu Command**. For example, "choose File I Open" means to choose File from the menu bar and Open from the drop-down menu. To close a menu without choosing a command, either click the mouse outside the menu or press the Esc key on the keyboard.

Drop-down menus can have the following attributes:

- with a check mark (✔) in front of it—to indicate an option that is turned on in a group where more than one choice is permitted
- without a check mark (✔)—to indicate that the option is turned off
- with a dot (●) in front of it—to indicate the option that is turned on in a group where only one choice is permitted
- grayed-out—to indicate it is not available at the present time
- followed by a right-pointing arrow (➤)—to indicate that pointing to it opens a submenu
- followed by an ellipsis (…)—to indicate that clicking it opens a dialog box like the one shown in Figure 1.12

DIALOG BOXES

Dialog boxes are windows in which you provide PowerPoint with information needed to perform a task. Some dialog boxes, like the one in Figure 1.12, use tabs, with each tab containing a group of similar options.

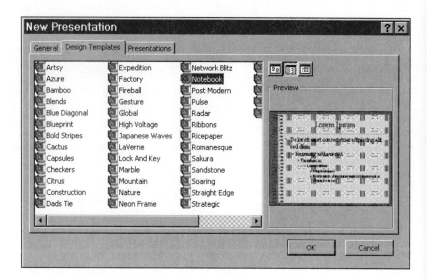

FIGURE 1.12   A Sample Dialog Box

Dialog boxes contain **command buttons** that allow you to issue commands. Two common command buttons are the OK button and the Cancel button. When you have made the desired selections in a dialog box, click the OK button. If you simply want to close the dialog box, click the Close button or the Cancel button. If you are uncertain of an option in a dialog box, click the question mark button in the title bar and click on that option to receive help.

POINTER

Moving a Dialog Box

When a dialog box opens on the screen and you need to see the text that it has covered, click and drag the title bar of the dialog box to move it on the screen.

TOOLBARS AND RULER

PowerPoint has more than a dozen toolbars with buttons you can click to perform actions. Some toolbars display by default; others appear only when needed; and you can display some manually by choosing View | Toolbars. You will use several of the toolbars in this book and will find that they save you time.

Clicking a toolbar button has the same effect as choosing a command from the menu bar but is quicker. Besides buttons, toolbars can contain list boxes. Clicking the downward-pointing arrow at the right edge of the box opens a list from which you can make a choice.

The **Standard**, **Formatting**, and **Drawing toolbars** display by default. The Standard toolbar contains buttons for commands from the File and Edit menus and other buttons that start some of PowerPoint's special features. The Formatting toolbar contains buttons for commands from the Format menu. These toolbars normally appear below the menu bar, but you can move them, as explained in the pointer box "Moving a Toolbar." The two toolbars can share a single row or can be displayed on separate rows. When the toolbars are separate, each displays its complete set of buttons. When the toolbars share a row, PowerPoint keeps track of which buttons have been used recently and displays those buttons, displacing buttons that haven't been used. To display the missing buttons, click the double arrows at the right end of the toolbar. Figure 1.13a shows the Standard and Formatting toolbars sharing a row.

POINTER

Moving a Toolbar

You can move a toolbar to its own row or other location on the screen by dragging its move handle. If you double-click a toolbar that is docked at an edge of the screen, it floats freely on the screen and displays a title bar. You can resize a floating toolbar by dragging an edge or move it by dragging its title bar. Double-click it again to redock it.

The Drawing toolbar displays by default along the bottom of the slide window. Figure 1.13d shows the Drawing toolbar.

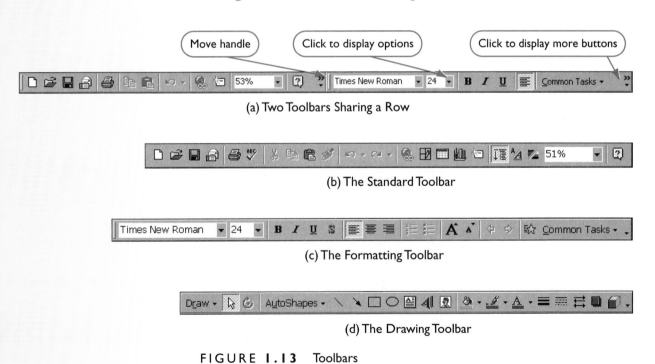

(a) Two Toolbars Sharing a Row

(b) The Standard Toolbar

(c) The Formatting Toolbar

(d) The Drawing Toolbar

FIGURE 1.13   Toolbars

The **drawing ruler** displays along the top and left edge of the slide pane. To display or hide the ruler, choose View | Ruler. The numbers on the ruler change depending on the feature you are using. If you are aligning text, the origin (or zero position) is located at the left edge of the horizontal ruler. However, if you are aligning a graphic, then the origin is in the center of the slide.

NORMAL VIEW

By default, your presentation is shown in **Normal view**, which allows you to work on and view your presentation all on one screen. For ease of use, Normal view contains three panes:

- **outline pane**—displays the slide number, icon, title of the slide, and the slide's text
- **slide pane**—displays the slide selected in the outline pane
- **notes pane**—allows you to create speaker notes as you create slides

 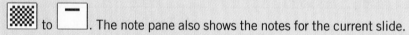
Scroll bars appear at the right edge of the outline, notes, and slide panes, and along the bottom of the outline pane, allowing you to move through a document using the mouse. The following describes how to use a scroll bar:

- Click the up arrow and down arrow on the vertical scroll bar on the slide pane to move the display up or down one slide at a time. Notice that the outline pane moves also.
- Click the up arrow and down arrow on the vertical scroll bar on the outline pane to move up or down through the outline text.
- Click the double upward-pointing arrow on the slide pane to move to the previous slide and the double downward-pointing arrow to move to the next slide.
- Click and drag the **scroll box** down or up to quickly scroll down or back up a window.

The horizontal scroll bar contains buttons that allow you to change the view of your document. Table 1.3 describes the view buttons. (You will learn to change and use views in Unit 2.)

Button	Name	Description
⊟	Normal View	Displays the three panes described above
≣	Outline View	Enlarges the outline pane of the presentation
▭	Slide View	Shows slides individually
⊞	Slide Sorter View	Displays the entire presentation as miniature slides
⬛	Slide Show	Displays the slides full screen in a slide show

TABLE 1.3   View Buttons

STATUS BAR

The bottom of the window contains the **status bar**. The left end of the status bar displays information about the location of your insertion point in the slide presentation, for example, Slide 2 of 8. The middle of the status bar contains the name of the wizard or template used to create the slide show. The right end displays the Spelling status button.

TASKBAR

The Windows 98 **taskbar**, which appears along the bottom of the screen, contains the Start button and buttons for all open programs and files. When you have two or more presentations open in PowerPoint, the taskbar displays a button for each of them. You will use these buttons to switch from one presentation to another.

SHORTCUT MENU

Like other Windows programs, PowerPoint provides quick access to often-used tasks by means of **shortcut menus**. To open a shortcut menu, point to an object and click the right mouse button. The content of the menu varies with the object you click. Figure 1.14 shows a shortcut menu that opens if you right-click the slide pane.

FIGURE 1.14   A Shortcut Menu

1. Choose **Tools** | **Customize**.
The Customize dialog box opens on the screen.

2. Click the **Options tab**.
The Options tab moves to the front and becomes active. It displays the current settings for the toolbars as well as other interface options you can customize.

3. Click the **Close button**.
The dialog box closes.

4. Choose **View** | **Ruler**.
The ruler disappears if it was displayed, or reappears if it was not displayed.

5. Move the mouse pointer over any toolbar button and hold it there.
A ScreenTip shows the name of the button.

6. Click the **Minimize button** on the title bar.
Windows reduces PowerPoint to a button on the taskbar.

7. Click the **PowerPoint button** on the taskbar.
Windows restores the PowerPoint window to its former size.

8. Keep PowerPoint running for use in the next exercise.

TASK 4 | *Getting Help*

What: Use PowerPoint's Online Help.

How: Click the Office Assistant or choose Help | Microsoft Power-Point Help.

Why: PowerPoint provides extensive online documentation that is easy to use.

Tip: Press the F1 key on the keyboard to launch PowerPoint Help.

If the **Office Assistant** is visible on the screen, then Help is just a click away. Click the cartoon character to open the Help bubble shown in Figure 1.15. To get help, complete the following steps:

1. Type a question into the text box. For example, if you want help on creating a presentation, type *"How do I create a presentation?"*
2. Click the Search button. PowerPoint provides a list of Help topics to choose from, as shown in Figure 1.16.

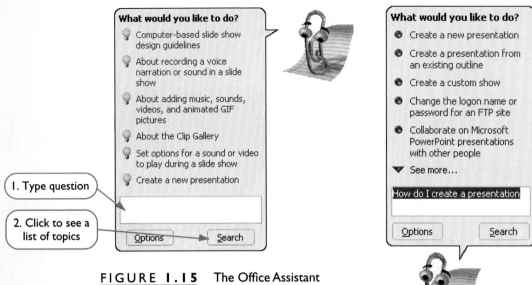

1. Type question

2. Click to see a list of topics

FIGURE 1.15 The Office Assistant Offering to Help

FIGURE 1.16 Choose the Appropriate Topic

3. Select a topic from the list to display the Help document, as shown in Figure 1.17.

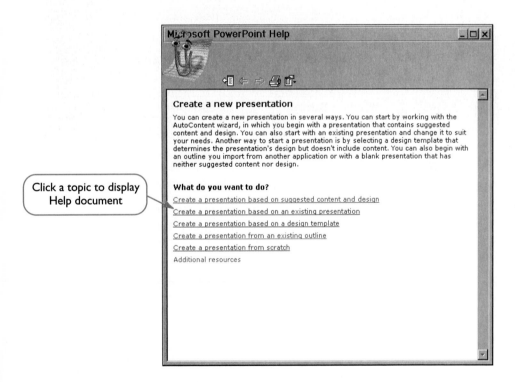

Click a topic to display Help document

FIGURE 1.17 The Help Document Displayed

4. To display the entire Help window, click the Show button. The window expands to include the Contents, Answer Wizard, and Index tabs, along with the Help buttons shown in Figure 1.18. Table 1.4 describes these buttons.

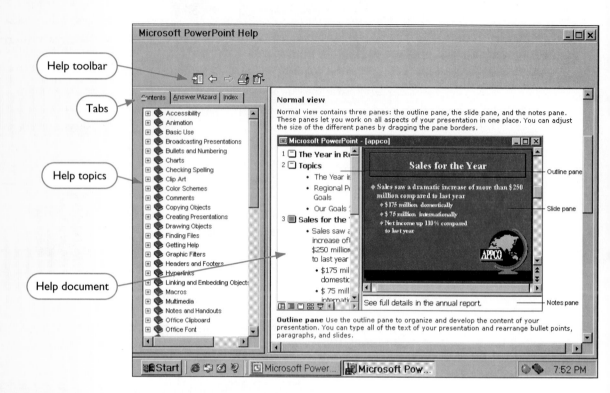

FIGURE 1.18 The Complete Help Window Displaying the Contents Tab

Button	Description
	Reduces the Help window to hide the tabs
	Increases the size of the Help window
	Returns to the previous Help topic
	If you have used the Back button, you can click the Forward button to return to the previous topic
	Prints the current Help topic
	Provides the options on a drop-down list

TABLE 1.4 Help Buttons

To use other help options, follow these steps:

- To use Help Contents, click the Contents tab. Click the plus sign before the topic to display the list of subtopics. Click a topic to display the Help document.
- To use the Answer Wizard, click the Answer Wizard tab. Type a question in the text box and click the Search button. PowerPoint displays a list of Help topics.
- To use the Help Index, click the Index tab. Type a topic in the keywords text box and click the Search button. PowerPoint displays a list of topics.

The default Office Assistant character, Clipit, though nothing more than a thin metal wire, helps find what you need and keeps it all together. If the Office Assistant isn't displayed on the screen, choose Help | Microsoft PowerPoint Help, or press the F1 key on the keyboard.

If Clipit gets in the way, drag it to another part of the screen or choose Help | Hide the Office Assistant. If you would prefer a different Assistant, right-click Clipit and choose Choose Assistant from the shortcut menu.

The Office Assistant provides tips to help with using keyboard shortcuts or software features more effectively. A light bulb appears along with Clipit when a tip is available. Click the light bulb to display the tip. If a tip is available, but Clipit isn't displayed, the PowerPoint Help button displays a light bulb along with the question mark.

Other help features are available using the following methods:

- To get help on screen features, choose Help | What's This? The mouse pointer changes to the Help pointer, with a question mark. Click any part of the screen to get help on that feature.

- To link to up-to-date help, choose Help | Office on the Web. PowerPoint opens your browser and connects you to Microsoft's Web site.

POINTER

Connecting to Microsoft on the Web

You must have a **modem** and an **Internet Service Provider** to successfully log on to the Web from your home, or be attached to a network with a gateway to the Internet at work or in a computer lab. (Check the Glossary for definitions of these terms.)

- To get help while using a dialog box, click the [?] in the dialog box title bar. The pointer changes to the Help pointer, with a question mark. Click the option in the dialog box that you want explained. PowerPoint displays an explanation in a ScreenTip, as shown in Figure 1.19.

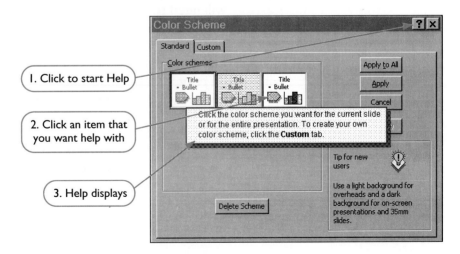

FIGURE 1.19   Help in a Dialog Box

EXERCISE 4 | *Getting Help*

1. Click the **Office Assistant**.
The Help bubble appears.

2. Type **How do I create presentations?** and click the **Search button**.
A list of topics displays in the Help bubble.

3. Click **Create a new presentation**.
The Microsoft PowerPoint Help window opens and displays the page you selected.

4. Click **Create a presentation based on suggested content and design**.
The Help window displays this document.

5. Click the Help window's **Print button**.
The Print dialog box opens.

6. Click the **OK button**.
The Help topic prints.

7. After reading the contents, click the **Close button** in the Help window.
The Help window closes.

8. Keep the presentation on the screen for use in the next exercise.

TASK 5 | *Printing the Slides and the Outline*

What: Print the slides and the outline.

How: Choose File | Print.

Why: To have a hard copy of the presentation, you must print it.

Tip: To create overhead transparencies, choose the Overhead option in the *Slides Sized For* option of the Page Setup dialog box. You will need to adjust the size accordingly. Before you print, load transparency film into the printer.

You will want to print out various views of your presentation. In this task, you will learn to print both the slides and the outline. Before you print, you should check the page setup by choosing File | Page Setup. The dialog box shown in Figure 1.20 displays.

The default setup for slides is landscape orientation, 10 inches wide by 7.5 inches high, with each page numbered starting with the number 1. Notice that PowerPoint has a second orientation option already set up in portrait orientation for printing the outline and notes.

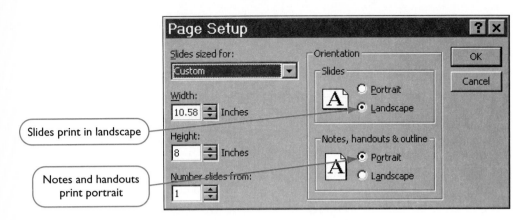

Slides print in landscape

Notes and handouts print portrait

FIGURE 1.20   Page Setup Dialog Box

To print slides do one of the following:

- Click the Print button on the Standard toolbar to print on the default printer.
- Choose File | Print—the Print dialog box displays, as shown in Figure 1.21.

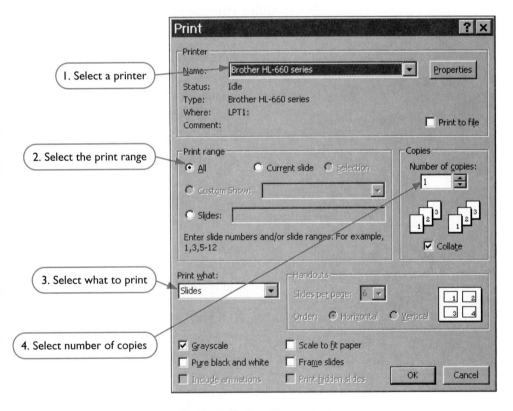

1. Select a printer

2. Select the print range

3. Select what to print

4. Select number of copies

FIGURE 1.21   The Print Dialog Box

When the Print dialog box appears, complete the following steps:

1. Check the Printer Name to see which printer will actually print the document. To change printers, click the down arrow in the Name list box and select a different printer from the list.

2. Change the Page range option, if necessary, by clicking an option button as shown in Table 1.5.

Page Range	Description
All	Prints all the slides (the default)
Current slide	Prints the slide that is displayed
Selection	Prints the selected outline text
Custom show	Prints a custom slide show
Slides	Prints several slides in a range

TABLE 1.5   Page Range Options

3. Change the Copies option to change the number of copies that PowerPoint prints.
4. Change the Print What option to one of the following:

- **Slides** (the default) places each slide on a separate piece of paper with a landscape orientation (11 x 8½)
- **Handouts** prints the audience notes—you choose how many slides should appear on each page and how they should be ordered
- **Notes Pages** prints the speaker notes
- **Outline View** prints the outline in portrait orientation (8½ by 11)

5. Select from the following options:

- Grayscale optimizes color slides for a black-and-white printout
- The Pure Black & White option prints the color slides in black and white without gray tones
- Include animations prints animations as an icon on the slide
- Scale to fit paper reduces or enlarges slides to fit the printed page
- Frame slides places a border around the slides on the printed page
- Print Hidden slides prints slides you have hidden

6. Click OK.

The presentation prints on the selected printer.

EXERCISE 5 | *Printing the Slides and the Outline*

1. With your presentation on the screen, choose **File | Print**.
   The Print dialog box displays.
2. Select the correct printer and select **All** in the Print Range section.
3. Select **Slides** in the Print what section.
4. Make sure **Grayscale** is selected.

5. Click **OK**.

The slides print in black and white.

6. To print the outline, choose **File | Print**.

7. Under Print What, select **Outline View**.

8. Click **OK**.

The outline prints.

9. Leave the slides on the screen for use in the next exercise.

TASK 6 | *Exiting PowerPoint*

What: Exit correctly from PowerPoint.

How: Choose File | Exit.

Why: You must exit the software correctly to keep your files from becoming corrupted.

Tip: Never turn off the computer while you have programs running.

You should always exit from Microsoft PowerPoint when you are finished working with the application. To exit, you can use either of these methods:

- Choose File | Exit.
- Click the close button on the title bar.

If you have not saved the file you were working on, PowerPoint prompts you to do so, as shown in Figure 1.22.

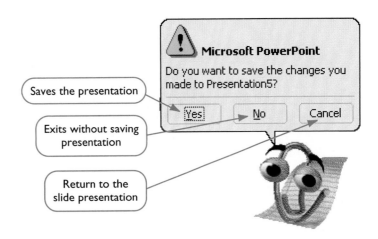

FIGURE 1.22   PowerPoint Prompts You to Save Your Work

You can do one of the following:

- Choose **Yes** to save the presentation.
- Choose **No** to exit without saving the presentation.
- Choose **Cancel** to return to the presentation.

When you exit PowerPoint, you return to the Windows desktop.

EXERCISE 6 | *Exiting PowerPoint*

1. Choose **File | Exit**.

2. If PowerPoint asks to save your file, select **No**.
PowerPoint closes and Windows displays.

REVIEW

SUMMARY

After completing this unit, you should be able to
- start PowerPoint 2000 (page 2)
- create a presentation using the AutoContent Wizard (page 4)
- use the PowerPoint Interface (page 9)
- use Microsoft Help (page 16)
- print slides (page 21)
- print the presentation outline (page 23)
- exit from PowerPoint (page 23)

KEY TERMS

Close button (page 10)
command button (page 12)
dialog box (page 12)
Drawing ruler (page 14)
Drawing toolbar (page 13)
Formatting toolbar (page 13)
graphical user interface (GUI)
  (page 9)
Internet Service Provider (page 19)
Maximize button (page 10)
menu bar (page 10)
Minimize button (page 10)
modem (page 19)
Normal view (page 14)
notes pane (page 14)

Office Assistant (page 16)
outline pane (page 14)
presentation software (page 2)
Restore button (page 10)
ScreenTip (page 14)
scroll bar (page 14)
scroll box (page 14)
shortcut menu (page 15)
slide pane (page 14)
Standard toolbar (page 13)
Start button (page 2)
status bar (page 15)
taskbar (page 15)
title bar (page 10)

TEST YOUR SKILLS

True/False

1. The status bar displays the number of the current slide with the total number of slides in the presentation.
2. You can create 35mm slides using PowerPoint.
3. You should never turn off the computer before you have correctly exited PowerPoint.
4. PowerPoint's primary use is for spreadsheets.
5. You can create overhead transparencies using PowerPoint.

Multiple Choice

1. The Office Assistant
   a. can't be turned off
   b. allows you to type questions to ask for help
   c. is the only way to access help in Microsoft PowerPoint
   d. all of these answers

2. Normal view displays
   a. the current slide
   b. the presentation outline
   c. the notes pane
   d. all of these answers

3. When you are using a dialog box and need help, you
   a. must cancel the operation and use the Office Assistant
   b. must cancel the operation and use the Help menu
   c. click the [?] in the dialog box and then click on the option you want help for
   d. exit the dialog box and initiate a help search

4. The ruler
   a. displays across the entire screen in Normal view
   b. displays across the top and to the left of the slide pane in Normal view
   c. always has the origin on the left.
   d. both answers b and c

5. The scroll bars
   a. let you view other slides in your presentation
   b. let you view other parts of the outline
   c. are both horizontal and vertical
   d. all of these answers

Short Answer

Match the letter of the correct word with the correct location in Figure 1.23:

   ___ a. Windows task bar   ___ b. slide pane
   ___ c. Title bar   ___ d. outline pane
   ___ e. notes pane   ___ f. slide number

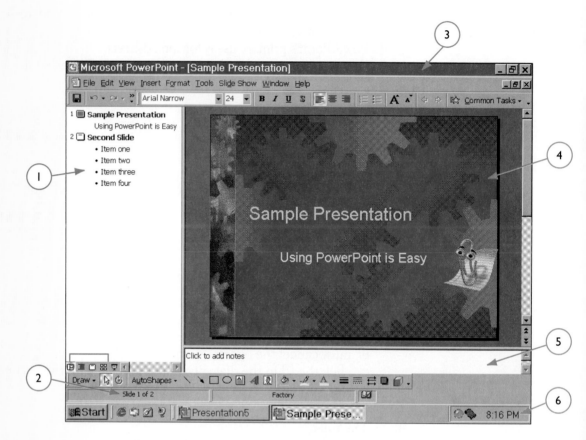

FIGURE 1.23   PowerPoint Screen

What Does This Do?

Write a brief description of the function of the following:

1.	✖	6.	▨
2.	Next >	7.	▬
3.	Carnegie Coach	8.	Finish
4.	Search	9.	▣
5.	◻	10.	▶?

On Your Own

1. Create a new presentation using the AutoContent Wizard. Choose a different style presentation to see other options.
2. With the sample presentation open, search Help for information on a topic that isn't clear to you.
3. With the sample presentation open, move to different slides and explore the outline contents.
4. Print the slides.
5. Print the outline.

PROJECTS

1. Start Microsoft PowerPoint. Use the AutoContent Wizard to create a sample presentation based on Recommending a Strategy, which is under the General category. Place your name in the footer of every slide. Print the slides. Print the outline. Exit PowerPoint without saving the presentation.

2. Use Help Contents. Choose Using—Accessibility Features. Print the resulting Help document—Accessibility for people with disabilities.

3. Use Help Index. Choose *Key Information*. Then, choose *How to get started using PowerPoint 2000*. Display the results and print the help information.

4. Start PowerPoint. Use the AutoContent Wizard to create a sample presentation based on the Generic presentation in the General category. Place your name in the footer of every slide. Print the slides. Print the outline. Exit PowerPoint without saving the presentation.

Creating and Viewing Presentations

UNIT OBJECTIVES

- Create a presentation using a template
- Insert and delete text
- Change views
- Check the spelling and style of a presentation
- Save the presentation
- Close and open a presentation

In Unit 1, you used the AutoContent Wizard to automatically create a presentation. In this unit, you will use one of PowerPoint's built-in templates to create a presentation. After creating presentations, you will insert text, add new slides, and save the presentation for future use. You will also want to open saved presentations and close presentations that you are finished using. As described in Unit 1, PowerPoint provides various views of your presentation to help you to create, edit, and enhance your presentations. You learn to use each of the views in this unit.

What: Use a built-in template to create a presentation.

How: Choose File | New.

Why: Templates format your content on slides.

Tip: Templates format your presentations with professionally designed styles.

To create a presentation with your own content, but have PowerPoint format the slides, you can use **design templates**. Choose File | New, and then select the Design Templates tab. PowerPoint presents you with design templates, which are professionally formatted presentations that you can use to enhance your own information. Figure 2.1 shows the Design Templates tab of the New Presentation dialog box with a sample design in the Preview window. Click different templates to preview them in the dialog box.

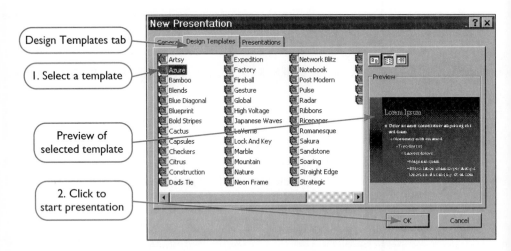

FIGURE 2.1   Design Templates Tab of the New Presentation Dialog Box

POINTER

Getting Assistance with Presentations

PowerPoint provides three levels of assistance for creating presentations:

- AutoContent Wizard provides content and formatting for a presentation with the step-by-step help of a wizard.

- Presentation templates include both a design and suggested content for a presentation.

- Design templates supply the formatting, but no content, for the presentation.

To use one of the design templates, follow these steps:

1. Select a design name and click OK.

The New Slide dialog box appears presenting layout options for slides, as shown in Figure 2.2.

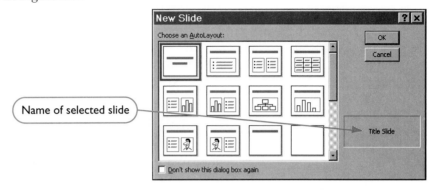

FIGURE 2.2   New Slide Dialog Box

POINTER

Layout Options

The choices for the layout of slides is the same for all templates; that is, the **layout** controls the positioning of elements on the individual slides regardless of the template used to format the presentation. For example, a Title Slide has a title centered on the slide with a subtitle below it, but if you choose a bulleted slide, the title is located at the top of the slide to allow space for a bulleted list.

2. Click a layout to display the option name in the bottom right corner of the dialog box. Figure 2.3 shows the elements of the Title Slide.

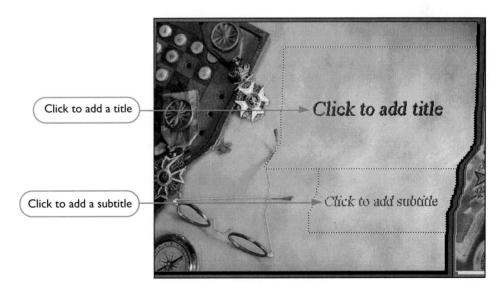

FIGURE 2.3   The Title Slide with Placeholders

3. Click OK to use the layout to create a slide.
4. Place text on the slide by clicking the **placeholder** box and typing the desired text.

1. Start PowerPoint. On the opening dialog box, choose **Design Template** and click **OK**.
   This reveals a list of design template names.

2. Click various names in the list and preview how they appear.

3. Choose **Network Blitz** and click **OK**.
   This brings up the dialog box asking you to choose an AutoLayout.

4. Select **Title Slide** and click **OK**.
   Now you are ready to work on the text.

5. Click in the top placeholder and type the title **Linking to the World**.
   The title appears on the slide and in the outline.

6. Click in the bottom placeholder and type the subtitle **Our Web Presence**.
   The subtitle appears as shown in Figure 2.4.

7. Keep the presentation on the screen for use in the next exercise.

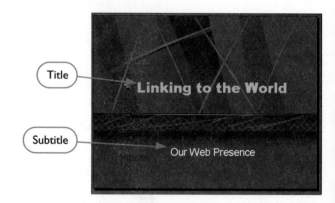

FIGURE 2.4   The Title Slide with Text

TASK 2 | *Inserting and Deleting Text*

What: Insert and delete text from slides.

How: Select text, and press the Delete key.

Why: You will want to edit presentations.

Tip: Using these editing techniques, you can modify the content of presentations created with the AutoContent Wizard or presentation templates to fit your specific needs.

In the last task, you added text to a slide by clicking the placeholder and typing the title text and subtitle text. As you create more types of slides, you will want to add and change text.

To insert text, follow these steps:

1. In either the slide pane or the outline pane, click the mouse at the location in the text where you want the new text to appear.
2. Type the desired text.

PowerPoint inserts the text on the slide and in the outline.

To delete text, follow these steps:

1. Select text using your mouse in either the slide pane or the outline pane by clicking and dragging the mouse.
2. Press the Delete key on the keyboard or choose Edit | Clear just as you would in your word processing software.

PowerPoint deletes the selected or highlighted text from the slide.

To undo an operation, such as a deletion, either choose Edit | Undo or click the Undo button on the Standard Toolbar.

EXERCISE 2 | *Inserting and Deleting Text*

1. Place the insertion point before the word *Web* in the subtitle either on the slide or in the outline.
2. Type **World Wide** and press the **spacebar**.
   The words *World Wide* appear in the subtitle before the word *Web* both in the outline and on the slide.
3. Select the text *World Wide* in the Outline pane.
4. Press the **Delete** key on the keyboard.
   PowerPoint deletes the words from the outline and the slide. But maybe you need to be more specific, so you decide to put it back in.
5. Click the **Undo button**.
   PowerPoint restores the words *World Wide* to the slide subtitle, as shown in Figure 2.5.
6. Keep the slide on the screen for use in the next exercise.

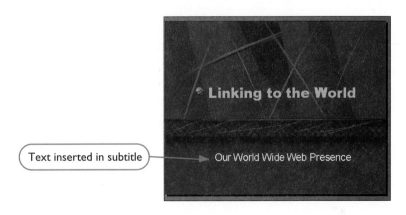

FIGURE 2.5 The Title Slide with Inserted Text

TASK 3 | *Changing Views*

What: Change the way the presentation displays on the screen.

How: Use commands on the View menu (Normal, Slide Sorter, Notes Page, Slide Show) or the view buttons.

Why: Each view gives you different ways to work with your presentation.

Tip: You can change the size of any of the panes in Normal view by pointing to a pane border until you see the two-headed pointer, then dragging the border to adjust the size of the pane.

When you create or view a presentation in PowerPoint 2000, it displays in Normal view, which Unit 1 describes. PowerPoint provides other options or views for working with and viewing presentations.

To change the view of a presentation, use one of the following methods:

- Choose a different view from the View menu.
- Click the view buttons on the horizontal scroll bar.

    Figure 2.6a shows the buttons on the scroll bar, and Figure 2.6b shows the View menu.

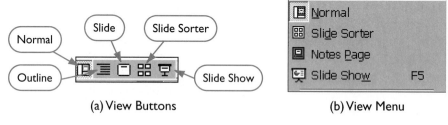

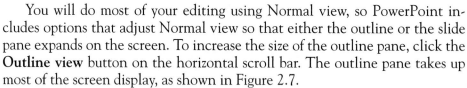

FIGURE **2.6** View Options

You will do most of your editing using Normal view, so PowerPoint includes options that adjust Normal view so that either the outline or the slide pane expands on the screen. To increase the size of the outline pane, click the **Outline view** button on the horizontal scroll bar. The outline pane takes up most of the screen display, as shown in Figure 2.7.

To increase the size of the slide pane, click the **Slide view** button on the horizontal scroll bar. Now, the slide pane takes up most of the screen display, as shown in Figure 2.8.

    After creating several slides in a presentation, you might want to view all the slides at one time. To change to **Slide Sorter view**, use one of the following methods, either choose View | Slide Sorter or click the Slide Sorter button.

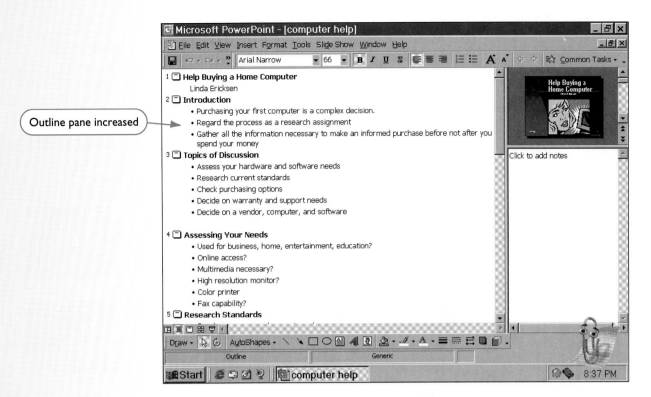

Outline pane increased

FIGURE 2.7   Outline View

Outline collapsed

Slide pane increased

FIGURE 2.8   Slide View

As you see in Figure 2.9, when you change to Slide Sorter view, you can see all the slides in the presentation as miniatures or **thumbnails**, just as if you were viewing actual 35-mm slides on a light table. In Slide Sorter view, you can rearrange or delete slides and use the tools found on the Slide Sorter toolbar. (You will learn to use the Slide Sorter in Unit 3.)

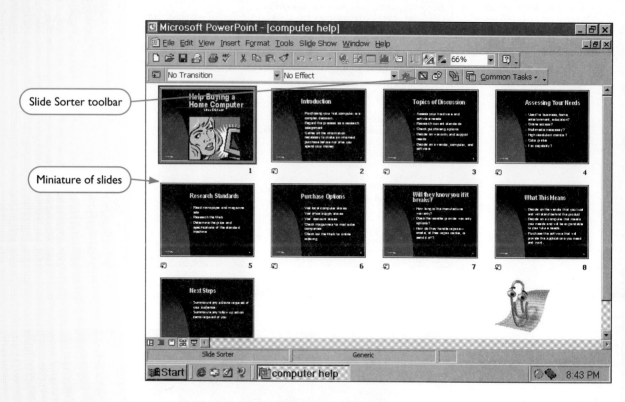

Slide Sorter toolbar

Miniature of slides

FIGURE 2.9   Slide Sorter Window

The third pane of Normal view is the notes pane, used to create speaker's notes. You type what you will say as you conduct the presentation in the notes pane. Because the notes pane is quite small when viewed in Normal view, PowerPoint provides an option for viewing the notes as a whole page. To view the slide notes on separate pages, choose View | Notes Page; PowerPoint displays the individual slides one by one with a text box for typing notes. Figure 2.10 shows the **Notes Page**.

When you have created a presentation, you will want to play it as a slide show. To see the presentation in its final form as a **Slide Show**, choose View | Slide Show or click the Slide Show button on the horizontal scroll bar. Power-Point displays each slide full screen, as shown in Figure 2.11.

To display the next slide, click the mouse any place on the screen, and the next slide in the presentation displays. When you run slides as a slide show, PowerPoint places a button in the bottom left corner of the screen. When you click the button, PowerPoint displays the shortcut menu shown in Figure 2.12.

Choose End Show from the shortcut menu to end the show with the current slide and restore the previous view.

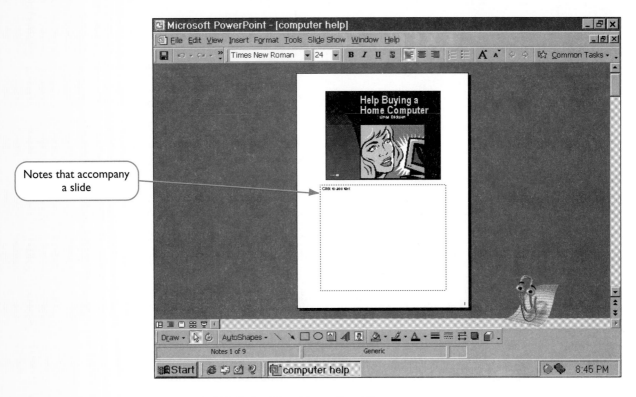

FIGURE 2.10 Notes Page View

FIGURE 2.11 Slide Show

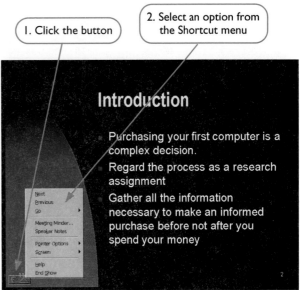

FIGURE 2.12 Slide Shortcut Menu

1. Click the **Outline View button** on the horizontal scroll bar.
The outline pane gets larger, though you can still see a miniature slide and have room to type notes.

2. Click the **Slide View button** on the horizontal scroll bar.
PowerPoint enlarges the slide pane, but you can still see part of the outline.

3. Choose **View | Notes Page**.
The slide displays with the text box for notes you type.

4. Choose **View | Slide Sorter**.
PowerPoint displays the slides in miniature.

5. Choose **View | Slide Show**.
The slide displays full screen with a button in the bottom left corner.

6. Click the mouse several times to end the slide show.
The presentation returns to the last selected view.

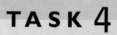

7. Click the **Normal View button** on the horizontal scroll bar.
The presentation displays the three panes.

8. Click in the notes pane and type: **Introduce my department and staff**.
The note appears in the Notes pane as a reminder.

9. Keep the presentation on your screen for use in the next exercise.

TASK 4 | *Checking the Spelling and Style of the Presentation*

What: Check the spelling and style of text in the presentation.

How: Choose Help | Microsoft PowerPoint Help and Tools | Spelling.

Why: You have to eliminate every spelling mistake, or you will make a bad impression on your audience.

Tip: Never give a presentation until you have carefully proofread for spelling, punctuation, and style.

CHECKING THE STYLE

PowerPoint offers tools to help ensure that your presentation represents you in the way that you want. When you have the Office Assistant running, PowerPoint automatically provides help and suggestions. One type of help it provides is to check the style of text that you type. When PowerPoint encounters an error, a light bulb appears on the slide next to the text with an error, as you see in Figure 2.13a.

When you click the bulb to open the Office Assistant Tip box, as in Figure 2.13b, you get a brief explanation of the tip and the following options:

- have PowerPoint change the text

- ignore this style rule in this presentation
- change the style checker options for all presentations you create

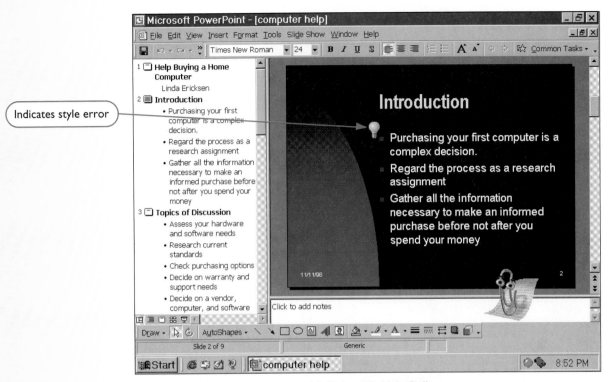

(a) Slide with Help Bulb

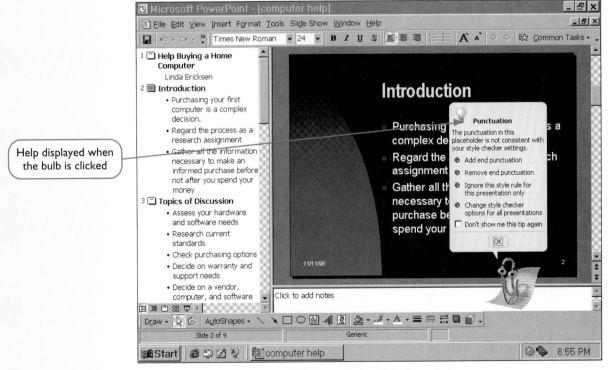

(b) PowerPoint Help Provided

FIGURE 2.13   Checking the Style of the Presentation

Clicking the change style checker options lets you customize the style checker. The two tabs of the Style Options dialog box are shown in Figures 2.14a and 2.14b.

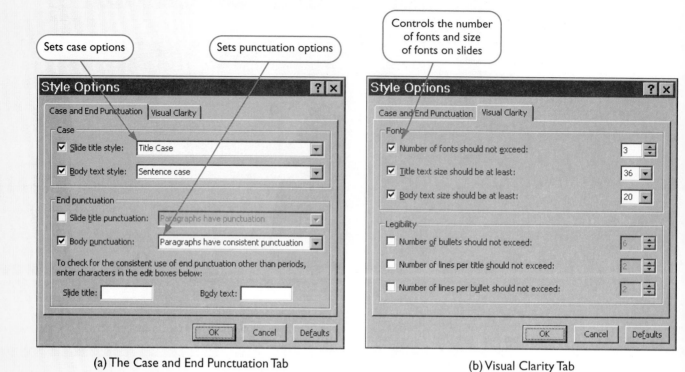

(a) The Case and End Punctuation Tab

(b) Visual Clarity Tab

FIGURE 2.14 Style Options Dialog Box

To change options for case and end punctuation on slides, make selections on the Case and End Punctuation tab of the Style Options dialog box. To change the number and size of fonts or the legibility of slides, make selections on the Visual Clarity tab of the Style Options dialog box.

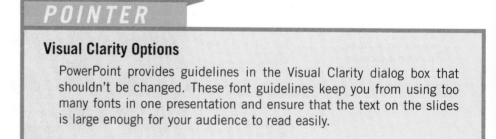

POINTER

Visual Clarity Options

PowerPoint provides guidelines in the Visual Clarity dialog box that shouldn't be changed. These font guidelines keep you from using too many fonts in one presentation and ensure that the text on the slides is large enough for your audience to read easily.

CHECKING SPELLING

As you type text onto slides in PowerPoint, you will notice that some words appear with a red wavy underline. These are words that don't appear in the Office dictionary, so PowerPoint flags them as spelling errors. To correct the spelling of the word, follow these steps:

1. Point to the word that appears with the red wavy underline.
2. Right-click the mouse on the word.
3. Choose the correct spelling from the shortcut menu, as shown in Figure 2.15.

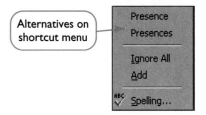

FIGURE 2.15   Spelling Shortcut Menu

POINTER

PowerPoint Doesn't Check Context

Not every misspelled word is flagged by the spelling checker. For example, you might misspell "from" as "form." For this reason, you must be sure to carefully proofread your slides and not merely rely on the Spell Checker.

You can also ignore the wavy red underlines as you work and later run the Spell Checker for the entire presentation. You can do this by choosing Tools | Spelling. Figure 2.16 shows the Spelling dialog box.

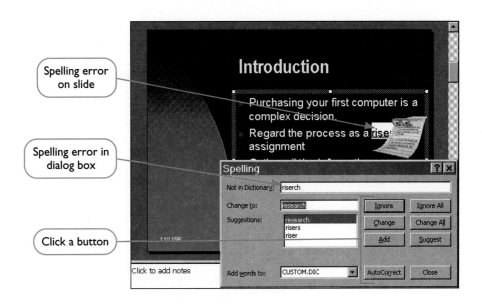

FIGURE 2.16   The Spelling Dialog Box

1. If the Office Assistant isn't on the screen, choose **Help | Microsoft PowerPoint Help**.
The Office Assistant displays on the screen.

2. Delete the first character of the first word in the subtitle (the O in *Our*).
The light bulb appears on the screen, and the word displays with a red wavy underline.

3. Point to the *ur* and right-click the mouse.
The shortcut menu appears.

4. Choose **our** from the list.
PowerPoint replaces the spelling with your choice.

5. Click the light bulb.
The Capitalization tip displays.

6. Click the **Change the text to title case** option.
PowerPoint capitalizes the O in *our*.

7. Keep the presentation open for use in the next exercise.

TASK 5 | *Saving the Presentation*

What: Save the presentation to a disk.

How: Choose File | Save.

Why: To keep a permanent copy of your presentation, you must make a copy of it on disk or on your hard drive.

Tip: It's a good idea to save your presentation every 10 to 15 minutes to avoid losing your work if your computer shuts down unexpectedly.

To save a presentation, choose File | Save. When you first save a presenta-
tion, the Save As dialog box opens, as shown in Figure 2.17.

FIGURE 2.17   The Save As Dialog Box

/	.
\	?
>	|
<	:
*	;

PowerPoint suggests a name for the presentation in the File name text box. The suggested name is the title of the presentation, but you can type another name you prefer. Give files meaningful names that represent their content so that finding them later will be easy.

When naming files, you can make the names up to 255 characters long, but you can't use any of the following characters noted in the chart in the margin.

Always check the location in the **Save in** list box of the Save dialog box. This dialog box shows the disk drive where PowerPoint saves the file. If you wish to save it on a different disk, click the down arrow in the list box and select the one you want—such as the 3 1/2 Floppy (A:) drive to save the file on a floppy disk, as shown in Figure 2.18.

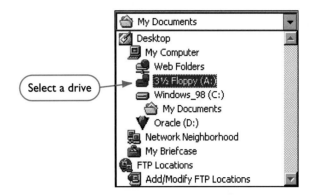

Select a drive

FIGURE 2.18 Choosing a Drive in Which to Save a File

PowerPoint's Save dialog box includes the **Places bar** along the left edge to help you organize your files into folders. Table 2.1 describes the buttons on the Places bar. When you click a button on the bar, that folder name appears in the Save in list box. This is a quick way to select the folder.

Button	**Name**	**Folder Description**
My Documents	History	List of documents that were used recently; you can't save a file here, but can find a recently used file to open it
History	My Documents	The default folder for storing Office files
Desktop	Desktop	Saves the file to the desktop for quick access
Favorites	Favorites	Folder where you can store files you use often
Web Folders	Web Folders	Folder where you can store files that you want to publish on the Web

TABLE 2.1 Places Bar

Formatted Disk Needed

You will need a formatted 3$\frac{1}{2}$" disk inserted in the A drive in order to save files on the 3$\frac{1}{2}$ floppy (A:) drive.

EXERCISE 5 | *Saving the Presentation*

1. Choose **File | Save**.
The dialog box appears.

2. Type **Web**.
The name appears in the File name text box. Let's save it to a floppy disk.

3. Insert a floppy disk into the computer's floppy drive (drive A).

4. Click the down arrow at the right of the Save in text box.

5. Choose 3$\frac{1}{2}$ **Floppy (A:)**.

6. Click the **Save** button in the dialog box to complete the operation.
PowerPoint saves the file on the disk in drive A.

TASK 6 | *Closing and Opening a Presentation*

What: Close presentations that you are finished using, and open presentations that are saved on a disk.

How: Choose File | Close and choose File | Open.

Why: To edit or present saved presentations, you must open them.

Tip: When you close down all open presentations, PowerPoint displays a gray background. Simply create a new presentation or open an existing one.

CLOSING PRESENTATIONS

When you are finished editing and saving a presentation, you will close it. To close the presentation, follow these steps:

1. Choose File | Close or click the Close button in the top-right corner of the window.
2. The Office Assistant tip appears, as shown in Figure 2.19, if the presentation hasn't been saved since your last edits.

FIGURE 2.19 PowerPoint Prompts You to Save Changes

In this dialog box, you can choose to do any of the following:

* Save the presentation and close the file.
* Close the file without saving it.
* Cancel the operation and return to the presentation.

OPENING SAVED PRESENTATIONS

When you first start PowerPoint, you must choose to create or open a presentation. To open a presentation as you start PowerPoint, follow these steps:

1. Select *Open an Existing Presentation*.
2. Click OK to display the Open dialog box—see Figure 2.20.

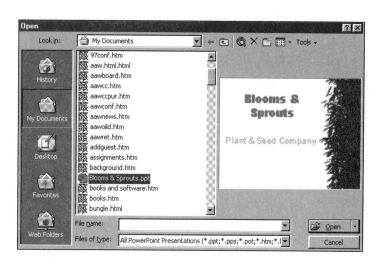

FIGURE 2.20 The Open Dialog Box

If you are already working in PowerPoint and want to open an existing file, either choose File | Open or click the Open button. The Open dialog box appears. It looks very similar to the Save As dialog box, as you can see in Figure 2.20, with the same folders down the left side and so on.

To open a file listed in the Open dialog box, follow these steps:

1. Change the drive in the Look in text box if necessary.
2. Change the folder you want to look in if necessary.
3. Click the desired file to select it—notice the selected file displays in the preview section.
4. Click the Open button.

The presentation opens on the screen.

EXERCISE 6 | *Closing and Opening a Presentation*

1. Choose **File | Close**.
2. If the tip appears, click **Yes** to save the changes.
   The file closes and the gray background appears.
3. Choose **File | Open**.
   The Open dialog box appears.
4. Change the *Look in* option to the *3¹/₂ Floppy (A:)* if necessary.
5. Click the file **Web**.
   The file becomes selected and appears in the preview section.
6. Click the **Open button**.
   The file opens on the screen.
7. Choose **File | Exit** to close the file and exit from PowerPoint.

REVIEW

SUMMARY

After completing this unit, you should be able to
- create a presentation using a template (page 30)
- insert and delete text (page 32)
- change views (page 34)
- check the spelling and style of a presentation (page 38)
- save the presentation to a disk (page 42)
- close a presentation (page 44)
- open a presentation saved on a disk (page 45)

KEY TERMS

design template (page 30)

layout (page 31)

Notes Page (page 36)

Outline view (page 34)

placeholder (page 31)

Places bar (page 43)

Save in (page 43)

Slide Show (page 36)

Slide Sorter view (page 34)

Slide view (page 34)

thumbnails (page 36)

TEST YOUR SKILLS

True/False

1. You must have the Office Assistant turned on in order to check the spelling of words on slides.
2. You must have the Office Assistant turned on in order to check the style of the text that appears on slides.
3. The Slide Sorter view displays all the slides in a presentation as miniatures.
4. The view buttons are located on the horizontal scroll bar.
5. You click a Placeholder to type text on slides.

Multiple Choice

1. You can create presentations in PowerPoint by using
   a. templates
   b. Notes Page
   c. Slide Sorter view
   d. all of these answers

2. To view single slides, you would choose
   a. Slide Sorter view
   b. Outline view
   c. Slide view
   d. all of these answers

3. To view multiple slides at one time, you would use the
   a. Notes Page view
   b. Slide Sorter view
   c. Slide view
   d. all of these answers

4. PowerPoint's automatic style checker recommends that you
   a. capitalize titles
   b. use no more than three fonts per slide presentation
   c. make titles 36 point
   d. all of these answers

5. To create speaker's notes, you would use the
   a. Slide view
   b. Slide Sorter view
   c. Notes Page view
   d. Outline view

Short Answer

Match the following:

    ___ a. Slide view   ___ b. Normal view

    ___ c. Notes Page   ___ d. Slide Show view

    ___ e. Slide Sorter view

1. The default view with three panes
2. Enlarges the Slide pane in Normal view
3. Displays the slide and a text box
4. Displays all the slides at once as miniatures
5. Displays slides one after the other

What Does This Do?

Write a brief description of the function of the following:

1.		6.	My Documents
2.		7.	History
3.		8.	Desktop
4.		9.	Favorites
5.		10.	Web Folders

On Your Own

1. Use the AutoContent Wizard to create a slide presentation.
2. Use the Blends template to create a presentation and create a title slide. Type text on the title slide.
3. Use the Nature template to create a presentation and create a title slide. Type text on the title slide.
4. Open an existing presentation and edit text.
5. Search Help for information on the various PowerPoint view options.

PROJECTS

1. Use the AutoContent Wizard to create a presentation. Select Motivating a Team under Carnegie Coach as the type of presentation. Insert and delete text to change the content of at least two slides. Run the Spell Checker. Save the presentation as Motivation. Print the slides. Print the outline.

2. Use the AutoContent Wizard to create a presentation. Select Business Plan under Corporate as the type of presentation. Insert and delete text to change the content of at least two slides. Run the Spell Checker. Save the presentation as Business Plan. Print the slides. Print the outline.

3. Use the AutoContent Wizard to create a presentation. Select Project Overview under Projects as the type of presentation. Insert and delete text to change the content of at least two slides. Run the Spell Checker. Save the presentation as Project. Print the outline.

4. Use a Design Template to create a title slide. Include a title for a presentation that you are interested in creating. If necessary, insert and delete text. Run the Spell Checker. Save the presentation. Print the slide.

PROJECTS

1. As the owner of Soup's On, a soup cart that sells soup and bread on the university campus, you want to expand your business to include cookies and pastries.

   You decide to create a PowerPoint presentation to help sell your idea to your banker and other financial backers.

   Using the AutoContent Wizard, create the presentation using the Product / Services Overview, which is under the Sales / Marketing category.

   The Title slide (1) should contain the text:
   - Soup's On
   - Your name
   - Expanding our services

   The Overview slide (2) should contain the text:
   - Provide cookies and pastries
   - Continue to provide soups and bread

   The Features and Benefits slide (3) should contain the text:
   - Increase cash flow
   - Interest new customers
   - Sell more soup

   Leave the Applications slide unchanged (4).

   The Specifications slide (5) should contain the text:
   - Existing cart sufficient
   - Existing personnel sufficient
   - Investment in food needed

The Pricing slide (6) should contain the text:

- Competitive pricing
- Better than average service
- Convenient location

The Availability slide (7) should contain the text:

- Available spring of 1999

Run the Spell Checker.
Save the presentation as Soup's On.
Run the slide show.
Print the slides and the outline.

2. You have been asked to create a presentation for your computer class that will help people who are buying their first computer. Using the AutoContent Wizard, create the presentation using the Generic presentation, which is under the General category.

The Title slide (1) should contain the text:

- Help Buying a Home Computer
- your name

The Introduction slide (2) should contain the text:

- Purchasing your first computer is a complex decision
- Regard the process as a research assignment
- Gather all the information necessary to make an informed purchase before, not after, you spend your money

The Topics of Discussion slide (3) should contain the text:

- Assess your software and hardware needs
- Research the current standards
- Check purchasing options
- Decide on warranty and support needed
- Decide on a vendor, computer, and software

For the Topic One slide (4),

- Change the title to Assessing Your Needs

Insert the following text:

- Used for business, home, entertainment, education?
- Online access?
- Multimedia necessary?
- High resolution monitor?
- Color printer?
- Fax capability?

For the Topic Two slide (5),

- Change the title to Research Standards

Insert the following text:

- Read newspaper and magazine ads
- Research the Web
- Determine the price and specifications of the standard machine

For the Topic Three slide (6),

- Change the title to Purchase Options

Insert the following text:

- Visit local computer stores
- Visit office supply stores
- Visit discount stores
- Check magazines for mail order companies
- Check the Web for online shopping

For the Real Life slide (7),

- Change the title to Will they know you if it breaks?

Insert the following text:

- How long is the manufacturer's warranty?
- Does the reseller provide warranty options?
- How do they handle repairs—onsite, at their repair center, or send it off?

The What this Means slide (8) should include the following text:

- Decide on the vendor that you trust and who will stand behind the product
- Decide on a computer that meets your needs and will be expandable to your future needs
- Purchase the software that will provide the applications you need and want

Leave the last slide (9) unchanged.

Run the Spell Checker.
Save the presentation as Computer Help.
Run the slide show.
Print the slides and the outline.

Edit the Presentation

UNIT OBJECTIVES

- Add a slide to the presentation
- Delete a slide from the presentation
- Change the order of slides
- Change the layout of a slide
- Move text
- Change the bullets in a list
- Create subtopics in a bulleted list

In the previous units, you created slide presentations using the Auto-Content Wizard and design templates. You added one type of slide to a presentation—title slide. In this unit, you will learn to add other types of slides to a presentation and to edit the presentation by deleting slides, moving slides, moving text to different slides, and creating customized bulleted lists. These tasks will allow you the freedom to edit any presentation whether you create it from scratch or use one of PowerPoint's tools.

What: Add a new slide to a presentation.

How: Choose Insert | New Slide.

Why: You will want to add new information to presentations using other types of layouts.

Tip: If you want to add a new slide that is based on another slide, you can copy or duplicate that slide by placing your insertion point on the slide and choosing Insert | Duplicate Slide.

As you create slide presentations, you will need to add more slides of different types to a presentation. PowerPoint makes adding slides easy because it supplies numerous layout options for ease of use.

1. Place the insertion point on the slide preceding where you want the new slide to appear. The new slide appears after the current slide.
2. Use one of the following methods to insert the slide:

• Choose Insert | New Slide.

• Click the New Slide button on the Standard Toolbar.

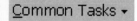

• Choose New Slide in the Common Tasks toolbar.

The New Slide dialog box displays showing the first 12 layout options, as shown in Figure 3.1.

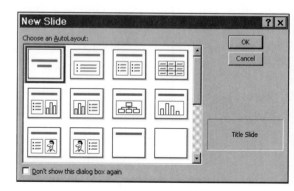

FIGURE 3.1   New Slide Dialog Box

3. Determine the type of slide to insert by considering the content you want to include.
4. Select the desired slide layout and click OK.

New slides contain **placeholders** that you click to include text, bulleted lists, graphics, charts, tables, media, and other objects. You will learn to include these elements in your presentations in this and subsequent units. Table 3.1 describes the slide options.

New Slide	Description
	Title Slide
	Bulleted List
	Two Column Text
	Table
	Text and Chart
	Chart and Text
	Organizational Chart
	Chart
	Text and Clip Art
	Clip Art and Text
	Title Only
	Blank
	Text and Object
	Object and Text
	Large Object
	Object
	Text and Media Clip
	Media Clip and Text
	Object over Text
	Text over Object
	Text and Two Objects
	Two Objects and Text
	Two Objects over Text
	Four Objects

TABLE 3.1 New Slide Options

I. Choose **File | New**.
The New dialog box displays.

2. Choose the Design Templates tab, select the **Sunny Days** template and click **OK**.
The New Slide dialog box displays.

3. With the **Title** slide selected, click **OK**.
The Title slide appears in the slide pane.

4. Add the following title and subtitle:
Title: **Welcome to the Southwest**
Subtitle: **Land of the Enchanted Sun**

5. Choose **Insert | New Slide**.
The New Slide dialog box displays.

6. Select the second slide—the **Bulleted List** slide, and click **OK**.
The new bulleted slide displays.

7. Click the Title box and type **Land of History and Myth**.

8. Click the text box, type **American Indian Cultures** and press the **Enter** key.
The second bullet automatically displays.

9. Type the following, pressing **Enter** after each one to display the text on separate lines with bullets:

Mexican Ancestors
Pioneers
Ancient Ruins
Sacred Places
Land of Traditions

Your presentation should look like the one in Figure 3.2.

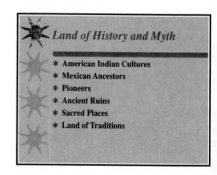

1   2

FIGURE 3.2   The Presentation with Two Slides

10. Click the **Common Tasks button** and choose **New Slide**.

II. Choose the **Bulleted List** slide and click **OK**.
PowerPoint adds the slide to the presentation.

12. Save the presentation as **Southwest**.

13. Keep the presentation on the screen for use in the next exercise.

What: Delete an entire slide from a presentation.

How: Choose Edit | Delete Slide.

Why: You may find it necessary to remove slides from a presentation.

Tip: If you are preparing a slide presentation to be viewed on screen in color and to be printed out in black and white, you can see what your color slides will look like in black and white. In the Slide Sorter view, choose View | Black and White. The slides appear in black and white.

As you create presentations, you may find that you have created slides that you no longer want as part of the presentation. You can delete slides from a presentation using several methods. Select the slide that you want to delete and do one of the following:

- In Normal view, choose Edit | Delete Slide.
- In Slide Sorter view, choose Edit | Delete Slide or press the Delete key.
- In Outline view, click the slide icon and choose Edit | Delete Slide or press the Delete key.

   If you decide to undo the deletion, choose Edit | Undo Delete Slide or use the Undo button on Standard Toolbar.

EXERCISE 2 | *Deleting Slides*

1. Use the Southwest presentation in Normal view, making the third slide the current slide.

2. Choose **Edit | Delete Slide**.
   PowerPoint deletes the slide.

3. Choose **Edit | Undo Delete Slide**.
   PowerPoint restores the slide to the presentation.

4. Switch to Slide Sorter view.

5. With the third slide selected, press the **Delete** key.
   PowerPoint deletes the slide.

6. Choose **Edit | Undo Delete Slide**.
   PowerPoint restores the slide to the presentation.

7. Switch to Outline view.

8. Select the third slide and click the **Delete** key.
   PowerPoint deletes the slide.

9. Click the **Undo button**.
   PowerPoint restores the slide to the presentation.

10. Keep the presentation on the screen for use in the next exercise.

What: Move slides to change the order of the presentation.
How: Click and drag the slides to the desired location.
Why: Edit the presentation by changing the order of the slides.
Tip: If you are using Slide Sorter view and you want to return to the previous view with the selected slide displayed, double-click the slide.

As you create presentations, you might want to move slides around for greater clarity, emphasis, or just to make the content flow better. You can move slides to change the order of the presentation in Outline view or in the Slide Sorter view.

> ## POINTER
>
> ### Slide Numbering
>
> Whatever method you use to move slides in a presentation, PowerPoint renumbers the slides to keep the presentation up-to-date.

To move a slide in either the Slide Sorter or the Outline view, click the slide that you want to move and drag it to the new location.

> ## POINTER
>
> ### Another Method for Moving Slides
>
> If you want to move a slide in a large presentation to a location far from the present location, you might find it easier to select the slide and choose Edit | Cut. Windows places the slide on the **Clipboard**, a memory location. Then, place the insertion point where you want the slide to appear and choose Edit | Paste.

EXERCISE 3 | *Moving Slides in a Presentation*

1. View the presentation in the Slide Sorter view.
2. Click and drag the third slide to the beginning of the presentation. The slide becomes the first slide, and the slides renumber, as shown in Figure 3.3.
3. Switch to Normal view and select the first slide by clicking the slide icon in the outline pane.

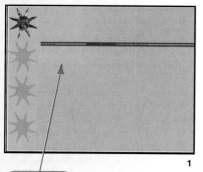

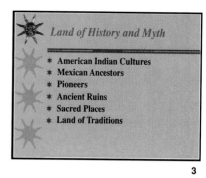

1   2   3

Slide moved to beginning of presentation

FIGURE 3.3 The Presentation in the New Order

4. Click and drag the slide to the end of the presentation.
The slide becomes the third slide, and the slides renumber.

5. Leave the presentation on the screen for use in the next exercise.

TASK 4 | *Changing the Layout of a Slide*

What: Change the layout of a slide in a presentation.

How: Choose Format | Slide Layout.

Why: If you want to add another element to a slide, you can do so by changing the slide's layout.

Tip: Keep text clear and concise on slides—a cluttered slide will not get read.

After creating many slides, you might want to consolidate slide information, add something else to an existing slide, or just change the look of a slide. To change what appears on a slide, you would change the layout of the slide.

To change the layout of a slide, follow these steps:

1. Select the slide, and do one of the following:

 • Choose Format | Slide Layout.
 • Choose Common Tasks | Slide Layout.

2. Choose the desired layout in the Slide Layout dialog box.
3. Click the Apply button.

The slide appears using the new layout. To undo the layout change, choose Edit | Undo Slide Layout or click the Undo button.

EXERCISE 4 | *Changing the Layout of a Slide*

1. View the Southwest presentation in Normal view.

2. Select the second slide.

3. Choose **Format | Slide Layout**.
The Slide Layout dialog box displays.

4. Select the first layout, the **Title** slide.

5. Click the **Apply button**.
The slide displays as a Title Slide, as shown in Figure 3.4.

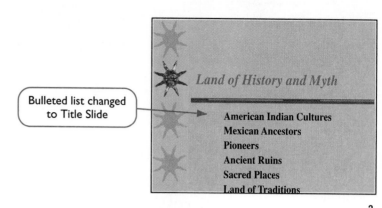

Bulleted list changed
to Title Slide

Land of History and Myth

American Indian Cultures
Mexican Ancestors
Pioneers
Ancient Ruins
Sacred Places
Land of Traditions

2

FIGURE 3.4   The Slide Changed to a Title Slide

6. Choose **Edit | Undo Slide Layout**.
The slide returns to its original layout.

7. Keep the presentation on the screen for use in the next exercise.

TASK 5 | *Moving and Copying Text*

What: Move or copy text from one slide to another slide.
 How: Click and drag the text.
 Why: To edit the presentation, you may want to move or copy text.
 Tip: To copy a slide from another presentation, choose Insert | Slides from Files. Select the presentation file and then choose the slide to copy or choose Insert All to copy all the slides to the current presentation.

As you type text onto slides in a presentation, you may want to rearrange the flow of the text by moving the text to a different slide. If text appears on one slide and you want to **move** it or **copy** it to another slide, follow these steps:

1. View the presentation in Normal view or Outline view.
2. Select the text to move in the outline.
3. Point to the selected text, right-click, and drag it to the desired location.
4. When you lift up on the mouse button, the shortcut menu shown in Figure 3.5 displays.

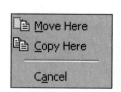

Move Here

Copy Here

Cancel

FIGURE 3.5   Shortcut Menu

5. Choose Move Here to move the text to the new location or choose Copy Here to copy the text to the new location.

If the new location is many slides away, you might find it easier to cut or copy the text. To cut or copy the text, follow these steps:

1. Select the text that you want to cut or copy.
2. Choose Edit | Cut to move the text to the Clipboard, choose Edit | Copy to make a duplicate of the text on the Clipboard, or use the cut or copy buttons.

3. Move the insertion point to the desired location.
4. Choose Edit | Paste or click the paste button.

If you decide to undo the move or copy, use Edit | Undo or click the Undo button on the Standard Toolbar.

EXERCISE 5 | *Moving and Copying Text*

1. View the Southwest presentation in Normal view.

2. Select the text *Ancient Ruins* in the outline.

3. Right-click the text, drag it to the third slide, and then lift up on the mouse.
   The shortcut menu appears.

4. Choose **Move Here**.
   The text moves from the second to the third slide.

5. Click the **Undo button**.
   The text returns to the second slide.

6. Select all the text on the second slide, except the title of the slide.

7. Click the **Copy button**.

8. Select the third slide, click in the second placeholder, and click the **Paste button**.
   PowerPoint copies the text to the third slide.

9. Keep the presentation on the screen for use in the next exercise.

TASK 6 | *Changing the Bullets in a List*

What: Change the bullets that appear on a bulleted list.

How: Choose Format | Bullets and Numbering.

Why: To add to the presentation's formatting, you can change the bullets that automatically display on bulleted lists.

Tip: If you discover that you want to change the order of a bulleted list, point to the bullet at the beginning of the line you want to move. When the four-headed pointer displays, click and drag up or down to move the item up or down in the list.

When you create a presentation, you might have several slides that contain bulleted lists. To get some variety using the same layout, you can change the bullets that display in a bulleted list.

To change bullets, follow these steps:

1. View the slide that you want to edit in Normal view.
2. Place the insertion point in a line of the bulleted list to change one bullet or select the entire list if you want the same bullet in front of every item in the list.
3. Choose Format | Bullets and Numbering.

The Bulleted tab of the Bullets and Numbering dialog box displays, as shown in Figure 3.6.

4. Click the desired bullet and click OK.

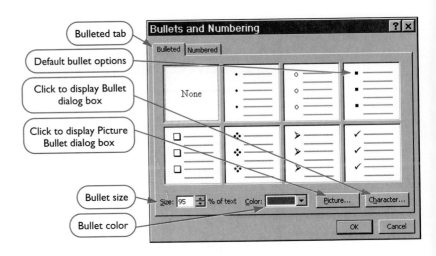

FIGURE 3.6 Bullets and Numbering Dialog Box

The item or the list will change to the new bullet. If you don't see any bullets that you want to use displayed in the dialog box, you can insert other symbols, by following these steps:

Character...

1. Click the Character button on the Bulleted tab of the Bullets and Numbering dialog box.

The Bullet dialog box displays.

2. Click the down arrow on the Bullets from text box to display other fonts.
3. Click the down arrow on the Color box to change the color. If the desired color is not displayed, click More Colors. The Colors dialog box displays, as shown in Figure 3.7.

More Colors...

4. Click the desired color on the color wheel and click OK.
5. Use the increment and decrement buttons on the size box to change what percentage of the text the bullet will be.
6. Click a bullet to view it enlarged.
7. Click OK.

PowerPoint places the bullet in the slide.

8. Repeat these steps to change the bullet or the color of the bullet for each line in the bulleted list.

Figure 3.8 shows various bullet changes.

Picture...

Other bullets are also available by clicking the Pictures button on the Bulleted tab of the Bullets and Numbering dialog box. The Picture Bullet dialog box displays, as shown in Figure 3.9.

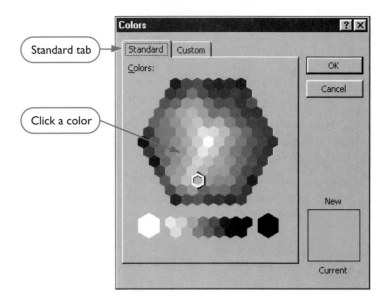

Standard tab

Click a color

FIGURE 3.7   The Colors Dialog Box

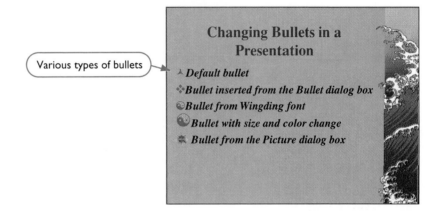

Various types of bullets

FIGURE 3.8   Example Bullets

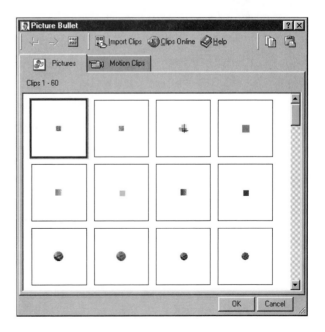

FIGURE 3.9   The Picture Bullet Dialog Box

To insert a picture bullet, follow these steps:
1. Click the desired bullet to select it.
   The Clip toolbar displays, as shown in Figure 3.10.
2. Click the Insert Clip button.
   PowerPoint places the bullet on the slide.

FIGURE **3.10**   Clip Toolbar

EXERCISE 6 | *Changing the Bullets in a List*

1. Make the third slide in the Southwest presentation the current slide in Normal view.

2. Place the insertion point in the first line of the bulleted list.

3. Choose **Format | Bullets and Numbering**.
The Bulleted tab of the Bullets and Numbering dialog box displays.

4. Click the **Character button**.
The Bullet dialog box displays.

Character...

5. Click the down arrow on the **Bullets from:** box and choose **Webdings**.
The symbols available in the Webdings font display.

6. Choose the tenth bullet in the second row—the cactus and sun icon.

7. Click **OK**.
PowerPoint inserts the icon next to the first item in the bulleted list.

8. Place the insertion point on the second item in the bulleted list.

9. Choose **Format | Bullets and Numbering**.
The Bullets and Numbering dialog box displays.

10. Click the **Character button**.
The Bullet dialog box displays.

11. Select the thirteenth bullet in the first line of the Webdings symbols.
The pepper becomes selected.

12. Click the down arrow under the **Color** box.
The Color drop-down box displays.

13. Click **More Colors**.
The Colors dialog box displays.

14. Click on the red area and click **OK**.
The Bullet dialog box displays with the color red in the Color box.

15. Click the increment button on the size box until it reads 135.

16. Click **OK**.
The pepper displays on the slide in red and increased in size.

17. Place your insertion point in the third line of the bulleted list.

18. Choose **Format | Bullets and Numbering**.
The Bullets and Numbering dialog box displays.

19. Click the **Picture button**.
The Picture Bullet dialog box displays.

20. Select a bullet by clicking it.

21. Click the **Insert Clip button** on the Clip toolbar.
PowerPoint inserts the bullet on the slide.

22. Place the insertion point on the fourth line of the bulleted list.

23. Choose **Format | Bullets and Numbering**.

24. Select one of the bullets from the list.

25. Click the **Color** down arrow and select a color, or click **More Colors button** and choose one from the color wheel.

26. Click **OK**.
PowerPoint inserts the bullet in the list.

27. Insert bullets for the last two items in the list, repeating steps from above.
Your bulleted list should look similar to the one in Figure 3.11.

28. Save the presentation with the same name and keep it on the screen for use in the next exercise.

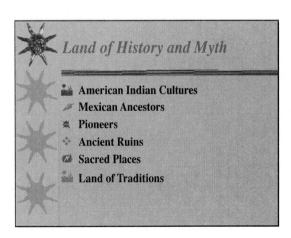

FIGURE 3.11 The Slide with Bullets

What: Indent subtopics in a bulleted list.

How: Click the Demote button on the Formatting toolbar.

Why: Many topics in a bulleted list have subtopics that should appear indented for clarity.

Tip: You can change the bullet or the color of the existing bullet supplied for the indented subtopic, just as you did for the main bullets.

You might want to create a bulleted list that contains subtopics under the main headings. These **subtopics** should be indented and should be preceded by a different or smaller sized bullet than the main topic for clarity. Figure 3.12 shows an example.

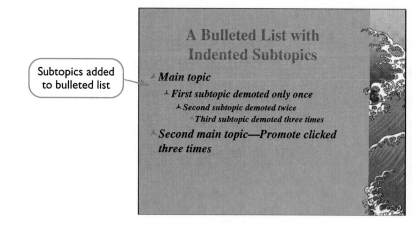

FIGURE 3.12   A Bulleted List with Subtopics

To create a subtopic in a bulleted list, follow these steps:

1. Place the insertion point at the end of a main topic in the bulleted list.
2. Press the Enter key to create a new bullet and blank line.
3. Click the **Demote** button on the Formatting toolbar to indent the subtopic. You can click the Demote button more than once to increase the indentation. PowerPoint reduces the font size of the text and reduces the size of the bullet each time you demote the text (see Figure 3.12).
4. Type the text of the subtopic and press Enter.

After typing one or more subtopics, you may want to move back to the left to type another main topic. To move the insertion back to the left, follow these steps:

1. Place the insertion point on the line that you want to move to the left.
2. Click the **Promote** button on the Formatting toolbar. You can click the Promote button more than once if necessary.
3. Type the desired text for the topic.

Using Promote and Demote

If you change your mind about indenting text, you can use the Promote or **Demote buttons** on lines that already contain text just as you do for blank lines.

EXERCISE 7 | *Creating Subtopics in a Bulleted List*

1. Make the second slide of the Southwest presentation the active slide in Normal view.

2. Place the insertion point at the right end of the first item in the bulleted list on the slide.

3. Press the **Enter** key.
   A new blank line appears with a bullet.

4. Click the **Demote button** twice.

5. Type **Navajo, Hopi, Zuni**.

6. Press **Enter**.
   The text appears indented, and a new bullet appears on the next line.

7. Click the **Promote button** twice.
   The original style bullet appears.

8. Press the **Backspace** key twice to remove the bullet and the blank line.
   Your slide should look similar to the one in Figure 3.13.

9. Save the presentation with the same name and close the file.

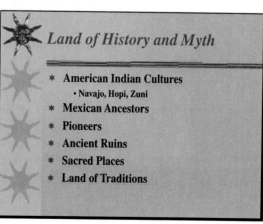

FIGURE 3.13   The Bulleted List with a Subtopic

SUMMARY

After completing this unit, you should be able to
- add a slide to a presentation (page 54)
- delete a slide (page 57)
- change the order of slides in a presentation (page 58)
- change the layout of a slide (page 59)
- move text (page 60)
- copy text (page 60)
- change the bullets in a list (page 61)
- create subtopics in a bulleted list (page 66)

KEYWORDS

Clipboard (page 58)   **placeholder** (page 55)
copy (page 60)   **Promote button** (page 66)
Demote button (page 66)   **subtopic** (page 66)
move (page 60)

TEST YOUR SKILLS

True/False

1. If you delete a slide, you can't use Edit | Undo to bring the slide back.
2. When you add new slides to a presentation, you select what type of slide to add.
3. If you move slides in a presentation, PowerPoint renumbers all the slides.
4. You can change the bullets that appear in a bulleted list.
5. To stop indenting in a bulleted list, click the Promote button.

Multiple Choice

1. You can delete slides using the
   a. Outline view
   b. Slide Sorter view
   c. Normal view
   d. all of these answers
2. To move a slide in a presentation, you
   a. must delete it first
   b. must demote it first
   c. can click and drag it to the new location
   d. all of these answers

3. If you want to change the order of items in a bulleted list, you
   a. drag the four-headed arrow
   b. promote the item
   c. demote the item
   d. change the bullet for the item

4. You can change bullets
   a. for each line in a list
   b. only for the entire list
   c. only in Outline View
   d. all of these answers

5. When you edit a presentation, you can
   a. change the order of slides
   b. delete slides
   c. add new slides
   d. all of these answers

Short Answer

Match the letter of the correct word with the correct location in Normal view in Figure 3.14.

_____ a. slide number   _____ b. style checker

_____ c. slide title   _____ d. design template used

_____ e. name of file

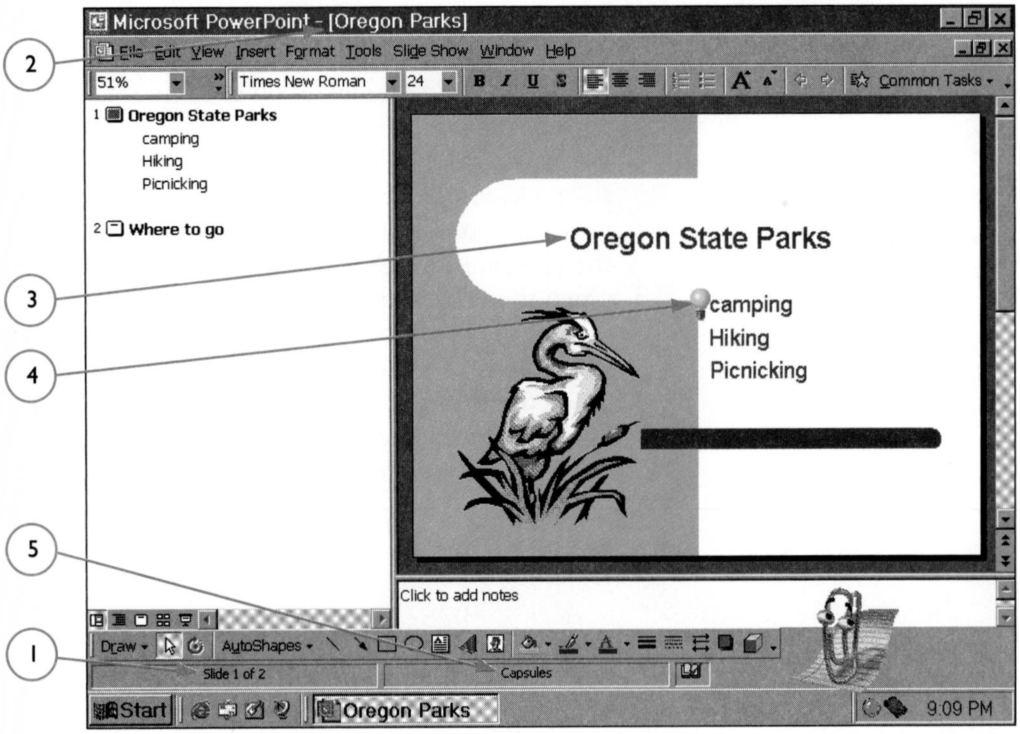

FIGURE 3.14

Write a brief description of the function of the following:

1.	▤	6.	▬
2.	Character...	7.	⇨
3.	↶ ▾	8.	More Colors...
4.	Common Tasks ▾	9.	▤
5.	☷	10.	⇦

On Your Own

1. Create a new slide presentation using a design template.
2. Add several slides to the presentation, and place text on them.
3. Move slides within the presentation.
4. Change the bullets on a bulleted list.
5. Create subtopics on the bulleted list.

PROJECTS

1. Open the Motivation presentation. View the second slide in Normal view. Change the bullet that appears before each item in the list. Use a different color and bullet on each line. Save the file. Print the current slide only.
2. Using the Motivation presentation, insert a new slide after the third slide. Delete the first slide. Move the second slide to the end of the presentation. Copy text from the fifth slide to the fourth slide. Print the presentation. Close the presentation without saving it.
3. Open the Project presentation. Move the last two slides to the beginning of the presentation. Delete the new last slide in the presentation. Print the slides. Close the presentation without saving it.
4. Open the Business Plan presentation. Insert a new slide before the fifth slide in the presentation. Type information of your own on the slide. Print the slides. Close the presentation without saving it.

Changing the Look of the Presentation

UNIT OBJECTIVES

- Change the color of the presentation or just one slide
- Change the presentation design
- Use the slide master
- Change font, font size, and color
- Format text
- Change text alignment
- Add AutoShapes
- Add ClipArt

After creating a presentation, you might decide to change the look of some or all of the slides. You can change the color of one slide or all slides. You can change the design that the presentation is based on, or you can format text by including special formatting or change the font, font color, and font size. You can also add elements to the entire slide presentation using the slide master, which controls elements on slides in the presentation. Graphics can also be added to slides to make the presentation more friendly. In this unit, you will learn to place AutoShapes and ClipArt on slides.

TASK 1 | *Changing the Color of the Presentation or Just One Slide*

What: Apply a color scheme to the presentation or to a slide.

How: Choose Format | Slide Color Scheme.

Why: To change the colors of slides but leave the design of the slide intact.

Tip: Use complementary colors on your slides so that they are easy to read.

When you create presentations using the presentation template, design templates, or the AutoContent Wizard, PowerPoint applies color to the slides. Each design template has assigned colors to each of the slide elements, such as one color for text, another color for the background, another color for lines, and so on. These groups of colors are called a **color scheme**. Color schemes use colors that are complementary to each other and therefore produce pleasing slide presentations.

POINTER

Blank Presentations

To apply your own color scheme to all slide elements, choose the Blank Presentation option in the New dialog box. A blank presentation has no colors assigned to the slide elements.

To change a color scheme, follow these steps:

1. Choose Format | Slide Color Scheme. The Color Scheme dialog box displays, as shown in Figure 4.1.

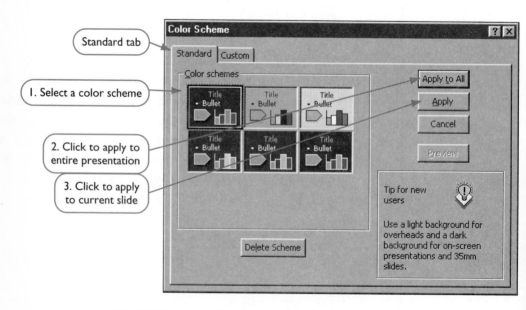

FIGURE 4.1   Color Scheme Dialog Box

Alternative color schemes for the current design template display in the Color schemes section of the dialog box. The displayed color schemes are often variations of the same color scheme. That is, these schemes use the same basic colors, but they apply the colors to different screen elements.

2. Select one of the alternative color schemes.
3. Click one of the following buttons:

- Apply to All button to apply the colors to the entire presentation.
- Apply button to apply the color change to the current slide only.

To change colors beyond what the Color schemes section of the dialog box presents, click the Custom tab of the Color Scheme dialog box. The Custom dialog box displays, as shown in Figure 4.2.

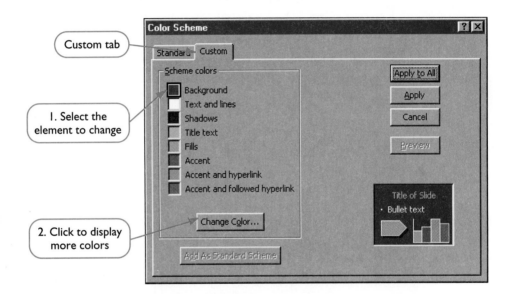

FIGURE 4.2 Custom Color Schemes

For example, to change the color of the background, follow these steps:

1. Select the Background option.

2. Click the desired color on the color wheel.

3. Click OK.

The Custom dialog box displays, showing the new background color.

4. Follow the same steps to individually change the color of other screen elements.

5. Click the Apply to All button or the Apply button.

If you only want to change the background color of slides and add special effects, choose Format | Background. The Background dialog box displays, allowing you to change the color of one slide or all the slides in the presentation. Click the arrow on the color drop-down box to display the More Colors and Fill Effects options. Use the More Colors option following the steps outlined above. To create special effects with colors on slides, click the Fill Effects option. The Fill Effects dialog box displays, as shown in Figure 4.3.

To change the fill effects used on the slide's background, follow these steps:

1. Choose the number of colors and shading styles on the Gradient tab, as shown in Figure 4.3a.

2. Choose a texture on the Texture tab, as shown in Figure 4.3b.

3. Choose a pattern on the Pattern tab, as shown in Figure 4.3c.

4. Choose a graphic on the Picture tab to place a graphic in the background of a slide.

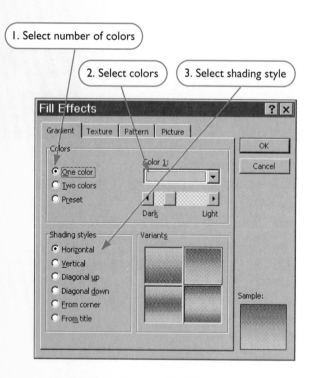

(a) Gradient Tab of the Fill Effects Dialog Box

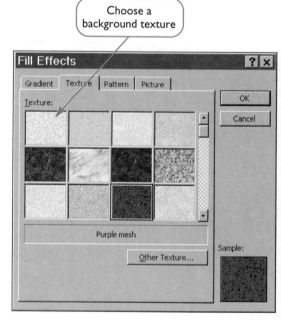

(b) Texture Tab of the Fill Effects Dialog Box

FIGURE 4.3

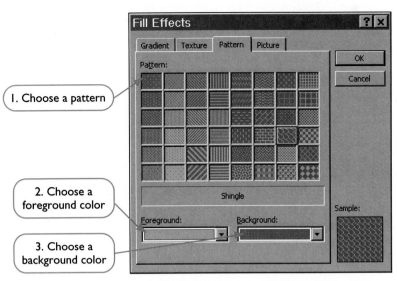

(c) Pattern Tab of the Fill Effects Dialog Box

FIGURE 4.3 (continued)

These effects are fun to work with and can create some nice backgrounds for your presentations. However, remember not to make the background of your slides too busy, causing viewers to have a hard time reading the text.

EXERCISE 1 | *Changing the Color Scheme*

1. Open the Southwest file with the Title Slide displayed.
The Title Slide displays in Normal view.

2. Choose **Format | Slide Color Scheme**.
The Color Scheme dialog box displays.

3. Select an alternative color scheme, such as purple.

4. Click the **Apply button**.
The Title Slide appears with the new color scheme, as shown in Figure 4.5.

5. Select the second slide in the presentation.
The second slide displays in Normal view.

6. Choose **Format | Slide Color Scheme**.
The Color Scheme dialog box displays.

7. Click the **Custom** tab.
The Custom tab of the Color Scheme dialog box displays.

8. Select the **Background** option.

9. Click the **Change Color button**.
The Background Color dialog box displays.

10. Select a light green from the color wheel and click **OK** to return to the custom tab.

11. Click the **Apply button**.

PowerPoint applies the new background color to the second slide, as shown in Figure 4.4.

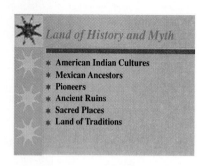
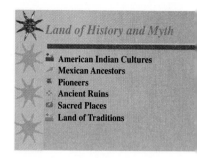

1   2   3

FIGURE 4.4   Slide Sorter View

12. Select the third slide.

13. Choose **Format | Background**.

14. Click the down arrow on the color box and choose **Fill Effects**.
The Fill Effects dialog box displays.

15. Apply a pattern, gradient, or texture to the slide.

16. Close the file without saving it.

TASK 2 | *Changing the Presentation Design*

What: Change the design of the presentation.

How: Choose Format | Apply Design Template.

Why: To change the overall appearance of the presentation, you can change the design.

Tip: Make sure the design you apply to slides helps to convey the message of the presentation by setting the tone.

When you create your presentation, PowerPoint applies a design template to the presentation, unless you use the Blank Presentation option. If you decide that you want a different design for the entire presentation, you can change the design template.

To change the design template, follow these steps:

1. Use one of the following methods to start changing the design template:

   • Choose Format | Apply Design Template.
   • Click the Apply Design button on the Standard toolbar.
   • Choose Apply Design Template from the Common Tasks toolbar.

The Apply Design Template dialog box displays, as shown in Figure 4.5.

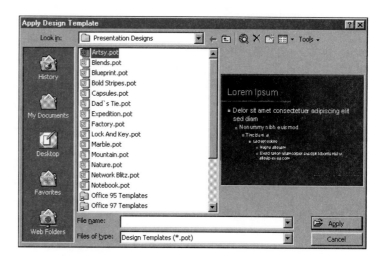

FIGURE 4.5 Apply Design Template Dialog Box

2. Select a design and it will display in the preview section of the dialog box.

3. Click the Apply button.

PowerPoint applies the design to the entire presentation. If you decide that you want the original design template applied to the presentation instead, choose Edit | Undo Design Template.

EXERCISE 2 | *Changing the Design of the Presentation*

1. Display the Southwest presentation in the Slide Sorter view.

2. Choose **Format | Apply Design Template**.
   The Apply Design Template dialog box displays.

3. Select the **Nature** design template.

4. Click the **Apply button**.
   All the slides in the Slide Sorter view display the new design.

Your presentation should look like the one in Figure 4.6.

1   2   3

FIGURE 4.6 The Nature Design Template Applied to the Presentation

5. Click **Edit | Undo Apply Design Template**.
The original design template replaces the Nature design on all slides.

6. Keep the presentation on the screen for use in the next exercise.

TASK 3 | *Using the Slide Master*

What: Change the presentation by changing the slide master.
How: Choose View | Master | Slide Master.
Why: To add the same elements to every slide, use the slide master.
Tips: You can also change the title master, and all slides that are based on the Title Slide will change automatically.

If you want to add an element to every slide, except Title Slides, you can do so by changing the slide master. The **slide master** controls the formatting on slides, as shown in Figure 4.7.

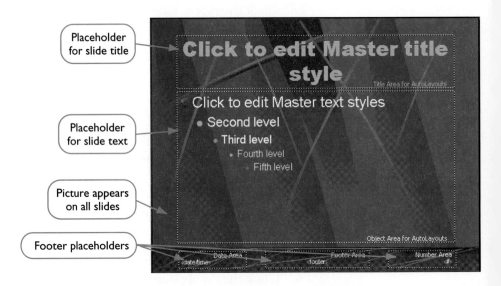

FIGURE 4.7   PowerPoint Help Diagram of Slide Master

Suppose, for example, that you want to include your company logo in the background of slides in the presentation, you could modify the slide master to include the logo in the background. The logo would then appear on every slide in the presentation except slides based on the Title Slide. Figure 4.8 shows the Southwest presentation with a graphic added to the background of every slide except the Title Slide.

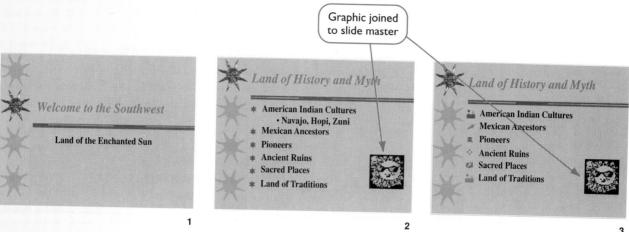

FIGURE 4.8 Slide Presentation with Background Graphic

You can make numerous other changes to presentations using the slide master, such as adding footers to each slide or changing the bullets for every bulleted list in the presentation by editing the slide master.

POINTER

Text on Every Slide

To include text on every slide of the presentation, open the slide master and choose Insert | Text Box. Click and drag to draw the text box and then type the text you want in the text box. Move and size the text box to place it where you want it to appear on every slide in the presentation.

To edit the slide master, follow these steps:

1. Choose View | Master | Slide Master.

The slide master displays, as shown in Figure 4.9.

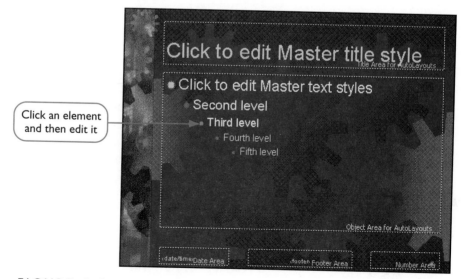

FIGURE 4.9 A Slide Master

2. Make the desired editing changes to the slide master.

3. Click the Slide Sorter view button.

The change is made on all the slides in the presentation—except the Title Slide and any slides in the presentation based on the Title Slide. To change the Title Slide and all slides based on the Title Slide, choose View | Master | Title Master and follow the same steps outlined above for the slide master.

EXERCISE 3	*Using the Slide Master to Make Changes in a Presentation*

1. With the Southwest presentation open, choose **View | Master | Slide Master**.
   The slide master displays.

2. Click on the bullet.
   The list becomes selected.

3. Choose **Format | Bullets and Numbering**.
   The Bullets and Numbering dialog box displays.

4. Click the **Character button**.
   The Bullet dialog box displays.

5. Display the Wingdings font.
   The bullets available in the Wingdings font display.

6. Click the fifth button from the left in the bottom row—the right pointing arrow.

7. Change the color to red in the Color drop-down box.

8. Click **OK**.
   The slide master displays with the red arrow displayed in the bulleted list.

9. Switch to the Slide Sorter view.
   All slides with bulleted lists reflect the bullet change, except those bullets that were placed individually on a slide, as shown in Figure 4.10.

10. Close the file without saving it.

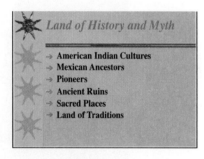
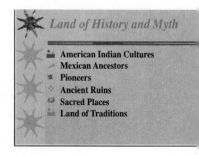

FIGURE **4.10** The Presentation Reflecting the Change to the Slide Master

What: Change the font, font size, and color of text on slides.
How: Choose Format | Font.
Why: Format text to emphasize it on slides.
Tips: Title text should be at least 36 points, and body text should be at least 24 points, so that an audience can read the slides easily.

You can change the **font**—the set of characters used, its size, and the color of text on slides. If you want to make changes to the entire presentation, you do so by changing text on the slide master, but to change text on an individual slide, follow these steps:

1. Select the text to be formatted.
2. Choose Format | Font.

The Font dialog box displays, as shown in Figure 4.11.

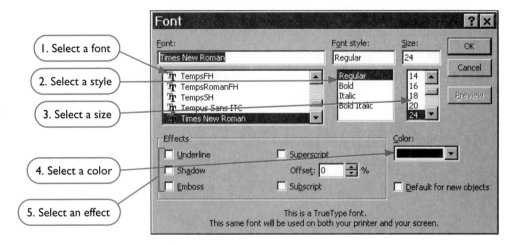

FIGURE 4.11 Font Dialog Box

3. Select a different font in the Font section.
4. Change the style of the font in the Font style section, for example, choose Bold Italic.
5. Change the size of the text in the Size section.
6. Add effects to the text. Table 4.1 describes the different effects that are available.

Effect	Result
Underline	Selected text appears underlined
Shadow	Adds a shadow to the right and below the selected text
Emboss	The selected text appears raised off the slide
Superscript	Raises selected text above the baseline, such as 2^2
Subscript	Lowers selected text below the baseline, such as H_2O

TABLE 4.1 Text Effects

7. Change the color of text using the Color drop-down box.

8. Click OK to apply the formatting to the selected text.

PowerPoint formats the selected text on the slide.

Alternately, you can use buttons on the Formatting toolbar. To use
toolbar for formatting, follow these steps:

1. Select the text to be formatted.

2. Click the Font button and select a different font.

3. Choose one of the following buttons to change the font size:

   • Click the Font Size button and select the desired size.

   • Click the Increase Font Size button to increase the selected tex
     the next larger size listed in the Font Size box.

   • Click the Decrease Font Size button to decrease the selected tex
     the next smaller size listed in the Font Size box.

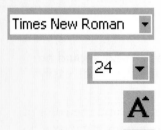

EXERCISE 4 | *Changing the Font, Style, and Color*

1. Open Southwest presentation and view the Title Slide in Normal v

2. Select the subtitle text.

3. Choose **Format | Font**.
   The Font dialog box displays.

4. Choose **Arial Rounded MT Bold**.

5. Click **Emboss** in the Effects section.

6. Change the font size to 36.

7. Click **OK**.
   The Title Slide displays with the changes to the subtitle, as shown i
   Figure 4.12.

FIGURE 4.12   The Presentation Reflecting the Changes Made in Exercis

8. Close the file without saving it.

What: Format text in a presentation.

How: Use the Formatting toolbar.

Why: Format text to create effects on slides.

Tip: If a toolbar isn't displayed, choose View | Toolbars and select the one you want from the menu.

If you want to format text on a slide for greater impact, you can use buttons that appear on the Formatting toolbar. If the button you want is not displayed, click the double-arrow at the right edge of the toolbar to display all the buttons.

To format text using the buttons, follow these steps:

1. Select the text to be formatted.
2. Use one of the Formatting toolbar buttons that Table 4.2 describes.

Button	Name	Description
B	Bold	**Boldfaces selected text**
I	Italic	*Italicizes selected text*
<u>U</u>	Underline	<u>Underlines selected text</u>
S	Shadow	Places a shadow to the right and under selected text

TABLE 4.2 Formatting Buttons

To place more than one formatting attribute on text, leave the text selected as you click other buttons.

EXERCISE 5 | *Formatting Text*

1. Open the Southwest presentation with the Title Slide displayed.
2. Select the subtitle text.
3. Click the **Bold button**.
   The subtitle appears boldfaced.
4. Click the **Italic button**.
   The subtitle appears boldfaced and italicized.
5. Click the **Underline button**.
   The subtitle appears boldfaced, italicized, and underlined.
6. Select the title.

7. Click the **Shadow button**.

The title appears with the shadow effect, as shown in Figure 4.13.

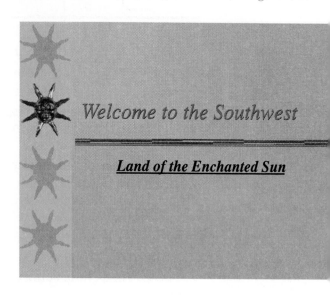

Welcome to the Southwest

Land of the Enchanted Sun

FIGURE 4.13   The Presentation with the Formatting Changes

8. Close the file without saving it.

TASK 6 | *Changing Text Alignment on Slides*

What: Change the way text lines up on a slide.

How: Choose Format | Alignment.

Why: To control how text appears on a slide, change the way it is align

Tips: If you want to control the spacing between lines of text and paragraphs, choose Format | Line Spacing. In the Line Spacing dialog box, change the line spacing option or change the amou of space before and after paragraphs.

Text appears on slides aligned in specific locations. For example, titles subtitles are centered on the slide, bulleted lists are aligned at the left mar and so on. You can change the alignment of text using the three alignm options that Table 4.3 describes.

Button	Alignment	Description
	Align Left	Text lines up at the left with a jagged right edge
	Center	Text is centered on the slide
	Align Right	Text lines up at the right with a jagged left edge

TABLE 4.3   Alignment Options

To change the horizontal alignment of text on a slide, follow these steps:

1. Place the insertion point in the text you want to change or select several lines of text.
2. Use one of the following methods to change the alignment of the selected text:

   - Choose Format | Alignment and choose one of the alignment options.
   - Click the Align Left, Center, or Align Right button on the Formatting toolbar.

If you want to change the alignment for all slides, make your changes on the slide master, instead of on individual slides.

EXERCISE 6 | *Changing the Alignment of Text*

1. Open the Southwest presentation with the Title Slide displayed in Normal view.

2. Select the title and click the **Align Right button**.
The title appears aligned at the right of the slide.

3. Display the second slide and select the bulleted list.

4. Choose **Format | Alignment | Center**.
The bulleted list appears center aligned.

5. Close the file without saving it.

TASK 7 | *Adding AutoShapes to Slides*

What: Adding shapes that are included with PowerPoint to your slides.

How: Choose Insert | Picture | AutoShapes.

Why: Slides should include visual content to keep the viewer interested.

Tip: When using AutoShapes, include shapes that help the content of the slides. Don't include objects that have no relevance to the presentation and actually detract from the presentation.

You can add shapes to a slide presentation that help keep the viewer's attention, point to important information, or help illustrate a point. Microsoft PowerPoint 2000 includes several types of **AutoShapes**, that is, built-in graphic shapes. Once you create a shape, you can move it, size it, and change the fill color.

To place a shape on the current slide, follow these steps:

1. Either choose Insert | Picture | AutoShapes or click the AutoShap[
   button on the drawing toolbar.
2. Click an AutoShape button to open the drop-down menu.
3. Click the desired shape.
4. Point to the slide.
5. Click and drag to size the shape.

When you lift up on the mouse the shape appears on the sl
Figure 4.14 shows a slide containing two AutoShapes.

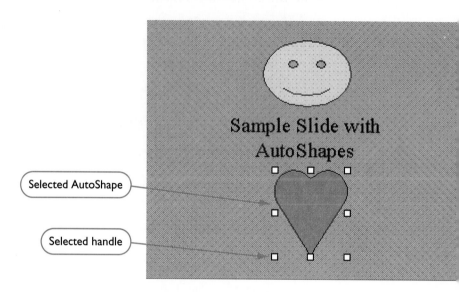

FIGURE 4.14 Slide with AutoShapes

Notice that one has boxes around it. These boxes are the **sizing hand**
The shape containing the handles is selected, which means that anything
do, such as sizing, coloring, moving, and so on will apply to the selected grap

To size the graphic, follow these steps:

1. Point to one of the selection handles.
2. Click and drag the handle, which accomplishes the following:

   - drag toward the center of the shape to decrease the size of the ima
   - drag away from the center of the shape to increase the size of the im
   - click and drag selection handles located on the corners of the grap
     to keep the graphic in proportion
   - click and drag a selection box that isn't on a corner to distort the im

To move the image to a different location on the same slide, follow these st

1. Point to the center of the selected graphic until the four-hea
   arrow appears.
2. Click and drag the four-headed arrow to move the graphic.

Notice that a color fills the image. To change the color of the selec
AutoShape, follow these steps:

1. Click the down-arrow on the Fill Color button on the Drawing tool
2. Choose a color from the Color menu or choose More Fill Colors to disp
   more choices.

The AutoShape changes to the color that you click.
To delete an unwanted shape from a slide, follow these steps:

1. Select the shape.
2. Press the Delete key.

PowerPoint removes the AutoShape from the slide.

You are the owner of JRT Kennels, which breeds Jack Russell Terriers and other small mixed-breed dogs along with boarding dogs. You recently opened a dog grooming business as part of your expanding operation. You want to feature the grooming and boarding kennels in a presentation to help advertise your business.

EXERCISE 7 | *Using AutoShapes*

1. Choose **File | New** and click the **General** tab.
The General tab of the New Presentation dialog box displays.

2. Choose **Blank Presentation** and click **OK**.
The New Slide dialog box displays.

3. Choose the **Bulleted List** slide and click **OK**.
The blank slide displays.

4. Type the following information on the slide.

Title:	**JRT Kennels**
Bullets:	**Grooming**
	Boarding
	Breeding

5. Change the size of the title to **66**-point type and the bulleted list to **48**.
The size of the text increases.

6. Place the insertion point at the beginning of the first bullet in the list and press **Enter**.
PowerPoint inserts white space above the list.

7. Change the bullets to a purple scissors, purple airplane, and a purple dog, using the Bullets and Numbering dialog box. Size the bullets if necessary.

8. Place the insertion point at the beginning of the text of each item in the list and press the **spacebar** twice.
Each item in the list moves to the right, creating space between the bullet and the text.

9. Choose **Insert | Picture | AutoShape**.
The AutoShapes toolbar displays.

10. Point to the **Basic Shapes button**.
The Basic Shapes menu displays.

11. Click the sun shape.

12. Point to the top right corner of the slide, and click and drag to place the sun image on the slide.

13. Use the sizing handles to size and move the sun shape as necessary.

14. Click the **Fill Color button** on the Drawing toolbar.
The Colors menu displays.

15. Choose a **bright yellow** to change the color of the sun. If necessary, click **More Fill Colors** to find a bright yellow.
The sun changes to yellow.

16. Choose **Format | Slide Color Scheme**.
The Color Scheme dialog box displays.

17. On the Custom tab, select **Background**.

18. Click the **Change Color button**.
The Background Color dialog box displays.

19. Choose a **light green** and click **OK**.
The Color Scheme dialog box redisplays.

20. Click the **Apply to All button**.
The slide displays as shown in Figure 4.15.

21. Save the presentation as **Kennel** and keep it open for use in the next exercise.

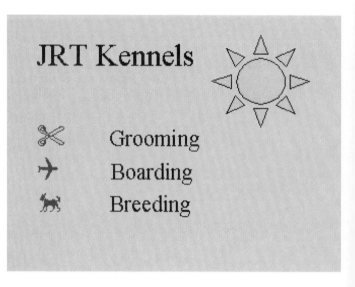

FIGURE 4.15 JRT Kennels Slide

TASK 8 | *Adding Clip Art to Slides*

What: Adding ClipArt to a slide.

How: Choose Insert | Picture | ClipArt.

Why: To add interest to your slides.

Tip: To have access to more clipart, click the Clips on the Web button in the ClipArt dialog box. If you have a modem and an Internet Service Provider, PowerPoint connects to Microsoft's Web site so that you can download more graphics.

You will want to include images on your slides that enliven your presentation.

You can use the clip art library that comes with Microsoft Office—don't forget that the CD contains more images. You can also scan images on a scanner, or you can create images in a graphics program.

To include a clip art graphic on the current slide, follow these steps:

1. Choose Insert | Picture | ClipArt.

The Microsoft Clip Gallery dialog box displays, as shown in Figure 4.16.

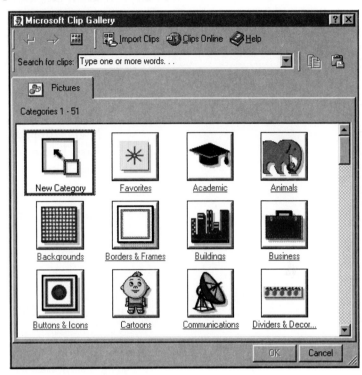

FIGURE 4.16 Clip Art Dialog Box

2. Browse the images by category.
3. Select the desired image.

The ClipArt toolbar displays.

4. Click the Insert Clip button on the ClipArt toolbar.

PowerPoint places the clip art image on the slide.

5. Close the dialog box to display the slide with the clip art image.

An alternative method used to insert graphics on a slide is to use a slide layout that includes placeholders for ClipArt.

To use a slide with a clip art placeholder, follow these steps:

1. Choose Common Tasks | New Slide.

The New Slide dialog box displays.

2. Select one of the Text and ClipArt slides and click OK.

The new slide displays.

3. Double-click the clip art button that appears on the slide.
4. Follow the same procedure outlined above to add the clip art image to the slide.

Once you place the clip art on your slide, you will notice that it is selected. You can size, move, and delete the clip art using the same methods you used to adjust the AutoShapes. Click outside the clip art to deselect it.

1. Choose **Common Tasks** | **New Slide**.
The New Slide dialog box displays.

2. Select the **Text and ClipArt** slide and click **OK**.
The new slide displays, with the green background.

3. Type **JRT Grooming** for the title and make it **54** point.

4. Type the following bulleted list:

> **Gentle Care**
> **No Sedatives**
> **Professional Cutting**
> **Nails Clipped**
> **Ears Trimmed**
> **Flea Dip**

5. Change the font size to **40** for the list.

6. Make all the bullets in the list the scissors bullet and make them pur
The bulleted list appears with the scissors bullets.

7. Double-click the image to add clip art.
The Microsoft Clip Gallery dialog box displays.

8. Under the Animals category, find a dog image. Select the dog image
and click the **Insert Clip button**.
PowerPoint inserts the clip art image onto the slide.

9. Move and size the image as necessary.
Your slide should look similar the one in Figure 4.17; however, your
image will probably be different.

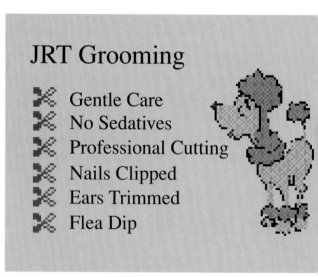

FIGURE 4.17   JRT Grooming Slide

10. Choose **Common Tasks** | **New Slide**.

11. In the New Slide dialog box, choose the **Bulleted List slide**.
The new slide displays.

12. Type **JRT Boarding Kennels** for the title and make it **54** point.

13. Type the following bulleted list:

> **Individual rooms**
> **Air conditioned**
> **24 hour care**
> **Daily walks**
> **Soothing music playing**
> **Fresh cooked meals**

14. Change the font size to **40** for the list.

15. Make all the bullets in the list the airplane bullet and make them purple.

16. Choose **Insert | Picture | ClipArt**.

17. Under the Animals category, find a dog image. Select the dog image and click the Insert button, or click the **Clips on the Web button** and find more images on the Microsoft Online Gallery.

18. Move and size the image as necessary.
Your slide should look similar to Figure 4.18; however, your clip art image will probably be different.

FIGURE **4.18**   JRT Boarding Slide

19. Save the presentation, your slide presentation should look like the Slide Sorter view shown in Figure 4.19.

1

2   3

FIGURE **4.19**   Presentation in Slide Sorter View

S U M M A R Y

After completing this task, you should be able to
- change the color of the presentation (page 72)
- change the color of one slide in a presentation (page 72)
- change the presentation design (page 76)
- use the slide master (page 78)
- change the font, font size, and color (page 81)
- format text (page 83)
- change text alignment on slides (page 84)
- add AutoShapes (page 85)
- add ClipArt (page 88)

K E Y   T E R M S

bold (page 83)
color scheme (page 72)
font (page 81)
italic (page 83)
shadow (page 83)

slide master (page 78)
underline (page 83)
AutoShape (page 85)
sizing handles (page 86)

T E S T   Y O U R   S K I L L S

True/False

1. The slide master controls formatting on all slides except those based on the Title Slide.
2. Color schemes are based on the design template used to create the presentation.
3. You can change the horizontal alignment of text on slides.
4. You can apply color changes to a slide or to the presentation.
5. You can't change the layout of a slide once you have saved the presentation.

Multiple Choice

1. You can change the design template
   a. for one slide
   b. for the entire presentation
   c. only before you have placed text on the slides
   d. all of these answers
2. The slide master
   a. can never be changed
   b. can be changed only before you have placed text on the slides
   c. controls the display of Title Slides only
   d. allows you to add elements to every slide in the presentation

3.   The Custom Color Scheme option allows you to
       a. change the color of individual elements on the slide
       b. choose colors from a color wheel
       c. create your own effects
       d. all of these answers
4.   Text on a slide can appear
       a. bold
       b. italicized
       c. shadowed
       d. all of these answers
5.   You can add a logo to the Title Slide by adding it to
       a. the slide master
       b. the presentation design
       c. the title master
       d. all of these answers

Short Answer

1. The _____ _____ controls the display of the entire presentation.
2. The _____ _____ is the group of complementary colors based on the presentation design.
3. _____ allow you to move a graphic on a slide.
4. Unless you used the Blank Presentation option to create a presentation, the _____ _____ will determine the look of the design.
5. To format text on a slide, you must first _____ it.

What Does This Do?

Write a description of the function of the following:

No.		No.	
1.	**B**	6.	*I*
2.	≣	7.	≣
3.	**A**	8.	A
4.	⬙	9.	24
5.	Times New Roman	10.	

On Your Own

1. Create a new presentation and choose a different template from the one you have used so far.
2. Change the color of the background, text, and other elements.
3. Change the design template that the presentation is based on.
4. Edit the slide master and the title master.
5. Change the size, font, color, and effects of text.

PROJECTS

1. Create a new presentation based on the Blueprint Design Template.
    Place the following text on the Title Slide
    >   Title—Blueprint for Success
    >   Subtitle—Attitude Counts More Than You Think!

    Center the subtitle on the slide.
    Change the subtitle font to Algerian.
    Add a bulleted list slide to the presentation.
    Place the following text on the bulleted list.
    >   Title—You Are What You Think
    >   List—If you think you can't, you can't.
    >   >   If you keep an open mind, you are more likely to succeed.
    >   >   Positive thoughts have changed many negative situations.

    Print the slides.
    Add an AutoShape to the slide.
    Change the presentation design to Radar.
    Print the presentation a second time, and save it as Success.

2. Using the Success presentation, use the slide master to change the bullets to the style and color of your choice.
    Add a third slide that is a bulleted list slide.
    Add the following text:
    >   Title—How Do You Measure Success?
    >   List—Money
    >   >   Free time
    >   >   Career advancement
    >   >   Peace
    >   >   Good relationships
    >   >   Fame

    Add a ClipArt image to the slide.
    Change the font of the bulleted list and boldface it.
    Print and save the presentation.

3. Using the Success presentation, change the color scheme of the slides. Select your own colors for various elements from the Custom option. Print the slides. Save the file with the same name and close it.

4. Create a personal slide presentation. Use PowerPoint to create a slide presentation of at least four slides. They should contain information for a topic you are interested in. Format the slides using any techniques you have learned so far. Save the presentation. Run the slide show. Print the slides. Print the outline.

1. As the owner of Plant Wonders, a small plant distribution company, you want to create a presentation that you will use at the local home show.

   Create a new presentation based on the Bamboo Design Template.

   Slide 1: Title Slide

       Title—Plant Wonders

       Subtitle—Distributors of Hard-to-Find Plants

   Add a ClipArt image.

   Slide 2: Bulleted List

       Title—Currently Available

       List—Sun Plant

           Baby Blue Eyes

           Monkey Flower

           Livingstone Daisy

           Toadflax

           Poached-Egg Flower

           Blazing Star

   Italicize the items in the list.

   Change the bullets that appear before the items for this list only.

   Slide 3: Bulleted List

       Title—Special Order

       List—Harlequin Flower

           Corn Lily

           Sword Lily

           Snowdrop

           Dog's-tooth Violet

           Glory of the Snow

           Indian Shot

   Use the slide master to center the bulleted lists on the slides.

   Move the third slide before the second slide.

   Check the spelling of the presentation.

   Save the presentation as Plant Wonders.

   Play the slide show.

   Print the slides.

   Print the outline.

2. Travel Beyond is a small travel agency that has asked you to develo
   PowerPoint presentation.

   Create a new presentation using the Neon Frame Design Template.

   Slide 1: Title Slide

   > Title—Travel Beyond

   > Subtitle—Expand Your Horizons

   Add an AutoShape or ClipArt image.

   Slide 2: Bulleted List

   > Title—Leave Your Stress at Home

   > List— Visit famous spots

   >> Visit secluded locations

   >> Wander through history

   >> Visit ancient cultures

   Change the bullets for the list and the color to bright purple.

   Slide 3: Bulleted List

   > Title—Get Away from It All

   > List— Take a cruise to magical islands

   >> Retreat to the ends of civilization

   >> Hike into the wilderness

   >> Raft down a whitewater river

   >> Climb a mountain

   >> See unusual animals

   Slide 4: Bulleted List

   > Title—Our Services

   > List— Low-fare flights

   >> Cruise bookings

   >> Unique lodging options

   >> Alternative tours

   >> Tips on restaurants

   >> Wilderness adventures

   Use the slide master to center the bulleted lists on the slides.

   Move the third slide before the first slide.

   Check the spelling of the presentation.

   Save the presentation as Travel Beyond.

   Play the slide show.

   Print the slides.

   Print the outline.

Integrating the Parts

Merging Documents and Linking to the World Wide Web

You have learned to use Microsoft Office 2000 by becoming proficient with the individual applications. You have mastered Word, Excel, Power-Point, and Access and become familiar with Internet Explorer and the World Wide Web. You know a tremendous amount about Office. But now you are ready to use it as one entity in which all parts work together. You may be amazed at the results you can achieve, avoiding duplication of effort and duplication of data.

Integration can consist of using information from one application in another application, such as using an Access database in a Word mail merge or a Word table in a PowerPoint presentation. You have already seen some of the ways in which this is accomplished. In the Word section of this book, you embedded WordArt and Microsoft Graph objects in a Word document. In the Excel section, you copied and linked an Excel worksheet into a Word document.

Integration can also include hyperlinks to documents in other applications or to documents located on the World Wide Web, providing in-depth information on your topic.

MERGING FILES

When you created a mail merge in Microsoft Word 2000, you created the data source in Word. Sometimes it is more efficient to use Access. When you are ready to create a data source for your own data, you should analyze the data to see which program is better suited to the task. If the list of names and addresses will not be very large and the data will not need much editing, Word should be your choice. It's quicker and simpler. However, if the list of names and addresses will be very large and will need a lot of editing to keep it up to date, Access will definitely be more efficient.

PASTING, EMBEDDING, AND LINKING

Other integrative methods include placing an object created in one program in another program's document. You can do this by simple pasting, by embedding, or by linking. All three methods start by copying the data from a source file in one application. The process you use for pasting the data into the destination file determines whether the data are simply pasted, embedded, or linked in the new location.

- You can *paste* data from the Windows clipboard directly into any Office application. Place the insertion point in the destination file where you want the new data to appear and issue the Paste command. The clipboard data from the source file are placed in the destination file. This is quick and simple, but the pasted object can no longer be edited using the source application. Instead, it takes on properties of the destination application. An Excel worksheet pasted into Word becomes a Word table, for instance. You can edit it like any other Word table, but you can't calculate with it, as you could when it was an Excel worksheet. And if the data in the source document change, the pasted data will not be updated.

- You can use the Edit menu's Paste Special command and *embed* an object into a destination file in any Office application. The object becomes part of the destination file, but it is still the same object it was. An Excel worksheet embedded in a Word document remains an Excel worksheet. When you want to edit the embedded object, double-click it to activate it, and the toolbar changes to show commands for the application that created the object. You are able to edit the object from the destination document using the source application, making use of any of its features. You can add formulas and functions to the worksheet within Word, for instance. Because the information embedded in the destination document is stored with the destination document, any changes made there are not carried back to the source document, and changes in the source are not carried forward to the destination.

- Using the Paste Special command, you can *link* an object from the original application to a destination document in another Office application. When you do this, a representation of the object is placed in the destination file, along with a shortcut, or link, to its original location. If the original document in the source application is updated, the linked image will be updated automatically. Linked objects must be edited in their source software application because that is where the data are saved. If you double-click a linked object, the source application launches so that you can edit the object.

The technology whereby an object created in one application is embedded or linked in another application's document is known as Object Linking and Embedding, or OLE, pronounced "OH-lay."

CREATING HYPERLINKS

Yet another method to link information between files is a hyperlink. A hyperlink can link data in the same or different applications, and it can also link to Web documents located on servers anywhere in the world. To create a hyperlink, place the insertion point in the file where you want the hyperlink to appear, and use the Insert Hyperlink command in the application to create the link. You specify the name of the file and path where it's located if the document is another Office document, or you specify the URL for a document located on the World Wide Web. When a person reading the document on a computer clicks the hyperlink, he or she is transferred to the linked document.

INTEGRATING FILES

You are an employee for the Seeds & Sprouts Company that specializes in vegetable and flower seeds for the home gardener. You want to use Office 2000 more efficiently by integrating information between applications. Complete the following exercises to help learn about integration.

EXERCISE 1 | *Merging Between Applications*

1. Use Access to create a database called **Current Customers**.
2. Create the **Customer** table shown in Table 1.

Field	Type	Size
Title	text	4
First_name	text	15
Last_name	text	20
Address1	text	20
Address2	text	20
City	text	20
State	text	2
Postal_code	text	5

TABLE I   Customer Table for the *Current Customers* Database

3. Add the following records to the **Customer** table:

Mr. James Long 200 W. 5th Place Apt 101 Seattle, WA 98650	Ms. Mary Farmer P. O. Box 1901 Eugene, OR 97403	Mrs. Sue Fields 1331 Monument Rd Jefferson, KY 40305
Mr. John Howard 189 N. 34th Ave Trenton, NJ 07654	Mrs. April Jones 34 N. Shore Drive Apt 303 Fort Lauderdale, FL 30089	Ms. Rose Jeffery 567 Cherry Lane Toledo, OH 87654

4. Save the table without setting a primary key, print the table, close the database, and exit from Access.

5. Start Word and run the Mail Merge Helper. Use the **Customer** table of the **Current Customer** database as the data source by changing the file type to **MS Access Databases** in the Open Data Source dialog box, selecting the correct file, and selecting the correct table.

6. Create the main document shown in Figure 1, inserting a graphic of your choice.

Seeds & Sprouts
725 Garden Way
Arcadia, ME 34567

<insert merge codes for inside address>

<insert current date>

Dear <insert title and last name merge codes>:

Thank you for your interest in Seeds & Sprouts. We have recently developed many new varieties of seeds that are hardier and will produce a higher yield of fruit in your garden. At Seeds & Sprouts, customer satisfaction is our first priority, so feel free to contact us at any time.

The enclosed catalog has many specials for the home gardener, and if you order before March 1st, you will receive a 20% discount on orders over $25.

We hope you enjoy the enclosed catalog, and we look forward to hearing from you.

Sincerely,

Your Name

FIGURE 1

7. Save the form letter as **Customer Letter** and print it.

8. Run the merge and print the letters.

9. Run the merge a second time, merging to mailing labels.

10. Print the labels and close Word without saving the labels.

EXERCISE 2 | *Linking, Embedding, and Pasting Data*

1. Start Excel 2000 and create the worksheet shown in Figure 2, inserting a graphic of your choice.

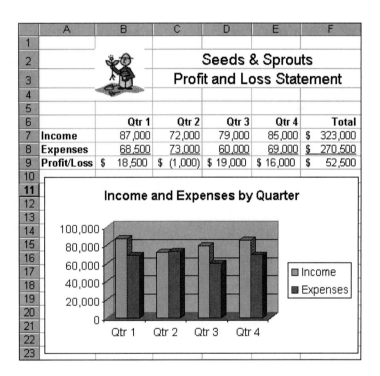

FIGURE 2

2. Save the workbook as **Profit**, print the worksheet, and keep Excel open on the desktop.

3. Select the range that includes the cells occupied by the worksheet data and the chart, and then choose **Edit | Copy**. This copies the worksheet and the chart to the clipboard.

4. Start Word and create the document shown in Figure 3, inserting a graphic of your choice.

**Seeds & Sprouts
Annual Report**

<insert a page break>

Financial Report

Seeds & Sprouts has had a very successful year overall. Although we fell into the red for one quarter, we were able to overcome those losses and show a strong profit for the year. Despite severe weather that caused disruption of the seed crop, we were able to increase our sales by 5 percent over the preceding year. As you can see by the figures below, we experienced extremely strong first and third quarters, with profits over $18,000 for each quarter.

FIGURE 3

5. With the insertion point at the end of the document, choose **Edit | Paste Special**.
   The Paste Special dialog box opens.

6. Choose **Paste Link** as **Microsoft Excel Worksheet Object** and click **OK**.
   The worksheet, graphic, and chart appear in the Word document as a linked object.

7. Double-click the linked object to start Excel, and change the Expenses for Qtr 2 to **$100,000**.
   The worksheet formulas are recalculated, and the chart refreshes to show the new expenses for Qtr 2. Save the Excel workbook.

8. Switch back to Word.
   The worksheet and chart have changed to reflect the edit you made in Excel.

9. Save the document as **Annual Report** and print the document.

10. Select the linked object and press **Delete** to delete it from the Word document.

11. Switch to Excel and copy the worksheet and chart to the clipboard again.

12. Switch to Word and choose **Edit | Paste Special**.
    The Paste Special dialog box opens.

13. Choose **Paste** as **Microsoft Excel Worksheet Object** and click **OK**.
    This time the worksheet, graphic, and chart are embedded in the Word document as an Excel object. There is no link to the original.

14. Double-click the embedded object.
    The toolbars change to those of Excel. You will be able to edit the worksheet using Excel from within Word.

15. Change the income for Qtr 3 to **$100,000**.
    The worksheet formulas are recalculated, and the chart refreshes to reflect the change.

16. Click outside the selected object.
    The embedded object is deselected, the toolbars change back to Word's, and the changes you made are shown.

17. Select the embedded object again and press the **Delete key**.
    The object is deleted from the Word document.

18. Switch to Excel.
    The changes you made in the embedded object were not carried back to the original worksheet.

19. Copy the worksheet and chart to the clipboard once again.

20. Switch to Word and choose **Edit | Paste**.
    The worksheet and chart are pasted into the Word document as a Word table and a picture. They can no longer be edited in Excel, but you can edit the table as a Word table, and you can move, size, and edit the picture.

21. Close both applications.

22. If you have access to e-mail, attach the **Annual Report** document to an e-mail message and send it to your instructor at the address he or she provides.

1. Start Word and create the document shown in Figure 4, using WordA to create a title, which is an embedded object, and inserting a graphic your choice.

If you want to increase your vitality, feel better, and eat more nutritious food, you should consider growing a garden. Don't let time or lack of space keep you from this pursuit. You can grow a garden in a container or in the ground, on a deck or in the yard, in about any situation you can think of.

You will not only be in control of any additives to your food, you will also be eating fresh, tasty food filled with vitamins and minerals. The larger the garden, the more you will benefit. You will be outside more, getting more exercise, and feeling better.

The USDA provides nutrition information to help you eat a healthy diet. You can find this information on the World Wide Web by clicking here.

For information about gardening, contact:

Seeds & Sprouts
725 Garden Way
Arcadia, ME 34567
garden@seeds.com

FIGURE **4**

2. Select the the words **by clicking here** near the end of the document, choose **Insert | Hyperlink**, and insert a hyperlink to the following Web address:

www.nal.usda.gov/fnic/Fpyr/pyramid.gif

3. Test the link to be sure it works.

The link should take you to the food pyramid, shown in Figure 5.

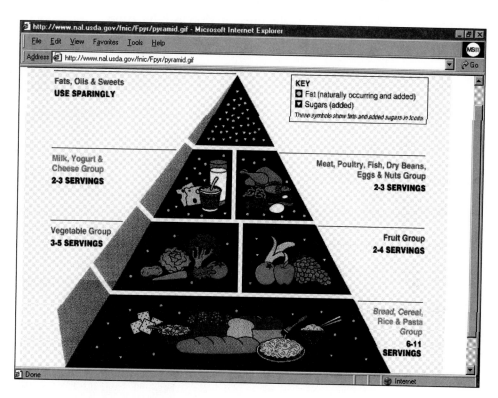

FIGURE 5 The Hyperlink from Figure 4

4. Save the document as **Nutrition** and print the document.

5. Choose **File | Save as Web Page** and save the document as **Good Eats**.

The document is resaved as a Web page.

6. Exit from Word.

7. Start your browser and open the Web document.

You will find a folder and a file named *Good Eats*. Click the file named *Good Eats*.

8. Print the document in your browser, and then exit from the browser.

1. Start PowerPoint and create the slides shown in Figures 6, 7, and 8 to help educate children about the benefits of growing a garden. Format the slides as shown and include graphics of your own choosing. Save the presentation as **Education**.

FIGURE 6   Slide 1 in the *Education* Presentation

FIGURE 7   Slide 2 in the *Education* Presentation

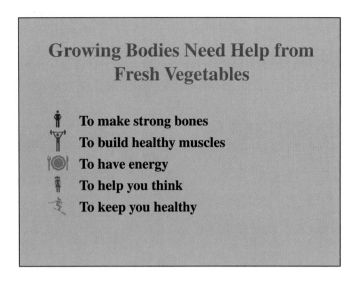

Growing Bodies Need Help from Fresh Vegetables

- To make strong bones
- To build healthy muscles
- To have energy
- To help you think
- To keep you healthy

FIGURE 8 Slide 3 in the *Education* Presentation

2. On the second slide, make the text *Click here for reasons to eat well* a hypertext link to the following URL:

http://www.ars.usda.gov/is/kids

When you test the link, you should open the site shown in Figure 9.

FIGURE 9 The Hyperlink for Slide 2

3. Start Word and create a table like that in Figure 10, formatting it as shown.

Food Group	USDA Recommended Servings
Milk, Yogurt, and Cheese	2-3 servings
Vegetables	3-5 servings
Meat, Poultry, Fish, Beans, Eggs	2-3 servings
Fruit	2-4 servings
Bread, Cereal, Rice, and Pasta	6-11 servings

FIGURE 10   The Table for the *Education* Presentation

4. Copy the table to the clipboard.

5. Switch to PowerPoint and add a new **title-only slide**, titling it USDA Recommendations.

6. Choose **Edit | Paste Special**.

7. In the Paste Special dialog box, **Paste** the object as a **Microsoft Word Document Object**.

8. Double-click the table to edit it as an embedded object using Word. Increase the size of the text in the table to **22-point**. Click outside the table to return to PowerPoint.

Your new slide will look somewhat like Figure 11.

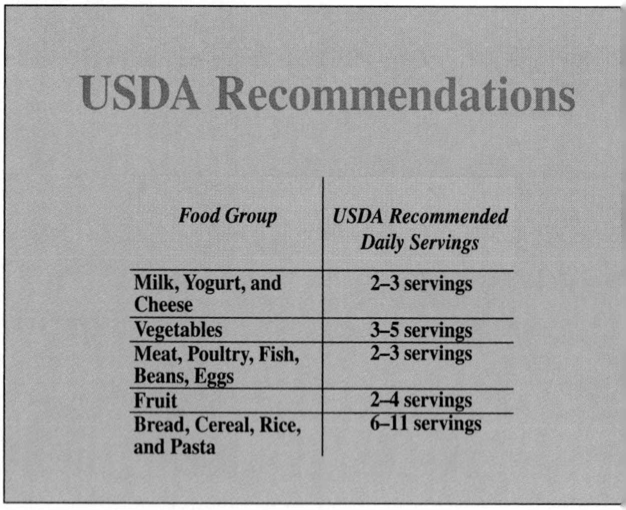

USDA Recommendations

Food Group	USDA Recommended Daily Servings
Milk, Yogurt, and Cheese	2–3 servings
Vegetables	3–5 servings
Meat, Poultry, Fish, Beans, Eggs	2–3 servings
Fruit	2–4 servings
Bread, Cereal, Rice, and Pasta	6–11 servings

FIGURE 11   Slide 4 in the *Education* Presentation

9. Print slide handouts.

10. Exit from PowerPoint.

You are working for the utility service in your area, and you are responsible for a new program called *Save the Planet*. Your job is to create materials to provide information to your customers on such topics as saving energy by conserving consumption and using alternative energy sources such as solar.

- Search the World Wide Web for information.
- Create a Web site for Save the Planet with links to government agencies or other organizations.
- Create a letterhead for Save the Planet.
- Create a worksheet using statistics that you find on the Web showing the advantages of consuming less energy.
- Create a database of five customers in Access.
- Create a report summarizing the information you have found. Include graphics, charts, a title page, and formatting, plus a link to the worksheet.
- Create a letter to accompany the report and address it to the customers in the Access database. Print the letters on the letterhead you created.
- Create a slide presentation pulling together information from all your sources.
- Print all documents.

Task	Commands

MICROSOFT WINDOWS 98

Active Desktop	Control Panel | Display | Web tab
Add a screen saver	Control Panel | Display | Screen Saver tab
Add sounds to events	Control Panel | Sounds
Arrange files by date	View | Arrange Icons | by Date
Arrange files by name	View | Arrange Icons | by Name
Arrange files by size	View | Arrange Icons | by Size
Arrange files by type	View | Arrange Icons | by Type
Arrange icons	Shortcut menu | Arrange Icons | Auto Arrange
Capture the active window	Alt+Print Screen key
Capture the screen	Print Screen key
Cascade windows	Shortcut menu | Cascade Windows
Change colors	Control Panel | Display | Appearance tab
Change date or time	Control Panel | Date/Time
Change mouse to single clicks	View | Folder Options | single click
Change the background	Control Panel | Display | Background tab
Check system files	Start | Programs | Accessories | System Tools | System Tile Checker
Close a program	File | Exit
Close a window	Close button
Connect to the Internet	Start | Programs | Internet Explorer | Connection Wizard
Copy a disk	File | Copy disk
Copy data	Edit | Copy
Create a folder	File | New | Folder
Delete a file	File | Delete
Find files	Start | Find | Files or Folders
Format a disk	File | Format
Help	Start | Help
Install a new program	Control Panel | Add/Remove Programs
Install new hardware	Control Panel | Add New Hardware
Maximize window	Maximize button

Task	Commands
MICROSOFT WINDOWS 98 (continued)	
Minimize window	Minimize button
Modify keyboard	Control Panel | Keyboard
Modify mouse	Control Panel | Mouse
Modify Start menu	Start | Settings | Taskbar & Start menu
Move a window	Drag by title bar
Move data	Edit | Cut, Edit | Paste
Open Control Panel	My Computer | Control Panel
Paste data	Edit | Paste
Preview a document	File | Preview
Print a file	File | Print
Refresh the screen	View | Refresh
Rename a file	File | Rename
Restore a deleted file	Open Recycle Bin right-click file
Save a file	File | Save
Select a list of contiguous files	Shift+left click the mouse
Select all files	Edit | Select all
Select noncontiguous files	Ctrl+left click the mouse
Shut down a frozen program	Ctrl+Alt+Delete
Shut down the computer	Start | Shut down
Size window	Drag the two-headed arrow
Switch between programs	Click button on taskbar
System Information	Start | Programs | Accessories | System Tools | System Info
Tile windows horizontally	Shortcut menu | Tile Windows Horizontally
Tile windows vertically	Shortcut menu | Tile Windows Vertically
Tune up the hard disk	Start | Programs | Accessories | System Tools | Tune-Up
Undo Cascade windows	Shortcut menu | Undo Cascade
Undo Tiled windows	Shortcut menu | Undo Tile
View file details	View | Details
View file list	View | List

Task	Commands
View large icons	View | Large Icons
View small icons	View | Small Icons

MICROSOFT WORD 2000

Task	Commands
Alignment of text	Format | Paragraph
All caps	Format | Font
AutoCorrect	Tools | AutoCorrect
AutoFormat	Format | AutoFormat
AutoText	Insert | AutoText
Bold	Format | Font
Bookmarks	Insert | Bookmark
Borders	Format | Borders and Shading
Bulleted list	Format | Bullets and Numbering
Characters or special symbols	Insert | Symbols
Chart	Insert | Picture | Chart
Clip Art	Insert | Picture | Clip Art
Close a document	File | Close
Color of text	Format | Font
Copy text	Edit | Copy
Create a new document	File | New
Double-strikethrough text	Format | Font
Emboss text	Format | Font
Engrave text	Format | Font
Envelopes	Tools | Envelopes and Labels
Font	Format | Font
Font size	Format | Font
Footnote	Insert | Footnote
Format a Web document	Format | Themes
Header and Footer	View | Header Footer
Help	Help | Contents and Index
Hidden text	Format | Font

Task | Commands

MICROSOFT WORD 2000 (continued)

Task	Commands
Hypertext link	Insert | Hyperlink
Indent text from margins	Format | Paragraph
Italic	Format | Font
Line spacing	Format | Paragraph
Mail merge	Tools | Mail Merge
Mailing labels	Tools | Envelopes and Labels
Margins	File | Page Setup
Move text	Edit | Cut
Numbered list	Format | Bullets and Numbering
Open a document	File | Open
Outline text	Format | Font
Page break	Insert | Break
Page numbers	Insert | Page Numbers
Paste as Hyperlink	Edit | Paste as Hyperlink
Paste text	Edit | Paste
Preview a Web page	File | Web Page Preview
Preview a document	File | Print Preview
Print a document	File | Print
Save a document as a Web document	File | Save as Web Page
Save a file	File | Save As
Shading text	Format | Borders and Shading
Shadow text	Format | Font
Small caps	Format | Font
Spelling and Grammar	Tools | Spelling and Grammar
Strikethrough text	Format | Font
Styles	Format | Style
Subscript text	Format | Font
Superscript text	Format | Font
Tab change	Format | Tabs
Table—create	Table | Insert Table

Task	Commands
Table—format	Table | AutoFormat
Template	File | New
Underline	Format | Font
Undo a task	Edit | Undo
View a toolbar	View | Toolbar
View the ruler	View | Ruler
WordArt	Insert | Picture | WordArt

MICROSOFT EXCEL 2000

Align cells	Format | Cells | Alignment tab
AutoCorrect	Tools | AutoCorrect
AutoFormat	Format | AutoFormat
Bold	Format | Cells | Font tab
Borders	Format | Cells | Border tab
Chart	Insert | Chart
Clip Art	Insert | Picture | Clip Art
Close a workbook	File | Close
Color	Format | Cells | Font tab or Patterns tab
Column width	Format | Column | Width
Copy	Edit | Copy
Copy a worksheet	Edit | Move or Copy Sheet
Create a new workbook	File | New
Currency format	Format | Cells | Number tab | Currency
Delete cell contents	Edit | Clear | Contents
Delete a worksheet	Edit | Delete Sheet
Delete cell contents and formatting	Edit | Clear | All
Delete cell formatting	Edit | Clear | Formats
Delete column	Edit | Delete | Entire Column
Delete row	Edit | Delete | Entire Row
Display the formula bar	View | Formula Bar
Display the status bar	View | Status Bar
Fill	Edit | Fill

Task | Commands

MICROSOFT EXCEL 2000 (continued)

Task	Commands
Font	Format | Cells | Font tab
Font size	Format | Cells | Font tab
Format numbers	Format | Cells | Number tab
Go to	Edit | Go To
Header and footer	File | Page Setup | Header/Footer tab
Help	Help | Contents and Index
Hypertext link	Insert | Hyperlink
Insert column	Insert | Columns
Insert row	Insert | Row
Italic	Format | Cells | Font tab
Margins	File | Page Setup | Margins tab
Move a sheet	Edit | Move or Copy Sheet
Move data	Edit | Cut, Edit | Paste
Open a workbook	File | Open
Paste	Edit | Paste
Paste link	Edit | Paste Special
Preview a worksheet	File | Print Preview
Print	File | Print
Print gridlines	File | Page Setup | Sheet tab
Print landscape orientation	File | Page Setup | Page tab
Save a file	File | Save As
Save as Web document	File | Save As Web Document
Shading	Format | Cells | Patterns tab
Show formulas	Alt+~
Spelling	Tools | Spelling
Subscript	Format | Cells | Font tab
Superscript	Format | Cells | Font tab
Underline	Format | Cells | Font tab
Undo a task	Edit | Undo
View a toolbar	View | Toolbars

Task	Commands
MICROSOFT ACCESS 2000	
Change field properties	Table Design view | General tab | Field Properties
Change object properties	right-click object | Properties
Copy records	Edit | Copy
Copy a table	Edit | Copy
Create a database	File | New
Create a query in Design view	Queries object | New | Design View
Create a query using a wizard	Queries object | New | Simple Query Wizard
Create a table in Datasheet view	Tables object | New | Datasheet View
Create a table in Design view	Tables object | New | Design View
Create a table with the Table Wizard	Tables object | New | Table Wizard
Create a relationship	Tools | Relationships
Define a primary key	Edit | Primary Key
Delete a field	right-click row selector | Delete Rows
Delete a record	Edit | Delete
Exit Microsoft Access	File | Exit
Filter records by form	Records | Filter | Filter by Form
Filter records by selection	Records | Filter | Filter by Selection
Filter records excluding selection	Records | Filter | Filter Excluding Selection
Format the datasheet	Format | Font
Insert a field	right-click row selector | Insert Rows
Insert a new record	Insert | New Record
Locate a record	Edit | Find
Modify a query	select in Queries object | Design
Modify a table's design	select in Tables object | Design
Move records	Edit | Cut
Open a database	File | Open
Open a form	double-click in Forms object in Database window
Open a query	double-click in Queries object in Database window
Open a report	double-click in Reports object in Database window
Open a table	double-click in Tables object in Database window

Task	Commands
MICROSOFT ACCESS 2000 (continued)	
Print the table design	Tools | Analyze | Documenter
Print relationships	File | Print Relationships
Replace a field's content	Edit | Replace
Save the design	File | Save
Sort the table	Records | Sort
Start Access	Start | Programs | Microsoft Access
Switch to Datasheet view	View | Datasheet View
Switch to Design view	View | Design View
Unhide a column	Format | Unhide Columns
Use a Lookup table	choose Lookup Wizard under Field Type
MICROSOFT POWERPOINT 2000	
Alignment of text	Format | Alignment
Change a bullet	Format | Bullets and Numbering
Change slide layout	Format | Slide Layout
Change the color scheme	Format | Color Scheme
Change the design	Format | Apply Design
Clip Art	Insert | Picture | Clip Art
Close a document	File | Close
Color of text	Format | Font
Copy text	Edit | Copy
Create a new presentation	File | New
Delete a slide	Edit | Delete Slide
Emboss text	Format | Font
Font	Format | Font
Font size	Format | Font
Help	Help | Microsoft PowerPoint Help
Insert a duplicate slide	Insert | Duplicate Slide
Insert a new slide	Insert | New Slide

Task	Commands
Insert an AutoShape	Insert | Picture | AutoShapes
Move text	Edit | Cut
Notes Master	View | Master | Notes Master
Open a presentation	File | Open
Paste text	Edit | Paste
Play a slide show	View | Slide Show
Print a presentation	File | Print
Save a document as a Web document	File | Save as Web Page
Save a file	File | Save As
Shadow text	Format | Font
Spell Checker	Tools | Spelling
Subscript text	Format | Font
Superscript text	Format | Font
Title master	View | Master | Title Master
Undo a task	Edit | Undo
View a toolbar	View | Toolbar
View Normal view	View | Normal
View notes page	View | Notes Page
View slide master	View | Master | Slide Master
View slide show	Slide Show | View Show
View slide sorter	View | Slide Sorter
View speaker notes	View | Speaker Notes

MICROSOFT WINDOWS 98 STANDARD TOOLBAR

 Moves back to the previous screen

 Moves forward to the next screen if the Back button has been used

 Moves up one level in the folder structure

 Cuts the selection and places it on the Clipboard

 Copies the selection to the Clipboard

 Pastes the Clipboard contents

 Reverses the last action

 Deletes the selection

 Displays the Properties dialog box

 Changes the view of the file list

MICROSOFT WINDOWS 98 INTERNET EXPLORER STANDARD TOOLBAR

 Returns to the previously viewed page

If you have gone back to a page, takes you forward again

Stops the current page from loading

Reloads the current page

Displays the page designated as your home page

Allows you to search for documents on the World Wide Web

Keeps track of pages you want to return to

Keeps track of pages you have visited

Allows you to read and send mail

Prints the Web document

Opens the Web document in the designated editor

Connects to discussion server

MICROSOFT WINDOWS 98 DIALOG BOX BUTTONS

Provides help on an object in a dialog box

Applies the settings without closing the dialog box

MICROSOFT WINDOWS 98 DIALOG BOX BUTTONS (continued)

Provides choices on a drop-down list

☑ Stri**k**eout
☑ **U**nderline

Allows user to check more than one option in the group

◉ **Q**uick (erase)
○ **F**ull

Allows user to select only one option in the group

14

Allows user to increment the number with the up arrow, decrement the number with the down arrow, or type the option in the text box

Slow .... Fast

Allows user to increase or decrease option

Yes

Implements the changes

No

Does not implement the changes

Next >

Proceeds to the next step of a wizard

< **B**ack

Returns to the previous step of a wizard

MICROSOFT WINDOWS 98 OTHER BUTTONS ON THE DESKTOP

Connects to the Internet

Opens the Start menu

MICROSOFT WORD 2000 STANDARD TOOLBAR

Opens a new blank document

Opens a document from the disk

Saves the current document

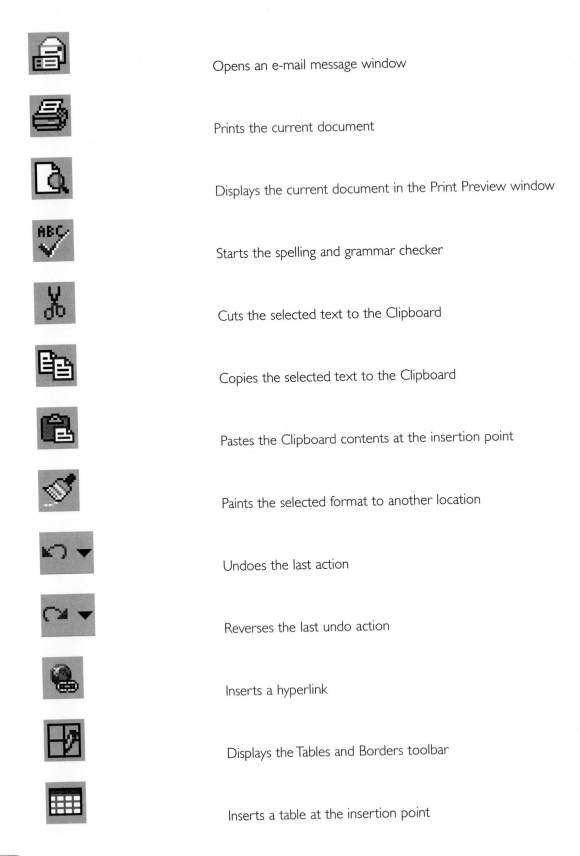

Opens an e-mail message window

Prints the current document

Displays the current document in the Print Preview window

Starts the spelling and grammar checker

Cuts the selected text to the Clipboard

Copies the selected text to the Clipboard

Pastes the Clipboard contents at the insertion point

Paints the selected format to another location

Undoes the last action

Reverses the last undo action

Inserts a hyperlink

Displays the Tables and Borders toolbar

Inserts a table at the insertion point

MICROSOFT WORD 2000 STANDARD TOOLBAR *(continued)*

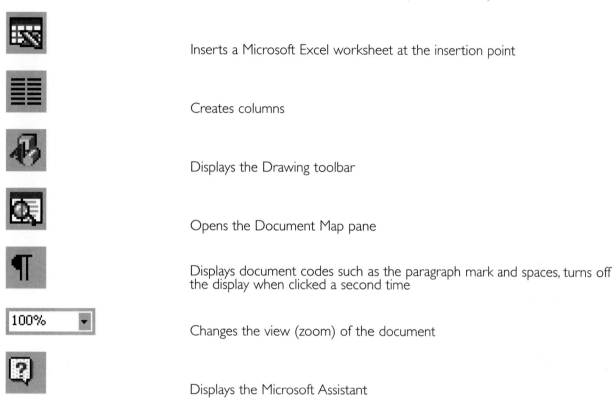

Inserts a Microsoft Excel worksheet at the insertion point

Creates columns

Displays the Drawing toolbar

Opens the Document Map pane

Displays document codes such as the paragraph mark and spaces, turns off the display when clicked a second time

Changes the view (zoom) of the document

Displays the Microsoft Assistant

MICROSOFT WORD 2000 FORMATTING TOOLBAR

Formats text using styles

Changes the font

Changes the font size

Applies bold font style

Applies italic font style

Underlines the selected text

 Left-aligns text

 Centers text

 Right-aligns text

 Justifies text

 Creates a numbered list

 Creates a bulleted list

 Decreases indentation

 Increases indentation

 Places a border around text

 Highlights text in the color designated

 Changes the color of the text

MICROSOFT EXCEL 2000 STANDARD TOOLBAR

 Opens a new blank workbook

Opens a file from the disk

MICROSOFT EXCEL 2000 STANDARD TOOLBAR (continued)

 Saves the current workbook

 Sends the workbook as an e-mail attachment

 Prints the active worksheet

 Displays the current worksheet in the Print Preview window

 Starts the spelling checker

 Cuts the selected text to the Clipboard

 Copies the selected text to the Clipboard

 Pastes the Clipboard contents at the insertion point

 Paints the selected format to another location

 Reverses the last action

 Reverses the last undo action

 Inserts a hyperlink

 Inserts the Sum function

Opens the Paste Function dialog box

Sorts the selected column in ascending order

Sorts the selected column in descending order

Starts the Microsoft ChartWizard

Opens the Drawing toolbar

88%　　　Changes the view of the document

Opens the Microsoft Assistant

MICROSOFT EXCEL 2000 FORMATTING TOOLBAR

Times New Roman　　　Changes the font

12　　　Changes the font size

B　　　Formats the selection as bold

I　　　Formats the selection as italic

U　　　Underlines the selection

Left-aligns selection

MICROSOFT EXCEL 2000 FORMATTING TOOLBAR (continued)

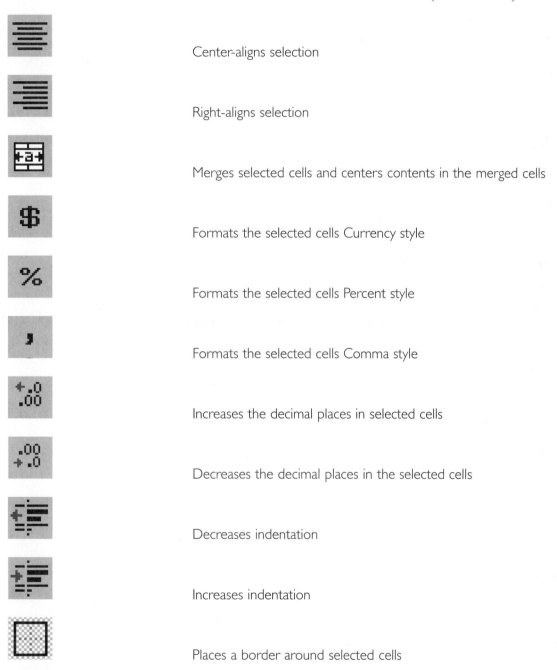

Center-aligns selection

Right-aligns selection

Merges selected cells and centers contents in the merged cells

Formats the selected cells Currency style

Formats the selected cells Percent style

Formats the selected cells Comma style

Increases the decimal places in selected cells

Decreases the decimal places in the selected cells

Decreases indentation

Increases indentation

Places a border around selected cells

Fills the selected object with the specified color

Changes the color of the text

MICROSOFT ACCESS 2000 DATABASE WINDOW

 Opens selected object

 Designs selected object

 Creates a new object

 Deletes selected object

MICROSOFT ACCESS 2000 STANDARD TOOLBAR

 Opens a new database

 Opens a file from the disk

 Saves the current object

 Prints the active object

 Displays the current object in the Print Preview window

 Starts the spelling checker

 Cuts the selected text to the Clipboard

 Copies the selected text to the Clipboard

 Pastes the Clipboard contents at the insertion point

MICROSOFT ACCESS 2000 STANDARD TOOLBAR (continued)

Paints the selected format to another location

Undo

Office links with other Office applications

Analyze

Opens the properties window

Opens the Relationships window

Creates a new object

MICROSOFT ACCESS 2000 TABLE TOOLBAR

Changes view form with data from the table

Edits hyperlink

Sorts in ascending order

Sorts in descending order

Filters the table by selection

Filters the table by form

Apply filter to the selection

Finds matching data in the table

Inserts a new record in the table

Deletes record

Database window

Creates a new object

MICROSOFT POWERPOINT 2000 STANDARD TOOLBAR

Opens a new blank document

Opens a file from the disk

Saves the current file

Provides the options to attach the entire presentation or a slide to an e-mail message

Prints the current file

Starts the Spell Check

Cuts the selected text to the Clipboard

MICROSOFT POWERPOINT 2000 STANDARD TOOLBAR (continued)

Copies the selected text to the Clipboard

Pastes the Clipboard contents at the insertion point

Paints the selected format to another location

Reverses the last action

Reverses the last undo action

Inserts a hyperlink

Opens the Tables and Borders toolbar

Inserts a table at the insertion point

Inserts a chart at the insertion point

Opens the Insert Slide dialog box

Toggle that expands the outline to show all the text on slides or only the headings

Toggle that shows formatting of text in the outline or showing plain text

Toggle that displays the slides in grayscale for printing on a black and white printer

`33%` ▼	Click the down arrow to display other zoom options
[?]	Displays the Office Assistant

MICROSOFT POWERPOINT 2000 FORMATTING TOOLBAR

`Times New Roman` ▼	Changes the font
`12` ▼	Changes the font size
B	Formats the selection as bold
I	Formats the selection as italic
U	Underlines the selection
S	Formats the text with a shadow
≡	Left-aligns selection
≡	Center-aligns selection
≡	Right-aligns selection
≔	Creates a numbered list
≔	Creates a bulleted list

MICROSOFT POWERPOINT 2000 FORMATTING TOOLBAR (continued)

Increases the font one size

Decreases the font one size

Moves the bulleted or numbered item to the left

Increases the indent of a bulleted or numbered item

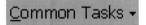

Drop-down box provides list of often used tasks

Opens the Animation toolbar

MICROSOFT POWERPOINT 2000 DRAWING TOOLBAR

Opens the Draw menu

Selects objects

Rotates the selected object

Draws a Word AutoShape in the document

Draws a line in the document

Draws an arrow in the document

Draws a rectangular object in the document

Draws an oval object in the document

Creates a text box in the document

Inserts a ClipArt image

Opens Microsoft WordArt

Fills the selected object with the specified color

Changes the color of the selected line

Changes the color of the selected text

Changes the line style

Changes the style of dashes

Changes the style of arrows

Places a shadow behind the selected object

Opens the 3-D setting options

GLOSSARY

A

absolute cell reference—in a worksheet, a reference to a specific cell that, when copied to a different location, does not change; indicated in a formula by a dollar sign

active cell—in a worksheet, the current cell; it contains a heavy border to differentiate it from the surrounding cells

Active desktop—dynamic desktop environment that can display and automatically update information from Web sites

And criteria—in a database, an expression where both values must be true for the expression to be true

application program—a software program that performs a specific task; examples are word processing, spreadsheet, database, and presentation programs

argument—the constants, cell addresses including ranges, or operations that Excel uses to perform the predefined calculation designated by the function name

asset—property owned by a person or business

AutoComplete—provides the full text of dates and AutoText entries as you begin to type them; to accept the AutoComplete tip (displayed in a yellow box at the insertion point), press Enter

AutoCorrect—automatically replaces text as you type, using a built-in list of corrections that you can edit

AutoShapes—built-in graphic shapes

AutoText—stores text or other items that you use frequently so that you can insert them with a single command

B

boilerplate text—text that is used over and over

browser—software, such as Internet Explorer, for viewing documents on the World Wide Web

bullets—small icons or characters at the beginning of each line in a list

byte—equals one character

C

cache—a folder that holds temporary files

caption—a name used in Access reports to identify field contents

cascade delete—Access automatically deletes all records in the secondary table when the record with the matching primary key is deleted from the primary table

cascade update—Access automatically updates related fields in the secondary table when the primary table is edited

cascaded windows—two or more windows displayed together on the screen so that they overlap

cell address (cell reference)—the location of a cell on a worksheet, designated by the column letter and row number

cell location math—in a worksheet, the use of cell references rather than cell contents in formulas, making the formulas independent of the cell contents; if the contents change, the formula still calculates accurately

cell—intersection of a column and row in a worksheet or table

character formatting—formatting that affects individual characters or selected text, including font, font size, font style, and font effects

check box—a square box you click to select or deselect an option in a group where more than one selection is permitted

circular reference—the inclusion in a formula of the cell that shows the formula's result

click and drag—hold down the left mouse button while moving the mouse, to move a selected object on the screen

Clipboard—a temporary storage location for data; place data there by choosing Cut or Copy; place an image of the screen there by pressing the Print Screen key

Close button—The button at the right end of a window's title bar or menu bar which closes the window when you click it

color scheme—groups of related colors

column—a vertical division of a worksheet or table grid

command button—a button you can click to execute a command

condition—a logical test in an argument in a worksheet function; A1>=B2

conditional operators—establish a criteria by setting up conditions for the data to meet

consolidation worksheet—a worksheet used to consolidate information, such as monthly reports, drawn from other sheets

constant—text and numbers you type into the worksheet; anything that doesn't start with an equal sign or contain a formula

contiguous files—files that are next to each other in the file list

copy—place a duplicate on the Clipboard while leaving the original in place

criteria—a set of conditions in a query or filter that determines the records to be selected from a table

cursor—the pointer on the screen, which moves when you move the mouse on a flat surface; it most often takes the form of an arrow

cut—move to the Clipboard

D

data series—a group of data points in the row or column of the worksheet that is plotted in the chart

data source—the Word document or other file that contains the records used in a mail merge

data type—in Access, a property that determines the type of data a field can hold

database management system—software used to collect and manage data in a database

database object—in Access, a component of the database such as tables or forms

Database window—a window in Access where database objects are available

database—in Access, a collection of tables, queries, forms, reports, and other objects

Datasheet view—a view of an Access table that displays data in rows and columns

data—the raw material such as a name or part number stored in a database table

daylight saving time—moving the clock forward one hour in the spring and back one hour in the fall

dead link—an invalid Web address or other nonfunctioning hyperlink

default value—a value automatically entered into a field

demote—indent an element in a PowerPoint list

depreciation—the amount an asset will decrease in value over a set period

design template—slide-show formatting provided by PowerPoint

Design view—in Access, a view used to design or edit objects such as tables, forms, queries, or reports

desktop—the background area displayed on your screen

detail report—in Access, report that prints both the records and summary information

dialog box—a window where you provide information needed to perform a task

disk capacity—the amount of information that can be stored on a disk: 1.44 Mb for a standard floppy disk

Documenter—an Access tool for printing documentation of your table's design

domain name—the server containing a Web docum

drawing ruler—in PowerPoint, the ruler that is displ along the top and left edge of the slide pane

E

electronic spreadsheet—an electronic grid columns and rows into which you can enter text, numb and formulas for purposes of calculation and data anal

embedded object—a copy in one application of an ject that has been created in another application; it ca edited in the application that contains it but is not li to the original

emboss—a font effect in which text appears raise the surface

extension—the three letters following a file name a period, indicating the file type and the software that ated the file; the extension is automatically assigned t file by the software

F

field name—a category of information in the data s of a database

field property—attributes of a field

field size—defines the maximum size of the dat can be entered into a field

field—in Access, a data category; in Word, a code th structs Word to insert information into a document

File Allocation Table (FAT)—the table of conte a disk located at track zero

file—a document that has been given a name and to disk

fill handle—in Excel, the small square at the b right corner of the selected cell; when dragged, it the number in the active cell to the adjacent cells, o increment a series of numbers or dates

Filter by Form—the criteria is typed into an Acce

Filter by Selection—in Access, a filter in wl records that match the criteria are selected

Filter Excluding Selection—in Access, a filter displays all records except those containing the crit

floppy disk—the 3 ½″ disk

folder—a named division of the space on a disk, u organize files

font—a typeface, a complete set of type characte its own design and name

footer—text at the bottom of every page

footnote—a note placed at the bottom (foot) of a page; used extensively in research to cite sources; a superscript number in the text is repeated at the beginning of the note to designate the spot being referenced

foreign key—in Access, the primary key of the primary table when it is in the secondary table

form—a database object that is used to view and edit data

format a disk—electronically place tracks and sectors on a disk

format property—in Access, a field property setting to control how the data is displayed

Formatting toolbar—a toolbar containing buttons for commands from the Format menu

formatting—the structure and layout of a document and its individual parts

formula bar—in Excel a bar, located below the toolbars and above the worksheet, that identifies the cell location of the active cell and displays the contents of the active cell

formula—a statement of the steps used to make a calculation; it can contain numbers, cell references, and mathematical operators such as multiplication and division signs

freenet—community-based volunteer Internet service provider

function—a predefined calculation built into Excel, such as AutoSum

G

gigabyte (GB)—equals a billion bytes

graphical user interface (GUI)—a screen display in which you issue commands by pointing to graphical elements on the screen

gridlines—(1) in a chart, lines that run vertically and horizontally through the plot area from points (tick marks) on the *x* and *y* axes (2) in a worksheet, the lines between the columns and rows

H

hanging indent—a paragraph indent in which all lines after the first line are indented

hard copy—a printed copy of the document

hard disk drive—a built-in disk drive, also called a fixed disk drive; usually drive C

hardware—a physical component of a computer system

header row—the first row of cells in the data table of a mail merge, containing the field names

header—text at the top of every page

hyperlink—text or a graphic that contains a link to another object

HyperText Markup Language (HTML)—the language used for documents on the World Wide Web

hypertext—text that contains a link to a document—usually appears blue and underlined; clicking the link starts the browser (if necessary) and displays the document

I

icon—a small graphic; it can represent a document, a Web site, a command, or a program

information superhighway—the Internet

information—an organized collection of data

input device—hardware that allows you to enter information into a computer system

input mask—a database field property that assists with entering data by automatically adding formatting and special characters, such as for phone numbers

Insert mode—Word's default editing mode, where text automatically moves to the right to make room for new text as you type

insertion point—a blinking vertical line that marks your current location in a document

inside address—the delivery address of a letter

interest—rate charged for a loan

Internet Service Provider (ISP)—a company that provides dial-up access to the Internet to individuals who purchase accounts with it

Internet—a worldwide network of computers

J

justify—align lines of type evenly at both the left and right edges

K

keyword—a word used to describe what you want to search for on the World Wide Web

kilobyte (KB)—equals a thousand bytes

L

label—text in a worksheet used to identify the numbers

landscape orientation—the page setup orientation in which the long edge of the paper is at the top

layout—positioning of elements on a document or slide

leader—a line of dots, dashes, or other marks leading the reader's eye across the page; used in the space before a tab

legend—a box that identifies the colors used for the data series or categories in a chart

linked object—an image in one application of an object created in another application, plus a pointer to the original object; changes in the original are carried to the linked image

list box—a box displaying mutually exclusive options; you select an option by clicking it

M

mail merge—a personalized form letter, label, or envelope address created from a main document and a data source

main document—a document used in a mail merge, containing the text or other elements that remain the same, plus merge fields taken from the data source

maximize—enlarge a window to fill the desktop

megabyte (MB)—equals a million bytes

menu bar—a bar at the top of a window that displays names of pull-down menus

merge field—in a mail merge, codes in the main document drawn from the field names in the data source, indicating the information to be merged

minimize—display an open window only as a button on the taskbar

modem—a hardware device that converts a computer signal so that your computer can use the phone lines to send and receive data

mouse—a hand-held input device

move—cut to the Clipboard and paste in another spot, or drag and drop in another spot

multitask—keep two or more programs open at the same time and switch between them

N

Name box—in Excel, a section of the formula bar that identifies the cell location of the current or active cell

noncontiguous files—files that are not listed next to each other in the file list

Normal view—default view in Word and PowerPoint; in Word, does not show margins; in PowerPoint, contains three frames: outline pane, slide pane, and notes pane

normalization—in Access, eliminating redundancy in table data

Notes Page—in PowerPoint, a layout that places one slide on a page with a text box for typing speaker notes

O

object linking and embedding—see **OLE**

Office Assistant—cartoon character that provides H

Office Clipboard—a temporary storage location material cut or copied from Office applications; displa as a toolbar, it holds the last 12 items that have b copied or cut

OLE (object linking and embedding)—inclu objects created in one application in another applicat document; see **linked object** and **embedded obje**

operating system—the software that enables a c puter to start up and run other programs; Windows an operating system

operator—a symbol that represents a mathematica eration, such as addition or multiplication

option button (radio button)—a button indic mutually exclusive options where one must be chose

Or criteria—in Access, an expression whereby only part of the expression needs to be true for the expre to be true

order of operations—order in which Excel perf calculations

outline pane—in PowerPoint, displays the slide nu icon, title of the slide, and the slide's text

Outline View—in PowerPoint, a view that increase size of the outline pane from that of Normal vie Word, a view that displays a document's structure

Overtype mode—the editing mode in which replaces existing text as you type, character for char

P

paragraph formatting—formatting that affects cor paragraphs, including alignment, indents, line spacing, ar

payment—amount due per period on a loan

placeholder—containers for text, bulleted lists, gr charts, tables, and so on

Places bar—the bar at the left side of the Ope Save As dialog boxes, containing shortcuts to folder a button to move to the folder

plot area—the central area of a chart, where valu represented as lines, bars, columns, slices of the pie,

point—a unit of measure for type, 1/72nd of an in is generally set in 10-to-13-point type

pointer (cursor)—a mark that moves on the scr you move the mouse on the desktop; it assumes d shapes, depending on its location

portrait orientation—the page setup orientation in which the short edge of the paper is at the top

presentation software—program used primarily to create slide shows

primary key—a field or fields that uniquely identify a record in a database

primary table—in Access, the main table in a relationship

principal—the amount of a loan

promote—undo indentation in a bulleted list by moving the item toward the left margin

protocol—a communication standard

Q

query—a database object that provides a set of specific records you want to work with

R

radio button—same as option button

range—a group of two or more cells

record—a set of data concerning a single item in a database table or the data source in a mail merge

Recycle Bin—a temporary storage location for files that have been deleted from a hard disk drive

referential integrity—rules Access enforces to maintain consistency between related tables

relational design—designing tables in a database to eliminate redundant data

relationships—an association between two or more database tables with matching values

relative cell reference—in Excel, a reference to a cell relative to its position in a formula; when copied to a different location, it adjusts to preserve the same relative position

report—a database object used to format, summarize, and present data suitable for printing

restore—display an open window at a size smaller than the desktop

row selector—selects a row in Excel or an Access record in Datasheet view

row—a horizontal division of a worksheet or table grid

S

salvage—amount that an asset will be worth at the end of the period

screen burn—image etched onto the screen from having been displayed for too long on a monitor; not a problem with today's monitors

screen saver—software that displays images on the screen after a designated interval during which neither the keyboard nor mouse has been used

ScreenTip—a small yellow box that appears when the mouse is held over a button to provide help with the button

scroll bar—a bar at the right edge or bottom of a window or frame that allows you to move through a window using a mouse

scroll box—a small square box inside a scroll bar; dragging it allows you to move quickly through a window

ScrollTip—a ScreenTip that identifies the location you are scrolling past when using the scroll bar

secondary table—in Access, the table that contains the primary key of the primary table as a foreign key

selected text—text that has been highlighted in order to have some action performed on it

serial number—Excel's internal designation of dates, where January 1, 1900, is day 1

shadow—a font effect in which text has a shadow to the right and below

sheet tab—tab at the bottom of a worksheet that displays the name of the worksheet; click a tab to move to the sheet

shortcut menu—a small menu that appears when you right-click a screen element; it provides access to commands specific to the element clicked

shortcut—an icon that, when clicked (or double-clicked, in the Classic style), will open a file or folder that is located elsewhere on the system.

sizing handles—boxes that appear around selected objects, which can be used to resize the object when they are clicked and dragged

slide master—in PowerPoint, controls the formatting on slides

slide pane—in PowerPoint, displays the slide selected in the outline pane

Slide Show—in PowerPoint, plays the slides one at a time full screen

Slide Sorter view—in PowerPoint, shows all slides as miniatures

Slide view—in PowerPoint, increases the size of the slide pane from that of normal view

software—a computer program; the two basic types are operating system software and application software

sort—ordering records in a list or table on the contents of a field

Standard toolbar—a toolbar that contains buttons for commands from the File and Edit menus and other buttons that start some of the application's special features

Start button—the taskbar button that opens the Start menu

status bar—a bar at the bottom of a window that displays information about the status of the window or the selected command or the operation that you are performing

straight-line depreciation—a depreciation method in which the asset decreases in value by the same amount every period

style—a group of stored formatting options identified by a name, e.g., Heading 1

subscript—text placed below the base line in a reduced size

subtopic—indented information under a main topic

summary report—in Access, prints only the summary information, not the records

superscript—text placed above the base line in a reduced size

surf—browse Web documents

system files—files necessary to start the computer and run application programs

T

tab stop—a horizontal position within a paragraph that you can set for placing and aligning text

tabbed dialog box—a dialog box with separate tabs containing groups of options

table—a collection of data organized into columns (fields) and rows (records)

taskbar—a Windows screen element containing the Start button and buttons for all open programs; it is displayed at the bottom of the desktop by default but may be moved to any edge of the screen

template—in Word, a model for the text and formatting of a document, which can be opened, customized or completed, and saved under a new name; in Excel, a worksheet that contains labels, formatting, and formulas but not any specific data; saved with the extension .xlt; in PowerPoint, built-in color schemes that help you format your presentations

text box—a box with space where you type data

text-editing window—the area of the screen that displays the text you type

three-letter extension— three characters, preceded by a period, added to file names by the software; the .xls tension designates a file as a Microsoft Excel workbook; designates a Word document; .ppt designates a PowerP presentation; and .mbd designates an Access database

thumbnails—miniature display of all slides in Slide Sorter v

tilde (~) key—the key on the keyboard that, w pressed with the Ctrl key, toggles the Excel worksheet play between showing the results of formulas and show the formulas

tiled windows—two or more open windows displa together on the screen side by side or one above the o

title bar—a bar across the top of every window; it tains the name of the window and, where applicable, name of the open document; it always contains a Close ton and usually contains a Maximize and Minimize butto

toolbar—a screen element containing buttons you click to execute commands

U

Uniform Resource Locator (URL)—Web add the location of a document on the World Wide Web

URL—see **Uniform Resource Locator**

utility program—software program that perf housekeeping tasks

V

virus—a program that can corrupt the system file keep your system from working correctly

W

Web address—the Uniform Resource Locator, or that is unique to each document on the World Wide V consists of the communication protocol, the domain (and any subdomain names), and the document name

window—a rectangular frame on the desktop tha contain programs, documents, or icons

Windows 98—the current version of Microsoft's popular operating system software

Windows Clipboard—a temporary storage lo for the last item to have been cut or copied fro Windows application

wizard—a series of dialog boxes in which you pro program with information it uses to to help you preformatted documents

word processing software—a program used primarily to create text documents such as letters, memos, and reports

word wrap—the feature whereby a word processor automatically moves text to the next line of a paragraph when a line becomes full

workbook—the file in which Excel stores worksheets

worksheet—Excel's term for a spreadsheet, the grid of vertical columns and horizontal rows

World Wide Web—the hypertext documents available on the Internet using a browser

X

x axis—the horizontal axis of a chart, usually containing data labels

Y

y axis—vertical axis along the left edge of a chart, usually containing numeric values

INDEX

A = Access; E = Excel; IP = Integrating the Parts; MO = Introduction to Microsoft Office; P = PowerPoint; U = Using Computers; W = Word; WN = Windows 98